GUIDE TO
LEAGUE OF NATIONS
PUBLICATIONS

GUIDE TO
LEAGUE OF NATIONS
PUBLICATIONS

A BIBLIOGRAPHICAL SURVEY OF THE WORK

OF THE LEAGUE, 1920-1947

By HANS AUFRICHT

1951

COLUMBIA UNIVERSITY PRESS

NEW YORK

The Rockefeller Foundation has generously provided funds
to meet part of the cost of preparation and publication
of this work

FOREWORD

D R. HANS AUFRICHT'S *Guide to League of Nations Publications* will be of immense service both to the historian seeking to assess the lessons of the past and to the statesman seeking guidance for the future.

The author of this Foreword, who has been privileged to serve both the League of Nations throughout its entire history and the United Nations from its inception, would unhesitatingly venture the opinion that the records compiled by the League during the quarter century of life permitted to it constitute the most complete and the most compact international documentation in existence. There, in a single packet, as it were, is to be found the whole story, from smallest embryo through full flowering to final tragic ending, of mankind's first effort at permanent, organized, world-wide international cooperation to prevent war and promote human well-being.

This period was, and, in the nature of things, always will be, unique. The League began at the very beginning, with a paucity of experience or precedent to guide it and the necessity of constantly opening new roadways in a human society become unprecedentedly complex in the modern technological world about it. It passed through two very illuminating periods, the first a decade of almost uninterrupted growth and progress, and the second, an almost equal period of steady decline and eventual extinction in the fires of World War II. In it, as in a laboratory, can be found and analyzed all the forces which contribute to fulfilling, and, inversely, to negating, mankind's age-old desire for peace. It is an ironic fact that the strongest testimony to the richness of this experience came from none other than the Secretary of State of that great country which had passionately championed and then irresponsibly abandoned the League, Cordell Hull, who, on February 2, 1939, as the world was standing on the verge of a second World War, wrote in an official communication to Geneva that the League "has been responsible for the development of mutual exchange and discussion of ideas and methods to a greater extent and in more fields of humanitarian and scientific endeavor than any other organization in history."

Yet the records of the League have been strangely neglected. The course of historical study and analysis was rudely broken by the war. The first "Great Experiment," as Lord Robert Cecil described it, had not been permitted to succeed; the high hopes with which it had been launched had been sapped and corroded; a second World War had broken out in a vacuum of defeatism and neglect; and when, at its conclusion, a shattered world got around to a second effort to prevent still another cataclysm, its lessons were largely blacked out. Some of the leaders were new and did not want to hear of efforts that had "failed"; others were tired or made cynical by the war; all had their eyes on the future rather than the past. Moreover, there was the political necessity to accommodate the United States and the Soviet Union; almost by tacit agreement the world's statesmen chose to start off anew rather than pick up where they had left off. Yet without willing it, often without realizing it, and sometimes while positively denying it, the architects of the new world organization came out almost exactly where the architects of the previous one had come out, when they agreed on a voluntary association of sovereign states, far greater in size than the League but with much the same form of organization and not greatly different constitutional power. While incorporating in the membership the two isolationist states of the inter-war period, they paralleled the League far more than they knew but benefited from its lessons far less than they might.

Dr. Aufricht's *Guide* allows history to get back into its continuous flow. Up to the Korean action, its pages are almost startling in their parallelism with today; with just the slightest changes in terminology, we can see in the League of Nations the same problems and activities as we see in the United Nations. We find, for instance, comparable debates on aggression and use of force, collective security, voting power, universality of membership, national sovereignty, regionalism, and the like. The catalogue of activities is almost the same except for the heretofore undreamed-of problem of atomic energy and the first instance in history of collective security action in Korea; most of the activity of the United Nations in its first years had been along conventional lines, to take over, revivify, and expand the manifold activities of the League, from the status of women to disarmament. Even the great specialized agencies which now have autonomous status find their roots in their more modest League counterparts: the Food and Agriculture Organization in the nutrition work; the World Health Organization in the Health Section; the International Bank in the League's loans; UNESCO in the International Institute of Intellectual Cooperation; while the Court and the International Labor Organization have been continued practically unchanged. The student of the current organizations and of their necessarily manifold and still growing documentation can be enlightened by examining their predecessors through the comparatively simple and well-catalogued documents of the League.

Fortunately for the historian, whatever else the League was able or unable to do, it kept its documents extraordinarily well. A vast amount was made available to the public, and in as clear and orderly a way as possible with an organization as complex as the League had to be. The Secretariat made special efforts to spread this material in key centers around the world by various devices of depositary libraries, an extensive sales and subscription service, and free distribution. It is a curious fact that much of this work was done by Americans, despite American non-membership in the League. The depositary libraries system was largely worked out by an American, Miss Florence Wilson; the global subscription system was evolved by the World Peace Foundation in Boston; far and away the best cataloguing of League documents has been carried out by the Woodrow Wilson Foundation in cooperation with the Library of Congress and the Rockefeller Foundation; and the most complete unofficial collection of multilateral instruments drafted under the auspices of the League is to be found in Manley O. Hudson's nine-volume *International Legislation* (Washington, 1931–1950). Now the first full history of the League has been completed in Geneva with the assistance of the Rockefeller Foundation.

Despite these efforts, however, two great difficulties confronted the user of this rich material. First was its mass, which, while incomparable with that of the publications which the United Nations is now issuing, is nevertheless formidable and almost overwhelming to all but the most redoubtable researcher. A recent private estimate from Geneva put the total number of League documents issued during its twenty-seven years at well over the hundred thousand mark. The second difficulty has been the intricacy of the material and the necessity of following a given problem or activity roundabout through all the various agencies where it might appear from time to time: Assembly, Council, Secretariat, committee, and special conference.

Dr. Aufricht's *Guide* meets both these difficulties to a considerable degree, and from several different angles. It is the only such effort to cover the whole League period from the start in 1920 till the end in 1947. It includes all types of documents, not only those put on sale and included in the sales catalogue, but also documents not put on sale. It is arranged by subject, so that if one is interested in double taxation, for instance, or child welfare, or disarmament, he can find listed in one place all the important documents on the subject. It is selective and descriptive, omitting many publications which are ephemeral and drawing special attention to those which have proved to be basic. Finally, it includes the major documents not only of the League proper but of its principal autonomous organs: the Permanent Court, International Labor Organization, International Institute of Intellectual Cooperation, International Cinematographic Institute, and International Institute for the Unification of Private Law.

Dr. Aufricht's *Guide* is, in fact, far more than a bibliography; it is a concise historical outline of the League and its principal agencies. Its systematic layout, explanatory notes, and cumulative lists and tables give a picture of the League as a whole and show perhaps more vividly than could continuous text the sweep of its interests. Its material constitutes one of the treasure houses of history, complete and unitary in itself and worthy of being worked and reworked as regards both the specific problems of a tragic period and the beginnings of world organization. It is difficult to see how anyone would be safe in writing on these problems or assessing the forces which alternately pull the world together and apart without consulting this *Guide*. With its aid, historians will find it possible to write more objectively and in longer perspective. The *Guide* is, in sum, an indispensable instrument for any analysis of world organization.

ARTHUR SWEETSER

July, 1951

ACKNOWLEDGMENTS

HAVING TRAVERSED the arduous path through the jungle of League of Nations documents, I find it pleasant to stop and thank those whose assistance and encouragement contributed to the completion of this undertaking.

Mr. Arthur Sweetser showed a most understanding and active interest in the project during every phase of the preparation of this *Guide* from its inception. Mr. Denys P. Myers, probably the greatest living connoisseur of the style and content of League of Nations documents, was kind enough to read the entire work in galley proof and to make many valuable suggestions. Mr. Egon F. Ranshofen-Wertheimer, in personal conversations as well as through his book, *The International Secretariat*, facilitated greatly the selection and arrangement of League documents pertaining to the Secretariat. Constructive criticism and helpful advice from Professor Clyde Eagleton and from Mr. Malcolm W. Davis are most gratefully acknowledged.

My thanks are also due to the officials and staff of Columbia University Press, in particular to Mr. Raymond J. Dixon, who consistently and efficiently edited the major part of the *Guide;* to Mrs. Miriam Bergamini, who conscientiously completed the editing; and to Dr. William Bridgwater, whose extraordinary experience as historian and editor proved most helpful. Moreover, I am indebted to Dr. Konrad Gutman, who prepared the Index, for his thorough and systematic approach.

The major part of the *Guide* was completed at the Woodrow Wilson Memorial Library in New York prior to the transfer of this Library to the United Nations on July 1, 1950. Beginning in 1920 the Woodrow Wilson Library—through the good offices of Mr. Raymond B. Fosdick, the first Under-Secretary-General of the League, and of Mr. Arthur Sweetser, then a member of the Secretariat of the League in Geneva—received all of the League sale and non-sale publications on the same basis as member governments. This collection of League documents is no doubt one of the most comprehensive and best organized collections in existence. Miss Harriet van Wyck, in her capacity as Librarian of the Woodrow Wilson Memorial Library, assisted with enthusiasm and imagination in overcoming many obstacles which were encountered in the preparation of the *Guide*.

Miss Ragnhild F. Luhnenschloss and Miss Dora Hesse cooperated by checking a number of entries, as did Mrs. Eleanor F. Steiner-Prag. Dr. Elisabeth M. Langer contributed some helpful suggestions.

Special thanks are also due to Miss Helen L. Scanlon, who, in her capacity as Librarian of the Carnegie Endowment for International Peace in Washington, D. C., rendered valuable assistance; in particular, her card index relating to the Supervisory Commission of the League proved extremely useful.

Finally, I wish to express my gratitude to The Rockefeller Foundation, which generously provided financial assistance toward the preparation and publication of this volume.

HANS AUFRICHT

Washington, D. C.
July, 1951

CONTENTS

Appendix One: Documents Relating to
the League of Nations

Appendix Two: Documents Relating to the
International Labor Organization and
the Permanent Court of International Justice

Part One
INTRODUCTION

I. THE PLAN AND SCOPE OF THE GUIDE

1. WHAT IS A LEAGUE OF NATIONS DOCUMENT?

FOR THE PURPOSES of this *Guide* every official and unofficial[1] publication issued on behalf of the League of Nations is considered a League of Nations document. A League document is, furthermore, one issued by the League of Nations proper as distinct from an affiliated international organization such as the International Labor Organization or the Permanent Court of International Justice. Selected publications of several of these international organizations have been included, however.

2. TYPES OF DOCUMENTS

LEAGUE DOCUMENTS

In general, three types of League documents are to be distinguished: "documents on public sale," "documents not on public sale," and "classified," that is, confidential and secret documents.[2]

Beyond the fact that documents other than those on public sale were circulated exclusively to members of the League and to a few depository libraries like the Woodrow Wilson Memorial Library[3] in New York City, the distinction between the documents on public sale and those that were not is more or less arbitrary. The fact that an individual document was not on public sale did not preclude its publication in the *Official Journal*, provided it was not "classified." And it would be erroneous to assume that publication of a document for sales purposes was a test of its significance. Actually, several documents of primary importance, which were not confidential, were never on public sale. This was particularly true in the first and last phases of the League, 1920–1926, 1939–1946. Before 1926, the year

[1] That is, documents issued by the Information Section or the Library of the League.
[2] On the Classification, Registry, and Index Branch of the Secretariat, see Catherine Pastuhova, "The Filing System of the Secretariat," in Egon F. Ranshofen-Wertheimer, *The International Secretariat* (Washington, 1945), p. 454–457.
[3] The Woodrow Wilson Memorial Library, with the co-operation of the Library of Congress and the Rockefeller Foundation, has completed a cataloguing project which aims at an exhaustive card catalogue of all League documents, including confidential ones. See Harriet van Wyck, "Documents in Search of a Catalogue," *Library Journal*, LXXI (September 15, 1946), 1177–1181.

the League adopted sales numbers for its publications, the distinction between "sales" and "non-sales" documents was not at all clear. After that it was clear that any document bearing a sales number was on public sale. From 1939 to 1946, several important documents, especially the Reports of the Supervisory Commission, were not on public sale.

Some of the classified documents, which were so designated in the checklists distributed exclusively to members of the League were subsequently declassified. Several of these confidential documents are included in the *Guide*. The League's *Catalogue of Publications, 1920–1935*[4] contains this sweeping statement: "All League of Nations documents are accessible to the public *in their final form.*" Since confidential documents were circulated only to members of the League and were never published, this statement requires qualification.

The archives and files of the League contained, of course, numerous documents, letters, and reports which were never published. The minutes of the secret meetings of the Council, for instance, were kept in secret files by the Registrar.[5]

Although this *Guide* is designed to give a selective rather than a complete list of League documents, it is hoped that it constitutes a fuller and more systematic survey of League publications than has been available heretofore. Unlike the League's *Catalogue of Publications* and Marie J. Carroll's *Key to League of Nations Documents Placed on Public Sale, 1920–1929*[6] which, with their respective supplements, are confined to documents on public sale, the *Guide* lists documents which were never on public sale, at least not as separate documents.

NON-LEAGUE DOCUMENTS

In principle this *Guide* is limited to selected publications issued by or concerning the League of Nations proper. It has been thought advisable, however, to include selected documentation of the several autonomous organizations which co-operated with the League. Complete lists of the conventions and recommendations adopted by the International Labor Conferences from 1919 to 1947 and of the judg-

[4]Geneva, 1935, p. 9; hereafter cited: League Catalogue.
[5]See Catherine Pastuhova, in Ranshofen-Wertheimer, *The International Secretariat*, p. 458.
[6]This volume, the First-Second Supplements, 2 vols., covering the years 1930–1931, and the Third Supplement, 1932–1933, were published by the World Peace Foundation, Boston, in 1930, 1931–1933, and 1934 respectively. The Fourth Supplement, 1934–1936, was published by Columbia University Press in 1938. On League documents, see also Th. F. Currier, "The League of Nations Publications—A Simplified Treatment," *Library Journal*, LV (March 15, 1930), 255; M. Ginsberg, "Economic and Financial Documentation (at the League Library)," in International Federation of Documentation, XIVth Conference, 1938, *Transactions*, II, 174; A. Loveday,

ments, orders, and advisory opinions of the Permanent Court of International Justice should prove useful. These are contained in Part Five, which is exclusively devoted to selected publications by or concerning the International Labor Organization and the Permanent Court of International Justice. In Part Four, Section X, "Intellectual Co-operation," are listed publications of the International Institute of Intellectual Co-operation and of the International Educational Cinematographic Institute. Documents relating to or issued by the International Institute for the Unification of Private Law are included in Part Four, Section VII, "Legal Questions."[7]

3. LISTING OF INDIVIDUAL DOCUMENTS

ORDER

The pertinent bibliographical data on each document entered in the *Guide* are listed in the following order: the title of the document; the place and date of publication; and the number of pages. To facilitate the identification of a document, one or all of the following numbers, when they exist, are indicated at the end of the entry: the official number, in square brackets [ ]; the committee or conference number, in pointed brackets < >; and the sales number, in parentheses ( ).[8] Mimeographed documents are especially designated as such.

LANGUAGE

Most League documents appeared both in English and French, either as separate publications or in bilingual editions. In general only English editions are entered in the *Guide*; a French document is listed only in case no English edition is extant.

Bilingual publications of the League, numbered either *seriatim* or "double-paged," are indicated thus: "49 p., bilingual" or "49 p. + 49 p., bilingual."

In 1920–1921, the *Official Journal* was published in a bilingual edition. Beginning in January, 1922, two editions were issued, one in English and one in French.

"Geneva as a Centre of Economic Information," in the Index published monthly by Svenska Handelsbanken, Stockholm (September, 1934), p. 195; D. P. Myers, "League of Nations Documents," in *Proceedings of the Fifth Conference of Teachers of International Law* (Washington, 1933), p. 148; P. B. Potter, "League Publicity: Cause or Effect of League Failure?" *Public Opinion Quarterly*, II (July, 1938), 399; A.C. Breycha-Vauthier, *Sources of Information: A Handbook on the Publications of the League of Nations* (New York, 1939).

[7]For the five international bureaus placed under the direction of the League of Nations, see below, p 25, 630.

[8]For an explanation of these numbers, see below, p. 9–11.

It is no exaggeration to say that the wide circulation of League documents in English was perhaps the strongest factor in placing English on an equal footing with French as a diplomatic language.[9]

4. MULTIPLE PUBLICATION OF DOCUMENTS

Many League documents were first printed or mimeographed as separate publications and subsequently reprinted in more comprehensive documents, for instance, in the *Official Journal*.[10] The fact that most of these documents were designed primarily for the use of the organs of the League rather than for the public at large and had to be circulated to delegates on very short notice during sessions justified this practice.

In general only documents of a comparatively small number of pages were published more than once and in different places. Naturally, 500-page books and 700-page conference proceedings were not printed twice. In 1928 it became the declared policy of the League to reduce multiple publication as much as possible.[11]

In this *Guide* documents, even if published in more than one place, are usually listed only once. Some important documents, however, are not easily available, and it has been thought advisable to cite their publication in more accessible documents, particularly the *Official Journal*, in footnotes. General conventions concluded under the auspices of the League are also listed twice: in the regular bibliographical entries, and in footnotes citing their publication in the *Treaty Series of the League of Nations* and including the dates on which the conventions entered into force.

5. ANNOTATIONS

Annotations to some of the documents listed in this *Guide* are designed to furnish concise information on the significance or content of the documents. Three types of annotation are used: (1) Brief commentaries indicate the special importance of some documents, for example: "This so-called Bruce Report is indispensable for an understanding of the provisions of the United Nations Charter (Articles 61–72) on the Economic and Social Council." (2) Tables of contents of other documents are reproduced, sometimes in full to indicate exactly what the documents contain, sometimes only in part to note

[9]For the translation services of the League, see Ranshofen-Wertheimer, *The International Secretariat*, p. 138–139.
[10]When the official or sales number of a document published between 1925 and 1939 is known, it will be advisable for the reader to consult the Numerical Index which first appeared in the *Official Journal* in 1925. From 1925 to 1930 the Index listed official numbers only; from 1931 on it listed both official and sales numbers.
[11]See *Second Annual Report of the Publications Committee*, p. 9. [A.5.1929.X.]

the sections of particular interest. These two types of annotation, when they pertain to a single document, are set immediately after the regular bibliographical entry, in smaller type. When the first or commentary type of annotation concerns a series of related documents, it is set in ordinary text form. (3) Footnotes contain cross references to related documents, articles, or books and other pertinent information. In Part Four, Section IX, "Political Questions," the bibliographical pattern used throughout the greater part of the book has been abandoned in favor of concise statements of facts, issues, or procedures, accompanied by footnotes which indicate the principal documents related to these questions.

6. CLASSIFICATION

The arrangement of this *Guide*, in particular its classification system, is designed to supplement the necessarily limited information contained in the annotations.

The sections of the parts of the *Guide* which are devoted to League documents proper (Parts Two, Three, and Four) do not always correspond to the Roman numerals[12] used in the official and sales numbers. In Part Four, Section IV, "Social and Humanitarian Problems," for instance, there are listed documents bearing the classmarks I.B. (Minorities), XII.(Refugees), VI.B.(Slavery), IV.(Social Questions, including Traffic in Women and Children). In Part Four, Section VII, "Legal Questions," publications of the International Institute for the Unification of Private Law are listed, in addition to League documents marked V.(Legal).

The League sometimes treated the same subject under more than one Roman numeral. Thus, documents relating to the Saar Territory were originally published under the classmark I.A.(Administrative Commissions) and later under VII.(Political Questions). All documents relating to the Saar Territory are listed in Part Four, Section I, "Administration of Territory."

7. COMMITTEE DOCUMENTS

In view of the importance of the work of League committees, documents pertaining to them include references to the authorizing Assembly Resolution, Council Resolution, or International Convention or the appropriate rules of procedure, such as the Rules of Procedure of the Permanent Mandates Commission [C.404(2).M.295(2).1921. VI.] <C.P.M.8(2).> and other basic documents such as the *Statute of the Organisation for Communications and Transit* [C.95.M.48.1938. VIII.] (1938.VIII.1.).

[12]See below, p. 9, 10, 86.

Periodic reports and major *ad hoc* reports of the committees are included in the *Guide*. In the case of periodic reports, only first and last reports are given for the most part.

The printing of committee minutes, except those of Assembly committees, the European Union Commission, the Permanent Mandates Commission, the Committee for Communications and Transit, and the Advisory Committee on Traffic in Opium and Other Dangerous Drugs was discontinued in 1931.[13] The minutes of committee sessions issued prior to 1932 are listed by reference to the first and last recorded session.

8. CONFERENCE DOCUMENTS

In general the proceedings of the numerous conferences held under the auspices of the League of Nations[14] are listed throughout the *Guide*, with special reference to the final acts and draft conventions adopted by the conferences. At times preliminary documentation was published in advance of the meeting of a conference, for instance, the reports by the Preparatory Committee of the International Economic Conference, 1927.[15] Collections of conference documents were also published, such as those issued in connection with the Disarmament Conference, 1932–1936.[16] After the International Financial Conference, held in Brussels in 1920, a review of the recommendations and their applications was published in 1923.[17]

9. CUMULATIVE LISTS

Cumulative lists of publications relating to Assembly and Council sessions, Assembly committee meetings, reports of the Secretary-General, League budgets, and ratifications of the general conventions concluded under the auspices of the League have been included to facilitate access to these, at times widely scattered, sources and to furnish the documentary background for a historical survey of League activities.

[13]See below, p. 14f. The Minutes of the nineteenth to thirty-first Sessions of the Health Committee were published from 1932 to 1940 by the Health Organization as <C.H.> documents. For a list of these Minutes see *Bulletin of the Health Organisation*, Vol. XI (1945), p. 14–15.

[14]On these conferences, see Vladimir D. Pastuhov, *A Guide to the Practice of International Conferences* (Washington, 1945), p. 22–28; Norman L. Hill, *The Public International Conference: Its Function, Organization and Procedure* (Stanford University, 1929); and Frederick S. Dunn, *The Practice and Procedure of International Conferences* (Baltimore, 1929).

[15]See below, p. 220–221.

[16]See below, p. 299, especially Documents (1932.IX.63.), (1935.IX.4.), (1936.IX.4.).

[17]See below, p. 219.

II. NUMBERING AND CLASSIFICATION

OF LEAGUE DOCUMENTS

As PREVIOUSLY INDICATED most League documents may be identified by one or all of the following numbers: official number, committee or conference number, and sales number. Among documents which cannot be identified by any of these numbers are publications issued during the formative period of the League, such as the Proceedings of the International Financial Conference, Brussels, 1920,[1] and the periodicals of the League, for example, the *Official Journal*, *Monthly Bulletin of Statistics*, and *Bulletin of the Health Organisation*.

1. OFFICIAL NUMBERS

The official number in the upper right-hand corner of the title page of a document refers for the most part to a Council and/or Assembly document, that is, to a document distributed to members of the Council and/or Assembly. The constituent elements of the official number [C.340.M.98.1928.II.] may be explained as follows: "1928." is the year in which the document was distributed; "C.340." designates the three hundred and fortieth document distributed to Council members in 1928; "M.98." means that it was the ninety-eighth document distributed in 1928 to members of the League who were not members of the Council; the Roman numeral "II."[2] is the classmark for the Economic and Financial Section of the Secretariat, where the document was prepared. A document bearing the official number [A.3.1939.] would be the third one distributed to the Assembly in 1939. Some "A." documents which periodically covered the same subject appeared under the same number each year, except, of course, for the date. The annual reports to the Assembly on the work of the League, for instance, were numbered [A.6.1926.] [A.6.1927.], and so on.

OFFICIAL NUMBERS PRIOR TO 1921

From 1920 to April, 1921, the League used a different system for its official numbers. In the typical official number [20/29/1], "20"

[1]See below, p. 218–219.
[2]See below, p. 86.

stands for the year 1920, "29" is an arbitrary symbol for the Council, and "1" designates the first document distributed in 1920 to members of the Council. Assembly documents followed the same pattern, with "48" being the symbol for the Assembly.

2. SALES NUMBERS

In 1926 a sales number appeared in the lower right-hand corner of the title page of a League document on public sale. Thus, beginning with that year the great majority of sales documents were marked by both official and sales numbers.[3] The sales number in the broader sense is exemplified by the following box:

> Series of Publications of the League of Nations
> V.Legal
> 1945.V.2.

For purposes of bibliographical identification the bottom line, "1945.V.2.," which might be called the sales number in the narrow sense, is sufficient. Beginning in 1931 this bottom line was used in the *Numerical List of Documents* published or mentioned in the *Official Journal* and at times in the sales catalogues issued by the official sales agents of the League.[4]

3. COMMITTEE AND CONFERENCE NUMBERS

A document which was meant primarily for the use of members of a League committee or delegates to a conference held under the auspices of the League was marked with a committee or conference number. For instance, Document <C.H.197.> is a publication of the Health Committee, and <C.E.I.16.> is the numerical symbol for the *Memorandum on the Electrical Industry*, distributed to the International Economic Conference, 1927. The abbreviations within these numbers are those of the French names for the committee or confer-

[3]In some cases only sales numbers were used, *e.g.*, *Statistical Yearbook of the League of Nations* (1945.II.A.5.). It is noteworthy that it took the United Nations more than a year before it adopted its own sales number system, which, by the way, is patterned for the most part after the sales number system of the League. For instance, the Roman numeral "II" stands for "Economic and Financial," the Roman numeral "V" for "Legal Affairs," and so on. For an explanation of the Roman numeral and the sales number system of the United Nations, see *United Nations Index* vol. 1, No. 11 (November 1950) p. 4.

[4]See, *e.g.*, the catalogues of the International Documents Service, Columbia University Press.

ence.[5] The committee or conference number appears either alone or in combination with the official number in the upper right-hand corner of the title page of a document.

4. REGISTRATION NUMBERS

Under Article 18 of the Covenant treaties or international engagements entered into by members of the League were registered with the Secretariat and published in the *Treaty Series of the League of Nations*. In all, 4,834 treaties and international engagements were registered. The registration is useful in connection with listing signatures, ratifications, denunciations, and so forth.[6] No reference is made in the *Guide* to the registry numbers designed only for the internal use of the Secretariat.

5. REVISED EDITIONS AND SUPPLEMENTS

The printed first issue of a document was not always the final one. To indicate a revised version an arabic figure was added in parentheses within the official number, for example, [C.153(1).M.59(1). 1929.]. A supplement to a document is indicated by the addition of "Addendum" or "Supplement" to the official number. At times, supplements to a document are indicated by inserting (a) (b) (c) into the official number, for instance, [A.6(a).1932.].

6. CHECKLISTS

From 1922 to 1931 eight subject lists of "Documents Distributed to the States Members of the League,"[7] covering the years 1921–1928, were prepared by the Distribution Branch. The lists covering the years 1923–1928 inclusive indicate whether or not a document was

[5]"C.H." is the abbreviation for Comité d'Hygiène, "C.E.I." for Conférence Economique Internationale. For an explanation of the various committee symbols and abbreviations and a list of the French names of these committees, with their English equivalents, see Marie J. Carroll, *Key to League of Nations Documents Placed on Public Sale, 1920–1929* (Boston, 1930), p. 227–232, and its First Supplement (Boston, 1931), p. 35.

[6]See, *e.g.*, 205 *Treaty Series* (1944–1946), p. 192–220; see also United Nations, *Treaty Series*, I (1946–1947), 269.

[7]The titles of these subject lists varied slightly over the years. Their numbers and the periods covered are as follows: [C.450.M.267.1922.], May to December, 1921; [C.250. M.141.1923.], 1922; [C.300.M.111.1924.], 1923; [C.260.M.96.1925.], 1924; [C.400.M. 141.1926.], 1925; [C.400.M.134.1927.] (General 1927.6.), 1926; [C.112.M.33.1930.] (General 1930.1.), 1927; [C.400.M.300.1930.] (General 1931.4.), 1928.

reprinted in the *Official Journal*. For reasons of economy the printing of these subject lists was discontinued in 1932. Only mimeographed lists were circulated to members of the League in 1929–1946.[8] These lists, which were never generally available, contain the comparatively most complete records of League publications. They include sales, non-sales, and confidential documents. However, for bibliographical purposes the listing of individual items as well as the enumeration of entries is incomplete in several respects.[9]

[8] See, *e.g.*, *Numerical List of Documents*, 5 p., mimeographed. [C.61.M.61.1945.]
[9] The lists covering the years 1925 to 1928 were on public sale and therefore contained no references to confidential material.

III. THE PRODUCTION, DISTRIBUTION, AND SALE OF LEAGUE DOCUMENTS

1. LEGAL BASIS

THE COVENANT of the League of Nations contains but one reference to League publications, namely, Article 18, which provides for the registration and publication of "every treaty or international engagement entered into hereafter by any member of the League." In accordance with this provision and subsequent authoritative interpretations by the League, 205 volumes of the *Treaty Series of the League of Nations* were published from 1920 to 1946.

Additional references to League documentation and publication are to be found in the Rules of Procedure of the Assembly (Rule 10), Rules of Procedure of the Council (Rule XI),[1] Assembly Resolutions,[2] and in recommendations of the Supervisory Commission[3] and of the Publications Committee.[4]

For the most part, expenses for the publications of the League were financed out of the regular budget. The cost of League publications entailed, apart from printing costs, the salaries of the members of the Publication and Printing Department,[5] of interpreters, translators, précis-writers, and index officers.

Several publications were financed, at least in part, by grants-in-aid of the Rockefeller Foundation, for instance, the publications of the Health Organization and of the Economic and Financial Organ-

---

[1]Rule XI of the Rules of Procedure of the Council provides that the Minutes of the meetings of the Council shall be kept by the Secretariat and that they shall be published. However, the Council may decide not to have published Minutes. In this case, a summary record in a single copy shall be kept in the Secretariat of the League of Nations. Representatives of the Governments which took part in the meeting shall at all times have the right to consult the record at the Secretariat.

[2]See, *e.g.*, Assembly Resolution of September 25, 1926, *Official Journal*, Special Supplement No. 43, p. 18–19.

[3]See, *e.g.*, *The Publications of the League. Report of the Supervisory Commission to the Assembly*. [A.13.1928.X.]

[4]See below, p. 15, 107–108.

[5]On the organization of the Internal Administrative Services of the Secretariat in reference to League documentation, see Egon F. Ranshofen-Wertheimer, *The International Secretariat* (Washington, 1945), p. 134–143.

ization. Others were financed out of the James J. Forstall Revolving Fund for Special Publications.[6]

2. PUBLICATIONS POLICY AND THE PUBLICATIONS COMMITTEE

The question of League of Nations publications was frequently discussed by the Assembly. In 1926, for instance, the Assembly adopted a resolution[7] requesting the advisory committees and the conferences convened by the League to consider whether publication of their discussions would not in many instances be better effected by means of detailed reports giving as exact accounts as possible of their work. At the same time it was decided that minutes of subcommittees should not be published, unless the Secretary-General gave express consent to a formal request in advance. In 1931 the Assembly resolved to discontinue the printing of committee minutes, except those of the Assembly, the European Union Commission, and the Permanent Mandates Commission, the Committee for Communications and Transit, and the Advisory Committee on Traffic in Opium and Other Dangerous Drugs.[8]

By far the greater part of all printed documents was placed on public sale, either as individual documents or as part of a more comprehensive document, such as the *Official Journal*. In the years 1928 and 1938 sales receipts averaged about one third of production costs. Strangely enough, in the war years 1939 to 1941, when the prestige of the League as a political factor reached perhaps the lowest point in its history, the ratio of sales receipts to production costs improved considerably. In 1941 there was even a surplus of 13,578 Swiss francs,[9] which dispelled a widespread belief that League publications necessarily entailed a budgetary loss. It cannot be denied, however, that in general League publications constituted a considerable burden on three services of the League (Budget, Staff, Printing and Supplies).[10] The Supervisory Commission, therefore, carefully examined the publications policy and practice with a view to reducing production costs.[11]

[6]On the James J. Forstall Revolving Fund, see *Official Journal*, Special Supplement No. 194, p. 170–171.
[7]*Official Journal*, Special Supplement No. 43, p. 18–19.
[8]*Official Journal*, Special Supplement No. 92, p. 29. See also "Fifth Annual Report of the Publications Committee of the Secretariat for 1931," in Document [A.5.1932.X.], p. 14: "The Minutes of the Committees will be roneod [mimeographed], but the Sections [*i.e.*, of the Secretariat] have been asked to note that no revised version of minutes may be duplicated in view of the stringent need for economy and in order to avoid spending on roneo work the money saved for printing."
[9]Sales receipts amounted to 108,808 Swiss francs, production costs, 95,230.
[10]See *Report of the Supervisory Commission on the Work of Its Forty-first Session*, p. 9. [A.5.1931.X.]. Also in *Official Journal*, Special Supplement No. 97, p. 74.
[11]See *The Publications of the League. Report of the Supervisory Commission*, p. 1. [A.

Upon the recommendation of the Supervisory Commission a Publications Committee was set up by Assembly Resolution of 1926[12] to serve as an advisory committee to the Secretary-General. The Committee[13] was presided over by the Director of the Internal Administrative Services and was composed of a representative of the Treasury, the Chief of the Document Service, the head of the Publications Service of the Secretariat, and a representative of the section from which the document originated.

The Publications Committee issued 12 annual reports,[14] covering the years 1928 to 1938. These reports constitute the most authoritative source on the publications policy and practice of the League.

Many proposals to improve the publications practice and to reduce production costs were advanced by the Publications Committee. On the whole, its recommendations or pertinent Assembly Resolutions based on these recommendations resulted in greater efficiency. Especially after 1930, the year of the greatest deficit, did production costs decrease, while sales receipts increased and, in 1941, resulted in a surplus.

The Publications Committee recommended the placing of printing orders outside Switzerland whenever printing prices abroad were lower. Accordingly, 23.4 percent of League publications were printed outside Switzerland in 1928, 38 percent in 1936, and 50 percent in 1941.[15]

The number of "reprints" of the same document was reduced after 1928.[16] For example, the budget as adopted by the Assembly was thereafter regularly inserted in the October issue of the *Official Journal*. In 1933 it was decided that the reports of advisory committees and certain documents which were circulated to all the members of the League would no longer be reprinted in the *Official Journal*, which would simply make a detailed reference to them.[17] Similarly,

---

13.1928.X.]. See also Assembly Resolution of September 29, 1931, *Official Journal*, Special Supplement No. 92, p. 29, which reads in part as follows: "When proposals involving publication not immediately required for work already undertaken by the League are made by a League body, no final decision shall be taken until the Secretary-General has been consulted regarding the financial and administrative consequences of these proposals."

[12]See Supervisory Commission, *Report of the Commission on the Work of Its Thirty-second Session.* [A.5.1929.X.]. See also *supra*, footnote 7.

[13]On the Publications Committee, see also Ranshofen-Wertheimer, *The International Secretariat*, p. 147, 219–221.

[14]These reports form part of the Reports of the Supervisory Commission, which are listed below, p. 108–116.

[15]During World War II, numerous League documents were printed in the United States and Canada irrespective of printing costs.

[16]See "Second Annual Report of the Publications Committee," in Document [A.5. 1929.X.], p. 9.

[17]See "Seventh Annual Report of the Publications Committee of the Secretariat," in Document [A.5.1934.X.], p. 14.

beginning in the middle of March, 1934, the great majority of documents were roneographed (mimeographed) in "single spacing" and on both sides of the paper,[18] a procedure which obviously was designed to save time and paper.

The foregoing measures adopted at the advice of the Publications Committee are recalled here for two reasons: first, they explain certain changes in the publications practice of the League; second, these changes were not merely accidental, but in many instances the result of a deliberate policy to reduce costs.

To increase the circulation and sales of documents several positive measures were resorted to. Authorized sales agents, located in member and nonmember states, were selected.[19] In 1935 there were 51 agents.

A sales catalogue, *Catalogue of Publications, 1920–1935*,[20] was published. Subsequently five supplements appeared, covering the years 1936–1939 inclusive. A list of League publications issued from 1940–1945 is contained in the Report of the Secretary-General on the Work of the League during the War [A.6.1946], p. 151–167. The *Catalogue* contained a useful index and the list prices of individual documents.

Review copies of books and documents were sent out, and the resulting reviews were carefully traced.[21]

In the course of time the "legal-size" format for documents was occasionally abandoned in favor of more convenient formats. An ever-increasing number of publications of the Economic and Financial Section in particular appeared in regular book or pamphlet form.

There are very few libraries, with the exception of the libraries of foreign offices, which have complete sets of League of Nations documents. This is not surprising when one recalls that the all-inclusive subscriptions averaged 142 in the years 1928–1938; the maximum of 156 was reached in 1930.[22] Apparently the high costs of binding and cataloguing the documents as well as the extraordinary shelf space required to house the legal-size documents were deterrents to the acquisition of complete League collections.

[18]See "Eighth Annual Report of the Publications Committee of the Secretariat," in Document [A.5.1935.X.], p. 11.

[19]For the authorized sales agent in the United States, see "Eleventh Annual Report of the Publications Committee of the Secretariat," in Document [A.15.1938.X.], p. 14, footnote 3: "At the end of 1936, the agency for the United States was transferred from Boston (World Peace Foundation) to New York, N. Y. (Columbia University Press)."

[20]Previous editions as well as supplements appeared in 1929 and 1934.

[21]On the review copy service, see Document [A.5.1938.X.], p. 14.

[22]The following figures, with the years in parentheses, indicate the number of all-inclusive subscriptions (the source for 1928 and 1929 is [A.5.1930.X.], p. 18; for 1930 and 1931, [A.5.1933.X.], p. 14; for 1932 through 1938, [A.5.1939.X.], p. 17): 97 (1928), 117 (1929), 156 (1930), 150 (1931), 150 (1932), 152 (1933), 144 (1934), 148 (1935), 149 (1936), 150 (1937), 150 (1938).

Although the number of all-inclusive subscriptions was surprisingly small, many single publications had a wide circulation and are still in demand. Beginning with 1937 the Publications Committee included in its report a list of "best sellers."[23] The list is headed by Gottfried von Haberler's *Prosperity and Depression*, which in 1937 and 1938 had sold 6,845[24] copies, 2,325 of them in 1938. Several serial publications followed in popularity. The *World Economic Survey* was second with a total of 5,570, of which 2,200 were sold in 1938. The *Statistical Yearbook of the League of Nations* ranked third, having sold 2,800 copies in 1938 to make a total of 5,515. In 1937 and 1938 more than 3,000 copies of Volume I and 3,000 copies of Volume II of *Money and Banking* were sold. The *Review of World Trade* sold 2,900 copies in 1937 and 1938.

According to American standards these figures are rather modest. But considering the highly technical character of the material, the figures compare favorably with related publications.

Among the periodicals, the *Monthly Bulletin of Statistics* with 1,603 subscriptions in 1938 and the *Bulletin of the Health Organisation* with 905 subscriptions in the same year had the widest circulation.[25]

A publication of the Information Section, which is generally not considered as "official," entitled *Essential Facts about the League of Nations*, sold altogether about 20,000 copies.[26]

No official figures have been published since 1938. But the demand for certain League publications has increased during recent years, and it is to be expected that certain League publications will have to be reprinted or will have to be published in revised editions by the United Nations as soon as the present stock is exhausted.

[23]For first list, see Document [A.5.1937.X.], p. 21.
[24]These and the following figures are quoted from Documents [A.5.1938.X.] and [A.5.1939.X.].
[25]See Document [A.5.1939.X.], p. 17.
[26]Up to the end of 1937, 17,000 copies were sold; see Document [A.5.1938.X.], p. 15

IV. THE POLITICAL FUNCTIONS
OF THE LEAGUE

1. THE LEAGUE AS A "BODY POLITIC"

THE PRIMARY POLITICAL FUNCTION of the League was "to promote international co-operation and to achieve international peace and security." Although there is general agreement on this basic objective of the League, there is considerable disagreement concerning the League as a "body politic" and concerning the adequacy of its constitutional structure to safeguard peace and security.

Many lawyers will agree that the existence and character of a corporate person is to a considerable extent independent of its membership. This principle applies also to the League of Nations, since technically the League existed as the same legal entity from January 10, 1920, to April 18, 1946, despite far-reaching changes in its membership during this period. From a political viewpoint, however, the changing political complexion of the League caused by changes in its membership is highly significant.

With regard to decisive changes in its membership, three major phases in the political history of the League can be distinguished. During the first phase, 1920–1926, the League included all major powers, except Germany, the Union of Soviet Socialist Republics, and the United States. The admission of Germany to membership in 1926 marked the beginning of the second phase, which ended with the withdrawal of Germany and Japan from the League in 1933. The third and last phase began with the adherence of Soviet Russia in 1934 and ended in 1939 on the outbreak of World War II.

The internal political structures of the member states were also subject to changes that could not be or were not anticipated at the time the League was established. Above all, the change from the pacifist idealism of the 1920's to the aggressive militarism of the 1930's could not fail to have its repercussions on League policies towards its members and nonmembers.

But even faithful members like France and the United Kingdom, who stayed in the League till the end and whose governments were not exposed to the same violent changes as were those of other nations, advocated "peace strategies which were almost continually in conflict"[1] and failed to harmonize their League policies. Thus League action was repeatedly paralyzed by the joint irresolution of its members. There have been, therefore, critiques of the League which maintained that the League was at times a "body politic" without a policy[2]—a phenomenon not unknown in domestic politics.

League policy was finally dependent upon the attitude of nonmembers towards the League, attitudes which ranged from mere indifference to open hostility. The lack of universality was felt time and again as a regrettable shortcoming, the more so since the authority of the League vis-à-vis nonmembers was rather limited in law[3] and fact. Nevertheless, almost all States, in the sense of international law, were members of the League between 1920 and 1939. A complete list of the 63 League members is contained in Appendix I, Section XI. On April 18, 1946 there were altogether 44 League members. It is controversial whether Austria was a League member at that time. Assuming that Austria did not lose its League membership as a consequence of the events of March 13, 1938 and the ensuing temporary incorporation into the German Reich, there were 45 members. It should be recalled that not all 63 members participated simultaneously in the League. Soviet Russia, for instance, joined the League after Germany and Japan had declared their intention to withdraw. Leichtenstein, Monaco, San Marino were not considered eligible for membership.

Of the "original" members only the United States and Hedjaz,[4] respectively Saudi Arabia, the successor of Hedjaz, failed to join the League.

It is unrealistic, then, to speak of the League as a "body politic" without taking into consideration its changing membership, the relationship among its members, the relationship between members and nonmembers, and those policy decisions which were responsible for League action and inaction.

2. A COERCIVE OR NONCOERCIVE LEAGUE?

In the discussion of League procedures for the prevention or repression of war, the term "sanction"—though it is not to be found in the Covenant—has been widely used, implying that the League had the authority automatically to impose coercive measures on recalcitrant members.

[1] Arnold Wolfers, *Britain and France between Two Wars* (New York, 1940), p. 8; see also p. 380–390.
[2] See, *e.g.*, Edward H. Carr, *The Twenty Years' Crisis, 1919–1939*, (London, 1940), p. 38–53, especially p. 40.
[3] See Art. 17 and Art. 16, Par. 1 of the Covenant.
[4] For a list "States Members of the League," see below, p. 505–508.

Article 16, Paragraph 1 of the Covenant, it is true, provides for economic measures against any member resorting to war in disregard of its covenants under Articles 12, 13, or 15,[5] especially for the severance of all trade and financial relations between the nationals of the covenant-breaking state and the nationals of any other member.[6] By contrast, Paragraph 2 of the same article authorizes the Council to *recommend* adequate military measures to the members to protect the covenants of the League. Hence, economic measures against recalcitrant members were deemed "compulsory," military measures "optional."

Only once in the history of the League, in the Italo-Ethiopian "dispute," was Article 16, Paragraph 1 applied—and then in an incomplete and hesitating fashion. Subsequently, a report on the application of the principles of the Covenant,[7] submitted to the Assembly in 1938, even cast doubt on the compulsory character of economic measures. It reads in part as follows:

There is general agreement that the military measures contemplated in Article 16 are not compulsory. As regards the economic and financial measures, many Members of the League have stated that they could not in present conditions consider themselves bound automatically to apply such measures in any conflict. Some other Members expressed the contrary view.

In the light of League practice it was felt by many after the "sanctions" experiment of 1935–1936 that, the unmistakable language of the Covenant notwithstanding, not only military but also economic measures under Article 16 should be considered optional rather than compulsory.[8] Similarly, in Article 10, no automatic obligation, except consultation, was provided for in case of external aggression or threat of aggression against the territorial integrity and existing political independence of any member of the League.[9]

[5]The question of who determines the covenant-breaking state and who decides on the application of economic measures was discussed in connection with the economic measures against Italy.
[6]For the so-called Chaco Embargo, see below, p. 318–319.
[7]Document [A.74.1938.VII.], in *Records of the Nineteenth Ordinary Session of the Assembly. Minutes of the Sixth Committee*, p. 102; see Assembly Resolution of September 30, 1938, *ibid.*, which reads as follows: "The Assembly decides to communicate the present report, together with its annexes, to all the Members of the League."
[8]See especially the United Kingdom declaration of September 22, 1938, in *Records of the Nineteenth Ordinary Session of Assembly. Minutes of the Sixth Committee*, p. 25. See also S. Engel, *League Reform: An Analysis of Official Proposals and Discussions, 1936–1939* (Geneva, 1940), p. 154; Engel states that of the 36 members who expressed themselves on this point at the 19th Assembly "only eleven still considered the League to be of the coercive type," namely, China, Colombia, Iran, Spain, Ecuador, the Union of Soviet Socialist Republics, Mexico, Argentina, Rumania, New Zealand, and Turkey.
[9]This interpretation of Art. 10 is controversial; see Document [A.7.1938.VII.], p. 95, 97–98. "The remarkable elasticity of the Covenant makes it possible to interpret

In 1938, in the course of the discussion on the "coercive" or "non-coercive" nature of the League, Mr. Unden (Sweden) invited the members of the League to face honestly the difference between the theory and practice of the League, when he said: "By maintaining ... the fiction of a system of automatic and compulsory sanctions we do not bring about the realisation of such a system."[10] Mr. Gorgé (Switzerland) remarked that "by recognizing that Article 16 is facultative, as indeed it is already . . . the League . . . would be increasing its chances of consolidating its work."[11]

It is probably not incidental that Articles 41 and 42 of the United Nations Charter, which correspond to Article 16, Paragraphs 1 and 2 of the League Covenant, are not mandatory but permissive.[12] Here, the Security Council *may* decide what measures not involving the use of armed force are to be employed to give effect to its decisions, and it *may* call upon the members of the United Nations to apply such measures (Article 41). Furthermore, should the measures provided for in Article 41 be, in the opinion of the Security Council, inadequate, it *may* take such action by air, sea, or land forces as may be necessary to maintain or restore international peace and security.

3. DISARMAMENT

The provisions of the Covenant concerning the reduction and limitation of armaments (Articles 8 and 9) were never put into effect by League action. The temporary disarmament of the Central Powers was a consequence of the peace treaties with these powers rather than the result of special obligations towards the League. Again, the Washington Conference on the Limitation of Armaments (1921–1922), which resulted in agreement among the major naval powers on naval disarmament, was convened independently of the League.

However that may be, the elaborate documentation prepared by the League with a view to universal reduction and limitation of armaments should still prove valuable in any attempt to reach multilateral agreement on disarmament.[13]

Article 10 as desired. *The tendency has been to treat it as a simple declaration of principle; but there is nothing to prevent it being treated as the basis of an independent procedure, if thought desirable. The general and categorical terms of Article 10 make it perfectly possible, with the approval of the Council, to organize the most effective resistance to aggression.*" This quotation is from the report by M. Entezam, p. 97. Italics added.
[10]Document [A.7.1938.VII.], p. 10.
[11]*Ibid.*, p. 13.
[12]On the permissive character of Arts. 41 and 42 of the United Nations Charter, see Leland M. Goodrich and Edvard Hambro, *The Charter of the United Nations: Commentary and Documents* (Boston, 1946), p. 160–161.
[13]See below, Part Four, Section VIII.

4. PACIFIC SETTLEMENT OF DISPUTES

In numerous cases the League of Nations successfully contributed to the pacific settlement of "disputes" and "incidents." Its achievements in this field should by no means be belittled.

No attempt has been made to list all League documents relating to political questions. These questions are discussed in Part Four, Section IX. Concise statements of facts, issues, or procedures, accompanied by footnotes that list the major documents bearing on these questions, are designed to furnish, in addition to bibliographical information, a brief survey of the major phases of League procedure in 26 incidents and disputes that were dealt with by the League.

In addition to the League proper, the Permanent Court of International Justice, independently of the League or upon the request of the League, rendered judgments, orders, and advisory opinions bearing on political questions. A complete list of these is to be found in Part Five, Section II.

5. WHO FAILED—THE LEAGUE OR ITS MEMBERS?

It has been said time and again, and especially at the last Assembly of the League in 1946, that the failure of the League, if failure there was, is not attributable to the League of Nations, but to the Nations of the League.[14]

This statement is undoubtedly correct—if it means that the members of the League did not always live up to the ideals of the League, that not all the members settled their disputes peacefully, that several members violated the political and territorial integrity of fellow members, that the members were often unable to agree on common principles of economic policy and of disarmament, and that members withdrew from the League whenever they considered such action in their national interests.

But if it means that the "machinery" of the League was a sufficient safeguard of peace and that the mere threat of economic measures would have been sufficient to prevent and repress war, the statement seems unrealistic in the light of League practice. Recall that in 1938 the principle of the mandatory character of economic measures was discarded by several members in favor of voluntary participation in economic measures against the covenant-breaking state.[15] When this stage was reached in the interpretation of the Covenant, the League machinery to safeguard peace by automatic economic

[14]See, e.g., the remarks of M. Costa du Rels, in *Official Journal*, Special Supplement No. 194, p. 28.
[15]See above, footnote 8.

"sanctions" had been weakened to a point where aid was to be granted to other members only if such action appeared clearly advantageous to the aiding member. Thus collective obligation gave way to individual discretion.[16]

It would be unfair, however, to attribute the failure of the League to prevent World War II exclusively to League members. The absence of the United States[17] from the League reduced its effectiveness from the outset. And it should be remembered that in 1939, the Axis powers were no longer members but, on the contrary, the most ardent enemies of the League.

[16]See, *e.g.*, the views of Maxim Litvinov in *Records of the Nineteenth Ordinary Session of the Assembly: Plenary Meetings, Official Journal*, Special Supplement No. 183, p. 76. Mr. Litvinov advocated a coercive League.

[17]Although not a member of the League, the United States participated in many of its activities through official delegations or individual officials and experts. See Ursula P. Hubbard, "The Cooperation of the United States with the League of Nations and the International Labour Organization," *International Conciliation*, No. 274 (November, 1931), and "The Cooperation of the United States with the League of Nations, 1931–1936," *ibid.*, No. 329 (April, 1937), p. 291; Arthur Sweetser, "The Nonpolitical Achievements of the League," *Foreign Affairs*, XIX (October, 1940), 179, and "The United States and the League, the International Labour Organisation, and the World Court during 1940," in Geneva Research Centre, *Geneva Special Studies*, Vol. XI, No. 8 (December, 1940); this survey by Mr. Sweetser is the last in a series covering the years 1930–1934, 1935–1936, 1937, 1938, and 1939 which was previously published under varying titles by the Geneva Research Centre. See also Harriet E. Davis, ed., *Pioneers in World Order* (New York, 1944).

V. THE NONPOLITICAL FUNCTIONS
OF THE LEAGUE

1. PRINCIPAL FIELDS

THE SO-CALLED nonpolitical functions of the League, though less conspicuous than the political functions, constituted the greater part of the League's activities. They covered the following principal fields: administration of territory; health; traffic in opium and other dangerous drugs; social and humanitarian problems, such as the protection of minorities, refugees, slavery, traffic in women and children, child welfare, improvement in penal administration; economic and financial questions; communications and transit; legal questions; intellectual co-operation.

Actually, many of these activities had direct or indirect political effects. For example, the administration of territories, such as the Saar and Danzig, or economic and financial measures taken by the League involved at times major political decisions or policy recommendations. Moreover, the Economic and Financial Organization of the League co-operated with the Council and other organs in matters which were primarily political in nature.[1] Nevertheless, it became customary to designate the foregoing functions as technical[2] or nonpolitical even in official League of Nations,[3] and later in United Nations,[4] terminology.

The activities of the League in these fields were authorized by Articles 22 to 24 of the Covenant, by special international conventions,[5] and by Assembly or Council Resolutions. They were carried on, for the most part, by various organs of the League in co-operation with the competent section of the Secretariat. The League organs charged with nonpolitical functions had various names.[6] One was a

[1] See Martin Hill, *The Economic and Financial Organization of the League of Nations* (Washington, 1946), p. 103, and Article 65 of the United Nations Charter.
[2] On the origin of the technical organizations of the League, see the *Procès-Verbal of the Fifth Session of the Council of the League of Nations*, Annex 51, p. 187.
[3] See, *e.g.*, *Report on the Work of the League during the War Submitted to the Assembly by the Acting Secretary-General*, p. 16. [A.6.1946.]
[4] See below, p. 33, 599–600, 609–610, 629–631.
[5] See *List of Conventions with Indication of Relevant Articles Conferring Powers on the Organs of the League of Nations*, p. 13–81. [C.100.M.100.1945.V.]
[6] See *The Committees of the League of Nations: Classified List and Essential Facts.* [C.99.M.99.1945.V.] (1945.V.2.)

"Commission" (Permanent Mandates Commission), others were "Committees" (Financial Committee of Statistical Experts), and others "Organizations" (Health Organization).

In addition, numerous conferences[7] were held under the auspices of the League of Nations to agree on common policies or procedures in the nonpolitical field or to draft general conventions. In 1931 a special procedure for conferences convoked for the purpose of drafting general international conventions was adopted by the Assembly.[8]

Nonpolitical functions were also entrusted to several "autonomous" organizations: the International Labor Organization, the International Institute of Intellectual Co-operation, the International Institute for the Unification of Private Law, the International Educational Cinematographic Institute.

Five bureaus were placed under the direction of the League in accordance with Article 24 of the Covenant: the International Bureau for Information and Enquiries Regarding Relief to Foreigners (Paris); the International Hydrographic Bureau (Monaco); the Central International Office for the Control of the Liquor Traffic in Africa (Brussels); the International Commission for Air Navigation (Paris); the International Exhibitions Bureau (Paris).[9]

It is probably correct to say that the Permanent Court of International Justice, though primarily a judicial organ, indirectly performed nonpolitical as well as political functions.

[7]On League of Nations conferences, see Norman L. Hill, *The Public International Conference: Its Function, Organization and Procedure* (Stanford University, 1929), p. 110-131, especially p. 123-131; Frederick S. Dunn, *The Practice and Procedure of International Conferences* (Baltimore, 1929), p. 30-34; and Vladimir D. Pastuhov, *A Guide to the Practice of International Conferences* (Washington, 1945), *passim*. On the League of Nations technique in editing conference documents, see *ibid.*, p. 165-166. For a chronological list of major conferences held under the auspices of the League, see *Essential Facts about the League of Nations* (10th ed., revised, Geneva, 1939), p. 325-338.
[8]*Official Journal*, Special Supplement No. 92, p. 11-12. The text of this resolution is reprinted below, p. 498 f. For a list of international conventions concluded under the auspices of the League, see *Essential Facts*, p. 339-344, and *The Treaty of Versailles and After: Annotations of the Text of the Treaty*, Dept. of State Publication 2724 (Washington, 1947), p. 107-122. See also "List of Ratifications," below, p. 278-279.
[9]On April 18, 1946, the last Assembly of the League adopted a resolution whereby the relationship to these five bureaus was severed. The resolution reads in part as follows: "1. The Assembly directs the Secretary-General to thank the international bureaux and other organisations named in this resolution for their collaboration with the League of Nations in the past, and to inform them that the relation with the League which was established in accordance with Article 24 of the Covenant must be regarded as coming to an end on the dissolution of the League, with effect from the day following the close of the present session of the Assembly... 2. The Assembly directs the Secretary-General to address a similar communication to the International Relief Union (Geneva), which, though it was not placed under the direction of the League, was brought into relation with the League under the Convention of July 12th, 1927, which created the Union." *Official Journal*, Special Supplement No. 194, p. 279; see also p. 238.

2. SPECIAL FUNCTIONS

Besides the convening of conferences and the drafting of conventions the nonpolitical activities of the League entailed such special functions as the supervision of treaties, fact-finding, and research and publication.

SUPERVISION OF TREATIES

The League served as the depository of signatures, ratifications, accessions, and denunciations of all general conventions concluded under the auspices of the League. Beginning with 1927 the Secretary-General prepared annually an official list of these conventions. The list indicated the states which became parties to these agreements by ratification or accession; the states which signed but had not yet ratified them; and, finally, the states which neither signed nor acceded, although they had taken part in the conferences at which the agreements were drawn up or had been invited to become parties thereto.[10]

By special provisions, the authority to supervise was conferred either upon the League without further specifications or on special organs of the League. In the great majority of conventions, even those of a technical nature, the Council was designated as the supervisory organ.[11] Besides the Council and the Secretary-General, the Assembly or special commissions or committees such as the Committee for Communications and Transport or the Supervisory Body, set up under the 1931 Convention for Limiting the Manufacture and Regulating the Distribution of Narcotic Drugs, were charged with the supervision of treaties.[12]

The authority of the Council to settle any difference as to interpretation was expressly recognized by several conventions or arrangements.[13] Another clause which appeared in several arrangements empowered the Council to designate trustees who themselves acted in a supervisory capacity.[14]

Perhaps the broadest regulatory and supervisory functions were

[10]For official lists of ratifications issued from 1927 to 1946, see below, p. 278 f.; on the "administrative" powers of the League in reference to these general conventions, see *List of Conventions with Indication of the Relevant Articles Conferring Powers on the Organs of the League of Nations*, p. 13. [C.100.M.100.1945.V.]

[11]See *ibid.*, p. 13–87.

[12]The general provisions of Art. 23 (d) and (e) of the Covenant were subsequently modified through special conventions so that the authority of the League to supervise was delegated to special organs of the League.

[13]See, *e.g.*, the clauses quoted in Document [C.100.M.100.1945.V.], p. 48.

[14]See the pertinent provisions of the Austrian Government Guaranteed Loan (1934–1959), *ibid.*, p. 51.

entrusted to the special organs charged with the control of the production, distribution, and manufacture of narcotic drugs.[15] They included the authority to receive annual estimates of the world requirements of dangerous drugs and national requirements, as well as recommendatory powers in case a country exceeded its internationally determined quota.

FACT-FINDING

The supervisory functions of the League were frequently related to fact-finding on an international scale, a field in which the League devised new methods of research and presentation. On the assumption that a sound policy decision should be based on an objective evaluation of the facts, the League of Nations carried on fact-finding activities in many fields. Questionnaires submitted by the League to the governments of member states, and even nonmember states, brought back periodic reports on developments in certain fields. The serial publication *Summary of Annual Reports . . . Received from Governments Relating to the Traffic in Women and Children*, first issued in 1924, was based on such a survey. Moreover numerous special enquiries were undertaken, as evidenced by the Report of the International Commission of Enquiry in Liberia,[16] the Report of the Commission of Enquiry into the Production of Opium in Persia,[17] and the Report on Enquiries into the Economic, Administrative, and Legal Situation of International Air Navigation.[18]

Among the periodicals primarily devoted to fact-finding, the *Weekly Epidemiological Record* and the *Monthly Bulletin of Statistics* deserve special attention.[19]

By approaching fact-finding on a worldwide scale and by using new methods of selecting and comparing data, a better-balanced view of many questions was attained than was possible heretofore.

Of course, there was the usual gap between information *per se* and the willingness on the part of the member governments to act on the basis of such information. But irrespective of the immediate purpose and use of the League's fact-finding activities, the information contained in its numerous reports, monographs, and periodicals is still of interest to the historian, the social scientist, and the statesman.

[15]See below, p. 178–180.
[15]See below, p. ∞.
[16]Document [C.658.M.272.1930.VI.] (1930.VI.B.6.).
[17]Document [A.7.1927.XI.] (1926.XI.10.).
[18]Document [C.339.M.139.1930.VIII.] <R.R.C.T.3.> (1930.VIII.6.).
[19]In addition to the *Monthly Bulletin of Statistics*, the following publications of the Economic Intelligence Service of the League are considered to be primarily fact-finding in character: *Statistical Yearbook, International Trade Statistics, International Trade in Certain Raw Materials and Foodstuffs*. See Martin Hill, *The Economic and Financial Organization of the League of Nations*, p. 98.

RESEARCH AND PUBLICATION

As previously indicated, "publication" constituted a considerable part of the League's activities. The records of the League reflect the structure and proceedings of the organs of the League. They contain factual information on numerous subjects which can be obtained nowhere else and include the results of research conducted on the highest scholarly level.

Two organs of the League were especially active in the field of research, the Health Organization and the Economic and Financial Organization. Their publications differ in many respects from other League publications, but they are particularly outstanding because they frequently contain substantial and original contributions to medicine, including public health, and economics.

In the health field the publications of the League on the biological standardization of vitamins, sera, insulin, and penicillin are standard works in the literal sense of the word. They appeared partly as conference reports, partly as individual documents, and partly in the *Bulletin of the Health Organisation.* Numerous other contributions to medicine and public health are also to be found in the publications of the Health Organization. An excellent classified guide to the pertinent documentation is the "Bibliography of the Technical Work of the Health Organisation of the League of Nations, 1920–1945," in Volume XI of the *Bulletin of the Health Organisation.*

By far the most extensive research and publications activity was carried on by the Economic and Financial Organization.

In the year 1938, for example, the Economic Intelligence Service published the following serial publications: *Monthly Bulletin of Statistics, Statistical Yearbook, International Trade Statistics, International Trade in Certain Raw Materials and Foodstuffs, World Production and Prices, Review of World Trade, Balances of Payments, Money and Banking, World Economic Survey, Survey of National Nutrition Policies.*

Prior to the Great Depression of 1929–1933, the economic work of the League centered on two questions: the financial reconstruction of several Central and Eastern European countries,[20] and tariff problems,[21] with special reference to the economic consequences of the peace settlement. Beginning in the early 1930's[22] the scope of economic studies was broadened considerably. The investigations covered, not

[20]See below, p. 231 f., especially *The League of Nations Reconstruction Schemes in the Inter-War Period.* [C.59.M.59.1945.II.A.]
[21]See below, p. 241 f., especially *Commercial Policy in the Inter-War Period. International Proposals and National Policies.* (1942.II.A.6.)
[22]On the new tasks and methods in the 1930's, see Martin Hill, *The Economic and Financial Organization of the League of Nations,* p. 72–94.

including fields which had been surveyed previously: business cycle; commercial arbritration; commercial propaganda; foreign buyers; pacific settlement of economic disputes between states; commercial policy and international trade, including trade controls, clearing agreements, and exchange controls; double taxation and tax evasion; monetary questions; nutrition; raw materials; statistics and statistical methods. Special studies were also published on cartels, demographic questions, industrialization and trade, housing, public finance, and tourist traffic.

Sixteen conferences dealing with economic matters were convened by the League from 1919 to 1937. The Conference on Rural Life, scheduled to meet in 1939, did not take place. The documentation prepared in connection with these conferences furnished a noteworthy cross section of the economic thought of this period.

Numerous memoranda, pamphlets, and monographs prepared by outstanding economists who were regular members of the staff of the Secretariat or were invited by the Secretariat to investigate particular subjects appeared under the imprint of the League. Some studies were prepared in co-operation with other sections of the Secretariat or with *ad hoc* experts. An outstanding example of such co-operation is the *Final Report of the Mixed Committee of the League of Nations on the Relation of Nutrition to Health, Agriculture and Economic Policy*.[23]

The so-called Princeton Mission, that is, the Economic, Financial, and Transit Department of the Secretariat which enjoyed the hospitality of the Institute for Advanced Study and of Princeton University at Princeton, New Jersey, from August, 1940, to 1946,[24] published most valuable economic studies. In addition to continuing several of the traditional serial publications of the League, among them the *World Economic Survey* and the *Statistical Yearbook*, the Mission undertook numerous studies on various aspects of economics, including studies on war economics and postwar reconstruction.

The International Labor Organization was also engaged in the drafting and supervision of international labor conventions, in fact-finding, in labor statistics, and in research and publication. Thus its activities and procedures resemble in many respects the nonpolitical activities of the League; its publications supplement those of the League, especially League publications in the economic field.[25]

[23]Document [A.13.1937.II.A.] (1937.II.A.10.).
[24]On the Princeton Mission, see Martin Hill, *The Economic and Financial Organization of the League of Nations*, p. 122–134; and *Report on the Work of the League During the War Submitted to the Assembly by the Acting Secretary-General*, p. 22–23. [A.6.1946.]
[25]For the publications of the International Labor Organization, see below, Part Five.

VI. LEAGUE OF NATIONS AND UNITED NATIONS

1. COVENANT AND CHARTER

THE COVENANT of the League of Nations and the Charter of the United Nations resemble each other in many respects. But a comparison of the text of the Charter with the text of the Covenant as such is apt to be misleading, because the Charter, which is a much more elaborate document than the Covenant, contains many rules which were characteristic of League practice, but which are not to be found in the Covenant. Thus the impact of League tradition upon the Charter can be adequately appraised only if one examines the Charter in the light of the practice of the League of Nations.

In the Covenant, for instance, there was no provision authorizing the Assembly and the Council to adopt their own rules of procedure. However, in practice, these organs agreed on rules of procedure *praeter legem*. In contrast, Articles 22 and 30 of the United Nations Charter expressly empower the General Assembly and the Security Council to adopt their own rules of procedure.[1] Although the Secretary-General of the League of Nations made annual reports[2] to the Assembly, this was not required by the Covenant. Article 98 of the United Nations Charter, however, obligates the Secretary-General of the United Nations to submit an annual report to the General Assembly on the work of the organization. In both of these cases the Charter legalizes League practice.

The staff of the League Secretariat was subject to Staff Regula-

[1]For the texts of the Rules of Procedure of the Assembly and of the Council, see below, Appendix One, Sections II and III. For the Rules of Procedure of the General Assembly and of the Security Council, see *Provisional Rules of Procedure for the General Assembly, as Amended during the First Part of the First Session*, United Nations Document A/71, September 6, 1946, and *Provisional Rules of Procedure of the Security Council, Adopted by the Security Council at Its First Meeting and Amended at Its Forty-eighth Meeting, June 24, 1946*, United Nations Document S/96,—Rev. 3. Jan. 27, 1948. (1948.I.2.).

[2]See the cumulative list of reports, below, p. 126f. See also *Report of the Secretary-General on the Work of the Organization*, United Nations Document A/65, June, 1946, and "Oral Report of the Secretary-General to the General Assembly on the Work of the Organization, July-October 1946," in *Journal of the United Nations*, No. 15 (October 26, 1946), Supplement A-A/P.V./35, p. 17-28.

tions,[3] although these were not mentioned in the Covenant. But Article 101 of the Charter provides that the staff of the United Nations shall be appointed by the Secretary-General under regulations established by the General Assembly. On the other hand, neither the Covenant nor the Charter contains an express reference to financial regulations, but when the Preparatory Commission of the United Nations convened in London in 1945 to draft supplementary rules to the Charter, it adopted "Draft Provisional Financial Regulations for the United Nations," patterned after the Financial Regulations of the League.[4]

On the whole, the principal organs of the United Nations, with the exception of the Economic and Social Council, correspond to the principal or related organs of the League. The General Assembly of the United Nations corresponds to the Assembly of the League, the Security Council of the United Nations to the Council of the League, the Trusteeship Council to the Permanent Mandates Commission, the United Nations Secretariat to the Secretariat of the League, the International Court of Justice, the principal judicial organ of the United Nations, to the Permanent Court of International Justice. Yet, despite this similarity or even identity of the structure of the United Nations, the powers and functions of the principal United Nations organs differ in many respects from the powers and functions of the corresponding League organs.[5]

These comparisons may serve to illustrate the fact that the United Nations has adopted the administrative pattern of the League in many more respects than could be surmised by simply comparing the texts of the Covenant and the Charter. To bring out these simi-

[3]Reprinted below, Appendix One, Section IV. For United Nations Staff Regulations, see *Provisional Staff Regulations*. United Nations Document A/64. p. 18–19. See also *Codification of Staff Rules*, United Nations Document A/551. May 14, 1948. 43p.

[4]See *Report of the Preparatory Commission of the United Nations*, United Nations Document PC/20, December 23, 1945, p. 111. See Appendix One, Section XII, for Regulations for the Financial Administration of the League of Nations.

[5]For comparative evaluations of the League and the United Nations, see James L. Brierly, *The Covenant and the Charter* (Cambridge, 1947); Clyde Eagleton, "Covenant of the League of Nations and Charter of the United Nations: Points of Difference," *Department of State Bulletin*, XIII (August 19, 1945), 263; Leland M. Goodrich, "From League of Nations to United Nations," *International Organization*, February, 1947, p. 3; Leland M. Goodrich and Edvard Hambro, *Charter of the United Nations: Commentary and Documents* (Boston, 1946); William E. Rappard, "The United Nations as Viewed from Geneva," *American Political Science Review*, XL (June, 1946), 545; Hans Wehberg, "Historische und grundsätzliche Betrachtungen zur Völkerbundfrage: Zugleich ein Beitrag zur Struktur und Fortbildung von Dumbarton Oaks," *Die Friedenswarte*, XLV (1945), 1–120, and "Einführung in die Satzung der Vereinten Nationen," *ibid.*, p. 329–393, especially p. 332. For a list of major publications on the League of Nations, see Hans Aufricht, *War, Peace, and Reconstruction: A Classified Bibliography* (New York, 1943), p. 13–16, and the section, "Unofficial Collections, Guides, and Major Publications Relating to League Activities," below p. 398–401.

larities of structure and procedure, documentary appendices have
been attached to the *Guide*. They include those rules and regulations
which are essential for an understanding of League administration in
action and which also served as prototypes for corresponding rules
adopted by the United Nations.

2. LEAGUE REFORM PROPOSALS AND UNITED NATIONS CHARTER

Several proposals on League reform which were not adopted by
the League have been incorporated in the Charter.

On September 30, 1938, the Assembly adopted a resolution placing
on record the independence of the Covenant from the peace treaties
of 1919–1920,[6] thus reversing President Wilson's intention of making
the Covenant an integral part of the treaties. Article 107 of the
United Nations Charter reads:

Nothing in the present Charter shall invalidate or preclude action, in relation to any state which during the Second World War has been an enemy of
any signatory to the present Charter, taken or authorized as a result of that
war by the Governments having responsibility for such action.

This article was obviously designed to "separate" the Charter from
the peace treaties, or the peace treaties from the Charter. It probably
had the effect of facilitating the ratification of the Charter, but it
may also have contributed to the delay in the conclusion of peace
treaties after World War II.[7]

In August, 1939, the "Bruce Committee" met in Paris to consider
the possible reorganization of the economic and social work of the
League. Its report, entitled *The Development of International Co-operation in Economic and Social Affairs*,[8] popularly called the Bruce Report, recommended an agency, to be both effective and representative
to supervise the economic and social work of the League and to co-
ordinate the activities of the different international administrative
agencies. The Bruce Report suggested the establishment of a "Central Committee for Economic and Social Questions," to be composed
of 24 government representatives and not more than eight co-opted
members, appointed in their personal capacities because of their special competence and authority.

The Central Committee was to assume the function which the
Council of the League had hitherto performed in economic and social

---

[6]For text of the resolution, see *Official Journal*, Special Supplement No. 183, p. 143.
[7]On the implications of Article 107 of the United Nations Charter, see *The Charter of
the United Nations. Hearings before the Committee on Foreign Relations. United States
Senate. Seventy-ninth Congress. First Session*. Washington, 1945, p. 303 and 322.
[8]Document [A.23.1939.] (General 1939.).

matters. It should publish a separate annual report to the Assembly, and the committees which heretofore had reported to the Council[9] should address their reports to the Central Committee.

The relationship of the Bruce Report to Chapters IX and X of the United Nations Charter is obvious. The Economic and Social Council under the authority of the General Assembly of the United Nations is authorized to co-ordinate the policies and activities of specialized agencies. It also operates through commissions,[10] whose terms of reference are subject to the approval of the Council. The Commissions report to the Council, [11] and the Council reports to the General Assembly.[12]

It was one aim of the Bruce Report to secure the co-operation of nonmembers in the economic and social work of the League. Membership in the Economic and Social Council of the United Nations, and its commissions and subcommissions, is confined to member states. Membership in the specialized agencies, however, is, in principle, independent of membership in the United Nations.[13]

3. TRANSFER OF NONPOLITICAL FUNCTIONS TO THE UNITED NATIONS

On February 4, 1946, the First General Assembly of the United Nations requested the Economic and Social Council "to survey the functions and activities of a non-political character which have hitherto been performed by the League of Nations in order to determine which of them should, with such modifications as are desirable, be assumed by organs of the United Nations or be entrusted to specialized agencies which have been brought into relationship with the United Nations."[14]

[9]See, *e.g.*, the Reports of the Health, Economic, Financial, and Fiscal Committees to the Council.
[10]See Art. 68 of the United Nations Charter.
[11]See, *e.g.*, *Report of the Commission on Human Rights to the Economic and Social Council*, United Nations Document E/259, February 11, 1947.
[12]*Report by the Economic and Social Council to the General Assembly, January 23–October 3, 1946*, United Nations Document A/125, October 2, 1946.
[13]See, *e.g.*, Art. II of the Constitution of the United Nations Educational, Scientific, and Cultural Organization.
[14]See United Nations Document A/28, February 4, 1946; the complete text of this resolution is reprinted below, Appendix Three, Section I. On the nonpolitical activities of the League, see also Arthur Sweetser, "The Nonpolitical Achievements of the League," *Foreign Affairs*, XIX (October, 1940), 179; "Transfer to the United Nations of Certain Nonpolitical Functions and Activities of the League of Nations, Other than Those Pursuant to International Agreements," Document A/243, in *Official Records of the Second Part of the First Session of the General Assembly. Plenary Meetings of the General Assembly. Verbatim Record. 23 October–16 December 1946*, p. 1579, and in *Resolutions Adopted by the General Assembly*, p. 78–79.

LEAGUE COMMITTEES—UNITED NATIONS COMMISSIONS

In the course of 1946 the Economic and Social Council of the United Nations established the following commissions:[15] Fiscal Commission, Narcotics Commission, Populations Commission, Social Commission, Statistical Commission, Transport and Communications Commission, Commission on Human Rights, Commission on the Status of Women, Economic and Employment Commission. These commissions are for the most part patterned after League committees.

The Fiscal Commission, under its terms of reference,[16] combines functions of the Fiscal[17] and the Financial[18] Committees of the League of Nations.

The Narcotics Commission is expressly authorized to carry out such functions entrusted to the League of Nations Advisory Committee on Traffic in Opium and Other Dangerous Drugs[19] by the international conventions on narcotic drugs as the Economic and Social Council may find necessary to assume and continue.[20]

The Populations Commission [21] corresponds to the League's Committee of Experts for the Study of Demographic Problems.[22]

The work of the Social Commission[23] is related to the work of the Advisory Commission on Social Questions.[24]

[15]For a chart on the commission and committee structure of the Economic and Social Council, see *United Nations Weekly Bulletin*, Vol. 1, No. 16 (November 18, 1946), 24–25.
[16]For terms of reference of the Fiscal Commission, see United Nations Document E/237, October 1, 1946, in E/245, October 25, 1945, p. 3–4. See also United Nations Document E/440, 29 May 1947, especially p. 5, 8, and 9.
[17]For the Fiscal Committee of the League, see *The Committees of the League of Nations*, p. 53–55. [C.99.M.99.1945.V.]
[18]For the Financial Committee, see *ibid.*, p. 37–38.
[19]See *ibid.*, p. 60–61.
[20]See *Journal of the Economic and Social Council*, First Year, No. 12 (April 10, 1946), p. 129. See also Commission on Narcotic Drugs, *Report to the Economic and Social Council on the Second Session of the Commission, Held at Lake Success, New York, from 24 July to 8 August 1947*, United Nations Document E/575, 12 September 1947, p. 4–5, and the *Protocol of December 11, 1946, Amending the Agreements, Conventions and Protocols on Narcotic Drugs Concluded at The Hague on 23 January 1912, at Geneva on 11 February 1925, 19 February 1925 and 13 July 1931, at Bangkok on 27 November 1931, and at Geneva on 26 June 1936, and Transferring to the United Nations and World Health Organization the Functions Vested in the League of Nations under These Instruments.* See also United Nations Documents (1947.XI.3.), (1947.XI.5.), (1947.XI.6.), (1947.XI.7.), and (1947.I.20.), p. 55.
[21]For the terms of reference of the Populations Commission, see United Nations Documents E/190/Rev.2., E/223, E/229, October 3, 1946, in E/245, October 25, 1946, p. 5–6, United Nations Document E/267, February 25, 1947, p. 2–3, and United Nations Document E/571, August 29, 1947, p. 6–7.
[22]See *The Committees of the League of Nations*, p. 58–59. [C.99.M.99.1945.V.]
[23]For the terms of reference of the Social Commission, see *Journal of the Economic and Social Council*, First Year, No. 29, p. 523–525, and United Nations Document E/260, February 11, 1947, p. 2–3; see *ibid.*, p. 3, for transfer of League functions to the United Nations. See also United Nations Document E/578, September 23, 1947, p. 11–12.
[24]See *The Committees of the League of Nations*, p. 65–66. [C.99.M.99.1945.V.]. See also

The Statistical Commission[25] is designed to carry on activities similar to those of the League's Committee of Statistical Experts.[26]

The Transport and Communications Commission[27] assumes functions previously entrusted to the Transport and Communications Organization of the League.[28]

In their reports to the Second Session of the Economic and Social Council, held in New York, 1946, the Statistical Commission, the Temporary Social Commission, and the Temporary Transport and Communications Commission submitted proposals to the Council regarding the assumption of functions formerly performed by the League of Nations in their respective fields. These proposals have been approved in part by resolutions of the Economic and Social Council.[29]

There was no League committee that corresponded exactly to the Commission on Human Rights as set up by the United Nations,[30] but there can be no doubt that its creation was inspired by the various proposals to establish a Permanent Minorities Commission in the League.[31] The Subcommission on Prevention of Discrimination and for Protection of Minorities,[32] aiming at universal rather than regional or bilateral safeguards, is broader in scope, but far less

---

Transfer to the United Nations of Functions and Powers Exercised by the League of Nations under the International Convention of 30 September 1921 on Traffic in Women and Children, the Convention of 11 October 1933 on Traffic in Women of Full Age, and the Convention of 12 September 1923 on Traffic in Obscene Publications, United Nations Document A/372, 2 September 1947. See also A/372, Add. 1; Economic and Social Council Resolution of 14 August 1947, "Unification of the International Agreements and Conventions for the Suppression of the Traffic in Women and Children," in United Nations Document (1947.I.20.), p. 53; see also *ibid.*, p. 45, and General Assembly Resolution 126 (II) of October 20, 1947.

[26]For the terms of reference of the Statistical Commission, see *Journal of the Economic and Social Council*, First Year, No. 29, p. 518–520, and United Nations Document E/264, February 18, 1947; for transfer of League functions, see *ibid.*, p. 8–9. See also United Nations Document E/705, February 26, 1948, especially p. 1–2; for "Draft Protocol to Amend the International Convention Relating to Economic Statistics, Signed at Geneva on 14 December 1928," see *ibid.*, p. 2–4.

[26]See *The Committees of the League of Nations*, p. 41. [C.99.M.99.1945.V.]

[27]For the terms of reference of the Transport and Communications Commission, see *Journal of the Economic and Social Council*, First Year, No. 29, p. 515–518, and United Nations Document E/270, February 24, 1942, p. 7–8.

[28]See *The Committees of the League of Nations*, p. 33–35. [C.99.M.99.1945.V.]

[29]See *The Report of the Secretary-General on the Transfer to the United Nations of Non-Political Functions and Activities of the League of Nations, Other than Those Belonging to the League under International Agreements*, United Nations Document E/177/Rev.1, October 11, 1946, and *Report by the Economic and Social Council to the General Assembly*, United Nations Document A/125, October 21, 1946, p. 90–91.

[30]For the consolidated terms of reference of the Commission on Human Rights, see United Nations Document E/248, December 5, 1946. See also Report of the Commission on Human Rights, Second Session, United Nations Document E/600, December 17, 1947.

[31]On the proposed Permanent Minorities Commission, see P. de Azcárate, *League of Nations and National Minorities* (Washington, 1945), p. 132, 188, 202–203.

[32]See United Nations Document E/259, February 11, 1947, p. 5–6.

powerful than the Minorities Committee of the Council and the other organs provided for in the League's system for the protection of minorities. The Subcommission on Freedom of Information and the Press[33] is designed to foster mutual understanding among nations and to carry on and expand the activities of the League of Nations and of the International Institute of Intellectual Co-operation in this field.

The Commission on the Status of Women corresponds to the League Committee for the Study of the Legal Status of Women, established by Assembly Resolution of September 30, 1937.[34] The United Nations Commission is a new agency, but it is guided in its work, in part at least, by the preparatory work of the League relating to the codification of international law.[35]

The Economic and Employment Commission had no counterpart in the League system, but its own work and that of its subcommissions on Employment and Economic Stability and on Economic Development will undoubtedly benefit from the study on *Economic Stability in the Post-War World*,[36] published by the League in April, 1945.

AUTONOMOUS ORGANIZATIONS AND SPECIALIZED AGENCIES

The Permanent Court of International Justice (PCIJ) and the International Labor Organization (ILO) were the two major "autonomous" organizations in the League system.

The Permanent Court of International Justice was dissolved by Assembly Resolution of April 17, 1946,[37] as of the following day. It has been replaced by the International Court of Justice (ICJ), which, according to Article 92 of the United Nations Charter, is "the principal judicial organ of the United Nations," and whose Statute forms an integral part of the Charter. Actually, "the institution has merely changed its name . . . its structure has not changed, its mission is similar and, finally, its Statute has been only slightly modified."[38]

[33]For terms of reference of the Subcommission on Freedom of Information and the Press, see *Journal of the Economic and Social Council*, First Year, No. 14 (Friday 24 May 1946), p. 167–168, and the Economic and Social Council Resolution of March 28, 1947, in United Nations Document (1947.I.14), p. 32–33. For the resolution on "International Conference on Freedom of Information and the Press," see Resolution 132 (II), adopted by the Second Session of the General Assembly on November 17, 1947. See also United Nations Document E/Conf.6/4, February 11, 1948, especially p. 10–14 on "The League of Nations and the Press."
[34]See *Report on the Work of the League during the War Submitted to the Assembly by the Acting Secretary-General*, p. 135. [A.6.1946.]
[35]See below, p. 276–277.
[36]Document [C.1.M.1.1945.II.A.].
[37]Text in *Official Journal*, Special Supplement No. 194, p. 256; reprinted below, Appendix Three.
[38]From the address prepared by M. Guerrero, last President of the Permanent Court

While, in the terms of the Charter, the Court is more closely related to the United Nations than its predecessor was, the International Labor Organization became, upon the dissolution of the League,
a truly independent organization. This change of status is clearly recognized in the new Constitution of the International Labor Organization adopted in Montreal in 1946.[39]

The International Institute of Intellectual Co-operation was dissolved as of December 31, 1946. The property rights of the League
in the Institute were transferred by the Assembly Resolution of April
18, 1946,[40] to the United Nations, which, in turn, transferred these
rights to the United Nations Educational, Scientific, and Cultural
Organization (UNESCO), in order to ensure, under the auspices of
UNESCO, the continuity of work performed hitherto by the International Institute of Intellectual Co-operation.[41]

Similarly, the functions and activities of the League's Health Organization, which temporarily had been assumed by the United
Nations, were transferred to the newly established World Health Organization (WHO) through its Interim Commission.[42]

The resolution for the dissolution of the League[43] provided that

---

of International Justice and first President of the International Court of Justice,
ibid., p. 227. For drafting of the Statute of the International Court of Justice by the
United Nations Committee of Jurists, which met in Washington from April 9 to 20,
1945, see *The International Court of Justice. Selected Documents Relating to the Drafting
of the Statute.* Department of State Publication 2491, Conference Series 84, Washington, 1946. See also International Court of Justice, Series D, *Acts and Documents Concerning the Organization of the Court*, No. 1, Second Edition—*Charter of the United
Nations, Statute and Rules of Court and Other Constitutional Documents.* May, 1947.
See also International Court of Justice, *Yearbook 1946–1947.*

[39]See "Instrument for the Amendment of the Constitution of the International Labour
Organisation," in International Labor Office, *Official Bulletin*, XXIX (November 15,
1946), 203–253.

[40]See *Official Journal*, Special Supplement No. 194, p. 279; reprinted below, Appendix
Three.

[41]See *Utilization by UNESCO of Property Rights of League of Nations in the International Institute of Intellectual Cooperation.* United Nations Document A/64.Add.1, p.
133. For the Constitution of UNESCO, see Department of State Publication 2545,
Executive Agreement Series 506; the draft agreement between UNESCO and the International Institute of Intellectual Co-operation was approved on December 6, 1946,
at the First General Conference of UNESCO; see *Journal of the General Conference of
UNESCO*, First Session, No. 17 (December 7, 1946), p. 160. For the liquidation of
the International Institute of Intellectual Co-operation, see also League of Nations,
Board of Liquidation, *Final Report*, p. 17–18. [C.5.M.5.1947.] (General.1947.1.)

[42]See *Establishment of the World Health Organization.* United Nations Document A/64.
Add.1, p. 96–97. See *ibid.*, for the dissolution of the Office International d'Hygiène
Publique. For text of the Constitution of the World Health Organization, see United
Nations Document E/155, October, 1946, p. 9–32; see also "Protocol Concerning the
Office International d'Hygiène Publique," *ibid.*, p. 45–53. See also *Report of the Activi-
ties of the Interim Commission of the World Health Organization in 1947*, United Nations
Document E/593, January 14, 1948.

[43]See *Official Journal*, Special Supplement No. 194, p. 282. The appointment of the

the High Commissioner for Refugees should remain in office until the end of 1946 or until such a time as might appear desirable to the Board of Liquidation. The Nansen Office had been in liquidation since January 1, 1939, but the liquidation was not terminated at the time of the last Assembly of the League. In place of these two agencies the United Nations agreed upon a new specialized agency, the International Refugee Organization, recognizing that "genuine refugees and displaced persons constitute an urgent problem which is international in scope and character."[44]

In 1937, a Mixed Committee, including agricultural, economic, and health experts, prepared a report on the relation of nutrition to health, agriculture, and economic policy[45] which influenced to a considerable extent the decisions of the founders of the Food and Agriculture Organization.

The International Civil Aviation Organization (ICAO)[46] is designed to combine functions previously exercised by the International Commission for Air Navigation (Paris),[47] whose Bureau had been placed under the direction of the League in accordance with Article 24 of the Covenant, and by the Committee of Air Navigation[48] of the Communications and Transit Organization of the League.

The League's activities in the field of public finance and economic reconstruction,[49] especially the several loans issued under the auspices of the League,[50] have undoubtedly influenced the decision to establish the International Bank for Reconstruction and Development,[51] which is to carry on, on a much larger scale, activities very

High Commissioner for Refugees was terminated on December 31, 1946; see League of Nations, Board of Liquidation, *Final Report*, p. 16.

[44]See Constitution of the International Refugee Organization, United Nations Document A/64.Add.1, p. 98–110. For the liquidation of the former Nansen Office, see . League of Nations, Board of Liquidation, *Final Report*, p. 19.

[45]Document [A.13.1937.II.A.]. See also the *Constitution of the Food and Agriculture Organisation of the United Nations* (Washington, 1945), and *Report on the Work of the League during the War Submitted to the Assembly by the Acting Secretary-General*, p. 40. [A.6.1946.]

[46]For the Constitution of the International Civil Aviation Organization, see "The Convention on International Civil Aviation," in International Civil Aviation Conference, *Final Act and Related Documents*, Department of State Publication 2282, Conference Series 64, p. 59–86.

[47]On the Commission, see *Official Journal*, Special Supplement No. 194, p. 238.

[48]See Art. 10 of the *Statute of the Organisation for Communications and Transit*, p. 11–12. [C.95.M.48.1938.VIII.]

[49]See *The League of Nations Reconstruction Schemes in the Inter-War Period*. Geneva, 1945. [C.59.M.59.1945.II.A.] <F.1696(1).> (1945.II.A.8.)

[50]For a list of loans issued under the auspices of the League, see *ibid.*, p. 164–171. See also Margaret G. Myers, "The League Loans," *Political Science Quarterly*, LX (December, 1945), 492–526. On the International Loans Contract Committee see *The Committees of the League of Nations*, Geneva, 1945. [C.99.M.99.1945.V.] (1945.V.2.), p. 42–43.

[51]For "Articles of Agreement of the International Bank for Reconstruction and Development," see United Nations Monetary and Financial Conference, *Final Act and*

INTRODUCTION 39

similar to those of the Financial Committee of the League. Furthermore, there is ample evidence that the authors of the Constitution
of the International Monetary Fund[52] were familiar with the League
study, *International Currency Experience: Lessons of the Inter-War
Period.*[53]

In the 1930's the League undertook elaborate studies on the pre-
requisites of sound international trade relations and the principles of
commercial policy.[54] A report published by the League in 1945
stressed the need for return to multilateral trading[55] and advocated
international machinery to prepare multilateral agreements to study
and analyze the essential factors affecting international trade, to advise and to promote trade, and to mediate trade conflicts which
might arise between states.[56] Similarly, the proposed International
Trade Organization is designed to study, regulate, and promote international trade with a view to increasing the international volume
of trade for the benefit of its members.[57]

To summarize, the effective transfer of the nonpolitical functions
of the League was a matter of more than a purely formal resolution;[58]
it presupposed the establishment of appropriate agencies (commissions, committees, or specialized agencies), a competent research
staff in the United Nations Secretariat, and, in certain instances, the
renegotiation of existing international conventions, in others, the conclusion and ratification of new conventions. An adequate division of
labor among the agencies concerned is desirable, and it is to be hoped
that the Economic and Social Council of the United Nations will be

Related Documents, Department of State Publication 2187, Conference Series 55,
Washington, 1944, p. 68–97.
[52]For "Articles of Agreement of the International Monetary Fund," see *ibid.*, p. 28–67.
[53]Document (1944.II.A.4.). See also *Report on the Work of the League during the War
Submitted to the Assembly by the Acting Secretary-General*, p. 41. [A.6.1946.]
[54]See especially *Commercial Policy in the Inter-War Period* (1942.II.A.6.), and *Commercial Policy in the Post-War World* (1945.II.A.7.); see also *The Network of World
Trade*. (1942.II.A.3.)
[55]*Commercial Policy in the Post-War World*, p. 33. (1945.II.A.7.)
[56]*Ibid.*, p. 56–66.
[57]See the *Havana Charter for an International Trade Organisation* in United Nations
Publication Sales No. 1948.II.D.4.
[58]On this point, see United Nations Document E/177/Rev.1, October 11, 1946, p. 4:
"This process of transfer and assumption of activities can, however, take place but
gradually and will not be completed for some time. In the meanwhile, the conveyance
on 1 August 1946 of the assets of the League of Nations including premises, archives,
working documents and library to the United Nations has made it possible for the
Secretariat of the United Nations to assume provisionally, and to the extent it is
called for, the work previously performed by the various branches of the League
Secretariat dealing with non-political activities. At the same time, use has been made
of the expert services of a number of individuals who had acquired in the League
Secretariat special competence in the tasks assumed by the United Nations. This
measure, together with the use of the facilities existing in Geneva for research and
other purposes, has contributed to smooth transfer of activities in the social and
economic fields."

successful in effectively co-ordinating the activities of the major international agencies. In this connection the following statement by the first Secretary-General of the United Nations, Mr. Trygve Lie, may be recalled: "This task, to make life richer for ordinary human beings everywhere, must occupy us throughout our lifetime as it will occupy those who follow us for time to come."[59]

[59] *Journal of the United Nations*, No. 15 (October 26, 1946), Supplement A—A/P.V./35, p. 28.

Part Two
THE COVENANT — TEXT AND AMENDMENTS

I. TEXT OF THE COVENANT

THE CONSTITUTION of the League of Nations was contained in the 26 articles of the "Covenant,"[1] which formed an integral part of the Treaties of Peace with Germany (signed at Versailles, June 28, 1919), with Austria (signed at St. Germain, September 10, 1919), with Bulgaria (signed at Neuilly, November 27, 1919), and with Hungary (signed at Trianon, June 4, 1920).[2] The Information Section of the Secretariat distributed numerous copies of an unofficial edition.[3]

Both the French and English texts of the Covenant are authentic, but due to the fact that the final version was based primarily on Anglo-American drafts,[4] the English text at times reflects more clearly the intention of the authors of the Covenant. For example, the English text of the Preamble reads in part: "The High Contracting Parties . . . agree to this Covenant of the League of Nations"; in the French, the term "Pacte" instead of "Covenant"[5] is used. Similarly, Article 22 of the Covenant invokes the principle that "the well-being and development of such peoples form a sacred trust of civilization," whereas the French text uses "mission" instead of "trust."

Under Article 26 amendments to the Covenant took effect "when ratified by the Members of the League whose Representatives compose the Council and by a majority of the Members of the League whose Representatives compose the Assembly." The proposed amendments to the Covenant, in contradistinction to the Covenant itself,

[1]The text of the Covenant, including amendments in force and proposed, is reprinted below, Appendix One, Section I.

[2]For the genesis of the Covenant, see David Hunter Miller, *The Drafting of the Covenant* (2 vols., New York, 1928), and Florence Wilson, *The Origins of the League Covenant: Documentary History of Its Drafting* (London, 1928).

[3]On this point, see "Report Adopted on September 29th, 1937, by the Committee of Ten Jurists" <C.S.P.24(1).>, *Official Journal*, Special Supplement No. 189, p. 93: ". . . there is not at present any authentic official edition of that instrument" (*i.e.*, the Covenant.

[4]See Miller, *The Drafting of the Covenant*, I, 127–128, and Margaret E. Burton, *The Assembly of the League of Nations* (Chicago, 1941), p. 13.

[5]On Woodrow Wilson's emphasis on the religious implications of the term "Covenant," see his Kansas City Address (September, 1919), quoted in Ray Stannard Baker, *Woodrow Wilson and World Settlement* (3 vols., New York, 1922), I, 213: "My ancestors were troublesome Scotchmen and among them were some of that famous group that were known as Covenanters. Very well, there is the Covenant of the League of Nations. I am a Covenanter."

were distributed as official League documents, and several of the amendments were published as individual documents, as well as in the *Official Journal* and/or in the *Treaty Series*.

The Covenant of the League was adopted by the Paris Peace Conference at the Plenary Session of April 28, 1919. It came into effect on January 10, 1920, with the deposit of the required ratifications of the Treaty of Versailles. The Assembly Resolution of April 18, 1946 on the dissolution of the League was presumably designed to terminate also the effectiveness of the Covenant, although no express reference to the validity of the Covenant or to its termination is made in the Resolution. Actually, the provisions on Mandates, for instance, were deemed applicable even after April 18, 1946. The League of Nations was liquidated as of August 1, 1947.

II. AMENDMENTS TO THE COVENANT

1. AMENDMENTS ADOPTED

Article Amended	Entry into Force	Title of Document	Source
4	July 29, 1926	Protocol of an Amendment to Article 4 of the Covenant. Geneva, October 5, 1921.	51 *Treaty Series*, p. 361–366. [C.L.100.1921.V.Annexe 1.]
6	August 13, 1924	Protocol of an Amendment to Article 6 of the Covenant. Geneva, October 5, 1921.	27 *Treaty Series*, p. 349–354. [C.L.100.1921.V.Annexe 3.]
12	September 26, 1924	Protocol of an Amendment to Article 12 of the Covenant. Geneva, October 5, 1921.	29 *Treaty Series*, p. 68–72. [C.L.100.1921.V.Annexe 5.]
13	September 26, 1924	Protocol of an Amendment to Article 13 of the Covenant. Geneva, October 5, 1921.	29 *Treaty Series*, p. 73–78. [C.L.100.1921.V.Annexe 6.]
15	September 26, 1924	Protocol of an Amendment to Article 15 of the Covenant. Geneva, October 5, 1921.	29 *Treaty Series*, p. 79–83. [C.L.100.1921.V.Annexe 7.]

2. AMENDMENTS PROPOSED, NOT ADOPTED

Article	Resolution Adopted	Title of Document	Source
10		Amendment to Article 10 of the Covenant Proposed by the Canadian Delegation to the Third Assembly. Replies of Albania, etc. Geneva, 1923.	[A.17.1923.V.]

Article	Resolution Adopted	Title of Document	Source
10		Amendment to Article 10 of the Covenant Proposed by the Canadian Delegation at the Third Assembly. Replies of Denmark, etc. Geneva, 1923.	[A.39.1923.V.]
10		Amendment to Article 10 of the Covenant Proposed by the Canadian Delegation at the Third Assembly. Geneva, 1923.	[A.52.1923.V.]
10		Interpretation of Article 10 of the Covenant. Report Presented by the First Committee.	[A.85.1923.V.]
16	October 4, 1921	Amendments to Article 16 of the Covenant (latter part of the first paragraph to be amended).	*Official Journal*, Special Supplement No. 6, p. 14. [C.L.100.1921.V.Annexe 8.]
16	October 4, 1921	Amendments to Article 16 of the Covenant (second paragraph to be inserted after the first amended paragraph of Article 16).	*Official Journal*, Special Supplement No. 6, p. 14. [C.L.100.1921.V.Annexe 9.]
16	October 4, 1921	Amendments to Article 16 of the Covenant (third paragraph to be inserted).	*Official Journal*, Special Supplement No. 6, p. 15. [C.L.100.1921.V.Annexe 10.]
16	October 4, 1921	Amendments to Article 16 of the Covenant (fourth paragraph to be inserted).	*Official Journal*, Special Supplement No. 6, p. 15. [C.L.100.1921.V.Annexe 11.]
16		Proposals of the British Government for the Amendment of Article 16 of the Covenant.	[A.26.1923.V.]
16		Proposals of the British Government for the Amendment of Article 16 of the Covenant. Report Presented by the First Committee, Geneva, 1923.	[A.86.1923.V.]
16	September 27, 1924	Amendments to Article 16 of the Covenant.	*Official Journal*, Special Supplement No. 21, p. 9. [A.131.1924.]

Article	Resolution Adopted	Title of Document	Source
16	September 21, 1925	Amendments to the Covenant. Protocol of an Amendment to Article 16 (second paragraph of the original text).	*Official Journal*, Special Supplement No. 32, p. 9.[1] [A.95(1).1925.V.]
16		Reports and Resolutions on the Subject of Article 16 of the Covenant. Geneva, 1927.	[A.14.1927.]
16		Questions Relating to Article 16 of the Covenant. Geneva, 1938.	[C.244.M.287.1938.VII.2.]
26	October 3, 1921	(Assembly Resolution to replace the first paragraph of Article 26 of the Covenant by a new paragraph).	*Official Journal*, Special Supplement No. 6, p. 9. [C.L.100.1921.V.Annexe 12.]
26	October 3, 1921	(Assembly Resolution adding a new paragraph after the first paragraph).	*Official Journal*, Special Supplement No. 6, p. 9. [C.L.100.1921.V.Annexe 13.]
26	October 3, 1921	(Assembly Resolution to replace the second paragraph of Article 26 by two new paragraphs).	*Official Journal*, Special Supplement No. 6, p. 9. [C.L.100.1921.V.Annexe 14.]

[1]The heading in the *Official Journal* reads: "Amendment to Article 16 of the Covenant (Paragraph 2 of the Original Text Which Becomes Paragraph 5 of the Text as Amended in 1921)."

III. LEAGUE REFORM

1. INDIVIDUAL DOCUMENTS

Proposed Amendments to the Covenant and Other Matters Referred by the Assembly to the Committee on Amendments. Geneva, 1921. 32 p.+32 p., bilingual. [21/68/47] [A.C.1.]

Arbitration, Security and Reduction of Armaments. Protocol for the Pacific Settlement of International Disputes. Geneva, 1925. 22 p. [A.25.1925.IX.]

Arbitration, Security and Reduction of Armaments. Draft Resolution Submitted by the Spanish Delegation. Geneva, 1925. 1 p.+ 1 p., bilingual. [A.113.1925.IX.]

Replies of the Special Committee of Jurists Appointed under the Council Resolution of September 28, 1923. Observations by the Governments of the States Members of the League. Geneva, 1926. 19 p. [C.212.M.72.1926.V.] (1926.V.12.)

Amendment of the Covenant of the League of Nations as a Result of the General Adhesion of the Members of the League to the Pact of Paris for the Renunciation of War. Geneva, 1929. 23 p. [C. 499.M.163.1929.V.]

Committee for the Amendment of the Covenant of the League of Nations in Order to Bring It into Harmony with the Pact of Paris (Geneva, February 25th to March 5th, 1930). Minutes. Geneva, 1930. 126 p. [C.160.M.69.1930.V.] (1930.V.10.)

Amendment of the Covenant of the League of Nations in Order to Bring It into Harmony with the Pact of Paris. Geneva, 1930. 38 p. [C.623.M.245.1930.V.]

Amendment of the Covenant of the League of Nations in Order to Bring It into Harmony with the Pact of Paris. Observations Submitted by Governments. Series No. 1. Geneva, 1931. 10 p. [A.11. 1931.V.] (1931.V.3.)

Amendment of the Covenant of the League of Nations in Order to Bring It into Harmony with the Pact of Paris. Observations Submitted by Governments. Series No. 2. Geneva, 1931. 2 p. [A. 11(a).1931.V.] (1931.V.5.)

Amendment of the Covenant of the League of Nations in Order to Bring It into Harmony with the Pact of Paris. Observations Submitted by Governments. Series No. 3. Geneva, 1931. 2 p. [A. 11(b).1931.V.] (1931.V.8.)

Amendment of the Covenant of the League of Nations in Order to Bring It into Harmony with the Pact of Paris. Report of the First Committee to the Assembly. Rapporteur: Mr. Henri Rolin. Geneva, 1931. 5 p. [A.86.1931.V.]

Application of the Principles of the Covenant. Report Submitted by the General Commission to the Assembly. Rapporteur: The Right Honourable S. M. Bruce; Australia). Geneva, 1936. 3 p. [A.83. 1936.VII.]

Report of the Special Committee Set up to Study the Application of the Principles of the Covenant. Adopted by the Committee on February 2nd, 1938. Geneva, 1938. 123 p. [A.7.1938.VII.] (1938. VII.1.)

An extremely revealing document on the nature of the League and the possibilities of League reform. Contains: Annex 1. Minutes of the Third Session of the Special Committee Set up to Study the Application of the Principles of the Covenant. Annexes 2 to 5: Question of the Universality of the League of Nations. 2. Participation of All States in the League: Report by Lord Cranborne. 3. Co-operation between the League and Non-member States: Report by Lord Cranborne. 4. Coordination of Covenants: Report by M. Carlos A. Pardo. 5. Regional or Continental Organisation of the League of Nations: Report by M. Boris Stein. Annex 6. Choice of Methods: Report by M. F. Umaña-Bernal. Annex 7. Article 10 of the Covenant: Report by M. N. Entezam. Annex 8. Article 11 of the Covenant: Report by M. Undén. Annexes 9 and 10: Article 16 of the Covenant. 9. General Obligations: Report by M. Rutgers. 10. Regional Pacts of Mutual Assistance: Report by M. J. Paul-Boncour.

Application of the Principles of the Covenant. Question of the So-called Separation of the Covenant from the Peace Treaties. Report Submitted by the Sixth Committee to the Assembly. Rapporteur: The Representative of the United Kingdom. Geneva, 1938. 3 p. [A. 78.1938.VII.]

Amendments to the Covenant. Protocol for the Amendment of the Preamble, of Articles 1, 4 and 5, and of the Annex. Geneva, 1938. 4 p., bilingual; in part double-paged. [A.79.1938.V.]

Amendments to the Covenant. Protocol for the Amendment of the Preamble, of Articles 1, 4 and 5, and of the Annex. Geneva, 1938. 10 p., bilingual; in part double-paged. [A.79(1).1938.V.]

The Development of International Co-operation in Economic and Social Affairs. Report of the Special Committee. Geneva, 1939. Annotated. 22 p. [A.23.1939.] (General 1939.)[1]

[1]See below, p. 93. For other documentary material concerning League reform, see S. Engel, "League Reform: An Analysis of Official Proposals and Discussions, 1936–1939," in Geneva Research Center, *Geneva Studies*, Vol. XI, Nos. 3–4 (1940), p. 265–270. On League reform in general, see also Hans Kelsen, "Legal Technique in International Law: A Textual Critique of the League Covenant," in Geneva Research Center, *Geneva Studies*, Vol. X, No. 6 (1939).

2. *SINGLE ISSUES OF THE* OFFICIAL JOURNAL *ON LEAGUE REFORM*

Documents Relating to the Question of the Application of the Principles of the Covenant.[2] *Official Journal*, Special Supplement No. 154. Geneva, 1936. 97 p.

> Contains: I. Circular Letter 124.1936.VII.(July 7th, 1936) Recalling the Text of the Recommendation Adopted by the Assembly on July 4th, 1936. II. Communication from Governments in Reply to Circular Letter 124.1936.VII. III. Report and Resolution Submitted by the Special Main Committee and Adopted by the Assembly on October 10th, 1936. IV. Study of the Proposals Presented and the Statements Made by the Members of the League of Nations.

Minutes of the Special Main Committee (Question of the Application of the Principles of the Covenant). *Official Journal*, Special Supplement No. 162. Geneva, 1936. 30 p.

> Includes, on p. 28–30, Annex on Application of the Principles of the Covenant of the League of Nations and Problems Connected Therewith: Report of the Special Main Committee to the Assembly.

Records of the Nineteenth Ordinary Session of the Assembly . . . Minutes of the Sixth Committee (Political Questions). *Official Journal*, Special Supplement No. 189. Geneva, 1938. 110 p.

> This issue of the *Official Journal* is primarily, although not exclusively, devoted to the question of the application of the principles of the Covenant.

[2]For a "List of Official Documents Relating to the Question of the 'Application of the Principles of the Covenant,'" covering the years 1934–1939, see S. Engel, "League Reform: An Analysis of Official Proposals and Discussions, 1936–1939," in Geneva Research Center, *Geneva Studies*, Vol. XI, Nos. 3–4 (1940), p. 265–270.

Part Three
PRINCIPAL ORGANS AND
ORGANIZATION OF THE LEAGUE

I. ASSEMBLY

1. INTRODUCTORY NOTE

UNDER Article 2 of the Covenant the Assembly,[1] in addition to the Council and the Secretariat, was one of the main organs of the League of Nations.

The Assembly had exclusive jurisdiction concerning the admission of new members (Article 1, Paragraph 2); the selection of nonpermanent members of the Council (Article 4, Paragraphs 1 and 2 *bis*); the reconsideration by members of the League of treaties which became inapplicable and the consideration of international conditions whose continuance might endanger the peace of the world (Article 19); and the approval of the budget and the allocation of the contributions of its members (Article 6, Paragraph 5).

Joint Council and Assembly action was required on any increase of the members of the Council (Article 4, Paragraph 2); on the appointment of the Secretary-General (Article 6, Paragraph 2); and for the purpose of amending the Covenant (Article 26, Paragraph 1).

A concurrent jurisdiction, authorizing either the Assembly or the Council to act, was provided for in reference to any matter within the sphere of action of the League or affecting the peace of the world (Article 3, Paragraph 3); the friendly right of each member of the League to bring to the attention of the Assembly or the Council any circumstance whatever affecting international relations which threatened to disturb international peace or the good understanding between nations upon which peace depends (Article 11, Paragraph 2); the right to request advisory opinions from the Permanent Court of International Justice (Article 14). Finally, the Council was authorized to refer any dispute under Article 15 to the Assembly (Article 15, Paragraph 9).[2]

All members of the League were represented in the Assembly (Article 3, Paragraph 1). The number of participants in Assembly meetings varied between 41 members in 1920 and 55 members in 1935.

---

[1]See Margaret E. Burton, *The Assembly of the League of Nations* (Chicago, 1941); on the development of the concept of the Assembly, see especially p. 1–60.

[2]It should be noted that Article 23 of the Covenant conferred authority upon the "League" without specifically mentioning any League agency charged with exercising such authority.

The Assembly met at least once a year in ordinary session, usually in September.[3]

Each member had one vote. Voting on substantive matters required unanimity; a majority vote was sufficient on procedural matters (Article 5, Paragraphs 1 and 2).[4] A *voeu* could also be adopted by a majority vote.[5] A party to a dispute had no vote, either in the Council (Article 15, Paragraph 6) or in the Assembly. Representatives who abstained from voting were not considered present.[6]

The resolutions[7] of the Assembly appeared in Special Supplements of the *Official Journal*.[8]

The Assembly met in plenary sessions and in committees. The Records of the first three Assembly meetings appeared as separate publications. Beginning with the Fourth Session, all proceedings of the Assembly, plenary and committee, were published in Special Supplements of the *Official Journal*.[9]

An important part of the work of the Assembly was entrusted to its committees.[10] Its six main committees[11] were: First Committee—Constitutional and Legal Questions; Second Committee—Technical Organizations; Third Committee—Reduction of Armaments; Fourth Committee—Budget and Financial Questions; Fifth Committee—General and Humanitarian Questions; Sixth Committee—Political Questions.

In addition to these committees there was the General Committee,[12] composed of the President of the Assembly, the eight vice presidents of the Assembly, the chairmen of the six[13] main committees of the Assembly, and the chairmen of the Agenda Committee, the Credentials Committee, and the Nominations Committee.

The Assembly's part in the pacific settlement of international disputes is discussed in Part Four, Section IX, "Political Questions."

[3]See Rule 1 of the Rules of Procedure which defined the term "stated intervals" of Art. 3, Par. 2 of the Covenant.

[4]On voting, see especially Cromwell A. Riches, *The Unanimity Rule and the League of Nations* (Baltimore, 1933).

[5]See Burton, *The Assembly of the League of Nations*, p. 105.

[6]On this point and also on what constituted a quorum, see Rule 19 of the Rules of Procedure.

[7]See also Rule 17 of the Rules of Procedure.

[8]See below, p. 68-69.

[9]On the duty of the Secretariat to receive, print, circulate, and translate documents, reports, and resolutions, see Rule 10 of the Rules of Procedure.

[10]On the committees, see Marcel-Henri Prévost, *Les Commissions de l'Assemblée de la Société des Nations* (Paris, 1936), and Burton, *The Assembly of the League of Nations*, p. 135-174.

[11]The names of the main committees varied slightly; see below, p. 62-68.

[12]On the General Committee, see Rules 7, 7(a), 7(b), and 24 of the Rules of Procedure; see also Howard B. Calderwood, "The General Committee and Other Auxiliary Committees of the League Assembly," *American Journal of International Law*, XXXVIII (January, 1944), 74-94.

[13]For the Seventh Committee (Various Technical Questions), see below, p. 64, footnote 53.

2. *RULES OF PROCEDURE*

"Rules of Procedure of the Assembly: Final Text," in *The Records of the First Assembly: Plenary Meetings*, Geneva, 1920, p. 236–241, bilingual.[14]

Rules of Procedure of the Assembly.[15] Geneva, 1921. 8 p.+8 p., bilingual. [C.409.M.287.1921.V.]

Rules of Procedure of the Assembly. Geneva, May, 1923. 6 p.+ 6 p., bilingual. [C.356.M.158.1923.V.]

Contains all amendments adopted by the Second and Third Assemblies and replaces any preceding edition.

Rules of Procedure of the Assembly. Geneva, 1923. 9 p.+9 p., bilingual. [C.356(1).M.158(1).1923.V.]

Edition published in October, 1923, containing the amendments adopted by the Second, Third, and Fourth Assemblies. Includes: Annex I. Recommendations as to the Arrangements for the Debates in the Assembly on the Annual Report by the Council, p. 7. Annex II. Procedure of Adoption of the Budget at Plenary Meetings of the Assembly, p. 8. Annex III. Extract from the Regulations for the Financial Administration of the League of Nations, p. 8–9.

Rules of Procedure of the Assembly. Geneva, 1929. 11 p.+11 p., bilingual. [C.615.M.192.1928.X.]

Edition published in January, 1929, containing the amendments adopted at the Second, Third, Fourth, and Ninth Ordinary Sessions of the Assembly. Includes: Annexes I–III of the 1923 edition. Annex IV. Rules Dealing with the Election of the Nine Non-Permanent Members of the Council (September 15th, 1926), p. 10–11.

Rules of Procedure of the Assembly. Geneva, 1931. 22 p.+22 p., bilingual. [C.220.M.92.1931.V.] (1931.V.2.)

Edition published in April, 1931, containing the amendments adopted at the Second, Third, Fourth, Ninth, and Eleventh Ordinary Sessions of the Assembly. Includes: Annexes I–III of the 1923 edition and Annex IV of the 1929 edition.

Rules of Procedure of the Assembly with Annexes. Geneva, 1934. 28 p.+28 p., bilingual. [C.472.M.204.1934.V.] (1934.V.5.)

Edition published in November, 1934, containing the amendments adopted at the Second, Third, Fourth, Ninth, Eleventh, Thirteenth, and Fifteenth Ordinary Sessions of the Assembly. Includes: Annexes I–III of the 1923 edition and Annex IV of the 1929 edition. Annex V. Adoption of Decisions by a Majority in Committees of the Assembly: Minority Reports, p. 26–28.

Rules of Procedure of the Assembly. Geneva, 1937. 33 p.+33 p. +11 p. Index, bilingual. [C.144.M.92.1937.] (1937.1.)

Revised edition, April, 1937. Includes: Annexes I–III of the 1923 edition, Annex IV of the 1929 edition, and Annex V of the 1934 edition. Appendix VI. Rules Con-

---

[14]See also p. 58–63, 66–85. On the Rules of Procedure of the Assembly, see Burton, *The Assembly of the League of Nations, passim.*

[15]The title page carries this statement: "The present copy of the Rules of Procedure of the Assembly contains the amendments to Rules 4, 14 and 20, adopted by the Second Assembly."

cerning the Election of the Members of the Permanent Court of International Justice, p. 29–33. Contains also the following amendment to Article 1, Paragraph 1 of the Rules of Procedure of the Assembly: "The Assembly shall meet in general session every year at the seat of the League of Nations, commencing on the Monday which falls in the period September 10th to September 16th inclusive." Since this rule was adopted on September 29, 1938, it was never put into effect.

3. RECORDS OF THE PLENARY MEETINGS[16]

The Records of the First Assembly. Plenary Meetings (Meetings Held from the 15th of November to the 18th of December 1920). Geneva, 1920. 771 p.

The Records of the Second Assembly. Plenary Meetings (Meetings Held from the 5th of September to the 5th of October 1921). Geneva, 1921. 904 p.

The Records of the Third Assembly. Plenary Meetings. Volume I. Text of the Debates (Meetings Held from September 4th to 30th 1922). Geneva, 1922. 231 p.

The Records of the Fourth Assembly. Plenary Meetings. Text of the Debates. *Official Journal*, Special Supplement No. 13, 1923. 420 p.[17]

Records of the Fifth Assembly. Text of the Debates. *Official Journal*, Special Supplement No. 23, 1924. 506 p.

Records of the Sixth Assembly. Plenary Meetings. Text of the Debates. *Official Journal*, Special Supplement No. 33, 1925. 443 p.

Records of the Special Session of the Assembly (March 1926). Plenary Meetings and Meetings of Committees. *Official Journal*, Special Supplement No. 42, 1926. 78 p.

Records of the Seventh Ordinary Session of the Assembly. Plenary Meetings. Text of the Debates. *Official Journal*, Special Supplement No. 44, 1926. 435 p.

Records of the Eighth Ordinary Session of the Assembly. Plenary Meetings. Text of the Debates. *Official Journal*, Special Supplement No. 54, 1927. 493 p.

Records of the Ninth Ordinary Session of the Assembly. Plenary Meetings. Text of the Debates. *Official Journal*, Special Supplement No. 64, 1928. 544 p.

Records of the Tenth Ordinary Session of the Assembly. Plenary Meetings. Text of the Debates. *Official Journal*, Special Supplement No. 75, 1929. 522 p.

[16]From 1920 to 1938 a *Journal* was issued during the sessions of the Assembly for the benefit of the delegates and the public. In all 19 volumes appeared: First Volume: *Journal of the First Assembly of the League of Nations*. Geneva, 1920. 324 p. Last Volume: *Journal of the Nineteenth Assembly*. Geneva, 1938. 292 p. A *List of Delegates* was also circulated in connection with Assembly meetings.

[17]Beginning with the Fourth Session, all proceedings of the Assembly, plenary and committee, were published in Special Supplements of the *Official Journal*.

Records of the Eleventh Ordinary Session of the Assembly. Plenary Meetings. Text of the Debates. *Official Journal*, Special Supplement No. 84, 1930. 608 p.

Records of the Twelfth Ordinary Session of the Assembly. Plenary Meetings. Text of the Debates. *Official Journal*, Special Supplement No. 93, 1931. 268 p.

Records of the Special Session of the Assembly Convened in Virtue of Article 15 of the Covenant at the Request of the Chinese Government. *Official Journal*, Special Supplements, 1932: No. 101, 292 p.; No. 102, 52 p.; No. 111, 192 p.; No. 112, 105 p.; No. 113, 16 p.[18]

Records of the Thirteenth Ordinary Session of the Assembly. Plenary Meetings. Text of the Debates. *Official Journal*, Special Supplement No. 104, 1932. 190 p.

Records of the Fourteenth Ordinary Session of the Assembly. Plenary Meetings. Text of the Debates. *Official Journal*, Special Supplement No. 115, 1933. 98 p.

Dispute between Bolivia and Paraguay. Appeal of the Bolivian Government under Article 15 of the Covenant. Extracts from the Records of the Fifteenth Ordinary Session of the Assembly. Special Supplement No. 124, 1934. 175 p.[19]

Records of the Fifteenth Ordinary Session of the Assembly. Plenary Meetings. Text of the Debates. *Official Journal*, Special Supplement No. 125, 1934. 106 p.

Dispute between Bolivia and Paraguay. Records of the Special Session of the Assembly Convened in Virtue of Article 15 of the Covenant and in Accordance with the Assembly of September 27th, 1934. *Official Journal*, Special Supplement No. 132, 1934. 89 p.[20]

Records of the Sixteenth Ordinary Session of the Assembly. Plenary Meetings. Text of the Debates. *Official Journal*, Special Supplement No. 138, 1935. 136 p.

Records of the Sixteenth Ordinary Session of the Assembly. Plenary Meetings (June 30th to July 4th, 1936). Text of the Debates. Part II. *Official Journal*, Special Supplement No. 151, 1936. 108 p.

Records of the Seventeenth Ordinary Session of the Assembly. Plenary Meetings. Text of the Debates. *Official Journal*, Special Supplement No. 155, 1936. 148 p.

Records of the Special Session of the Assembly Convened for the Purpose of Considering the Request of the Kingdom of Egypt for Admission to the League of Nations (May 26th–27th, 1937). *Official Journal*, Special Supplement No. 166, 1937. 47 p.

Records of the Eighteenth Ordinary Session of the Assembly. Plenary

[18]See also below, p. 319.
[19]See also below, p. 319.
[20]See also below, p. 319.

Meetings. Text of the Debates. *Official Journal*, Special Supplement No. 169, 1937. 151 p.

Records of the Nineteenth Ordinary Session of the Assembly. Plenary Meetings. Text of the Debates. *Official Journal*, Special Supplement No. 183, 1938. 155 p.

Records of the Twentieth Ordinary Session of the Assembly (December 11th–14th, 1939). Plenary Meetings. Geneva, 1940. 53 p., bilingual.

4. DOCUMENTS PERTAINING TO THE TWENTIETH (CONCLUSION) AND TWENTY-FIRST ORDINARY SESSIONS OF THE ASSEMBLY, GENEVA, APRIL 8–17, 1946

OF THE INDIVIDUAL DOCUMENTS which were issued in connection with the sessions of the Assembly held in April, 1946, only Document [A.10.1946.XII.] was placed on public sale. All 1946 Assembly documents were published in the *Records of the Twentieth (Conclusion) and Twenty-first Ordinary Sessions of the Assembly*, which is Special Supplement No. 194 of the *Official Journal*, with the exception of Document [A.9.1946.] and the *Report on the Work of the League during the War Submitted to the Assembly by the Acting Secretary-General [A.6. 1946.]*.

In this section 34 individual documents are listed, including Documents [A.1.1946.] through [A.35.1946.]. Document [A.21.1946.] does not exist.[21] Most of these documents were printed; the rest were mimeographed. The titles of several of them as reprinted in the *Official Journal*, Special Supplement No. 194 (*Records of the Twentieth (Conclusion) and Twenty-first Ordinary Sessions of the Assembly*) vary slightly from the originals.

Convocation of the Assembly. Geneva, February 4th, 1946. 2 p., mimeographed. [A.1.1946.][22]

Annotated Provisional Agenda of the Assembly Convened to Meet in Geneva on Monday, April 8th, 1946 at 11 a.m. Geneva, March 2nd, 1946. 2 p. [A.2.1946.][23]

Report of the Board of Management of the Staff Provident Fund. Geneva, September 7th, 1945. 2 p. [A.3.1946.X.]

[21]According to a communication from the League of Nations to the Library of the Carnegie Endowment for International Peace, Washington, D. C.

[22]Also in *Official Journal*, Special Supplement No. 194, p. 9.

[23]Also *ibid.*, p. 143, with the inclusion of a supplementary item under the heading "Mandate of the Acting Secretary-General," adopted by the Assembly on April 10, 1946.

Administrative Board of the Staff Pensions Fund. Tenth Report to the Assembly. Geneva, October 8th, 1945. 4 p. [A.4.1946.X.]

Supervisory Commission. General Summarised Report on Its Work during the Period of Emergency, 1940–1946. Geneva, March 14th, 1946. 13 p. [A.5.1946.X.][24]

Includes statement showing Working Capital Fund, p. 8; balances of special funds, p. 9; and statement of actual expenditure for the years 1939–1945, p. 12–13.

Report on the Work of the League during the War Submitted to the Assembly by the Acting Secretary-General. Geneva, 1945. 167 p. [A.6.1946.] (General 1945.2.)

Includes a list of League of Nations Publications, January 1st, 1940–October 31st, 1945, p. 151–167.

Actuarial Valuation of the League of Nations Staff Pensions Fund as at December 31st, 1944. Report by Dr. H. Wyss, Consulting Actuary to the Pensions Fund. Geneva, October, 1945. 8 p. [A.7.1946.X.][25]

Supervisory Commission. Report on Discussions with the Representatives of the United Nations on Questions of the Transfer of League of Nations Assets. Geneva, March 14th, 1946. 4 p. [A.8.1946.X.][26]

Annex contains: Common Plan for the Transfer of League of Nations Assets Established by the United Nations Committee and the Supervisory Commission of the League of Nations, p. 3–4.

Transfer of the Assets of the League. Note by the Acting Secretary-General. Geneva, March 14th, 1946. 4 p. [A.9.1946.]

Includes: Report of the Committee set up by the Preparatory Commission of the United Nations (United Nations Document A/18, dated January 28th, 1946).[27]

International Assistance to Refugees. Report Submitted by Sir Herbert Emerson, G.C.I.E., K.C.S.I., C.B.E., High Commissioner for Refugees. Geneva, April, 1946. 10 p. [A.10.1946.XII.] (1946.XII.B.1.)[28]

Transfer of the Assets of the League. Proposals by the Government of the Dominican Republic. Geneva, March 14th, 1946. 2 p., bilingual. [A.11.1946.][29]

Administrative Board of the Staff Pensions Fund. Eleventh Report to the Assembly. Geneva, March 14th, 1946. 2 p. [A.12.1946.X.][30]

[24] Also *ibid.*, p. 149–159.
[25] Also *ibid.*, p. 187–194.
[26] Also *ibid.*, p. 217–220, p. 273–274. See below, Appendix Three, Section II, p. 601–608.
[27] See below, Appendix Three, Section II, p. 601–608.
[28] Also in *Official Journal*, Special Supplement No. 194, p. 228–237.
[29] Also *ibid.*, p. 220.
[30] Also *ibid.*, p.185–187.

Decisions of the United Nations Concerning Certain Functions, Powers and Activities of the League. Geneva, March 20th, 1946. 4 p. [A.13.1946.][31]

Includes: United Nations Document A/28, dated February 4th, 1946.

Report of the Supervisory Commission on the Work of Its Ninety-ninth Session. Geneva, March 22nd, 1946. 7 p. [A.14.1946.X.][32]

Complaint of Certain Former Officials of the Governing Commission of the Saar Territory (MM. Danzebrink, Ritzel, Machts, Lehnert and Lauriolle). Report by the Supervisory Commission. Geneva, March 18th, 1946. 4 p. [A.15.1946.V.][33]

Administrative Tribunal: Note by the Acting Secretary-General on the Judgments Pronounced by the Administrative Tribunal on February 26th, 1946 Concerning Certain Officials Discharged in Application of the Emergency Measures Adopted by the 1939 Assembly. Geneva, March 22nd, 1946. 6 p. [A.16.1946.][34]

Mandate of the Acting Secretary-General. Geneva, March 28th, 1946. 2 p., mimeographed. [A.17.1946.][35]

Dissolution of the Permanent Court of International Justice. Geneva, March 30th, 1946. 1 p., mimeographed. [A.18.1946.V.][36]

Report of the Supervisory Commission on the Work of Its One-hundredth Session. Geneva, April 3rd, 1946. 8 p. [A.19.1946.X.][37]

Financial Situation on March 31st, 1946. Memorandum by the Acting Secretary-General. Geneva, April 3rd, 1946. 3 p. [A.20.1946. X.][38]

Includes: Statement of Current Contributions for the Twenty-eighth Financial Period (1946) as at March 31st, 1946, p.2.

Communication from the Austrian Federal Government. Geneva, April 11th, 1946. 3 p., mimeographed. [A.22.1946.][39]

Telegram from the Acting Director of the International Labour Office. Geneva, April 8th, 1946. 1 p., mimeographed. [A.23.1946.][40]

Mandate of the Acting Secretary-General. Report of the General Committee to the Assembly. Genève, le 9 avril 1946. 1 p., bilingual; mimeographed. [A.24.1946.][41]

[31]Also *ibid.*, p. 221–224.
[32]Also *ibid.*, p. 160–165.
[33]Also *ibid.*, p. 241–244.
[34]Also *ibid.*, p. 245–249.
[35]Also *ibid.*, p. 213–214.
[36]Also *ibid.*, p. 225, with the addition of the following subtitle: "Text of Report Adopted on December 18th, 1945, by the Preparatory Commission of the United Nations."
[37]Also *ibid.*, p. 166–173; see especially p. 167 on League publications.
[38]Also *ibid.*, p. 209–211.
[39]Also *ibid.*, p. 49.
[40]Also *ibid.*, p. 216.
[41]Also *ibid.*, p. 214.

Report of the Supervisory Commission on the Work of Its Hundred and First Session. Geneva, April 10th, 1946. 9 p., mimeographed. [A.25.1946.X.][42]

Attribution to the Assembly of the Responsibilities of the Council. Report by the General Committee to the Assembly. Geneva, April 11th, 1946. 1 p., mimeographed. [A.26.1946.][43]

Communication from the Italian Government to the President of the Assembly. Geneva, April 11th, 1946. 2 p., mimeographed. [A.27. 1946.][44]

Report of the Supervisory Commission on the Work of Its Hundred and Second Session. Geneva, April 12th, 1946. 3 p., mimeographed. [A.28.1946.X.][45]

Telegram from the Austrian Federal Government. Geneva, April 13th, 1946. 1 p., mimeographed. [A.29.1946.][46]

Dissolution of the Permanent Court of International Justice. Note by the Acting Secretary-General. Geneva, April 16th, 1946. 5 p., mimeographed. [A.30.1946.][47]

> Contains the text of an address prepared by M. Guerrero, President of the Permanent Court of International Justice.

Mandate of the Acting Secretary-General. Report by the General Committee to the Assembly. Geneva, April 16th, 1946. 1 p., mimeographed. [A.31.1946.]

> Resolution confirming Mr. Sean Lester as Secretary-General of the League of Nations as from September 1, 1940.[48]

Financial and Administrative Questions: General Report of the Finance Committee to the Assembly (Second Committee). Rapporteur: Madame C. A. Kluyver (Netherlands). Geneva, April 17th, 1946. 17 p. [A.32.1946.X.][49]

General Questions: Report of the First Committee to the Assembly. Rapporteur: Professor K. H. Bailey (Australia). Geneva, April 17th, 1946. 6 p. [A.33.1946.][50]

[42]Also *ibid.*, p. 174–178.
[43]Also *ibid.*, p. 212; see also p. 48, 277.
[44]Also *ibid.*, p. 48–49.
[45]Also *ibid.*, p. 179–180.
[46]Also *ibid.*, p. 215.
[47]Also *ibid.*, p. 225–227.
[48]Also *ibid.*, p. 214. See also p. 277 for a resolution, in substance identical, adopted by the Assembly on April 18, 1946; it reads in part as follows: "The Assembly, in accordance with paragraph 2 of Article 6 of the Covenant, appoints Mr. Sean Lester Secretary-General of the League of Nations as from September 1st, 1940."
[49]Also *ibid.*, p. 258–274. This document appears here in revised form as [A.32(1). 1946.X.]. See especially "Resolution for the Dissolution of the League of Nations," p. 269–272. For the Assembly Resolution approving the Report of the Finance Committee, see *ibid.*, p. 280.
[50]Also *ibid.*, p. 250–255.

Annexes A-D contain resolutions concerning the assumption by the United Nations of functions and powers hitherto exercised by the League under international agreements; the assumption of the nonpolitical activities of the League; mandates; the international bureaus and other organizations placed under the direction of the League; the International Institute of Intellectual Co-operation.

Letter from the Observers of the Austrian Federal Government. Geneva, April 17th, 1946. 1 p., mimeographed. [A.34.1946.][51]

Report and Resolution of the First Committee on the Dissolution of the Permanent Court of International Justice. Rapporteur: Professor K. H. Bailey (Australia). Geneva, April 17th, 1946. 2 p. [A.35.1946.][52]

5. MINUTES OF THE SIX MAIN COMMITTEES

FIRST COMMITTEE

"Minutes of the First Committee (Constitutional Questions)," in *The Records of the First Assembly: Meetings of the Committees*, Geneva, 1920, Volume I, p. 1-110, bilingual.

"Minutes of the First Committee (Constitutional Questions)," in *The Records of the Second Assembly: Meetings of the Committees*, Geneva, 1921, Volume I, p. 3-201, bilingual.

Minutes of the First Committee (Constitutional Question). *Records of the Third Assembly: Meetings of the Committee*. Geneva, 1922. 110 p.+2 p.

Minutes of the First Committee (Constitutional Questions). *Official Journal*, Special Supplement No. 14, 1923. 60 p.

Minutes of the First Committee (Constitutional Questions). *Official Journal*, Special Supplement No. 24, 1924. 140 p.

Minutes of the First Committee (Constitutional and Legal Questions). *Official Journal*, Special Supplement No. 34, 1925. 57 p.

Minutes of the First Committee (Constitutional and Legal Questions). *Official Journal*, Special Supplement No. 45, 1926. 54 p.

Minutes of the First Committee (Constitutional and Legal Questions). *Official Journal*, Special Supplement No. 55, 1927. 58 p.

Minutes of the First Committee (Constitutional and Legal Questions). *Official Journal*, Special Supplement No. 65, 1928. 139 p.

Minutes of the First Committee (Constitutional and Legal Questions). *Official Journal*, Special Supplement No. 76, 1929. 100 p.

Minutes of the First Committee (Constitutional and Legal Questions). *Official Journal*, Special Supplement No. 85, 1930. 169 p.

Minutes of the First Committee (Constitutional and Legal Questions). *Official Journal*, Special Supplement No. 94, 1931. 153 p.

[51]Also *ibid.*, p. 215; see also p. 277.
[52]Also *ibid.*, p. 277-278.

Minutes of the First Committee (Constitutional and Legal Questions). *Official Journal*, Special Supplement No. 105, 1932. 73 p.
Minutes of the First Committee (Constitutional and Legal Questions). *Official Journal*, Special Supplement No. 116, 1933. 48 p.
Minutes of the First Committee (Constitutional and Legal Questions). *Official Journal*, Special Supplement No. 126, 1934. 59 p.
Minutes of the First Committee (Constitutional and Legal Questions). *Official Journal*, Special Supplement No. 139, 1935. 107 p.
Minutes of the First Committee (Constitutional and Legal Questions). *Official Journal*, Special Supplement No. 156, 1936. 88 p.
Minutes of the First Committee (Constitutional and Legal Questions). *Official Journal*, Special Supplement No. 170, 1937. 56 p.
Minutes of the First Committee (Legal Questions). *Official Journal*, Special Supplement No. 184, 1938. 30 p.

SECOND COMMITTEE

"Minutes of the Second Committee (Technical Organisations)," in *The Records of the First Assembly: Meetings of the Committees*, Geneva, 1920, Volume I, p. 113–271, bilingual.
"Minutes of the Second Committee (Technical Organisations)," in *The Records of the Second Assembly: Meetings of the Committees*, Geneva, 1921, Volume I, p. 205–278, bilingual.
Minutes of the Second Committee (Technical Organisations). Geneva, 1922. 80 p.
Minutes of the Second Committee (Technical Organisations). *Official Journal*, Special Supplement No. 15, 1923. 68 p.
Minutes of the Second Committee (Technical Organisations). *Official Journal*, Special Supplement No. 25, 1924. 61 p.
Minutes of the Second Committee (Technical Organisations). *Official Journal*, Special Supplement No. 35, 1925. 104 p.
Minutes of the Second Committee (Technical Organisations). *Official Journal*, Special Supplement No. 46, 1926. 88 p.
Minutes of the Second Committee (Technical Organisations). *Official Journal*, Special Supplement No. 56, 1927. 110 p.
Minutes of the Second Committee (Technical Organisations). *Official Journal*, Special Supplement No. 66, 1928. 78 p.
Minutes of the Second Committee (Technical Organisations). *Official Journal*, Special Supplement No. 77, 1929. 121 p.
Minutes of the Second Committee (Technical Organisations). *Official Journal*, Special Supplement No. 86, 1930. 126 p.
Minutes of the Second Committee (Technical Organisations). *Official Journal*, Special Supplement No. 95, 1931. 101 p.

Minutes of the Second Committee (Technical Organisations). *Official Journal*, Special Supplement No. 106, 1932. 68 p.

Minutes of the Second Committee (Technical Organisations). *Official Journal*, Special Supplement No. 117, 1933. 52 p.

Minutes of the Second Committee (Technical Questions). *Official Journal*, Special Supplement No. 127, 1934. 60 p.

Minutes of the Second Committee (Technical Questions). *Official Journal*, Special Supplement No. 140, 1935. 89 p.

Minutes of the Second Committee (Technical Questions). *Official Journal*, Special Supplement No. 157, 1936. 112 p.

Minutes of the Second Committee (Technical Questions). *Official Journal*, Special Supplement No. 171, 1937. 134 p.

Minutes of the Second Committee (Economic, Financial and Transit Questions). *Official Journal*, Special Supplement No. 185, 1938.[53] 77 p.

THIRD COMMITTEE

"Minutes of the Third Committee (Permanent Court of International Justice)," in *Records of the First Assembly: Meetings of the Committees*, Geneva, 1920, Volume I, p. 273–617, bilingual.

"Minutes of the Third Committee (Armaments, Economic Weapon)," in *Records of the Second Assembly: Meetings of the Committees*, Geneva, 1921, Volume I, p. 279–422, bilingual.

Minutes of the Third Committee (Reduction of Armaments). Geneva, 1922. 163 p.

Minutes of the Third Committee (Reduction of Armaments). *Official Journal*, Special Supplement No. 16, 1923. 217 p.

Minutes of the Third Committee (Reduction of Armaments). *Official Journal*, Special Supplement No. 26, 1924. 239 p.

Minutes of the Third Committee (Reduction of Armaments). *Official Journal*, Special Supplement No. 36, 1925. 43 p.

Minutes of the Third Committee (Reduction of Armaments). *Official Journal*, Special Supplement No. 47, 1926. 51 p.

Minutes of the Third Committee (Reduction of Armaments). *Official Journal*, Special Supplement No. 57, 1927. 84 p.

Minutes of the Third Committee (Reduction of Armaments). *Official Journal*, Special Supplement No. 67, 1928. 123 p.

Minutes of the Third Committee (Reduction of Armaments). *Official Journal*, Special Supplement No. 78, 1929. 126 p.

Minutes of the Third Committee (Reduction of Armaments). *Official Journal*, Special Supplement No. 87, 1930. 102 p.

[53]See also *Minutes of the Seventh Committee (Various Technical Questions: Health, Opium, Intellectual Co-operation, etc.) and Minutes of Meetings of the Seventh Committee Held Jointly with Members of the Second Committee. Official Journal*, Special Supplement No. 190, 1938. 108p.

Minutes of the Third Committee (Reduction of Armaments). *Official Journal*, Special Supplement No. 96, 1931. 65 p.

Minutes of the Third Committee (Reduction of Armaments). *Official Journal*, Special Supplement No. 158, 1936.[54] 29 p.

Minutes of the Third Committee (Reduction of Armaments). *Official Journal*, Special Supplement No. 172, 1937. 20 p.

Minutes of the Third Committee (Reduction of Armaments). *Official Journal*, Special Supplement No. 186, 1938. 52 p.

FOURTH COMMITTEE

"Minutes of the Fourth Committee (Secretariat and Budget)," in *The Records of the First Assembly: Meetings of the Committees*, Geneva, 1920, Volume II, p. 3–151, bilingual.

"Minutes of Committee No. IV (Finances and Internal Questions of the League)," in *The Records of the Second Assembly: Meetings of the Committees*, Geneva, 1921, Volume II, p. 1–324, bilingual.

Minutes of the Fourth Committee (Budget and Financial Questions). Geneva, 1922. 291 p.

Minutes of the Fourth Committee (Budget and Financial Questions). *Official Journal*, Special Supplement No. 17, 1923. 312 p.

Minutes of the Fourth Committee (Budget and Financial Questions). Geneva, 1924. 334 p.

Minutes of the Fourth Committee (Budget and Financial Questions). *Official Journal*, Special Supplement No. 37, 1925. 258 p.

Minutes of the Fourth Committee (Budget and Financial Questions). *Official Journal*, Special Supplement No. 48, 1926. 260 p.

Minutes of the Fourth Committee (Budget and Financial Questions). *Official Journal*, Special Supplement No. 58, 1927. 273 p.

Minutes of the Fourth Committee (Budget and Financial Questions). *Official Journal*, Special Supplement No. 68, 1928. 198 p.

Minutes of the Fourth Committee (Budget and Financial Questions). *Official Journal*, Special Supplement No. 79, 1929. 144 p.

Minutes of the Fourth Committee (Budget and Financial Questions). *Official Journal*, Special Supplement No. 88, 1930. 434 p.

Minutes of the Fourth Committee (Budget and Financial Questions). *Official Journal*, Special Supplement No. 97, 1931. 147 p.

Minutes of the Fourth Committee (Budget and Financial Questions). *Official Journal*, Special Supplement No. 107, 1932. 260 p.

Minutes of the Fourth Committee (Budget and Financial Questions). *Official Journal*, Special Supplement No. 118, 1933. 176 p.

Minutes of the Fourth Committee (Budget and Financial Questions). *Official Journal*, Special Supplement No. 128, 1934. 84 p.

[54]The Third Committee did not meet in 1932–1935. See below, p. 697f., for documents pertaining to the Conference for the Reduction and Limitation of Armaments.

Minutes of the Fourth Committee (Budget and Financial Questions). *Official Journal*, Special Supplement No. 141, 1935. 107 p.

Minutes of the Fourth Committee (Budget and Financial Questions). *Official Journal*, Special Supplement No. 159, 1936. 100 p.

Minutes of the Fourth Committee (Financial Questions). *Official Journal*, Special Supplement No. 173, 1937. 164 p.

Minutes of the Fourth Committee (Budgetary and Administrative Questions). *Official Journal*, Special Supplement No. 187, 1938. 128 p.

FIFTH COMMITTEE

"Minutes of the Fifth Committee (Admission of New Members into the League)," in *The Records of the First Assembly: Meetings of the Committees*, Geneva, 1920, Volume II, p. 155–242, bilingual.

"Minutes of Committee No. V (Humanitarian Questions)," in *The Records of the Second Assembly: Meetings of the Committees*, Geneva, 1921, Volume II, p. 327–508, bilingual.

Minutes of the Fifth Committee (Social and General Questions). *Official Journal*, Special Supplement No. 18, 1922. 168 p.

Minutes of the Fifth Committee (Social and General Questions). 1923. 159 p.

Minutes of the Fifth Committee (General and Humanitarian Questions). *Official Journal*, Special Supplement No. 28, 1924. 118 p.

Minutes of the Fifth Committee (General and Humanitarian Questions). *Official Journal*, Special Supplement No. 38, 1925. 202 p.

Minutes of the Fifth Committee (General and Humanitarian Questions). *Official Journal*, Special Supplement No. 49, 1926. 147 p.

Minutes of the Fifth Committee (General and Humanitarian Questions). *Official Journal*, Special Supplement No. 59, 1927. 102 p.

Minutes of the Fifth Committee (General and Humanitarian Questions). *Official Journal*, Special Supplement No. 69, 1928. 108 p.

Minutes of the Fifth Committee (General and Humanitarian Questions). *Official Journal*, Special Supplement No. 80, 1929. 84 p.

Minutes of the Fifth Committee (General and Humanitarian Questions). *Official Journal*, Special Supplement No. 89, 1930. 114 p.

Minutes of the Fifth Committee (General and Humanitarian Questions). *Official Journal*, Special Supplement No. 98, 1931. 63 p.

Minutes of the Fifth Committee (General and Humanitarian Questions). *Official Journal*, Special Supplement No. 108, 1932. 57 p.

Minutes of the Fifth Committee (General and Humanitarian Questions). *Official Journal*, Special Supplement No. 119, 1933. 48 p.

Minutes of the Fifth Committee (General and Humanitarian Questions). *Official Journal*, Special Supplement No. 129, 1934. 97 p.

Minutes of the Fifth Committee (General and Humanitarian Questions). *Official Journal*, Special Supplement No. 142, 1935. 92 p.

Minutes of the Fifth Committee (General and Humanitarian Questions). *Official Journal*, Special Supplement No. 160, 1936. 72 p.

Minutes of the Fifth Committee (General and Humanitarian Questions). *Official Journal*, Special Supplement No. 174, 1937. 94 p.

Minutes of the Fifth Committee (Social Questions). *Official Journal*, Special Supplement No. 188, 1938. 59 p.

SIXTH COMMITTEE

"Minutes of the Sixth Committee (Mandates, Armaments, the Economic Weapon)," in *The Records of the First Assembly: Meetings of the Committees*, Geneva, 1920, Volume II, p. 245–397, bilingual.

"Minutes of Committee No. VI (Enquiry into Applications for Admission of States to the League: Political Questions)," in *The Records of the Second Assembly: Meetings of the Committees*, Geneva, 1921, Volume II, p. 509–604, bilingual.

Minutes of the Sixth Committee (Political Questions). Geneva, 1922. 68 p.

Minutes of the Sixth Committee (Political Questions). *Official Journal*, Special Supplement No. 19, 1923. 41 p.

Minutes of the Sixth Committee (Political Questions). *Official Journal*, Special Supplement No. 29, 1924. 25 p.

Minutes of the Sixth Committee (Political Questions). *Official Journal*, Special Supplement No. 39, 1925. 56 p.

Minutes of the Sixth Committee (Political Questions). *Official Journal*, Special Supplement No. 50, 1926. 48 p.

Minutes of the Sixth Committee (Political Questions). *Official Journal*, Special Supplement No. 60, 1927. 30 p.

Minutes of the Sixth Committee (Political Questions). *Official Journal*, Special Supplement No. 70, 1928. 46 p.

Minutes of the Sixth Committee (Political Questions). *Official Journal*, Special Supplement No. 81, 1929. 42 p.

Minutes of the Sixth Committee (Political Questions). *Official Journal*, Special Supplement No. 90, 1930. 89 p.

Minutes of the Sixth Committee (Political Questions—Questions Concerning Refugees). *Official Journal*, Special Supplement No. 99, 1931. 57 p.

Minutes of the Sixth Committee (Political Questions—Questions Concerning Refugees). *Official Journal*, Special Supplement No. 109, 1932. 77 p.

Minutes of the Sixth Committee (Political Questions). *Official Journal*, Special Supplement No. 120, 1933. 76 p.

Minutes of the Sixth Committee (Political Questions). *Official Journal*, Special Supplement No. 130, 1934. 117 p.

Minutes of the Sixth Committee (Political Questions). *Official Journal*, Special Supplement No. 143, 1935. 88 p.

Minutes of the Sixth Committee (Political Questions). *Official Journal*, Special Supplement No. 161, 1936. 75 p.

Minutes of the Sixth Committee (Political Questions). *Official Journal*, Special Supplement No. 175, 1937. 99 p.

Minutes of the Sixth Committee (Political Questions). *Official Journal*, Special Supplement No. 189, 1938. 110 p.

6. *ASSEMBLY RESOLUTIONS AND RECOMMENDATIONS*

Resolutions Adopted by the Assembly during Its First Session (November 15th to December 18th, 1920). *Official Journal*, Special Supplement, janvier 1921. 34 p.+34 p., bilingual.

Resolutions and Recommendations Adopted by the Assembly during Its Second Session (September 5th to October 5th, 1921). *Official Journal*, Special Supplement No. 6, October, 1921. 41 p.+41 p., bilingual.

Resolutions and Recommendations Adopted by the Assembly during Its Third Session (September 4th to 30th, 1922). *Official Journal*, Special Supplement No. 9, October, 1922. 40 p.+40 p., bilingual.

Resolutions and Recommendations Adopted by the Assembly during Its Fourth Session (September 3rd to 29th, 1923). *Official Journal*, Special Supplement No. 11, October, 1923. 34 p.+34 p., bilingual.

Resolutions and Recommendations Adopted by the Assembly during Its Fifth Session (September 1st to October 2nd, 1924). *Official Journal*, Special Supplement No. 21, October, 1924. 48 p.+48 p., bilingual.

Resolutions and Recommendations Adopted by the Assembly during Its Sixth Session (September 7th to 26th, 1925). *Official Journal*, Special Supplement No. 32, October, 1925. 34 p.+31 p., bilingual.

Resolutions and Recommendations Adopted by the Assembly during Its Seventh Ordinary Session (September 6th to 25th, 1926). *Official Journal*, Special Supplement No. 43, October, 1926. 30 p.+30 p., bilingual.

Resolutions and Recommendations Adopted by the Assembly during Its Eighth Session (September 5th to 27th, 1927). *Official Journal*, Special Supplement No. 53, October, 1927. 36 p.+36 p., bilingual.

Resolutions and Recommendations Adopted by the Assembly during Its Ninth Ordinary Session (September 3rd to 26th, 1928). *Official Journal*, Special Supplement No. 63, October, 1928. 71 p.+71 p., bilingual.

Resolutions and Recommendations Adopted by the Assembly during Its Tenth Ordinary Session (September 2nd to 25th, 1929). *Official*

Journal, Special Supplement No. 74, October, 1929. 45 p.+45 p., bilingual.

Resolutions and Recommendations Adopted by the Assembly during Its Eleventh Ordinary Session (September 10th to October 4th, 1930). *Official Journal*, Special Supplement No. 83, October, 1930. 52 p.+52 p., bilingual.

Resolutions and Recommendations Adopted by the Assembly during Its Twelfth Ordinary Session (September 7th to 29th, 1931). *Official Journal*, Special Supplement No. 92, October, 1931. 42 p.+ 42 p., bilingual.

Resolutions and Recommendations Adopted by the Assembly during Its Thirteenth Ordinary Session (September 26th to October 17th, 1932). *Official Journal*, Special Supplement No. 103, November, 1932. 33 p.+33 p., bilingual.

Resolutions Adopted by the Assembly during Its Fourteenth Ordinary Session (September 25th to October 11th, 1933). *Official Journal*, Special Supplement No. 114, October, 1933. 26 p.+26 p., bilingual.

Resolutions Adopted by the Assembly during Its Fifteenth Ordinary Session (September 10th to 27th, 1934. *Official Journal*, Special Supplement No. 123, October, 1934. 25 p.+25 p., bilingual.

Resolutions Adopted by the Assembly during Its Sixteenth Ordinary Session (September 9th to October 11th, 1935). *Official Journal*, Special Supplement No. 137, October, 1935. 34 p.+34 p., bilingual.

Resolutions Adopted by the Assembly during Its Seventeenth Ordinary Session (September 21st to October 10th, 1936). *Official Journal*, Special Supplement No. 153, October, 1936. 43 p.+43 p., bilingual.

Resolutions Adopted by the Assembly during Its Eighteenth Ordinary Session (September 13th to October 6th, 1937). *Official Journal*, Special Supplement No. 168, October, 1937. 36 p.+36 p., bilingual.

Resolutions Adopted by the Assembly during Its Nineteenth Ordinary Session (September 12th to 30th, 1938). *Official Journal*, Special Supplement No. 182, October, 1938. 39 p.+39 p., bilingual.

II. COUNCIL

1. INTRODUCTORY NOTE

IN ARTICLE 2 of the Covenant, the Council[1] is expressly mentioned as one of the "instrumentalities" through which League action was to be effected.

By various provisions of the Covenant exclusive jurisdiction was conferred on the Council.[2] Special functions were entrusted to the Council by numerous bilateral and multilateral treaties which enlarged the authority of the Council with respect to the parties to these treaties and which strengthened the Council at the expense of the Assembly.[3] Procedural rules and regulations concerning the principal and subsidiary organs of the League also affected the role of the Council within the League system. In short, a fair appraisal of the legal status of the Council[4] in the light of the League practice is possible only on the basis of these sources of its power, namely, the Covenant, treaties and other international understandings, Rules of Procedure of the Council, and regulations concerning other League organs.

As previously indicated, the Covenant in several instances conferred joint or concurrent jurisdiction upon the Council and the Assembly.

[1]For the first suggestion to establish a Council which should be responsible "for the real work of the League," see Lieut.-Gen. The Rt. Hon. J. C. Smuts, P.C., "The League of Nations: A Practical Suggestion," in David Hunter Miller, *The Drafting of the Covenant* (2 vols., New York, 1928), II, 23–60, especially p. 41.

[2]For joint and concurrent jurisdiction of Council and Assembly, see above, p. 53.

[3]See *List of Conventions with Indication of the Relevant Articles Conferring Powers on the Organs of the League of Nations*, Geneva, 1945, especially p. 17. [C.100.M.100. 1945.V.] (1945.V.1.)

[4]On the Council, see Otto Göppert, *Organisation und Tätigkeit des Völkerbundes* (Stuttgart, 1938); Jean Ray, *Commentaire du Pacte de la Société des Nations selon la politique et la jurisprudence des organes de la Société* (Paris, 1930); Hans Wehberg, *Die Satzung des Völkerbundes* (2d ed., Berlin, 1924); T. P. Conwell-Evans, *The League Council in Action: A Study of the Methods Employed by the Council of the League of Nations to Prevent War and to Settle International Disputes* (London, 1929); A. H. Philipse, *Le Rôle du Conseil de la Société des Nations dans le règlement pacifique des différends internationaux* (La Haye, *1929*); Felix Morley, *The Society of Nations: Its Organization and Constitutional Development* (Washington, 1932), p. 338–499; Paul Barandon, *Le Systéme Juridique de la Societe des Nations pour la prévention de la guerre* (Paris, 1933).

The character of the League as a political entity was determined to a great extent by the composition of the Council. Any historical analysis of the League's role in international political relations from 1920 to 1939 should consider the different power constellations resulting from the changing membership in the Council. The admission to and withdrawal from membership in the Council on the part of its "permanent" members is of particular significance in this connection.

The major phases in the composition of the Council are illustrated by reference to pertinent documents.[5] The number of the nonpermanent members increased from four in 1920 to eleven in 1936, whereas the number of permanent members varied between 1920 and 1939.

Under its Rules of Procedure the Council[6] met in ordinary session four times in each year; it also met in extraordinary sessions. A chronological list of the 107 ordinary and extraordinary sessions held from 1920 to 1939[7] may serve to facilitate access to the widely scattered records of the Council.

The proceedings of the first fifteen sessions of the Council appeared as separate documents. Beginning with the Sixteenth Session (January 10–14, 1922), the Council Minutes appeared in the *Official Journal*.[8]

Voting in the Council was controlled by Article 5, Paragraphs 1 and 2 of the Covenant and by Article IX of the Rules of Procedure, which added to the voting rules of the Covenant: "in counting the votes, abstentions from voting shall be disregarded." A majority of the Council members constituted a quorum.

The decisions and resolutions of the Council, unlike those of the Assembly, did not appear in Special Supplements of the *Official Journal*, but may be ascertained by consulting the indices to the Council Minutes.[9]

The Council's part in the pacific settlement of individual disputes between members of the League is discussed in Part Four, Section IX, "Political Questions."[10]

[5]See below, p. 72–73.
[6]See Art. I of the *Rules of Procedure of the Council. Adopted by the Council on May 26th, 1933*, p. 2. [C.197.M.106.1938.] (1938.3.). Reprinted below, Appendix One, Section III.
[7]See below, p. 78–85.
[8]For minutes, summary records, and communiqués on private meetings, see Art. XI of the *Rules of Procedure of the Council*.
[9]An excellent list of Council Resolutions is to be found in *Annuaire de la Société des Nations, 1920–27; préparé sous la direction de Georges Ottlik* (Genève, 1927), p. 947–963.
[10]See also the books cited in footnote 4 above.

2. COMPOSITION OF THE COUNCIL

Documents[11]

The Council of the League of Nations: Composition. Competence. Procedure. Information Section, Geneva, 1938. 141 p.

> Annexes contain: 1. Chronological Table of Council Sessions. 2. States That Have Sat as Non-permanent Members of the Council. 3. List of Those Who Have Sat on the Council. 4. Evolution and Enlargement of the Council. 5. Rules of Procedure of the Council. 6. Report of the Committee on Council Procedure. 7. Extract from the Report Presented by the First Committee to the First Ordinary Session of the Assembly. 8. Index of Matters Dealt with by the Council (1920–1937).

Permanent Members[12]

1920–1926: United Kingdom, France, Italy, Japan.

> See Article 4, Paragraph 1 of the Covenant.[13]

1926–1933: United Kingdom, France, Germany, Italy, and Japan.

> Germany became a permanent member of the Council on September 8, 1926. See Assembly Resolution of September 8, 1926, which reads in part as follows: "The Assembly approves the proposals put forward by the Council in its resolution of September 4th, 1926, regarding: (a) The nomination of Germany as a Permanent Member of the Council..." *Official Journal*, Special Supplement No. 43, p. 29. On October 19, 1933, Germany announced its intention of withdrawing from the League. See the letter from Baron Konstantin von Neurath of the German government to the Secretary-General of the League, dated October 19, 1933, in *Official Journal*, January, 1934, p. 16.[14] On March 27, 1933, Japan announced its intention of withdrawing from the League. See the telegram from the Japanese Minister of Foreign Affairs, Count Yosuga Uchida, to the Secretary-General of the League, in *Official Journal*, May, 1933, p. 657–658.[15]

[11]The following documents concerning the composition of the Council are listed here by their official numbers: [C.207.1926.]; [C.L.41(a).1926.]; [C.357.1926.]; [C.394.M.137.1926.] <C.C.C.1.>; [C.504.1926.] <C.C.C.27.>; [C.505.1926.] <C.C.C.25(1).>; [C.122.M.43.1927.]; [C.553.1933.]; [A.8.1933.V.]; [C.L.149.1935.V.]. The reports and minutes of the Committee which studied the question of the composition of the Council in 1926 were published as documents [C.299.M.139.1926.V.] (1926.V.6.) and [C.597.M.234.1926.VII.]. For additional documents see below, p. 77–78.

[12]Art. 1, Par. 3 of the Covenant provided that any member of the League could withdraw after two year's notice of its intention to do so.

[13]The Covenant had originally envisaged five permanent and four nonpermanent members. Failure of the United States to ratify the Covenant resulted at the outset in the above-listed distribution of "permanent" seats at the Council table.

[14]Document [C.605.M.282.1933.V.]. In accordance with Art. 1, Par. 3 of the Covenant, Germany ceased to be a member of the League on October 19, 1935. For pertinent documentary material, see also *Documents on International Affairs, 1934*, ed. by J. W. Wheeler-Bennett and S. Heald (London, 1935), p. 321–336.

[15]Document [C.211.M.103.1933.VII.]. See also the Imperial Rescript of the same date, in *Documents on International Affairs, 1932*, ed. by J. W. Wheeler-Bennett (London, 1933), p. 395–396. In accordance with Art. 1, Par. 3 of the Covenant, Japan ceased to be a member of the League on March 27, 1935.

1933–1934: United Kingdom, France, Italy.

1934–1937: United Kingdom, France, Italy, Union of Soviet Socialist Republics.

The Union of Soviet Socialist Republics became a permanent member of the League on September 18, 1934. See Assembly Resolution of September 18, 1934: "I. The Assembly decides to admit the Union of Soviet Socialist Republics to the League of Nations. II. The Assembly approves the proposal put forward by the Council in its resolution of September 15th, 1934, regarding the nomination of the Union of Soviet Socialist Republics as a Permanent Member of the Council." *Official Journal*, Special Supplement No. 122, p. 18. On December 11, 1937, Italy announced its intention of withdrawing from the League. See the telegram, dated December 11, 1937, from the Italian Minister of Foreign Affairs, Count Galeazzo Ciano, to the Secretary-General of the League: "In consequence of the decisions of the Grand Council of Fascism, I hereby inform you that Italy withdraws from the League of Nations on December 11th, 1937 . . ." *Official Journal*, January, 1938, p. 10.[16]

1937–1939: United Kingdom, France, Union of Soviet Socialist Republics.

On December 14, 1939, the Union of Soviet Socialist Republics was excluded from the League under Article 16, Paragraph 4 of the Covenant. For the Council Resolution of December 14, 1939, see *Official Journal*, November-December, 1939, p. 505-508, especially p. 506. For the pertinent Assembly Resolution, see *Records of the Twentieth Ordinary Assembly (December 11th-14th, 1939): Plenary Meetings*, p. 53.

1939–1946: United Kingdom and France.

On April 19, 1941, France announced its withdrawal from the League. But on April 16, 1943, General Charles de Gaulle, supported by General Henri Giraud, repudiated the Vichy declaration of withdrawal, intimating that France still considered itself a member of the League.[17]

[16]See Documents [C.572.M.407.1937.VII.] and [C.572(a).M.407(a).1937.]. See also the following Assembly Resolution in *Official Journal*, October, 1938, p. 700: "Having considered the first, second and third reports of the Supervisory Commission to the 1938 Assembly . . . the Assembly . . . (b) Decides that the shares of Paraguay, Guatemala, Honduras, Nicaragua, Italy and Salvador in the Working Capital Fund shall be refunded to them at the moment when their notice of withdrawal takes effect, provided that they have at that time fully discharged their obligations as to League contributions."

[17]On April 19, 1941, Admiral Jean François Darlan, in his capacity as Foreign Minister of France, sent the following telegram to the Secretary-General: "I have the honour to inform you that the French Government, availing itself of the right which it is entitled to exercise under Article 1, Paragraph 3, of the Covenant, has decided to withdraw from the League of Nations. The French Government reserves the right to take a decision later as to whether it will continue its participation in the International Labour Organisation and the institutions of a purely technical character connected with the League of Nations . . ." See Document [C.26.M.23.1941.], mimeographed. On April 18, 1943, General Charles de Gaulle made this statement to the League of Nations: "Referring to my public statement on October 27, 1940, as well as to the French National Committee's memorandum of February 23, 1943, and in agreement with General Giraud, I have the honour to inform you that those Frenchmen who are still at liberty to choose, cannot permit the notice that was sent to you on April 19,

Nonpermanent Members

By virtue of Article 4, Paragraph 1 of the Covenant, the number of nonpermanent members of the Council was set at four, to "be selected by the Assembly from time to time in its discretion." Belgium, Brazil, Spain, and Greece were named until the Assembly made its own selections. The number of nonpermanent members was increased to six by Assembly Resolution of September 25, 1922, which reads as follows: "The Assembly approves the decision of the Council to increase the number of Members of the League chosen by the Assembly for representation on the Council from four to six. This decision shall go into force immediately."[18] In 1926 the membership was increased to nine by virtue of Assembly Resolution of September 15, 1926.[19]

On October 2, 1933, the Assembly resolved to approve "the recommendation of the Committee for the provisional creation of one new non-permanent seat on the Council, and accordingly declares that it is desirable that for the period commencing with the election of the non-permanent Members of the Council at the Assembly Session of 1933 and ending with the election of the said non-permanent Members in the year 1936, the number of non-permanent seats on the Council should be provisionally increased from nine to ten."[20] A further increase to eleven was approved by Assembly Resolution of

1941, to become effective until the remainder of the French people, who are at present deprived of their rights, become able to express their wishes about France's position in regard to the League of Nations through legal representatives. The French National Committee has always considered that it was bound by its pledged word and that it still enjoys its privileges as a member of the League of Nations. It is with this understanding that we have kept you informed of all measures taken in the territories of the Cameroons and the Levant by virtue of, and within the bounds of, the mandate entrusted to France." Text from *Fighting France Year Book, 1944* (published by France Forever, the Fighting French Committee in the United States, New York, 1944), p. 69. See also the letter by M. Georges Bidault, Minister for Foreign Affairs of the Provisional Government of the French Republic, dated October 26, 1944, which reads in part as follows: "I would recall . . . that this Government does also not recognise the notice of withdrawal of France from the League of Nations, which was notified to Geneva on April 19th, 1941. Before the expiration of the period fixed by the notice, General de Gaulle, had, moreover, taken up position in a letter addressed to you under date of April 18th, 1943." Document [C.32.M.32.1944.XII.], mimeographed.

[18] *Official Journal*, Special Supplement No. 9, p. 14. See also Assembly Recommendation of September 29, 1922: "It is desirable that the Assembly, in electing the six nonpermanent Members of the Council, should make its choice with due consideration for the main geographical divisions of the world, the great ethnical groups, the different religious traditions, the various types of civilization and the chief sources of wealth." *Ibid.*, p. 15. For this so-called group system, which was never sanctioned by any amendment to the Covenant, see *The Council of the League of Nations*, p. 17–18.

[19] *Official Journal*, Special Supplement No. 43, p. 9–10.

[20] Assembly Resolution of October 2, 1933, *Official Journal*, Special Supplement No. 114, p. 10–11.

October 1, 1936, which reads in part as follows: "The Assembly, having considered the report of the Committee appointed to study the composition of the Council [Doc. A.9.1936.V.] approves the recommendation of the Committee for the provisional creation of two non-permanent seats on the Council, and accordingly, declares that it is desirable that, for the period commencing with the election of the non-permanent members of the Council at the Assembly's Session of 1936, and ending with the election of the said non-permanent members in the year 1939, the number of non-permanent seats should be provisionally increased to eleven."[21]

States That Have Sat as Nonpermanent Members of the Council

	Date of election	Period of office
Argentina	Oct. 2, 1933	Oct. 2, 1933–Sept. 28, 1936
Australia	Oct. 2, 1933	Oct. 2, 1933–Sept. 28, 1936
Belgium	In virtue of Art. 4, Par. 1 of the Covenant	Jan. 10–Dec. 31, 1920
	Dec. 15, 1920	Jan. 1–Dec. 31, 1921
	Oct. 5, 1921	Jan. 1–Dec. 31, 1922
	Sept. 30, 1922	Jan. 1–Dec. 31, 1923
	Sept. 29, 1923	Jan. 1–Dec. 31, 1924
	Oct. 2, 1924	Jan. 1–Dec. 31, 1925
	Sept. 26, 1925	Jan. 1–Sept. 16, 1926
	Sept. 16, 1926	Sept. 16, 1926–Sept. 15, 1927
	Sept. 28, 1937	Sept. 28, 1937–1940 election
Bolivia	Sept. 28, 1936	Sept. 28, 1936–1939 election
Brazil	In virtue of Art. 4, Par. 1 of the Covenant	Jan. 10–Dec. 31, 1920
	Dec. 15, 1920	Jan. 1–Dec. 31, 1921
	Oct. 5, 1921	Jan. 1–Dec. 31, 1922
	Sept. 30, 1922	Jan. 1–Dec. 31, 1923
	Sept. 29, 1923	Jan. 1–Dec. 31, 1924
	Oct. 2, 1924	Jan. 1–Dec. 31, 1925
	Sept. 26, 1925	Jan. 1–Sept. 16, 1926
Canada	Sept. 15, 1927	Sept. 15, 1927–Sept. 17, 1930
Chile	Sept. 16, 1926	Sept. 16, 1926–Sept. 9, 1929
	Sept. 17, 1934	Sept. 17, 1934–Sept. 20, 1937
China	Dec. 15, 1920	Jan. 1–Dec. 31, 1921
	Oct. 5, 1921	Jan. 1–Dec. 31, 1922
	Sept. 30, 1922	Jan. 1–Dec. 31, 1923
	Sept. 16, 1926	Sept. 16, 1926–Sept. 10, 1928
	Sept. 14, 1931	Sept. 14, 1931–Sept. 17, 1934
	Oct. 8, 1936	Oct. 8, 1936–1939 election
Colombia	Sept. 16, 1926	Sept. 16, 1926–Sept. 10, 1928
Cuba	Sept. 15, 1927	Sept. 15, 1927–Sept. 17, 1930
Czechoslovakia	Sept. 29, 1923	Jan. 1–Dec. 31, 1924
	Oct. 2, 1924	Jan. 1–Dec. 31, 1925
	Sept. 26, 1925	Jan. 1–Sept. 16, 1926
	Sept. 16, 1926	Sept. 16, 1926–Sept. 15, 1927
	Oct. 3, 1932	Oct. 3, 1932–Sept. 16, 1935

[21]*Official Journal*, Special Supplement No. 153, p. 10; see also p. 43.

	Date of election	Period of office
Denmark	Oct. 2, 1933	Oct. 2, 1933–Sept. 28, 1936
Ecuador	Sept. 16, 1935	Sept. 16, 1935–1938 election
Finland	Sept. 15, 1927	Sept. 15, 1927–Sept. 17, 1930
Greece	In virtue of Art. 4, Par. 1 of the Covenant	Jan. 10–Dec. 31, 1920
Guatemala	Sept. 17, 1930	Sept. 17, 1930–Oct. 2, 1933
Iran	Sept. 10, 1928	Sept. 10, 1928–Sept. 14, 1931
	Sept. 20, 1937	Sept. 20, 1927–1940 election
Irish Free State	Sept. 17, 1930	Sept. 17, 1930–Oct. 2, 1933
Latvia	Oct. 8, 1936	Oct. 8, 1936–1939 election
Mexico	Oct. 3, 1932	Oct. 3, 1932–Sept. 16, 1935
Netherlands	Sept. 16, 1926	Sept. 16, 1926–Sept. 10, 1928
New Zealand	Sept. 28, 1936	Sept. 28, 1936–1939 election
Norway	Sept. 17, 1930	Sept. 17, 1930–Oct. 2, 1933
Panama	Sept. 14, 1931	Sept. 14, 1931–Sept. 17, 1934
Peru	Sept. 9, 1929	Sept. 9, 1929–Oct. 3, 1932
	Sept. 20, 1937	Sept. 20, 1937–1940 election
Poland	Sept. 16, 1926	Sept. 16, 1926–Sept. 9, 1929
	Sept. 9, 1929	Sept. 9, 1929–Oct. 3, 1932
	Oct. 3, 1932	Oct. 3, 1932–Sept. 16, 1935
	Sept. 16, 1935	Sept. 16, 1935–1938 election
Portugal	Oct. 9, 1933	Oct. 9, 1933–Sept. 28, 1936
Roumania	Sept. 16, 1926	Sept. 16, 1926–Sept. 9, 1929
	Sept. 16, 1935	Sept. 16, 1935–1938 election
Salvador	Sept. 16, 1926	Sept. 16, 1926–Sept. 15, 1927
Spain	In virtue of Art. 4, Par. 1 of the Covenant	Jan. 10–Dec. 31, 1920
	Dec. 15, 1920	Jan. 1–Dec. 31, 1921
	Oct. 5, 1921	Jan. 1–Dec. 31, 1922
	Sept. 30, 1922	Jan. 1–Dec. 31, 1923
	Sept. 29, 1923	Jan. 1–Dec. 31, 1924
	Oct. 2, 1924	Jan. 1–Dec. 31, 1925
	Sept. 26, 1925	Jan. 1–Sept. 16, 1926
	Sept. 10, 1928	Sept. 10, 1928–Sept. 14, 1931
	Sept. 14, 1931	Sept. 14, 1931–Sept. 17, 1934
	Sept. 17, 1934	Sept. 17, 1934–Sept. 20, 1937
Sweden	Sept. 30, 1922	Jan. 1–Dec. 31, 1923
	Sept. 29, 1923	Jan. 1–Dec. 31, 1924
	Oct. 2, 1924	Jan. 1–Dec. 31, 1925
	Sept. 26, 1925	Jan. 1–Sept. 16, 1926
	Sept. 28, 1936	Sept. 28, 1936–1939 election
Turkey	Sept. 17, 1934	Sept. 17, 1934–Sept. 20, 1937
Uruguay	Sept. 30, 1922	Jan. 1–Dec. 31, 1923
	Sept. 29, 1923	Jan. 1–Dec. 31, 1924
	Oct. 2, 1924	Jan. 1–Dec. 31, 1925
	Sept. 26, 1925	Jan. 1–Sept. 16, 1926
Venezuela	Sept. 10, 1928	Sept. 10, 1928–Sept. 14, 1931
Yugoslavia	Sept. 9, 1929	Sept. 9 1929–Oct. 3, 1932

Composition of the Council, December 13, 1939–April 18, 1946

Members	Date of election
Belgium	September 28, 1937
Bolivia	December 13, 1939 (re-elected)[22]
China	December 14, 1939 (re-elected)[23]
Dominican Republic	September 21, 1938
Egypt	December 14, 1939
Finland	December 13, 1939
France	Permanently represented
Greece	September 21, 1938
Iran	September 20, 1937
Peru	September 20, 1937[24]
Union of South Africa	December 13, 1939
United Kingdom of Great Britain and Northern Ireland	Permanently represented
Yugoslavia	September 21, 1938

3. RULES OF PROCEDURE

Rules of Procedure of the Council of the League of Nations.[25] No date. 7 p., bilingual. [20/31/39A]

Resolved at the meeting of the Council in Rome on May 17, 1920.

Rules of Procedure of the Council. Adopted by the Council on May 26th, 1933.[26] Geneva, 1933. 6 p.+6 p., bilingual. [C.393.M.200. 1933.V.] (1933.V.4.)

Editions of this document published after 1935 include Document [C.393.M.200. 1933.V.Addendum], containing the principles formulated by the Council on January 11, 1935, for the guidance of its President in the application of Article I, Paragraph 5.

Rules of Procedure of the Council. Adopted by the Council on May 26th, 1933. No date. 13 p.+13 p., bilingual. [C.197.M.106.1938.] (1938.3.)[27]

[22]Bolivia was elected on September 28, 1936.
[23]China was elected on October 8, 1936.
[24]Peru's membership in the League expired in 1941 in accordance with the "Notification by the Government of Peru of Its Intention to Withdraw from the League of Nations," Document [C.117.M.71.1939.VII.], dated April 8, 1939, *Official Journal,* March-April, 1939, p. 204.
[25]Also in *Official Journal,* July-August, 1920, p. 272–274, bilingual.
[26]Also in *Official Journal,* July, 1933, p. 900–902.
[27]Reprinted below, Appendix One, Section III.

Includes: Annex I. Resolutions Concerning the Procedure of the Council Which
Have Not Been Included in the Rules of Procedure. Annex II. Report[28] of the
Committee on Council Procedure, Adopted by the Council on September 29th, 1937.

4. COUNCIL SESSIONS, INCLUDING
MINUTES OF SESSIONS

1. Paris, January 16, 1920. 1 meeting. Procès-Verbal [sic] of the
First Meeting of the Council of the League of Nations . . . 7 p.,
bilingual. [20/29/1][29]
2. London February 11 and 13, 1920. 6 meetings. Procès-Verbal
of the First Meeting of the Second Session of the Council of the
League of Nations . . . 5 p., bilingual. [20/29/2/1]. Procès-
Verbal of the Second Meeting . . . 17 p., bilingual. [20/29/3].
Procès-Verbal of the Third Meeting . . . 67 p., bilingual. [20/
29/4]. Procès-Verbal of the Fourth Meeting . . . 45 p., bilingual. [20/29/5]. Verbatim Report of the Fifth Meeting . . .
23 p., bilingual. [20/33/1]. Verbatim Report of the Sixth Meeting . . . 27 p., bilingual. [20/33/2][30]
3. Paris, March 12–13, 1920. 5 meetings. Procès-Verbal of the
Third Session of the Council of the League of Nations . . . 33 p.,
bilingual. [20/29/6][31]
4. Paris, April 9–11, 1920. 4 meetings. Procès-Verbal of the Fourth
Session . . . 57 p., bilingual. [20/29/7–10][32]
5. Rome, May 14–19, 1920. 9 meetings. Procès-Verbal of the Fifth
Session . . . 283 p., bilingual. [20/29/11][33]
6. London, June 14–16, 1920. 4 meetings. Procès-Verbal of the
Sixth Session . . . 79 p., bilingual. [20/29/12][34]
7. London, July 9–12, 1920. 6 meetings. Procès-Verbal of the Seventh Session . . . 79 p., bilingual. [20/29/13][35]
8. San Sebàstian, July 30–August 5, 1920. 10 meetings. Procès-
Verbal of the Eighth Session . . . 242 p., bilingual. [20/29/14][36]
9. Paris, September 16–20, 1920. 10 meetings. Procès-Verbal of the
Ninth Session . . . 121 p., bilingual. [20/29/15][37]

[28]This report was also published in *Official Journal*, December, 1937, p. 1167–1170,
under the official number: [C.395.1937.].
[29]See also *Official Journal*, February, 1920, p. 17–25, bilingual. Prior to 1922 the
Official Journal contained only excerpts from or abstracts of Council Minutes.
[30]See also *Official Journal*, March, 1920, p. 29–59, bilingual.
[31]See also *ibid.*, p. 60–69, bilingual.
[32]See also *Official Journal*, April-May, 1920, p. 80–87, bilingual.
[33]See also *Official Journal*, June, 1920, p. 115–190, bilingual.
[34]See also *Official Journal*, July-August, 1920, p. 213–225, bilingual.
[35]See also *ibid.*, p. 246–251, bilingual.
[36]See also *Official Journal*, September, 1920, p. 304–345, bilingual.
[37]See also *Official Journal*, October, 1920, p. 391–413, bilingual.

10. Brussels, October 20–28, 1920. 12 meetings. Procès-Verbal of the Tenth Session . . . 283 p., bilingual. [20/29/16][38]

11. Geneva, November 14–December 18, 1920. 15 meetings. Procès-Verbal of the Eleventh Session . . . 151 p.+151 p., bilingual. [20/29/17][39]

12. Paris, February 21–March 4, 1921. 18 meetings. Minutes of the Twelfth Session of the Council of the League of Nations . . . 205 p.+205 p.+1 p., bilingual.[40]

13. Geneva, June 17–28, 1921. 21 meetings. Minutes of the Thirteenth Session . . . 282 p.+282 p., bilingual.[41]

14. Geneva, August 30–October 12, 1921. 14 meetings. Minutes of the Fourteenth Session . . . First Part: August 30th–September 3rd, 1921. 75 p.+75 p., bilingual. Second Part: September 12th–October 12th, 1921. 197 p.+197 p., bilingual.[42]

Extraordinary. Geneva, August 29–October 12, 1921. 2 meetings. Minutes of the Extraordinary Session of the Council of the League of Nations Held at Geneva from August 29th to October 12th, 1921 to Consider the Question of Upper Silesia. 24 p.+24 p., bilingual.

15. Paris, November 16–19, 1921. 6 meetings. Minutes of the Fifteenth Session of the Council of the League of Nations . . . 42 p.+42 p., bilingual.[43]

Beginning in 1922 (with those of the Sixteenth Session), the Council Minutes were published in the *Official Journal.*

16. Geneva, January 10–14, 1922. 13 meetings. Minutes of the Sixteenth Session of the Council. *Official Journal*, February, 1922, p. 87–196.

17. Paris, March 24–28, 1922. 6 meetings. Minutes of the Seventeenth Session . . . *Official Journal*, May, 1922, p. 371–420.

18. Geneva, May 11–17, 1922. 12 meetings. Minutes of the Eighteenth Session . . . *Official Journal*, June, 1922, p. 513–707.

19. London, July 17–24, 1922. 13 meetings. Minutes of the Nineteenth Session . . . *Official Journal*, August, 1922, p. 781–1020.

20. Geneva, August 31 and October 4, 1922. 2 meetings. Minutes of the Twentieth Session . . . *Official Journal*, November, 1922, p. 1147–1154.

[38]See also *Official Journal*, November-December, 1920, p. 4–36, bilingual.
[39]See also *Official Journal*, January-February, 1921, p. 4–27, bilingual.
[40]See also *Official Journal*, March-April, 1921, p. 106–186, 312, bilingual.
[41]See also *Official Journal*, September, 1921, p. 640–705, bilingual.
[42]See also *Official Journal*, December, 1921, p. 1073–1180.
[43]See also *Official Journal*, December, 1921, p. 1181–1232, bilingual. The following indices have been issued in reference to the first 15 sessions of the Council: *Index to the Council 1920 (Sessions I–XI)*, 98p.; *Index to the Minutes and Sessions of the Council 1921 (Sessions XII–XV and the Extraordinary Session on the Question of Upper Silesia*, *Official Journal*, Special Supplement No. 8, July, 1922, 80p.

21. Geneva, August 31–October 4, 1922. 19 meetings. Minutes of the Twenty-first Session . . . *Official Journal*, November, 1922, p. 1155–1437.

22. Geneva, August 31–October 4, 1922. 8 meetings. Minutes of the Twenty-second Session . . . *Official Journal*, November, 1922, p. 1441–1479.

23. Paris, January 29–February 3, 1923. 14 meetings. Minutes of the Twenty-third Session . . . *Official Journal*, March, 1923, p. 193–405.

24. Geneva, April 17–23, 1923. 14 meetings. Minutes of the Twenty-fourth Session . . . *Official Journal*, June, 1923, p. 547–708.

25. Geneva, July 2–7, 1923. 13 meetings. Minutes of the Twenty-fifth Session . . . *Official Journal*, August, 1923, p. 849–1056.

26. Geneva, August 31–September 29, 1923. 24 meetings. Minutes of the Twenty-sixth Session . . . *Official Journal*, November, 1923, p. 1261–1513.

27. Paris, December 10–20, 1923. 12 meetings. Minutes of the Twenty-seventh Session . . . *Official Journal*, February, 1924, p. 319–431.

28. Geneva, March 10–15, 1924. 11 meetings. Minutes of the Twenty-eighth Session . . . *Official Journal*, April, 1924, p. 497–744.

29. Geneva, June 11–17, 1924. 7 meetings. Minutes of the Twenty-ninth Session . . . *Official Journal*, July, 1924, p. 895–1030.

30. Geneva, August 29–October 3, 1924. 20 meetings. Minutes of the Thirtieth Session . . . *Official Journal*, October, 1924, p. 1277–1642.

31. Brussels, October 27–31, 1924. 4 meetings. Minutes of the Thirty-first (Extraordinary) Session . . . *Official Journal*, November, 1924, p. 1645–1680.

32. Rome, December 8–13, 1924. 11 meetings. Minutes of the Thirty-second Session . . . *Official Journal*, February, 1925, p. 111–294.

33. Geneva, March 9–14, 1925. 12 meetings. Minutes of the Thirty-third Session . . . *Official Journal*, April, 1925, p. 429–628.

34. Geneva, June 8–11, 1925. 8 meetings. Minutes of the Thirty-fourth Session . . . *Official Journal*, July, 1925, p. 847–1026.

35. Geneva, September 2–28, 1925. 17 meetings. Minutes of the Thirty-fifth Session . . . *Official Journal*, October, 1925, p. 1299–1548.

36. Paris, October 26–30, 1925. 5 meetings. Minutes of the Thirty-sixth (Extraordinary) Session[44] . . . *Official Journal*, November, 1925, p. 1693–1720.

37. Geneva, December 7–16, 1925. 15 meetings. Minutes of the

[44]This session considered the "Appeal of the Bulgarian Government under Articles 10 and 11 of the Covenant."

Thirty-seventh Session . . . *Official Journal*, February, 1926, p. 103–366.

38. Geneva, February 12, 1926. 1 meeting. Minutes of the Council. Thirty-eighth Session (Extraordinary Meeting).[45] *Official Journal*, April, 1926, p. 497–498.

39. Geneva, March 8–18, 1926. 7 meetings. Minutes of the Council. Thirty-ninth Session. *Official Journal*, April, 1926, p. 499–642.

40. Geneva, June 7–10, 1926. 5 meetings. Minutes of the Fortieth Session of the Council . . . *Official Journal*, July, 1926, p. 849–1013.

41. Geneva, September 2–7, 1926. 5 meetings. Minutes of the Council. Forty-first Session. *Official Journal*, October, 1926, p. 1217–1398.

42. Geneva, September 16–20, 1926. 3 meetings. Minutes of the Council. Forty-second Session . . . *Official Journal*, October, 1926, p. 1399–1474.

43. Geneva, December 6–11, 1926. 6 meetings. Minutes of the Forty-third Session of the Council . . . *Official Journal*, February, 1927, p. 109–281.

44. Geneva, March 7–12, 1927. 8 meetings. Minutes of the Forty-fourth Session . . . *Official Journal*, April, 1927, p. 339–608.

45. Geneva, June 13–17, 1927. 6 meetings. Minutes of the Forty-fifth Session . . . *Official Journal*, July, 1927, p. 739–956.

46. Geneva, September 1–15, 1927. 7 meetings. Minutes of the Council. Forty-sixth Session . . . *Official Journal*, October, 1927, p. 1093–1376.

47. Geneva, September 17–28, 1927. 8 meetings. Minutes of the Council. Forty-seventh Session . . . *Official Journal*, October, 1927, p. 1377–1493.

48. Geneva, December 5–12, 1927. 8 meetings. Minutes of the Forty-eighth Session of the Council . . . *Official Journal*, February, 1928, p. 105–266.

49. Geneva, March 5–10, 1928. 10 meetings. Minutes of the Forty-ninth Session . . . *Official Journal*, April, 1928, p. 363–592.

50. Geneva, June 4–9, 1928. 9 meetings. Minutes of the Fiftieth Session . . . *Official Journal*, July, 1928, p. 849–1131.

51. Geneva, August 30–September 8, 1928. 7 meetings. Minutes of the Council. Fifty-first Session. *Official Journal*, October, 1928, p. 1427–1639.

52. Geneva, September 12–26, 1928. 6 meetings. Minutes of the Council. Fifty-second Session . . . *Official Journal*, October, 1928, p. 1641–1773.

53. Lugano, December 10–15, 1928. 7 meetings. Minutes of the

[45]The questions discussed at this session included that of convening a special session of the Assembly following the request of Germany for admission to the League.

Fifty-third Session of the Council . . . *Official Journal*, January, 1929, p. 3–256.

54. Geneva, March 4–5, 1929. 7 meetings. Minutes of the Fifty-fourth Session . . . *Official Journal*, April, 1929, p. 497–780.

55. Madrid, June 10–15, 1929. 5 meetings. Minutes of the Fifty-fifth Session . . . *Official Journal*, July, 1929, p. 969–1263.

56. Geneva, August 30–September 6, 1929. 3 meetings. Minutes of the Council. Fifty-sixth Session . . . *Official Journal*, November, 1929, p. 1441–1665.

57. Geneva, September 13–25, 1929. 3 meetings. Minutes of the Council. Fifty-seventh Session . . . *Official Journal*, November, 1929, p. 1667–1767.

58. Geneva, January 13–16, 1930. 7 meetings. Minutes of the Fifty-eighth Session of the Council . . . *Official Journal*, February, 1930, p. 55–250.

59. Geneva, May 12–15, 1930. 4 meetings. Minutes of the Fifty-ninth Session . . . *Official Journal*, June, 1930, p. 491–812.

60. Geneva, September 8–12, 1930. 3 meetings. Minutes of the Council. Sixtieth Session . . . *Official Journal*, November, 1930, p. 1289–1489.

61. Geneva, September 17–October 3, 1929. 8 meetings. Minutes of the Council. Sixty-first Session . . . *Official Journal*, November, 1930, p. 1491–1681.

62. Geneva, January 19–24, 1931. 9 meetings. Minutes of the Sixty-second Session of the Council . . . *Official Journal*, February, 1931, p. 135–534.

63. Geneva, May 18–23, 1931. 6 meetings. Minutes of the Sixty-third Session . . . *Official Journal*, July, 1931, p. 1061–1531.

64. Geneva, September 1–14, 1931. 4 meetings. Minutes of the Sixty-fourth Session . . . *Official Journal*, November, 1931, p. 2025–2237.

65. Geneva, September 19–30, October 13–24, 1931; Paris, November 16–December 10, 1931. 20 meetings. Minutes of the Sixty-fifth Session . . . *Official Journal*, December, 1931, p. 2241–2594.

66. Geneva, January 25–February 29, April 12–15, 1932. 16 meetings. Minutes of the Sixty-sixth Session . . . *Official Journal*, March, 1932. Part I:[46] p. 323–428; Part II: p. 431–911; Part III:[47] p. 915–944; Part IV: p. 1017–1095. (May, 1932.)

67. Geneva, May 9–July 15, 1932. 10 meetings. Minutes of the Sixty-seventh Session . . . *Official Journal*, July, 1932, p. 1157–1472.

68. Geneva, September 23–October 3, 1932. 4 meetings. Minutes of

[46]Subtitle: Appeal by the Chinese Government.
[47]Subtitle: Appeal by the Chinese Government.

the Sixty-eighth Session . . . *Official Journal*, November, 1932, p. 1711–1862.

69. Geneva, October 3–December 19, 1932. 26 meetings. Minutes of the Sixty-ninth Session . . . *Official Journal*, December, 1932. Part I:[48] p. 1865–1915; Part II: p. 1917–2308.

70. Geneva, January 24–February 3, 1933. 7 meetings. Minutes of the Seventieth Session . . . *Official Journal*, February, 1933, p. 175–381.

71. Geneva, February 21–March 18, 1933. 5 meetings. Minutes of the Seventy-first (Extraordinary) Session . . . *Official Journal*, April, 1933. Part I:[49] p. 489–614; Part II: p. 617–647.

72. Geneva, May 15–20, 1933. 2 meetings. Minutes of the Seventy-second (Extraordinary) Session of the Council[50] . . . *Official Journal*, June, 1933, p. 749–789.

73. Geneva, May 22–June 6, 1933. 7 meetings. Minutes of the Seventy-third Session . . . *Official Journal*, July, 1933. Part I: p. 793–935; Part II:[51] p. 939–979.

74. Geneva, July 3, 1933. 2 meetings. Minutes of the Council. Seventy-fourth (Extraordinary) Session . . . *Official Journal*, September, 1933. Part I: p. 1055–1065; Part II:[52] p. 1069–1079.

75. Geneva, August 3, 1933. 1 meeting. Minutes of the Council. Seventy-fifth (Extraordinary) Session[53] . . . *Official Journal*, September, 1933, p. 1081–1099.

76. Geneva, September 22–29, 1933. 4 meetings. Minutes of the Seventy-sixth Session of the Council . . . *Official Journal*, November, 1933. Part I: p. 1297–1545; Part II:[54] p. 1549–1554.

77. Geneva, October 4–26, 1933. 6 meetings. Minutes of the Seventy-seventh Session . . . *Official Journal*, November, 1933. Part I:[55] p. 1555–1593; Part II: p. 1597–1841.

78. Geneva, January 15–20, 1934. 5 meetings. Minutes of the Seventy-eighth Session . . . *Official Journal*, February, 1934. Part I: p. 97–236; Part II:[56] p. 239–271.

79. Geneva, May 14–19, 1934. 5 meetings. Minutes of the Seventy-ninth Session . . . *Official Journal*. Part I: June, 1934, p. 489–632; Part II: July, 1934, p. 747–766; Part III: July, 1934, p. 871–949.[57]

[48]Subtitle: Appeal of the Chinese Government.
[49]Subtitle: Dispute between Colombia and Peru.
[50]Subtitle: Dispute between Bolivia and Paraguay.
[51]Subtitle: Dispute between Colombia and Peru.
[52]Subtitle: Dispute between Bolivia and Paraguay.
[53]Subtitle: Dispute between Bolivia and Paraguay.
[54]Subtitle: Dispute between Bolivia and Paraguay.
[55]Subtitle: Dispute between Bolivia and Paraguay.
[56]Subtitle: Dispute between Bolivia and Paraguay.
[57]Subtitle: Dispute between Colombia and Peru.

80. Geneva, May 30–June 7, 1934. 6 meetings. Minutes of the Eightieth (Extraordinary) Session of the Council . . . *Official Journal.* Part I: June, 1934, p. 635–739; Part II: July, 1934, p. 767–867.[58]

81. Geneva, September 7–15, 1934. 3 meetings. Minutes of the Eighty-first Session . . . *Official Journal,* November, 1934. Part I: p. 1373–1423; Part II: p. 1529–1532.

82. Geneva, September 19–28, 1934. 5 meetings. Minutes of the Eighty-second Session . . . *Official Journal,* November, 1934. Part I: p. 1424–1521; Part II: p. 1533–1611.[59]

83. Geneva, December 5–11, 1934. 7 meetings. Minutes of the Eighty-third (Extraordinary) Session . . . *Official Journal,* December, 1934, p. 1689–1842.

84. Geneva, January 11–21, 1935. 9 meetings. Minutes of the Eighty-fourth Session . . . *Official Journal,* February, 1935, p. 83–435.

85. Geneva, April 15–17, 1935. 4 meetings. Minutes of the Eighty-fifth (Extraordinary) Session . . . *Official Journal,* May, 1935, p. 543–583.

86. Geneva, May 20–25, 1935. 6 meetings. Minutes of the Eighty-sixth Session . . . *Official Journal,* June, 1935, p. 587–886.

87. Geneva, July 31–August 3, 1935. 2 meetings. Minutes of the Eighty-seventh (Extraordinary) Session . . . *Official Journal,* August, 1935, p. 961–976.

88. Geneva, September 4–13. 5 meetings. Minutes of the Eighty-eighth Session . . . *Official Journal,* November, 1935, p. 1131–1172.

89. Geneva, September 17–October 7, December 18–19, 1935. 10 meetings. Minutes of the Eighty-ninth Session . . . *Official Journal.* Part I: November, 1935, p. 1173–1632; Part II: January, 1936, p. 3–47.

90. Geneva, January 20–24, 1936. 6 meetings. Minutes of the Ninetieth Session . . . *Official Journal,* February, 1936, p. 51–267.

91. London, March 14–24, 1936; Geneva, April 20, 1936. 11 meetings. Minutes of the Ninety-first (Extraordinary) Session . . . *Official Journal,* April, 1936. Part I: p. 309–351; Part II: p. 355–488.

92. Geneva, May 11–13, June 26–July 4, 1936. 5 meetings. Minutes of the Ninety-second Session . . . *Official Journal.* Part I: June, 1936, p. 529–743; Part II: July, 1936, p. 747–903.

93. Geneva, September 18–26, 1936. 4 meetings. Minutes of the Ninety-third Session . . . *Official Journal,* November, 1936, p. 1133–1184.

[58] Subtitle: Dispute between Bolivia and Paraguay.
[59] Subtitle: Dispute between Bolivia and Paraguay.

94. Geneva, October 2–10, 1936. 4 meetings. Minutes of the Ninety-fourth Session . . . *Official Journal*, November, 1936, p. 1185–1396.

95. Geneva, December 10–16, 1936. 7 meetings. Minutes of the Ninety-fifth (Extraordinary) Session . . . *Official Journal*, January, 1937, p. 3–55.

96. Geneva, January 21–27, 1937. 5 meetings. Minutes of the Ninety-sixth Session . . . *Official Journal*, February, 1937, p. 59–248.

97. Geneva, May 24–29, 1937. 6 meetings. Minutes of the Ninety-seventh Session . . . *Official Journal*, May–June, 1937, p. 281–589.

98. Geneva, September 10–16, 1937. 3 meetings. Minutes of the Ninety-eighth Session . . . *Official Journal*, December, 1937, p. 883–919.

99. Geneva, September 29–October 5, 1937. 3 meetings. Minutes of the Ninety-ninth Session . . . *Official Journal*, December, 1937, p. 921–1324.

100. Geneva, January 26–February 2, 1938. 6 meetings. Minutes of the One Hundredth Session . . . *Official Journal*, February, 1938, p. 73–227.

101. Geneva, May 9–14, 1938. 8 meetings. Minutes of the Hundred and First Session . . . *Official Journal*, May–June, 1938, p. 297–601.

102. Geneva, September 9–19, 1938. 4 meetings. Minutes of the Hundred and Second Session . . . *Official Journal*, November, 1938, p. 829–865.

103. Geneva, September 26–30, 1938. 2 meetings. Minutes of the Hundred and Third Session . . . *Official Journal*, November, 1938, p. 867–1115.

104. Geneva, January 16–20, 1939. 5 meetings. Minutes of the Hundred and Fourth Session . . . *Official Journal*, February, 1939, p. 49–192.

105. Geneva, May 22–27. 5 meetings. Minutes of the Hundred and Fifth Session . . . *Official Journal*, May–June, 1939, p. 241–332.

106. Geneva, December 9, 1939. 2 meetings. Minutes of the Hundred and Sixth Session . . . *Official Journal*, November–December, 1939, p. 493–497.

107. Geneva, December, 14, 1939. 2 meetings. Minutes of the Hundred and Seventh Session . . . *Official Journal*, November–December, p. 499–542.

III. THE SECRETARY-GENERAL
AND HIS STAFF

1. INTRODUCTORY NOTE

THE COVENANT, in Article 6, referred to the Secretariat of the League of Nations in very general terms. In the course of time the Secretariat developed a unique type of international administrative service and performed its multifarious functions through its General and Special Sections.

For the purpose of bibliographical identification it is expedient to distinguish 13 sections which correspond to the Roman numerals of the official numbers and of the sales numbers of League documents. They are as follows:

I.A.—Administrative Commissions (Saar Basin, Free City of Danzig)
I.B.—Protection of Minorities
II.—Economic and Financial Section[1]
III.—Health
IV.—Social Questions (Traffic in Women and Children, Child Welfare, Refugees, Suppression of Obscene Publications)
V.—Legal Section (Legal Adviser to the Secretariat, Codification of International Law)
VI.A.—Mandates
VI.B.—Slavery
VII.—Political Section
VIII.—Communications and Transit
IX.—Disarmament
X.—Financial Administration of the League
XI.—Traffic in Opium and Other Dangerous Drugs
XII.A.—Intellectual Co-operation
XII.B.—International Bureaus
XIII.—Refugees[2]

According to another, more systematic, approach, the sections of the Secretariat may be classified under two categories: the General and the Special Sections.[3] The Central, the Political (VII.), the Legal (V.), and the Information Sections were the principal General Sec-

[1]In 1931 this was divided into two sections, the Financial Section and Economic Intelligence Service, and the Economic Relations Section. Accordingly, from 1931 on, the symbols II.A. and II.B. were used.
[2]After 1933 no documents were issued bearing the Roman numeral XIII, but some libraries bind in with XIII material on refugees which is actually numbered XII.B. See below, p. 190-191.
[3]See Egon F. Ranshofen-Wertheimer, *The International Secretariat* (Washington, 1945), p. 90f.

tions. The Library and the Treasury, serving the League as a whole, were also considered General Sections.[4]

The personnel of the Secretariat included 121 officials in 1919, 707 in 1931 (maximum), 94 in 1942, and 99 in April, 1946.[5] In 1938, 50 nationalities were represented on the staff.

The Secretary-General was the head of the administrative services of the League. By virtue of the Covenant or special rules and agreements the Secretary-General also performed some political or quasi-political functions.

During the 26 years of its existence the League was under the direction of only three Secretaries-General. Sir James Eric Drummond[6] (United Kingdom) served from the inception of the League until his resignation in June, 1933, when he was succeeded by M. Joseph Avenol (France). Avenol resigned in 1940.[7] On August 31, 1940, Mr. Sean Lester (Ireland), who since 1937 had served as Deputy Secretary-General, assumed the office of Acting Secretary-General.[8] By Assembly Resolution of April 16, 1946, in accordance with Article 6, Paragraph 2 of the Covenant, Lester was confirmed as Secretary-General of the League as from September 1, 1940.[9]

In addition to the Secretary-General there were a varying number of Deputy Secretaries-General, Under Secretaries-General, and other officers.[10] In 1938 there were one Deputy Secretary-General; one Under Secretary-General in charge of the Political Section; eight Directors in charge of the following sections: Information Section, Minorities Questions Section, Financial Section and Economic Intelligence Service, Economic Relations Section, Health Section, Mandates Section, Disarmaments Section, Opium Traffic and Social Questions Section; one Acting Director (Communications and Transit Section); one Legal Adviser (Legal Section); one Treasurer; one Librarian; one Chief of Section (Central Section).[11]

---

[4] *Ibid.*

[5] See *Budget for the Twenty-eighth Financial Period (1946): General Budget of the League and Part I—Secretariat.* Geneva, November 20th, 1945, p. 9. [C.102.M.102.1945.X.]

[6] Art. 6, Par. 2 of the Covenant reads: "The first Secretary-General shall be the person named in the Annex; thereafter the Secretary-General shall be appointed by the Council with the approval of the majority of the Assembly." M. Joseph Avenol was the only Secretary-General appointed by the Council with the approval of the Assembly in accordance with Art. 6, Par. 2.

[7] The following documents, though at times mutually contradictory, bear upon M. Avenol's resignation: [C.121.M.111.1940.], [C.127.M.116.1940.], [C.131.M.120.1940.], [C.134.M.123.1940.]. See also *Report of the Supervisory Commission for the Year 1940*, p. 6. [C.152.M.139.1940.X.]. For comment on M. Avenol's resignation, see Ranshofen-Wertheimer, *The International Secretariat*, p. 378–381.

[8] On the sequence of events after the resignation of M. Avenol, see especially Document [A.17.1946.], *Official Journal*, Special Supplement No. 194, p. 213–214.

[9] See Document [A.31.1946.], *Official Journal*, Special Supplement No. 194, p. 214.

[10] See Ranshofen-Wertheimer, *The International Secretariat*, p. 61–65.

[11] *Ibid.*, Chart between p. 90–91.

When engaged on business of the League representatives of the members of the League and League officials were entitled to diplomatic privileges and immunities under Article 7, Paragraph 4 of the Covenant. To carry out this provision of the Covenant a *modus vivendi* concerning the diplomatic immunity of League officials was concluded between the Swiss Federal Government and the League in 1926.[12]

The Secretariat operated under Staff Regulations[13] which were repeatedly revised. The text of the Staff Regulations was not placed on public sale. The Office Rules[14] of the League were designed primarily for the internal use of the Secretariat and therefore were not placed on public sale.

2. STAFF REGULATIONS AND OFFICE RULES

Provisional Statutes for the Staff of the International Secretariat. Geneva, June 1, 1921. 19 p.+19 p., bilingual.

Staff Regulations.[15] Edition Issued in March, 1933. Geneva, 1933. 69 p.

Amendments No. 1–19, 1933–1939, issued separately.

Staff Regulations. Edition Issued in September, 1945, and Incorporating Amendments in Force on the Date of Issue. No date. 74 p.

Contains: Articles 1–80 of Staff Regulations, p. 5–45. Annex I. Divisions and Categories of Staff and Salary Scales, p. 47. Annex II. Rules as to Compensation for Overtime, p. 57. Annex III. Rules as to Travelling and Removal Expenses and Subsistence Allowances, p. 60. Annex IV. Publications, Lectures and Speeches by Members of the Secretariat: Abstention from Political Activities, p. 71.

Office Rules. Secretariat Office Rules. Geneva, 1936. 143 p.

3. ORGANIZATION OF THE SECRETARIAT

Staff of Secretariat. Memorandum by the Secretary-General.[16] No date. 11 p., bilingual. [Council Document 6] [29/1083/1083]

[12]Reprinted below, Appendix One, Section V, 2. For the so-called provisional *Modus Vivendi* of 1921 see: *Letter of July 19, 1921, from the Head of the Federal Political Department to the Secretary-General of the League of Nations.* (Unofficial English translation in Martin Hill, *Immunities and Privileges of International Officials*, Washington, 1947, p. 121–127; for original French text see *ibid.*, p. 129–135); and *Reply of October 25, 1921, from the Secretary-General* (unofficial English translation *ibid.*, p. 127–129; for original French text see *ibid.*, p. 135–137).
[13]Reprinted below, Appendix One, Section IV.
[14]See Section 2, this page.
[15]See Ranshofen-Wertheimer, *The International Secretariat*, p. 256.
[16]For comment on this document, see *ibid.*, p. 82–85. See also Annex to Council Document No. 6. [111A]. 1p. + 1p., bilingual.

Staff of the Secretariat. Report Presented by the British Representative, Mr. A. J. Balfour. *Official Journal*, June, 1920, p. 136–139, bilingual.

Staff and Organisation of the Secretariat. Memorandum by the Secretary-General. No date. 7 p., bilingual. [Document de l'Assemblée 32] [20/48/32]

Staff and Organisation of the Secretariat. Report by Sir James Allen. December 16, 1920. 2 p., bilingual. [Document de l'Assemblée 229] [20/48/229]

Minor Staff Appointments. Memorandum by the Secretary-General. Geneva, February 9, 1921. 2 p., bilingual. [Document du Conseil 137] [21/4/35]

Organisation of the Secretariat and of the International Labour Office. Report Submitted by the Fourth Committee and Adopted by the Second Assembly on October 1st, 1921, on the Conclusions and Proposals of the Committee of Experts Appointed in Accordance with the Resolutions Approved by the First Assembly at Its Meeting of December 17th, 1920. Rapporteur: Mr. Georges Noblemaire.[17] Geneva, 1921. 28 p.+21 p., bilingual. [C.424.M.305.1921. X.] [A.140.1921.]

This document is usually cited as the Noblemaire Report.

Committee of Enquiry on the Organisation of the Secretariat, the International Labour Office and the Registry of the Permanent Court of International Justice (Committee of Thirteen). Report of the Committee.[18] Geneva, 1930. 63 p. [A.16.1930.] (General 1930.3.)

Contains several charts on the organization of the Secretariat.

Committee Appointed to Give Further Consideration to Certain Questions Relating to the Organisation of the Secretariat, the International Labour Office and the Registry of the Permanent Court of International Justice (New Committee of Thirteen). Report and Minutes of the Committee. Geneva, 1931. 40 p. [A.8.1931.X.] (1931.X.2.)

Present Activities of the Secretariat and Special Organisations of the League. Geneva, 1932. 34 p. [A.21.1932.] (General.1932.6.)

Technical Concentration of the Activities of the League of Nations

---

[17]Also in the *Records of the Second Assembly: Plenary Meetings*, Geneva, 1921, p. 595–626.
[18]See also Document [A.16.(Addendum).1930.], including Annex A, "Draft Amended Staff Regulations of the Secretariat," p. 2–16; Document [A.16.(Second Addendum). 1930.], containing "Staff Regulations for the Registry of the Permanent Court of International Justice," p. 3–5; Document [A.16.(Third Addendum).1930.]; and Document [A.16.(Fourth Addendum).1930.].

and Rationalisation of the Services of the Secretariat and the International Labour Office. Geneva, 1933. 18 p. [A.10.1933.X.][19]

4. PENSIONS

STAFF PROVIDENT FUND[20]

Regulations of the Staff Provident Fund. Report to the Assembly by the Supervisory Commission. Geneva, 1924. 7 p. [A.6.1924.X.]

Regulations of the Staff Provident Fund. Geneva, 1924. 5 p.+5 p., bilingual. [A.6(a).1924.X.]

Administrative Rules of the Staff Provident Fund. Geneva, 1925. 3 p. [A.48.1925.X.]

Staff Provident Fund. Report Submitted by the Chairman of the Board Management. Geneva, 1926. 4 p. [A.7.1926.X.]

Amendment to Article 6 of the Staff Provident Fund Regulations. Memorandum by the Secretary-General. Geneva, 1926. 3 p. [A. 72.1926.X.] [C.38(1).1926.X.] (1926.X.19.)

PENSIONS[21]

Staff Pensions Regulations Submitted by the Fourth Committee to the Assembly for Adoption.[22] Geneva, 1930. 9 p. [A.25(1).1930.X.]

Staff Pensions Fund. Staff Pensions Regulations. Administrative Rules. Rules of Procedure of the Administrative Board of the Staff Pensions Fund. [Edition issued in June, 1933, incorporating amendments in force on the date of issue.]. 20 p., mimeographed.

Contains: Staff Pensions Regulations, p. 1–11; Administrative Rules, p. 12–19; Rules of Procedure of the Administrative Board of the Staff, p. 20.

5. ADMINISTRATIVE TRIBUNAL

Establishment of an Administrative Tribunal. Report by the Fourth Committee to the Assembly. Rapporteur: H. E. M. César Zumeta (Venezuela). Geneva, 1927. 1 p.+1 p., bilingual. [A.72.1927.V.]

Statute and Rules of Court of the Administrative Tribunal of the League of Nations [T.A.4.]. *Official Journal*, May, 1928, p. 751–756.

[19]Also in *Official Journal*, Special Supplement No. 118, p. 99–115.
[20]On the Staff Provident Fund, see Ranshofen-Wertheimer, *The International Secretariat*, p. 310–312.
[21]See *ibid.*, p. 312–315.
[22]Also in *Official Journal*, Special Supplement No. 84, p. 585–592, and Special Supplement No. 88, p. 381–389.

Contains: Resolution Adopted by the Assembly of the League of Nations on September 26th, 1927, p. 751; Statute[23] of the League of Nations Administrative Tribunal Adopted by the Assembly on September 26th, 1927, p. 751; Rules of Court[24] Drawn up by the League of Nations Administrative Tribunal on February 2nd, 1928, p. 753; Annex, p. 756.

6. IMMUNITIES AND PRIVILEGES

Communications from the Swiss Federal Council Concerning Diplomatic Immunities to Be Accorded to the Staff of the League of Nations and of the International Labour Office. Report by M. Titulesco, Adopted by the Council on September 20th, 1926. [C. 558.1926.V.]. *Official Journal*, October, 1926, p. 1422–1424.[25]

This document is usually designated as the *modus vivendi* between Switzerland and the League.

Circular Regarding the Rights Conferred and the Obligations Imposed upon the Members of the Secretariat by Article 7 of the Covenant. Third edition. Geneva, May 1st, 1928. 7 p.

[23]Reprinted below, Appendix One, Section VI. Also in Manley O. Hudson, *International Legislation* (7 vols., Washington, 1931–1941), I, 212–216. On administrative tribunals of international organizations, see Hudson, *International Tribunals: Past and Future* (Washington, 1944), p. 220–222.

[24]The Rules were promulgated by the Tribunal at its First Session under the authority of Art. 11 of its Statute. See Hudson, *International Tribunals*, p. 220–222.

[25]Reprinted below, Appendix One, Section V, 1. Also in *Official Journal*, October, 1926, p. 1422–1424, and in Hudson, *International Tribunals*, p. 226, footnote 1. For text of 1921 *modus vivendi* see Martin Hill, *Immunities and Privileges of International Officials: the Experience of the League of Nations* (Washington, 1947), p. 121–137.

IV. COMMITTEES OF THE LEAGUE

OF NATIONS

1. INTRODUCTORY NOTE

IN ADDITION to the principal organs of the League, namely the Council, the Assembly, and the Secretariat, the major "Committees" of the League performed many of its most essential functions. This section lists only those major League documents which refer to "League Committees" in general.[1]

In League practice the term "Committee" was not always used consistently. Several "Committees" were styled "Commissions," for instance, the Permanent Mandates Commission and the Permanent Advisory Commission for Military, Naval, and Air Questions, both of which were provided for in the Covenant.

The rather complex committee structure of the League almost defies classification. Apart from classification according to function, the committees may be listed according to their legal basis, in other words, whether their existence was based upon the Covenant, Council or Assembly Resolutions, or special international conventions. They also have occasionally been classified in accordance with the legal character of their members, that is to say, whether members served as government representatives subject to instructions or as experts in their individual capacities.

The following documents, referred to more fully below, are indispensable for an understanding of the committee structure of the League: *Committees of the League of Nations* [C.287.M.125.1934.]; General Regulations on Committees, 1936;[2] *The Development of International Co-operation in Economic and Social Affairs* [A.23.1939.], also called the Bruce Report; *The Committees of the League of Nations* [C.99.M.99.1945.V.].

It is expected that the previously mentioned card catalogue prepared by the Woodrow Wilson Memorial Library will include complete entries for all Standing Committees and for most of the *ad hoc* Committees of the League as well as their publications.

[1]See also above, p. 54.
[2]Reprinted below, Appendix One, Section VII.

2. NATURE AND COMPOSITION OF LEAGUE COMMITTEES[3]

Relations between Technical Organisations and the Council and Assembly of the League: Resolution Adopted by the Council of the League of Nations. *Official Journal*, June, 1920, p. 151–152, bilingual.

"General Report by M. Gabriel Hanotaux on the Technical Organisations," in *Records of the First Assembly: Plenary Meetings*, p. 337–351, 371–382.

Committees of the League of Nations. Report by the Secretary-General. Drawn up in Pursuance of the Council's Decision of January 17th, 1934.[4] Geneva, 1934. 105 p. [C.287.M.125.1934.] (General 1934.4.)

This document contains (Annex 1) an extremely useful "Table Showing the Main Features of the League of Nations Commissions."

Report of the Committee Appointed to Study the Constitution, Procedure and Practice of Committees of the League of Nations. Geneva, 1935. 6 p. [A.16.1935.] (General 1935.3.)

Committees of the League of Nations. Report Submitted by the Second Committee to the Assembly.[5] Rapporteur: M. F. Van Langenhove (Belgium). Geneva, 1935. 2 p. [A.70.1935.]

Constitution, Procedure and Practice of Committees of the League of Nations (Massigli Report).[6] *Official Journal*, February, 1936, p. 129–137.

Contains: General Regulations on Committees,[7] p. 131–133.

The Development of International Co-operation in Economic and Social Affairs: Report of the Special Committee. Geneva, August 22nd, 1939. 22 p. [A.23.1939.] (General 1939)

This so-called Bruce Report is indispensable background material for an understanding of the Social and Economic Council provided for in Articles 61–72 of the United Nations Charter.

[3]See especially Vladimir D. Pastuhov, *Memorandum on the Composition, Procedure and Functions of Committees of the League of Nations* (Washington, 1943), No. 1 in the Series *Experience in International Administration: Preliminary Materials and Monographs*. See also Harold R. G. Greaves, *The League Committees and World Order* (New York, 1931). Useful information on the committees is also found in Marie J. Carroll, *Key to League of Nations Documents Placed on Public Sale, 1920–1936* (5 vols., Boston, 1930–1935, New York, 1938).

[4]See Assembly Resolution of September 27, 1934, *Official Journal*, Special Supplement No. 123, p. 24.

[5]Adopted by Assembly Resolution of September 28, 1935, *Official Journal*, Special Supplement No. 137, p. 17.

[6]Document [C.71.1936.].

[7]For a critical analysis of the Regulations, see Pastuhov, *Memorandum on the Composition . . . of the Committees of the League of Nations*, p. 28–66. The General Regulations are reprinted below, Appendix One, Section VII.

The Committees of the League of Nations: Classified List and Essential Facts. Geneva, 1945. 73 p. [C.99.M.99.1945.V.]

Contains information on about 40 committees, including specialized organizations such as the International Institute for the Unification of Private Law, and on the following items: legal basis, purposes, expert or official character of members, number of members, terms of office, and subcommittees.

3. LIST OF MEMBERS OF COMMITTEES[8]

Committees of the League of Nations (List of Members of Committees). Geneva, 1937, 10 p. [C.193.M.138.1937.] Corrigendum No. 1–7. 12 p.

Committees of the League of Nations (List of Members of Committees). Geneva, 1938, 10 p. [C.80.M.35.1938.] Corrigendum No. 1–6. 7 p.

Committees of the League of Nations (List of Members of Committees). Geneva, 1939. 11 p. [C.74.M.35.1939.] Corrigendum No. 1–5. 5 p.

[8]The lists were never placed on public sale. Prior to 1937 they were mimeographed. See, e.g., Special Circular 46. List of Committees and Commissions under the League of Nations, Prepared by Dr. Hawkling Yen. Unpaged (33p.), mimeographed. Geneva, 1921. Committees of the League of Nations. List of Members. Geneva, 1934. 22 p., mimeographed. [C.287(a).M.125(a).1934.]. Committees of the League of Nations. List of Members. Geneva, 1936. 24 p., mimeographed. [C.24.M.16.1936.]

V. FINANCIAL ADMINISTRATION AND BUDGET OF THE LEAGUE

1. INTRODUCTORY NOTE

ARTICLE 6 of the Covenant provided originally that "the expenses of the Secretariat shall be borne by the members of the League in accordance with the apportionment of the expenses of the International Bureau of the Universal Postal Union." The application of this rule encountered difficulties from the outset.[1]

As early as 1921 the Joint Sub-Committee of the First and Fourth Committees of the Assembly suggested that the last paragraph of Article 6 be amended as follows: "The expenses of the League shall be borne by the members of the League in the proportion decided by the Assembly."[2] This amendment came into force on August 13, 1924.

The Committee on the Allocation of Expenses, which met for the first time in September, 1920, was charged with determining the individual contributions of League members in accordance with their capacity to pay. Various tentative solutions are referred to in *Allocation of the Expenses. Report Submitted by the Fourth Committee to the Assembly* [A.179.1921.]. On September 26, 1925, the Sixth Assembly adopted the following resolution: "The Assembly, I. Requests the Council to ask the Committee on the Allocation of Expenses to follow the economic development of the various Member States with a view to submitting a revised scale to the Assembly of 1928. II. Approves for the years 1926, 1927 and 1928 the scale for the allocation of the expenses of the League annexed to the present resolution."[3]

On the whole, the need for reallocating the contributions to the League's budget arose time and again for various reasons: (1) changes in the capacity of members to pay, necessitating the reduction or increase of the number of basic units to be paid; (2) changes in the number of members; (3) necessity for reallocating a budget surplus;

[1]See Document [20/48/41], listed below, especially p. 5, 9, 11.
[2]See Document [A.179.1921.], p. 4. See also Art. 17, par. 2 of the United Nations Charter.
[3]For the full text of this resolution, see *Official Journal*, Special Supplement No. 32, p. 22–23. Also in Document [C.614.M.198.1925.X.].

(4) necessity for reallocation because of failure of several members to contribute their annual dues.[4]

In addition to the Committee on the Allocation of Expenses there was also a Special Committee on Arrears of Contributions.[5]

The annual budget estimates were examined by the Supervisory Commission in accordance with the Regulations for the Financial Administration of the League of Nations.[6] After examination by the Commission the estimates were circulated to all the members of the League not less than three months before the regular meeting of the Assembly. After scrutiny by the Fourth Committee (Budget and Financial Questions) of the Assembly, the budget was submitted to the Assembly for approval.[7]

In 1938 the powers of the Supervisory Commission were considerably increased, since the financial and administrative powers of the Assembly,[8] and later of the Council, were delegated to it.

Other offices and agents concerned with budgetary matters were the League Treasury[9] and the auditor who verified the accounts of the League.[10]

From 1920–1946, 28 budgets, covering 28 financial periods, were published. The budgets for the Eleventh (1929) through the Twenty-second Financial Periods (1940) were published in the *Official Journal*.[11]

A survey of the League budgets from 1920 to 1946 reveals that the maximum annual expenditures of the League of Nations, including the expenditures of the International Labor Organization and the Permanent Court of International Justice, amounted to 29,932,779 Swiss francs or $5,777,015 in 1933. The budget authorization for the year 1933 amounted to Swiss francs 33,429,132, or $6,450,151. It should be noted that the 1932 authorized budget of 33,687,994 Swiss francs was the largest budget ever voted on, but that the actual expenditures of 27,290,281 Swiss francs were smaller than the actual expenditures in 1933.[12] These amounts seem rather modest, if compared with the cost of mechanized warfare during World War II.

---

[4]For the scale of contributions in force for the years 1937, 1938, and 1939, originally approved by the Assembly in 1936, see *Essential Facts about the League of Nations* (10th ed., revised, Geneva, 1939), p. 34–37.

[5]See, *e.g.*, Document [C.76.M.32.1935.II.A.].

[6]Reprinted below, Appendix One, Section XII.

[7]For the budget of the League, see Denys P. Myers, *Handbook of the League of Nations* (Boston, 1935), p. 76–88, and Egon F. Ranshofen-Wertheimer, *The International Secretariat* (Washington, 1945), p. 223–228.

[8]See *Report of the Supervisory Commission for the Year 1940* [C.152.M.139.1940.X.]. See also below, p. 106–107.

[9]On the functions of the League Treasury, see Ranshofen-Wertheimer, *The International Secretariat*, p. 105.

[10]For a list of audited accounts, see below, p. 100–101.

[11]For a list of League budgets, see below, p. 102–105.

[12]For a year to year survey of League expenditures, see Appendix One, Section XIII. The budget of the United Nations for 1948, exclusive of the budget of the specialized

In 1942, for example, it was "estimated that eight million dollars would take care of the . . . war expenditures of the United States Government for approximately forty-five minutes."[13]

2. REGULATIONS FOR THE FINANCIAL ADMINISTRATION OF THE LEAGUE

Regulations for the Administration of the Finances of the League. Memorandum by the Secretary-General. Geneva, 1921. 2 p.+ 2 p., bilingual. [C.245.M.181.1921.X.]

Regulations for the Financial Administration of the League of Nations. Report of the Fourth Committee. Rapporteur: M. Mélot.[14] Geneva, 1922. 1 p.+1 p., bilingual. [A.153.1922.X.]

Regulations for the Financial Administration of the League of Nations. Adopted by the Third Assembly. Text as Amended by the Fourth Assembly. Geneva, 1923. 15 p.+15 p., bilingual. [C.663. M.266.1923.X.]

Regulations for the Financial Administration of the League of Nations. Edition Published January, 1929, Containing the Amendments Adopted at the Fourth, Sixth, and Ninth Ordinary Sessions of the Assembly.[15] Geneva, 1929. 21 p.+21 p., bilingual. [C.614. M.191.1928.X.] (1928.X.3.)

Regulations for the Financial Administration of the League of Nations. Edition Published January, 1931, Containing the Amendments by the Fourth, Sixth, Ninth, Tenth and Eleventh Ordinary Sessions of the Assembly. Geneva, 1931. 21 p.+21 p., bilingual. [C.3.M.3.1931.X.] (1931.X.1.)

Regulations for the Financial Administration of the League of Nations. Edition Published November, 1935, Containing the Amendments Adopted at the Fourth, Sixth, Ninth, Tenth, Eleventh, Thirteenth, Fourteenth and Sixteenth Ordinary Sessions of the Assembly. Geneva, 1935. 23 p.+23 p., bilingual. [C.461.M.241. 1935.X.]

---

agencies amounted to $34,825,195; the Budget of the United Nations plus those of the specialized agencies (ILO, UNESCO, FAO, ICAO, WHO), but exclusive of IBRD and IMF, amounted to $59,109,495.

[13]See Raymond B. Fosdick, in *The Rockefeller Foundation: Annual Report for 1942*, p. 5–6.

[14]See also Assembly Resolution of September 29, 1922, on Regulations for the Financial Administration of the League of Nations, *Official Journal*, Special Supplement No. 9, p. 30; and Assembly Resolution of October 4, 1921, *Official Journal*, Special Supplement No. 6, p. 28.

[15]For a discussion of the Regulations, see Felix Morley, *The Society of Nations; Its Organization and Constitutional Development* (Washington, 1932), p. 512–525. See also *Report of the Fourth Committee to the Assembly. Rapporteur: Prof. W. Rappard (Switzerland)*. [A.54.1929.X.]

Regulations for the Financial Administration of the League of Nations. Edition Published November, 1936, Containing the Amendments Adopted at the Fourth, Sixth, Ninth, Tenth, Eleventh, Thirteenth, Fourteenth, Sixteenth and Seventeenth Ordinary Sessions of the Assembly. Geneva, 1936. 24 p.+24 p., bilingual. [C.480.M.293.1936.X.]

Regulations for the Financial Administration of the League of Nations. Edition Published November, 1937, Containing the Amendments Adopted at the Fourth, Sixth, Ninth, Tenth, Eleventh, Thirteenth, Fourteenth, Sixteenth, Seventeenth and Eighteenth Ordinary Sessions of the Assembly. Geneva, 1937. 24 p.+24 p., bilingual. [C.536.M.373.1937.X.]

Regulations for the Financial Administration of the League of Nations. Amendment of Article 23, Paragraph 1. Geneva, 1938. 1 p., bilingual. [C.536.M.373.1937.X.Amendment.]

Regulations for the Financial Administration of the League of Nations. Edition Published in 1945, Containing the Amendments Adopted at the Fourth, Sixth, Ninth, Tenth, Eleventh, Thirteenth, Fourteenth, Sixteenth, Seventeenth and Eighteenth Ordinary Sessions of the Assembly. Geneva, 1945. 30 p.+30 p., bilingual. [C.81.M.81.1945.X.][16]

3. ALLOCATION OF EXPENSES

Allocation of Expenses of the League of Nations for 1919–1920. Memorandum by the Secretary-General. No date. 13 p., bilingual. [31/1344/X] Council Document 15.

Method of Apportionment of the Expenses of the Secretariat. Memorandum by the Secretary-General. No date. 9 p., bilingual. [13/1653/X] Council Document 16.

Allocation of the Expenses of the League of Nations. Brussels, October 7th, 1920. 11 p., bilingual. [20/40/41] Council Document 41.

Allocation of the Expenses. Report Submitted by the Fourth Committee to the Assembly. Rapporteur: Sir Rennell Rodd. Geneva, 1921. 8 p.+8 p., bilingual. [A.179.1921.]

Allocation of Expenses of the League for the Fourth Fiscal Period (1922). Memorandum by the Secretary-General. November 15th, 1921. [C.477.M.326.1921.X.]. *Official Journal*, January, 1922, p. 32–35.

Committee on Allocation of Expenses. Report Submitted to the Nineteenth Session of the Council. Geneva, 1922. 5 p.+5 p., bilingual. [C.458.1922.II.]

[16]Reprinted below, Appendix One, Section XII.

Allocation of the Expenses for the Fifth Fiscal Period. Geneva, 1922.
3 p.+3 p., bilingual. [C.715.M.427.1922.X.]

Allocation of Expenses of the League. Report to the Council by the
Committee on Allocation of Expenses. Geneva, 1923. 8 p., bilingual. [C.396.1923.II.]

Allocation of the Expenses for the Sixth Financial Period (1924).
Memorandum by the Secretary-General. Geneva, 1923. 2 p. [C.
677.M.274.1923.X.]

Allocation of the Expenses for the Seventh Financial Period (1925).
Memorandum by the Secretary-General. Geneva, 1924. 4 p. [C.
629.M.228.1924.X.]

Allocation of the Expenses for the Eighth Financial Period (1926).
Memorandum by the Secretary-General. Geneva, 1925. 3 p. [C.
614.M.198.1925.X.]

Allocation of the Expenses for the Ninth Financial Period (1927).
Memorandum by the Secretary-General. Geneva, 1926. 4 p. [C.
593.M.229.1926.X.]

Allocation of the Expenses for the Tenth Financial Period (1929).
Memorandum by the Secretary-General. Geneva, 1927. 2 p. [C.
526.M.184.1927.X.]

Beginning with the Eleventh Financial Period (1929), the Allocation of the Expenses appeared in the *Official Journal* as part of the
budget. See, for instance, *Official Journal*, November, 1928, pages
1855–1856. Beginning with the Seventeenth Financial Period (1935),
the corresponding statement is listed under "Summary of Ordinary
Contributions."

Contributions Fixed for 1939. Geneva, 1938. 2 p. [C.L.206.1938.X.
Annexe.]

Contributions Fixed for 1940.[18] Geneva, 1939. 2 p. [C.L.178.1939.X.
Annexe.]

STATES IN DEFAULT OF THEIR CONTRIBUTIONS

Legal Positions of States Which Do Not Pay Their Contributions to
the League.[19] Geneva, 1927. 4 p. [A.10.1927.V.]

[18]For the contributions scale for the years 1940 to 1946, see the budgets for the Twenty-
third (1941) through the Twenty-eighth Financial Periods (1946). On contributions,
see also Document [A.5.1946.], *Official Journal*, Special Supplement No. 194, p. 154.
[19]See especially the following statement from the Report by the Secretary-General to
the Council (March 9, 1927), p. 3: "Apart from the somewhat theoretical possibility
of the application of Article 16 of the Covenant, it appears certain that the strictly
legal rights (including, for example, the right to vote in the Assembly and eligibility
for membership of the Council) which a state derives from membership in the League
cannot suffer any diminution as the result of default in payment of contributions."
See also Walter Schiffer, *Repertoire of Questions of General International Law before the
League of Nations, 1920–1940* (Geneva, 1942), Nos. 708, 757, 759, 818, 824, 854.

4. AUDITED ACCOUNTS

Accounts of the League of Nations for the Fiscal Period Ending 31st March 1920. No date. 17 p., bilingual. [20/4/205]

Audited Accounts of the League of Nations for the Second Period Ending 31st December, 1920. Memorandum by the Secretary-General. Geneva, 1921. 6 p., bilingual. [21/31/45]

Audited Accounts for the Third Fiscal Period (1921). Memorandum by the Secretary-General.[20] Geneva, 1922. 40 p., bilingual. [C. 237.M.133.1922.X.]

Audited Accounts for the Fourth Fiscal Period (1922). Memorandum by the Secretary-General. Geneva, 1923. 71 p. [A.5.1923.X.]

Audited Accounts for the Fifth Financial Period (1923). Memorandum by the Secretary-General and Report by Commendatore A. Ceresa (Auditor). Geneva, 1924. 67 p. [A.1.1924.X.]

Audited Accounts for the Sixth Financial Period (1924) and Report Thereon by Dr. F. Vivaldi, Auditor (Substitute). Geneva, 1925. 64 p. [A.3.1925.X.]

Audited Accounts for the Seventh Financial Period (1925) and Reports Thereon by Commendatore A. Ceresa, Auditor. Geneva, 1926. 81 p. [A.3.1926.X.] <C.C.208.> (1926.X.6.)

Audited Accounts for the Eighth Financial Period (1926) and Reports Thereon by Commendatore A. Ceresa, Auditor. Geneva, 1927. 72 p. [A.3.1927.X.]

Audited Accounts for the Ninth Financial Period (1927) and Reports Thereon by M. A. Ceresa, Auditor. Geneva, 1928. 79 p. [A.3. 1928.X.] (1928.X.1.)

Audited Accounts for the Tenth Financial Period (1928) and Reports Thereon by M. A. Ceresa, Auditor. Geneva, 1929. 84 p. [A.3. 1929.X.] (1929.X.1.)

Audited Accounts for the Eleventh Financial Period (1929) and Reports Thereon by M. A. Ceresa, Auditor. Geneva, 1930. 92 p. [A.3.1930.X.] (1930.X.1.)

Audited Accounts for the Twelfth Financial Period (1930) and Reports Thereon by M. A. Ceresa, Auditor. Geneva, 1931. 109 p. [A.3.1931.X.] (1931.X.3.)

Audited Accounts for the Thirteenth Financial Period (1931) and Reports Thereon by M. A. Ceresa, Auditor. Geneva, 1932. 104 p. [A.3.1932.X.] (1932.X.1.)

Audited Accounts for the Fourteenth Financial Period (1932) and Reports Thereon by M. A. Ceresa, Auditor. Geneva, 1933. 126 p. [A.3.1933.X.] (1933.X.1.)

[20]See also *Audited Accounts for the Third Fiscal Period (1921) Approved by the Third Assembly at Its Twenty-third Meeting, Held on September 29th, 1922.* Geneva, 1922. 40 p. + 40 p., bilingual. [A.13(1).1922.X.] [C.237(1).M.1333(1).1922.X.]

Audited Accounts for the Fifteenth Financial Period (1933) and Reports Thereon by M. A. Ceresa, Auditor. Geneva, 1934. 132 p. [A.3.1934.X.] (1934.X.1.)

Audited Accounts for the Sixteenth Financial Period (1934) and Reports Thereon by M. A. Ceresa, Auditor. Geneva, 1935. 123 p. [A.3.1935.X.] (1935.X.1.)

Audited Accounts for the Seventeenth Financial Period (1935) and Reports Thereon by M. A. Ceresa, Auditor. Geneva, 1936. 135 p. [A.3.1936.X.] (1936.X.1.)

Audited Accounts for the Eighteenth Financial Period (1936) and Reports Thereon by M. A. Ceresa, Auditor. Geneva, 1937. 147 p. [A.3.1937.X.] (1937.X.1.)

Audited Accounts for the Nineteenth Financial Period (1937) and Reports Thereon by M. U. A. J. Brunskog, Auditor. Geneva, 1938. 127 p. [A.3.1938.X.] (1938.X.1.)

Audited Accounts for the Twentieth Financial Period (1938) and Report Thereon by M. U. A. J. Brunskog, Auditor. Geneva, 1939. 135 p. [A.3.1939.X.]²¹

Audited Accounts for the Twenty-first Financial Period (1939) and Report Thereon by M. U. A. J. Brunskog, Auditor. Geneva, 1940. 125 p. [C.158.M.144.1940.X.] (1940.X.1.)

Audited Accounts for the Twenty-second Financial Period (1940) and Reports Thereon by M. U. A. J. Brunskog, Auditor. Geneva, 1941. 96 p. [C.93.M.90.1941.X.]

Audited Accounts for the Twenty-fourth Financial Period (1942) and Reports Thereon by M. U. A. J. Brunskog, Auditor. [C.4.M.4. 1944.X.] 1944. 95 p.

Audited Accounts for the Twenty-fifth Financial Period (1943) and Reports Thereon by M. U. A. J. Brunskog, Auditor. [C.9.M.9. 1945.X.] 1945. 87 p.

Audited Accounts for the Twenty-sixth Financial Period (1944) and Reports Thereon by M. U. A. J. Brunskog, Auditor. [C.83.M.83. 1945.X.] 1945. 91 p.

Audited Accounts for the Twenty-seventh Financial Period (1945) and Reports Thereon by M. U. A. J. Brunskog, Auditor. [C.15.M. 15.1946.X.] 1946. 97 p.

Audited Accounts for the Six Months Ended June 30th, 1946 (Twenty-eighth Financial Period, 1946) and Reports Thereon by M. U. A. J. Brunskog, Auditor. [C.82.M.82.1946.X.] 1946. 39 p.

Audited Accounts for the Twenty-eighth Financial Period (1946) and Reports Thereon by M. U. A. J. Brunskog, Auditor. [C.2.M.2. 1947.X.] 1947. 91 p.

²¹See also Document [A.3.1939.X.Erratum.]. 2 p.

5. THE BUDGET OF THE LEAGUE OF NATIONS

GENERAL

The Finances of the League of Nations. Report Presented by the Spanish Representative, Mr. Quinones de Léon, and Adopted by the Council of the League of Nations, Meeting in Rome, on May 19th, 1920.[22] No date. 11 p., bilingual. [20/31/37]

The Finances of the League of Nations. Resolutions Adopted by the Council of the League of Nations, Meeting in Rome, on 19th May 1920.[23] No date. 1 p.+1 p., bilingual. [31/4435/4435]

CHRONOLOGICAL LIST OF LEAGUE BUDGETS

1. Estimate for the Organisation Period. Memorandum Submitted by the Secretary-General.[24] No date. 7 p., bilingual. [31/1793/291]

2. Estimate for the Second Fiscal Period, April 1st-December 31st, 1920. Memorandum by the Secretary-General. No date. 9 p.+7 p., bilingual; mimeographed.[25] [20/4/138/1]

3. Third Budget of the League of Nations. Memorandum by the Secretary-General.[26] No date. 7 p., bilingual. [20/4/275]

4. Budget for the Fourth Fiscal Period, 1922. Passed by the Second Assembly on October 3rd, 1921. *Official Journal*, November, 1921, p. 1034-1065, bilingual.

5. Budget for the Fifth Fiscal Period (Supplementary Credits Included) (1923). Adopted by the Third Assembly on September 29th, 1922. Geneva, 1922. 78 p. [C.713.M.425.1922.X.]

6. Budget for the Sixth Financial Period (1924) and General Report on Financial Questions. Adopted by the Fourth Assembly on September 28th, 1923. Geneva, 1923. 76 p. [C.668.M.268.1923.X.]

7. Budget for the Seventh Financial Period (1924) and General Report on Financial Questions. Adopted by the Fourth Assembly on September 29th, 1924. Geneva, 1924. 77 p. [C.618.M.1924.X.]

8. Budget for the Eighth Financial Period (1926) and General Re-

---

[22]Also in Council Minutes, 5th Sess., p. 238–247, bilingual.
[23]Also in Council Minutes, 5th Sess., p. 272–273, bilingual.
[24]This memorandum was approved by the Council on May 19, 1920. It covers the period to March 31, 1920, and includes estimates for April, May, and June, 1920. Also in Council Minutes, 5th Sess., p. 248–253, bilingual.
[25]Also in Council Minutes, 8th Sess., p. 210–233; see also p. 204–209.
[26]Covers the period January 1–December 31, 1921. Also in *Official Journal*, October, 1920, p. 453–456. The figures listed here do not always coincide with those contained in the above documents; see also Georges Ottlik, *Annuaire de la Société des Nations* p. 234.

port on Financial Questions. Adopted by the Sixth Assembly on September 26th, 1925. Geneva, 1925. 69 p. [C.619.M.1925.X.]

9. Budget for the Ninth Financial Period (1927) and General Report on Financial Questions. Adopted by the Assembly at Its Seventh Ordinary Session on September 25th, 1926. Geneva, 1926. 72 p. [C.581.M.220.1926.X.] (1926.X.25.)

10. Budget for the Tenth Financial Period (1928) and General Report on Financial Questions. Adopted by the Assembly at Its Eighth Ordinary Session on September 27th, 1927. Geneva, 1927. 66 p. [C.520.M.178.1927.X.] (1927.X.5.)

Beginning with the Eleventh Financial Period (1929) the budget of the League was published in the *Official Journal*.

11. Budget for the Eleventh Financial Period (1929) and General Report on Financial Questions. Adopted by the Assembly at Its Ninth Ordinary Session on September 26th, 1928. *Official Journal*, November, 1928, p. 1775–1885.

   Contains: 1. General Report on Financial Questions Adopted by the Assembly at Its Ninth Ordinary Session on September 26th, 1928. 2. General Budget for the Eleventh Financial Period (1929), Adopted by the Assembly at Its Ninth Ordinary Session on September 26th, 1928. 3. Allocation of the Expenses for the Eleventh Financial Period (1929). 4. Staff Lists of the Secretariat of the League of Nations and of the International Labour Office.[27]

12. Budget for the Twelfth Financial Period (1930) and General Report on Financial Questions. Adopted by the Assembly at Its Tenth Ordinary Session on September 25th, 1929. *Official Journal*, October, 1929, p. 1319–1431.

13. Budget for the Thirteenth Financial Period (1931) and Report on Financial Questions. Adopted by the Assembly at Its Eleventh Ordinary Session on October 3rd, 1930. *Official Journal*, October, 1930, p. 1169–1280.

14. Budget for the Fourteenth Financial Period (1932) and Report on Financial Questions. Adopted by the Assembly at Its Twelfth Ordinary Session on September 29th, 1931. *Official Journal*, October, 1931, p. 1903–2021.

15. Budget for the Fifteenth Financial Period (1933) and Report on Financial Questions. Adopted by the Assembly at Its Thirteenth Ordinary Session on October 17th, 1932. *Official Journal*, October, 1932, p. 1591–1710.

16. Budget for the Sixteenth Financial Period (1934) and Report on Financial Questions. Adopted by the Assembly at Its Fourteenth

---

[27]From 1928 on the publication of the budget and related material usually followed this pattern.

Ordinary Session on October 11, 1933. *Official Journal*, October, 1933, p. 1179–1293.

17. Budget for the Seventeenth Financial Period (1935) and Report on Financial Questions . . . Adopted by the Assembly at Its Fifteenth Ordinary Session on September 27th, 1934. *Official Journal*, October, 1934, p. 1255–1369.

18. Budget for the Eighteenth Financial Period . . . (1936) and Report on Financial Questions. Adopted by the Assembly at Its Sixteenth Ordinary Session on September 28th, 1935. *Official Journal*, October, 1935, p. 1003–1121.

19. Budget for the Nineteenth Financial Period (2937) and Report on Financial Questions. Adopted by the Assembly at Its Seventeenth Ordinary Session on October 10th, 1932. *Official Journal*, October, 1936, p. 1005–1130.

20. Budget for the Twentieth Financial Period (1938) and Report on Financial Questions. Adopted by the Assembly at Its Eighteenth Ordinary Session on October 5th, 1937. *Official Journal*, October, 1937, p. 693–821.

21. Budget for the Twenty-first Financial Period (1939) and Report on Financial Questions. Adopted by the Assembly at Its Nineteenth Ordinary Session on September 30th, 1938. *Official Journal*, October, 1938, p. 693–821.

22. Budget for the Twenty-second Financial Period (1940) and Report on Financial Questions. Adopted by the Assembly at Its Twentieth Ordinary Session on December 14th, 1939. *Official Journal*, November-December, 1939 (Part I), p. 417–488.

23. Budget for the Twenty-third Financial Period (1941). General Budget of the League and Part I—Secretariat. Geneva, October 31st, 1940. 21 p. [C.153.M.140.1940.X.]. Part II—International Labour Organisation. Geneva, April 17th, 1941. 11p. [C.153(a). M.140(a).1940.X.]. Part III—Permanent Court of International Justice. Geneva, December 26th, 1940. 10 p. [C.153(b).M.140(b). 1940.X.]

24. Budget for the Twenty-fourth Financial Period (1942). General Budget of the League and Part I—Secretariat. Geneva, October 31st, 1941. 20 p. [C.54.M.51.1941.X.]. Part II—International Labour Organisation. Geneva, October 31st, 1941. 11 p. [C. 54(a).M.51(a).1941.X.]. Part III—Permanent Court of International Justice. Geneva, October 31st, 1941. 8 p. [C.54(b).M. 51(b).1941.X.]

25. Budget for the Twenty-fifth Financial Period (1943). General Budget of the League and Part I—Secretariat. Geneva, October 15th, 1942. 19 p. [C.81.M.81.1942.X.]. Part II—International Labour Organisation. Geneva, October 15th, 1942. 16 p. [C.

81(a).M.81(a).1942.X.]. Part III—Permanent Court of International Justice. Geneva, October 15th, 1942. 8 p. [C.81(b).M. 81(b).1942.X.]

26. Budget for the Twenty-sixth Financial Period (1944). General Budget of the League and Part I—Secretariat. Geneva, 1943, 16 p. [C.24.M.24.1943.X.]. Part II—International Labour Organisation. Geneva, 1943. 12 p. [C.24(a).M.24(a).1943.X.]. Part III—Permanent Court of International Justice. Geneva, 1943. 8 p. [C.24(b).M.24(b).1943.X.]

27. Budget for the Twenty-seventh Financial Period (1945). General Budget of the League and Part I—Secretariat. Geneva, October 31st, 1944. 17 p. [C.28.M.28.1944.X.]. Part II—International Labour Organisation. No date. 14 p. [C.28(a).M.28(a).1944.X.]. Part III—Permanent Court of International Justice. Geneva, October 31st, 1944. [C.28(b).M.28(b).1944.X.]

28. Budget for the Twenty-eighth Financial Period (1946). General Budget of the League and Part I—Secretariat. Geneva, November 20th, 1945. 16 p. [C.102.M.102.1945.X.]. Part II—International Labour Organisation. Geneva, November 20th, 1945. [C.102(a).M.102(a).1945.X.]. Part III—Permanent Court of International Justice. Geneva, November 20th, 1945. 8 p. [C.102(b).M.102(b).1945.X.]

For detailed statements and tables on League of Nations assets, liabilities, and schedules of contributions at the time of liquidation of the League, see the reports of the Board of Liquidation listed below, Appendix Three.

6. SUPERVISORY COMMISSION

The Supervisory Commission (Commission de Contrôle), originally styled Commission of Control, was established by Assembly Resolution of October 4, 1921.[28] It met for the first time from May 16 to 22, 1922.[29] From 1922 to 1928 its members were appointed by the Council of the League in accordance with the aforesaid Assembly Resolution and with Article 1, Paragraph 2 of the Regulations for the Financial Administration of the League of Nations.[30] In 1928 the authority to appoint the members of the Supervisory Commission was transferred to the Assembly on the motion of Mr. C. J. Hambro (Norway).[31]

[28]See Official Journal, Special Supplement No. 6, p. 28f.
[29]See Document [A.7.1922.X.] [C.350(1).M.201(1).1922.].
[30]See Document [C.663.M.266.1923.X.], Official Journal, January, 1924, p. 78–99. In force since January 1, 1923.
[31]See Official Journal, Special Supplement No. 68, p. 89–90. On the constitutional

The powers of the Supervisory Commission were enlarged to a considerable extent in 1938 when the Assembly passed the following resolution:

Until the next ordinary session of the Assembly, the Secretary-General and, as regards the International Labour Organisation, the Director of the International Labour Office, acting with the approval of the Supervisory Commission, which may take all decisions by a majority vote, shall have power in their discretion to take any exceptional administrative or financial measures or decisions which appear necessary (including the amendment of administrative or financial regulations) and such measures and decisions shall have the same force and effect as if they had been taken by the Assembly.[32]

In 1939 the Assembly resolved:

During the year 1940, all the powers and functions conferred on the Council of the League of Nations by the Regulations for the Financial Administration of the League or by the Regulations of the Staff Provident Fund may be exercised by the Supervisory Commission with the same force and effect as if they were exercised by the Council itself.[33]

By several resolutions adopted by the Supervisory Commission at its Eighty-seventh and subsequent sessions, the Supervisory Commission reaffirmed its increased authority pending the conclusion of the Twentieth and the convening of the Twenty-first Ordinary Session of the Assembly.[34]

In exercising its emergency powers the Supervisory Commission was charged with maintaining the League as a going concern in the face of a considerable reduction in the League's budget. Expenditures of the League decreased from Swiss francs 28,193,045 in 1939 to Swiss francs 13,238,244 in 1940 and to an average amount of about Swiss francs 8,000,000 in the years 1941–1944.[35] Moreover, the Commission was responsible for all major administrative and financial measures taken by the League during World War II; finally, it carried on negotiations with the United Nations concerning the transfer of functions and assets of the League and its affiliated "autonomous" organizations to the United Nations.[36]

In its *General Summarized Report on the Work of the Supervisory Commission during the Period of Emergency, 1940–1946*, the Commission stated its general objectives as follows: "Broadly speaking the

implications of this amendment to the Financial Regulations, see Felix Morley, *The Society of Nations* (Washington, 1932), p. 525–527. The amendment came into force on January 1, 1929, after approval by the Assembly on September 26, 1928. See Document [A.78.1928.X.].

[32]*Official Journal*, October, 1938, p. 701.
[33]*Official Journal*, November-December, 1939, p. 423.
[34]See, *e.g.*, Document [A.5.1946.] in *Official Journal*, Special Supplement, No. 194, p. 149.
[35]See *Official Journal*, Special Supplement No. 194, p. 159.
[36]See Document [A.8.1946.X.], *ibid.*, p. 217–220.

purpose which has guided the Commission has been to keep intact the framework of the League Organisation and to continue its non-political work at the lowest practicable cost to States Members."[37] The aim of the Commission was to keep alive the economic and social work of the League and to maintain all nonpolitical activities "for the use of whatever authority might be entrusted with these matters after the war."

Under the Regulations for the Financial Administration of the League[38] the Supervisory Commission was composed of five members, of whom at least one had to be a financial expert. The Assembly was directed to select as members of the Commission nationals of countries which were not represented on the Council. Pursuant to Assembly Resolutions adopted in 1938[39] and 1939[40] the number of members of the Commission was raised to seven.[41]

The Reports on the Work of the Supervisory Commission are of particular interest. Strangely enough, none of these reports were placed on public sale as individual documents, but several of them appeared in the *Official Journal*, in the *Records of the Assembly: Plenary Meetings*, or in the *Minutes of the Fourth Committee*. The last reports (Ninety-ninth to One Hundred and Second Sessions) were published in *Official Journal*, Special Supplement No. 194, pages 160–180.[42]

In addition to the Reports on the Work of the Supervisory Commission, *ad hoc* reports were issued, for example, *Pensions and Deferred Pay Scheme* [A.1.1923.X.].

Reports of the Fourth Committee to the Assembly very often contain references to or quotations from Reports on the Work of the Supervisory Commission.

In the following pages Reports on the Work of the Supervisory Commission during its 102 sessions have been listed. Both the titles and the contents vary. The reports are usually neither proceedings, nor mere recommendations, but frequently a mixture of both. Thus, they almost defy classification. In several instances no reports were issued on individual sessions; there was merely a summary reference that a meeting was held and a certain question discussed.

For the student of League publications one feature of the reports is of particular interest, namely, the Annual Reports of the Publica-

[37]Document [A.5.1946.], *ibid.*, p. 149.
[38]See, *e.g.*, text of "Regulations for the Financial Administration of the League of Nations," *Official Journal*, January, 1924, p. 78. For a later edition of the Financial Regulations, see Appendix One, Section XII.
[39]*Official Journal*, October, 1938, p. 701.
[40]*Official Journal*, November-December, 1939, p. 424.
[41]For a complete list of the members of the Supervisory Commission in 1946, see Document [A.25.1946.X.]; also in *Official Journal*, Special Supplement No. 194, p. 174.
[42]See also *ibid.*, p. 149, 217.

tions Committee, which furnish a unique insight into the publications policy and practice of the League.

REPORTS ON THE WORK OF THE SUPERVISORY COMMISSION

1st Session: First Report of the Commission of Control. Geneva, July 10th, 1922. 15 p. [A.7.1922.X.] [C.350(1).M.201(1).1922.X.][43]

2d Session: No published records.

3d Session: Supplementary Report of the Commission of Control. Genève, le 15 septembre 1922. 7 p.+6 p., bilingual. [A.7b.1922. X.][44]

4th Session: Work of the Supervisory Commission. Report on the Work of the Fourth Session, Held at Geneva in February, 1923, Submitted to the Council on April 17th, 1923. [C.193.1923.X.]. *Official Journal*, June, 1923, p. 613–628.

Includes Rules of Procedure of the Supervisory Commission, p. 617–619.

5th Session: Second Annual Report of the Supervisory Commission. In Assembly Records, 4th Assembly, Fourth Committee, p. 97–116.

6th Session: Supervisory Commission: Report on the Work of the Sixth Session. Geneva, July 10th, 1923. 5 p. [A.14.1923.X.][45]

7th Session: Supervisory Commission: Report on the Work of the Seventh Session (August 29th to 31st, 1923). Geneva, September 1st, 1923. 11 p. [A.43.1923.X.][46]

8th Session: No published records.

9th Session: Supervisory Commission: Report on the Work of the Ninth Session (January 9th–12th, 1924). Geneva, January 15th, 1924. 20 p. [C.19.M.9.1924.X.][47]

10th Session: Supervisory Commission: Report of the Commission on the Work of Its Tenth Session. Geneva, August 20th, 1924. 9 p. [A.7(1).1924.X.] [C.214.1924.X.][48]

11th to 13th Sessions: No published records.

14th and 16th Sessions: Supervisory Commission: Report of the Commission on the Work of Its Fourteenth and Sixteenth Sessions. Geneva, May 16th, 1925. 15 p. [A.5.1925.X.][49]

17th Session: No published records.

[43]Also in Assembly Records, 3d Assembly, Fourth Committee, p. 119–132.
[44]Also *ibid.*, p. 133–139.
[45]Also in Assembly Records, 4th Assembly, Fourth Committee, p. 193–196.
[46]Also *ibid.*, p. 197–208.
[47]Also in Assembly Records, 5th Assembly, Fourth Committee, p. 241–260.
[48]Also *ibid.*, p. 261–269.
[49]Also in Assembly Records, 6th Assembly, Fourth Committee, p. 66–76, 76–80. There are no records of the 15th Session, which was devoted entirely to an exchange of views on the question of the revision of the Staff Regulations.

18th and 19th Sessions: Supervisory Commission: Report of the Commission on Its Eighteenth and Nineteenth Sessions. Geneva, May 1st, 1926. 11 p. [A.5.1926.X.] (1926.X.8.)

20th and 21st Sessions: No published records.

22d and 23d Sessions: Supervisory Commission: Report of the Commission on the Work of Its Twenty-second and Twenty-third Sessions. Geneva, May 6th, 1927. 12 p. [A.5.1927.X.][50]

24th Session: Supervisory Commission: Report of the Commission on the Work of Its Twenty-fourth Session. Geneva, July 6th, 1927. 6 p. [A.5(a).1927.X.][51]

25th Session: Supervisory Commission: Report of the Supervisory Commission to the Fourth Committee. Geneva, September 22nd, 1927. 12 p. [C.518.M.177.1927.X.][52]

26th Session: No published records.

27th Session: Supervisory Commission: Report of the Commission on the Work of Its Twenty-seventh Session. Geneva, May 5th, 1928. 9 p. [A.5.1928.X.][53]

28th Session: Supervisory Commission: Report of the Commission on the Work of Its Twenty-eighth Session. Geneva, June 20th, 1928. 8 p. [A.5(a).1928.X.][54]

29th Session: Supervisory Commission: Report of the Commission on the Work of Its Twenty-ninth Session. Geneva, August 1st, 1928. 20 p. [A.5(b).1928.X.][55]

30th Session: Ninth Ordinary Session of the Assembly: Report of the Supervisory Commission to the Fourth Committee. Geneva, September 20th, 1928. 9 p. [C.522.M.152.1928.X.][56]

31st and 32d Sessions: Supervisory Commission: Report of the Commission on the Work of Its Thirty-second Session. Geneva, May 5th, 1929. 10 p. [A.5.1929.X.][57]

Includes Second Annual Report of the Publications Committee, p. 7–10.[58]

33d Session: Supervisory Commission: Report of the Commission on the Work of Its Thirty-third Session. Geneva, July 31st, 1929. 7 p. [A.5(a).1929.X.][59]

34th Session: Tenth Ordinary Session of the Assembly: Report of the

[50]Also in Assembly Records, 8th Assembly, Fourth Committee, p. 73–80, 81–84.
[51]Also ibid., p. 84–89.
[52]Also ibid., p. 258–269.
[53]Also in Assembly Records, 9th Assembly, Fourth Committee, p. 120–128.
[54]Also ibid., p. 129–136.
[55]Also ibid., p. 137–157.
[56]Also ibid., p. 173–181.
[57]Also in Assembly Records, 10th Assembly, Fourth Committee, p. 91–101.
[58]See also *The Publications of the League: Report of the Supervisory Commission to the Assembly.* Geneva, June 16th, 1928. 5 p. [A.13.1928.X.]
[59]Also in Assembly Records, 10th Assembly, Fourth Committee, p. 101–108.

Supervisory Commission to the Fourth Committee. Geneva, September 24th, 1929. 12 p. [C.488.M.153.1929.X.][60]

35th and 36th Sessions: No published records.

37th Session: Supervisory Commission: Report of the Commission no the Work of Its Thirty-seventh Session. Geneva, May 6th, 1930. 19 p. [A.5.1930.X.][61]

Includes Third Annual Report of the Publications Committee, p. 16-19.

38th Session: Supervisory Commission: Report of the Commission on the Work of Its Thirty-eighth Session (Held on September 15th and 16th, 1930). Geneva, September 17th, 1930. 4 p. [A.5(a). 1930.X.][62]

39th Session: Reports Adopted by the Supervisory Commission at Its Thirty-ninth Session. Geneva, September 29th, 1930. 7 p. [C.609.M.236.1930.X.][63]

40th and 41st Sessions: Supervisory Commission: Report of the Commission on the Work of Its Forty-first Session. Geneva, May 2nd, 1931. 19 p. [A.5.1931.X.][64]

Includes Fourth Annual Report of the Publications Committee of the Secretariat, p. 13-17.

42d Session: Twelfth Ordinary Session of the Assembly: Report by the Supervisory Commission to the Fourth Committee. Geneva, 28 September 1931. 21 p. [C.646.M.260.1931.X.][65]

43d to 45th Sessions: Construction of the New Buildings: Report by the Supervisory Commission to the Council. Geneva, January 25th, 1932. 10 p. [C.97.M.50.1932.X.][66]

46th Session: Supervisory Commission: Report of the Commission on the Work of Its Forty-sixth Session. Geneva, May 2nd, 1932. 16 p. [A.5.1932.X.][67]

Includes Fifth Annual Report of the Publications Committee of the Secretariat, p. 14-16.

47th to 49th Sessions: Supervisory Commission: Report of the Commission on the Work of Its Forty-seventh, Forty-eighth and Forty-ninth Sessions. Geneva, September 21st, 1932. 8 p. [A.5(b).1932. X.][68]

47th to 49th Sessions: Report of the Supervisory Commission to the

[60]Also *ibid.*, p. 124-134.
[61]Also in Assembly Records, 11th Assembly, Fourth Committee, p. 256-274.
[62]Also *ibid.*, p. 275-278.
[63]Also *ibid.*, p. 389-393.
[64]Also in Assembly Records, 12th Assembly, Fourth Committee, p. 66-84.
[65]Also *ibid.*, p. 99-119; see also p. 145-146 for the "Supplementary Report by the Supervisory Commission to the Fourth Committee."
[66]Also in *Official Journal*, March, 1932, p. 755-764.
[67]Also in Assembly Records, 13th Assembly, Fourth Committee, p. 216-231.
[68]Also *ibid.*, p. 232-238.

Fourth Committee. Geneva, October 19th, 1932. 2 p. [C.737.M. 348.1932.X.][69]

49a to 53d Sessions: Technical Concentration of the Activities of the League of Nations and Rationalisation of the Services of the Secretariat and the International Labour Office. Report by the Supervisory Commission to the Assembly. Geneva, July 20th, 1933. 18 p. [A.10.1933.X.][70]

52d Session: Report of the Supervisory Commission to the 1933 Assembly. Geneva, May 13th, 1933. 15 p. [A.5.1933.X.][71]

Includes Sixth Annual Report of the Publications Committee of the Secretariat, p. 12–15.

54th Session: Supplementary Report by the Supervisory Commission to the 1933 Assembly. Geneva, September 25th, 1933. 7 p. [A. 5(a).1933.X.][72]

54th Session: Second Supplementary Report by the Supervisory Commission to the Assembly. Geneva, October 7th, 1933. 3 p.[73]

55th and 56th Sessions: No published records. These sessions dealt mainly with the question of the new buildings of the League.

57th Session: First Report of the Supervisory Commission to the 1934 Assembly. Geneva, May 28th, 1934. 16 p. [A.5.1934.]

Includes Seventh Annual Report of the Publications Committee of the Secretariat, p. 13–16.

58th Session: Second Report of the Supervisory Commission to the 1934 Assembly. Geneva, June 20th, 1934. 12 p. [A.5(a).1934.X.]

59th to 61st Sessions: No published records.

62d Session: First Report of the Supervisory Commission to the Assembly of 1935. Geneva, May 12th, 1935. 16 p. [A.5.1935.X.][74]

Includes Eighth Annual Report of the Publications Committee of the Secretariat, p. 10–13.

[69]Also *ibid.*, p. 239–240.

[70]Also in Assembly Records, 14th Assembly, Fourth Committee, p. 99–111. See also *Questions Referred to the Supervisory Commission by the Council at Its Meeting on May 21st, 1932.* Geneva, September 20th, 1932. 42 p. [A.5(a).1932.X.]. This document, also in Assembly Records, 13th Assembly, Fourth Committee, p. 122–133, deals with the internal organization of the League; reforms designed to increase the efficiency of the organizations; staff salaries; and control of expenditures and limitation of budgets. In addition, see *Thirteenth Ordinary Session of the Assembly: Report of the Supervisory Commission to the Fourth Committee.* Geneva, December 19th, 1932. 2 p. [C.737.M.348.1932.X.]. Also in Assembly Records, 13th Assembly, Fourth Committee, p. 239–240.

[71]Also in Assembly Records, 14th Assembly, Fourth Committee, p. 122–136.

[72]Also *ibid.*, p. 115–121.

[73]Also *ibid.*, p. 156–158.

[74]The 60th Session (November, 1934) dealt exclusively with the question of the new buildings. At the 61st Session certain questions referred to the Commission by the previous Assembly were considered, and these are referred to in Document [A.5.1935. X.].

63d Session: Second Report of the Supervisory Commission to the 1935 Assembly. Geneva, August 16th, 1935. 11 p. [A.5(a).1935.X.][75]
64th Session: Report of the Supervisory Commission to the Fourth Committee of the Sixteenth Assembly. Geneva, September 30th, 1935. 7 p. [A.5(b).1935.X.]
65th Session: No published records.
66th to 67th Sessions: First Report of the Supervisory Commission to the Assembly of 1936. Geneva, May 25th, 1936. 19 p. [A.5. 1936.X.][76]

Includes Ninth Annual Report of the Publications Committee of the Secretariat, p. 16-19.

68th Session: Second Report of the Supervisory Commission to the Assembly of 1936. Geneva, September 24th, 1936. 7 p. [A.5(a). 1936.X.]

Appendix III contains Correspondents: Model Rules of Engagement, p. 7.

68th Session: Third Report of the Supervisory Commission to the 1936 Assembly. Geneva, October 12th, 1936. 5 p. [A.5(b).1936.X.]
69th to 71st Sessions: First Report of the Supervisory Commission to the 1937 Assembly. Geneva, May 28th, 1947. 23 p. [A.5.1937.X.][77]

Includes Tenth Annual Report of the Publications Committee of the Secretariat, p. 19-23.

72d Session: Second Report of the Supervisory Commission to the 1937 Assembly. Geneva, September 13th, 1937. 10 p. [A.5(a). 1937.X.][78]
72d Session: Second Report of the Supervisory Commission to the 1937 Assembly (Continuation). Geneva, September 14th, 1937. 2 p. [A.5(a).1937.X.(continuation)][79]
73d Session: Third Report of the Supervisory Commission to the 1937 Assembly. Geneva, October 5th, 1937. 10 p. [A.5(b).1937.X.][80]

Includes Item (10), Means of Spreading Information at the Secretariat's Disposal, p. 6-7.

74th Session: Technical Collaboration with China. Scheme of Anti-epidemic Action. Report by the Supervisory Commission. Geneva, October 22nd, 1937. 4 p. [C.524.M.363.1937.X.]
75th Session: Participation of the League of Nations in the New York

[75]See also the 4 p. Addendum [A.5(a).1935.X.Addendum].
[76]The Commission had met twice since the 1935 Assembly. The 65th Session (November, 1935) was entirely devoted to the question of the new buildings. At the 66th Session (January, 1936) certain questions referred to the Commission by the previous Assembly were considered, and these are dealt with in this document.
[77]Also in Assembly Records, 18th Assembly, Fourth Committee, p. 79-101.
[78]See especially "Payments to the League Budget by Non-Member States," p. 8-10.
[79]Also in Assembly Records, 18th Assembly, Fourth Committee, p. 111-112.
[80]Also *ibid.*, p. 113-121.

World's Fair (1939). Geneva, February 8th, 1938. 3 p. [A.5(c). 1938.X.]

76th Session: No published records.

77th Session: First Report of the Supervisory Commission to the 1938 Assembly. Geneva, May 12th, 1938. 16 p. [A.5.1938.X.][81]

Includes Eleventh Annual Report of the Publications Committee of the Secretariat, p. 13–16.

78th Session: Second Report of the Supervisory Commission to the 1938 Assembly. Geneva, July 13th, 1938. 10 p. [A.5(a).1938.X.][82]

79th Session: Third Report of the Supervisory Commission to the 1938 Assembly. Geneva, September 26th, 1938. 5 p. [A.5(b). 1938.X.][83]

80th Session: Technical Collaboration with China. Scheme of Anti-epidemic Action. Report of the Supervisory Commission. Geneva, November 21st, 1938. 4 p. [C.468.M.311.1938.X.][84]

81st Session: No published records.

82d Session: First Report of the Supervisory Commission to the 1939 Assembly. Geneva, May 31st, 1939. 19 p. [A.5.1939.X.]

Includes Twelfth Annual Report of the Publications Committee of the Secretariat, p. 14–19.

83d Session: Second Report of the Supervisory Commission to the 1939 Assembly. Paris, June 27th, 1939. 3 p. [A.5(a).1939.X.]

84th and 85th Sessions: Third Report of the Supervisory Commission to the 1939 Assembly. Geneva, October 19th, 1939. 8 p. [A.5(b). 1939.X.]

Contains: I. Functions of the Commission in Time of Emergency, p. 1. II. Decisions Reached by the Commission, at Its September Session, in Virtue of the Special Powers Conferred upon It by the Resolution of the 1938 Assembly, p. 2. III. Financial Position of the League, p. 3. IV. Emergency Measures: Administrative, p. 3. V. Rectified and Reduced Budget for 1940, p. 4. VI. Miscellaneous Financial Recommendations, p. 5. VII. Re-opening in 1940 of the New York World's Fair, p. 6. Annex I. Special Measures Applicable to the Staff during the Emergency Period. Annex II. Financial Position of the League of Nations.

86th Session: Fourth Report of the Supervisory Commission (1939). Geneva, December 5th, 1939. 8 p. [A.5(c).1939.X.]

Contains: A. Budget for 1939 [i.e., comments on the budget for 1939], p. 1. B. Budget for 1940, p. 2. C. Amendment of Article 29 of the Financial Regulations, p. 3. D. Voluntary Contribution from Salaries, p. 4. E. Emergency Measures: Ad-

[81]Also in Assembly Records, 19th Assembly, Fourth Committee, p. 59–71.
[82]Also ibid., p. 77–80.
[83]Also ibid., p. 86–90. See also Participation of the League of Nations in the New York World's Fair (1939). Second Report of the Supervisory Commission. Geneva, September 28th, 1938. 4 p. [A.5(d).1938.]. Also in Assembly Records, 19th Assembly, Fourth Committee, p. 107–110.
[84]On technical collaboration with China see also Assembly Records, 19th Assembly, Fourth Committee, p. 41–43, and Official Journal, November, 1938, p. 1112–1114.

ministrative, p. 4. F. Amendments Proposed in the Pensions Regulations, p. 6. G. Transfer of the Financial Functions of the Council, p. 8.

87th to 88th Sessions: Report of the Supervisory Commission for the Year 1940. Geneva, November 4th, 1940. 12 p. [C.152.M.139. 1940.X.][85]

89th Session: First Report of the Supervisory Commission for the Year 1941. Geneva, October 15th, 1941. 10 p. [C.53.M.50.1941.X.]

Contains: A. Introductory Remarks, p. 1. B. General Considerations, p. 2. C. Accounts for 1939 and 1940, p. 2. D. Contributions, p. 3. E. Allocation of the Expenses for 1942, p. 4. F. Financing of the Organisations, p. 4. G. Budget for 1942, p. 5. H. Publicity for the Work of the League Organisations, p. 7. I. Miscellaneous Grants for League Work in the United States of America, p. 8. J. Wireless Station, p. 8.[86] Annex A. Expenditure Budget for 1942, p. 9. Annex B. Resolutions, p. 9.

90th Session: First Report of the Supervisory Commission for the Year 1942. Geneva, October 15th, 1942. 38 p. [C.L.11.1942.X. Annex II.]

Contains: A. Introductory Remarks, p. 1. B. Activities of the Organisations, p. 2. C. Accounts for 1940 and 1941, p. 3. D. Allocation of the Expenses for 1943, p. 4. E. International Labour Organisation, p. 4. F. Financial Situation, p. 5. G. Contributions, p. 5. H. Budget for 1943, p. 5. I. Permanent Central Opium Board, p. 8. J. Eastern Bureau of the International Health Organisation at Singapore, p. 8. K. Transfers in the Budget, p. 9. L. Wireless Station, p. 9. M. Grants by the Rockefeller Foundation, p. 9. N. Administrative Board of the Staff Pensions Fund, p. 9. O. Pension Fund for Members of the Court, p. 9. Annex A. Expenditure Budget for the Year 1943 as Passed by the Supervisory Commission, p. 11. Annex B. Budget Allocation, Showing Proportion of Individual Budgets to Total Budget in Terms of Percentage, p. 11. Annex C. Resolutions, p. 12. Annex D. Permanent Court of International Justice: Vacancies Created by the Resignations of M. Urrutia and M. Nagaoka, p. 13. Annex E. League of Nations Wireless Station (Radio-Nations), p. 15. Annex F. Administrative Board of the Staff Pensions Fund. Report to the Supervisory Commission by the Sub-Committee of the Administrative Board of the Staff Pensions Fund, p. 21.

91st and 92d Sessions: First Report of the Supervisory Commission for the Year 1943.[87] Geneva, September 20th, 1943. 31 p. [C.23. M.23.1943.X.]

Contains: A. Introductory Remarks, p. 1. B. Activities of the Organisations, p. 2. C. Situation of League Offices, p. 6. D. Accounts for 1941 and 1942, p. 6. E. Allocation of the Expenses for 1944, p. 7. F. Communications Received Regarding the Membership of France, p. 7. G. Financial Situation, p. 7. H. Contributions, p. 8. I. Budget for 1944, p. 8. J. Eastern Bureau of the International Health Organisation at Singapore, p. 10. K. Request by the International Red Cross for the Temporary Loan of the Premises of the International Labour Organisation in Geneva, p. 11. L. Transfers in the Budget, p. 11. M. Grants by the Rockefeller Foundation,

[85]See especially the resolutions adopted by the Supervisory Commission, p. 10–11.
[86]This refers to the denunciation by the Swiss government of the agreement with the League concerning Radio-Nations on January 27, 1940.
[87]See also *Addendum to the First Report of the Supervisory Commission for the Year 1943*. Geneva, March 18th, 1944. 1 p., mimeographed. [C.23.M.23.1943.X(Addendum)]

p. 11. N. Administrative Board of the Staff Pensions Fund, p. 11. O. Pension Fund for Members of the Court, p. 11. P. Settlement of the Claim by the "Entreprise du Palais des Nations" (E.P.N.) against the League of Nations, p. 12. Q. Resolutions, p. 12. Annexes include: F. Summary of Report by the Acting Secretary-General on the Publishing Activities of the Secretariat during the Year 1942, p. 28. G. Publications of the Economic and Financial Department, August, 1942–July, 1943, p. 30.

93d and 94th Sessions: First Report of the Supervisory Commission for the Year 1944. Geneva, October 31st, 1944. 42 p. [C.27.M.27.1944.X.]

Contains: A. Introductory Remarks, p. 1. B. Activities of Organisations, p. 6. C. Financial Situation, p. 11. D. Allocation of Expenses, p. 11. E. Contributions, p. 11. F. Budget for 1945, p. 12. G. Accounts for 1942 and 1943, p. 15. H. Supplementary International Labour Office Credit in 1944 to Provide for the Convening of a Conference, p. 13. I. Regulations for the Financial Administration of the League, p. 16. J. Transfers in the Budget, p. 16. K. Settlement of the Assyrians of Iraqu, p. 17. L. Grant by the Rockefeller Foundation, p. 17. M. Grant by the Milbank Memorial Fund, p. 17. N. Prolongation of Contracts, p. 18. O. Income Tax Payable by Officials on Mission in the United States, p. 18. P. Special Temporary Allowances to Members of the Staff of the Secretariat and the International Labour Office, p. 18. Q. Administrative Board of the Staff Pensions Fund, p. 19. R. Board of Management of the Staff Provident Fund, p. 13. S. Resolutions, p. 16. Annexes include: H. Report by the Acting Secretary-General on the Publishing Activities of the Secretariat during the year 1943, p. 36. I. Recent Publications of the Economic, Financial and Transit Department on Post-War Problems, p. 40. J. Publications of the Economic and Financial Department in 1943–1944, p. 41–42.

95th and 96th Sessions: First Report of the Supervisory Commission for the Year 1945. Geneva, November 20th, 1945. 24 p. [C.118.M.118.1945.X.]

Contains: A. Introductory Remarks, p. 1. B. Activities of Organisations, p. 4. C. Financial Situation, p. 7. D. Allocation of Expenses, p. 7. E. Contributions, p. 7. F. Budget for 1946, p. 8. G. Accounts for 1943 and 1944, p. 11. H. Regulations for the Financial Administration of the League, p. 11. I. Transfers in the Budget, p. 11. J. Grant by the Rockefeller Foundation, p. 11. K. Income Tax Payable by Officials on Mission in the United States, p. 11. L. Special Temporary Allowances to Members of the Staff of the Secretariat, the International Labour Office and the Permanent Court of International Justice, Residing at Geneva or at the Hague, p. 12. M. Administrative Board of the Staff Pensions Fund, p. 12. N. Administrative Tribunal, p. 12. O. Board of Management of the Staff Provident Fund, p. 12. P. Resolutions, p. 12. Annexes include: C. Statement of Actual Expenditure for the Years 1939–1944, p. 16. Annex D: 1. Report by the Acting Secretary-General on the Publishing Activities of the Secretariat during the Year 1944, p. 17. 2. Interim Report by the Acting Secretary-General on the Publishing Activities of the Secretariat during the Period January-August, 1945, p. 20.

Reports of the 79th to 102d Sessions of the Supervisory Commission are in *Official Journal*, Special Supplement No. 194. 293 p. The page numbers refer to that volume.

97th and 98th Sessions: General Summarised Report on the Work of

the Supervisory Commission during the Period of Emergency, 1940–1946. [A.5.1946.]. p. 149–159.

Contains: I. General, p. 149. II. Constitution, p. 152. III. The Permanent Court of International Justice, p. 153. IV. Financial Situation, p. 153.

99th Session: Report of the Supervisory Commission on the Work of Its Ninety-ninth Session. Geneva, March 22nd, 1946. [A.14.1946. X.]. p. 160–165.

Contains: A. Introductory Remarks, p.160. B. Indemnities to Staff, p. 161. C. Administrative Tribunal, p. 162. D. Repatriation Expenses of Officials and/or Removal of Their Furniture, p. 162. E. Grant of a Winter Allowance to the Lower Categories of the Geneva Staff, p. 163. F. International Labour Organisation Balances for 1941, 1943 and 1944, p. 163. G. Financial Situation, p. 163. Appendix: Extracts from the Staff Regulations, p. 163.

100th Session: Report of the Supervisory Commission on the Work of Its One-hundredth Session. Geneva, April 3rd, 1946. [A.19.1946. X.]. p. 166–173.

Contains: A. Introductory Remarks, p. 166. B. Activities of Organisations, p. 166. C. Audited Accounts for 1945, p. 168. D. Liquidation of the Nansen International Office, p. 168. E. Contributions, p. 168. F. Staff Pensions Fund, p. 169. G. Staff Provident Fund, p. 169. Appendix, p. 169.

101st Session: Report of the Supervisory Commission on the Work of Its Hundred-and-first Session. Geneva, April 10th, 1946. [A.25. 1946.X.]. p. 174–178.

Contains: A. Staff Provident Fund, p. 174. B. Staff Pensions Fund and Judges' Pensions Fund, p. 174. C. Claim of the Carnegie Foundation for Payment of Maintenance Charges during the War Years from the Permanent Court of International Justice, p. 175. D. Voluntary Contribution of the Staff, p. 175. E. Indemnities to Employees, p. 176. F. Termination of the League: Measures to Be Taken for the Disposal of League Assets, p. 176. Appendix: Memorandum by the Rapporteur on the Future Administration of the League Pensions Funds, p. 177.

102d Session: Report of the Supervisory Commission on the Work of Its Hundred-and-second Session. Geneva, April 12th, 1946. [A.28. 1946.X.]. p. 179–180.

Contains: A. Draft Assembly Resolution for the Dissolution of the League of Nations, p. 179. B. Liquidation of the Nansen International Office, p. 180.

VI. INFORMATION SECTION

1. INTRODUCTORY NOTE

THE INFORMATION SECTION of the Secretariat was designed to inform the general public about the activities of the League, and, in turn, to inform the Secretariat and the League members about public opinion towards the League.[1] In addition to these liaison activities, the Information Section prepared for the use of the Secretariat a daily synopsis of the press, covering about 200 newspapers. It is a controversial point whether the publications of the Information Section were "official" publications of the League. They did not, however, bear either official or sales numbers.

2. SERIAL PUBLICATIONS

THE LEAGUE FROM YEAR TO YEAR

First Volume: The League of Nations from Year to Year (October 1926–October 1927). Geneva, 1927. 158 p.
Last Volume: The League from Year to Year (1938). Geneva, 1938. 214 p.
This was an annual publication covering the period from October, 1926 to 1938.[2]

ESSENTIAL FACTS ABOUT THE LEAGUE OF NATIONS

First Edition: Essential Facts about the League of Nations. Geneva, 1933. 140 p.
Last Edition: Essential Facts about the League of Nations. Tenth edition (revised). Geneva, 1939. 359 p.

MONTHLY SUMMARY OF THE LEAGUE OF NATIONS

First Number: No. 1, April, 1921. 12 p.
Last Number: Vol. XX, Nos. 1–2, January–February, 1940. 35 p.
This was a popular survey of the League's work during the preceding month, published in five languages: English, French, German, Italian, and Spanish. It included a calendar of events, a listing of conferences, committees, meetings, etc. Special Supplements, for

[1]On the work of the Information Section, see Egon F. Ranshofen-Wertheimer, *The International Secretariat* (Washington, 1945), p. 199–222.
[2]For the period 1920–1926, see *The League of Nations: A Survey (January 1920–December 1926)*. Revised edition. Geneva, 1926. 117 p.

instance, "Books on the League of Nations Received in the Library of the Secretariat," enhance the usefulness of the series. The last Special Supplement, "The Health Work of the League of Nations, Thirty-first Session of the Health Committee," appeared in January, 1940.

The Information Section was also responsible for several unofficial editions of the Covenant of the League of Nations.

3. INDIVIDUAL PAMPHLETS

From 1923 to 1927 the Information Section issued the following publications: *The League of Nations: A Survey; The League of Nations: Constitution and Organisation; The League of Nations and Mandates; Social and Humanitarian Activities; The League of Nations and the Protection of Minorities of Race, Language and Religion; Work of the Financial and Economic Organisation; The League of Nations and Intellectual Co-operation;* and *The Permanent Court of International Justice.* Virtually all of these pamphlets appeared in several editions which were revised from time to time.

Other pamphlets include:

Financial Administration and Apportionment of Expenses, by Sir Herbert Ames (Financial Director). Geneva, 1923. 42 p.

Financial Administration and Apportionment of Expenses. Revised edition. Geneva, 1928. 41 p.

The Financial Reconstruction of Austria. Geneva, 1923. 36 p.

Communications and Transit. Geneva, 1924. 41 p.

Saar Basin and Free City of Danzig. Geneva, 1924. 34 p.

Political Activities. Geneva, 1925. 130 p.

Political Activities. Geneva, 1927. 88 p.

The League of Nations and the Reform of the Calendar. Geneva, no date. 29 p.

The League of Nations and the Press. International Press Exhibition. Cologne, May to October, 1928. Geneva, 1928. 65 p.

The League of Nations. A Vital Necessity in the Modern World: Addresses Delivered on the Occasion of the 100th Session of the Council, January 27th, 1938. Geneva, 1938. 45 p.

The Council of the League of Nations. Composition. Competence. Procedure. Geneva, 1938. 141 p.

The League Hands Over. Geneva, 1946. 126 p. (General.1946.1.)

A readable summary of the proceedings of the Twentieth (Conclusion) and Twenty-first Assemblies on the liquidation of the League and the transfer of its assets and functions to the United Nations.

4. LEAGUE OF NATIONS QUESTIONS

No. 1. The Saar Plebiscite. Geneva, 1935. 41 p.

No. 2. Facts and Figures: Production, Trade and Prices To-day. Geneva, 1935. 13 p.

No. 3. The Economic Interdependence of States. Geneva, 1935. 33 p.

No. 4. Nutrition Considered in Relation to Public Health and to Economic Conditions. Geneva, 1935. 24 p.

No. 5. The Settlement of the Assyrians: A Work of Humanity and Appeasement. Geneva, 1935. 46 p.

No. 6. Intellectual Co-operation. Geneva, 1937. 69 p.

No. 7. New Technical Efforts towards a Better Nutrition. Geneva, 1938. 36 p.

No. 8. Traffic in Women in the East. Work of the Bandoeng Conference. Geneva, 1938. 86 p.

No. 9. The Refugees. Geneva, 1938. 54 p.

No. 10. The League of Nations Library. Geneva, 1938. 45 p.

No. 11. Towards a Better Economic World. Geneva, 1939. 90 p.

No. 12. World Health and the League. Geneva, 1939. 43 p.

5. PICTORIAL SURVEY

The League of Nations. A Pictorial Survey. No date. Unpaged.

"The Information Section of the League Secretariat has found that its Exhibit of Charts and Photographs concisely outlining in 25 placards the character and main achievements of the League, the International Labour Organisation, and the Permanent Court of International Justice, has met a definite requirement in schools and various organisations. It was therefore decided to reproduce them for individual use and interest in the form of this present volume." The volume covers developments up to 1929.

6. THE PALACE OF THE LEAGUE OF NATIONS

The Palace of the League of Nations. Text by Louis Cheronet. Paris, 1938. Published by *L'Illustration*. 72 p.

A lavishly illustrated guidebook. Distributed by the Information Section.

VII. THE LIBRARY

1. INTRODUCTORY NOTE

THE LIBRARY of the League of Nations grew from very modest beginnings in 1920 to a unique reference center[1] on international relations. Within the general field of international relations it specialized, of course, in League of Nations questions.

It was first housed in London (1920), at 117 Piccadilly. Together with the Secretariat it was subsequently moved to the Hotel National in Geneva. In the fall of 1936 it was transferred to a new building which later formed a wing of the Palace of the League of Nations.

In 1927 a sum of two million dollars was offered for the construction and endowment of a League Library by a group of American citizens.[2] No conditions were attached to the gift. The League was entirely free to decide what proportion should be devoted to construction and what to endowment and to take whatever measures seemed appropriate for the establishment of an efficient library service and for the building up of a collection which would serve the purposes of the League.

Besides the Secretariat Building and Assembly Hall the Library constituted the most valuable tangible asset of the League. In 1946 it was transferred together with other assets of the League to the United Nations. At that time it was decided that the Library should continue to function in Geneva until the whole question could be considered in connection with the permanent headquarters of the United Nations.

Several League publications were issued on behalf of the Library.

[1] See A. C. Breycha-Vauthier, *La Société des Nations centre d'étude d'information* (Paris 1937).

[2] See "Offer by a Group of American Citizens for the Construction and Endowment of the League of Nations Library," *Official Journal*, October, 1927, p. 1132-1134. See also *Report by the Executive Committee to the Preparatory Commission of the United Nations* (PC/EX/113/Rev.1, 12 November 1945), p. 114: "It is noted that Mr. J. D. Rockefeller, Jr., gave an endowment for erecting the library building and for the upkeep of a library of international value. It will, therefore, be proper to consult Mr. Rockefeller on any arrangement for the transfer of the library." See also League of Nations, Board of Liquidation, *Final Report* [C.5.M.5.1947.] (General.1947.1.), p. 12: "The Library Endowment Fund, the balance of which amounted on the date of transfer, April 15th, 1947, to Swiss francs 2,177,486.18, was constituted from funds given by Mr. Rockefeller. The Board accordingly decided to hand it with the building to the United Nations. Subsequently it added to the Endowment Fund an amount of Swiss francs 217,735.38, representing the balance of the Library Building Fund." See also Board of Liquidation, *Fourth Interim Report*, Annex 3, p. 10.

Like the publications of the Information Section, the publications of the Library were not marked with official or sales numbers.

The major publications of the Library are listed below.

2. GENERAL

The Library. A Report on Its Progress, Aims, Scope, Methods, Details of Work and Personnel. Prepared for the Committee on the Library Appointed by the Secretary-General. No date. 48 p., mimeographed.

Marked: Florence Wilson 10/2/22

Libraries of the Secretariat and the International Labour Office. Report by the Commission of Experts. Geneva, 1923. 5 p. [C.204. M.120.1923.]

The League of Nations Library. Geneva, 1938. 45 p.

Published by the Information Section as *League of Nations Questions No. 10*.

3. FORTNIGHTLY LIST OF SELECTED ARTICLES

First Issue: League of Nations. Library. Fortnightly List of Selected Articles. 1st Year, Volume 1, Nos. 1–2. Genève, 1929. 14 p.

Last Issue: League of Nations. Library. Fortnightly List of Selected Articles. Volume 1, Nos. 23–24. Genève, December 15th, 1929, p. 253–271.

4. MONTHLY LIST OF SELECTED ARTICLES

First Issue: League of Nations Library. Monthly List of Selected Articles. 2nd Year, Volume 2, No. 1. January 15th, 1930. Genève, 1930. p. 1–22.

This issue was the first in the monthly series, notwithstanding the imprint "Volume 2."

Last Issue: League of Nations. Monthly List of Selected Articles. Volume 18, Nos. 4–7. March 16th–July 31st, 1946. Genève, 1946. p. 25–53.

The series is being continued by the United Nations. The first issue was published under the imprint: United Nations Library. Vol. XVIII, Nos. 8–9. August 1st–September 30th, 1946.

5. CHRONOLOGY OF INTERNATIONAL TREATIES AND LEGISLATIVE MEASURES

First Issue: League of Nations Library. Chronology of International

Treaties and Legislative Measures. 1930, No. 1. 15 janvier 1930. 12 p.

Last Issue: League of Nations Library. Chronology of International Treaties and Legislative Measures. 11th Year, Nos. 1–2. December 16th, 1939–February 15th, 1940. 20 p.

The object of this publication was to provide particulars of the latest treaties and conventions concluded and of the most recent legislative documents (laws, bills, decrees, orders, etc.) of the various countries which had any connection with the different activities of the League of Nations. The texts were from the official gazettes of nearly all countries of the world.

6. BOOKS ON THE LEAGUE IN THE LIBRARY

League of Nations. Books on the Work of the League of Nations Catalogued in the Library of the Secretariat. Genève, 1928. 274 p.

League of Nations Library. Books on the Work of the League of Nations Catalogued in the Library of the Secretariat. First Supplement, January, 1928–October, 1931. Genève, 1931. 156 p.

7. MONTHLY LIST OF BOOKS CATALOGUED IN THE LIBRARY

First Issue: League of Nations Library. Monthly List of Books Catalogued in the Library of the League of Nations. 1st Year–Volume 1, January–February, 1928. Nos. 1–2. Genève, 1928. 32 p.

Last Issue: League of Nations Library. Monthly List of Books Catalogued in the Library of the League of Nations. 18th–19th Years, January, 1945–July, 1946. Genève, 1946. 162 p.

The series is being continued by the United Nations. The first issue was published under the imprint: United Nations Library. 19th–20th years, Nos. 8–9, August 1946–December 1947.

8. BIBLIOGRAPHY ON MANDATES

League of Nations Library. List of Works Relating to the Mandates System and the Territories under Mandate Catalogued in the Library of the League of Nations. Genève, 1930. 106 p.

League of Nations Library. List of Works Relating to the Mandates System and the Territories under Mandate Catalogued in the Library of the League of Nations. First Supplement. Genève, 1934. 55 p.

9. BIBLIOGRAPHY ON DISARMAMENT

League of Nations Library. Annotated Bibliography on Disarmament and Military Questions. Geneva, 1931. 163 p.

10. MISCELLANEOUS BIBLIOGRAPHIES

[1]. League of Nations Library. Material Relating to China and Japan Received in the Library from January 1st to September 30, 1933. Geneva, 1933. 21 p.

[2]. League of Nations Library. Material Relating to the Corporative Movement. Genève, mars 1934. 32 p., mimeographed.

3. League of Nations Library. List of Works Relating to Slavery Catalogued in the Library of the League of Nations. Genève, 1935. 48 p.[3]

4. League of Nations Library. Analysis of Material Published Regularly in Official Gazettes. Genève, 1935. 24 p., mimeographed.

5. League of Nations Library. List of Works on Hashish Catalogued in the Library of the League of Nations. Genève, 1935. 12 p., mimeographed.

6. League of Nations Library. List of Selected Works on Raw Materials, Colonies and Allied Problems Catalogued at the Library of the League of Nations. Genève, 1937. 24 p., mimeographed.

7. League of Nations Library. List of Economic and Financial Periodicals Regularly Received in the League of Nations Library. Genève, 1936. 148 p., mimeographed.

8. League of Nations Library. Annotated Bibliography on Legal Questions Concerning International Loans. Genève, 1937. 23 p., mimeographed.

9. League of Nations Library. Documentation Relating to the Economic Aspects of War. Genève, septembre 1939. 74 p., mimeographed.

10. League of Nations Library. War-time Legislation 1939: Economic, Financial and Transport Questions. Genève, novembre 1939. 51 p., mimeographed.

11. League of Nations Library. War-time Legislation 1939/40: Economic, Financial and Transport Questions. Genève, février 1940. 71 p., mimeographed.

11. GUIDE TO LEAGUE OF NATIONS PUBLICATIONS

Brief Guide to League of Nations Publications. Revised edition. Genève, 1930. 32 p.

[3]Beginning with No. 3 these bibliographies are numbered *seriatim:* "League of Nations Library Miscellaneous Bibliographies."

VIII. RADIO-NATIONS[1]

Communications of Importance to the League of Nations at Times of Emergency. Geneva, 1927. 3 p. <C.C.T.310.>

Report submitted to the Council by the Advisory and Technical Committee for Communications and Transit.

Establishment of a League of Nations Radio-Telegraphic Station. Geneva, 1928. 9 p. [C.141.M.32.1928.VIII.] <C.C.T.356.>

Radio-Telegraphic Station for the Purpose of Ensuring Independent Communications for the League of Nations at Times of Emergency. Note and Memorandum from the Swiss Federal Government. Geneva, 1928. 5 p. [A.31.1928.VIII.] (1928.VIII.5.)

Agreement between the Swiss Federal Council and the Secretary-General of the League of Nations Concerning the Establishment and Operation in the Neighbourhood of Geneva of a Wireless Station. Geneva, 1930. 3 p. [C.191.M.91.1930.VIII.] (1930.VIII.2.)

Translation from the original French text published under the same official and sales number. Reprinted below, Appendix One, Section X.

Convention between the Secretary-General of the League of Nations and the Radio-Suisse Incorporated Wireless Telegraph and Telephone Company, Berne, Concerning the Establishment and Operation in the Neighbourhood of Geneva of a Wireless Station. Geneva, 1930. 7 p. [C.192.M.92.1930.VIII.] (1930.VIII.3.)

Systematic Survey of the Regime of Communications of Importance to the Working of the League of Nations at Times of Emergency. Geneva, 1934. 101 p. [C.348.M.161.1934.VIII.] (1934.VIII.6.)

Radio-Nations Code for the Announcement or Organisation of the Transmission of Radiotelegraphic Communiqués by the Secretary-General of the League of Nations to the Governments, and Rules to Be Followed for These Transmissions. (This Code Will Come into Force on September 21st, 1936). No date. 16 p. [C.L.131. 1936.VIII.Annex]

The Radio-Nations Code intended to be used for announcing or organizing the transmission of radiotelegraphic communiqués sent to governments by the Secretary-General of the League of Nations came into force on September 21, 1936.[2]

[1]"Radio-Nations" was the official name of the wireless station operated by the League designed chiefly to meet the needs of the League in normal times and to ensure independent communications to the League in times of emergency.
[2]See also the covering Circular Letter, Document [C.L.131.1936.VIII.]. No date.

League of Nations Wireless Station (Radio-Nations). Note by the Acting Secretary-General. Geneva, 1941. 6 p., mimeographed. [C.56.M.53.1941.VIII.]

This document, dated September 15, 1941, contains information and supplementary material related to the letter of January 27, 1940, by which the Swiss Federal Council denounced with effect as from February 2, 1942, the agreement concluded on May 21, 1930, between the Swiss Federal Council and the Secretary-General of the League of Nations concerning the establishment and operation of a wireless station.[3] This denunciation automatically involved the cancellation of the Convention concluded on May 21, 1930, between the Secretary-General of the League of Nations and Radio-Suisse[4].

---

3 p., mimeographed. Circular Letter dated December 28th, 1935, Document [C.L. 212.1935.VIII.] 3 p., mimeographed, together with the 6 p. mimeographed Annex, Document [C.L.212.1935.VIII.Annex].

[3]See above, Document [C.191.M.91.1930.VIII.].

[4]See above, Document [C.192.M.92.1930.VIII.]. See also *League of Nations Wireless Station (Radio-Nations). Note by the Acting Secretary-General.* Geneva, February 2nd, 1942. 12 p. + 12 p., mimeographed, bilingual. For the text of the agreement between the United Nations and the Swiss Federal Government concerning radio frequencies formerly used by the League of Nations, see United Nations Document A/C.5/207, 8 November 1947. Reprinted below, Appendix Three, Section VIII.

IX. THE LEAGUE IN GENERAL

1. ANNUAL REPORTS BY THE SECRETARY-GENERAL

Report by the Secretary-General to the First Assembly of the League on the Work of the Council. No date. [1920] 59 p., bilingual. [Document de l'Assemblée 37] (20/48/37)[1]

Report to the Second Assembly of the League on the Work of the Council and on the Measures Taken to Execute the Decisions of the First Assembly. Geneva, 1921. 83 p.+83 p., bilingual. [A.9. 1921.]

Supplementary Report to the Second Assembly of the League on the Work of the Council and on the Measures Taken to Execute the Decisions of the First Assembly. Geneva, 1921. 8 p.+8 p., bilingual. [A.9(1).1921.]

Report to the Third Assembly . . . Geneva, 1922. 84 p.+84 p., bilingual. [A.6.1922.]

Supplementary Report to the Third Assembly . . . Geneva, 1922. 22 p.+22 p., bilingual. [A.6(a).1922.]

Report to the Fourth Assembly . . . Geneva, 1923. 96 p. [A.10.1923.]

Supplementary Report to the Fourth Assembly . . . Geneva, 1923. 46 p. [A.10(a).1923.]

Annex to the Supplementary Report to the Fourth Assembly . . . Geneva, 1923. 16 p. [A.10(a).Annex 1923.]

Report to the Fifth Assembly . . . Geneva, 1924. 93 p. [A.8.1924.]

Supplementary Report to the Fifth Assembly . . . Geneva, 1924. 50 p. [A.8(a).1924.]

Annex to the Supplementary Report . . . to the Fifth Assembly . . . Geneva, 1924. 27 p. [A.8(a).1924.Annex.]

Report to the Sixth Assembly of the League . . .[2] Geneva, 1925. 120 p. [A.7.1925.]

Supplementary Report to the Sixth Assembly . . . Geneva, 1925. 50 p. [A.7(a).1925.]

Annex to the Supplementary Report . . . to the Sixth Assembly . . . Geneva, 1925. 30 p. [A.7(a).1925.Annex]

Report to the Seventh Assembly . . . Geneva, 1926. 125 p. [A.6. 1926.] (General Questions.1926.3.)

Supplementary Report to the Seventh Assembly . . . Geneva, 1926. 71 p. [A.6(a).1926.] (General Questions.1926.9.)

[1]Also listed in the League's *Catalogue of Publications*, p. 34, as Document [A.37.1920.].
[2]See also Document [A.7.1925.Erratum]. 1 p.

Annex to the Supplementary Report . . . to the Seventh Assembly . . . Geneva, 1926. 37 p. [A.6(a).1926.Annex.] (General.1926.7.)

Report to the Eighth Ordinary Session of the Assembly . . . Geneva, 1927. 96 p. [A.13.1927.] (General Questions.1927.3.)

Supplementary Report to the Eighth Ordinary Session of the Assembly . . . Geneva, 1927. 52 p. [A.13(a).1927.] (General.1927.7.)

Annex to the Supplementary Report . . . to the Eighth Ordinary Session of the Assembly . . . Geneva, 1927. 40 p. [A.13(a).1927.Annex.]

Report to the Ninth Ordinary Session of the Assembly . . . Geneva, 1928. 120 p. [A.6.1928.] (General.1928.3.)

Supplementary Report to the Ninth Ordinary Session of the Assembly . . . Geneva, 1928. 64 p. [A.6(a).1928.] (General.1928.4.)

Annex to the Supplementary Report . . . to the Ninth Ordinary Session of the Assembly . . . Geneva, 1928. 54 p. [A.6(a).1928.Annex.] (General.1928.5.)

Report on the Work of the League of Nations since the Last Session of the Assembly. Geneva, 1929. 129 p. [A.6.1929.] (General.1929.2.)

Supplementary Report on the Work of the League since the Last Session of the Assembly. Geneva, 1929. 51 p. [A.6(a).1929.] (General.1929.3.)

Annex to the Supplementary Report . . . to the Tenth Ordinary Session of the Assembly . . . Geneva, 1929. 62 p. [A.6(a).1929.Annex.] (General.1929.4.)

Report on the Work of the League since the Last Session of the Assembly . . . Geneva, 1930. 115 p. [A.6.1930.] (General.1930.2.)

Supplementary Report on the Work of the League since the Tenth Session of the Assembly. Geneva, 1930. 48 p. [A.6(a).1930.] (General.1930.5.)

Annex to the Supplementary Report . . . to the Eleventh Ordinary Session of the Assembly of the League. Geneva, 1930. 91 p. [A.6(a).1930.Annex.] (General.1930.6.)

Report on the Work of the League since the Last Session of the Assembly. Geneva, 1931. 161 p. [A.6.1931.] (General.1931.3.)

Supplementary Report on the Work of the League since the Eleventh Session of the Assembly. Geneva, 1931. 47 p. [A.6(a).1931.] (General.1931.5.)

Annex to the Supplementary Report . . . to the Twelfth Ordinary Session of the Assembly . . . Geneva, 1931. 115 p. [A.6(a).1931.V.Annex.] (General.1931.6.)

Report on the Work of the League since the Twelfth Session of the Assembly.[3] Geneva, 1932. 113 p. [A.6.1932.] (General.1932.3.)

Supplementary Report on the Work of the League since the Twelfth Session of the Assembly. Geneva, 1932. 56 p. [A.6(a).1932.] (General.1932.5.)

[3]See also Document [A.6.1932.Erratum]. 1 p.

Annex to the Supplementary Report . . . to the Thirteenth Ordinary Session of the Assembly . . . Geneva, 1932. 112 p. [A.6(a).1932. V.Annex.] (1932.V.1.)

Report on the Work of the League since the Thirteenth Session of the Assembly. Geneva, 1933. 122 p. [A.6.1933.] (General.1933.2.)

Supplementary Report on the Work of the League since the Thirteenth Session of the Assembly. Geneva, 1933. 69 p. [A.6(a). 1933.] (General.1933.3.)

Annex to the Supplementary Report . . . to the Fourteenth Ordinary Session of the Assembly . . . Geneva, 1933. 119 p. [A.6(a).1933. V.Annex.] (1933.V.5.)

Report on the Work of the League since the Fourteenth Session of the Assembly. Part I: Geneva, 1934. 108 p. [A.6.1934.] (General. 1934.3.I.). Part II: Geneva, 1934. 79 p. [A.6(a).1934.] (General. 1934.3.II.)

Annex to the Report . . . to the Fifteenth Ordinary Session of the Assembly . . . Geneva, 1934. 125 p. [A.6(a).1934.V.Annex.] (1934. V.1.)

Report on the Work of the League since the Fifteenth Session of the Assembly. Part I: Geneva, 1935. 117 p. [A.6.1935.] (General. 1935.2.). Part II: Geneva, 1935. 70 p. [A.6(a).1935.] (General. 1935.4.)

Annex to the Report . . . to the Sixteenth Ordinary Session of the Assembly . . . Geneva, 1935. 122 p. [A.6(a).1935.V.Annex.] (1935. V.3.)

Report on the Work of the League 1935/36. Part I:[4] Geneva, 1936. 247 p. [A.6.1936.] (General.1936.5.). Part II: Geneva, 1936. 105 p. [A.6(a).1936.] (General.1936.6.)

Annex to the Report . . . to the Seventeenth Ordinary Session of the Assembly . . . Geneva, 1936. 131 p. [A.6(a).1936.Annex I(V).] (1936.V.4.)

Annex to the Report on the Work of the League 1935/36, Part II: Note by the Secretary-General on the Economic Situation. Geneva, 1936. 16 p. [A.6(a).1936.Annex II] (General.1936.7.)

Report on the Work of the League 1936/37. Part I: Geneva, 1937. 240 p. [A.6.1937.] (General.1937.3.). Part II: Geneva, 1937. 75 p. [A.6(a).1937.] (General.1937.4.)

Annex to the Report on the Work of the League 1936/37. Part II: Note by the Secretary-General on the Economic Situation. Geneva, 1937. 15 p. [A.6(a).1937.Annex II.] (General.1937.6.)

Annex to the Report . . . to the Eighteenth Ordinary Session of the Assembly. Geneva, 1937. 133 p. [A.6(a).1937.Annex.I.V.] (1937. V.4.)

[4]See also Document [A.6.1936.Addenda]. 4 p.

Report on the Work of the League 1937/38. Part I. Geneva, 1938. 216 p. [A.6.1938.] (General.1938.4.). Part II: Geneva, 1938. 92 p. [A.6(a).1938.] (General.1938.5.)

Annex to the Report . . . to the Nineteenth Ordinary Session of the Assembly . . . Geneva, 1938. 139 p. [A.6(a).1938.Annex.I.V.] (1938.V.4.)

Annex to the Report on the Work of the League 1937/38. Part II: Note by the Secretary-General on the Economic Situation. Geneva, 1938. 18 p. [A.6(a).1938.Annex.II.] (General.1938.6.]

Report on the Work of the League 1938/39.[5] Geneva, 1939. 194 p. [A.6.1939.] (General.1939.2.)

Report on the Work of the League (Continuation) July-Mid-November 1939. Geneva, 1939. 62 p. [A.6(a).1939] (General.1939.4.)

Annex to the Report . . . to the Twentieth Ordinary Session of the Assembly.[6] Geneva, 1939. 144 p. [A.6.1939.Annex.I.V.] (1939.V.2.)

Brief Statement on the Activities of the League of Nations and Its Organs in 1940 and 1941. Submitted by the Acting Secretary-General. Geneva, 1941. 26 p. [C.41.M.38.1941.] (General.1941.1.)

Report on the Work of the League 1941–1942. Submitted by the Acting Secretary-General. Geneva, 1942. 87 p. [C.35.M.35.1942.] (General.1942.1.)

Report on the Work of the League 1942–1943. Submitted by the Acting Secretary-General. Geneva, 1943. 103 p. [C.25.M.25.1943.] (General.1943.1.)

Annex to the Report on the Work of the League for the Year 1942–1943. Geneva, 1944. 197 p. [C.25.M.25.1943.V.Annex.] (1944.V.2.)

Report on the Work of the League 1943–1944. Submitted by the Acting Secretary-General. Geneva, April, 1945. 100 p. [C.14.M.14.1945.] (General.1945.1.)

Report on the Work of the League during the War. Submitted to the Assembly by the Acting Secretary-General. Geneva, October, 1945. 167 p. [A.6.1946.] (General.1945.2.)

Contains a list of League of Nations Publications, January 1st, 1940–October 31st, 1945, p. 151–167.

2. GENERAL SURVEYS ON THE ACTIVITIES OF THE LEAGUE

MONOGRAPHS

Ten Years of World Co-operation. Secretariat of the League of Nations. 1930. 467 p.

[5]See introductory note.
[6]See also Document [A.6.1939.Annex V.Addendum].

Contains: Foreword by Sir Eric Drummond. Chapter I. The Peaceful Settlement of Disputes. Chapter II. The Organisation of Peace and Disarmament. Chapter III. International Justice. Chapter IV. Codification of International Law. Chapter V. Financial and Economic Co-operation. Chapter VI. International Transit and Communications. Chapter VII. Health. Chapter VIII. Social and Humanitarian Activities. Chapter IX. Intellectual Co-operation. Chapter X. The Mandates System. Chapter XI. Protection of Minorities. Chapter XII. The Saar Territory and the Free City of Danzig. Chapter XIII. The Financial Administration of the League. Chapter XIV. The League and Public Opinion. Annexes: I. The Covenant of the League of Nations. II. Short Bibliography of the Publications of the League of Nations. III. Annotated Bibliography of the Principal Works on the League of Nations Catalogued in Secretariat Library. The following chapters were published as separate pamphlets: The Organisation of Peace and Disarmament; Financial and Economic Co-operation; Health Organisation; Social and Humanitarian Activities; The Mandates System; Protection of Minorities.

The Aims, Methods and Activity of the League of Nations. Secretariat of the League of Nations. Geneva, 1935. 221 p.

This little book, due largely to the joint efforts of the Information and Intellectual Co-operation Sections of the Secretariat of the League of Nations, represents an attempt to carry out the recommendations made by the Advisory Committee on League of Nations Teaching at its two meetings on July 10, 1935. It is also an attempt to supply the general public with a useful, though by no means exhaustive, account of the League's origins, organization, methods and achievements. Though published by the Secretariat, it should not be regarded as an official document involving the responsibility of the League of Nations.

Powers and Duties Attributed to the League of Nations by International Treaties. Geneva, 1944. 48 p. [C.3.M.1.1944.V.] (1944.V.3.)

Discusses, in addition to the so-called Secretarial or Ministerial Functions, League functions that form part of the operation of international treaties, conventions, or other instruments. Thus it serves to indicate the gap which would be caused by its disappearance.

3. LIQUIDATION OF THE LEAGUE OF NATIONS AND TRANSFER OF ASSETS AND FUNCTIONS TO THE UNITED NATIONS

In accordance with the Assembly Resolution of April 18, 1946 the League of Nations ceased to exist, except for the sole purpose of liquidation on and after April 18, 1946. A [Board of Liquidation composed of nationals of Bolivia, China, Czechoslovakia, France, India, Norway, South Africa, Switzerland, and the United Kingdom was charged with the liquidation of the League of Nations from April 23, 1946 to July 31, 1947. The Final Report of the Board of Liquidation [C.5.M.5.1947] (General.1947.1.) constitutes the last League document published on behalf of the League. Subsequently, however, the United Nations published in its own name, but giving due credit to the League, several studies prepared by the League, for instance, the volume on *Balances of Payments, 1939–1945*. In addition, several measures and reports concerning the transfer of League functions and assets appeared exclusively in United Nations documents; see, for instance, United Nations document A/604, August 10, 1948 entitled: *Transfer of the Assets of the League of Nations: Report of the Secretary-General*. Appendix III of this *Guide* contains the text of the major documents relating to the transfer to the United Nations of League assets and functions. On the liquidation of the League see Denys P. Myers, "Liquidation of League of Nations Functions," *American Journal of International Law* (April 1948), p. 320–354, and Henry Reiff, *Transition from League of Nations to United Nations* (U.S. Department of State Publication No. 2542, Washington, 1946).

The League Hands Over. Geneva, 1946. 126 p. (General.1946.1.)

A readable summary of the proceedings of the Twentieth (Conclusion) and Twenty-first Assemblies.

Board of Liquidation. First Interim Report Presented in Accordance with Paragraph 9 of the Assembly Resolution of April 18th, 1946. Geneva, September 1st, 1946. 23 p. [C.83.M.83.1946.]

Includes: Chapter 1. Transfers Effected as at August 31st, 1946; Chapter 2. Transfers Pending as at August 31st, 1946; Chapter 3. Non-transferable Services, Funds, etc., Liquidated; Chapter 4. Non-transferable Services, Funds, etc., under Liquidation; Chapter 5. Work of League Commissions and Committees; Chapter 6. Staff Questions; Chapter 7. Claims; Chapter 8. Financial Questions. Annexes: 1 (i) Resolution for the Dissolution of the League of Nations, Adopted by the Assembly on April 18th, 1946; 2 (i) Agreement Concerning the Execution of the Transfer to the United Nations of Certain Assets of the League of Nations, Signed July 19th, 1946; (ii) Protocol Concerning the Execution of Various Operations in the Transfer to the United Nations of Certain Assets of the League of Nations, Signed August 1st, 1946. 3. Agreement between the League of Nations and the International Labour Organisation for the Transfer of Certain Properties; 4 (i) Resolution on the Assumption by the United Nations of Functions and Powers Hitherto Exercised by the League under International Agreements Adopted by the Assembly on April 18th, 1946; (ii) Resolution on the Assumption by the United Nations of Activities Hitherto Performed by the League, Adopted by the Assembly on April 18th, 1946; (iii) Resolution Concerning the International Institute of Intellectual Co-operation Adopted by the Assembly on April 18th, 1946; 5. Protocol Concerning the Transfer of Certain Services by the League of Nations to the United Nations, Signed August 1st, 1946; 6. Statement of Contributions Outstanding as at August 31st, 1946; 7. Position of Contributions Received as at August 31st, 1946.

Board of Liquidation. Second Interim Report. Geneva, December 1st, 1946. 10 p. [C.89.M.89.1946.]

Includes: Chapter 1. Transfers Effected since August 31st, 1946; Chapter 2. Transfers Pending as at November 30th, 1946; Chapter 3. Non-transferable Services, Funds, etc., Liquidated since August 31st, 1946; Chapter 4. Non-transferable Services, Funds, etc., under Liquidation; Chapter 5. Work of League Commissions and Committees; Chapter 6. Staff Questions; Chapter 7. Claims; Chapter 8. Financial Questions. Annexes: 1. Statement of Contributions Outstanding as at November 30th, 1946; 2. Position of Contributions Received as at November 30th, 1946.

Board of Liquidation. Third Interim Report (Covering the Period December 1st, 1946–February 28th, 1947). Presented in Accordance with the Assembly Resolution of April 18th, 1946. Geneva, March 1st, 1947. 48 p. [C.3.M.3.1947.]

Includes: Chapter 1. Transfers Effected since November 30th, 1946; Chapter 2. Transfers Pending as at February 28th, 1947; Chapter 3. Non-transferable Services, Funds, etc., Liquidated since November 30th, 1946; Chapter 4. Non-transferable Services, Funds, etc., under Liquidation; Chapter 5. Staff Questions; Chapter 6. Claims; Chapter 7. Financial Questions. Annexes: 1. Actuarial Valuation of the League of Nations Staff Pensions Fund as at July 31st, 1946: Report by Dr. H. Wyss, Consulting Actuary to the Pensions Fund; 2(a) Administrative Board of the Staff Pensions Fund: Twelfth Report to the Liquidation Board as Successor to the Assembly; (b) Thirteenth Report to the Liquidation Board as Successor to the Assembly, and to the Governing Body of the International Labour Office; 3. Accounts for the Financial Year 1946 of the Staff Pensions Fund, Staff Provident Fund, and the Pensions Fund of the Members of the Former Permanent Court of International Justice; 4. Audit of the Accounts of the Staff Pensions Fund for the 1946 Financial Period: Report by M. U. A. J. Brunskog, Auditor; 5(a) Pensions Fund of the Members of the Former Permanent Court of International Justice (Judges' Pensions Fund): Consulting Actuary's Report, Dated May 11th, 1946, on the Position of the Fund; (b) Supplementary Report Dated January 27th, 1947, by the Consulting Actuary; 6(a) Request Addressed to M. Plinio Bolla, President of the Swiss Federal Tribunal, for a Legal Opinion on the Right Claimed by Mr. Manley O. Hudson, a Former Member of the Permanent Court of International Justice, to Reimbursement by the League of Nations of the Taxes Due by Him in the United States on the Salary Which He Received from the League of Nations for the Period January 1st, 1941, to January 31st, 1946; (b) Legal Opinion Given by M. Plinio Bolla, President of the Swiss Federal Tribunal; 7. Statement of Contributions Received in 1947 and Contributions Outstanding as at February 28th, 1947.

Board of Liquidation. Fourth Interim Report (Covering the Period March 1st–April 30th, 1947). Geneva, May 1st, 1947. 15 p. [C.4.M. 4.1947.]

Includes: Chapter 1. Transfers Effected since February 28th, 1947; Chapter 2. Transfers Pending as at April 30th, 1947; Chapter 3. Non-transferable Services, Funds, etc., Liquidated since February 28th, 1947; Chapter 4. Staff Questions; Chapter 5. Claims; Chapter 6. Financial Questions. Annexes: 1. Note on the Transfer of the Working Capital Fund to the International Labour Organisation; 2. Protocol Concerning the Transfer of the Custody of the International Press House Fund; 3. Protocol Concerning the Transfer of the Library Endowment Fund; 4. Correspondence with the United Nations Concerning the Care and Disposal of League Archives; 5. Provisional Protocol Concerning the Final Schedule to the "Common Plan." 6. Statement of Contributions Received during the period January 1st to April 30th, 1947, and of Contributions Outstanding as at April 30th, 1947.

Board of Liquidation. Final Report Presented to States Members of the League of Nations in Accordance with the Requirement of the Final Article of the Resolution for the Dissolution of the League

of Nations Adopted by the Assembly on April 18th, 1946, at Its Twenty-first Ordinary Session. Geneva, July 31st, 1947. [C.5.M. 5.1947.] (General.1947.1.)

Contains: Part I. General. Part II. Chapter 1. Disposal of Material Assets; Chapter 2. Disposal of Various Special Funds; Chapter 3. Assumption of Activities by the United Nations and Specialised Agencies; Chapter 4. Disposal of Non-transferable Activities, Funds and Services; Chapter 5. Staff Questions; Chapter 6. Settlement of Claims against the League; Chapter 7. Miscellaneous Financial Questions; Chapter 8. Contributions; Chapter 9. Distribution of Assets among States Members; Chapter 10. Arrangements Made for the Settlement of Questions Outstanding on the Dissolution of the Board. Annexes: 1. Resolution Concerning the Dissolution of the League of Nations, Adopted by the Assembly on April 18th, 1946; 2. "Common Plan": Final Schedule Approved by the Board of Liquidation of the League of Nations and by the Advisory Committee on Administrative and Budgetary Questions and the Secretary-General of the United Nations; 3. Letter from the Secretary-General of the League of Nations to the Secretary-General of the United Nations Communicating to Him the List Showing the States Members of the United Nations Entitled to Participate in the Material Assets, and Their Respective Shares in These Assets; 4. Protocols Concerning the Transfer of the Léon Bernard Fund and the Darling Foundation to the United Nations; 5. Audited Accounts for the Period January 1st, 1947, to the Close of the Liquidation: Report of the Auditor Thereon; 6. Tables Showing the Calculations Made in Accordance with the Scheme of Distribution Approved on April 18th, 1946, by the Assembly on the Recommendation of the Second (Finance) Committee, in Order to Arrive at the Final Figures for the Apportionment of the Assets of the League among the States Members Entitled to Participate; 7. Report of the Auditor on the Audit of the Financial Accounts of the Administrative Fund of the Nansen International Office for Refugees (in Liquidation); 8. Report of the Auditor on the Final Audit of the Accounts of the League of Nations Staff Pensions Fund.

4. THE OFFICIAL JOURNAL

INTRODUCTORY NOTE

The *Official Journal* appeared in three parts: (1) the *Official Journal* proper; (2) the Special Supplement; (3) the Index.

In 1920–1921, the *Official Journal* was published in a bilingual edition. Beginning in January, 1922, two editions were issued, one in English and one in French. From its inception in February, 1920, the *Official Journal* was considered a "monthly" publication notwithstanding the fact that from time to time the records of two months were combined in one issue, for instance, April–May, 1920.

For each year the pagination of the *Official Journal* is *seriatim*. Accordingly any reference to the *Journal* proper is complete if page number and year are indicated, for example, *Official Journal*, 1938, p. 24. However, references in the annual Index to the *Journal* are to "Number" and pages. The 1931 Index gives the following example: "9:1807" = "Number 9 of *Official Journal*, p. 1807." The complete title of Number 9 of the *Journal* is: League of Nations, *Official Journal*, 12th Year, No. 9, September, 1931.

In Index entries which refer to the Council Minutes, the number of the Council Session is indicated by a Roman numeral, thus "7 (LXIII):1203" stands for "Number 7 of *Official Journal*, 63d Session of Council, page 1203."

The individual issues of the Special Supplements to the *Official Journal* are identifiable by number and title, for instance,, "No. 1. Correspondence Relating to the Question of the Aaland Islands."

In the course of time the arrangement of the contents of the *Journal* followed a more and more systematic pattern. This pattern may be illustrated by reference to the following features:

(1) Beginning with the Sixteenth Session (1922), the Proceedings of the Council and the Council Resolutions appeared regularly in the *Official Journal*.

(2) From the 11th to 22d Financial Periods (1929–1940), the approved budgets were not published as separate documents, but were issued annually in the *Official Journal*.[7]

(3) From 1927 to 1944 lists of ratifications of international conventions concluded under the auspices of the League were published either in the *Official Journal* or in Special Supplements.

Although it was at times incidental, as in the case of lists of ratifications, whether a particular type of document was published either in the *Official Journal* or in Special Supplements, Assembly Resolutions and Recommendations were published exclusively in Special Supplements and, beginning with the Fourth Assembly (1923), Assembly Proceedings and Assembly Committee Proceedings appeared regularly as Special Supplements.

In addition numerous individual documents which are listed in this *Guide* as separate documents were reprinted in the *Official Journal*. Whether or not a particular document was included in the *Journal* was not subject to consistent rules. Therefore it is more a matter of luck than of principle whether one succeeds in encountering an individual document in the *Official Journal*. Actually, numerous highly significant documents were published exclusively in the *Official Journal*. In any case there is no doubt that the central organ of the League was the *Official Journal* and its Special Supplements.

Because of limitations of space it was possible only in several instances to include a special reference to the fact that an individual document had been reprinted in the *Official Journal*.

Up to and including 1929 the *Subject List of Documents Distributed to the Council and the Members of the League . . .*[8] contained detailed

[7]See above, p. 103–104.
[8]The first Subject List is entitled: *Subject List of Documents Distributed to States Mem-*

information on reprinting of individual documents in the *Official Journal*.

Beginning with 1925 the Index to the *Official Journal* contained a Numerical Index listing the official numbers of the documents reproduced in the *Official Journal*; beginning with 1931 a Numerical Index listing the Sales Numbers has been added.

OFFICAL JOURNAL

First Issue: League of Nations. *Official Journal*, Number 1, February, 1920. 26 p.

Last Issue: League of Nations. *Official Journal*. 21st Year, Nos. 1–3, January–February–March, 1940. 50 p.

Special Supplements and Indices to the *Journal*.

OFFICIAL JOURNAL: SPECIAL SUPPLEMENTS

No. 1. Correspondence Relating to the Question of the Aaland Islands. The Finnish Case; the Swedish Case . . . 1920. 67 p.

No. 2. . . . Draft Scheme for the Institution of the Permanent Court of International Justice . . . 1920. 14 p.

No. 3. Report of the International Committee of Jurists Entrusted by the Council of the League of Nations with the Task of Giving Advisory Opinion upon the Legal Aspects of the Aaland Islands Question . . . 1920. 19 p.

No. 4. Documents Concerning the Dispute between Poland and Lithuania . . . 1920. 155 p.

Supplement spécial. Resolutions Adopted by the Assembly during Its First Session (November 15th–December 18th, 1920). 1921. 34 p.

No. 5. Resolutions Adopted by the Council of the League of Nations at Its Thirteenth Session in Geneva (June 17th–28th, 1921). 1921. 38 p.

No. 6. Resolutions and Recommendations Adopted by the Assembly during its Second Session (September 5th–October 5th, 1921). 1921. 41 p.

No. 7. Constitution of the Free City of Danzig. German text, with translation in English and French. 1922. 20 p.+20 p.+20 p.

No. 8. Index to the Minutes of the Sessions of the Council 1921 . . . 1922. 80 p.

No. 9. Resolutions and Recommendations Adopted by the Assembly during Its Third Session (September 4th–30, 1922) . . . 1922. 40 p.

No. 10. Index to the *Official Journal* for the Years 1920 and 1921 (First and Second Years) . . . 1923. 184 p.

---

bers from May to December 1921 Inclusive (Prepared by the Distribution Branch). Gèneve, 30 juin 1922. [C.450.M.267.1922.]. The last Subject List is the *Répertoire Analytique No. 128 des documents distribués aux membres de la Société au cours du mois decembre 1931* (Elaboré par le Service de la Distribution.) Gèneve, 4 janvier 1932. [C.42.M.24.1932.]

No. 11. Resolutions and Recommendations Adopted by the Assembly during Its Fourth Session (September 3rd–29th, 1923) . . . 1923. 34 p.

No. 12. Part I: Index to the Minutes of the Council Sessions XVI–XXII Contained in the *Official Journal* of 1922. Part II: Index to the *Official Journal* of 1922 (Exclusive of Those Numbers Which Contain the Minutes of the Council Sessions) . . . 1923. 98 p.

Nos. 13–20. Records of the Fourth Assembly (1923).

No. 21. Resolutions and Recommendations Adopted by the Assembly during Its Fifth Session (September 1st–October 2nd, 1924) . . . 1924. 48 p.

No. 22. Index to the *Official Journal* 1923. Part I: Index to the Minutes of the Council Sessions XXIII–XXVII. Part II: Index to the *Official Journal* of 1923 (Exclusive of Those Numbers Which Contain the Minutes of the Council Sessions) . . . 1924. 46 p.

Nos. 23–30. Records of the Fifth Assembly (1924).

No. 31. Index to the *Official Journal* 1924 . . . 1925. 48 p.

No. 32. Resolutions and Recommendations Adopted by the Assembly during Its Sixth Session (September 7th–26th, 1925). 1925. 34 p.

Nos. 33–40. Records of the Sixth Assembly (1925).

No. 41. Index to the *Official Journal* 1925 (Including Minutes of Council Sessions XXXII–XXXVI) . . . 1925. 40 p.

No. 42. Records of the Special Session of the Assembly (March, 1926).

No. 43. Resolutions and Recommendations Adopted by the Assembly during Its Seventh Ordinary Session (September 6th–25th, 1926). 1926. 30 p.

Nos. 44–51. Records of the Seventh Ordinary Session of the Assembly (1926).

No. 52. Index to the *Official Journal* 1926 (Including Minutes of Council Sessions XXXVII–XLII) . . . 1927. 41 p.

No. 53. Resolutions and Recommendations Adopted by the Assembly during Its Eighth Ordinary Session (September 5th–27th, 1927) . . . 1927. 36 p.

Nos. 54–61. Records of the Eighth Ordinary Session of the Assembly (1927).

No. 62. Index to the *Official Journal* 1927 (Including Minutes of Council Sessions XLIII–XLVII) . . . 1927. 44 p.

No. 63. Resolutions and Recommendations Adopted by the Assembly during Its Ninth Ordinary Session (September 3rd–26th, 1928) . . . 1928. 71 p.

Nos. 64–71. Records of the Ninth Ordinary Session of the Assembly (1928).

No. 72. Index to the *Official Journal* 1928 (Including Minutes of Council Sessions XLVIII–LII) . . . 1928. 60 p.

No. 73. Documents Relating to the Protection of Minorities by the League of Nations (Published in Accordance with the Council Resolution of June 13th, 1929) . . . 1929. 87 p.

No. 74. Resolutions and Recommendations Adopted by the Assembly during Its Tenth Ordinary Session (September 2nd–25th, 1929) . . . 1929. 45 p.

Nos. 75–82. Records of the Tenth Ordinary Session of the Assembly (1929).

No. 83. Resolutions and Recommendations Adopted by the Assembly during Its Eleventh Ordinary Session (September 10th–October 4th, 1930) . . . 1930. 52 p.

Nos. 84–91. Records of the Eleventh Ordinary Session of the Assembly (1930).

No. 92. Resolutions and Recommendations Adopted by the Assembly during Its Twelfth Ordinary Session (September 7th–29th, 1931) . . . 1931. 42 p.

Nos. 93–100. Records of the Twelfth Ordinary Session of the Assembly (1931).

Nos. 101 and 102. Records of the Special Session of the Assembly (1932).

No. 103. Resolutions and Recommendations Adopted by the Assembly during Its Thirteenth Ordinary Session (September 26th–October 17th, 1932) . . . 1932. 33 p.

Nos. 104–110. Records of the Thirteenth Ordinary Session of the Assembly (1932).

Nos. 111–113. Records of the Special Session of the Assembly (1932).

No. 114. Resolutions Adopted by the Assembly during Its Fourteenth Ordinary Session (September 25th–October 11th, 1933) . . . 1933. 26 p.

Nos. 115–121. Records of the Fourteenth Ordinary Session of the Assembly (1933).

No. 122. Ratification of the Agreements and Conventions Concluded under the Auspices of the League of Nations. Fifteenth List . . .

Bears the number [A. 6 (a). 1934. V. Annex.] (1934. V.1.).

No. 123. Resolutions Adopted by the Assembly during Its Fifteenth Ordinary Session (September 10th–27th, 1934) . . . 1934. 25 p.

No. 124. Dispute between Bolivia and Paraguay. Appeal of the Bolivian Government under Article 15 of the Covenant. 1934. 175 p.

Nos. 125–131. Records of the Fifteenth Ordinary Session of the Assembly (1934).

No. 132. Dispute between Bolivia and Paraguay. Records of the Special Session of the Assembly (1934).

No. 133. Dispute between Bolivia and Paraguay. Appeal of the Bolivian Government under Article 15 of the Covenant. Documentation Communicated to Members of the League of Nations since December 31st, 1934 . . . 1935. 52 p.

No. 134. Dispute between Bolivia and Paraguay. Appeal of the Bolivian Government under Article 15 of the Covenant. Documentation Communicated to the Members of the League of Nations for the Special Session of the Assembly Convened at Geneva for Monday, May 20th, 1935. Geneva, 1935. 74 p.

No. 135. Dispute between Bolivia and Paraguay. Pt. 1. Records of the Special Session of the Assembly. Pt. 2. Documentation (Including the Minutes of the Meetings of the Advisory Committee Held on May 16th and 17th, 1935). Geneva, 1935. 50 p.

No. 136. Ratification of Agreements and Conventions Concluded under the Auspices of the League of Nations. Sixteenth List. 1935. 122 p.

Bears the sales number (1935.V.3.).

No. 137. Resolutions Adopted by the Assembly during Its Sixteenth Ordinary Session (September 9th–October 11th, 1935). 1935. 34 p.

Nos. 138–144. Records of the Sixteenth Ordinary Session of the Assembly (1935).

No. 145. Dispute between Ethiopia and Italy. Co-ordination of Measures under Article 16 of the Covenant. Co-ordination Committee. Committee of Eighteen and Sub-Committees. Minutes of the First Session (October 31st–November 6th, 1935). 1935. 155 p.

No. 146. Dispute between Ethiopia and Italy. Co-ordination of Measures under Article 16 of the Covenant. Co-ordination Committee. Committee of Eighteen and Sub-Committees. Minutes of the Second Session (October 11–19, 1935). 1935. 83 p.

No. 147. Dispute between Ethiopia and Italy. Co-ordination of Measures under Article 16 of the Covenant. I. Committee of Eighteen. Minutes of the Third Session (December 12th–19th, 1935). II. Committee of Experts Appointed under the Terms of the Resolution Adopted by the Committee of Eighteen on November 6th, 1935. Minutes of the First Session (November 27th–December 12th, 1935). 1935. 62 p.

No. 148. Dispute between Ethiopia and Italy. Co-ordination of Measures under Article 16 of the Covenant. I. Committee of Eighteen. Minutes of the Fourth Session (January 22nd, 1936). II. Committee of Experts Created to Follow the Application of Sanctions (Resolution of the Committee of Eighteen, Dated November 6th, 1935). Minutes of the Second Session (January 29th–February 1st, 1936). III. Committee of Experts for the Technical Examination of the Conditions Governing the Trade in and Transport of Petroleum and Its Derivatives, By-products and Residues (Resolution of the Committee of Eighteen, Dated January 22nd, 1936). Minutes of the First Session (February 3rd–12th 1936). 1936. 85 p.

No. 149. Dispute between Ethiopa and Italy. Co-ordination of Measures under Article 16 of the Covenant. I. Committee of Eighteen. Minutes of the Fifth Session (March 2nd–4th, 1936.) II. Committee of Experts for the Technical Examination of the Conditions Governing the Trade in and Transport of Petroleum and Its Derivatives, By-products and Residues (Resolution of the Committee of Eighteen, Dated January 22nd, 1936). Minutes of the Second Session (March 4th–7th, 1936). III. Committee of Experts Created to Follow the Application of Sanctions (Resolution of the Committee of Eighteen, Dated November 6th, 1935). Minutes of the Third and Fourth Sessions (March 4th–9th, and April 21st, 1936). IV. Co-ordination Committee. Minutes of the Third Session (July 6th, 1936). 1936. 65 p.

No. 150. Dispute between Ethiopia and Italy. Co-ordination of Measures under Article 16 of the Covenant. Proposals and Resolutions of the Co-ordination Committee and the Committee of Eighteen and Official Correspondence and Communications Relating Thereto. 1936. 359 p.

No. 151. Records of the Sixteenth Ordinary Session of the Assembly 1936 (continued).

No. 152. Ratification of Agreements and Conventions Concluded under the Auspices of the League of Nations. Seventeenth List. 1936. 131 p.

Bears the sales number (1936.V.4.).

No. 153. Resolutions Adopted by the Assembly during Its Seventeenth Ordinary Session (September 21st–October 10th, 1936). 1936. 43 p.

No. 154. Documents Relating to the Question of the Application of the Principles of the Covenant. 1936. 97 p.

Nos. 155–163. Records of the Seventeenth Ordinary Session of the Assembly (1936).

No. 164. Dispute between Ethiopia and Italy. Co-ordination of Measures under Article 16 of the Covenant. General Index to Special Supplements Nos. 145–150. 1937. 63 p.

No. 165. Appeal by the Spanish Government. White Book Published by the Spanish Government and Presented to the Council on May 28th, 1937. (See Minutes of the Ninety-seventh Session of the Council, Fifth Meeting, *Official Journal*, May–June, 1937). 1937. 140 p.

No. 166. Records of the Special Session of the Assembly Convened for the Purpose of Considering the Request of the Kingdom of

Egypt for Admission to the League of Nations (May 26th–27th, 1937). 1937. 47 p.

No. 167. Ratification of Agreements and Conventions Concluded under the Auspices of the League of Nations. Eighteenth List. 1937. 133 p.

Bears the sales number (1937.V.4.).

No. 168. Resolution Adopted by the Assembly during Its Eighteenth Ordinary Session (September 13th to October 6th, 1937). 1937. 36 p.

Nos. 169–176. Records of the Eighteenth Ordinary Session of the Assembly (1937).

No. 177. Sino-Japanese Conflict. Appeal by the Chinese Government. Extract from the Minutes of the Third Meeting of the Ninety-eighth Session of the Council (September 16th, 1937). Minutes of the Third Session of the Far-East Advisory Committee Set up by the Assembly Resolution of February 24th, 1933 (September 21st to October 5th, 1937). Extracts from the Verbatim Record of the Eighteenth Ordinary Session of the Assembly. Reports Adopted by the Far-East Advisory Committee on October 5th and by the Assembly on October 6th, 1937. Invitation Addressed by the President of the Assembly to the Members of the League Who Are Parties to the Nine Power Treaty, Signed at Washington on February 6th, 1922. Documentation Received up to October 31st, 1937. 1937. 59 p.

No. 178. Texts Adopted by the Inter-American Conference for the Maintenance of Peace (Buenos Aires, December 1st to 23rd, 1936) and Transmitted to the League of Nations in Accordance with a Decision of the Conference. 1937. 71 p.

No. 179. Communication from the Government of the United States of America. Statement in Regard to the International Situation Made on July 16th, 1937, by Mr. Cordell Hull, Secretary of State of the United States of America, and Comments on That Statement from Various Governments. 1937. 34 p.

No. 180. Report of the Special Committee Set up to Study the Application of the Principles of the Covenant Adopted by the Committee on February 2nd, 1938. Annexes: 1. Minutes of the Third Session of the Committee (January 31st–February 2nd, 1938). 2 to 10. Reports Communicated for Information to the Members of the League of Nations. 1938. 123 p.

No. 181. Ratification of Agreements and Conventions Concluded under the Auspices of the League of Nations. Nineteenth List. 1938. 139 p.

Bears the sales number (1938.V.4.).

No. 182. Resolutions Adopted by the Assembly during Its Nineteenth Ordinary Session (September 12th–30th, 1938). 1938. 39 p.

Nos. 183–191. Records of the Nineteenth Ordinary Session of the Assembly (1938).

No. 192. Ratification of Agreements and Conventions Concluded under the Auspices of the League of Nations. Twentieth List. 1939. 144 p.

Bears the sales number (1939.V.2.).

No. 193. Signatures, Ratifications and Accessions in Respect of Agreements and Conventions Concluded under the Auspices of the League of Nations. Twenty-first List. 1944. 197 p.

Bears the sales number (1944.V.2.).

No. 194. Records of the Twentieth (Conclusion) and Twenty-first Ordinary Sessions of the Assembly (1946). 1946. 293 p.

No. 195. Signatures, Ratifications and Accessions in Respect of Agreements and Conventions Concluded under the Auspices of the League of Nations. Supplement to the Twenty-first List. 1946. 38 p.

Bears the sales number (1946.V.1.).

Part Four

DOCUMENTS RELATED TO
THE MAIN ACTIVITIES
OF THE LEAGUE

I. ADMINISTRATION OF TERRITORY

1. THE SAAR TERRITORY

Governing Commission

THE LEGAL BASIS of the administration of the Saar Territory on behalf of the League of Nations was contained in the so-called Saar Annex, following Article 50 of the Treaty of Versailles.[1] According to Paragraph 17 of the Saar Annex, the Governing Commission of the Saar Territory included "one citizen of France, one native inhabitant of the Saar basin, not a citizen of France, and three members belonging to three countries other than France and Germany." The members of the Commission were appointed for a year by the Council of the League of Nations and could be reappointed. The Governing Commission administered the Saar Territory on behalf of the League of Nations.[2] Its decisions were taken by a majority vote.

The Governing Commission was, in principle, entitled to exercise "all the powers of government hitherto belonging to the German Empire, Prussia or Bavaria" (Saar Annex, Paragraph 19). However, the authority of the Governing Commission was limited not only by the Saar Annex and related legal measures but also subject to the instructions of the Council. The Governing Commission was bound to "report to the Council of the League of Nations, through the Secretary-General,[3] in order to keep the League informed on all questions of interest."[4]

Reports of the Governing Commission

From 1920 to 1927 the reports of the Governing Commission to the Council were published on behalf of the Commission or the Administrative Commissions Section of the Secretariat. In all, 32 periodical reports were on sale. After the thirty-second report, the

[1]On the Saar Annex, see Sarah Wambaugh, *The Saar Plebiscite* (Cambridge, Mass, 1940), p.58.
[2]For the problem as to whether the League of Nations acted as "trustee" in reference to the Saar, see *ibid.*, p. 58, and Walther Schücking and Hans Wehberg, *Die Satzung des Völkerbundes*, 3d ed. (Berlin, 1931), p.106–116.
[3]For the Administrative Commissions Section of the Secretariat, see above, p. 86.
[4]See Council Resolution of February 13,1920, Sec.VIII., *Official Journal*, March, 1920, p.52.

periodical reports ceased to be published as separate documents, but were included in the *Official Journal*.

First Report: First Report of the Saar Governing Commission, March 25, 1920. Document du Conseil B1. 25 p., bilingual. [20/4/65][5]

Last Report: Thirty-second Report of the Governing Commission (October 1st to December 31st, 1927) (Extract from *Official Journal*, March, 1928). Geneva, 1928. 12 p. [C.35.M.17.1928.I.] (1928. I.A.1.)

In addition to the periodical reports, the Governing Commission issued special reports which appeared either in mimeographed form or were inserted into the *Official Journal*.

Petitions from the Inhabitants of the Saar

The inhabitants of the Saar were authorized to address petitions to the Council of the League of Nations. The petition procedure was controlled by the report to the Council (by Mr. Coromitas) of May 15, 1920. This report read in part as follows: "All petitions from the inhabitants of the Saar to the Council of the League of Nations should be sent to the Governing Commission. The Commission will duly forward these petitions, with or without comment, to the Secretary-General for the information of the Council."[6]

The text of these petitions were made available in mimeographed form to the members of the Council as well as to the recipients of the States Members Service by the Administrative Commission. Several petitions were also published in the *Official Journal*; others are classified under classmark VII (Political Questions).

PLEBISCITE

Article 34 of the Saar Annex provided that 15 years after the coming into force of the Treaty of Versailles the population would decide by plebiscite for one of the following: (a) maintenance of the League of Nations regime in the Saar; (b) union with France; (c) union with Germany. The plebiscite took place on January 13, 1935, under the supervision of a special Plebiscite Commission and in the presence of an international police force. The result of the vote was: for union with Germany, 477,119; for the *status quo*, 46,613; for union with France, 2,124.[7]

Functions and Composition of the Plebiscite Commission

Saar Territory: Preparatory Measures in View of the Plebiscite.I: Preliminary Report of the Council, Dated May 15th, 1934. [C.199.

[5]Also numbered [3/3670/2].
[6]Council Minutes, 5th Sess., p.191.
[7]On the vote, see Wambaugh, *The Saar Plebiscite*, p.295-322.

1934.VII.]. II: Final Report by the Committee of the Council, Dated June 2nd, 1934. [C.209.1934.VII.]. *Official Journal*, June, 1934, p. 644-650.

This report suggested the establishment of a Plebiscite Commission and Plebiscite Tribunals as "Organs of the Plebiscite." The Plebiscite Commission, constituted under the authority of the Council, had "powers of organization, direction and supervision in regard to the plebiscite". In addition, the Plebiscite Commission was authorized to issue ordinances.[8]

Saar Territory: Preparatory Measures in View of the Plebiscite: Appointment of the Plebiscite Commission. Geneva, July 17, 1934. *Official Journal*, July, 1934, p. 978. [C.313.1934.VII.]

Formal appointment of the three members of the Plebiscite Commission—Mr. Victor Henry (Switzerland), Mr. Daniel de Jongh (Netherlands), Mr. A. E. Rodhe (Sweden)—and of the technical adviser, Miss Sarah Wambaugh (United States of America).[9]

Reports of the Plebiscite Commission

First Monthly Report of the Plebiscite Commission (July 1st to 31st, 1934). Geneva, 1934. 12 p. [C.356.M.166.1934.VII.] (1934.VII.8.)

Annex 2 contains the Regulations for the Plebiscite in the Territory of the Saar Basin.

Second Monthly Report of the Plebiscite Commission (August 1st to 31st, 1934). Geneva, 1934. 3 p. (Extract No. 91 from the *Official Journal*). [C.384.M.168.1934.VII.] (1934.VII.12.)

Third Report of the Plebiscite Commission (September 1st to October 31st, 1934). Saarbruck, October 31, 1934. *Official Journal*, December, 1934, p. 1660-1671. [C.500.M.221.1934.VII.]

The Annex contains the decree setting up a Supreme Plebscite Court and District Tribunals in the Territory of the Saar Basin and establishing Rules of Procedure.

Fourth Report of the Plebiscite Commission (November 1st to 15th, 1934). Saarbruck, November 15, 1934. *Official Journal*, December, 1934, p. 1671-1672. [C.501.M.222.1934.VII.]

Fifth Report of the Plebiscite Commission (November 16th to 30th, 1934). Saarbruck, November 30, 1934. *Official Journal*, December, 1934, p. 1672-1673. [C.525.M.240.1934.VII.]

Sixth Report of the Plebiscite Commission (December 1st to 31st, 1934). Saarbruck, December 31, 1934. *Official Journal*, January, 1935, p. 31-38. [C.18.M.9.1935.VII.]

Annex I contains the Ordinance Amending the Plebiscite Regulations of July 7, 1934.

Seventh Report of the Plebiscite Commission[10] (January 1st to 15th,

---

[8]See *Official Journal*, June, 1934, p.648.
[9]For the Plebiscite Commission, see also Wambaugh, *The Saar Plebiscite*, p.183-292.
[10]The Third to Seventh Reports of the Plebiscite Commission (September 1, 1934—January 15, 1935) were also published as one document, Extract No.97 from the *Official Journal*, under the classmark (1935.VII.7.).

1935). Saarbruck, January 15, 1935. *Official Journal*, January, 1935, p. 38–40. [C.51.M.23.1935.VII.]

Supreme Plebiscite Court and District Courts

Third Report of the Plebiscite Commission (September 1st to October 31st, 1934). Saarbruck, October 31, 1934. *Official Journal*, December, 1934, p. 1660–1671. [C.500.M.221.1934.VII.]

The Plebiscite Tribunals had jurisdiction in the following matters: (1) disputes concerning entries in the registers of persons entitled to vote and the validity of the voting; (2) offences covered by the Plebiscite Regulations; (3) breaches of ordinary criminal law, in so far as they were connected with the purpose of the plebiscite, committed before, during, and after the plebiscite proceedings.[11] For the Rules of Procedure of the Plebiscite Tribunals (October 31, 1934), see Document [C.500.M. 221.1934.VII.], *Official Journal*, December, 1934, p.1667–1671.[12]

International Police

Saar Territory: Preparatory Measures in View of the Plebiscite: Maintenance of Order in the Territory. Council Resolution of December 8, 1934. Council Minutes, Eighty-third Session, p. 1.

Invited the governments of the United Kingdom, Italy, the Netherlands, and Sweden to take part in the establishment of an international force to be charged, under the authority of the Governing Commission of the Saar Territory, with the maintenance of order in the Territory before, during, and after the plebiscite.[13]

Saar Territory: Preparatory Measures in View of the Plebiscite: Maintenance of Order in the Territory. Council Resolution of December 11, 1934. Council Minutes, Eighty-third Session, p. 2–3.

Requested the States Members of the League of Nations concerned to grant every facility for the transit through their territories of the national contingents forming the international force despatched to the Saar Territory and for their supply. The command of the international force, its organs and services, and the members of the said force were to be exempt from the jurisdiction of the Courts of the territory.[14]

Result of the Plebiscite

Saar Territory: Result of the Plebiscite. Geneva, January 15, 1935. 7 p., bilingual. [C.44(1).M.19(1).1935.VII.] (1935.VII.4.)

Saar Territory: Report of the Council Committee. Geneva, March 5, 1935. 32 p., bilingual. [C.103.M.48.1935.VII.] (1935.VII.6.)

Saar Territory: Report of the Council Committee. Geneva, May 8, 1935. 1 p., bilingual. [C.103.M.48.1935.VII.Erratum.] (1935.VII. 6.Erratum)

Saar Territory: German Text of the Agreements and Declarations Annexed to the Report of the Council Committee, Adopted at

[11] *Official Journal*, June, 1934, p.649.
[12] See also Wambaugh, *The Saar Plebiscite, passim*.
[13] See *ibid.*, p.283.
[14] *Ibid.*, p.282.

Naples on February 19th, 1935, Concerning the Change of Regime in the Saar Territory. Geneva, March 5, 1935. 27 p. [C.103.M. 48.1935.Annexe.]

General Information

Information Section. The Saar Plebiscite. No. 1 of *League of Nations Questions*. Geneva, 1935. 41 p.

2. FREE CITY OF DANZIG

INTRODUCTORY NOTE

A unique regime for the Free City of Danzig was established by the Treaty of Versailles. Under Article 103 of the Treaty, the Constitution of the Free City of Danzig was "placed under the guarantee of the League of Nations." The League as a guarantor of the Constitution was concerned not merely with the text of the Constitution but also with the proper application of it.[15] The League, in practice, exercised its function as a guarantor of the Constitution through the Council. Moreover, a High Commissioner of the League of Nations at Danzig was entrusted with special functions. Under Article 102 the Free City of Danzig was "placed under the protection of the League of Nations."[16] In several instances the Council asked the Permanent Court of International Justice for advisory opinions on matters concerning Danzig.

LEGAL STATUS OF THE FREE CITY OF DANZIG

The Free City of Danzig. Decision Establishing the City of Danzig as a Free City. Council Document C.5.[17] Geneva, November 24, 1920. No date. 4 p., mimeographed. [20/4/389.]
Treaty Between Poland and the Free City of Danzig, Concluded at Paris, the 9th November, 1920.[18] 10 p.+10 p., bilingual. [20/4/365/1A]

[15]See Advisory Opinion No.27 of the Permanent Court of International Justice. Series A/B, Fasc. No.65, p.49.
[16]For the meaning of the "protection of the League of Nations," see *The Future of the City of Danzig. Report to the Council by His Excellency Viscount Ishii, Japanese Representative*, Geneva, November 13, 1920, p. 2. [20/48/98].
[17]This decision was taken by the Conference of Ambassadors in Paris on October 27, 1920, and was signed by the duly authorized representative of the Free City of Danzig on November 9, 1920. For the role of the Conference of Ambassadors in reference to Danzig, see Gerhard P. Pink, "The Conference of Ambassadors (Paris 1920–1931)," in Geneva Research Center, *Geneva Studies*, Vol.XII,Nos.4–5 (1942), p.53–68.
[18]Also in 6 *Treaty Series*, p.190. Both documents, *i.e.* [20/4/389] and [20/4/365/1A], came into force on November 15,1920. See Pink, in *Geneva Studies*, XII,61.

The Future of the City of Danzig. Report to the Council by His
Excellency Viscount Ishii, Japanese Representative. Geneva, No-
vember 13, 1920.[19] 8 p.+8 p., bilingual. [20/48/98.]
Constitution of the Free City of Danzig (German Text, with English
and French Translations). *Official Journal*, Special Supplement
No. 7,[20] July, 1922.
Free City of Danzig. Amendment to the Constitution of Danzig:
Valorization of Claims. Geneva, November 5, 1926. 18 p. [C.605.
1926.I.] (1926.I.A.4.)

THE HIGH COMMISSIONER OF THE LEAGUE OF NATIONS AT DANZIG

Under Article 103 of the Treaty of Versailles and supplementary
arrangements, a High Commissioner for Danzig was appointed by
the Council of the League of Nations. His main functions were: (1)
to deal in the first instance with all differences arising between Poland
and the Free City of Danzig;[21] (2) to report to the Council of the
League of Nations through the Secretary-General on all matters
within his jurisdiction as High Commissioner.
The High Commissioner had to observe directives issued by the
League of Nations and was responsible to the League of Nations.

Functions of the High Commissioner

Free City of Danzig. Memorandum by the Secretary-General. Council Document 3. No date. 1 p.+1 p., bilingual. [4/1872/4][22]
The Future of the City of Danzig. Report to the Council by His
Excellency Viscount Ishii, Japanese Representative. Geneva, November 13, 1920. 8 p.+8 p., bilingual. [20/48/98.]

Reports

No consistent publication procedure regarding reports by the High
Commissioner can be ascertained. Originally, they were only mimeo-

[19]Adopted by Council Resolution of November 17, 1920. See Council Minutes, 11th
Sess., p.7.
[20]The Constitution of Danzig came into effect on May 11, 1922, after approval by the
High Commissioner for Danzig. See Pink, in *Geneva Studies*, XII,64–65. Cf., however,
Art.104 of the Treaty of Versailles.
[21]See Art.39 of the Convention between Poland and the Free City of Danzig, signed at
Paris, November 9, 1920. Art.39 reads: "Any differences arising between Poland and the
Free City of Danzig in regard to the present Treaty or to any other subsequent agree-
ments, arrangements or conventions or to any matter affecting the relations between
Poland and the Free City, shall be submitted by one or the other party to the decision
of the High Commissioner, who shall, if he deems it necessary, refer the matter to the
Council of the League of Nations." The two parties retained the right of appeal to the
Council of the League of Nations.
[22]See also Council Minutes, 2d Sess. Fasc.4,p.22–24. See also *The Future of the City of
Danzig*. p.7–8. [20/48/98].

graphed, or, if printed, designed for limited circulation, for example, the *Report of the High Commissioner on the Economic Condition of Danzig*, Geneva, May 23, 1921. [C.61.1921.I.]. Later, general or special reports appeared, occasionally in the *Official Journal*, for example, General Reports by the High Commissioner of the League of Nations at Danzig [C.386.1933.I.], *Official Journal*, August, 1934, p. 988–994. After the outbreak of World War II, however, the following report appeared as a separate document:
Report of M. Carl Burckhart, High Commissioner of the League of Nations at Danzig. Geneva, March 19, 1940. 16 p. [C.42.M.38. 1940.VII.] (1940.VII.1.)

Petitions and Appeals

Under the Danzig regime a right of petition was granted to individuals and groups as well as a right of appeal against decisions of the High Commissioner.[23] For petitions, see especially:
Free City of Danzig. Procedure to Be Followed in Cases of Petitions Addressed to the League by Citizens of the Free City. Geneva, June 5, 1925. 2 p., mimeographed. [C.324.1925.I.]

ADVISORY OPINIONS OF THE PERMANENT COURT OF INTERNATIONAL JUSTICE ON QUESTIONS CONCERNING DANZIG

Polish Postal Service in Danzig. Advisory Opinion No. 11, May 16, 1925. Series B, No. 11, p. 6–45.
Jurisdiction of the Courts of Danzig (Pecuniary Claims of Danzig Railway Officials Transferred to the Polish Service). Advisory Opinion No. 15, March 3, 1928. Series B, No. 15, p. 4–47.
The Free City of Danzig and the International Labour Organisation. Advisory Opinion No. 18, August 26, 1930. Series B, No. 18, p. 4–36.
Access to, or Anchorage in, the Port of Danzig of Polish War Vessels. Advisory Opinion No. 22, December 11, 1931. Series A/B, Fascicule No. 43, p. 128–164.
Treatment of Polish Nationals and Other Persons of Polish Origin or Speech in the Danzig Territory. Advisory Opinion No. 23, February 4, 1932. Series A/B, Fascicule No. 44, p. 4–63.
Consistency of Certain Danzig Legislative Decrees with the Constitution of the Free City. Advisory Opinion No. 27, December 4, 1935. Series A/B, Fascicule No. 65, p. 41–73.[24]
It is notable that six out of the twenty-seven advisory opinions rendered by the Permanent Court of International Justice deal with Danzig.

[23]See above, footnote 21.
[24]The foregoing Court publications are double-paged, bilingual.

3. MANDATES

INTRODUCTORY NOTE

The mandates system, established under Article 22 of the Covenant, constituted a special technique of international supervision of territorial administration. Contrary to a widespread belief, the mandates system was not confined to "colonies," since the so-called A mandates were instituted on territory that previously had formed an integral part of the Turkish Empire (see Article 22, Paragraphs 1 and 4).

The Covenant, in Article 22, Paragraphs 4–6, determined rather vaguely those areas that were to be administered as "Mandates,"[25] and left open the question of who was to act as mandatory.

The territories to be administered as mandates were ceded to the Principal Allied and Associated Powers under Article 119 of the Treaty of Versailles and Article 16 of the Treaty of Lausanne of July 24, 1923,[26] respectively. Accordingly, the mandatory powers were designated by the Supreme Council and not by the League of Nations.

There were three classes of mandates:

(1) A mandates. By decision of the Supreme Council at San Remo of April 25, 1920,[27] France was designated as mandatory for Syria and Great Britain as mandatory for Palestine and Mesopotamia (Iraq).[28]

(2) B mandates. On May 7, 1919,[29] the Supreme Council assigned the mandates for Togoland and the Cameroons to France and Great Britain, who by agreement of July 10, 1919, defined their respective territorial jurisdiction in these areas. The mandate for German East Africa (Tanganyika Territory) was allotted to Great Britain. The northwestern part of Tanganyika Territory (the province of Ruanda-

[25]The term "Mandate" is not unequivocal. It denotes (1) a certain legal relationship, between the League of Nations, the mandatory power, and the inhabitants of a certain area; (2) the mandates "Charter," adopted by the Council, which defines the application of the general principles laid down in Art.22 of the Covenant to a special territory; (3) the territory itself; (4) the varying degree of authority, such as A mandates, B mandates, C mandates.

[26]Art.16 of the Treaty of Lausanne (1923) replaced Art.132 of the never-ratified Treaty of Sèvres of 1920.

[27]For the Conference of San Remo, April 19–26,1920, see Arnold J. Toynbee, *Survey of International Affairs,1920–1923* (London,1925), p.10–12.

[28]For details, see *The Mandates System: Origin-Principles-Application*, Geneva, 1945 p.18–21. (1945.VI.A.1.). See also Quincy Wright, *Mandates under the League of Nations* (Chicago, 1930) p.24–63.

[29]See League of Nations, *The Records of the First Assembly. Meetings of the Committees* (6th Committee), p.375.

Urundi) was entrusted to Belgium by decision of the Supreme Council of August 21, 1919.[30]

(3) C mandates. The mandatories for C mandates were selected on May 17, 1919, by the Supreme Council.[31] The mandate for South-West Africa was entrusted to the Union of South Africa; that for Western Samoa to New Zealand; that for the island of Nauru to the British Empire—by special agreement between the governments of the United Kingdom, Australia, and New Zealand, Nauru was administered by Australia;[32] that for the other German possessions in the Pacific south of the equator to Australia, and that for the German islands north of the equator to Japan.

The mandate "Charter,"[33] determined the authority of the mandatory, the rights and duties of the inhabitants of the mandated areas, the role of the Permanent Court of International Justice in the interpretation of the mandates,[34] and the role of the League Council as to the modification of the terms of the mandates. It should be recalled that the terms of the mandate for Iraq were never embodied into a formal "charter," but rather in a series of treaties and agreements[35] which were subsequently approved by the Council.[36]

The mandatory power was obliged to submit to the Council an annual report on the situation in the mandated area. In addition, the Permanent Mandates Commission[37] was to receive and examine the annual reports of the mandatories and to advise the Council on all matters relating to the observance of the mandates.[38] Although in principle a purely advisory organ, the Commission's recommendations did on various occasions decisively influence the actions of the Council and the mandatories. The Permanent Mandates Commission was also entitled to receive petitions from the inhabitants of the mandated territories, or from some other source.[39] The minutes as

[30]On the Belgian mandate for East Africa, see Council Minutes, 12th sess., p.10–11, and the Agreement between the Belgian and British governments approved by the Council on August 31, 1923, *Official Journal*, November, 1923, p.1273–1274, 1409–1410.
[31]See League of Nations, *The Records of the First Assembly. Meetings of the Committees* (6th Committee), p.375.
[32]See *ibid*.
[33]For a brief analysis of the major provisions of the mandates "Charter," see *The Mandates System*, p.24–32. (1945.VI.A.1.)
[34]For the jurisdiction of the Permanent Court of International Justice as to mandates, see Manley O. Hudson, *The Permanent Court of International Justice, 1920–1942* (New York,1943), p.441–442.
[35]See *The Mandates System*, p.31, footnote 5. (1945.VI.A.1.)
[36]*Ibid.*, p.31, footnote 6.
[37]The Permanent Mandates Commission is expressly provided for in Art.22, Par.9 of the Covenant.
[38]The Permanent Mandates Commission was called the "mainspring of the whole Mandates system," *The Mandates System*, p.35. (1945.VI.A.1.). See also *ibid.*, p.50.
[39]See *ibid.*, p.33.

well as the reports of the Permanent Mandates Commission furnish valuable information on the work of the Commission. Finally, to facilitate the preparation of the annual reports of the mandatory powers the Permanent Mandates Commission drew up special questionnaires.[40] A special procedure was adopted in the matter of petitions concerning mandates.[41]

It should be noted that Article 77(1)(a) of the United Nations Charter provides that "territories now held under mandate"—"now" refers presumably to the date of the signature of the Charter, June 26, 1945, or the date of its entry into force, October 24, 1945—may be placed under the trusteeship system by means of trusteeship agreements.

The General Assembly of the United Nations, by Resolution of February 9, 1946 (see United Nations Document A/64, July 1, 1946, page 13), invited the mandatory powers to place the mandated territories under trusteeship.

The Union of South Africa, however, which under the League regime acted as mandatory power for the former German colony of South-West Africa, proposed to incorporate the mandated territory in the territory of the Union. The General Assembly of the United Nations by Resolution of December 14, 1946, recommended "that the mandated territory of South West Africa be placed under the international trusteeship system" and invited the "Government of the Union of South Africa to propose for the consideration of the General Assembly a trusteeship agreement for the aforesaid territory." (See General Assembly, First Session: Text of Debates, *Journal* No. 75, Supplement A-64, Add. 1, page 883–884).

In the course of 1946 and 1947 the General Assembly of the United Nations approved trusteeship agreements for all other former B and C mandates. In other words, the trusteeship regime has replaced the mandate regime in these areas, except in Southwest Africa and Palestine.

With the exception of the former Japanese mandates, which were entrusted to the United States, the former mandatory powers became "administering authority" in the sense of Article 81 of the United Nations Charter.

Of the former A mandates Iraq became an independent state and was admitted to League membership on October 3, 1932. Syria and Lebanon became independent in the course of World War II, participated in the San Francisco Conference (April 25–June 26, 1945), and adhered to the United Nations as original members.

In 1946 the mandate for Transjordan was terminated. On March

[40]See, *e.g.* Document [A.14.1926.VI.] (1926.VI.A.16.).
[41]See "Summary of the Procedure to Be Followed in the Matter of Petitions Concerning Mandated Territories" <C.P.M.558(1).>, in Permanent Mandates Commission, *Minutes of the Twelfth Session*, Geneva, 1927, p.176–178. [C.545.M.194.1927.VI.]

22, 1946, a Treaty of Alliance was signed in London between the governments of the United Kingdom and Transjordan, whereby Great Britain recognized Transjordan as a sovereign independent State (see the Preamble and Article 1 [Cmd. 6779]).

For the texts of trusteeship agreements in force as of March 15, 1948, see United Nations, *Official Records of the Second Part of the First Session of the General Assembly*, Supplement No. 5. *Text of Agreements for Trust Territories as Approved by the General Assembly on 13 December 1946* (New York, 1946), contains trusteeship agreements concerning Western Samoa, Tanganyika, Ruanda-Urundi, Cameroons under British administration, Cameroons under French administration, Togoland under British administration, Togoland under French administration, and New Guinea.

For *Trusteeship Agreement for the Former Japanese Mandated Islands, Approved at the Hundred and Twenty-fourth Meeting of the Security Council*, see United Nations Document S/318, April 2, 1947.

For *Trusteeship Agreement for the Territory of Nauru*, see United Nations Document (1947.VI.A.11.).

The first special session of the General Assembly was convened from April 28 to May 15, 1947, to discuss the future of Palestine after the termination of the mandate (see *Official Records of the First Special Session of the General Assembly*, 2 volumes, Lake Success, New York, no date). On November 29, 1947, the Second General Assembly adopted a recommendation on the partition of Palestine. According to this recommendation the United Kingdom was to withdraw as mandatory power from Palestine not later than August 1, 1948 (see United Nations Document A/516, November 25, 1947). Pursuant to Statute 11 and 12 Geo. VI, Palestine Act, 1948, all jurisdiction, except certain jurisdictions as to the British Army, Navy and Air Force, of the United Kingdom terminated on May 15, 1948. On June 30, 1948 the withdrawal of all British troops and officials was completed. See also the *Official Records of the Second Session of the General Assembly*, 2 vols., and Annex, Lake Success, 1948. On the status of German Southwest Africa as of 1950, see the Advisory Opinion of the International Court of Justice rendered on July 11, 1950.

Text of Mandates

A Mandates

Mandate for Syria and the Lebanon.[42] Geneva, August 12, 1922. 7 p.+7 p., bilingual. [C.528.M.313.1922.VI.]

[42] Also in *Official Journal*, August,1922, p.1013–1017. On the "termination" of the mandate for Syria and Lebanon, see the broadcast on behalf of General Charles de Gaulle, President of the French National Committee, London,June 8,1941, quoted in Louise W. Holborn, *War and Peace Aims of the United Nations* (Boston,1943), p.566. "People of Syria and the Lebanon! At this moment the forces of Free France, united to the forces

Mandate for Palestine.[43] Geneva, August 12, 1922. 8 p.+8 p., bilingual. [C.529.M.314.1922.VI.]

Article 25 of the Palestine Mandate: Territory Known as Trans-Jordan.[44] Geneva, September 23, 1922. 3 p., mimeographed. [C. 667.M.396.1922.VI.]

Iraqu. Decision of the Council of the League of Nations Relating to the Application of the Principles of Article 22 of the Covenant to Iraqu.[45] Geneva, October 4, 1924. 3 p.+3 p., bilingual. [C.586.M. 201.1924.VI.] <C.P.M.173.>

B Mandates

British Mandate for Togoland.[46] Geneva, August 1, 1922. 8 p.+8 p., bilingual. [C.449(1)b.M.345 (b).1922.VI.]

British Mandate for the Cameroons.[47] Geneva, August 1, 1922. 8 p. +8 p., bilingual. [C.449(1)(c).M.345(c).1922.VI.]

French Mandate for Togoland.[48] Geneva, August 1, 1922. 8 p.+8 p., bilingual. [C.449(1)(d).M.345(c).1922.VI.]

French Mandate for the Cameroons.[49] Geneva, August 1, 1922. 8 p. +8 p., bilingual. [C.449(1)(e).M.345(e).1922.VI.]

British Mandate for East Africa (Tanganyika).[50] Geneva, August 1, 1922. 6 p.+6 p., bilingual. [C.449(1)(a).M.345(a).1922.VI.]

Belgian Mandate for East Africa (Ruanda Urundi).[51] Geneva, August 1, 1922. 6 p.+6 p., bilingual. [C.449(1)(f).M.345(f).1922.VI.]

C Mandates

Mandate for German South-West Africa. Geneva, December 17, 1920, 5 p., bilingual. [20/31/96D][52]

---

of the British Empire, our ally, are entering your territory. I declare that I assume the powers, responsibilities and duties of the representative of 'La France au Levant.' I do this in the name of Free France, which identifies herself with the traditional and real France, and in the name of her chief, General de Gaulle. In this capacity I come to put an end to the mandatory regime and to proclaim you free and independent."

[43]Also in *Official Journal*, August,1922, p.1007–1012.

[44]Also in *Official Journal*, November,1922, p.1390–1391.

[45]Also in *Official Journal*, October,1924, p.1346–1347. The Council adopted the Draft Instrument submitted by the British government on September 27,1924. For the termination of the mandate for Iraq, see *Termination of the Mandatory Regime in Iraq: Report by the Representative of Yugoslavia.* Geneva,September 22,1932.1 p., mimeographed. This is also in the *Official Journal*, March,1932, p.471-479. See also "General Conditions Which Must Be Fulfilled before the Mandate Regime Can Be Brought to an End in Respect of a Country Placed under That Regime," in Permanent Mandates Commission, *Minutes of the Twentieth Session*, Geneva,1931, p.228–230.

[46]Also in *Official Journal*, August,1922, p.880–886. [C.449(1)b.1922.VI.]

[47]Also in *Official Journal*, August,1922, p.869–874. [C.449(1)c.1922.VI.]

[48]Also in *Official Journal*, August,1922, p.886–892. [C.449(1)d.1922.VI.]

[49]Also in *Official Journal*, August,1922, p.874–880. [C.449(1)e.1922.VI.]

[50]Also in *Official Journal*, August,1922, p.865–868. [C.449(1)a.1922.VI.]

[51]Also in *Official Journal*, August,1922, p.862–865. [C.449(1)f.1922.VI.]

[52]Also numbered [21/31/14D]. Also in *Official Journal*, January–February,1921,

Mandate for German Samoa. Geneva, December 17, 1920. 5 p., bilingual. [20/31/96B][53]

Mandate for Nauru. Geneva, December 17, 1920. 5 p., bilingual. [20/31/96C][54]

Mandate for German Possessions in the Pacific Ocean Situated South of the Equator Other than German Samoa and Nauru. Geneva, December 17, 1920. bilingual. [20/31/96D][55]

Mandate for the German Possessions in the Pacific Ocean Lying North of the Equator. Geneva, December 17, 1920. 5 p., bilingual. [20/31/96E][56]

PERMANENT MANDATES COMMISSION

Jurisdiction and General Procedure

Article 22, Paragraph 9 of the Covenant provided: "A permanent Commission shall be constituted to receive and examine the annual reports of the Mandatories, and to advise the Council on all matters relating to the observance of the mandates."

Permanent Mandates Commission. Constitution Approved by the Council on the 1st December, 1920.[57] Edition Embodying the Amendments Adopted by the Council on January 10th, 1922, and September 8th, 1927. 2 p. Geneva, December 12, 1928. <C.P.M. 368(1)>

Permanent Mandates Commission. Rules of Procedure.[58] Geneva, March 19, 1928. 2 p. [C.404(2).M.295(2).1921.VI.] <C.P.M.8(2)>

Petitions

Rules of Procedure in Respect of Petitions Concerning Inhabitants

---

p.89–90. The mandate for German South-West Africa was exercised by the Union of South Africa.

[53]Also numbered [21/31/14^B]. Also in *Official Journal*, January–Feburary,1921, p.91–92. The mandate for German Samoa was exercised by the Dominion of New Zealand.

[54]Also numbered [21/31/14^A]. Also in *Official Journal*, January–February, 1921, p.93–94. The mandate for Nauru was exercised by the Commonwealth of Australia.

[55]Also numbered [21/31/14^C]. Also in *Official Journal*, January-February,1921, p.85–86. This mandate was exercised by Australia.

[56]Also numbered [21/31/14^E]. Also in *Official Journal*, January-February,1921, p.87–88. This mandate was exercised by Japan.

[57]For the powers and functions of the Permanent Mandates Commission, see also *Committees of the League of Nations: Report by the Secretary-General Drawn up in Pursuance of the Council's Decision of January 17th, 1934*, p. 6–8. [C.287.M.125.1934.] (General.1934.4.)

[58]Approved by the Council of the League of Nations on October 10, 1921, January 10,1922, December 12,1923, September 8,1927, and March 5,1928. See also Permanent Mandates Commission, *Rules of Procedure*. Geneva, October 19,1921. 3 p.+3 p., bilingual. [C.404.M.295.1921.VI.] <C.P.M.8.>

of Mandated Territories. Adopted by the Council on January 31st, 1923. 1 p.+1 p., bilingual. <C.P.M.38(1)> (1927.VI.A.3.)

Mandates: Procedure Adopted in Replying to Petitions Concerning Mandated Territories. *Official Journal*, July, 1926, p. 988–990. [C.314.1926.VI.] <C.P.M.415.>

Minutes of Sessions, *1921–1939*

First Reported Session: Permanent Mandates Commission. Minutes of the First Session, Held in Geneva, October 4th-8th, 1921. Geneva, 1921. 49 p.+49 p., bilingual. [C.416.M.296.1921.VI.]

Last Reported Session: Permanent Mandates Commission. Minutes of the Thirty-seventh Session, Held at Geneva, from December 12th-21st, 1939, Including the Report of the Commission to the Council. Geneva, 1939. 135 p. [C.7.M.5.1940.VI.] (1940.VI.A.1.)

From 1921 to 1939 the Permanent Mandates Commission met in 37 sessions. For information on the minutes of these sessions, see the Indices to Sessions listed below.

Indices to Sessions

Index to the Records of the Permanent Mandates Commission. Sessions I–V, 1921–1924. 42 p. [C.686.M.245.1925.VI.]

Index to the Records of the Permanent Mandates Commission. Sessions VI–X, 1925–1926. 45 p. [C.359.M.132.1927.VI.] (1927.VI.A.14.)

General Index to the Records of the Permanent Mandates Commission, No. 3. Sessions XI–XX, 1927–1931. Geneva, 1931. 67 p. [C.918.M.483.1931.VI.] (1931.VI.A.4.)

General Index to the Records of the Permanent Mandates Commission, No. 4. Sessions XXI–XXX, 1932–1936. Geneva, 1937. 65 p. [C.170.M.117.1937.VI.] (1937.VI.A.1.)

QUESTIONNAIRES

Mandate for Syria and Lebanon: Questionnaire Intended to Assist the Preparation of the Annual Reports of the Mandatory Powers. Geneva, August 23, 1922. 2 p.+2 p., bilingual. [C.554.M.336.1922.VI.] (A.34.1922.VI.)

Mandate for Palestine: Questionnaire Intended to Assist the Preparation of the Annual Reports of the Mandatory Powers. Geneva, August 23, 1922. 6 p.+ 6 p., bilingual. [C.553.M.335.1922.VI.] (A.38.1922.VI.)

B and C Mandates

List of Questions Which the Permanent Mandates Commission Desires Should Be Dealt with in the Annual Reports of the Mandatory Powers. Geneva, June 25, 1926. 7 p. [A.14.1926.VI.] <C.P. M.407(1).> (1926.VI.A.16.)

STATISTICAL INFORMATION

Statistical Information Concerning Territories under Mandate. Geneva, May 21, 1928. 15 p., bilingual. [C.143.M.34.1928.VI.] <C. P.M.698> (1926.VI.A.4.)
Statistical Information Regarding Territories under Mandate. Geneva, October 5, 1933. 20 p., bilingual. [C.565.M.272.1933.VI.] <C.P.M.1387> (1933.VI.A.2.)

REPORTS

Annual Reports of the Mandatory Powers

Article 22, Paragraph 7 of the Covenant provided: "In every case of Mandate, the Mandatory shall render to the Council an annual report in reference to the territory committed to its charge."

The only reports of the mandatory powers published by the League Secretariat were those for 1924.[59] In order, however, to enable libraries and persons who are interested in obtaining without difficulty the other reports, published by seven different governments, the Publications Department of the League of Nations obtained a certain number of these reports[60] and supplied them at cost price.

Although the reports by the mandatory powers were not considered official League Documents, the translations of these reports prepared by the League were frequently classified in the same way as League Documents. For example:

Palestine Royal Commission Report. Presented by the Secretary of State for the Colonies to Parliament by Command of His Majesty. July, 1937. London, 1937. 404 p.

appeared in French as follows:

Mandats. Palestine: Rapport de la Commission Royale de Palestine presenté au Parlement de Royaume-Uni par le Secrétaire d'Etat pour les Colonies par ordre de Sa Majesté Britannique (juillet 1937). Genève, le 30 novembre 1937. 234 p. [C.495.M.336.1937. VI.] (1937.VI.A.5.)

Reports of the Commission to the Council, 1921–1925

Although only the mandatory powers were obliged by the Covenant to prepare annual reports (Article 22, Paragraph 9), the Permanent

[59] See League of Nations, *Catalogue of Publications, 1920–1935* (1935), p.171–172.
[60] For a listing of these reports, see *ibid.*, p.173–183.

Mandates Commission, according to administrative usage, also issued annual reports containing the views and the advice of the Permanent Mandates Commission on matters pertaining to mandates. On the whole, the reports of the mandatory powers were forwarded to the Council of the League of Nations, together with the observations of the Commission and the comments of the High Commissioners on those observations.

First Report: Permanent Mandates Commission. Report Submitted to the Council of the League of Nations on Behalf of the Commission by Its Chairman, the Marquis Theodoli. Geneva, 1921. 5 p. +5 p., bilingual. [C.395.M.294.1921.VI.]

Last Report: Permanent Mandates Commission. Report on the Work of the Seventh Session (October 19th-30th, 1925) Submitted to the Council of the League of Nations. Geneva, 1925. 11 p. [C.649.M. 238.1925.VI.] <C.P.M.330.>

From the Eighth Session onwards, all minutes included the report of the Commission to the Council. Besides, separate offprints of the First to Sixteenth Sessions inclusive were published.

MANDATES: GENERAL

The Responsibility of the League of Nations Arising out of Article XXII of the Covenant (Mandates). Memorandum by the Secretary-General. No date. 7 p., bilingual. [20/4/119] [20/48/106]

Tables of General International Conventions Applied to the Mandated Territories. Geneva, October 1, 1931. 18 p+18 p., bilingual. [C.735.M.340.1931.VI.] (1931.VI.A.2.)

The Mandates System: Origin-Principles-Application. Geneva, 1945. 120 p. (1945.VI.A.1.)

Prepared by Mr. P. M. Anker, who was a member of the Mandates Section from 1931.

II. HEALTH ORGANIZATION

1. INTRODUCTORY NOTE

THE STRUCTURE of the Health Organization of the League of Nations was more complex than that of most of the other so-called technical agencies of the League. The autonomous existence of the Office International d'Hygiène Publique in Paris[1] had to be respected when the Health Organization of the League was set up. After protracted negotiations a special Mixed Committee, composed of an equal number of members of the Provisional Health Committee of the League[2] and the Office International d'Hygiène Publique, drew up the scheme of the Health Organization that was subsequently approved by the Council and the Assembly.[3] It should be noted that the Health Organization was financed in part by the Rockefeller Foundation.[4]

[1]The Office International d' Hygiène Publique was originally established under the Rome agreement of December 9,1907. This agreement, as well as the provisions of the Sanitary Convention signed at Paris on January 17,1912, were subsequently modified by the "International Sanitary Convention, with Protocol of Signature, Signed at Paris, June 21,1926," 78 *Treaty Series*, p.229-349, bilingual. See especially Art.7 on the relationship between the Office International d'Hygiène Publique and the Health Committee of the League.

[2]The Provisional Health Committee was constituted by Council Resolution of June 21, 1921 (see Council Minutes, 13th Sess., p.21 and Annex 203), and Assembly Resolution of September 23,1921 (see *Official Journal*, Special Supplement No.6, October, 1921, p. 21-22); see also Assembly Resolution of December 10, 1920, *Official Journal*, Special Supplement, January, 1921, p. 15-19.

[3]See Council Resolution of July 7,1923, *Official Journal*, August,1923, p.936, 1045-1046, and Assembly Resolution of September 15,1923, *Official Journal*, Special Supplement No. 11, October, 1923, p. 11, in conjunction with Art. 23(f) of the Covenant. See also "Scheme for the Permanent Health Organization of the League of Nations," *Official Journal*, August,1923, p.1050-1052; this is also a separate document [C.391.1923.III.] <C.H.110>. See also Assembly Resolution of December 8,1920, regarding the establishment and working of the technical organizations of the League of Nations, *Official Journal*, Special Supplement, January,1921, p.12-13.

[4]For the co-operation between the Rockefeller Foundation and the Health Organization of the League, see Documents [C.435.M.300.1922.III.] <C.H.16.>, Annex 387a.; [C.594.F.374.1922.III.](sic);[C.40.1924.III.]. All the foregoing documents are mimeographed. See especially *Audit of the Accounts of the Rockefeller Foundation Grants to the Health Organization*. Geneva,1925.7p. [A.11.1925.X.] <C.319.1925.X>. For the contributions to the Health Organization by the League and the Rockefeller Foundation, see the table in Egon F. Ranshofen-Wertheimer, *The International Secretariat* (Washington,1945), p.158.

The main organs of the Health Organization were the General Advisory Health Council, which was identical with the Committee of the Office International d'Hygiène Publique, and the Standing Health Committee of the League, which directed the health work of the League. In addition, there was a special Health Section at the Secretariat of the League.[5]

Furthermore, an Advisory Committee of the Eastern Bureau of the Health Organization was set up by Assembly Resolution of September 20, 1924,[6] with the status of a committee of the Health Committee under Article 10 of the latter's Rules of Procedure.[7]

An International Center for Research on Leprosy was established in Rio de Janeiro under the auspices of the League in 1931.[8] The Governing Body of the International Center consisted of members of the Health Committee of the League, acting in their personal capacities, and the chairman of the Committee of Management.[9]

In the field of nutrition the Health Organization co-operated closely with the Economic Section of the League.[10] In the field of public health, interchange of public health personnel was encouraged, a Public Health Statistical Service was maintained, and individual countries obtained advice on the establishment or reform of their public health services.

The over-all Health Organization served as a center for biological standardization, that is to say, agreement on uniform standards based on generally accepted measurements of hormones, insulin, sera, and vitamins to render possible international understanding on these matters.[11] The Danish State Serum Institute at Copenhagen was chosen as the distributing center for international sera standards. The laboratories with which it was unable to communicate were supplied by the National Institute for Medical Research, Hempstead, United Kingdom. Epidemiological intelligence was another field of the Health Organization's activities. Information concerning epidem-

---

[5]For the organization of the Health Section of the Secretariat, see Ranshofen-Wertheimer, *The International Secretariat*, p.120–123.
[6]*Official Journal*, Special Supplement No.21, October,1924, p.12.
[7]For the work of the Advisory Committee of the Eastern Bureau, see also *Official Journal*, July, 1928, p. 966–967.
[8]See Document [C.475.1931.III], *Official Journal*, November,1931, p.2085–2087; for the "Organic Statute of the International Centre for Research on Leprosy," see *ibid*. p.2086–2087.
[9]For the composition of the Committee of Management, see Art.5 of the Organic Statute, *ibid*.
[10]See especially *Nutrition. Final Report of the Mixed Committee of the League of Nations on the Relation of Nutrition to Health, Agriculture and Economic Policy.* Geneva,1937. 327 p. [A.13.1937.II.A.] (1937.II.A.10.)
[11]See especially "Biological Standardisation," *Bulletin of the Health Organization*, Vol.10 (1942/43), p.77–154.

ics was supplied by radio[12] and by special serial publications on epidemics, such as the *Weekly Epidemiological Record*. In January 1945 major functions of the League in the field of epidemiological intelligence and public health were transferred to the Health Division of the United Nations Relief and Rehabilitation Administration (UNRRA) whose headquarters were in Washington, D. C. UNRRA published from January, 1945 through December, 1946 the *Epidemiological Information Bulletin*. (Vol. I, No. 1, January 1945–Vol. II, No. 23, December 15, 1946). As of December 1, 1946 the functions of UNRRA in this field were transferred to the Interim Commission of the World Health Organization, and subsequently to the World Health Organization (WHO) which came into existence on April 7, 1948. The following serial publications relating to public health, vital statistics, and epidemiology are now published by the World Health Organization: *Weekly Epidemiological Record*, (first issue: September 5, 1946); *Epidemiological and Vital Statistics Report* (first issue: June, 1947; monthly, designed to consolidate corresponding periodicals previously published by the League of Nations, the Office International d'Hygiène Publique, and UNRRA); the *Bulletin of the World Health Organization; Chronicle of the World Health Organization* (first issue: 1947); *International Digest of Health Legislation*, Vol. I, No. 1 (1948); *WHO Newsletter* (New Series, September, 1948–). For the transfer of functions formerly exercised by the Health Organization of the League, to the Interim Commission of the World Health Organization, respectively to the World Health Organization, see *Arrangement Concluded by the Governments Represented at the International Health Conference*, held in New York City from June 19 to July 22, 1946, in *Yearbook of the United Nations, 1946–1947*, p. 801–802. See also Resolution 61 (I) adopted by the General Assembly of the United Nations on December 14, 1946 (United Nations document A/64, Add. 1, p. 96–97).

2. CONSTITUTION AND RULES OF PROCEDURE

Scheme for the Permanent Health Organization of the League of Nations. Geneva, 1923. 5 p., bilingual. [C.391.1923.III.] <C.H. 110>[13]

For the 1936 revision of the Scheme, see *Official Journal*, November,1936, p.1175–1176.[14]

[12]See the Chart in Information Section, *Essential Facts about the League of Nations* (10th ed., revised, Geneva,1939), p.257.
[13]Also in *Official Journal*, August,1923, p.1050-1052, and in Document <C.H.197>, p.11-25.
[14]See also "Revision of the Constitution of the Health Organization" [C.235.1936.III.],

"Rules of Procedure of the Health Committee as Adopted on February 20, 1924" <C.H.22(3)>,[15] in Health Organisation, Rules of Procedure of the Health Committee, p. 30–41. <C.H.197.>

The title of Document <C.H.197>," Rules of Procedure," is misleading. Actually, the document includes: I. Article 23(f) of the Covenant of the League of Nations. II. The Resolution adopted by the Assembly on December 8th,1920, Regarding the Establishment and Working of the Technical Organisations of the League of Nations. III. Scheme for the Permanent Health Organisation of the League of Nations Drawn up by the Special Mixed Committee, June,1923[C.391.1923.III.]. IVa. Extract from Viscount Ishii's report on the Work of the Provisional Health Committee, Adopted by the Council on July 7th, 1923; IVb. Assembly Resolution of September 15th,1923.

3. MINUTES OF SESSIONS AND REPORTS

Minutes of Sessions of the Provisional Health Committee,[16] *1921–1923*

First Session: Provisional Health Committee. Minutes of the First Session Held in Geneva, August 25th to 29th, 1921. Geneva, 1921. 34 p.+34 p., bilingual. [C.400.M.280.1921.III.]
Last Session: Health Committee.[17] Minutes of the Sixth Session Held at Paris from May 26th to June 6th, 1923. No date. 126 p. [C. 424.M.187.1923.III.]

Minutes of Sessions of the Health Committee,[18] *1924–1931*

First Session: Health Committee. Minutes of the First Session Held at Geneva from February 11th to 21st, 1924. Geneva, 1924. 142 p. [C.10. M.7.1924.III.]
Last Recorded Session: Health Committee. Minutes of the Eighteenth Session Held in Paris on October 12th and 13th, 1931. Geneva, 33 p. [C.980.M.545.1931.III.] (1931.III.14.)
No minutes were published for the Nineteenth and subsequent sessions. For references covering the years 1932 to 1940, see, however, *Bulletin of the Health Organisation*, Vol. 11(1945), p. 14–15.

Official Journal, June,1936, p.738–741. For Council Resolution of September 26, 1936, see *ibid.*, November,1936,p.1178; for Assembly Resolution of October 10,1936,see *ibid.*, Special Supplement No.153, p.18.
[15]Also in Health Committee, *Minutes of the First Session,Held at Geneva from February 11th to 21st,1924*, Geneva,1924, p.140–142. [C.10.M.7.1924.III.]
[16]The Provisional Health Committee was established by Council Resolutions of March 2,1921 and June 21,1921, following Assembly Resolutions of December 10,1920. See *Official Journal*, March-April,1921, p.179–180; September,1921, p.709–710.
[17]This document is erroneously entitled "Health Committee," instead of "Provisional Health Committee."
[18]The definitive Health Committee was set up by Council Resolution of July 7, 1923 (*Official Journal*, August,1923, p.936, 1045–1046), and Assembly Resolution of September 15,1923 (*Official Journal*, Special Supplement No.11, October,1923, p.11).

Reports of the Health Organization, 1925–1939

From 1926 to 1931 six annual reports of the Health Organization, covering the years 1925–1930, were published as separate documents.

First Report: Annual Report of the Health Organization for 1925. Geneva, 1926. 44 p. <C.H.442> (1926.III.10.)

Last Report: Annual Report of the Health Organization for 1930. Geneva, 1931. 70 p. [A.7.1931.III.] (1931.III.3.)

From 1932 to 1939 reports on the work of the Health Organization, covering in part the years 1931–1939, appeared in the *Quarterly Bulletin of the Health Organisation:* January, 1931-September, 1932, in Vol. 1 (September, 1932), p. 362–424; October, 1932-September, 1933, in Vol. 2 (September, 1933), p. 495–549; June, 1937-May, 1938, in Vol. 7 (August, 1938), p. 622–665; June, 1938-April, 1939, in Vol. 8 (1939), p. 1–59. No reports were published for the periods September, 1933 to May, 1937 and May, 1939 to June, 1942. Reports for July, 1942 to June, 1943 and July, 1943 to June, 1944 are in *Chronicle of the Health Organisation*, Vol. 3 (October, 1943), p. 1–11, and Vol. 4 (April, 1945), p. 1–10.

Reports on the Work of the Health Committee to the Council, 1924–1939

First Report: Health Committee: Report on the Work of the First Session, February 11th to 21st, 1924. Geneva, 1924. 9 p. [C.63. 1924.III.] <C.H.192.>

Last Report:[19] Report to the Council on the Work of the Thirty-first Session of the Health Committee (Geneva, November 20th–24th, 1939). Geneva, 1939. 9 p. [C.364.M.277.1939.] <C.H.1445(1)> (1939.III.5.)

The Reports of the Rapporteur to the Council on the work of the sessions of the Health Committee did not appear as separate documents, but in the *Official Journal*. A bibliographical list covering thirty sessions (1924–1939) is contained in *Bulletin of the Health Organisation*, Vol. XI (1945), p. 15.

For Reports to the Council on the Work of the Provisional Health Committee, see the references to the *Official Journal*, 1921–1923, in *Bulletin of the Health Organisation*, Vol. 11 (1945), p. 16.

See also *Report by the Emergency Sub-Committee of the Health Committee on Its Meeting Held from March 4th–8th, 1940*. Geneva, March 11th, 1940. 4 p., mimeographed. <C.H.1449>

---

[19]In addition to these, several reports of the Health Committee were published as Assembly Documents. Several of these reports were addressed to the Assembly, *e.g.*, Document [A.70.1924.III]; others were addressed to the Permanent Committee of the Office International d'Hygiène Publique, *e.g.*, Document [A.22.1924.III.] <C.H.214>; others were addressed to the States Members of the League, *e.g.*, Document [A. 28.1923.III.].

4. CONFERENCES UNDER THE AUSPICES OF THE HEALTH ORGANIZATION

BIOLOGICAL STANDARDIZATION

Report of the Technical Conference for Consideration of Certain Methods of Biological Standardisation. Edinburgh, July 19th–21st, 1923. Geneva, 1924. 7 p. [C.4.M.4.1924.III.] <C.H.147.>

Second International Conference on the Biological Standardisation of Certain Remedies Convened by the Health Committee of the League of Nations and Held from August 31st-September 3rd, 1925, at Geneva. Geneva, 1925. 28 p.: 3–12, French; 13–22, English; 23–28, authentic text of the resolutions in German. [C.532. M.183.1925.III.] <C.H.350>

Report of the Permanent Standards Commission (Geneva, October 11th–13th, 1926). Geneva, 1926. 4 p. (1926.III.21.) <C.H.517.>

Report of the Permanent Commission on Standardisation of Sera, Serological Reactions and Biological Products. Frankfort-on-Main, April 25th to 28th, 1928. Geneva, 1928. 8 p. (1928.III.6.) <C.H. 717.>

Report of the Permanent Commission on Biological Standardisation (London, June 23rd, 1931). Geneva, 1931. 78 p. (1931.III.10.) <C.H.1056(1).>

Report of the Permanent Commission on Biological Standardisation. Session Held at Copenhagen from August 28th–30th, 1934. *Quarterly Bulletin of the Health Organisation*, Special Number, January, 1935, p. 1–120.

Report of the Permanent Commission on Biological Standardisation. Session Held at Geneva on September 30th and October 4th, 1935. *Quarterly Bulletin of the Health Organisation*, Special Number, November, 1936, p. 571–745.

Report on the Meeting of Serologists of the Permanent Commission on Biological Standardisation (Paris, October 19th–22nd, 1938). *Bulletin of the Health Organisation*, Vol. 7 (October, 1938), p. 683–899.

EUROPEAN HEALTH CONFERENCE, WARSAW, 1922

European Health Conference Held at Warsaw from March 20th to 28th, 1922. Geneva, 1922. 41 p.

Includes: Minutes of Plenary Session and General Report.

Resolutions Adopted by the European Health Conference at Its Meeting in Warsaw from 20th to 28th March, 1922. Geneva, 1922. 16 p.: 4–7, French; 8–11, English; 12–15, German. [C.177.M.96. 1922.]

PAN-AFRICAN HEALTH CONFERENCE, JOHANNESBURG, 1935

Report of the Pan-African Health Conference Held at Johannesburg, November 20th to 30th, 1935. *Quarterly Bulletin of the Health Organisation*, Vol. 5 (March, 1936), p. 1–209.

RABIES

International Rabies Conference. Held at the Pasteur Institute, Paris, from April 25th–29th, 1927. Organised by the Health Organisation of the League of Nations.[20] Reports by Messrs. A. C. Marie, P. Remlinger, H. Vallée to the Conference. Geneva, 1927. 164 p. <C.H.531(1)> (1927.III.14.)

RURAL HYGIENE IN EUROPE[21]

Report of the Preparatory Committee on the Principles Governing the Organisation of Medical Assistance, the Public Health Services and Sanitation in Rural Districts. Geneva, 1931, 62 p. <C.H. 1045> (1931.III.7.)
European Conference on Rural Hygiene (June 29th–July 7th, 1931). Proceedings. Volume I: Recommendations on the Principles Governing the Organisation of Medical Assistance, the Public Health Services and Sanitation in Rural Districts. Geneva, 1931. 59 p. [C.473.M.202.1931.III.] (1931.III.11'). Volume II: Minutes. Geneva, 1931. 187 p. [C.473.M.202.1931.III.(Vol.II)] (1931.III.11")

RURAL HYGIENE IN THE FAR EAST

Preparatory Committee

Intergovernmental Conference of Far-Eastern Countries on Rural Hygiene. Report by the Preparatory Committee. Geneva, 1937. 103 p. <C.H.1234> (1937.III.3.)

Preparatory Papers

Report of French Indo-China. Geneva, 1937. 135 p. <C.H.1235> (1937.III.4.)
1: Note on Public Health Organisation in Burma. 2: Note on Medical Organisation in Burma. Geneva, 1937. 49 p. <C.H.1235a> (1937. III.5.)

[20]See also Document [C.579.M.205.1927.III.], p.132, cited in Marie J. Carroll, *Key to League of Nations Documents Placed on Public Sale, 1920–1929* (Boston,1930), p.262.
[21]See also European Conference on Rural Life(1939), *Sickness Insurance and Rural Medical Assistance, Prepared by the International Labour Office.* Geneva,1939. 33 p. [C.87.M.47.1939.] <Conf. E.V.R. 15> <European Conference on Rural Life 15>

Preparatory Papers Relating to British India. Geneva, 1937. 414 p. <C.H.1235(b)> (1937.III.6.)

Report of the Malayan Delegation. Geneva, 1936. 38 p. <C.H.1235 (c)> (1937.III.7.)

Report on Health Organisation in Ceylon. Geneva, 1937. 60 p. <C.H.1235(d)> (1937.III.8.)

Report of the Philippines. Geneva, 1937. 26 p. <C.H.1235(e)> (1937.III.9.)

Report of China. Geneva, 1937. 109 p. <C.H.1235(f).> (1937.III. 11.)

Report of Japan. Geneva, 1937. 38 p. <C.H.1235(g).> (1937.III.12.)

Report of Siam. Geneva, 1937. 53 p. <C.H.1235(h).> (1937.III.13.)

I. A Brief Report on Rural Hygiene in the Colony of Hong-Kong. II. Memorandum on Conditions Prevailing in North Borneo. III. Note on the Medical and Health Services in Sarawak. IV. Memorandum Concerning the Colony of Fiji. V. Memorandum on Public Health Organisation of the Gilbert and Ellice Islands Colony. VI. Note on the Health Organisation of the British Solomon Islands Protectorate. VII. Report for the New Hebrides Condominium. VIII. Report for Tonga. Geneva, 1937. 125 p. <C.H.1235 (i)> (1937.III.14.)

Report of the Netherlands Indies. Prepared at the Head Office of the Netherlands Indies Public Health Service. Batavia-C. (Java), with the Collaboration of Many Authorities in the Fields of Administrative, Economic, Social, Educational, Health, Medical and Sanitary Matters. Geneva, 1937. 204 p. <C.H.1235(j)> (1937. III.15)

Report on the Conference

Report of the Intergovernmental Conference of Far-Eastern Countries on Rural Hygiene. Held at Bandoeng[22] (Java), August 3rd to 13th, 1937. Geneva, 1937. 119 p. [A.19.1937.III.] (1937.III.17.)

SCHOOLS OF HYGIENE

Report on the Work of the Conferences of Directors of Schools of Hygiene Held in Paris, May 20th to 23rd, 1930, and in Dresden, July 14th to 17th, 1930; with a Memorandum on the Teaching of Hygiene in Various European Countries, Submitted to the Dresden Conference by Professor Carl Prausnitz, and an Introduction by Professor Léon Bernard. Geneva, 1930. 115 p. <C.H.888.> (1930.III.10.)

22See also *Bulletin of the Health Organisation*, Vol. 7 (August,1938), p.623–627.

Report on the Meeting of Directors of Institutes and Schools of Hygiene Held at Geneva from November 22nd to 27th, 1937. *Bulletin of the Health Organisation*, Vol. 7 (April, 1938), p. 169–427.

SERODIAGNOSIS OF SYPHILIS

Investigations on the Serodiagnosis of Syphilis. Report of the Technical Laboratory Conference (Held at Copenhagen, November 19th to December 3rd, 1923) (with Two Annexes). No date. 183 p., bilingual. [C.5.M.5.1924.III] <C.H.148.>

Report of the Second Laboratory Conference on the Serodiagnosis of Syphilis, Held at Copenhagen, May 21st to June 4th, 1928. Geneva, 1928. 186 p. <C.H.726.> (1929.III.3.)

Report on the Meeting of the Third Laboratory Conference on Serodiagnosis of Syphilis, Held at Copenhagen August 4th to 5th, 1930. Geneva, 1930. 7 p. [C.627.M.248.1930.] <C.H.895.>

Report of the Laboratory Conference on the Serodiagnosis of Syphilis, Convened at Montevideo by the Institute for the Prevention of Syphilis of Uruguay (September 15th–26th, 1930). Geneva, 1931. 131 p. <C.H.968.> (1931.III.4.)

SLEEPING SICKNESS

Report of the Second International Conference on Sleeping Sickness,[23] Held in Paris, November 5th to 7th, 1928. Geneva, 1928. 90 p. <C.H.743.> (1928.III.18.)

STANDARDIZATION OF SERA AND SEROLOGICAL TESTS

International Conference on the Standardisation of Sera and Serological Tests, Convened by the Health Committee of the League of Nations and Held on December 12th to 14th, 1921, at the British Ministry of Health, London. Geneva, 1921. 12 p.+12 p., bilingual.

Annex 4, p.13–18, contains the Authentic Text of Memorandum and Resolutions in German, as Approved by the Conference.

Second International Conference on the Standardisation of Sera and Serological Tests Convened by the Health Committee of the League of Nations and Held from November 20th to 26th, 1922, at the Pasteur Institute, Paris. Geneva, 1922. 27 p.: 2–10, French; 11–19, English; 20–27, authentic text of the resolutions in German. [C.156.M.78.1923.III.] <C.H.48>

[23]The First Conference met in London, May 19-22,1925; see Carroll, *Key to League of Nations Documents . . . 1920-1929*, p. 260.

Reports on Serological Investigations Presented to the Second International Conference on the Standardisation of Sera and Serological Tests Held at the Pasteur Institute in Paris in November, 1922. No place of publication, 1923. 303 p. [C.168.M.98.1923.]

The papers submitted by several experts dealt with diphtheria and tetanus, antimeningococcus serum, antipneumococcus serum, antidysentery serum, serodiagnosis of syphilis.

STANDARDIZATION OF SEX HORMONES

Report of the Conference on the Standardisation of Sex Hormones, Held in London from July 30th to August 1st, 1932. *Quarterly Bulletin of the Health Organisation*, Vol. 4 (January, 1935), p. 121–127.

Report of the Second Conference on the Standardisation of Sex Hormones, Held in London, July 15th to 17th, 1935. *Quarterly Bulletin of the Health Organisation*, Vol. 4 (September, 1935), p. 618–630.

Report of the Third International Conference on the Standardisation of Sex Hormones (Geneva, August 11th to 13th, 1938). *Bulletin of the Health Organisation*, Vol. 7 (October, 1938), p. 887–899.

5. DISEASES

CANCER[24]

Report on the Results of Demographic Investigations in Certain Selected Countries. Geneva, 1925. 168 p. <C.H.333.Volume I.>. Volume II: Geneva, 1925. <C.H.333.Volume II.>

Considerations Regarding the Possible Relationship of Cancer to Race, Based on a Study of Anthropological and Medical Statistics of Certain European Countries, by Alfred Niceforo and Eugène Pittard. Geneva, 1926. 330 p. <C.H.492> (1926.III.24.)

Reports Submitted by The Radiological Sub-Commission. Geneva, 1929. 82 p. <C.H.788.> (1929.III.5.)

For other League publications on cancer see *Bulletin of the Health Organisation*, Vol. XI (1945), p. 29–37.

INFECTIOUS DISEASES

Handbook of Infectious Diseases with Notes on Prophylaxis, Serum

[24]On the work of the Cancer Commission, see also *Report on the Work of the Cancer Commission for the Years 1923 to 1927, Presented to the Health Committee on Behalf of the Commission by Sir George Buchanan (President), November, 1927.* Geneva,1927. 14p. <C.H.631(1)> <C.H./Cancer 42(2)> (1927.III.17.)

Treatment and Vaccination, by the Staff of the Cantacuzene Institute under the Direction of Professors C. Ionescu-Mihaesti and M. Ciuca. Geneva, 1945. 331 p. <C.H.1454> (1945.III.1.)

LEPROSY

The Principles of the Prophylaxis of Leprosy. First General Report of the Leprosy Commission. Geneva, 1931. 12 p. <C.H.970> (1931.III.2.)

For other League publications on leprosy see *Bulletin of the Health Organisation*, Vol. XI (1945), p. 71–72. For the publications of the International Centre for Leprosy Research (Rio de Janeiro) see *ibid.*, p. 72–73.

MALARIA

Principles and Methods of Antimalarial Measures in Europe. Second General Report of the Malaria Commission. Geneva, 1927. 95 p. <C.H./Malaria/73> (1927.III.5)

Enquiry into the Quinine Requirements of Malaria Countries and the World Prevalence of Malaria. Geneva, 1932. 89 p. <C.H. /Malaria/185> (1932.III.3.)

The Therapeutics of Malaria. Principles of Treatment Based on the Results of Controlled Experiments. Third General Report of the Malaria Commission. *Quarterly Bulletin of the Health Organisation*, Vol. 2 (June, 1933), p. 181–285.

For other League publications on malaria see *Bulletin of the Health Organisation*, Vol. XI (1945), p. 73–95.

PNEUMONIC PLAGUE

A Treatise on Pneumonic Plague, by Wu Lien-Teh. Geneva, 1926. 466 p. <C.H.474.> (1926.III.13.)

For other League publications on plague see *Bulletin of the Health Organisation*, Vol. XI (1945), p. 126–127.

RABIES

Analytical Review of Reports from Pasteur Institutes on the Results of Anti-Rabies Treatment, by Lt.-Col. A. G. McKendrick. Geneva, 1930. 158 p. <C.H.844> (1930.III.2.)

Additional reviews on rabies were published in the *Quarterly Bulletin of the Health Organisation:* Vol. 1 (March, 1932), p. 110–141; Vol. 1 (December, 1932), p. 725–755; Vol. 2 (December, 1933), p. 553–

599, Vol. 3 (December, 1934), p. 613–653; Vol. 4 (December 1935), p. 752–786; Vol. 6 (February 1937), p. 17–55; Vol. 7 (February 1938), p. 1–42; Vol. 8 (No. 1, 1940), p. 31–78.

For other League publications on rabies see *Bulletin of the Health Organisation*, Vol. XI (1945), p. 146–149.

SLEEPING SICKNESS

Final Report of the League of Nations International Commission on Human Trypanosomiasis. Geneva, 1928. 392 p. <C.H.629.> (1927.III.13.)

For other League publications on sleeping sickness (Trypanosomiasis) see *Bulletin of the Health Organisation*, Vol. XI (1945), p. 190–193.

SMALLPOX

Commission on Smallpox and Vaccination. Report on the Session Held at Geneva from August 22nd to 25th, 1928. Geneva, 1928. 12 p. <C.H.739> (1928.III.12.)

For other League publications on smallpox see *Bulletin of the Health Organisation*, Vol. XI (1945), p. 166–168.

SYPHILIS

Report on the Meeting of Experts on Syphilis and Cognate Subjects Held at Geneva, October 8th to 10th, 1928. Geneva, October, 1928. 7 p. <C.H.750.> (1928.III.15.)

For other League publications on syphilis see *Bulletin of the Health Organisation*, Vol. XI (1945), p. 183–186.

6. WELFARE

Report on the Welfare of the Blind in Various Countries Based on Replies Furnished to a Questionnaire Sent out by the Health Organisation of the League. Geneva, 1929. 284 p. <C.H.818.> (1929.III.8.)

Report on Maternal Welfare and the Hygiene of Infants and Children of Pre-school Age by the Reporting Committee Appointed to Deal with These Questions. Report Adopted by the Health Committee at Its Eighteenth Session, Held in October, 1931. Geneva, 1931. 75 p. <C.H.1060.> (1931.III.13.)

7. SPECIAL ENQUIRIES AND INVESTIGATIONS

ASIA (INCLUDING FAR EAST)

The Prevalence of Epidemic Disease and Port Health Organisation and Procedure in the Far East. Report Presented to the Health Committee of the League of Nations by F. Norman White. Geneva, 1923. 179 p. [C.167.M.43.1924.III.] <C.H.130.>

China:[25] Proposals of the National Government of the Republic of China for Collaboration with the League of Nations on Health Matters. Geneva, 1930. 51 p. [C.118.M.38.1930.III.] <C.H.842.> (1930.III.3.)

China: Collaboration with the Ministry of Health of the National Government of the Republic of China. Completion of the Survey of Chinese Ports and Report on the Reorganisation of the Port Health Services, in Conformity with the Request of the National Government of China. Geneva, 1930. 70 p. <C.H.906.> (1930. III.14.)

India: A Memorandum on the Epidemiology of Cholera, by Major A. J. H. Russell. Geneva, 1925. 46 p. <C.H.339.>

Iran (Persia): Report on an Investigation into the Sanitary Conditions in Persia Undertaken on Behalf of the Health Committee of the League of Nations at the Request of the Persian Government, by John Gilmour. Geneva, 1925. 64 p. <C.H.262.>

Japan: Studies of Cholera in Japan, by Rokuro Takano, Itsuya Ohtsubo, Zenjuro Inouye. Geneva, 1926. 121 p. <C.H.515.> (1926.III.22.)

EUROPE

The Present Menace of Typhus Fever in Europe and the Means of Combating it, by Dr. Yves Biraud. *Bulletin of the Health Organisation,* Vol. 10, No. 1 (1942/43), p. 1–76

SOUTH AMERICA

Enquiries into Infant Mortality in South America, by Robert Debré and O. E. W. Olsen. Report Approved by the Health Committee at its Sixteenth Session (September 29th to October 7th, 1930). Geneva, 1930. 20 p. <C.H.908(1)> (1930.III.15.)

[25]See also *Report on Medical Schools in China,* by Knud Faber. Geneva,1931. 47 p. <C.H. 961.> (1931.III.8.)

8. NUTRITION[26]

Report on the Physiological Bases of Nutrition by the Technical Commission Appointed by the Health Committee (Meeting Held in London, November 25th–29th, 1935). Geneva, 1935. 19 p. <C.H.1197.> (1935.III.6.)

Guiding Principles for Studies on the Nutrition of Populations, by Dr. E. J. Bigwood. Geneva, 1939. 281 p. <C.H.1401> <C.H. /Con.Exp.Alim./50(2)> (1939.III.1.)

Nutrition and Public Health, by Et. Burnet and W. R. Aykroyd. *Quarterly Bulletin of the Health Organisation*, Vol. 4 (June, 1935), p. 323–473.

9. BIOLOGICAL STANDARDIZATION[27]

Report of the Permanent Standards Commission (Geneva, October 11th–13th, 1926). Geneva, 1926. 4 p. <C.H.517.> (1926.III.21.)

Report of the Permanent Commission on Biological Standardisation. London, June 23rd, 1931. Geneva, 1931. 78 p. <C.H.1056(1)> (1931.III.10)

Bulletin of the Health Organisation, Vol. 10, No. 2 (1942/43), p. 77–154.

This issue of the *Bulletin* deals exclusively with biological standards. It contains: 1. International Biological Standards. 2. Standard Preparations for the Assay of the Gas-Gangrene-Anti-Toxins, cl. *perfringens*, cl. *vibrion septique* and cl. *oedematiens*, by P. Hartley and D. G. Evans. 3. Note on the Complexity of Tetanus Toxin by M. Llewellyn Smith. 4. Observation on the Variable Interactions of Tetanus Toxins and Antitoxins, by G.F. Petrie. 5. Heparin. 5a. The Biological Standardisation of Heparin, by F.C. MacIntosh. 5b. Memorandum on a Provisional Standard for Heparin (1942), Submitted by the Department of Biological Standards, the National Institute for Medical Research, Hampstead, London,N.W.3.

"The International Standard and Unit for Penicillin," *Bulletin of the Health Organisation*, Vol. XII, No. 2 (1945/46), p. 181–298.

See especially the Resolutions Adopted at the International Conference on the Standardisation of Penicillin, p. 189–191; and the International Penicillin Working Standard, p. 241–242.

For other League publications on international biological standardization see *Bulletin of the Health Organisation*, Vol. XI (1945), p. 172–181.

[26]On nutrition, see also the publications by the Section of Economic Relations (II). See also *Progress of the Science of Nutrition in Japan*, by Tadusu Saiki. Geneva,1926. 387 p. <C.H.523.> (1926.III.25.). *The Food of Japan*, by Egerton Charles Grey. Geneva,1928. 161 p. <C.H.681.> (1928.III.2.).

[27]See also above under Conferences and *The Biological Standardisation of Insulin Including Reports on the Preparation of the International Standard and the Definition of the Unit*. Geneva,1926. 71 p. <C.H. 398.> (1926.III.7.)

10. CABLE CODE

League of Nations: Health Section, Eastern Bureau. The AA Cable Code.[28] Compiled for the Bureau by Gilbert E. Brooke. Singapore, 1925. 45 p.

Second edition, Singapore, 1926. 84 p., bilingual. Brought up to date by successive appendices up to July 10, 1941.

11. GLOSSARY

Polyglot Glossary of Communicable Diseases. Contribution to the International Nomenclature of Diseases, by Dr. Yves Biraud. *Bulletin of the Health Organisation*, Vol. 10, No. 3 (1943/44), p. 202–556; introduction in English and French.

This glossary covers 25 languages. In addition to the official International List (in French) and the column of Latin terms, the various languages are given in the French alphabetical order as follows: German, English, Bulgarian, Danish and Norwegian, Spanish, Estonian, Finnish, French, Greek, Hungarian, Icelandic, Italian, Latvian, Lithuanian, Dutch, Polish, Portuguese, Romanian, Russian, Serbo-Croatian, Swedish, Czech, and Turkish.

In addition to this glossary the following publications aiming at uniformity of medical terminology are noteworthy:
Nomenclatures internationales des causes de décès 1938 (classification Bertillon). Cinquième revision décennale effectuée par la Conférence internationale de Paris du 3 au 7 octobre 1938. La Haye, 1940. 306 p.

This document, though published by the International Institute of Statistics, was prepared and edited by the Service of Epidemiological Intelligence and Public Health Statistics of the League of Nations.
League publications relating to the unification of pharmacopoeiae are listed in *Bulletin of the Health Organisation*, Vol. XI (1945), p. 122–125.

12. STATISTICAL HANDBOOK SERIES

From 1924 to 1930 the Health Organization published 14 volumes of the *Statistical Handbook Series*. These handbooks reported on the vital statistics in the following countries, enumerated in the order of publication: Netherlands, Belgium, England and Wales, Spain, Austria, Scandinavian Countries and Baltic Republics, Portugal, Czechoslovakia, France, Hungary, Irish Free State and Northern Ireland, Switzerland, Kingdom of Scotland, and Canada.

[28] The preparation of an Auxiliary Code (EE) was announced here, but it does not seem to have been published.

13. PERIODICAL PUBLICATIONS

WEEKLY RECORD
First Issue: April 1, 1926 <R.H.1>.
Last Issue: November 8, 1928 <R.H.141>.

WEEKLY EPIDEMIOLOGICAL RECORD
First Issue: November 25, 1928 <R.H.142>.
Last Issue: August 29, 1946 <R.H.1070>.

Since September 5, 1946, with Vol. 21, No. 36, the *Weekly Epidemiological Record* has been published by the Interim Commission of the World Health Organization, respectively by the World Health Organization.

EPIDEMIOLOGICAL REPORT OF THE HEALTH SECTION
First Issue: February 1, 1922 <R.E.1>.
Last Issue: June, 1940 <R.E.225>.

This publication appeared at irregular intervals: <R.E.1> to <R.E.51>, weekly; <R.E.52> to <R.E.159>, monthly; <R.E 160> to <R.E.176>, bi-monthly; <R.E.177> to <R.E.184>, quarterly; <R.E.185> to <R.E.225> monthly as Statistical Supplements to the *Weekly Epidemiological Report.* Continued as *Epidemiological and Vital Statistics Report*, Vol. I, No. 1 (June, 1947) by the Interim Commission of the World Health Organization, respectively by the World Health Organization. Monthly.

ANNUAL EPIDEMIOLOGICAL REPORT: CORRECTED STATISTICS OF NOTIFIABLE DISEASES
First Issue: for the year 1921 <E.I.7>.
Last Issue: for the year 1938 <E.I.23> (1941.III.1.).

BULLETIN OF THE HEALTH ORGANISATION[29]
First Issue: Quarterly Bulletin of the Health Organisation. Vol. I., No. 1 (March, 1932). 157 p.
Last Issue: Bulletin of the Health Organisation: The International Standard of Penicillin. Vol. XII, No. 2 (1945/46), p. 181–298.
The title of the *Bulletin* varied. Beginning with Vol. VI, No. 1 (February, 1937), it was called "Bulletin of the Health Organisation." Prior to that date it was styled "Quarterly Bulletin of the Health Organisation."

Beginning with Vol. XII, No. 3 (1945/46), the *Bulletin* appeared on behalf of the World Health Organization Interim Commission. Since 1947 published as *Bulletin of the World Health Organization.* Vol. I, No. 1 (1947/1948) issued on behalf of the Interim Commis-

---

[29]For periodical publications issued by the Eastern Bureau, see "Bibliography of the Technical Work of the Health Organisation of the League of Nations, 1920–1945," in *Bulletin of the Health Organisation*, Vol. XI (1945), p. 21–22; see also p. 20.

sion of the World Health Organization; Vol. I, No. 2 issued under the imprint of the World Health Organization.

CHRONICLE OF THE HEALTH ORGANISATION
First Issue: Vol. I, No. 1 (January 1, 1939).
Last Regular Issue: Vol. II, No. 4 (April, 1940).
Special numbers appeared in October, 1943, April, 1945, and December, 1945. See also *Chronicle of the World Health Organization.* Vol. I, Nos. 1–2, 1947–. Monthly.

14. BIBLIOGRAPHY

"Bibliography of the Technical Work of the Health Organisation of the League of Nations, 1920–1945," *Bulletin of the Health Organisation*, Vol. XI (1945). 235 p.

A comprehensive, carefully classified and indexed bibliography. It consists of five parts: I. The Health Organisation of the League of Nations, Its Origin and Constitution, the Examination of Its work by the Organs of the League of Nations, Its Chief Periodical Publications, the Operation of Its Epidemiological Service, etc., p. 13–22; II. Field Work Carried out by the Health Organisation in Various Countries, p. 23–25; III. Technical Studies and Publications Issued by the Health Organisation, Grouped by Subjects, p. 26–205; IV. Alphabetical Index of Authors, p. 206–227; V. A Geographical Index, p. 228–235.

III. TRAFFIC IN OPIUM AND OTHER DANGEROUS DRUGS

1. INTRODUCTORY NOTE

UNDER Article 23(c) of the Covenant the League was to be entrusted by its members with "the general supervision over the execution of agreements with regard to . . . the traffic in opium and other dangerous drugs." By virtue of subsequent conventions the scope of the League's competence as to drug control covered legitimate as well as illicit traffic, production, manufacture, and stocks of dangerous drugs.

Three agencies exercised drug control within the framework of the League:

(1) The Advisory Committee on Traffic in Opium and Other Dangerous Drugs. The "Advisory Committee on Traffic in Opium"—as it was originally styled—was set up under Assembly Resolution of December 15, 1920,[1] and Council Resolution of February 21, 1921.[2] During its Fifth Session (May to June, 1923), the Committee adopted its Rules of Procedure.[3] New Rules of Procedure were submitted to the Council for approval in 1936.[4] The Committee was composed of representatives of governments. It became "the principal policy-making organ of the League in the drug field."[5] It prepared international conferences and conventions on narcotics and served as an over-all supervisory organ concerned with the application of the narcotics conventions. Its jurisdiction as supervisory body was, in principle, unlimited, with the exception of those functions that by the international conventions were expressly entrusted[6] to the Permanent Central Opium Board and the Supervisory Body.

(2) The Permanent Central Opium Board. The Board operated by virtue of the pertinent 1925 and 1931 Conventions. The composi-

[1]Text in *Official Journal*, Special Supplement, January, 1921, p.21–22.
[2]Text in Council Minutes, 12th Sess., p.6, 55–56.
[3]Document <O.C.123(1)>.
[4]Document <O.C.1649(a)>, *Official Journal*, November,1936, p.1237; also in *Report to the Council on the Work of the Twenty-first Session* [C.278.M.168.1936.XI.] (1936.XI.-10.).
[5]Bertil A. Renborg, "Principles of International Control of Narcotic Drugs" *American Journal of International Law*, XXXVII (July, 1943), p. 450.
[6]See *ibid.*

tion and the character of the Board were defined in Article 19 of the 1925 Convention.[7] The members of the Permanent Central Opium Board acted in their private capacities and not as government officials, in contrast to the members of the Advisory Committee on Traffic in Opium. The expenses of the Board were included in those of the Secretariat; its staff was administratively part of the Secretariat. The Board was actually an independent body which carried out its duties on its own responsibility.[8] The 1931 Convention,[9] without affecting the structure of the Board, enlarged its powers. Accordingly, the Board was authorized to receive annual estimates of the total national requirements which the countries were not permitted to exceed (Articles 6–9).[10] In case a country exceeded the quota allotted to it, "the Board shall immediately notify the fact to all the High Contracting Parties, who will not, during the currency of the year in question authorize any new exports to that country" (Article 14). This provision was frequently interpreted as implying that mandatory sanctions would be imposed by the Permanent Central Opium Board under the 1931 Convention.[11] However, it is generally agreed that under the 1925 Convention the Board was only authorized to recommend economic measures against states which did not comply with the Convention.

(3) The Supervisory Body. The Supervisory Body, set up under Article 5, Paragraph 6 of the 1931 Convention, was authorized to examine the estimates of the yearly requirements submitted by individual governments and to publish authoritative estimates, for instance, *Estimated World Requirements of Dangerous Drugs in 1945: Statement Issued by the Supervisory Body under Article 5.*[12]

It is noteworthy that the League Health Committee was also entrusted with special functions by the 1925[13] and 1931[14] Conventions.

Since 1930, the Opium Traffic Section of the Secretariat served as the secretariat of the Advisory Committee and the Supervisory Body.

[7]"International Convention, Adopted by the Second Opium Conference (League of Nations), and Protocol Relating Thereto, Signed at Geneva, February 19, 1925," 81 *Treaty Series*, p. 317–358. In force since September 25, 1928.
[8]See especially Art.20 of the 1925 Convention and *Powers and Duties Attributed to the League of Nations by International Treaties*, p.16–170. [C.3.M.3.1944.V.] (1944.V.1.)
[9]"Convention for Limiting the Manufacture and Regulating the Distribution of Narcotic Drugs, and Protocol of Signature Signed at Geneva, July 13, 1931," 139 *Treaty Series*, p. 301–349, bilingual. In force since July 9, 1933.
[10]For statements of the preceding year, see Art.14, Par. 3.
[11]See, *e. g.*, Renborg, in *American Journal of International Law*, XXXVII (July,1943), 455, 456–458.
[12]Document [C.33.M.33.1944.XI.] (1944.XI.3.). See Art. 5, Par. 7 of the 1931 Convention.
[13]See especially Arts.8 and 10.
[14]See especially Art.11.

In 1939 the official name was changed to Drug Control Service.[15] The unique relationship between the Permanent Central Opium Board and the Secretariat has been described above.

To facilitate communication with non-European governments a branch office of the Permanent Central Opium Board and of the Supervisory Body was opened in Washington, D. C., February, 1941.[16] The Supervisory Body performed its functions in 1941 and 1942 primarily in Geneva, and in 1942, 1943 and 1944 in London. On November 19, 1946 the General Assembly approved Resolution 54(1) entitled: "Transfer to the United Nations of Powers exercised by the League of Nations under the International Agreements, Convention and Protocols on Narcotic Drugs." At the same time the General Assembly approved a Protocol, signed on December 11, 1946, which accompanies Resolution 54(1) as well as an Annex to the Protocol. (See United Nations document A/64/Add.1, p. 81–89; also United Nations *Treaty Series*, vol. 12, p. 180–239).

2. COMMITTEES AND BOARDS

ADVISORY COMMITTEE ON TRAFFIC IN OPIUM AND OTHER DANGEROUS DRUGS

Rules of Procedure

Rules of Procedure (as Amended by the Advisory Committee at Its Fifth Session, May-June, 1923). Geneva, 1923. 1 p.+1 p., bilingual. <O.C.123(1)>

Rules of Procedure for Submission to the Council under Article 18 of the General Regulations on Committees (Geneva, June 5, 1936). <O.C.1649(a)>. *Official Journal*, November, 1936, p. 1237.

Minutes of Sessions

First Session:[18] Procès-Verbal of the First Session, Held in Geneva, May 2nd to 5th, 1921. No date. 58 p.+58 p., bilingual. [C.77. M.39.1921.XI.]

[15]See Egon F. Ranshofen-Wertheimer, *The International Secretariat* (Washington,1945), p.123.
[16]For the transfer of functions to Washington, see also Herbert L. May, "Dangerous Drugs," in Harriet E. Davis, ed., *Pioneers in World Order* (New York,1944), p.192. For the transfer of functions to the United Nations see Herbert L. May, "Narcotic Drugs Control," *International Conciliation* (May 1948), No. 441, p. 3451.
[17]For a list of subcommittees of the Advisory Committee, see *The Committees of the League of Nations: Classified List and Essential Facts*, Geneva,1945, p.61. [C.99.M. 99.1945.V.] (1945.V.2.)
[18]Beginning with the Fifth Session the Minutes appeared on behalf of the Advisory Committee on Traffic in Opium and Other Dangerous Drugs.

For Rules of Procedure see p. 57.

Last Session: Minutes of the Twenty-fifth Session, Held at Geneva from May 13th to 17th, 1940. No date. 80 p., mimeographed. [C.162.M.147.1940.XI.] (1941.XI.1.)

Reports to the Council on the Work of the Committee

First Report: Advisory Committee on Traffic in Opium [Report on First Session] May 2nd to 5th, 1921. Geneva, 1921. 16 p.+16 p., bilingual. [A.38.1921.XI.] [C.28.M.157.1921.XI.]

Last Report: Report to the Council on the Work of the Twenty-fifth Session, Held at Geneva from May 13th to 17th, 1940. Geneva, 1940. 29 p. [C.125.M.114.1940.XI.] <O.C.1789(1)> (1940.XI.3.)

Summary of Annual Reports by Governments

First Report: Advisory Committee on Traffic in Opium and Other Dangerous Drugs. Summary of Annual Reports. Part I. Geneva, 1926. 54 p. <O.C.415.> (1926.XI.3.)

Last Report: Annual Reports of Governments for the Year 1943. Summary Prepared by the Secretariat. Geneva, 1947. 31 p. [C.92. M. 92.1946.XI.] <O.C.1814> (1946.XI.5.)

Illicit Transactions and Seizures Reported to the League of Nations

First List: Advisory Committee on Traffic in Opium and Other Dangerous Drugs. List of Seizures Reported to the League of Nations since 1921. Geneva, 1925. 104 p. <O.C.294.>

Last List: Summary of Illicit Transactions and Seizures during 1942. Reported to the Secretariat of the League of Nations. Geneva, February 16th, 1946. 68 p. [C.19.M.19.1946.XI.] <O.C.S.300 (w)>

This series is being continued by the United Nations. The first list issued by the United Nations, Document [C.57.M.57.1946.XI.] <O. C.S.300(x)>, dated July 1, 1946, has this note on page 2: "This document, which was prepared by the Secretariat of the League of Nations before July 31st, had to be printed after that date. The cost of printing it was therefore borne by the United Nations." The document covers the year 1943.

PERMANENT CENTRAL OPIUM BOARD

Reports to the Council on the Work of the Board

First Report: Report to the Council on the Work of the Central Board During Its Sixth and Seventh Sessions and on the Statistics for the Year 1929. Geneva, 1930. 68 p. [C.629.M.250.1930.XI.] <C.C.P.54.> (1930.XI.7.)

Last Report: Report to the Council on the Work of the Board. Geneva 1945. 5 p. [C.84.M.84.1945.XI.] (1945.XI.1.)

SUPERVISORY BODY ESTABLISHED UNDER ARTICLE
5 OF THE CONVENTION OF JULY 13, 1931

Estimated World Requirements of Dangerous Drugs

First Statement: Estimated World Requirements of Dangerous Drugs
in 1934. Statement Issued by the Supervisory Body under Article
5. Geneva, 1933. 76 p. [C.610.M.286.1933.XI.] <O.S.B./State-
ment 1934/1>

Annex II contains a sample of Statistical Form B(L).

Last Statement: Estimated World Requirements of Dangerous Drugs
in 1946. Statement Issued by the Supervisory Body under Article
5. Geneva, 1945. 38 p. [C.119.M.119.1945.XI.] <O.S.B./State-
ment 1946> (1945.XI.3.)

The following supplements were issued to the Last Statement.

First Supplement: Geneva, May 8, 1946. 7 p. [C.119(a).M.119(a).1945.
XI.] <O.S.B.1946/1stSupplement> (1946.XI.1.)

Second Supplement: Geneva, June 29, 1946. 6 p. [C.119(b).M.119(b).
1945.XI.] <O.S.B.1946/2nd Supplement> (1946.XI.2.)

This was the last issued on behalf of the League.

Third Supplement: Geneva, October 31, 1946. 8 p. E/DSB/1.

This is the first in the series now published by the United Nations.

3. CONFERENCES

FIRST OPIUM CONFERENCE, 1924–1925

First Opium Conference. Geneva, November 3rd, 1924–February
11th, 1925. Minutes and Annexes. No date. 176 p. [C.684.M.244.
1924.XI.]

Annex 13b, p.160-167, contains the Agreement, Protocol, and Final Act of the Conference [C.82.M.41.1925.XI.] <C.O.P.(1)>. Annex 13b was also published under the
classmark [C.82.M.41.1925.XI.] <C.O.P.(1)> as a separate document.

Index to the Records of the First Opium Conference. November
3rd, 1924–February 11th, 1925. Geneva, 1926. 16 p. [C.29.M.15.
1926.XI.] (1926.XI.1.)

SECOND OPIUM CONFERENCE, 1924–1925

Second Opium Conference. Geneva, November 17th, 1924–February
19th, 1925. Records of the Conference. Volume I: Plenary Meetings. Text of the Debates. Geneva, 1925. 539 p. [C.760.M.260.

1924.XI.] Volume II: Meetings of the Committees and Sub-committees. Geneva, 1925. 332 p. [C.760.M.260.1924.XI.Vol.II.]

Annex 31 of Volume I, p.501–539, contains the Convention-Protocol-Final Act. Geneva, February 19th,1925. In part bilingual. This is also a separate document [C.88.M.44.1925.XI.].

Index to the Records of the Second Opium Conference. November 17th, 1924–February 19th, 1925. Geneva, 1926. 42 p. [C.603.M. 237.1926.XI.] (1926.XI.9.)

CONFERENCE ON THE LIMITATION OF THE MANUFACTURE OF NARCOTIC DRUGS, 1931

Records of the Conference for the Limitation of the Manufacture of Narcotic Drugs. Geneva, May 27th–July 13th, 1931. Volume I: Plenary Meetings. Text of the Debates. Geneva, 1931. 421 p. [C.509.M.214.1931.XI.] (1931.XI.10^I). Volume II: Meetings of the Committees and the Sub-Committee on Control. Geneva, 1923. 135 p. [C.509.M.214.1931.XI. Volume II.] (1931.XI.10^{II})

Annex 35 of Volume I, p.367–421, contains the Convention for Limiting the Manufacture and Regulating the Distribution of Narcotic Drugs, Protocol of Signature, and Final Act, under the classmark [C.455.M.193.1931.XI.] < Conf.L.F.S.73(h)— (j).>

CONFERENCE ON THE SUPPRESSION OF OPIUM-SMOKING, 1931

Conference on the Suppression of Opium-Smoking Convened under Article XII of the Geneva Opium Agreement, 1925. Bangkok, November 9th–27th, 1931. Minutes of the Meetings and Documents Submitted to the Conference. Geneva, 1932. 127 p. [C.577.M. 284.1932.XI.] (1932.XI.5.)

Agreement and Final Act. Signed at Bangkok, November 27th, 1931. No date. 12 p., bilingual; in part double-paged. [C.70.M.36.1932. XI.] (1932.XI.1.)

CONFERENCE FOR THE SUPPRESSION OF THE ILLICIT TRAFFIC IN DANGEROUS DRUGS, 1936

Records of the Conference for the Suppression of the Illicit Traffic in Dangerous Drugs. Geneva, June 8th–26th, 1936. Geneva, 1936. 241 p. [C.341.M.216.1936.XI.] (1936.XI.20.)

Annexes include on p.216–241, the Text of the Convention of 1936 for the Suppression of the Illicit Traffic in Dangerous Drugs, Signed on June 26th,1936 [C.286.M. 174.1936.XI.]; the Protocol of Signature [C.286.(a)M.174(a).1936.XI.]; and the Final Act [C.286(b)M.174(b).1936.XI.]. The last two were published as separate documents.

4. CONVENTIONS AND AGREEMENTS

GENERAL DRUGS CONVENTIONS

International Opium Convention, Signed at The Hague, January 23rd, 1912. Protocols of Clôture, Signed at The Hague on January 23rd, 1912, July 9th, 1913, and June 25th, 1914. 29 p.+29 p., bilingual. <O. C.I.(I)>[19]

International Opium Convention, Adopted by the Second Opium Conference (League of Nations), Signed at Geneva on February 19th, 1925. 81 *Treaty Series*, p. 317–358, bilingual.[20]

By virtue of this Convention (Articles 19–27), the Permanent Central Opium Board was instituted.

Convention for Limiting the Manufacture and Regulating the Distribution of Narcotic Drugs, Protocol of Signature and Final Act.[21] Geneva, 1931. 36 p. [C.455.M.193.1931.XI.] (1931.XI.8.)

SUPPRESSION OF ILLICIT TRAFFIC

Convention of 1936 for the Suppression of the Illicit Traffic in Dangerous Drugs, Signed at Geneva, June 26th, 1936.[22] No date. 15 p., bilingual; in part double-paged. [C.286.M.174.1936.XI.] (1936.XI. 11.)

AGREEMENTS CONCERNING THE SUPPRESSION OF OPIUM SMOKING

Geneva Agreement of 1925

Agreement Concerning the Suppression of the Manufacture of, In-

[19]Also in 8 *Treaty Series*, p.187-239, bilingual. For dates of entry into force, see "Signatures, Ratifications and Accessions in Respect of Agreements and Conventions Concluded under the Auspices of the League of Nations, *Twenty-first List, 1944*, p.119. [C.25.M.25.1943.V.Annex] (1944.V.2.). For the powers and functions of the League of Nations in relation to this Convention, see *List of Conventions* . . ., Geneva,1945, p.67-68. [C.100.M.100.1945.V.] (1945.V.1.)

[20]The original document containing Convention-Protocol-Final Act is marked [C.88.M.44.1925.XI.]; also [C.88(1).M.44(1).1925.XI.] as a separate document. The Convention and the Protocol went into force on September 25,1928.

[21] Also in 139 *Treaty Series*, p.301-349, bilingual; in force since July 9, 1933. See also *Convention for Limiting the Manufacture and Regulating the Distribution of Narcotic Drugs of July 13,1931: Historical and Technical Study by the Opium Traffic Section of the Secretariat of the League of Nations.* Geneva,1937. 299 p. [C.191.M.136.1937.XI.] (1937.XI.3.). In addition, see *Model Administration Codes to the International Opium Conventions of 1925 and 1931.* Geneva,1932. 23 p. [C.774.M.365.1932.XI.] <O.C./M.C.11/2> (1932.XI.8.). These Model Codes were designed to supplement the International Opium Conventions.

[22]Also in 198 *Treaty Series*, p.299-319, bilingual; in force since October 26,1939. See also *Protocol of Signature*. No date. 6 p. [C.286(a).M.174(a).1936.XI.] (1936.XI.12). The Protocol is also in 198 *Treaty Series*, p.320-323, bilingual.

ternational Trade in and Use of, Prepared Opium, Adopted by the First Opium Conference of the League of Nations, with Protocol, Signed at Geneva, February 11th, 1925.[23] No date. 20 p., bilingual. [C.82.M.41.1925.XI.] <C.O.P.57(1)>

Bangkok Agreement of 1931

Agreement Concerning the Suppression of Opium-Smoking, Signed at Bangkok, November 27th, 1931.[24] No date. 12 p., bilingual; in part double-paged. [C.70.M.36.1932.XI.] (1932.XI.1.)

5. SPECIAL ENQUIRIES

ENQUIRY INTO THE PRODUCTION OF OPIUM IN PERSIA

Commission of Enquiry into the Production of Opium in Persia.[25] Report to the Council. Geneva, 1926. 57 p. [A.7.1927.XI.] (1926. XI.10.)

This report should be read in connection with Document [A.8.1927.XI], containing the observations of the Persian government and the relevant extract from the Council Minutes, Forty-fourth Session.

ENQUIRY INTO THE CONTROL OF OPIUM

Control of Opium

Smoking in the Far East: Proposal by the Government of Great Britain for a Commission of Enquiry. Geneva, 1928. 8 p. [A.40. 1928.XI.] [C.386.1928.XI.] (1928.XI.4.)

Commission of Enquiry into the Control of Opium-Smoking in the Far East. Report to The Council. Volume I: Report with Comparative Tables, Maps and Illustrations. Geneva, 1930. 158 p. [C.635.M.254.1930.XI.] (1930.XI.10.). Volume II: Detailed Memoranda on Each Territory Visited by the Commission. Geneva, 1931. 495 p. [C.635.M.254.1930.XI.Vol.II.] (1930.XI.10^{II}). Volume III: Collection of Laws and Regulations Governing the Control of Opium-Smoking in the Territories Visited by the Commission. Geneva, 1932. 304 p. [C.635.M.254.1930.XI.Vol.III.] (1930.XI. 10^{III})

[23] Also in 51 *Treaty Series*, p.337–347, bilingual. The Agreement and the Protocol came into force on July 28,1926.
[24] Also in 177 *Treaty Series*, p. 373–380, bilingual; in force since April 22, 1937.
[25] See also Documents [A.8.1927.XI.] and [A.16.1927.XI.].

6. MISCELLANEOUS DOCUMENTS

Conference on the Limitation of the Manufacture of Narcotic Drugs Covered by Article 4 (b) (c) and (g) of the Geneva Opium Convention. Analysis of the International Trade in Morphine, Diacetylmorphine and Cocaine for the Years 1925–1929. Part I: Geneva, 1931. 215 p. [C.587.M.228.1930.XI.] <Conf.L.F.S.3(1).> (1931.XI.5^{I}). Part II: General Analysis: Morphine and Diacetylmorphine. Geneva, 1931. 68 p. [C.587.M.228.1930.XI.] <Conf.L.F.S.3(1) (Part II)> (1931.XI.5^{II}). Part III: General Analysis: Cocaine. Geneva, 1931. 35 p. [C.587.M.228.1930.XI.Part III] <Conf.L.F.S.3(1) (Part III)> (1931.XI.5^{III})

Scheme for Limiting the Output of Manufactured Drugs, Submitted by Mr. C. K. Krane. Geneva, 1931. 13 p. [C.251.M.114.1931.XI.] <Conf.L.F.S.7.> (1931.XI.6.)

A B C of Narcotic Drugs, by Dr. O. Anselmino. Geneva, 1931. 48 p. <C.C.P.44(1)> (1931.XI.1.)

Studies and Documents Regarding the Working of the System of Import Certificates and Export Authorisations. Geneva, 1935. 14 p. [C.434.M.225.1935.XI.] <O.C.1535(g).> (1935.XI.11)[26]

Extradition under Existing Treaties for Offences against Drug Laws: Replies by Governments to the Circular Letter of February 8th, 1936 [C.L.22.1936.XI.]. Geneva, 1936. 16 p. <Conf.S.T.D.4.> (1936.XI.7.)

Studies and Documents Regarding the Working of the System of Import Certificates and Export Authorisations. Geneva, 1939. 38 p. [C.268.M.185.1939.XI.] <O.C.1535(n)> (1939.XI.7.)

Revised List of Drugs, Preparations and Proprietary Medicine Coming under the International Drug Conventions. Geneva, 1940. 149 p. [C.348.M.263.1939.XI.] <O.C.1778> (1940.XI.1.)

Pre-war Production and Distribution of Narcotic Drugs and Their Raw Materials. Geneva, 1944. 32 p. [C.24.M.240.1944.XI.] (1944. XI.1.).

List of Firms Authorized to Manufacture Drugs Covered by the Convention. Geneva, 1940. 32 p. [C.L.84.1940.XI.] <C.C.1793>

[26]See also Document (1935.XI.11.Addendum).

IV. SOCIAL AND HUMANITARIAN PROBLEMS

1. PROTECTION OF MINORITIES

INTRODUCTORY NOTE

AFTER 1919 numerous agreements were concluded under the auspices of the League of Nations with a view to protecting linguistic, racial, and religious minorities. These agreements declared the rights of linguistic, racial, and religious minorities matters of international concern to be placed under the guarantee of the League of Nations.[1]

The following organs of the League were entrusted with the supervision or interpretation of the minorities treaties:

Council: Under the minorities agreements[2] the Council was the main guarantor of the fair application of the minorities treaties. Since these treaties did not contain specific procedural rules, the Council, by resolution,[3] evolved the controlling legal principles.

Secretariat. According to the rules of procedure on the receivability of petitions, the Secretary-General[4] or the Minorities Section of the Secretariat[5] was authorized to pass upon the receivability of petitions,[6] subject to revision by the Council and the Minorities Com-

---

[1] Art.12 of the Treaty between the Principal Allied and Associated Powers (the United States of America, the British Empire, France, Italy, Japan) and Poland, June 28,1919.
[2] See below, p. 188–189.
[3] See below, p. 189–190.
[4] For the functions of the Secretary-General, see, *e.g.*, Council Resolution of June 13, 1929, in Document [C.8.M.1931.I.], p. 11.
[5] For the Minorities Section of the Secretariat, see P. De Azcárate, *League of Nations and National Minorities: An Experiment* (Washington,1945), p.123–130, 184, and Egon F. Ranshofen-Wertheimer, *The International Secretariat* (Washington,1945), p.109.
[6] On the receivability of petitions, see Council Resolution of September 5,1923, Document [C.8.M.5.1931.I], p.9. For the publication of petitions, see Council Resolution of June 13,1929, in Document [C.8.M.5.1931.I.], p.11., which reads in part as follows: "The Secretary-General will publish annually in the *Official Journal* of the League statistics of: (1) The number of petitions received by the Secretariat during the year; (2) The number of petitions declared to be non-receivable; (3) the number of petitions declared to be receivable and referred to Committees of Three; (4) The number of Committees and the number of meetings held by them to consider these petitions; (5) The number of petitions whose examination by a Committee of Three has been finished in the course of the year." See, *e. g.*, *Official Journal*, July-August,1939, p.370.

mittees[7] Until 1935 the Administrative Commissions and Minorities Questions Section was in charge of (1) questions concerning Danzig, the Saar, the exchange of Greek and Turkish populations, and Upper Silesia; and (2) minorities questions. This organizational setup explains the classification of the corresponding League documents as IA (Administrative Commissions) and IB (Minorities).[8]

Assembly. Although the Council was the organ of the League primarily designed to implement the League guarantee regarding minorities matters,[9] it was recognized time and again that the Assembly, especially the Sixth Committee, was also authorized to discuss questions of principle related to the protection of minorities.[10] Especially from 1922 to 1934 did the Assembly repeatedly take cognizance of minorities issues.[11]

Permanent Court of International Justice. Under the guarantee clause of Article 12 of the model treaty with Poland (June 28, 1919), the Permanent Court of International Justice was authorized to render final decisions on any question of law or fact pertaining to minorities. The Principal Allied and Associated Powers (the United States of America, the British Empire, France, Italy, and Japan) or any other member of the Council of the League of Nations was empowered to bring a dispute before the Court without special agreement. Accordingly, by Article 12 and related provisions of the minorities treaties, compulsory or obligatory jurisdiction was conferred upon the Permanent Court of International Justice in minorities matters.[12] At the request of the Council the Permanent Court of International Justice rendered several advisory opinions on minorities questions.[13]

SUBSTANTIVE PROVISIONS

Protection of Linguistic, Racial and Religious Minorities by the League of Nations: Provisions Contained in the Various International Instruments at Present in Force. Geneva, August, 1927. 111 p.+111 p., bilingual. [C.L.110.1927.I.Annexe] (1927.I.B.2.)

[7]For Minorities Committees, see Azcárate, *League of Nations and National Minorities,* p.112.
[8]In his statement on the Budget of the League the Secretary-General declared in 1939 with reference to the Political, Minorities, Disarmament, and Mandates Sections: "Of those four Sections only the Mandates Section had maintained all its former activities, which indeed had rather been increased." *Official Journal,* February, 1939, p. 94. See also Ranshofen-Wertheimer, *The International Secretariat,* p. 109.
[9]See Art.12 of the Treaty with Poland, June 28,1919.
[10]See Margaret E. Burton, *The Assembly of the League of Nations* (Chicago,1941), p.220.
[11]See Jacob Robinson and others, *Were the Minorities Treaties a Failure?* (New York, 1943), Chart 6 and p.130,133.
[12]See Manley O. Hudson, *The Permanent Court of International Justice, 1920-1942* (New York,1943), p.440-441.
[13]See below, p. 190, 396, 397.

Includes the primarily substantive provisions of international minorities protection under the auspices of the League of Nations. These international agreements, usually called minorities treaties, may be classified as follows:

(a) Agreements between the Principal Allied and Associated Powers (the United States of America, the British Empire, France, Italy, and Japan) on the one hand and individual countries on the other

    1.Poland, June 28,1919, p.41
    2.Czechoslovakia, September 10,1919, p.90
    3.Kingdom of the Serbs, Croats, and Slovenes, September 10,1919, p.59
    4.Roumania, December 9,1919, p.50
    5.Greece, August 10,1920, p.20

(b) Clauses in the peace treaties with Austria,Bulgaria, Hungary, Turkey

    1.Treaty of St. Germain, September 10,1919 (Articles62–69), p.7
    2.Treaty of Neuilly, November 27,1919 (Articles49–57), p.10
    3.Treaty of Trianon, June 4,1920 (Articles54–60), p.28
    4.Treaty of Lausanne, July 24,1923 (Articles37–45), p.96

(c) General declarations by individual states addressed to the Council of the League of Nations

    1.Albania, October 2,1921, p.3
    2.Lithuania, May 12,1922, p.33
    3.Latvia, July 7,1923, p.31
    4.Estonia, September 17,1923, p.13
    5.Memel, May 8,1924, p.37

(d) Special declaration by Finland addressed to the Council of the League of Nations
    The Aaland Islands: Guarantees to Be Given to the Population, Adopted by the Council of the League of Nations, June 27th,1919, p.16.

(e) Agreements concerning Upper Silesia and Danzig

    1.German-Polish Convention Relating to Upper Silesia, Geneva, May 15,1922, p.64
    2.Polish-Danzig Treaty, November 9,1920, p.100

(f) Reciprocal emigration and exchange of populations

    1.Greco-Bulgarian Convention Concerning Reciprocal Emmigration of November 27th,1919, p.102
    2.Greco-Turkish Convention on Exchange of Populations of January 30th,1923, p.106

PROCEDURAL PROVISIONS

Protection of Linguistic, Racial or Religious Minorities by the League of Nations. Resolutions and Extracts from the Minutes of the Council, Resolutions and Reports Adopted by the Assembly, Relating to the Procedure to Be Followed in Questions Concerning the Protection of Minorities. Geneva, February, 1929. 80 p. [C. 24.M.18.1929.I.] (1929.I.B.I.). 2d ed., Geneva, March, 1931. 247 p. [C.8.M.5.1831.I.] (1931.I.B.I.)

Contains: 1.Report Presented by Mr. Tittoni and Adopted by the Council of the League of Nations on October 22nd,1920, p.7
    States the right and duty of the Council to take action on minorities issues. Outlines the rights of others to submit petitions or reports which in themselves have not the legal effect of putting the matter before the Council.
2.Resolution Adopted by the Council on October 25th,1920, p.8
    Provides for the Minorities Committee of Three within the Council.
3.Resolution Adopted by the Council on June 27th,1921, p.8
    Regulates the petition procedure.

4.Resolution Adopted by the Council on September 5th,1923, p.9
  Establishes rules concerning the receivability of petitions.
5.Resolution Adopted by the Council on June 10th,1925, p.10
  Provisions concerning the composition of the Committee of Three.
6.Resolution Adopted by the Council on June 13th,1929, p.11
  Provides for a Committee of Five in exceptional cases and encourages publicity
  for the actions of the Minorities Committees.
Extracts from the Minutes of the Council, p.13–237, and Resolutions and Reports
Adopted by the Assembly, p.239–246, contain additional rules.[14]

General: Information Section. Protection of Minorities. Geneva, 1931.
27 p.

ADVISORY OPINIONS OF THE PERMANENT COURT
OF INTERNATIONAL JUSTICE CONCERNING
MINORITIES

German Settlers in Poland. Advisory Opinion No. 6, September 10,
1923. Series B, No. 6. 43 p.
Aquisition of Polish Nationality. Advisory Opinion No. 7, September
15, 1923. Series B, No. 7. 26 p.
Exchange of Greek and Turkish Populations. Advisory Opinion No.
10, February 21, 1925. Series B, No. 10. 28 p.
Interpretation of the Greco-Turkish Agreement of December 1st,
1926 (Final Protocol, Article IV). Advisory Opinion No. 16, Au-
gust 28, 1928. Series B, No. 16. 29 p.
The Greco-Bulgarian "Communities." Advisory Opinion No. 17,
July 31, 1930. Series B, No. 17. 46 p.
Access to German Minority Schools in Upper Silesia. Advisory
Opinion [No. 19], May 15, 1931. Series A/B, Fascicule No. 40. 32 p.
Minority Schools in Albania. Advisory Opinion [No. 26], April 6,
1935. Series A/B, Fascicule No. 64. 36 p.

2. REFUGEES

INTRODUCTORY NOTE

From 1921 to 1924 Dr. Fridtjof Nansen acted as High Commissioner for Refugees.[15] By the end of 1924 the Assembly approved in

[14]For the text of additional resolutions, see Otto Junghann, *Das Minderheitenschutz-
verfahren vor dem Völkerbund* (Tübingen,1934), *passim.*
[15]Originally Dr. Nansen was appointed to act "as High Commissioner on behalf of the
League in connection with the Problems concerning Russian Refugees in Europe." See
Dr. Nansen's letter of September 1,1921, in Document [C.337.M.239.1921.], mimeographed. See also Council Minutes,14th Sess., p.79. See, moreover, Council Resolution of April 10,1920, in Council Minutes, 4th Sess., p.13; see also *ibid.*, p.7,40–49,
especially p.43.

principle the Council's recommendation to transfer to the International Labor Organization the League's work on behalf of Russian and Armenian refugees.[16] The transfer of the High Commissariat to the International Labor Organization that took effect on January 1, 1925,[17] did not bring about a complete shifting of the related activities to the Organization. While the International Labor Organization concentrated on exploring employment and resettlement possibilities, the High Commissioner remained directly responsible to the Council[18] and was primarily concerned with the question of the legal status of refugees.

In 1928 the Governing Body of the International Labour Organisation resolved that the "1929 budget should be regarded as the last refugees budget to be administered by the International Labour Office."[19] On January 1, 1930, the Secretary-General assumed temporarily the responsibility for the refugee organization of the League.[20] Under Assembly Resolution of September 30, 1930, the autonomous Nansen International Refugee Office was established.[21] The Office began its work on April 1, 1931;[22] however, a time limit was provided.[23] The Nansen International Refugee Office was liquidated[24] at the end of 1938.[25]

[16]See Assembly Resolution of September 25,1924, *Official Journal*, Special Supplement No.21, October,1924, p.40–41; Council Resolution of September 30,1924, *Official Journal*, October,1924, p.1366; and the decision of the Governing Body of the International Labor Organization of October 10,1924, in Document [C.680.1924.XIII.], mimeographed; see also International Labor Conference, *Seventh Session* (Geneva,-1925), p.930–935.

[17]See Sir John Hope Simpson, *The Refugee Problem; Report of a Survey* (London,1939), p.205; see also p.203–204.

[18]*Ibid.*, p.198, 204.

[19]See *Russian, Armenian, Assyrian, Assyro-Chaldean, and Turkish Refugees. Report to the Ninth Ordinary Session of the Assembly*, p.19. [A.33.1928.VIII]

[20]See *Report by Secretary-General on the Future Organization of Refugee Work*, p.2. [A.28.1930.XIII.] At that time the administrative machinery of the League concerned with refugee questions was composed as follows: (1) the League of Nations High Commissioner for Refugees; (2) the Inter-Governmental Advisory Commission for Refugees; (3) the Central Service for Refugee Organizations; (4) the High Commissioner's Delegates; (5) the Advisory Committee of Private Organizations for Refugees. See *ibid.*, p.2–3.

[21]See *Official Journal*, Special Supplement No.83, October,1930, p.48.

[22]See Simpson, *The Refugee Problem*, p.210.

[23]See Nansen International Office for Refugees (under the Authority of the League of Nations), *Report by the Governing Body to the Twelfth Assembly of the League of Nations*, p.6–8. [A.27.1931.]

[24]See *Report on the Liquidation of the Office* [A.11.1937.XII.], and "Report to the Council Committee Appointed to Draw up a Plan for International Assistance to Refugees" [C.189.1938.XII.], *Official Journal*, May-June,1938, p.365–367.

[25]See Assembly Resolution of September 30,1938, *Official Journal*, Special Supplement No. 182, October,1938, p.26–28, and *Report by M. Michael Hansson, Former President of the Governing Body of the Nansen International Office for Refugees, on the Activities of the Office from July 1st to December 31st,1938*. [A.19.1939.XII.] (1939.XII.B.2.)

Basic Texts of the Nansen International Refugee Office

Statutes of the Nansen International Office for Refugees as Approved by the Council on January 19th, 1931. *Official Journal*, February, 1931, p. 309–311.
Rules of Procedure of the Nansen International Office for Refugees (under the Authority of the League of Nations), Adopted by the Governing Body on March 11th, 1931. *Official Journal*, April, 1931, p. 746–748.

High Commissioners for Refugees since 1933

In 1933 the office of High Commissioner for Refugees Coming from Germany (Jewish and Other) was created.[26] On October 26, 1933, the Council appointed Mr. James G. McDonald as High Commissioner.[27] Despite the fact that the High Commissioner was nominated by the Council, he was not to be considered a functionary of the League.[28] His reports were to be directed to the Governing Body of the "Commission" and not to the Council. By letter of December 27, 1935, Mr. McDonald tendered his resignation as of December 27, 1935.[29]

By Council Resolution of January 24, 1936, Major General Sir Neill Malcolm was appointed High Commissioner for Assistance to Refugees (Jewish and Other) from Germany.[30] Closer co-operation between the League and the new High Commissioner was envisaged, since, the foregoing Council Resolution states: "The High Commissioner will be provided with the assistance of the technical services of the League of Nations in such ways as will be agreed upon between him and the Secretary-General."[31] In September, 1938, Sir Herbert Emerson was appointed High Commissioner of the League of Nations for Refugees as from January 1, 1939.[32]

Reports by High Commissioners

Nansen Reports[33]

Russian Refugees.[34] General Report on the Work Accomplished up

[26]See Assembly Resolution of October 11,1933, *Official Journal*, Special Supplement No.114, p.13.
[27]See James G. McDonald, "Refugees," in Harriet E. Davis, ed., *Pioneers in World Order* (New York,1944), p.218.
[28]See *ibid.*, p.218–219.
[29]See below, p.197.
[30] See *Official Journal*, February,1936, p.127, and March,1936, p.296.
[31]*Ibid.*, February,1936, p.127.
[32]See Assembly Resolution of September 30,1938, *Official Journal*, Special Supplement No.182, October,1938, p.26–28.

to March 15th, 1922, by Dr. Fridtjof Nansen, High Commissioner
of the League of Nations. Geneva, 1922. 14 p.+14 p., bilingual.
[C.124.M.74.1922.]

Russian Refugees. Report Submitted to the Council by Dr. Nansen
on May 13th, 1922. *Official Journal*, June, 1922, p. 612-616. [C.
280.M.152.1922.]

Russian Refugees. Report by Dr. Nansen, High Commissioner of the
League of Nations, Submitted to the Council on July 20th, 1922.
Official Journal, August, 1922, p. 923-928. [C.472.M.297.1922.]

A sample form of the Certificate of Identity commonly known as Nansen Pass is
on p. 927.

Report on the Work of the High Commission for Refugees Presented
by Dr. Fridtjof Nansen to the Fourth Assembly. Geneva, 1923.
33 p. [A.30.1923.XII.]

Russian Refugees. Report by Dr. Nansen. No date. 5 p. Extract
No. 19 from the *Official Journal*. [C.473.1923.]

Reports by the High Commissioner for Refugees. Geneva, 1924.
19 p. Extract No. 25 from the *Official Journal*.

Conference on Russian and Armenian Refugee Questions. Report by
the High Commissioner. Geneva, 1926. 4 p. [C.327.1926.] (1926.
XIII.1.)

Armenian Refugee Settlement Commission. Report to the Council.
Geneva, 1926. 8 p. [C.328.1926.II.] (1926.II.19.)

Armenian and Russian Refugees. Refugee Questions. Report to the
Seventh Session of the Assembly by the High Commissioner of the
League of Nations.[35] Geneva, 1926. 35 p. [A.44.1926.] (1926.XIII.
2.)[36]

Armenian and Russian Refugees. Geneva, 1927. 16 p. [A.30.1927.]
(1927.XIII.1.)

Russian and Armenian Refugees. Report to the Eighth Ordinary
Session of the Assembly. Geneva, 1927. 33 p. [A.48.1927.XIII.]
(1927.XIII.3.)

Russian, Armenian, Assyrian, Assyro-Chaldean, and Turkish Refu-

[33]This listing of Nansen Reports is by no means complete; only a limited number appeared as separate documents, either mimeographed or in print. For additional Reports, consult *Official Journal*, 1922-1930 and Council Minutes, 1920-1922.

[34]See also *Russian Refugees. Summary of Documents Received by the Secretariat on This Subject since the 12th Session of the Council* [C.126.M.72.1921.VII.] and *Russian Refugees. Information Provided by Members of the Conference of Enquiry Held at Geneva from August 22nd-24th, 1921 and Memoranda Submitted to That Conference* [C.323.M.233.1921.VII.] <C.R.R.14.>.

[35]See also *Report by Dr. Fridtjof Nansen, President of the Commission Appointed to Study the Question of the Settlement of Armenian Refugees.* 24p.+24p., bilingual; issued on behalf of the International Labor Office, 1925.

[36]See also Document [A.44.1926.Erratum.].

gees. Report to the Ninth Ordinary Session of the Assembly.
Geneva, 1928. 25 p. [A.33.1928.VIII.] (1928.VIII.6.)

Inter-Governmental Conference on the Legal Status of Refugees.
Report by Dr. Fridtjof Nansen. . .[37] Geneva, 1928. 17 p., mimeographed. [C.392.M.183.1928.VIII.]

Russian, Armenian, Assyrian, Assyro-Chaldean, and Turkish Refugees. Memorandum by Dr. Fridtjof Nansen, High Commissioner
for Refugees, Submitted to the Council on December 14th, 1928.
Official Journal, January, 1929, p. 174–176. [C.575.1928.VIII.]

Emerson Reports

International Assistance to Refugees.[38] Report Submitted to the
Twentieth Ordinary Session of the Assembly of the League of Nations by Sir Herbert Emerson, G.C.I.E., K.C.S.I., C.B.E., High
Commissioner for Refugees. Geneva, 1939. 10 p. [A.18.1939.XII.]
(1939.XII.B.1.)

International Assistance to Refugees. Supplementary Report Sub-
mitted to the Twentieth Ordinary Session of the Assembly of the
League of Nations by Sir Herbert Emerson, G.C.I.E., K.C.S.I.,
C.B.E., High Commissioner for Refugees. Geneva, 1939. 5 p.
[A.18(a).1939.XII.] (1939.XII.B.4.)

Intermediate Report of the High Commissioner for Refugees. Geneva, 1940. 11 p., mimeographed: 1–5, English; 6–11, French. [C.
63.M.56.1940.XII.]

International Assistance to Refugees. Reports Submitted by Sir
Herbert Emerson, G.C.I.E., K.C.S.I., C.B.E., High Commissioner
for Refugees. Geneva, 1941. 11 p. [C.7.M.7.1941.XII.] (1941.XII.
B.1.)

International Assistance to Refugees. Report Submitted by Sir Her-
bert Emerson, G.C.I.E., K.C.S.I., C.B.E., High Commissioner for
Refugees. Geneva, 1942. 22 p. [C.25.M.25.1942.XII.] (1942.XII.
B.1.)

International Assistance to Refugees. Report Submitted by Sir Her-
bert Emerson, G.C.I.E., K.C.S.I., C.B.E., High Commissioner for
Refugees. Geneva, 1943. 11 p. [C.19.M.19.1943.XII.] (1943.XII.
B.1.)

International Assistance to Refugees. Report Submitted by Sir Her-
bert Emerson, G.C.I.E., K.C.S.I., C.B.E., High Commissioner for
Refugees. Geneva, 1944. 11 p. [C.23.M.23.1944.XII.] (1944.XII.
B.1.)

International Assistance to Refugees. Report Submitted by Sir Her-

---

[37]Dated August 15th,1928. This document appeared under a different heading, but
under the same official number in *Official Journal*, March,1929, p.483–488.
[38]See also Documents [A.18.1939.XII.Corrigendum] and [A.18.1939.XII.Corrigendum
II.].

bert Emerson, G.C.I.E., K.C.S.I., C.B.E., High Commissioner for Refugees. Geneva, 1945. 8 p. [C.79.M.79.1945.XII.] (1945.XII. B.1.)

International Assistance to Refugees. Report Submitted by Sir Herbert Emerson, G.C.I.E., K.C.S.I., C.B.E., High Commissioner for Refugees. Geneva, 1946. 10 p. [A.10.1946.XII.] (1946.XII.B.1.)

International Assistance to Refugees. Report Submitted by Sir Herbert Emerson, G.C.I.E., K.C.S.I., C.B.E., High Commissioner for Refugees. Geneva, 1946. 10 p. [A.10.1946.XII.] (1946.XII. B.1.)

CONFERENCES

Passports for Russian Refugees, 1922

Governmental Conference on Passports for Russian Refugees. Held at Geneva, July 3rd to 5th, 1922. 13 p.+9 p.+6 p.+6 p., mimeographed. [C.490.M.307.1922.]

This document contains the Minutes of the four meetings of the Conference.

Intergovernmental Conference on the Juridical Status of Refugees, 1928

Documents Préparatoires et Procès-Verbaux de la Conférence Intergouvernmentale pour le Statut Juridique de Réfugiés. 28–30 juin 1928. No date. 211 p. (1930.XIII.1.) French text only.

Intergovernmental Conferences on Refugees from Germany, 1936 and 1938.

Inter-Governmental Conference for the Adoption of a Statute for Refugees Coming from Germany. Geneva, July 2nd–4th, 1936. Final Act. Geneva, 1936. 5 p., bilingual; in part double-paged. [C.362(a).M.237.(a).1936.XII.] (1936.XII.B.5.)

International Conference for the Adoption of a Convention Concerning the Status of Refugees Coming from Germany. Geneva, February 7th–10th, 1938. Final Act. No date. 6 p., bilingual; in part double-paged. [C.75(a) M.30(a) 1938.XII.]

CONVENTIONS AND AGREEMENTS

Arrangement with Respect to the Issue of Certificates of Identity to Russian Refugees, Signed at Geneva, July 5, 1922. 13 Treaty Series, p. 237–242, bilingual.[39]

[39]The date of coming into force seems uncertain. See Manley O. Hudson, International Legislation (7 vols., Washington, 1931–1941), II, 873, footnote 1. See also Art. 9 of the Arrangement. See also 15 Treaty Series, p.322–323; 19 Treaty Series, p.284–285; 24 Treaty Series, p.178–179; 27 Treaty Series, p.420–421.

A sample form of the Identity Certificate, commonly known as Nansen Passport,[40] is on p.241.

Plan for the Issue of a Certificate of Identity to Armenian Refugees. Submitted for the Consideration of Interested Governments by Dr. Nansen, High Commissioner for Russian Refugees, in Execution of the Resolution of the Council of the League Adopted on September 28th, 1923.[41] No date. 4 p., mimeographed. [C.L.72(a) 1924.]

Arrangement Relating to the Issue of Identity Certificates to Russian and Armenian Refugees, Supplementing and Amending the Previous Arrangements Dated July 5, 1922, and May 31, 1924. Signed at Geneva, May 12, 1926. 89 *Treaty Series*, p. 47–52, bilingual.

Arrangement Relating to the Legal Status of Russian and Armenian Refugees. Signed at Geneva, June 30, 1928. 89 *Treaty Series*, p. 53–61., bilingual.

Arrangement Concerning the Extension to Other Categories of Refugees of Certain Measures Taken in Favour of Russian and Armenian Refugees. Signed at Geneva, June 30, 1928. 89 *Treaty Series*, p. 63–67, bilingual.

Agreement Concerning the Preparation of a Transit Card for Emigrants. Signed at Geneva, June 14, 1929. 94 *Treaty Series*, p. 277–285, bilingual.

Sample form of Carte de Transit on p.285.[42]

Convention Relating to the International Status of Refugees. Geneva, October 28th, 1933. Geneva, 1934. 8 p. [C.650(1).M.311(1) 1933.XIII.][43]

Provisional Arrangement Concerning the Status of Refugees Coming from Germany. Geneva, July 4th, 1936. Geneva, 1936. 7 p., bilingual; in part double-paged.[44]

Sample form of Identity Certificate for Refugees Coming from Germany on p.7.

Convention Concerning the Status of Refugees Coming from Germany. Geneva, February 10th, 1938. No date. 14 p., bilingual; in part double-paged.[45] [C.75.M.30(1).1938.XII.] (1938.XII.B.1.)

---

[40]The League as such was not authorized to issue passports; see on this question Item 145 in Walter Schiffer, *Repertoire of Questions of General International Law before the League of Nations, 1920-1940* (Geneva,1942), p.64–65.

[41]Also in *Official Journal*, July, 1924, p.969–971. Dr. Nansen's plan was adopted by Council Resolution of June 12,1924. See *ibid.*, p.907–908. Sample form of Certificate of Identity, *ibid.*, p.970.

[42]In force since September 12,1929.

[43]In force since June 13,1935. Text also in 159 *Treaty Series*, p.199–217., bilingual. Official text in French.

[44]In force since August 4,1936. Text also in 171 *Treaty Series*, p.75–87., bilingual.

[45]In force since October 26,1938. Text also in 192 *Treaty Series*, p.59–81., bilingual.

Sample form of Identity Certificate for Refugees Coming from Germany on p.18.

Additional Protocol to the Provisional Arrangement and to the Convention, Signed at Geneva on July 4th, 1936 and February 10th, 1938, Respectively, Concerning the Status of Refugees Coming from Germany. Geneva, September 14th, 1939. No date. 4 p., bilingual; in part double-paged.[46] [C.258.M.176.1939.XII.]

VARIOUS DOCUMENTS

Individual Documents[47]

Letter of Resignation of James G. McDonald, High Commissioner for Refugees (Jewish and Other), Addressed to the Secretary-General of the League of Nations. With an Annex Containing an Analysis of Measures in Germany against "Non-Aryans" and of Their Effects in Creating Refugees. London, 1935. 34 p.

It should be noted that this document is not to be considered as a League document in the technical sense, but its French version appeared under the numbers [C.13. M.12.1936.XII.Annexe] (1936.XII.B.2.).

International Assistance to Refugees. Geneva, 1938. 9 p. [A.27.1938. XII.] (1938.XII.B.3.)[48]

Contains: 1.Report of the Council Committee Appointed to Draw up a Plan for International Assistance to Refugees, Adopted by the Council on May 14th, 1938. 2.Replies from Governments. 3.Report by the Secretary-General on International Assistance to Refugees.

General

Information Section. The Refugees. No. 9 of League of Nations Questions. Geneva, 1938. 54 p.[49]

3. SLAVERY

INTRODUCTORY NOTE

The League's right to investigate the slavery question was derived from Article 23(b) of the Covenant whereby the members of the League "undertake to secure just treatment of the native inhabitants of territories under control."

By Council Resolution of September 26, 1922,[50] the Secretary-

[46]In force since September 14,1939. Text also in 198 Treaty Series, p.141–145.
[47]For a useful list of related documents, see Official Journal, February,1936, p.153–154.
[48]See also Document [A.27.1938.XII.Addendum.] (1938.XII.B.3.Addendum.).
[49]For the settlement of the Assyrians, see below, p.314–315. For developments up to, 1944, see also Arieh Tartakower and Kurt R. Grossmann, The Jewish Refugee (New York 1944), especially p.401–428.
[50]Official Journal, November,1922, p.1203, 1418.

General was authorized to request members of the League to inform the Council about the status of the slave question within their respective territories. On September 28, 1923, the Assembly, "having taken note of the information obtained up to the present from Members of the League and considering that it cannot form the basis of a sufficiently complete report,"[51] requested the Council to entrust to a competent body the task of enquiring into the slavery question and of proposing measures to facilitate the eradication of slavery. Accordingly, the Temporary Slavery Commission was set up on June 12, 1924.[52] Besides investigating the main problems involved in slavery the Temporary Slavery Commission paved the way for the Slavery Convention of 1926. The Temporary Slavery Commission was active from July, 1924 to about July 1925.[53]

The Committee of Experts on Slavery, later styled Advisory Committee of Experts on Slavery, was instituted by the Council on January 28, 1932.[54]

At the League's Secretariat questions related to slavery were handled in the Mandates Section.[55]

TEMPORARY SLAVERY COMMISSION

Minutes of Sessions

Minutes of the First Session, Held at Geneva from July 9th to 12th, 1924. Geneva, 1924. 31 p. [A.18.1924.VI.]

Minutes of the Second Session, Held at Geneva from July 13th to 25th, 1925. Geneva, 1925. 106 p. [C.426.M.157.1925.VI.]

Reports

Report to the Council.[56] Geneva, 1924. 3 p. [A.17.1924.VI.]

Letter from the Chairman of the Commission to the President of the Council and Report of the Commission.[57] Geneva, 1925. 15 p. [A.19.1925.VI.]

SLAVERY CONVENTION OF SEPTEMBER 25, 1926

Slavery Convention. Geneva, September 25, 1926. No date. 11 p.+ 11 p., bilingual. [C.586.M.223.1926.VI.] (1926.VI.B.7.)[58]

---

[51]*Official Journal*, Special Supplement No.11, October,1923, p.29.
[52]*Official Journal*, July,1924, p.909.
[53]See, *e. g.* Viscount Cecil's Report to the Council on the Draft Convention on Slavery of September 28,1925 [C.588.1925.VI.(1).], p.1: "The work of the Temporary Slavery Commission has come to an end."
[54]*Official Journal*, March,1932, p.482–484.
[55]See Ranshofen-Wertheimer, *The International Secretariat*, p.117.
[56]Covers the first session of the Temporary Slavery Commission.
[57]See also Documents [A.42(a).1924.VI.] and [A.39.1925.VI.].
[58]Text also in 60 *Treaty Series*, p.253–270, bilingual. In force since March 9,1927. Al-

ADVISORY COMMITTEE OF EXPERTS ON SLAVERY

Basic Texts

Assembly Resolution of September 25, 1931. *Official Journal,* Special Supplement No. 92, October, 1931, p. 36.

Council Resolution of September 25, 1931. *Official Journal,* December, 1931, p. 2295–2296.

Council Resolution of January 28, 1932. *Official Journal,* March, 1932, p. 482–484.

Assembly Resolution of October 12, 1932. *Official Journal,* Special Supplement No. 103, November, 1932, p. 24–26.

Rules of Procedure

Slavery. Advisory Committee of Experts. Rules of Procedure. Geneva, 1934. 4 p. Extract No. 86 from the *Official Journal.*

Contains: 1.Report of the Committee to the Council, Dated January 10th,1934. 2.Rules of Procedure. 3.Resolution of the Assembly of October 12th,1932.

Slavery. Advisory Committee of Experts. Rules of Procedure. Geneva, 1936. 4 p. <C.C.E.E.138.> (1937.VI.B.1.)

Contains: 1.Report of the Committee to the Council, Dated January 10th,1934. 2.Rules of Procedure. 3.Resolution of the Assembly of October 12th,1932, Interpreted by the Council's Decision of May 13th,1936.

Reports of the Advisory Committee of Experts on Slavery to the Council[59]

First Report: Report of the Committee of Experts on Slavery Provided for by the Assembly Resolution of September 25th, 1931. Geneva, 1932. 27 p. [C.618.1932.VI.] (1932.VI.B.1.)

Last Report: Report of the Advisory Committee of Experts. Fifth (Extraordinary) Session of the Committee. Held in Geneva, March 31st to April 5th, 1938. Geneva, 1938. 131 p. [C.112.M.98.1938. VI.] (1938.VI.B.1.)

ENQUIRY INTO LIBERIA

International Commission of Enquiry in Liberia. Communication by the Government of Liberia, Dated December 15th, 1930, Trans-

---

though the preamble to the Slavery Convention emphasizes the fact that "it is necessary to prevent forced labour from developing into conditions analogous to slavery," the Convention does not cover forced labor. On forced labor, see "Forced Labour Convention,1930" and "Forced Labour (Indirect Compulsion) Recommendation," in International Labor Organization, *International Labour Code, 1939* (Montreal,1941), p.476–489, 490–491.

[59]The title varies. The First Report appeared on behalf of the "Committee of Experts on Slavery," subsequent ones on behalf of the "Advisory Committee of Experts on Slavery." The title pages of the Second to Fifth Reports read: "Slavery. Report of the Advisory Committee of Experts."

mitting the Commission's Report. Geneva, 1930. 130 p. [C.658. M.272.1930.VI.] (1930.VI.B.6.)[60]

Contains on p.5–89 the Report of the International Commission of Enquiry into the Existence of Slavery and Forced Labour in the Republic of Liberia, Monrovia, Liberia, August,1930.

International Commission of Enquiry in Liberia. Communication from the Liberian Government, Dated January 9th, 1931. Geneva, 1931. 1 p.+1 p., bilingual. [C.50.M.27.1931.VI.] (1931.VI.B.1.)

International Commission of Enquiry in Liberia. Further Communication from the Liberian Government, Dated January 13th, 1931. Geneva, 1931. 1 p.+1 p., bilingual. [C.73.M.30.1931.VI.]

Slavery Convention of September 25th, 1926. Communication from the Government of the United States of America Regarding the Report of the International Commission of Enquiry into the Existence of Slavery and Forced Labour in Liberia. Geneva, 1931. 2 p. [C.L.3.1931.VI.] (1931.VI.B.2.)

4. TRAFFIC IN WOMEN AND CHILDREN

INTRODUCTORY NOTE

The League's authority to supervise the execution of agreements on the traffic in women and children can be traced back to Article 23(c) of the Covenant. The League in dealing with traffic in women and children, child welfare, and related questions acted through committees that have changed their names and were reorganized several times.

On January 14, 1922, the Council resolved[61] to set up the Advisory Committee on the Traffic in Women and Children, as suggested in Resolution XI of the Final Act of the International Conference on Traffic in Women and Children, which met in Geneva from June 30 to July 5, 1921.[62] The Committee was reconstituted under the title Advisory Committee on Traffic in Women and Protection of Children in 1924.[63] Shortly thereafter the Committee appeared under the new

[60]For the terms of reference of the International Commission, see p.94.
[61]Text in *Official Journal*, February,1922, p.186–187; see also p.112.
[62]See International Conference on Traffic in Women and Children, *Final Act*, p. 5-6. [C.223(1).M.162(1).1921.IV.] <C.T.F.E.52.>
[63]See Council Resolution of December 10,1924, *Official Journal*, February,1925, p. 135–136, 221–223; see also *ibid.*, July,1925, p.903. The Assembly, by its Resolution of September 20, 1924, adopted the Council's proposal and favored the reconstitution of the Advisory Committee on Traffic in Women and Children as effected by Council Resolution of December 10,1924. See also Assembly Resolution of September 26,1924, *Official Journal*, Special Supplement No. 21, October, 1924, p.42–43; this resolution contains the famous Declaration of Geneva on the rights of the child.

name, Advisory Committee for the Protection and Welfare of Children and Young People,[64] subdivided in two sections: (a) Traffic in Women and Children Committee, and (b) Child Welfare Committee.[65]

Previously, the Council had resolved that the work hitherto carried out by the International Association for the Protection of Children should henceforth be entrusted to the Secretariat of the League of Nations.

By Council Resolution of May 13, 1936,[66] the Committee on Traffic in Women and Children and the Child Welfare Committee, which had hitherto composed the Advisory Commission for the Protection and Welfare of Children and Young People, were merged into a single Committee, the Advisory Committee on Social Questions. The change in title did not imply, however, a change in the scope of the Committee's activities.

These repeated changes in the names of the committees are no doubt confusing; they are cited here to explain the varying titles of the related documents. Pertinent Rules of Procedure are listed below.

In 1931, upon recommendation of the Child Welfare Committee, the Council decided[67] to set up a special Committee of Experts to study the question of assistance to foreigners and to draft a preliminary international convention. The Committee met for the first time in December, 1933,[68] and worked out the Model Convention on Assistance to Indigent Foreigners, whose last published version is to be found in Document [C.105.M.57.1938.IV.].[69] The Committee had no rules of procedure.

CHILD WELFARE COMMITTEE

Rules of Procedure

"Rules of Procedure Adopted by the Child Welfare Committee, May, 1927," in *Report on the Work of the Third Session (May, 1927)*, p. 7–8. [C.228.M.90.1927.IV.] <C.P.E.123.>

Minutes of Sessions

First Reported Session: "Child Welfare," in Advisory Committee on the Traffic in Women and Protection of Children, *Report of the Fourth Session, May, 1925*, p. 2–5.[70] [C.293(1) 1925.IV.]

[64] See Council Resolution of June 9,1925, and the Chamberlain Report of the same date, *Official Journal*, July,1925, p.861, 903–904.

[65] See Advisory Committee on the Traffic in Women and Protection of Children, *Minutes of the Fourth Session*, p.28. [C.382.M.126.1925.IV.]

[66] See *Official Journal*, June,1936, p.557–558, 725–729. See also Assembly Resolution of October 10,1936, *Official Journal*, Special Supplement No.153, October,1936, p.29.

[67] See Council Resolution of May 20,1931, *Official Journal*, July,1931, p.1106–1107.

[68] See Document [C.10.M.8.1934.]; also in *Official Journal*, February,1934, p.188–189.

[69] See below, p.000.

[70] The pertinent section of this document is often referred to as "Minutes of the First Session," although actually, it is only a brief summary of the proceedings.

Last Reported Session: Child Welfare Committee. Minutes of the Seventh Session, Held at Geneva from Tuesday, April 14th to Monday, April 20th, 1931.[71] Geneva, 1931, 59 p. [C.297.M.139. 1931.IV.] <C.P.E./7th Session/P.V. revised> (1931.IV.7.)

Reports

First Report: In Advisory Committee on the Traffic in Women and Protection of Children, *Report of the Fourth Session, May, 1925,* p. 2–5. [C.293(1)1925.IV.]

Last Report: Child Welfare Committee. Report on the Work of the Eighth Session (Geneva, April 9th to 15th, 1932). Geneva, 1932. 16 p. [C.395.M.221.1932.IV.] <C.P.E.351.> (1932.IV.4.)

ADVISORY COMMISSION FOR THE PROTECTION AND WELFARE OF CHILDREN AND YOUNG PEOPLE

Rules of Procedure

"Rules of Procedure to Replace Existing Rules of Procedure, Dated May 16th, 1930," in *Report on the Work of the Commission in 1933,* p. 24–25. [C.247.M.129.1933.IV.] (1933.IV.1.)

Reports

First Report:[72] Report on the Work of the Commission in 1933. Geneva, 1933. 31 p. [C.247.M.129.1933.IV.] (1933.IV.1.)

Last Report: Report on the Work of the Commission in 1936. Geneva, 1936. 28 p. [C.204.M.127.1936.IV.] (1936.IV.3.)

TRAFFIC IN WOMEN AND CHILDREN COMMITTEE

Rules of Procedure

"Rules of Procedure," in Advisory Committee on the Traffic in Women and Children, *Report on the Work of the Committee at Its First Session, Held at Geneva from June 28th to July 1st, 1922, Approved by the Council on July 17th, 1922,* Geneva, 1922, p. 9–10. [A.9(1).1922.IV.] [C.438(1).1922.IV.]

The Rules of Procedure proper are marked <C.T.F.E.112>.

"Rules of Procedure Revised and Adopted by the Committee," in

[71]"The main report of the Committee is divided into two parts, the first dealing with Child Welfare and the second with Traffic in Women." p.2.

[72]Beginning with 1933 the Reports of the Advisory Commission for the Protection and Welfare of Children and Young People include Reports on the Sessions of the Child Welfare Committee, the Traffic in Women and Children Committee, and on Joint Sessions of the Traffic in Women and Children Committee and Child Welfare Committee.

Advisory Commission for the Protection and Welfare of Children and Young People, *Traffic in Women and Children Committee: Report on the Ninth Session,* Geneva, 1930, p. 11–12. [C.216.M.104. 1930.IV.] (1930.IV.2.)

Minutes of Sessions

First Session: Advisory Committee on the Traffic in Women and Children. Minutes of the First Session, Held at Geneva from June 28th to July 1st, 1922. Geneva, 1922. 70 p.+70 p., bilingual. [C.445.M.265.1922.IV.]

Last Reported Session:[73] Traffic in Women and Children Committee. Minutes of the Tenth Session, Held at Geneva from Tuesday, April 21st to Monday, April 27th, 1931. Geneva, 1931. 91 p. [C. 401.M.163.1931.IV.] (1931.IV.8.)

No Minutes were issued for the Eleventh and subsequent sessions.

Reports

First Report:[74] Advisory Committee on the Traffic in Women and Children. Report on the Work of the Committee at Its First Session, Held at Geneva from June 28th to July 1st, 1922, Approved by the Council on July 17th, 1922. Geneva, 1922. 13 p.+13 p., bilingual. [A.9(1) 1922.IV.] [C.438.(1) 1922.IV.]

Last Report:[75] Traffic in Women and Children Committee. Report on the Work of the Eleventh Session (Geneva, April 4th to 9th, 1932). Geneva, 1932. 10 p. [C.390.M.220.1932.IV.] <C.T.F.E.547(1)> (1932.IV.3.)

ADVISORY COMMITTEE ON SOCIAL QUESTIONS

Rules of Procedure

Rules of Procedure for the Advisory Committee on Social Questions.[76] *Official Journal,* June, 1936, p. 729–730.

[73]It should be noted that the Minutes of the First to Third Sessions appeared on behalf of the "Advisory Committee on the Traffic in Women and Children"; the Minutes of the Fourth Session, on behalf of the "Advisory Committee on the Traffic in Women and Protection of Children"; the Minutes of the Fifth to Ninth Sessions, on behalf of the "Advisory Commission for the Protection and Welfare of Children and Young People"; the Minutes of the Tenth Session, on behalf of the "Traffic in Women and Children Committee."

[74]This report contains a list of the states signatories of the Agreement of 1904 and of the Conventions of 1910 and 1921 as well as the ratifications and adhesions relating to these Conventions.

[75]For reports on the Twelfth and subsequent sessions, see *Reports on the Work of the Advisory Commission for the Protection and Welfare of Children and Young People.*

[76]Also published as an appendix to Document [C.192.M.121.1936.IV.], entitled "Reorganization of the Advisory Commission for the Protection and Welfare of Children and Young People."

Reports

First Report: Report on the Work of the Committee in 1937 (First Session). Geneva, 1937. 39 p. [C.235.M.169.1937.IV.] (1937.IV.5.)
Last Report: Report on the Work of the Committee in 1939 (Third Session). Geneva, 1939. 23 p. [C.214.M.142.1939.IV.] (1939.IV.11.)

SUMMARY OF ANNUAL REPORTS FROM GOVERNMENTS

Traffic in Women and Children and Obscene Publications[77]

First Report: Summary of Annual Reports for 1924 Received from Governments Relating to the Traffic in Women and Children. Geneva, 1924. 19 p. [C.164.M.40.1924.IV.]
Last Report: Advisory Committee on Social Questions. Summary of Annual Reports for 1944/45 Prepared by the Secretariat. Traffic in Women and Children. Geneva, 1946. [C.23.M.23.1946.IV.] (1926. IV.1.). Advisory Committee on Social Questions. Summary of Annual Reports for 1944/45 Prepared by the Secretariat. Circulation of and Traffic in Obscene Publications. Geneva, 1946. 4 p. [C.24.M.24.1946.IV.] (1946.IV.2.)

This report appeared in two sections, as indicated.

CONFERENCES ON TRAFFIC IN WOMEN AND CHILDREN

International Conference on Traffic in Women and Children. General Report on the Work of the Conference. Geneva, 1921. 33 p.+ 33 p., bilingual. [C.227.M.166.1921.IV.]

Records of the International Conference on Traffic in Women and Children. Geneva, 1921. 137 p.+137 p., bilingual. [C.484.M.339. 1921.IV.]

Records of the Diplomatic Conference Concerning the Suppression of Traffic in Women of Full Age. Held at Geneva, October 9th to 11th, 1933. Geneva, 1933. 29 p. [C.649.M.310.1933.IV.] (1933. IV.6.)

Includes on p.21–24 the Text of the International Convention for the Suppression of the Traffic in Women of Full Age, Adopted by the Conference on October 11th, 1933. [C.590.M.276.1933.IV.]

Traffic in Women and Children. Conference of General Authorities

[77]Reports covering the years 1922–1930 deal exclusively with Traffic in Women and Children. Reports covering the years 1931–1937 also include information on Obscene Publications. See Documents [C.68.M.30.1939.IV.] and [C.69.M.31.1939.IV.] for reports on Traffic in Women and Children and Obscene Publications for 1937–1938.

in Eastern Countries. Report. Bandoeng, 1937. 7 p. [C.228.M.
164.1937.IV.] (1937.IV.4.)
Conference of Central Authorities in Eastern Countries. Bandoeng
(Java), February 2nd to 13th, 1937. Minutes of Meetings. Geneva,
1937. 115 p. [C.476.M.318.1937.IV.] (1937.IV.10.)
The Work of the Bandoeng Conference. Geneva, 1937. 86 p. [C.516.
M.357.1937.IV.] (1937.IV.11.)

INTERNATIONAL CONVENTIONS

International Convention for Suppression of the Traffic in Women
and Children, Opened for Signature at Geneva from September 30,
1921, to March 31, 1922. 9 *Treaty Series*, p. 416–433, bilingual.[78]
International Convention for the Suppression of the Traffic in Women
of Full Age.[79] Geneva, 1933. 4 p.+4 p., bilingual; with 4 p. of
signatures. [C.590.M.276.1933.IV.] (1933.IV.5.)[80]

ENQUIRIES OF TRAFFIC IN WOMEN AND CHILDREN

General Enquiries

Report of the Special Body of Experts on Traffic in Women and
Children. Geneva, 1927. Part I: 50 p. [C.52.M.52.1927.IV.] <C.
T.F.E./Experts/55> (1927.IV.2^I. Part II: 226 p. [C.52(2)M.52(1)
1927.IV.] (1927.IV.2^{II}).

Part I contains the comments and conclusions of the experts based on the evidence
laid before them. Part II contains facts about traffic in 28 countries which were
studied, and the study was supplemented by investigations on the spot. It includes
[C.592.1927.IV.].

Commission of Enquiry into Traffic in Women and Children in the
East. Report to the Council. Geneva, December 10, 1932. 556 p.
[C.849.M.393.1932.IV.] <C.T.F.E./Orient 39(1)> (1932.IV.8.)
Commission of Enquiry into Traffic in Women and Children in the
East. Summary of the Report to the Council. Geneva, 1934. 41 p.
<C.T.F.E.606.> (1934.IV.3.)
Enquiry into Measures of Rehabilitation of Prostitutes. Part I:
Prostitutes: Their Early Lives. Geneva, July 1, 1938. 140 p. [C.
218.M.120.1938.IV.] (1938.IV.11.). Part II: Social Services and
Venereal Disease. Geneva, November 15, 1937 (?). 66 p. [C.6.M. 5.
1938.IV.] (1938.IV.1.). Part III and Part IV: Methods of Re-

[78]According to Art. 11 the Convention comes into force in respect to every party the
moment the party adheres to it. This is also a separate document [A.125.(3)1921.IV.].
[79]Signed at Geneva, October 11,1933. See also Document [C.590.M.276.1933.IV.Errat-
um] (1933.IV.5.Erratum).
[80]Also in 150 *Treaty Series*, p.432–443, bilingual; in force since August 24, 1934.

habilitation of Adult Prostitutes. Conclusions and Recommendations. Geneva, July 1, 1939. 157 p. [C.83.M.43.1939.IV.] (1939. IV.4.)

Special Questions

Traffic in Women and Children Committee. The Employment of Women in the Police. Geneva, 1927. 13 p. [C.374.M.144.1927.IV.] <C.T.F.E.331.> (1927.IV.7.)

Study of Laws and Regulations with a View to Protecting Order and Health in Countries Where the System of Licensed Houses Has Been Abolished. Geneva, 1930. 93 p. [C.380.M.164.1930.IV.] <C. T.F.E.466(1).> (1930.IV.5.)

Punishment of "Souteneurs." Draft Additional Protocol to the International Convention for the Suppression of Traffic in Women and Children from September 1921. Geneva, 1931. 2 p. [C.267.M. 122.1931.IV.Extract]

Concise Study of the Laws and Penalties Relating to "Souteneurs." Geneva, 1931. 30 p. [C.441.M.188.1931.IV.] <C.T.F.E.418(I).> (1931.IV.10.)

Traffic in Women and Children Committee. Central Authorities.[81] Geneva, 1932. 20 p. [C.504.M.245.1932.IV.] (1932.IV.6.)

Commission of Enquiry into Traffic in Women and Children in the East. Summary of the Report to the Council. Geneva, 1934. 41 p. +maps. <C.T.F.E.606.> (1934.IV.3.)

Abolition of Licensed Houses. No date. 96 p. [C.221.M.88.1934.IV.] <C.T.F.E.612(1)> (1934.IV.7.)

Position of Women of Russian Origin in the Far East. Geneva, 1935. 16 p. [A.12.1935.IV.] (1935.IV.3.)

5. OBSCENE PUBLICATIONS

CONFERENCE, 1923

Records of the International Conference for the Suppression of the Circulation of and Traffic in Obscene Publications, Held at Geneva from August 31st to September 12th, 1923. Geneva, 1923. 126 p. [C.734.M.299.1923.IV.]

CONVENTION

International Convention for the Suppression of the Circulation of and Traffic in Obscene Publications. Open for Signature at Ge-

[81]See also Document [C.504.M.245.1932.IV.Erratum]. 1p.

neva from September 12th, 1923 to March 31st, 1924. Geneva, 1924.[82] 7 p.+7 p., bilingual; with 3 p. of signatures. [C.202.M.64. 1924.IV.] [C.630.M.236.1923.IV.] <C.P.O.34(1).1923.>

International Convention for the Suppression of the Circulation of and Traffic in Obscene Publications. Methods of Transmission of Rogatory Commissions. No date. 10 p. [C.436.M.279.1938.IV.] (1938.IV.15.)[83]

6. CHILD WELFARE

CHILD WELFARE COMMITTEE[84]

Rules of Procedure Revised and Adopted by the Committee. Appendix to Document [C.223.M.110.1930.IV.] (1930.IV.3.). In Child Welfare Committee, *Minutes of the Sixth Session* (1930. IV.7.), p. 85.

JUVENILE COURTS AND AUXILIARY SERVICES

Enquiry into Juvenile Courts, Proposed by the Child Welfare Committee. Geneva, 1926. 1 p.+1 p., bilingual. [A.40.1926.IV.] (1926. IV.7.)

Auxiliary Services of Juvenile Courts. Geneva, 1931. 128 p. <C.P. E.238(1).> (1931.IV.1.)

Organisation of Juvenile Courts and the Results Attained Hitherto. Published by the League of Nations in Collaboration with the International Prison Commission. Geneva, 1932. 127 p. [C.975.M. 540.1931.IV.] (1931.IV.13.)

Institutions for Erring and Delinquent Minors. Geneva, 1934. 253 p. [C.I.M.I.1934.IV.] <C.P.E.430>. (1934.IV.1.)[85]

Organisation of Juvenile Courts and the Results Attained Hitherto.[86] Geneva, 1935. 151 p. [C.484.M.260.1935.IV.] <C.P.E.315> (1935. IV.5.)

This document takes the place of (1931.IV.13.)

Principles Applicable to the Functioning of Juvenile Courts and Similar Bodies. Auxiliary Services and Institutions. Geneva, 1937. 50 p. [C.375.M.252.1937.IV.] (1937.IV.9.)

---

[82]Also in 27 *Treaty Series* p. 213–233. In force since August 7, 1924.

[83]See also Document [C.436.M.279.1938.IV.Addendum.].

[84]For the establishment of the Child Welfare Committee, see above, p.201. For Declaration of Geneva, see *Official Journal*, Special Supplement No.129, 1934, p.68.

[85]See also Documents [C.247.M.129.1933.IV.] and [C.I.M.1.1934.IV.] <C.P.E.430>, 5 p., mimeographed.

[86]See also Document [C.484.M.260.1935.IV.Addendum] <C.P.E.315> (1935.IV.5. Addendum).

ILLEGITIMATE CHILDREN

Study of the Position of the Illegitimate Child Based on the Information Communicated by Governments.[87] Geneva, 1929. 107 p. <C.P.E.141(1).> (1929.IV.5.)

Official Guardianship of Illegitimate Children. Geneva, 1932. 16 p. [C.265.M.153.1932.IV.] <C.P.E.322> (1932.IV.1.)

Disclosure of Illegitimacy in Official Documents. Geneva, 1933. 8 p. [C.373.M.184.1933.IV.] <C.P.E.399(1)> (1933.IV.2.)

Study of the Legal Position of the Illegitimate Child. Geneva, 1939. 194 p. [C.70.M.24.1939.IV.] (1939.IV.6.)

PLACING OF CHILDREN IN FAMILIES

The Placing of Children in Families. Volume I: Fundamental Concept, Historical Development, Characteristic Features in Differing Systems, Principles and Procedures in the Organisation of Services. Geneva, 1938. 154 p. [C.260.M.155.1938.IV. Volume I] (1938. IV.14[1]). Volume II: Various Systems of Placing of Children in Families. Geneva, 1938. 241 p. [C.260.M.155.1938.IV. Volume II.] (1938.IV.14[II]).

SPECIAL QUESTIONS

The Age of Marriage and the Age of Consent. Geneva, 1928. 32 p. <C.P.E.90(2).> (1928.IV.20.)

Protection of Blind Children. Geneva, 1928. 22 p. <C.P.E.144.> (1928.IV.4.)

Report by the International Labour Office on Family Allowances in Relation to the Physical and Moral Well-being of Children. Geneva, 1928. 26 p. <C.P.E.150.> (1928.IV.10.)

Model Agreement Regarding the Return of Children and Young People to Their Homes. Geneva, April 27, 1931. 2 p. [C.264.M.119.1931.IV.] (1931.IV.5.)

Enquiry into the Question of Children in Moral and Social Danger. Report of Mlle. Chaptal. Geneva, 1934. 178 p. [C.285.M.123.1934.IV.] <C.P.E.445(1).> (1934.IV.8.).

Child Welfare Councils: Denmark, Norway, Sweden. Geneva, 1937. 96 p. [C.8.M.7.1937.IV.] (1937.IV.1.)

Prevention of Prostitution: A Study of Measures Adopted or under Consideration Particularly with Regard to Minors. Geneva, 1943. 182 p. [C.26.M.26.1943.IV.] (1943.IV.2.)

[87]Document <C.P.E.141(1)>, 4p., is the Index to this.

CHILD WELFARE INFORMATION CENTER

Summary of Annual Reports

Summary of Annual Reports Received from Governments between January 1st, 1936, and the First Session of the Advisory Committee on Social Questions (April 15th, 1937). Geneva, 1937. 98 p. [C.316.M.212.1937.IV.] <C.Q.S./B.3.> (1937.IV.6.)

Summary of Annual Reports Received from Governments between the Close of the First Session and the Close of the Second Session of the Advisory Committee on Social Questions (May 1st, 1937-May 5th, 1938). Geneva, 1938. 160 p. [C.81.M.36.1938.IV.] <C.Q.S./P.E./C.I.39.> (1938.IV.5.)

Annual Report on Child Welfare, for the Third Session of the Advisory Committee on Social Questions (June 19th, 1939). Geneva, 1939. 201 p. [C.91.M.50.1939.IV.] <C.Q.S./P.E./C.I.106.> (1939. IV.5.)

At this session, the Child Welfare Committee passed a resolution—approved by the Council on May 22 of the same year—the object of which was to obtain, each year, particulars of the progress made in child welfare in the various countries, both from the legislative and administrative points of view. To this end governments were asked to furnish reports to the Secretariat.

Annual Report on Child Welfare, for the Fourth Session of the Advisory Committee on Social Questions (June 24th, 1940). Geneva, 1940. 186 p. [C.41.M.37.1940.IV.] <C.Q.S./P.E./C.I.191.> (1940. IV.4.)

Annual Report on Child Welfare (Summarising Information Received from Governments between May 1940 and December 1941). Geneva, 1942. 122 p. [C.15.M.15.1942.IV.] <C.Q.S./P.E./C.I. 248.> (1942.IV.1.)

Annual Report on Child Welfare (Summarising Information Received from Governments in 1942). Geneva, 1943. 119 p. [C.12. M.12.1943.IV.] <C.Q.S./P.E./C.I.253.> (1943.IV.1.)

Annual Report on Child Welfare (Summarising Information Received from Governments in 1943 and 1944). Geneva, 1945. 76 p. [C.8.M.8.1945.IV.] <C.Q.S./P.E./C.I.259.>

Annual Report on Child Welfare (Summarising Information Received from Governments in 1943 and 1944). Geneva, 1945. 76 p. [C.8.M.8.1945.IV.] <C.Q.S./P.E./C.I.259.> (1945.V.1.)

Legislative and Administrative Series[88]

Summary of the Legislative and Administrative Series of Documents of the Child Welfare Information Centre to December 31st, 1937. Geneva, 1938. 52 p. [C.73.M.28.1938.IV.] (1938.IV.3.)

[88]See also mimeographed documents in the Series.

Summary of the Legislative and Administrative Series of Documents of the Child Welfare Centre Published in 1938. Geneva, 1939. 58 p. [C.72.M.33.1939.IV.] (1939.IV.1.)

Summary of the Legislative and Administrative Series of Documents of the Child Welfare Information Centre Published in 1939. Geneva, 1940. 77 p. [C.12.M.10.1940.IV.] <C.Q.S./P.E./C.I.180.> (1940.IV.1.)

Summary of the Legislative and Administrative Series of Documents of the Child Welfare Information Centre Published in 1940. Geneva, 1941. 52 p. [C.89.M.86.1941.IV.] <C.Q.S./P.E./C.I.247.> (1941.IV.3.)

7. IMPROVEMENTS IN PENAL ADMINISTRATION

Improvements in Penal Administration. Standard Minimum Rules for the Treatment of Prisoners Drawn up by the International Prison Commission. Geneva, 1930. 6 p. [C.620.M.241.1930.IV]. (1930.IV.10.)

Improvements in Penal Administration. Report by the Secretary-General to the Twelfth Assembly. Geneva, 1931. 17 p. [A.25. 1931.IV.] (1931.IV.11.)

Improvements in Penal Administration. Supplement to the Report of the Secretary-General to the Twelfth Assembly. 1931. 6 p. [A.25(a).1931.IV.] (1931.IV.12.)

Penal and Penitentiary Questions. Improvements in Penal Administration. Report of the Fifth Committee to the Assembly. Rapporteur: Professor V. V. Pella (Roumania). Geneva, 1931. 7 p. [A. 70.1931.IV.]

Penal and Penitentiary Questions. Joint Reply Submitted to the Secretary-General by the Seven Organisations Consulted on the Questions of the Gradual Unification of Criminal Law and the Co-operation of States in the Prevention and Suppression of Crime. Geneva, 1932. 6 p. [C.L.174.1932.Annex.] <A.P.4.>

Contains on p.3–6 a draft statute for the International Bureau for the Unification of Criminal Law.

Penal and Penitentiary Questions. Report of the Fifth Committee to the Assembly. Rapporteur: Professor V. V. Pella (Roumania). Geneva, 1932. 4 p. [A.58.1932.IV.]

Penal and Penitentiary Questions. Report Submitted by the Fifth Committee to the Assembly. Rapporteur: Mr. John J. Hearne (Irish Free State). Geneva, 1934. 8 p. [A.45.1934.IV.]

Contains on p.3–8 Standard Minimum Rules for the Treatment of Prisoners.

Penal and Penitentiary Questions. Report of the Secretary-General to the Assembly. 1934. 10 p. [A.14.1934.IV.] (1934.IV.9.)

Penal and Penitentiary Questions. Report Submitted by the Secretary-General to the Assembly. No date. 13 p. [A.21.1935.IV.] (1935.IV.4.)

Penal and Penitentiary Questions. Report by the Secretary-General to the Assembly. No date. 17 p. [A.25.1936.IV.] (1936.IV.4.)

Penal and Penitentiary Questions. Report by the Secretary-General to the Assembly. No date. 10 p. [A.23.1937.IV.] (1937.IV.7.)

Penal and Penitentiary Questions. Report by the Secretary-General to the Assembly. No date. 29 p. [A.20.1939.IV.] (1939.IV.12.)

8. ASSISTANCE TO INDIGENT FOREIGNERS

Committee of Experts[89] on Assistance to Indigent Foreigners and the Execution of Maintenance Obligations Abroad. Report to the Council on the Work of the Session Held from December 4th to 9th, 1933. Geneva, 1934. 8 p. [C.10.M.8.1934.] (1934.IV.6.)

Appendix contains a Draft Multilateral Convention on Assistance to Indigent Foreigners, p.7–8.

Committee of Experts on Assistance to Indigent Foreigners and the Execution of Maintenance Obligations Abroad. Report to the Council on the Work of the Second Session, from January 27th to February 1st, 1936. Geneva, 1936. 7 p. [C.94.M.37.1936.IV.] <A. E.33.> (1936.IV.2.)

Annex contains Second Draft Multilateral Convention on Assistance to Indigent Foreigners, p.5–6.

Observations of Governments on the Second Draft Multilateral Convention on Assistance to Indigent Foreigners. Geneva, 1937. 24 p. [C.341.M.231.1937.IV.] (1937.IV.8.)

Annex contains the First and Second Draft Multilateral Conventions, p.20–24.

Replies of Governments on the Questionnaire Concerning Methods at Present Applied in Different Countries in the Matter of Assistance to Indigent Foreigners. Geneva, 1937. 32 p. [C.552.M.389. 1937.IV.] (1937.IV.12.)

Committee of Experts on Assistance to Indigent Foreigners and the Execution of Maintenance Obligations Abroad: Report to the Council on the Work of the Third Session. Geneva, 1938. 9 p. [C.105.M.57.1938.IV.] (1938.IV.4.)

Annex contains Model Convention on Assistance to Indigent Foreigners, p.7–8.[90]

[89]By a decision of May 20,1931, the Council of the League of Nations set up a temporary Committee of Experts for the study of assistance to indigent foreigners and the execution of maintenance obligations abroad.

[90]For this Convention, see Elsa Castendyck, "Social Problems," in Davis, ed., *Pioneers in World Order*, p.236.

V. ECONOMIC AND FINANCIAL QUESTIONS

1. INTRODUCTORY NOTE

THE COVENANT carved out a rather limited field of economic activities for the League by concentrating on the "equitable treatment for the commerce of all Members of the League" (Article 23 (e)). "Equitable" in this connection meant presumably adherence to the most-favored-nations clause.[1]

Actually, the Economic and Financial Section of the League can look back on considerable achievements in theory and practice. It contributed to the financial reconstruction of several European countries; convoked and prepared a considerable number of international conferences—some of them leading to the drafting and adoption of general international conventions; devised new methods of statistical information[2] and other techniques of economic intelligence; and, finally, carried on economic research in fields other than statistics and economic intelligence. The broad scope of research and investigation entrusted to the Economic and Financial Organization can be illustrated by reference to Assembly Resolution of October 4, 1937, that suggested enquiries on: (a) measures of a national or international character for raising the standard of living; (b) measures which might be employed with a view to the prevention or mitigation of economic depressions; (c) the study of systems of agricultural credit and insurance; (d) existing economic and financial tendencies of which account should be taken by states in determining monetary systems; (e) the growth of the indebtedness of states, local authorities, and public undertakings; (f) methods for the suppression of fiscal evasion; (g) demographic problems; (h) permanent exhibition of graphs relating to current economic and financial conditions; (i) urban and rural housing.[3]

Within the Economic and Financial Organization of the League of

[1]See Wallace M. McClure, *World Prosperity as Sought through the Economic Work of the League of Nations* (New York,1933), p.88. "Economic equality gave way to a compromise: equitable treatment." On this point see also David Hunter Miller, *The Drafting of the Covenant*. (2vols., New York,1928), I, 19–22,33,46–47; II, 21–22,93.
[2]Actually, there existed a division of labor in the field of statistics between the League on the one hand and the International Labor Organization and the International Institute of Agriculture (Rome) on the other.
[3]See *Official Journal*, Special Supplement No.168, October,1937, p.12–14.

Nations, the four standing committees, namely, the Economic Committee, Financial Committee, Fiscal Committee, and Committee of Statistical Experts were of special significance.

In addition to several *ad hoc* committees,[4] the Second Committee of the Assembly discussed economic and financial questions on the basis of (1) the Annual Report by the Secretary-General on the Work of the League; (2) the Annual Report of the Co-ordination Committee; and (3) reports of the other committees of the Economic and Financial Organization.

Originally, the work of the Economic and Financial Organization of the League centered on the Provisional Advisory Financial and Economic Committee, established by Council Resolution of October 27, 1920.[5] After three years of successful work by the Committee the Council decided that "the word 'provisional' will be omitted in the appellation of the Commission."[6] Subsequently, the Economic Committee was separated from the Financial Committee. The latter operated throughout in a rather informal manner, and as late as 1934 the Council deemed it unnecessary "to contemplate the drafting of a statute for the Financial Committee similar, for example, to that under which the Fiscal Committee functions."[7] Later attempts to work out a precise statute for the Financial Committee[8] did not succeed. Until about 1935 the major part of the work of the Financial Committee was devoted to those countries for whose financial reconstruction it was so largely responsible in the twenties. After 1935 it was concerned with questions of a more general character.[9]

The Economic Committee, which, as previously indicated, formed at the outset part of the Financial and Economic Committee, became independent in the course of time. Until March, 1922, the Financial and Economic Committees submitted Joint Reports to the Council. From that date, each, in general, submitted a separate report at the end of each session.[10] The Economic Committee had no written rules of procedure,[11] but in 1927 the Council set forth at least some general rules concerning the composition and jurisdiction of the Committee.[12]

[4]See Document [C.169.1938.II.B.], *Official Journal*, May-June, 1938, p.552.
[5]Text in Council Minutes, 10th Sess., p.211; see also p.213–215.
[6]See Council Resolution of September 10,1923, *Official Journal*, November,1923, p. 1302–1303.
[7]*Official Journal*, February,1934, p.144. See also *ibid.*, February,1936, p.133; February, 1937, p.116; May-June,1937, p.299.
[8]See *Official Journal*, May-June,1938, p.553.
[9]See, however, Documents [C.52.M.52.1942.II.A.] and [C.1.M.1.1944.II.A.], listed below, p. 215.
[10]See *Committees of the League of Nations*, p.36. [C.287.M.125.1934.]
[11]See *Official Journal*, October, 1927, p. 1439–1440.
[12]See *ibid.*, p. 1455.

The Fiscal Committee was established in 1928 at the suggestion of the General Meeting of Government Experts on Double Taxation and Tax Evasion, which met in Geneva from October 22 to 31, 1928.[13] The General Meeting outlined the terms of reference of the Committee.[14] The primary function of the Fiscal Committee was to counteract double taxation by various means, such as the drafting of bilateral and collective model conventions, preparation of conferences, and the study of related questions of international law.[15] The Fiscal Committee, though in principle self-contained, maintained contact with the Financial Committee.

The Committee of Statistical Experts was set up under Article 8 of the 1928 International Convention relating to economic statistics.[16] The Committee had no written rules of procedure, but resorted in doubtful cases to the Rules of Procedure of the Assembly.[17] The specific functions to be performed by the Committee were defined by the pertinent sections of the 1928 Convention.[18]

The reorganization of the Economic and Financial Section of the League was under consideration in 1938 and 1939. While the *Report of the Committee to Consider the Structure and Functions of the Economic and Financial Organisation* suggested the creation of a Coordination Committee,[19] the Bruce Report favored a "Central Committee for Economic and Social Questions" composed of 24 government representatives and not more than 8 co-opted members, appointed in their personal capacity on the grounds of their special competence and authority.[20] Although the Central Committee for Economic and Social Questions was never set up, the underlying idea was a fruitful one and is directly related to Articles 61–72 of the United Nations Charter concerning the Economic and Social Council.

[13]See "Double Taxation and Tax Evasion. Report Presented by the General Meeting of Government Experts on Double Taxation and Tax Evasion. Submitted to the Council on December 14th,1928" [C.562.M.178.1928.II.], *Official Journal*, January, 1929, p.205–227.
[14]*Ibid.*, p. 224; see also Mitchell B. Carroll, "International Double Taxation," in Harriet E. Davis, ed., *Pioneers in World Order* (New York, 1944), p. 171–177.
[15]See Egon F. Ranshofen-Wertheimer, *The International Secretariat* (Washington,1945), p. 111–115, and Martin Hill, *The Economic and Financial Organization of the League of Nations* (Washington, 1946).
[16]Text in 110 *Treaty Series*, p.171–293,187.
[17]See *Committees of the League of Nations* [C.287.M.125.1934.], p.30, footnote 5.
[18]See also *Official Journal*, July,1929, p.1232, and E. Dana Durand," Standardizing World Statistics," in Davis, ed., *Pioneers in World Order*, p.178–181.
[19]Document [C.169.1938.II.B.], *Official Journal*, May-June,1938, p.551. The Coordination Committee was set up by the Council in May,1938, "to consider the structure and functions of the Economic and Financial Organisation of the League, more particularly with a view to extending the basis of international cooperation in the economic and financial spheres."
[20]Document [A.23.1939.] (General 1939).

Under the pressure of war and the gradual attrition of the League's work in Geneva two reorganizations ensued: the Communications and Transit Section of the Secretariat was merged with the Financial Section; and the Economic Intelligence Service and the Economic Relations Section were absorbed by the Economic, Financial, and Transit Department of the Secretariat.[21] In 1940 part of the Economic, Financial, and Transit Department was sent "on mission" to Princeton, New Jersey. In the words of the Acting Secretary-General the work was, in principle, "so divided that those at headquarters in Geneva are able to specialize on European developments, while those on mission follow the course of the events in the rest of the world."[22]

2. ECONOMIC WORK OF THE LEAGUE

Report on the Economic Work of the League of Nations. Geneva, 1927. 47 p. <C.E.I.41.> (1927.II.43.)

Document No. 41 submitted to the International Economic Conference, Geneva, 1927.

Structure and Functions of the Economic and Financial Organisation of the League of Nations. [C.169.1938.II.B.]. *Official Journal*, May-June, 1938, p. 551-555.

Report of the Committee appointed by the Council on January 29th, 1938, to consider the Question. Submitted to the Council on May 13th, 1938.

Information Section. Towards a Better Economic World. No. 11 of *League of Nations Questions*. Geneva, 1939. 90 p.

A readable description of the economic work of the League.

3. ECONOMIC AND FINANCIAL COMMITTEES

JOINT SESSIONS

Report to the Council on the Work of the Joint Session. London, April 27th-May 1st, 1942, Princeton, August 7th-8th, 1942. Geneva, 1942. 23 p. [C.52.M.52.1942.II.A.] (1942.II.A.4.)

Report to the Council on the Work of the 1943 Joint Session. Geneva, 1944. 81 p. [C.1.M.1.1944.II.A.] (1944.II.A.1.)

Appendices, p. 31-81, contain a summary of the Principal Conclusions from Recent League of Nations Publications on Post-war Problems.

[21] *Report on the Work of the League, 1941-1942, Submitted by the Acting Secretary-General*, Geneva, 1942, p. 14. [C.35.M.35.1942.] (1942.I.)
[22] *Ibid.*

BRUCE REPORT

The Development of International Co-operation in Economic and Social Affairs. Report of the Special Committee. Geneva, 1939. 22 p. [A.23.1939.] (General.1939.)

This so-called Bruce Report is indispensable for an understanding of the provisions of the United Nations Charter (Articles 61–72) on the Economic and Social Council.

PERIODICAL REPORTS TO THE COUNCIL[23] BY THE STANDING COMMITTEES

Economic Committee

First Report: Report of the Provisional Economic and Financial Committee of the Council. No date. 25 p.+25 p., bilingual. [20/48/267] [Document de l'Assemblée 267]

Last Report:[24] Economic Committee. Report to the Council on the Work of Its Fiftieth Session, Held at Geneva from June 15th to 20th, 1939. Geneva, 1939. 15 p. [C.178.M.107.1939.II.B.] (1939. II.B.2.)

Financial Committee[25]

First Report: Report of the Provisional Economic and Financial Committee of the Council. No date. 25 p.+25 p. [20/48/267] [Document de l'Assemblée 267]

Last Report: Financial Committee. Report to the Council on the Work of the Sixty-eighth Session of the Committee (Geneva, June 15th–20th, 1939). Geneva, 1939. 23 p. [C.176.M.105.1939.II.A. (Pt.I.)] <F.1689,Pt.I.>

Fiscal Committee

First Report: Report to the Council on the Work of the First Session of the Committee. Held in Geneva from October 17th to 26th, 1929. Geneva, 1929. 8 p. [C.516.M.175.1929.II.] <F./Fiscal/14.> (1929.II.44.)

Last Report: Report on the Work of the Tenth Session of the Committee, Held in London from March 20th to 26th, 1946. Geneva, 1946. 79 p. [C.37.M.37.1946.II.A.] (1946.II.A.4.)

[23]In addition to the periodical reports the Standing Committees released special reports; several of these special reports are cited below.
[24]See also the *Index to the Reports of the Economic Committee* (*First Session, November 1920 to Thirtieth Session, November 1929)and of the Economic Consultative Committee* (*First Session, May 1928, and Second Session, May 1929*). Geneva,1930. 33 p. [C.523.M.215.1930.II.] (1930.II.42.)
[25]See also *Work and Functions of the Financial Committee.* Geneva,1930. 7 p. [C.567.M.226.1930.II.] (1930.II.38.)

In Annex A the text of the 1943 Mexico and the 1946 London Model Conventions are given on opposite pages as follows: 1. Model Bilateral Convention for the Prevention of the Double Taxation of Income and Property, p. 16–43; 2. Model Bilateral Convention for the Prevention of the Double Taxation of Estates and Successions, p.44–57; 3. Model Bilateral Convention for the Establishment of Reciprocal Administrative Assistance for the Assessment and Collection of Taxes on Income, Property, Estates and Successions, p.58–75. Annex B contains a list of suggested studies in the field of international tax problems., p.77–79.

Committee of Statistical Experts

First Report: Committee of the Statistical Experts. Report. Geneva, 1931. 7 p. [C.215.M.90.1931.II.A.] <C.E.S.5.(1).> (1931.II.A.9.)
Last Report: Report to the Council on the Work of the Eighth Session. Held in Geneva from April 22nd to 27th, 1939. Geneva, 1939. 10 p. [C.133.M.85.1939.II.A.] <C.E.S.145.> (1939.II.A.5.)

International Loan Contracts Committee

Report of the Committee for the Study of International Loan Contracts. Geneva, 1939. 41 p. [C.145.M.93.1939.II.A.] (1939.II.A.10.)

Includes: Annex I. Relative Advantages of Currency Options and the Gold Clause, p. 28; Annex II. Note on the Machinery Required in Case of the Appointment of a Legal Bondholders' Representative in an International Loan Contract, p. 32; Annex III. Some Provisions of International Loan Contracts for the Settlement of Disputes, p. 38; Annex IV. International Loans Tribunal: Draft Convention Presented to the Committee, p. 40.

4. ECONOMIC CONFERENCES

CHRONOLOGICAL LIST

1919. Conference on International Co-operation in Statistics, London
1920. International Financial Conference, Brussels
1922. Genoa Conference
1923. International Conference on Customs and Other Similar Formalities, Geneva
1927. International Economic Conference, Geneva
1927–1929. International Conferences for the Abolition of Import and Export Prohibitions and Restrictions, Geneva
1928–1929. International Conferences on Hides, Skins, and Bones, Geneva
1928. International Conference on Economic Statistics, Geneva
1929. International Conference on the Treatment of Foreigners, Paris
1929. Counterfeiting Currency
1930–1931. International Conferences with a View to Concerted Economic Action, Geneva

1930–1931. International Conference for the Unification of Laws on Bills of Exchange, Promissory Notes, and Cheques, Geneva
1932. Stresa Conference
1933. Wheat Conference, London
1933. Monetary and Economic Conference, London
1937. Sugar, Geneva
1939. European Conference on Rural Life (prepared but not convened)

CONFERENCE ON INTERNATIONAL CO-OPERATION IN STATISTICS, LONDON, 1919

Conference on International Co-operation in Statistics. August 14th and 15th, 1919. London, no date. 41 p. <E.&F.1.>

The Economic and Financial Section of the provisional organization of the League of Nations invited members of the Institute of Agriculture at Rome, the International Statistical Institute at The Hague, and of the Bureau founded in connection with that Institute, to meet in London with other leading statisticians.

INTERNATIONAL FINANCIAL CONFERENCE, BRUSSELS, 1920

Records of the Conference

Proceedings of the Conference: Volume I: Report of the Conference. London, 1920. 47 p. Volume II: Verbatim Record of the Debates. London, 1920. 168 p., bilingual. Volume III: Statement on the Financial Situation of the Countries Represented at the Conference. London, 1920. 210 p. Documents of the Conference: Volume IV: Statistical Memoranda on Currency, Public Finance and Trade: Part I: Currency Statistics. 63 p., bilingual. Part II: Public Finance. 215 p., bilingual. Part III: International Trade. London, 1920. 83 p., bilingual. Volume V: Memoranda of Economic Experts. London, 1920. 129 p.[26]

Volume I includes the resolutions proposed by the Four Commissions of the Conference, namely, Commission on Public Finance, Commission on Currency and Exchange, Commission on International Trade, and Commission on International Credits. Volume V contains Monetary Problems: 1.Introduction and Joint Statement of Economic Experts. 2.Memorandum Prepared for the International Conference at Brussels, by Dr. G.W.J. Bruins. 3.Memorandum on the World's Monetary Problems, by Professor Gustav Cassel. 4.Memorandum on Credit, Currency and Exchange Fluctuations, by Professor A.C. Pigou. 5.Notes on the Financial and Monetary Situation, by Professor Charles Gide. 6.Memorandum Prepared for the International Conference at Brussels, by M. Pantaleoni.

[26]Vols. I and II were printed in Brussels, but published in London. Vols. III–V were printed and published in London by Harrison & Son, Ltd., for the League of Nations.

The Conference in Retrospect

Brussels Financial Conference, 1920. The Recommendations and Their Application: A Review after Two Years. Volume I: New and enlarged ed., Economics and Finance Section, December, 1922. 243 p. [C.10.M.7.1923.II.]. Volume II: Italy. Economics and Finance Section, December, 1922. 91 p. [C.10.M.7.1923.II.]. Volume III: Economics and Finance Section, March, 1923. 40 p. [C.10.M.7.1923.II.]. Volume IV: (Reports Concerning Bulgaria and France.) Economics and Finance Section, July, 1923. 70 p. [C.10.M.7.1923.II(Vol.IV).]

Includes replies to a request by the League of Nations on how far the states which took part in the Brussels Financial Conference in September,1920, had succeeded in putting its recommendations into practice. Volume I contains reports from 21 states. Volume II contains the reply from Italy. Volume III contains reports from Brazil, Latvia, and Poland. Volume IV contains reports from Bulgaria and France.

GENOA CONFERENCE, 1922

The Genoa Conference and the League of Nations. Memorandum by the Secretary-General. Geneva, 1922. 6 p.+6 p., bilingual. [C.423.M.257.1922.]

INTERNATIONAL CONFERENCE ON CUSTOMS AND OTHER SIMILAR FORMALITIES, GENEVA, 1923

International Conference on Customs and Other Similar Formalities. Geneva, October 15th to November 3rd, 1923. Proceedings of the Conference. Volume I: Geneva, 1924. 215 p. [C.66.M.24.1924.II.]. Volume II: Geneva, 1924. p. 220–321. [C.66.M.24.1924.II.]

Volume I contains: Part I. A. Introductions. B. Official Instruments Approved by the Conference.[27] Part II. Minutes of the Plenary Meetings. Part III. Annexes. Volume II contains: Part IV. Minutes of Committee-A. Part V. Minutes of Committee-B. Part VI. Minutes of Committee-C. Index.

[27]The Official Instruments include the International Convention Relating to the Simplification of Customs Formalities, and Protocol, p.6–31; also published in 30 *Treaty Series*, p.371–412, bilingual. In force since November 27,1924. See also *Application of the International Convention (Measures Taken by Governments to Give Effect to the Provisions of the Convention)* <E.268>: Nine Series of Summaries Communicated by Governments in Execution of Article 9, 1926–1936: [C.354.M.127.1927.II.], [C.180.M.56.1928.II.], [C.126.M.42.1929.II.], [C.539.M.193.1929.II.], [C.183.M.85.1930.II.], [C.557.M.223.1930.II.], [C.227.M.95.1931.II.B.], [C.270.M.140.1933.II.B.], [C.226.M.138.1936.II.B.] See also *Application of Articles 10 and 11 of the Convention* [C.198.M.75.1929.II.]: Seven Series of Summaries, 1929–1937: [C.563.M.224.1930.II.], [C.913.M.479.1931.II.B.], [C.698.M.335.1932.II.B.], [C.321.M.165.1935.II.B.], [C.478.M.254.1935.II.B.], [C.186.M.132.1937.II.B.]

INTERNATIONAL ECONOMIC CONFERENCE,
GENEVA, 1927[28]

Preparatory Work

PREPARATORY COMMITTEE

Preparatory Committee for the International Economic Conference. Report on the First Session of the Committee, Held at Geneva from April 26th to May 1st, 1926. Geneva, 1926. 16 p. [A.24. 1926.II.] [C.270.M.105.1926.II.] <C.E.C.P.17.> (1926.II.13.)

Preparatory Committee for the International Economic Conference. Report to the Council on the Second Session of the Committee, Held at Geneva from November 15th to 19th, 1926. Geneva, 1926. 10 p. [C.638.M.257.1926.II.] (1926.II.57.)

Work of the Preparatory Committee for the International Economic Conference. Report to the Assembly by the Second Committee. Rapporteur: M. Loucheur (Delegate of France). Geneva, 1926. 2 p. [A.76.1926.II.] (1926.II.39.)

MEMORANDA RELEASED FOR PUBLICATION BY THE PREPARATORY
COMMITTEE

Bowley, A. L. Estimates of the Working Population of Certain Countries in 1931 and 1941. Geneva, 1926. 19 p. <C.E.C.P.59(1).> (1926.II.67.)

Brunet, M. J. Stability of Customs Tariffs. Geneva, 1927. 11 p. <C.E.C.P.71(1).> (1927.II.17.)

Cassel, Gustav. Recent Monopolistic Tendencies in Industry and Trade: Being an Analysis of the Nature and Causes of the Poverty of Nations. Geneva, 1927. 48 p. <C.E.C.P.98.> (1927.II.36.)

Grossmann, Eugene. Methods of Economic Rapprochement. Geneva, 1926. 36 p. <C.E.C.P.24(1).> (1926.II.69.)

Hirsch, Julius. National and International Monopolies from the Point of Labour, the Consuming Public and Rationalisation. Geneva, 1926. 44 p. <C.E.C.P.99.>

Houston, David. Memorandum on Rationalisation in the United States. Geneva, 1926. 9 p. <C.E.C.P.20(1).> (1927.II.3.)

McGregor, D. H. International Cartels. Geneva, 1927. 7 p. <C.E. C.P.93.> (1927.II.16.)

Oualid, William. The Social Effects of International Industrial Agreements: The Protection of Workers and Consumers. Geneva, 1926. 35 p. <C.E.C.P.94.>[29]

---

[28]Usually referred to as the World Economic Conference.
[29] This monograph was prepared by the International Labor Office. Since it was sold through the Publications Department of that organization, there is no League sales number.

Page, W. T. Memorandum on Discriminatory Tariff Classifications. Geneva, 1927. 11 p. <C.E.C.P.96.> (1927.II.27.)

—————— Memorandum on European Bargaining Tariffs. Geneva, 1927. 14 p. <C.E.C.P.97.> (1927.II.28.)

Rousiers, Paul de. Cartels and Trusts and Their Development. Geneva, 1927. 24 p. <C.E.C.P.95.> (1927.II.21.)

Viner, Jacob. Memorandum on Dumping. Geneva, 1926. 19 p. <C.E.C.P.36(1).> (1926.II.63.)

Wiedenfeld, Kurt. Cartels and Combines. Geneva, 1927. 36 p. <C.E.C.P.57(1).> (1926.II.70.)

BIBLIOGRAPHY

Guide to the Preparatory Documents of the Conference. Geneva, 1927. 43 p. <C.E.I.40.> (1927.II.41.)

An annotated bibliography; notes by Sir Artur Salter.

Proceedings and Final Report

PROCEEDINGS

Report and Proceedings of the World Economic Conference, Held at Geneva, May 4th to 23rd, 1927. Volume I: Geneva, 1927. 246 p. [C.356.M.129.1927.II.] <C.E.I.46.> (1927.II.52.^{I}.). Volume II: Geneva, 1927. 250 p. [C.356.M.129.1927.II.] <C.E.I.46.> (1927. II.52.^{II}.)

Journal of the International Economic Conference, Geneva, 1927. Nos. 1–18. Geneva, 1927. 231 p., bilingual.

AGENDA

Agenda of the Conference. Report of the Preparatory Committee to the Council on Its Second and Last Session, Held at Geneva from November 15th to 19th, 1926, and Resolution Adopted by the Council on December 9th, 1926. Geneva, 1926. 22 p. <C.E.I.6.> (1926.II.64.)

FINAL REPORT

The World Economic Conference, Geneva, May, 1927. Final Report. Geneva, 1927. 76 p. <C.E.I.44(1).> (1927.I.46(a).)

World Economic Conference. Discussion and Declarations on the Report of the Conference at the Council of the League of Nations, on June 16th, 1927. Geneva, 1927. 14 p. <C.E.I.45.> (1927.II. 50.)

Official Declarations Concerning the Recommendations of the International Economic Conference Held at Geneva in May 1927. Geneva, 1928. 55 p. <C.E.I.45 (1)> (1928.II.4.)

EFFECT OF THE CONFERENCE[30]

Consultative Committee. Application of the Recommendations of the International Economic Conference. Report on the Period May 1928 to May 1929. Geneva, 1929. 65 p. [C.130.M.45.1929. II.] <C.C.E.53.> (1929.II.12.)

Documentation

GENERAL ECONOMIC SITUATION AND CONDITIONS

Principal Features and Problems of the World Economic Position from the Point of View of Different Countries. First Series: Austria, Finland, Great Britain, Luxemburg, Netherlands, Sweden. Geneva, 1927. 38 p. <C.E.I.29.1st Series.> (1927.II.31(a).). Second Series: Italy, Latvia, Norway, Portugal. Geneva, 1927. 34 p. <C.E.I.29.2nd Series.> (1927.II.31(b).). Third Series: Bulgaria, Estonia, Hungary, Kingdom of the Serbs, Croats and Slovenes. Geneva, 1927. 35 p. <C.E.I.29.3rd Series.> (1927.II.31(c).). Fourth Series: Czechoslovakia, Denmark, India, New Zealand. Geneva, 1927. 31 p. <C.E.I.29.4th Series.> (1927.II.31(d).). Fifth Series: Belgium, Brazil, Colombia, Greece, Poland, Union of South Africa. Geneva, 1927. 43 p. <C.E.I.29.5th Series.> (1927. II.31(e).)

Memorandum on the Balance of Payments and Foreign Trade Balances, 1911–1925. Volume I: Balance of Payments and Review of World Trade. Geneva, 1926. 239 p. <C.E.I.2.> (1926.II.51.I^{1}.). Volume II: Trade Statistics of Sixty-three Countries (Including Provisional Summary Figures for 1926). Geneva, 1927. 812 p. <C.E.I.2.> (1926.II.51.II^{11}.)

Memorandum on Currency and Central Banks, 1913–1925. Volume I: Geneva, 1926. 104 p. <C.E I.1.> (1926.II.28.). Volume II: Geneva, 1926. 214 p. <C.E.I.1.> (1926.II.28.)

Memorandum on Production and Trade. Geneva, 1926. 47 p. <C. E.I.3.> (1926.II.52.)

Memorandum on Public Finance (1922–1925). Geneva, 1927. 482 p. <C.E.I.34.> (1927.II.29.)

Natural Movement of Populations During the First Quarter of the Twentieth Century. Geneva, 1926. 7p. <C.E.I.4.(1).> (1926.II.61.)

Population and Natural Resources. Geneva, 1927. 70 p. <C.E.I. 39.> (1927.II.38.)

[30]See also *Report of the Economic Consultative Committee on Its First Session. Held in Geneva from May 14th to 19th,1928*. Geneva,1928. 28 p. [C.217.M.73.1928.II.] <C.C. E.49(1).> (1928.II.18.); and *Report of the Economic Consultative Committee on Its Second Session. Held in Geneva from May 6th to 11th,1929*. Geneva,1929. 37 p. [C.192. M.73.1929.II.] <C.C.E.87(1).> (1929.II.23.)

INDUSTRY

General: Summary Memorandum on Various Industries. Geneva, 1927. 40 p. <C.E.I.19.> (1927.II.10.)

Chemical: The Chemical Industry. Geneva, 1927. 134 p. <C.E.I. 10.> (1927.II.4.)

Coal: Memorandum on Coal. Volume I: Geneva, 1927. 75 p. <C.E. I.18.(Vol.I.).> (1927.II.9.^{I}). Volume II: Geneva, 1927. 56 p. <C. E.I.18.> (1927.II.9.^{II})

Cotton: Memorandum on Cotton. Geneva, 1927. 78 p. <C.E.I.9.> (1927.II.1.)

Electrical: Electrical Industry. Geneva, 1927. 121 p. <C.E.I.16.> (1927.II.7.)

Iron and Steel: Memorandum on the Iron and Steel Industry. Geneva, 1927. 113 p. <C.E.I.17.> (1927.II.8.)

Management: Scientific Management in Europe. Geneva, 1926. 15 p. <C.E.I.13.>
  Prepared by the International Labor Office.

Mechanical Engineering: Mechanical Engineering. Volume I: Geneva, 1927. 193 p. <C.E.I.15.Vol.I.> (1927.II.6^I). Volume II: Geneva, 1927. 92 p. <C.E.I.15.Vol.II.> (1927.II.6^{II})

Potash: Potash Industry. Geneva, 1927. 27 p. <C.E.21.> (1927.II. 12.)

Shipbuilding: Shipbuilding. Geneva, 1927. 48 p. <C.E.I.8.> (1927. II.2.)

Silk: The Artificial Silk Industry. Geneva, 1927. 51 p. <C.E.I.30.> (1927.II.25.)

Silk: Natural Silk Industry. Geneva, 1927. 34 p. <C.E.I.24.> (1927.II.15.)

LABOR CONDITIONS

Living Standards: Report on the Standard of Living of Workers in Various Countries. Geneva, 1926. 55 p. <C.E.I.26.>

Migration: Reports on Legislation Concerning the Movement of Labour and Migration in General. Geneva, 1926. 38 p. <C.E.I. 12.>

Migration: Migration in Its Various Forms. Geneva, 1926. 28 p. <C.E.I.25.>
  Documents/<C.E.I.26.>, <C.E.I.12.>, and <C.E.I.25.> were prepared by the International Labor Office.

Recruiting: Recruitment and Training of Skilled Workers and Technical Staff in Great Britain and Germany. From Information Supplied by Sir Arthur Balfour and M. C. Lammers. Geneva, 1927. 9 p. <C.E.I.38.> (1927.II.37.)

AGRICULTURE

Agricultural Problems and Their International Aspects. Rome, no date. 62 p. <C.E.I.36.>

Prepared by the International Institute of Agriculture, Rome.

Agriculture and the International Economic Crisis: Memorandum by Jules Gautier, Dr. Andreas Hermes, and Mr. H. A. F. Lindsey... Geneva, 1927. 26 p. <C.E.I.43.> (1927.II.39.)

Results of Certain of the Enquiries for Instituting a Comparison between the Retail Prices in Private Trade and Those of Distributive Co-operative Societies. Geneva, 1926. 31 p. <C.E.11.>

The Part Played by Co-operative Organisations in the International Trade in Wheat, Dairy Produce, and Some Other Agricultural Products. Geneva, 1926. 46 p. <C.E.14.>

The Relation of Labor Cost to Total Costs of Production in Agriculture. Geneva, 1926. 66 p. <C.E.I.27.>

Documents <C.E.I.11>, <C.E.I.14>, and <C.E.I.27> were prepared by the International Labor Office.

TRADE AND TRADE POLICIES

Cartels: Review of Legislation on Cartels and Trusts . . . by Clemens Lammers. Geneva, 1927. 40 p. <C.E.I.35.> (1927.II.33.)

Commercial Treaties: Commercial Treaties: Tariff Systems and Contractual Methods, by D. Serruys . . . Geneva, 1927. 15 p. <C.E.I.31.> (1927.II.26.)

Dumping: Memorandum on the Legislation of Different States for the Prevention of Dumping, with Special Reference to Exchange Dumping. Communicated by Dr. Trendelenburg . . . Geneva, 1927. 33 p. <C.E.I.7.> (1926.II.66.)

Export: Export Duties. I: Introduction by Hipolit Gliwic . . . II: List of Export Duties Established by the Economic and Financial Section. Geneva, 1927. 52 p. <C.E.I.23.> (1927.II.14.)

Export: 1: System of Fixing Export Prices. 2: Dependence of Trade on Control of Foreign Exchange. 3: Methods of Assessment for the Application of Ad Valorem Duties. 4: Variations in Tariffs in Accordance with the Origin of Goods, the Place Whence They Come, Their Destination, etc. 5: Consular Charges. Geneva, 1927. 44 p. <C.E.I.28.> (1927.II.20.)

Export: Marks of Origin. Part I: Obligation to Affix a Mark of Origin on Goods. Note . . . by the Secretariat of the League of Nations. Part II: Observations on Marks of Origin and the Various Laws Relating Thereto. Communication by Dr. Trendelenburg . . . Geneva, 1927. 59 p. <C.E.I.20.> (1927.II.11.)

Subsidies, etc.: 1. Direct and Indirect Subsidies. 2: Differential Taxes on Circulation, Consumption or Handling of Foreign Imported

Goods. 3: Regulation of Quantities of Imports and Exports Admitted. Geneva, 1927. 32 p. <C.E.I.42.> (1927.II.35.)

Tariffs: Abolition of Import and Export Prohibitions and Restrictions. Commentary and Preliminary Draft International Agreement Drawn up by the Economic Committee of the League of Nations to Serve as a Basis for an International Diplomatic Conference. Geneva, 1927. 33 p. <C.E.I.22.>

Tariffs: Customs Nomenclature and Customs Classification: Possibility of Unifying Customs Nomenclature. Transmitted by Dr. Trendelenburg. Geneva, 1927. 83 p. <C.E.I.32.> (1927.24.)

Tariffs: 1: Immunities of State Enterprise. 2: Railway Tariffs and Tolls as an Economic Factor. 3: National and Flag Discrimination with Regard to Communications and Transit. 4: Unfair Commercial Practices. Geneva, 1927. 36 p. <C.E.I.33.> (1927.II.32.)

Tariffs: Tariff Level Indices. Geneva, 1927. 38 p. <C.E.I.37.> (1927.II.34.)

Contains observations on the methods employed and the results of computation transmitted by MM. Schüller (Austria), Brunet (Belgium), Trendelenburg (Germany), the Hungarian Delegation to the League of Nations, M. di Nola (Italy), M. N. Sato (Japan), T. W. Page (United States of America).

Bibliography

Guide to the Documents of the Conference.[31] Geneva, 1927. 44 p. <C.E.I.40.(1).> (1927.II.41(a).)

Contains a complete list of documents, with indication of their contents, according to the Order of the program of the Conference Notes, by Sir Arthur Salter.

INTERNATIONAL CONFERENCES FOR THE ABOLITION OF IMPORT AND EXPORT PROHIBITIONS AND RESTRICTIONS, 1927–1929

International Conference for the Abolition of Import and Export Prohibitions and Restrictions. Geneva, October 17th to November 8th, 1927. Proceedings of the Conference. Geneva, 1928. 257 p. [C.21.M.12.1928.II.] (1928.II.7.)

See especially Commentary and Preliminary Draft International Agreement for the Abolition of Import and Export Prohibitions and Restrictions Submitted by the Economic Committee of the League of Nations, Annex I, p. 235; and Resolutions Relative to Import and Export Prohibitions and Restrictions Adopted by the Eighth Session of the Assembly of the League of Nations, the International Economic Conference, the Stockholm Congress of the International Chamber of Commerce, the Twenty-fourth Inter-Parliamentary Conference, Annex II, p. 235–237.

Second International Conference for the Abolition of Import and

[31]See also Eric C. Wendelin, *Subject Index to the Economic and Financial Documents of The League of Nations,1927-1930* (Boston, 1932), 190 p.

Export Prohibitions and Restrictions. Geneva, July 3rd to 19th, 1928. Proceedings of the Conference. Geneva, 1928. 131 p. [C. 611.M.187.1928.II.] (1929.II.9.)

See especially the Official Instruments of the Conference, p.9–36. 1.Supplementary Agreement to the Convention of November 8th,1927, for the Abolition of Import and Export Prohibitions and Restrictions. II. Protocol to the Supplementary Agreement. III. Final Act.

Third International Conference for the Abolition of Import and Export Prohibitions and Restrictions. Held in Paris from December 5th to 20th, 1929. Proceedings of the Conference. Geneva, 1930. 60 p. [C.176.M.81.1930.II.] (1930.II.13.)

See especially Annex 5, p. 59–60, Third Draft Protocol Concerning the Entry into Force of the International Convention of November 8th,1927, and of the Supplementary Agreement of July 11th,1928.[32]

INTERNATIONAL CONFERENCES ON HIDES, SKINS, AND BONES, GENEVA, 1928–1929

First International Conference on Hides, Skins, and Bones, Geneva, March 14–16, 1928

International Convention for the Abolition of Import and Export Prohibitions and Restrictions, November 8th, 1927. Execution of Recommendation No. 3 of the Final Act of the Conference, Signed November 8th, 1927. Protocols Concerning . . . the Export of Hides, Skins and Bones, Drawn up by the Meeting of Representatives of States Interested, Signatories to the International Convention of November 8th, 1927, Held at Geneva from March 14th to 16th, 1928. Geneva, 1928. 7 p. [C.149.M.39.1928.II.] (1928.II.11.)

Meeting of Government Representatives to Consider the Question of the Export of Hides, Skins and Bones. Held at Geneva from March 14th to 16th, 1928. Proceedings of the Meeting. Geneva, 1928. 46 p.; Annexes partly in French. [C.198.M.66.1928.II.] (1928.II.21.)

Second International Conference on Hides, Skins, and Bones, Geneva, June 29–July 11, 1928

Proceedings of the Conference. Geneva, 1928. 62 p. [C.524.M.154. 1928.II.] (1928.II.47.)

Contains: Part One: I: Note by the Secretary-General; II. Official Instruments of the Conference. Part Two: Minutes of the Meetings of the Conference.

International Agreement Relating to the Exportation of Hides and Skins,[33] and Protocol. Geneva, 1929. 19 p., bilingual; in part

[32]In force since 1930.
[33]Also in 95 *Treaty Series*, p.357–372; in force since October 1,1929.

double-paged. [C.11.M.8.1929.II.] <C.I.A.P./P.O.15.(2).> (1929.
II.2.)

International Agreement Relating to the Exportation of Bones (and
Protocol).[34] Geneva, 1929. 13 p., bilingual. [C.12.M.9.1929.II.] <C.
I.A.P./P.O.16.(2).> (1929.II.3.)

*Third International Conference on Hides, Skins, and Bones, Geneva,
August 29–September 11, 1929*

Proceedings of the Conference. Geneva, 1930. 35 p. [C.92.M.18.
1930.II.] (1930.II.4.)

> Contains: Part I: 1.Note by the Secretary-General; 2.Official Instruments of the
> Conference. Part II: Minutes of the Plenary Meetings of the Conference. Part III:
> Declarations Made on Behalf of Certain Countries on the Occasion of the Signature
> of the Protocol of September 11th,1929, and Concerning the Application of the Pro-
> visions of the Agreement of July 11th,1928, Relating to the Exportation of Bones.

Third International Conference Relating to the Exportation of
Hides and Skins and of Bones. Geneva, August 29th to September
11th, 1929. Final Act. Geneva, 1929. 6 p. [C.438.M.146.1929.II.]
<C.I.A.P./P.O.22.> (1929.II.38.)

INTERNATIONAL CONFERENCE ON ECONOMIC STATISTICS, GENEVA, 1928

International Conference on Economic Statistics. Geneva, 1928.
Preparatory Documents. Geneva, 1928. 101 p. Geneva, 1928.
<C.S.O.1.> (1928.II.6.)

Draft Convention Relating to Economic Statistics. Geneva, 1928.
63 p. [C.340.M.98.1928.II.] <C.S.O.2.>

Proceedings of the International Conference Relating to Economic
Statistics. Geneva, November 26th to December 14th, 1928. Geneva, 1929. 361 p. [C.163.M.64.1929.II.] (1929.II.21.)

> Includes International Convention Relating to Economic Statistics,[35] p.309–313;
> Protocol,[36] p. 314–315; and Final Act of the Conference,[37] p. 333–341.

INTERNATIONAL CONFERENCE ON THE TREAT-MENT OF FOREIGNERS, PARIS, 1929

International Conference on the Treatment of Foreigners. Prepara-

[34]Also in 95 *Treaty Series*, p.373–393, bilingual; in force since October 1,1929.
[35]Also published in 110 *Treaty Series*, p. 172–195, bilingual. In force since December
14,1930.
[36]Also published in 110 *Treaty Series*, 196–201, bilingual. For related questions see also
ibid., p. 203–283. In force since December 14,1930.
[37]The "International Convention Relating to Economic Statistics" was also published
as a separate document, [C.606(1).M.184(1).1928.II.] <C.S.O.73.> (1928.II.52.).
Geneva,1928. 79 p.

tory Documents. Draft Convention Prepared by the Economic Committee of the League of Nations to Serve as a Basis for Discussion at the International Conference. . . . Geneva, November 5th, 1929. Geneva, 1929. 97 p. [C.36.M.21.1929.II.] <C.I.T.E.1.> (1929.II.5.)[38]

Proceedings of the International Conference on the Treatment of Foreigners. First Session. Paris, November 5th–December 5th, 1929. Geneva, 1930. 573 p. [C.97.M.23.1930.II.] <C.I.T.E.62.> (1930.II.5.)

INTERNATIONAL CONFERENCES WITH A VIEW TO CONCERTED ECONOMIC ACTION, GENEVA, 1930–1931

Proceedings of the Preliminary Conference with a View to Concerted Economic Action. Held at Geneva from February 17th to March 24th, 1930. Geneva, 1930. 447 p., in part bilingual. [C.222.M.109. 1930.II.] (1930.II.17.)

Includes: 1. Commerical Convention, p. 15–26. 2. Protocol to the Commercial Convention, p.28–33. 3. Protocol Regarding the Programme of Future Negotiations, p. 34–55. 4. Final Act, p. 56–73.

Proceedings of the Second International Conference with a View to Concerted Economic Action. First Session. Held at Geneva from November 17th to 28th, 1930. Geneva, 1931. 263 p. [C.149.M. 48.1931.II.B.] (1931.B.3.)

The Final Act of the Conference is on p. 10–26.

Proceedings of the Second International Conference with a View to Concerted Economic Action. Second Session. Held at Geneva, from March 16th to 18th, 1931. Geneva, 1931. 38 p. [C.269.M. 124.1931.II.B.] (1931.II.B.10.)

INTERNATIONAL CONFERENCE FOR THE UNIFICATION OF LAWS ON BILLS OF EXCHANGE, PROMISSORY NOTES, AND CHEQUES, GENEVA, 1930–1931[39]

Records of the International Conference for the Unification of Laws on Bills of Exchange, Promissory Notes and Cheques. Geneva, May 13th–June 7th, 1930. First Session. Bills of Exchange and

---

[38]This document was released in Geneva, March 5,1929. The Conference met at Paris; see Document [C.97.M.23.1930.II.].

[39]For earlier phases of the League's work in this field, see Provisional Economic and Financial Committee, *Legislation Concerning Bills of Exchange. Questionnaire to be Addressed to Governments.* Geneva, 1921. 3 p., bilingual. <E.F.S.60.> <E.F.50(b).>. See also *Unification of Laws Relating to Bills of Exchange and Promissory Notes. General*

Promissory Notes. Geneva, 1930. 470 p., in part bilingual. [C.360. M.151.1930.II.] (1930.II.27.)

Includes: 1.Convention Providing a Uniform Law for Bills of Exchange and Promissory Notes (with Protocol and Annexes), p.21–63.[40] 2.Convention for the Settlement of Certain Conflicts of Laws in Connection with Bills of Exchange and Promissory Notes (with Protocol),[41] p.64–85. 3.Convention on the Stamp Laws in Connection with Bills of Exchange and Promissory Notes (with Protocol),[42] p.86–105. Final Act, p.106–117, bilingual.

Records of the International Conference for the Unification of Laws on Bills of Exchange, Promissory Notes and Cheques. Held at Geneva from February 23rd to March 19th, 1931. Second Session. Cheques. Geneva, 1931. 402 p. [C.294.M.137. 1931.II.B.] (1931.II.B.11.)

Includes: 1.Convention Providing a Uniform Law for Cheques (with Protocol and Annexes),[43] p.18–43. 2.Convention for the Settlement of Certain Conflicts of Laws in Connection with Cheques (with Protocol),[44] p.44–59. 3.Convention on the Stamp Laws in Connection with Cheques (with Protocol),[45] p.60–69. 4.Final Act of the Conference (Second Session),[46] p.70–87.

MONETARY AND ECONOMIC CONFERENCE,
LONDON, 1933[47]

Draft Annotated Agenda. Submitted by the Preparatory Commission of Experts. Geneva, 1933. 37 p. [C.48.M.18.1933.II.] <Conf. M.E.I.> (1933.II.Spec.1.)

Reports Approved by the Conference on July 27th, 1933, and Resolutions Adopted by the Bureau and the Executive Committee. London, 1933. 47 p. [C.435.M.220.1933.II.] <Conf.M.E.22(1).> (1933.II.Spec.4.)

Report and Individual Reports Submitted by Professor Josephus Jitta (Netherlands); Sir Mackenzie D. Chalmers, K.C.B. (Great Britain); Professor Dr. Franz Klein (Austria); Professor Ch. Lyon-Caen (France). Geneva, 1923. 150 p. [C.487.M.203.1923.II.] <E.106.>

[40]Also in 143 *Treaty Series,* p. 257–315, bilingual. In force since January, 1934.
[41]Also in 143 *Treaty Series,* p. 317–335, bilingual. In force since January, 1934.
[42]Also in 143 *Treaty Series,* p. 337–353, bilingual. In force since January, 1934.
[43]Also in 143 *Treaty Series,* p. 356–405, bilingual. In force since January, 1934.
[44] Also in 143 *Treaty Series,* p. 408–427, bilingual. In force since January, 1934.
[45]Also in 143 *Treaty Series,* p. 7–23, bilingual. In force since November 29, 1933. Also published as Document [C.460.M.197.1931.II.B.] (1931.II.B.18.), 11 p.; in part double-paged.
[46]Also published as Document [C.461.M.198.1931.II.B.] (1931.II.B.19.), 12 p.; in part double-paged.
[47]For President Franklin D. Roosevelt's attitude toward this conference, see *The Public Papers and Addresses of Franklin D. Roosevelt,* Vol. II: *The Year of Crisis, 1933* (New York, 1938), especially items 34, 43, 87, 88, 103. See also Arnold J. Toynbee, *Survey of International Affairs, 1933* (London, 1934), p. 35–81.

Journal of the Monetary and Economic Conference, London, 1933. Nos. 1–39, June 10th–July 28th, 1933. No date. 248 p.

Contains the only published record of the Proceedings of the Conference.

EUROPEAN CONFERENCE ON RURAL LIFE, 1939

Committee Report and Assembly Resolution

European Conference on Rural Life. Report Submitted by the Second and Seventh Committees to the Assembly. Rapporteur: Mr. Stoykovitch (Yugoslavia). No date. 3 p. [A.56.1938.]

European Conference on Rural Life. Resolution Adopted on September 29th, 1938 (Morning). *Official Journal*, Special Supplement No. 182, October, 1938, p. 13.

Technical Documentation

CONTRIBUTIONS BY THE INTERNATIONAL INSTITUTE OF AGRICULTURE

Population and Agriculture, with Special Reference to Agricultural Overpopulation. Contributions by the International Institute of Agriculture. (Document No. 1). No date. 63 p. [C.18.M.10.1939.] <Conf.E.V.R.6.> (European Conference on Rural Life 3)

The Land Tenure Systems in Europe. Contributions by the International Institute of Agriculture. (Document No. 2). No date. 71 p. [C.19.M.11.1939.] <Conf.E.V.R.7.> (European Conference on Rural Life 4)

The Capital and Income of Farms in Europe as They Appear from the Farm Accounts for the Years 1927–1928 to 1934–1935. Contributions by the International Institute of Agriculture. (Document No. 3). No date. 106 p. [C.20.M.12.1939.] <Conf.E.V.R.8.> (European Conference on Rural Life 5)

Land Reclamation and Improvement in Europe. Contributions by the International Institute of Agriculture. (Document No. 4). No date. 51 p. [C.21.M.13.1939.] <Conf.E.V.R.9.> (European Conference on Rural Life 6)

Conditions and Improvement of Crop Production, Stock-Raising and Rural Industries. Contributions by the International Institute of Agriculture. (Document No. 5). No date. 48 p. [C.22.M.14.1939.] <Conf.E.V.R.10.> (European Conference on Rural Life 7)

Government Action Concerned with Agricultural Market and Production. Contributions by the International Institute of Agriculture. (Document No. 6). No date. 44 p. [C.23.M.15.1939.] <Conf.E.V.R.11.> (European Conference on Rural Life 8)

SURVEYS PREPARED BY THE INTERNATIONAL LABOUR OFFICE

Co-operative Action in Rural Life: Survey Prepared by the Co-operation Service of the International Labour Office. Geneva, 1939.

42 p. [C.1.M.1.1939.] <Conf.E.V.R.2.> (European Conference on Rural Life 9)

Sickness Insurance and Rural Medical Assistance. Prepared by the International Labour Office. Geneva, 1939. 33 p. [C.87.M.47.1939.] <Conf.E.V.R.15.> (European Conference on Rural Life 15)

Recreation in Rural Areas. Report Prepared by the International Labour Office. Geneva, 1939. 34 p. [C.109.M.64.1939.] <Conf.E.V.R.17.> (European Conference on Rural Life 17)

SURVEY PREPARED BY THE INTERNATIONAL INSTITUTE OF INTELLECTUAL CO-OPERATION

Intellectual Aspects of Rural Life. Prepared by the International Institute of Intellectual Co-operation. Geneva, 1939. 56 p. [C.90. M.49.1939.] <Conf.E.V.R.16.> (European Conference on Rural Life 16)

SURVEY PREPARED UNDER THE AUSPICES OF THE HEALTH COMMITTEE

General Survey of Medico-social Policy in Rural Areas. Prepared under the Services of the Health Committee. Geneva, 1939. [C.60. M.22.1939.] <Conf.E.V.R.13.> (European Conference on Rural Life 13)

Rural Housing and Planning. Report Prepared under the Auspices of the Health Committee. Geneva, 1939. 58 p. [C.125.M.77.1939.] <Conf.E.V.R.20.> (European Conference on Rural Life 18)

Rural Dietaries in Europe. Annex: Report on Bread. Report Prepared under the Auspices of the Health Committee. Geneva, 1939. 84 p. [C.183.M.112.1939.] <Conf.E.V.R.25.> (European Conference on Rural Life 26)

TECHNICAL INSTRUCTION FOR AGRICULTURISTS

The Organisation of Technical Instruction for Agriculturists, by J. Van Der Vaeren, President of the International Commission for Instruction in Agriculture . . . . Geneva, 1939. 29 p. [C.75.M.36. 1939.] <Conf.E.V.R.14.> (European Conference on Rural Life 14)

5. ECONOMIC RECONSTRUCTION OF INDIVIDUAL COUNTRIES

AUSTRIA

Various Documents

Financial Committee. Report and Papers Relative to the Financial Reconstruction of Austria. Geneva, June 15, 1921. 98 p., bilingual; containing moreover several documents in German. [C.103.M.56. 1921.II.] <E.F-S.102.> [A.73.]

The Economic Situation of Austria. Report Presented to the Council of the League of Nations by W. T. Layton . . . and Charles Rist. Geneva, 1925. 213 p. [C.440(1).M.162(1).1925.II.]

Financial Reconstruction of Austria. Dates and Conditions of Termination of Control. Resolution Adopted by the Council of the League of Nations on September 10th, 1925. (With the Relevant Documents and Public Statements). Geneva, 1925. 10 p. [C.541. 1925.II.] <F.253.>

Financial Reconstruction of Austria. Termination of the Functions of the Commissioner-General. Geneva, 1926. 8 p. [C.385.1926.II.] <F.290.> (1926.II.22.)

The Financial Reconstruction of Austria. General Survey and Principal Documents. Geneva, 1926. 312 p. [C.568.M.232.1926.II.] (1926.II.30.)

See especially Protocols Containing the Scheme for the Financial Reconstruction of Austria: Elaborated by the Council of the League of Nations and Signed at Geneva, October 4th,1922, p.137–150. Chronology of Austrian Reconstruction, p.280–290. Principal Public League of Nations Documents Concerning the Financial Reconstruction of Austria, p. 291–295.

Austrian Protocol. Approved by the Council on July 15th, 1932.[48] Geneva, 1932. 6 p. [C.539.M.270.1932.II.A.] (1932.II.A.16.)

Reports: Monthly Reports by the Commissioner-General of the League of Nations for Austria

First Report: First Report by the Commissioner-General of the League of Nations at Vienna Submitted to the Council on February 1st, 1923. No date. 31 p. [C.41.1923.]

Last Report: Forty-second Report by the Commissioner-General of the League of Nations for Austria (Sixth Month of the Sixth Stage-Period May 15th–June 15th, 1926.) Geneva, 1926. 25 p. [C.412.1926.I.] (1926.II.26.)[49]

Reports: Quarterly Reports by the Representative in Austria of the Financial Committee

First Report: Financial Position of Austria in the Last Quarter of 1931. First Quarterly Report by M. Rost van Tonningen, the Representative in Austria of the Financial Committee. Geneva, 1932. 27 p. [C.34.M.18.1932.II.A.] <F.996.> (1932.II.A.2.)

Last Report: Financial Position of Austria in the Second Quarter of 1936. Nineteenth Quarterly Report by M. Rost van Tonningen,

[48]Also in *Official Journal*, July, 1932, p.1460.
[49]See also *Index to the 42 Reports by the Commissioner General of the League of Nations for Austria* (*December1922 to June1926*). Geneva,1927. 24 p. [C.26.1927.II.] (1927.II.5.)

the Representative of the League of Nations in Austria. Geneva, 1936. 23 p. [C.294.M.179.1936.II.A.] <F.1531.> (1936.II.A.11.)

Reports: Financial Organization

First Report by the Financial Organisation of the League of Nations. July-October, 1936. Geneva, 1936. 27 p. (1936.II.A.25.)

Second Report by the Financial Organisation of the League of Nations. November, 1936–March, 1937. Geneva, 1937. 36 p. (1937. II.A.2.)

Third Report by the Financial Organisation of the League of Nations. April-August, 1937. Geneva, 1937. 28 pp. (1937.II.A.15.)

BULGARIA

Various Documents

Convention between Greece and Bulgaria Respecting Reciprocal Emigration, Signed at Neuilly-sur-Seine, November 27, 1919. 1 *Treaty Series*, p. 68–72, bilingual.

The Settlement of Bulgarian Refugees. Scheme for an International Loan. Protocol Signed at Geneva on September 8th, 1926. Geneva, 1926. 15 p. [C.522.M.204.1926.II.] <F.332.> (1926.II.34.)

Scheme for the Settlement of Bulgarian Refugees. General Description and Principal Documents. Geneva, 1926. 43 p. [C.569.M.211. 1926.II.] <F.322.> (1926.II.53.)

Bulgaria and Greece. Financial Agreement on the Procedure to be Followed in Regard to the Compensation Payable to Exchanged Populations and the Settlement of the Debts of Both Governments under This Heading. Signed at Geneva, December 9, 1927. 87 *Treaty Series*, p. 199–209.

Bulgarian Stabilisation Loan. Protocol and Annexes. Approved by the Council of the League of Nations and Signed on Behalf of the Bulgarian Government on March 10th, 1928. With Relevant Public Documents.[50] Geneva, 1928. 57 p. [C.338.M.96.1928.II.] <F. 547.> (1928.II.32.)

Reports: Financial Committee

First Report: Report of the Financial Committee on the Work of Its Forty-fifth Session. Appendices on Bulgaria. Geneva, 1932. 23 p. [C.333.M.202.1932.II.A.] <F.1063.> (1932.II.A.6.)

Last Report: Financial Committee. Fifty-second Session, Paris, October 4th–7th, 1933. Report to the Council on Bulgaria. Geneva, 1933. 1 p.+1 p., bilingual. [C.568.M.273.1933.II.A.] <F.1289.> (1933.II.A.25.)

[50]For the Bulgarian Refugee Settlement, see Stephen P. Ladas, *The Exchange of Minorities: Bulgaria, Greece and Turkey* (New York,1932), p.27–331.

Reports: Reports by the Commissioner of the League of Nations

First Report: Settlement of Bulgarian Refugees. First Report of the Commissioner of the League of Nations. September 15th–November 15th, 1926. Geneva, 1926. 25 p. [C.629.M.246.1926.II.] (1926. II.58.)

Last Report: Cinquante-deuxième Rapport du Commissaire de la Société des Nations en Bulgarie. Période juillet-septembre 1939.[51] Genève, 1939. 15 p. [C.366.M.279.1939.II.A.] <F.1695.> (1939. II.A.23.)

DANZIG

Loan

Danzig Municipal Loan. Resolutions Adopted by the Council of the League of Nations on March 14th, 1925, with the Relevant Documents and Public Statements. Geneva, 1925. 16 p. [C.204. M.63.1925.II.]

Reports by the Trustees

First Report: Danzig Municipal Loan. First Report by the Trustee for the Municipality of Danzig Seven Per Cent Mortgage Loan of 1925, Covering the Period from March 15th, 1925 till March 15th, 1926. Geneva, 1926. 7 p. [C.281.1926.II.] <F.276.> (1926.II.16.)

Last Report: Fourteenth Report[52] of the Trustee of the Municipality of Danzig. 5% (Originally 7%) Mortgage Loan of 1925, Covering the Period from March 15th, 1938 to March 15th, 1939. Geneva, 1939. 2 p., mimeographed. [C.119.M.73.1939.II.A.] <F.1665.>

ESTONIA

Various Documents

Report of the Financial Committee of the League of Nations on the Economic and Financial Situation of Esthonia. Geneva, 1925. 32 p. [C.240.M.92.1925.II.] <F.227.>

Banking and Currency Reform in Estonia. Protocol Signed at Geneva on December 10th, 1926. With the Relevant Reports of the Financial Committee and Council Resolutions, Together with the Text of the Estonian Financial Laws of April 29th and May 3rd, 1927. Geneva, 1927. 26 p. [C.227.M.89.1927.II.] (1927.II.45.)

[51]Beginning with the Thirtieth Report [C.136.M.54.1934.II.A.] <F.1338.> (1934. II.A.7.), the reports appeared only in French.

[52]The numbering of the reports is somewhat confusing, because of the diversity of subjects covered. The Eleventh Report [C.239.M.138.1938.II.] <F.1642> and the French report *Douzième Rapport* [C.322.M.238.1938.II.A.] <F.1692> both deal with the tobacco monopoly, and the Thirteenth Report [C.111.M.61.1938.II.A.] <F.1626> and the Fourteenth both deal with the loan.

Reports by the Trustee

First Report: Republic of Estonia (Banking and Currency Reform) 7% Loan, 1927. First Annual Report by the Trustee Covering the Period from June 15th, 1927 to June 30th, 1928. Geneva, 1928. 24 p. [C.186.M.60.1928.II.] <F.514.> (1928.II.42.)

Last Report: Republic of Estonia (Banking and Currency Reform) 7% Loan, 1927. Twelfth Annual Report by the Trustee for the Period from July 1st, 1938 to June 30th, 1939. Geneva, 1939. 2 p., mimeographed. [C.265.M.182.1939.II.A.] <F.1691.>

GREECE

Exchange of Greek and Turkish Populations

Reciprocal Exchange of Racial Minorities between Greece and Turkey. Report by Dr. Nansen, High Commissioner of the League of Nations.[53] Geneva, 1922. Unpaged, mimeographed. [C.736.M.447.1922.]

Relief Measures for Refugees in Greece and Asia Minor. Report by Dr. Nansen, High Commissioner of the League of Nations.[54] Geneva, 1922. 12 p., mimeographed. [C.736(a).M.447.(a).1922.]

Convention Concerning the Exchange of Greek and Turkish Populations, Signed at Lausanne, January 30th, 1923.[55] 32 *Treaty Series*, p. 75–87, bilingual.

Only the French text is official.

International Loan and Refugee Settlement Commission

The Settlement of Greek Refugees. Scheme for an International Loan. Protocol of September 29th, 1923. Amended September 19th, 1924. With the Relevant Documents and Public Statements, Including the Statutes of the Refugee Settlement Commission. Geneva, 1924. 39 p. [C.524.M.187.1924.II.]

Greek Stabilisation and Refugee Loan. Protocol and Annexes. Approved by the Council of the League of Nations and Signed on Behalf of the Hellenic Government on September 15th, 1927. With the Relevant Report of the Financial Committee and Resolutions of the Council and the Assembly. Geneva, 1927. 43 p. [C. 556.M.198.1927.II.] (1927.II.74.)

[53]For the exchange of Greek and Turkish populations, see Ladas, *The Exchange of Minorities.*
[54]The title of the document is given here as later reproduced in *Official Journal*, January, 1923, p. 133–136.
[55]The title of the document is given here as later reproduced in *Official Journal*, November, 1923, p. 1468–1470. See also "Treaty of Peace Signed at Lausanne, July 24, 1923," 28 *Treaty Series*, p. 11–113.

Convention between the Hellenic Government and the Refugee Settlement Commission. Signed at Geneva on January 24th, 1930. Geneva, 1930. 6 p. [C.107.M.31.1930.II.] <F.730(2).> (1930.II.6.)

Report on the Liquidation of the Refugee Settlement Commission.[56] Geneva, 1931. 14 p. [C.67.M.28.1931.II.] <F.879.> (1931.II.A.3.)

Reports: Quarterly Reports on the Work of the Refugee Settlement Commission

First Report: Greek Refugees: Report on the Operations of the Refugee Settlement Commission for the First Three Months. Geneva, 1924. 6 p. [C.91.M.30.1924.II.]

Last Report: Twenty-seventh Quarterly Report of the Refugee Settlement Commission. Geneva, 1930. 20 p. [C.444.M.202.1930.II.] <F.831.> (1930.II.30.)

Reports: Financial Committee

Report of the Financial Committee on the Work of its Forty-fifth Session. Appendices on Greece. Geneva, 1932. 13 p. [C.334.M. 203.1932.II.A.] <F.1064.> (1932.II.A.7.)

Financial Committee. Extraordinary Session Held at London from June 6th to June 14th, 1933. Geneva, 1933. 48 p. [C.387.M.194. 1933.II.A.] <F.1259.> (1933.II.A.14.)

General Survey

L'Établissement des réfugiés en Grèce. Genève, 1926. 233 p. (1926. II.32.)

HUNGARY

Various Documents

Financial Reconstruction of Hungary. Agreements Drawn up by the League of Nations and Signed at Geneva on March 14th, 1924, Together with the Documents and Public Declarations Relating Thereto. Geneva, 1924. 45 p. [C.185.M.53.1924.II.]

Financial Reconstruction of Hungary. Termination of the Functions of the Commissioner-General. Resolution Adopted by the Council of the League of Nations on June 10th, 1926 (with the Relevant Documents and Public Statements). Geneva, 1926. 8 p. [C.392. 1926.II.] <F.293.> (1926.II.23.)

The Financial Reconstruction of Hungary. General Survey and Principal Documents. Geneva, 1926. 248 p. [C.583.M.221.1926. II.] (1926.II.54.)

[56]For the conclusion of the work of the Mixed Commission for the Exchange of Greek and Turkish populations, see also the Greek-Turkish Convention signed at Ankara, December 9,1933, *Official Journal*, April 1934, p.389–391, and February,1935, p. 103–106.

Reports: Monthly Reports by the Commissioner-General of the League of Nations for Hungary

First Report: First Report by the Commissioner-General of the League of Nations for Hungary. May 1st to 31st, 1924. Geneva, 1924. 9 p. [C.250.1924.II.]

Last Report: Twenty-fifth (Final) Report by the Commissioner-General of the League of Nations for Hungary. May 1st-June 30th, 1936. Geneva, 1926. 13 p. [C.421.1926.II.] (1926.II.27.)[57]

Reports: Quarterly Reports by the Financial Committee's Representative in Hungary

First Report: First Quarterly Report by Mr. Royall Tyler, the Representative in Hungary of the Financial Committee. Geneva, 1932. 27 p. [C.31.M.16.1932.II.A.] (1932.II.A.1.)

Last Report: Twenty-fifth and Final Report by Mr. Royall Tyler, the Representative in Hungary of the Financial Committee. Geneva, 1938. 22 p. [C.87.M.41.1938.II.A.] <F.1624.> (1938.II.A.1.)

General

Principles and Methods of Financial Reconstruction Work Undertaken under the Auspices of the League of Nations. Geneva, 1930. 73 p. (1930.II.16.)

The League of Nations Reconstruction Schemes in the Inter-War Period. Geneva, 1945. 172 p. [C.59.M.59.1945.II.A.] <F.1696(1)> (1945.II.A.8.)

6. VARIOUS QUESTIONS

BANKING

Agricultural and Industrial Credit

International Agricultural Mortgage Credit Company: Convention, Charter and Statutes Approved by the Council of the League of Nations and Signed on May 21st, 1931 and Other Relevant Documents . . . Geneva, 1931. 37 p. [C.375.M.155.1931.II.A.] (1931.II.A.13.)

Report on International Agricultural Mortgage Credit Company. Systems of Agricultural Credit and Insurance Submitted by M. Louis Tardy. Geneva, 1938. 116 p. [C.479.M.322.1938.II.A.] (1938.II.A.24.)

Agricultural Credit. Medium-term Credit to Industry. Geneva, 1939.

[57]See also *Index to the 25 Reports of the Commissioner-General of the League of Nations for Hungary* (*May 1924 to June 1926*). Geneva, 1927. 13p. [C.163.1927.II.] (1927.II.30.)

23 p. [C.176.M.105.1939.II.A.(Pt.II.)] <F.1689.Pt.II.> (1939.II.A. 15.)

Part II of the report to the Council on the work of Sixty-eighth Session of the Financial Committee.

Bank for International Settlements

Bank for International Settlements. Extracts from Minutes of the Tenth Ordinary Session of the Assembly and of the Second Committee of the Assembly, September, 1929. Geneva, 1929. 18 p. [C.494.M.158.1929.II.] <F.720.> (1929.II.41.)

Convention Respecting the Bank for International Settlements with Annex[58], Signed at The Hague, January 20, 1930. 104 *Treaty Series*, p. 441–471, bilingual.

Includes the Constituent Charter of the Bank and the Statutes of the Bank for International Settlements.

Commercial Banks

Memorandum on Commercial Banks. Geneva, 1931. 429 p. (1931. II.A.26.)

Commercial Banks, 1925–1933. Geneva, 1934. 336 p. (1934.II.A.5.)

Commercial Banks, 1929–1934. Geneva, 1935. 213 p. (1935.II.A.2.)

Currencies and Central Banks

Memorandum on Currency and Central Banks, 1913–1924.[59] Volume I: Geneva, 1925. 238 p. Volume II: Geneva, 1925. 314 p.

Memorandum on Currency and Central Banks, 1913–1925. Geneva, 1926. Volume I: 104 p. Volume II: 214 p. <C.E.I.I.> (1926.II. 28.)

Economic Intelligence Service. Monetary and Central Bank Laws. Edited by Paul Singer. Geneva, 1932.

Thirty numbers, printed in limited edition, primarily designed for States Members, Contains monetary and central bank laws for the following countries, etc.: No. 1. Albania; No. 2, Austria; No. 3, Belgium; No. 4, Bank for International Settlements; No. 5, Bulgaria; No. 6, Czechoslovakia; No. 7, Free City of Danzig; No. 8, Denmark; No. 9, Estonia; No. 10. Finland; No. 11, France; No. 12, Germany; No. 13, Great Britain; No. 14, Greece; No. 15, Hungary; No. 16, Irish Free State; No. 17, Italy; No. 18, Latvia; No. 19, Lithuania; No. 20, Grand Duchy of Luxemburg; No. 21, Netherlands; No. 22, Norway; No. 23, Poland; No. 24, Rumania; No. 25, Saar

[58]For the work of the Bank, see Eleanor Lansing Dulles, *The Bank for International Settlements at Work* (New York, 1932), and W. McClure, *World Prosperity as Sought through the Economic Work of the League of Nations*, p. 515–528. See also the Annual Reports of the Bank for International Settlements; the First Report covers the business year ended March 31, 1931; the Eighteenth Annual Report appeared in 1948.

[59]Prior to 1925 similar memoranda appeared under slightly varying titles, covering developments since 1913. The Memoranda on Central Banks appeared independently of the Memoranda on Currency.

Territory; No. 26, Denmark, Norway and Sweden; No. 27, Sweden; No. 28, Switzerland; No. 29, Union of Soviet Socialist Republics; No. 30, Vatican City.

For additional publications on Money and Banking see below, pages 240, 246-247, 255.

BUSINESS CYCLE

General

The Course and Phases of the World Economic Depression. Report Presented to the Assembly of the League of Nations. Geneva, 1931. 337 p.[60] [A.22.1931.II.A.] (1931.II.A.21.)

Report of the Delegation on Economic Depression. Part I: The Transition from War to Peace Economy. Geneva, 1943. 118 p. [C.6.M.6.1943.II.A.] (1943.II.A.3.). Part II: Economic Stability in the Post-War World. The Conditions of Prosperity after the Transition from War to Peace. Geneva, 1945. 319 p. [C.1.M.1.1945. II.A.] (1945.II.A.2.)

Business Cycle Theory

Haberler, Gottfried. Prosperity and Depression. 3d ed., Geneva, 1941. 532 p. (1943.II.A.2.)

Tinbergen, J. Statistical Testing of Business Cycle Theories. Geneva, 1939. Volume I: A Method and Its Application to Investment Activity. 164 p. (1938.II.A.23.). Volume II: Business Cycles in the United States of America, 1919–1932. 244 p. (1939.II.A.16.)

Agricultural Depression

Economic Committee. The Agricultural Crisis. Geneva, 1931. Volume I: 322 p. [C.239.M.105.1931.II.B.] (1931.II.12/¹.). Volume II: 113 p. [C.239.105.1931.II.B.Vol.II.] (1931.II.B.12/¹¹.)

Volume I contains I: Report of the Economic Committee on the Agricultural Crisis. II: The Position of Agriculture in Various Countries. Volume II contains Part I: The Position of Agriculture in Various Countries. Part II: The Spread between the Prices Paid to the Producers and the Prices Paid by the Consumers.

Economic Fluctuations in the Anglo-Saxon Countries

Economic Fluctuations in the United States and the United Kingdom, 1918–1922. Geneva, 1942. 93 p. (1942.II.A.7.)

CARTELS

International Cartels: A League of Nations Memorandum. (United Nations Publications: Sales No. 1948.II.D.2.)

Prepared by Gertrud Lovasy. This memorandum, prepared in connection with the

[60]There is also an American edition, bound, indexed, and distributed by the World Peace Foundation, Boston,1931. 355p.

study of post-war economic questions undertaken by the League department in Princeton, appeared under the imprint of the United Nations.

COMMERCIAL ARBITRATION

Protocol on Arbitration Clauses. Geneva, September 24th, 1923.[61] Edition Containing All Signatures Affixed to the Protocol and Ratifications Relating Thereto Deposited with the Secretariat up to January 31st, 1928. Geneva, 1928. 9 p. [A.83.1923.II.Annex.] (1928.II.5.)

Convention on the Execution of Foreign Arbitral Awards. Geneva, September 26th, 1927.[62] Geneva, 1929. 9 p., in part bilingual. [C.47.105.27.1929.II.] (1929.II.8.)

COMMERCIAL PROPAGANDA

Draft International Agreement for the Purpose of Facilitating Commercial Propaganda. Document Prepared for the Meeting Convened at Geneva for July 1st, 1935. Geneva, 1935. 22 p. <E. 881.> (1935.II.B.5.)

CURRENCY

Currencies after the War: A Survey of Conditions in Various Countries, Comp[iled] under the Auspices of the International Secretariat of the League of Nations. London, 1920, 254 p.

Preface signed: J. A. Salter

International Currency Experience. Lessons of the Inter-war Period. Princeton, 1944. 249 p. (1944.II.A.4.)

The greater part of this volume is the work of Ragnar Nurske. Chapter VI is by Professor Williams Adams Brown, Jr.

The Course and Control of Inflation. A Review of Monetary Experience in Europe after World War I. 1946. 132 p.+4 p. (1946.II.A.6.)

A study of the monetary disorders which swept over Europe after World War I. Part I by Ragnar Nurske.

CUSTOMS UNIONS

Customs Unions: A League of Nations Contribution to the Study of Customs Union Problems. Lake Success, 1947. 98 p. (United Nations Publications: Sales No. 1948.II.D.3.)

These studies, now presented as Parts 1–5 of the joint document, have been contributed by different members of the League department working in Princeton.

[61] See also *Official Journal*, July,1923, p. 835–836.
[62] See also Document[C.659.M.220.1927.II.] and [C.659(1).M.220(1).1927.II.(Erratum).].

FOREIGN BUYERS

Survey of the Direct and Indirect Means at the Disposal of Foreign Buyers to Enable Them in a Number of Countries to Ascertain the Quality of the Goods Acquired by Them.[63] Geneva, 1930. 153 p. [C.624.M.246.1930.II.] (1930.II.48.)

PACIFIC SETTLEMENT OF INTERNATIONAL ECONOMIC DISPUTES

Memorandum Relating to the Pacific Settlement of International Disputes Concerning Economic Questions in General and Commercial Customs Questions in Particular. Geneva, 1931. 74 p. <E.666.> (1931.II.B.1.)

A survey on the provisions in force on January 15,1931, in the various acts, treaties, conventions, and agreements concluded between the different powers, more especially in Europe.

Procedure for the Friendly Settlement of Economic Disputes between States. Set up by a Resolution of the Council of January 28th, 1932. Geneva, 1932. 5 p. [C.57.M.32.1932.II.B.] (1932.II.B.2.)

COMMERCIAL POLICY AND INTERNATIONAL TRADE

Economic Committee's Reports on International Relations

Remarks on the Present Phase of International Economic Relations. Geneva, 1935. 52 p. [C.344.M.174.1935.II.B.] (1935.II.B.11.)

Remarks on the Present Phase of International Economic Relations. Reconstruction of the Machinery of International Exchange as a Factor in Recovery and Appeasement. Together with Observations by the Financial Committee. Geneva, 1936. 10 p. [C.378.M.249.1936.II.B.] (1936.II.B.7.)

Remarks on the Present Phase of International Economic Relations (September 1937). The Carrying out of the Programme of the Tripartite Declaration of September 26th, 1936. Annex: Economic Appeasement. Memorandum Presented to the Committee by Mr. F. L. McDougall, C.M.G. Geneva, 1937. 28 p. [C.358.M.242.1937.II.B.] (1937.II.B.9.)

Observations on the Present Prospects of Commercial Policy. Geneva, 1939. 27 p. [C.179.M.108.1939.II.B.] (1939.II.B.3.)

General Survey of Commercial Policy

Commercial Policy in the Interwar Period: International Proposals and National Policies. Geneva, 1942. 164 p. (1942.II.A.6.)

[63]For treatment of foreigners in general, see p. 274, No. 4.

Part I: An Historical Survey. Part II: An Analysis of the Reasons for the Success or Failure of International Proposals.

Commercial Policy in the Post-war World. Report of the Economic and Financial Committees. Geneva, 1945. 124 p. [C.31.M.31. 1945.II.A.] (1945.II.A.7.)

See especially Annex I: Doctrine of the Economic Committee Relating to M[ost] F[avored]. N[ation]. Treatment (1929–1931). Annex II: Note by the Secretariat on Measures to Prevent the Growth of Vested Interests behind Quantitative Trade Controls during the Post-war Transitional Period of General Shortage. Annex III: Short List of Important League of Nations Documents Relating to Trade and Commercial Policy.

Most-Favored-Nation Clause

Committee of Experts for the Progressive Codification of International Law. The Most-Favoured-Nation Clause. Report Adopted by the Committee of Its Third Session, Held in March-April, 1927. Geneva, 1927. 15 p. [C.205.M.79.1927.V.] <C.P.D.I.97(1).> (1927.V.10.)

Recommendations of the Economic Committee Relating to Commercial Policy. Geneva, 1929. 14 p. [C.138.M.53.1929.II.] (1929. II.15.)

Recommendations of the Economic Committee Relating to Tariff Policy and the Most-Favoured-Nation Clause. Geneva, 1933. 23 p. <E.805.> (1933.II.B.1.)

Equality of Treatment in the Present State of International Commercial Relations. The Most-Favoured-Nation Clause. Geneva, 1936. 26 p. [C.379.M.250.1936.II.B.] (1936.II.B.9.)

International Trade Relations

INTERNATIONAL TRADE

Europe's Trade: A Study of the Trade of European Countries with Each Other and with the Rest of the World. Geneva, 1941. 116 p. (1941.II.A.1.)

The Network of World Trade. A Companion Volume to "Europe's Trade." Geneva, 1942. 172 p. (1942.II.A.3.)

Europe's Overseas Needs, 1919–1920, and How They Were Met. Geneva, 1943. 52 p. (1943.II.A.6.)

Industrialization and Foreign Trade, by Folke H. Hilgerdt. Geneva, 1945. 171 p. (1945.II.A.10.)

TRADE CONTROLS, CLEARING AGREEMENTS, EXCHANGE CONTROLS

Trade Relations between Free Market and Controlled Economies. Geneva, 1943. 92 p. (1943.II.A.4.)

Study prepared by Professor Jacob Viner.

Quantitative Trade Controls: Their Causes and Nature. Geneva, 1943. 45 p. (1943.II.A.5.)

Study prepared by Professor Gottfried Haberler and Mr. Martin Hill.

Enquiry into Clearing Agreements. Geneva, 1935. 154 p. [C.153. M.83.1935.II.B.] (1935.II.B.6.)

Report on Exchange Control Submitted by a Committee Composed of Members of the Economic and Financial Committees. Geneva, 1938. 53 p. [C.232.M.131.1938.II.A.] (1938.II.A.10.)

Customs Nomenclature

Sub-Committee of Experts for the Unification of Customs Tariff Nomenclature. Draft Customs Nomenclature. Edition Revised in Accordance with the Observations Forwarded by Governments.[64] Geneva, 1937. Volume I: 135 p. [C.295.M.194.1937.II.B.] (1937. II.B.5¹.). Volume II: 318 p. [C.295.M.194.1937.II.B.] (1937.II. B.5¹¹.)

Volume I contains, p.9–119, Draft Customs Nomenclature, including 991 classified items, and an alphabetical list of the products mentioned in basic items of the Draft Customs Nomenclature, p.121, 135. Volume II contains for the most part explanatory notes on the Draft Customs Nomenclature.

Demographic Questions

The Future Population of Europe and the Soviet Union. Population Projections, 1940–1970, by Frank Notestein. Geneva, 1944. 315 p. (1944.A.2.)

Economic Demography of Eastern and Southern Europe, by Wilbert E. Moore of the Office of Population Research, Princeton University. Geneva, 1945. 299 p. (1945. II.A.9.)

[64]The purpose of this document may best be explained in the words of its Introduction, p.5.: "The present volume contains the draft common Customs nomenclature prepared by the Special Sub-Committee of Experts set up in 1927. It is followed by a second volume, in which the classification of goods for tariff purposes as proposed by the experts is fully explained and annotated. The history of the draft common Customs nomenclature was given in the introduction to the 'Draft Framework for a Customs Tariff Nomenclature' published in 1928 [Doc.C.346.M.103.1928.II.] which is, as it were, the logical and necessary antecedent to the work now issued. It will suffice here to recall briefly that, following on a recommendation by the World Economic Conference in May 1927, the Council of the League of Nations referred the problem of establishing a systematic customs nomenclature to the Economic Committee. In making its recommendation, the World Economic Conference had in view the introduction of order, clearness and, above all, simplicity and uniformity into the nomenclature of Customs tariffs. All those who at present have occasion, in the course of business or study, to refer to these tariffs know from experience how difficult they are to consult and compare." See also International Conference on Customs Formalities (1923), and Document [C.678.M.241.1924.II.], containing: 1. International Convention Relating to the Simplification of Customs Formalities. 2. Protocol to the International Convention, Geneva, November 3rd,1923.

The Population of the Soviet Union: History and Prospects, by Frank Lorimer. Geneva, 1946. 289 p. (1946.II.A.3.)

Europe's Population in the Interwar Years, by Dudley Kirk. 302 p.+ maps. (1946.II.A.8.)

DOUBLE TAXATION AND TAX EVASION

Reports

Double Taxation and Tax Evasion. Report and Resolutions Submitted by the Technical Experts to the Financial Committee of the League of Nations. Geneva, 1925. 45 p. <F.212.>

Double Taxation and Tax Evasion. Report Presented by the Committee of Technical Experts on Double Taxation and Tax Evasion. Geneva, 1927. 33 p. [C.216.M.85.1927.II.] (1927.II.40.)

Double Taxation and Tax Evasion. Report Presented by the General Meeting of Government Experts on Double Taxation and Tax Evasion. Geneva, 1928. 39 p. [C.562.M.178.1928.II.] (1928. II.49.)

International Agreements and Internal Legal Provisions

Collection of International Agreements and Internal Legal Provisions for the Prevention of Double Taxation and Fiscal Evasion (Prepared by the Economic and Financial Section of the Secretariat of the League of Nations in Accordance with the Council Resolution of September 15th, 1927). Geneva, 1928. 278 p. [C. 345.M.102.1928.II.] (1928.II.45.). Supplement No. I: No date. 53 p. [C.365.M.134.1929.II.] (1929.II.34.). Volume III:[65] Geneva, 1930. 110 p. [C.585.M.263.1930.II.] (1930.II.50.). Volume IV: Geneva, 1931. 72 p. [C.791.M.385.1931.II.A.] (1931.II.A.29.). Volume V: No date. 136 p. [C.618.M.291.1932.II.A.] (1933.II.A.29.). Volume VI: No date. 119 p. [C.118.M.57.1936.II.A.] (1936.II.A. 10.)

Enterprises Operating in More Than One Country

Taxation of Foreign and National Enterprises: A Study of the Tax Systems and the Methods of Allocation of the Profits of Enterprises Operating in More Than One Country. Volume I: France, Germany, Spain, the United Kingdom and the United States of America. Geneva, 1932. 275 p. [C.73.M.38.1932.II.A.] (1932.II.A. 3.). Volume II: Austria, Belgium, Czecho-Slovakia, Free City of Danzig, Greece, Hungary, Italy, Latvia, Luxemburg, Netherlands, Roumania and Switzerland. Geneva, 1933. 467 p. [C.425.

[65]Volume I is the "Collection" [C.345.M.102.1928.II.]. Volume II is Supplement to the foregoing.

M.217.1933.II.A.] (1933.II.A.18.). Volume III: British India, Canada, Japan, Mexico, Netherlands East Indies, Union of South Africa, States of Massachusetts, of New York and Wisconsin. Geneva, 1933. 254 p. [C.425 (a).M.217 (a).1933.II.A.] (1933.II. A.19.). Volume IV: Methods of Allocating Taxable Income, by Mitchell B. Carroll. Geneva, 1933. 219 p. [C.425 (b).M.217 (b). 1933.II.A.] (1933.II.A.20.). Volume V: Allocation Accounting for the Taxable Income of Industrial Enterprises, by Ralph C. Jones. Geneva, 1933. 78 p. [C.425 (c).M.217 (c).1933.II.A.] (1933.II.A. 21.)

Second Regional Tax Conference, Mexico, 1943

Model Bilateral Convention for the Prevention of International Double Taxation and Fiscal Evasion. Second Regional Tax Conference, Mexico, D.F. July, 1943. Geneva, 1945. 85 p. [C.2.M.2. 1945.II.A.] (1945.II.A.3.)

Contains: I. Model Bilateral Convention for the Prevention of the Double Taxation of Income, p.9–19. II. Model Bilateral Convention for the Prevention of the Double Taxation of Succession, p.20–25. III. Model Bilateral Convention for the Establishment of Reciprocal Administrative Assistance for the Assessment and Collection of Direct Taxes, p.26–33. Commentary on the Model Bilateral Convention, p.35–85.

London and Mexico Model Tax Conventions

London and Mexico Model Conventions. Commentary and Text. Geneva, November, 1946. 117 p. [C.88.M.88.1946.II.A.]. (1946. II.A.7.)

Contains: I. Commentary on the Model Bilateral Convention on the Prevention of the Double Taxation of Income and Property, p.8–33; II. Commentary on the Model Bilateral Convention for the Prevention of the Double Taxation of Estates and Successions, p.34–43; III. Commentary on the Model Bilateral Convention for the Establishment of Reciprocal Administrative Assistance for the Assessment and Collection of Taxes on Income, Property, Estates and Successions, p.44–56. The Annex contains on opposite pages the texts of the foregoing Model Conventions.

General

Prevention of International Double Taxation and Fiscal Evasion: Two Decades of Progress under the League of Nations, by Mitchell B. Carroll.[66] Geneva, 1939. 53 p. <F./Fiscal/111.> (1939.II.A.8.)

INVESTMENT

Conditions of Private Foreign Investment. 1946. 45 p. [C.14.M.14. 1946.II.A.] (1946.II.A.1.)

Report by the Special Joint Committee of the Economic and Financial Organization.

[66]See also Mitchell B. Carroll, "International Double Taxation," in Davis, ed., *Pioneers in World Order*, p.171–177.

MONETARY QUESTIONS

General

International Currency Experience. Lessons of the Inter-war Period. Princeton, 1944. 249 p. (1944.II.A.4.)

Gold

Interim Report of the Gold Delegation of the Financial Committee. Geneva, 1930. 120 p. [C.375.M.161.1930.II.] (1930.II.26.)

Second Interim Report of the Gold Delegation of the Financial Committee. Geneva, 1931. 22 p. [C.75.M.31.1931.II.] (1931.II.A.2.)

Report of the Gold Delegation of the Financial Committee. Geneva, 1932. 83 p. [C.502.M.243.1932.II.A.] (1932.II.A.12.)

Legislation on Gold. Geneva, 1930. 375 p. [C.373.M.159.1930.II.] (1930.II.29.)

This publication is divided into three parts. Part I (p. 9–37) includes tables under the following headings: I. Legal Redemption Requirements; II. Countries Classified According to Legal Redemption Requirements; III. Legal Reserve Requirements; IV. Legal Requirements Regarding Place of Deposit of Gold Reserves; V. Legal Requirements to Purchase Gold and to Mint Gold; VI. Legal Restrictions on the Export and Import of Gold. Part II (p. 41–142) is entitled: Notes Summarising the Legislation on Gold in Various Countries. Part III (p. 145–375) is entitled: Extracts from Laws and Statutes.

The Functioning of the Gold Standard, by Dr. Felix Mlynarski. Geneva, 1931. 115 p. <F.979/F.Gold 67(1).> (1931.II.A.25.)

Selected Documents Submitted to the Gold Delegation of the Financial Committee. Geneva, 1930. 87 p. [C.374.M.160.1930.II.] (1930.II.34.)

Contains: Monetary Stability and the Gold Standard, by Sir Henry Strakosch; The Economic Consequences of Changes in the Value of Gold, by Sir Henry Strakosch; Price Stabilization, by O.M.W. Sprague; Undue Fluctuations of the Purchasing Power of Gold, by Jacques Rueff; The Functioning of the Gold Standard, by Dr. L. J. A. Trip; The Reform of the Gold Exchange Standard, by Dr. Felix Mlynarski; International Price Level Adjustments, by Dr.L.J.A.Trip.

Selected Documents on the Distribution of Gold Submitted to the Gold Delegation of the Financial Committee. Geneva, 1931. 67 p. [C.102.M.38.1931.II.A.] (1931.II.A.7.)

Contains: The Causes and Effects of the Movements of Gold into France, by Prof. Albert Aftalion; The Movements of Gold into and out of Germany since 1924, by Prof. G.W.J. Bruins; The Causes of Gold Movements into and out of Great Britain, 1925–1929, by Prof. Gregory; Gold Movement into and out of the United States, 1914–1929, and the Effect, by Mr. George E. Robert; Stastistics of Gold Movements, 1925–1930.

Counterfeiting Currency and Falsification of Securities

Counterfeiting Currency. Letter from M. Briand to the Secretary-General . . . Geneva, 1926. 4 p. <F.294.> (1926.II.24.)

Mixed Committee for the Suppression of Counterfeiting Currency. Report and Draft Convention. Geneva, 1927. 24 p. [C.523.M.181. 1927.II.] (1927.II.70.)

Summary of the Observations Received from Governments up to December 6th, 1928, on the Report of the Mixed Committee for the Suppression of Counterfeiting Currency, and on the Draft Convention Drawn up by the Committee, October, 1927. Geneva, 1928. 30 p. [C.607.M.185.1928.II.] (1928.II.54.)

International Conference for the Adoption of a Convention for Suppression of Counterfeiting Currency. Geneva, April 9th–20th, 1929. 1: International Convention for the Suppression of Counterfeiting Currency. 2: Protocol.[67] 3: Optional Protocol.[68] Geneva, 1930. 19 p., in part double-paged. [C.153 (1).M.59 (1).1929.II.] <C.F. M.12(1).>

Proceedings of the International Conference for the Adoption of a Convention for the Suppression of Counterfeiting Currency. Geneva, April 9th to 20th, 1929. Geneva, 1929. 302 p. [C.328.M. 114.1929.II.] (1929.II.48.)

Contains on p.8–41 the above-enumerated official instruments of the Conference.

Suppression of Counterfeiting Currency. First Conference of Central Offices. Report and Relevant Documents. Geneva, 1931. 15 p. [C.193.M.76.1931.II.A.] (1931.II.A.8.)

Committee of Jurists for the Suppression of the Falsification of Securities. Reports to the Council on the Work of the Meeting Held in Paris on October 29th and 30th, 1937. Geneva, 1937. 3 p. [C.542.M.379.1937.II.A.] (1937.II.A.22.)

Contains Draft Protocol for the Extension of the International Convention for the Suppression of Counterfeiting Currency, Dated April 20th,1929, to the Falsification of Certain Securities.

NUTRITION

General

The Problem of Nutrition. Volume I: Interim Report of the Mixed Committee on the Problem of Nutrition. Geneva, 1936. 98 p. [A.12.1936.II.B.] (1936.II.B.3.). Volume II: Report on the Physiological Bases of Nutrition Drawn up by the Technical Commission of the Health Committee at the Meeting Held in London (November 25th–29th, 1935), Revised and Amplified at the Meeting Held at Geneva (June 4th–8th, 1936). Geneva, 1936. 27 p. [A.

[67]The Convention and Protocol signed at Geneva on April 20,1929, are also published in 112 *Treaty Series*, p. 371–388, 389–393, bilingual. They came into force on February 22,1931.
[68]The Optional Protocol is also published in 112 *Treaty Series*, p.395–397; it came into force on August 30,1930.

12 (a).1936.II.B.] (1936.II.B.4.). Volume III: Nutrition in Various Countries. Geneva, 1936. 271 p. [A.12 (b).1936.II.B.] (1936.II.B. 5.). Volume IV: Statistics of Food Production, Consumption and Prices. Documentation Prepared by the International Institute of Agriculture. Presented to the Mixed Committee on the Problem of Nutrition at Its Second Session, June 4th, 1936. Geneva, 1936. 110 p. [A.12 (c).1936.II.B.] (1936.II.B.6.)

Nutrition Considered in Relation to Public Health and to Economic Conditions. Geneva, 1935. 24 p. (League of Nations Questions, No. 4.)

New Technical Efforts towards a Better Nutrition. Geneva, 1938. 36 p. (League of Nations Questions, No. 7.)

Report of the Mixed Committee

Final Report of the Mixed Committee of the League of Nations on the Relation of Nutrition to Health, Agriculture and Economic Policy. Geneva, 1937. 327 p. [A.13.1937.II.A.] (1937.II.A.10.)

Preliminary Investigation into Measures of a National or International Character for Raising the Standard of Living. Memorandum Prepared by Mr. N. F. Hall. Geneva, 1938. 91 p. [A.18.1938.II. B.] (1938.II.B.4.)

Survey of National Nutrition Policies, 1937/38. Geneva, 1938. 120 p. [C.478.M.321.1938.II.A.] (1938.II.A.25.)

Special Aspects of Nutrition

Rural Dietaries in Europe. Annex: Report on Bread. Report Prepared under the Auspices of the Health Committee. Geneva, 1939. 84 p. [C.183.M.112.1939.] (European Conference on Rural Life 26.)

Wartime Food Problems

Technical Commission on Nutrition. Report by a Special Commitee, Geneva, August, 1938. *Bulletin of the Health Organisation*, Vol. 7 (August, 1938), 666–678.

Wartime Rationing and Consumption. Geneva, 1942. 87 p. (1942. II.A.2.)

Food Rationing and Supply, 1943/44. Geneva, 1944. 101 p. (1944. II.A.3.)

Relief Deliveries and Relief Loans, 1919–1923. Geneva, 1943. 62 p. (1943.II.A.1.)

Agricultural Production in Continental Europe during the 1914–18 War and the Reconstruction Period. Geneva, 1943. 122 p. (1943. II.A.7.)

Food, Famine and Relief, 1940–1946. Geneva, 1946. 159 p. (1946.II. A.5.)

By John Lindberg.

RAW MATERIALS

General

Report on the Problem of Raw Materials and Foodstuffs, by Prof. Gini.[69] With Annexes Prepared under His Direction. No date. 251 p.

There is no official number or date for this document. The introductory report is dated "Geneva,1921." An attached slip reads: "The authors alone are responsible for the views and opinions expressed in this publication."

Provisional Economic and Financial Committee (Economic Committee). Report on Certain Aspects of the Raw Materials Problem (with the Relevant Documents Submitted to the Committee by Prof. Gini). Volume I: Geneva, 1921. 55 p. [C.51.M.18.1922.II.] <E.F.S.191.B.53.>. Volume II: No date. 175 p. [C.51.M.18.1922.II.] <E.F.S.191.B.53.>

Raw Materials and Foodstuffs. Production by Countries, 1935 and 1938. Geneva, 1939. 75 p. (1939.II.A.24.)

A statistical handbook on the production of raw materials and foodstuffs. Lists some 200 commodities produced by independent states, mandated territories, and colonies. Figures on net imports and exports for 1935 are included.

Raw Material Problems and Policies. Geneva, 1946. 110 p. (1946. II.A.2.)

Part I: Problems, Proposals and Policies. Part II: Lessons from the Past.

Committee for the Study of Raw Materials

Report of the Committee for the Study of the Problem of Raw Materials.[70] Geneva, 1937. 62 p. [A.27.1937.II.B.] (1937.II.B.7.)

Contains Examination of Complaints and Difficulties Experienced with Regard to the Supply of Raw Materials: I.Prohibition and Restrictions on the Export of Raw Materials; II.Export Duties; III. Development of Natural Resources; IV. International Regulation Schemes Relating to the Supply of Raw Materials; V. Monopolies and Examination of Complaints and Difficulties Experienced with Regard to the Acquisition of and Payment for Raw Materials. Annex I. Development of World Production of Raw Materials. Annex II. The Improvement of Regulation Schemes.

International Trade in Raw Materials and Foodstuffs

International Trade in Certain Raw Materials and Foodstuffs by Countries of Origin and Consumption, 1935. Geneva, 1936. 146 p.

[69]For the origin and nature of the Gini Report, see Karl W. Kapp, "The League of Nations and Raw Materials, 1919–1939," in Geneva Research Center, *Geneva Studies*, Vol. XII, No. 3 (1941), p. 25–29.
[70]See also the First and Second Interim Reports of the Committee for the Study of the Problems of Raw Materials [C.182.M.128.1937.II.B.] (1937.II.B.1.), 3p.; and [C.286.M. 187.1937.II.B.] (1937.II.B.4.), 2p. See also International Institute of Intellectual Co-operation, *International Raw Material Cartels: Causes, Effects, Regulation, by William Oualid . . . Assisted by L. Ballande* . . . Paris, 1938. 54 p.

(1936.II.A.26.). 1936: Geneva, 1937. 164 p. (1937.II.A.21.). 1937: Geneva, 1938. 176 p. (1938.II.A.20.). 1938: Geneva, 1939. 178 p. (1939.II.A.22.)

The object of these volumes is to show the sources from which countries do in reality obtain their raw materials and foodstuffs. The trade returns published by many countries fail to furnish this information or they indicate some intermediate country from which the goods have been sold or consigned and not the country from which they originated. Thirty-eight commodities are covered by the special returns made by governments. They were selected by the League Committee of Statistical Experts. The criteria employed in making this selection were mainly the importance of these commodities in world trade and their homogeneity.

Individual Raw Materials

Coal: The Coal Problem.[71] Geneva, 1932. 55 p. [C.405.M.224.1932. II.B.] (1932.II.B.4.)

Sugar: Sugar Memoranda Prepared for the Economic Committee by Dr. H. C. Prinsen Geerligs, Messrs. F. O. Licht and Dr. Gustav Mikusch. Geneva, 1929. 51 p. [C.148.M.57.1929.II.] <E/Sugar/ 23(1);24(1);25(1).> (1929.II.20.)

Sugar: The World Sugar Situation. Report by the Economic Committee of the League of Nations. Geneva, 1929. 32 p. [C.303.M. 104.1929.II.] (1929.II.30.)

Sugar: International Sugar Conference. Held in London from April 5th to May 6th, 1937.[72] Geneva, 1937. 83 p. [C.289.M.190.1937. II.B.] (1937.II.B.8.)

Timber: The Timber Problem. Geneva, 1932. 51 p. [C.493.M.239. 1932.II B.] (1932.II.B.6.)

INTERNATIONAL RELIEF UNION[73]

International Federation for Mutual Assistance in the Relief of Peoples Overtaken by Disaster. Documents Relating to the Scheme of Senator Ciraolo. Geneva, 1923. 19 p. [C.696.M.279. 1923.IV.]

International Relief Union: Note by the Secretary-General. Geneva, 1925. 3 p. [A.20 (a).1925.II.] [C.414.1925.II.]

[71]See also *The Problem of the Coal Industry. Interim Report on Its International Aspects by the Economic Committee of the League of Nations.* Geneva,1929. 49p. [C.150.M.58.1929. II.] (1929.II.19.)

[72]For the "Protocol to Enforce and to Prolong after August 31,1942, the International Agreement Regarding the Regulation of Production and Marketing of Sugar," signed at London, July 22,1942, see International Labor Office, *Intergovernmental Commodity Control Agreements* (Montreal, 1943), p.45–46. For a list of similar agreements concluded prior to 1937, see *ibid.,* p.26.

[73]For Council and Assembly Resolutions adopted in 1923 in reference to an International Federation for the Relief of Peoples Overtaken by Disaster, see also Documents [C.L.132.1932.IV.] and [C.L.133.1923.IV.].

Contains: Copy of a letter dated July 18th,1925, from the Director General of the League of Red Cross Societies, with Annexes, and copy of a letter dated July 23rd, 1925, from the President of the International Red Cross Committee.

International Relief Union (I.R.U.). Draft Statutes and Statement Drawn up by the Preparatory Committee for the Ciraolo Scheme. Geneva, 1926. 22 p. [C.618.M.240.1926.II.] <Conf.U.I.S.2.> (1926.II.1(a).)

Documents for the International Conference for the Formation of an International Relief Union. Geneva, July 4th, 1927. Geneva, 1927. 31 p. (1926.II.56.)[74]

International Conference for the Creation of an International Relie- Union. Geneva, July 4th to 12th, 1927. Official Instruments Approved by the Conference: Convention and Statute Establishing an International Relief Union. Final Act. Geneva, 1927. 24 p.+ 24 p., in part double-paged and bilingual. [C.364.M.137.1927. V.][75] (1927.V.17.)

Contains: Convention, p.2–7; Statute, p.9–11; Final Act, p.14–18.

STATISTICS AND STATISTICAL METHODS

Preliminary Documents

International Statistics. Memorandum by the Secretary-General. No date. 7 p., bilingual. [Council Document 28.] [10/2951/80.]

International Statistics. Report Presented by the Belgian Representative, Mr. Destrée, and Adopted by the Council of the League of Nations, Meeting in Rome, on 19th May, 1920. No date. 2 p., bilingual. [10/4433/80.]

International Statistical Commission. Report by M. Lucien March, with Annexes. No date. 35 p.+35 p., bilingual. (E.F.S.74.) [A.10.1921.]

International Convention and Protocol Relating to Economic Statistics, 1928

International Convention Relating to Economic Statistics with Protocol and Annexes. Signed at Geneva, December 14th, 1928.[76] 110 *Treaty Series*, p. 170–283.

[74]This document, published under the sales number (1926.II.56.), includes the following documents: <Conf. U.I.5.1.–4.>.
[75]The Convention and Statute, signed at Geneva, July 12, 1927, was also published as a separate document [C.364.M.137(1).1927.V.]; in force since December 27, 1932. See also *Official Journal*, February, 1933, p. 211–213, 303–305, for reprint of Documents [C.67.1933.II.B.] and [C.761.M.358.1932.II.B.].
[76]Also published as a separate document [C.606(1).M.184(1).1928.II.] (1928.II.52.).

Studies and Reports on Statistical Methods

The Committee of Statistical Experts has published the following statements and recommendations.

No. 1: Statistics of the Gainfully-occupied Population. Definitions and Classifications Recommended by the Committee of Statistical Experts. Geneva, 1938. 32 p. [C.226.M.128.1938.II.A.] <C.E.S. 127.Appendix I.> (1938.II.A.12.)

No. 2: Minimum List of Commodities for International Trade Statistics. Revised Edition Prepared by the Committee of Statistical Experts.[77] Geneva, 1938. 62 p. [C.226.M.128.1938.II.A.] <C.E. S.127.Appendix III.> (1938.II.A.14.)

No. 3: Timber Statistics. A Minimum Programme of Timber Statistics Drawn up by the Committee of Statistical Experts. Geneva, 1938. 17 p. [C.226.M.128.1938.II.A.] <C.E.S.127.Appendice V.> (1938.II.A.15.)

No. 4: Statistics Relating to Capital Formation. A Note on Methods. Geneva, 1938. 22 p. [C.226.M.128.1938.II.A.] <C.E.S.127.Appendix VI.> (1938.II.A.16.)

No. 5: Housing Statistics. A Minimum Programme of Housing Statistics. Geneva, 1939. 14 p. [C.133.M.85.1939.II.A.] <C.E.S. 145. Appendix I.> (1939.II.A.6.)

No. 6: Indices of Industrial Production. Report Drawn up by the Committee of Statistical Experts. Geneva, 1939. 16 p. [C.133.M. 85.1939.II.A.] <C.E.S.145.Appendix II.> (1939.II.A.7.)

No. 7: Measurement of National Income and the Construction of Social Accounts. Report of the Sub-Committee on National Income Statistics of the League of Nations Committee of Statistical Experts. Appendix: Definition and Measurement of the National Income and Related Totals. By Richard Stone. Geneva, 1947. 116 p. (United Nations Publications: Sales No. 1947.II.6.)

No. 8: Banking Statistics. Recommendations on Scope and Principles of Classification. Report of the Sub-Committee of the League of Nations Committee of Statistical Experts. Geneva, 1947. 42 p. (United Nations Publications: Sales No. 1947.II.7.)

No. 9: Note on Balance of Payments Statistics. Report drawn up by the Sub-Committee on Balance of Payments Statistics of the League of Nations Committee of Statistical Experts. Geneva, 1947. 26 p. (United Nations Publications: Sales No. 1947.II.8.)

[77]See Princeton Catalogue, p.39: "This list is intended to replace the classification of the Brussels Convention of 1913. Countries were requested to compile their foreign trade statistics—or at least a supplementary set of trade statistics—in accordance with this list, in order to secure greater comparability of international trade statistics. The list is accompanied by a discussion of the principles which have guided the Committee in preparing this list."

Reports of the Committee of Statistical Experts

The Committee of Statistical Experts, appointed by the International Convention on Economic Statistics of 1928, held eight sessions between 1931 and 1939.

First Report: Committee of Statistical Experts. Report. Geneva, 1931. 7p. [C.215.M.90.1931.II.A.] <C.E.I.S.(1).> (1931.II.A.9.)

Last Report: Committee of Statistical Experts. Report to the Council on the Work of the Eighth Session. Held in Geneva from April 22nd to 27th, 1939. [C.133.M.85.1939.II.A.] <C.E.S.145.> (1939.II.A.5.)

MISCELLANEOUS QUESTIONS

Housing

Urban and Rural Housing.[78] Geneva, 1939. 159 p. (1939.II.A.2.)

Public Finance

Public Finance, 1928–1935–1937.[79] Geneva, 1936–1938.

Published in the form of 62 monographs on public finance in individual countries.

Tourist Traffic

Survey of Tourist Traffic Considered as an International Economic Factor. Geneva, 1936. 47 p. [C.3.M.3.1936.II.B.] (1936.II.B.1.)

Veterinary Questions

International Convention for the Campaign against Contagious Diseases of Animals.[80] Geneva, 1936. 10 p., bilingual; in part double-paged. [C.77(1).M.33(1).1935.II.B.]

International Convention Concerning the Transit of Animals, Meat and Other Products of Animal Origin.[81] Geneva, 1936. 10 p. [C.78(1).M.34(1).1935.II.B.]

International Convention Concerning the Export and Import of Animal Products (Other than Meat, Meat Preparations, Fresh

[78]"The enquiry was entrusted to M.B. Helger of the Swedish Social Board, who has had special opportunities to familiarise himself with the problems of housing finance"; from the preface by Mr. A. Loveday. See also European Conference on Rural Life,1939, and the pertinent publications of the Health Section.

[79]See also *Memorandum on Public Finance, 1921; Memorandum on Public Finance, 1922; Memorandum on Public Finance, 1926.* <C.E.I.34.> (1927.II.29.). *Memorandum on Public Finance, 1926-1928.* (1929.II.50.)

[80]Also published in 186 *Treaty Series*, p. 173–190, bilingual. Signed at Geneva, February 20,1935; in force since March 23,1938.

[81]Also published in 193 *Treaty Series*, p.37–57, bilingual. Signed at Geneva, February 20,1935; in force since December 6,1938.

Animal Products, Milk and Milk Products).[82] Geneva, 1936. 9 p., bilingual; in part double-paged. [C.79(1).M.35(1).1935.II.B.]

Whaling

Convention for the Regulation of Whaling (Geneva, September 24th, 1931).[83] Geneva, 1932. 8 p., bilingual. [C.642(1).M.256(1).1931. II.B.]

7. SERIAL AND PERIODICAL PUBLICATIONS

BALANCES OF PAYMENTS

First Volume:[84] Balances of Payments 1931 and 1932, Including an Analysis of Capital Movements up to September 1933. Geneva, 1933. 191 p. (1933.II.A.26.)

Last Volume: Balances of Payments, 1938. Geneva, 1939. 148 p. (1939.II.A.20.)

In all, seven volumes appeared from 1933 to 1939. The statements given in these volumes on the balance of international payments and outstanding international assets and liabilities of particular countries were, with few exceptions, compiled by the competent authorities of the countries concerned, and were in the majority of cases in more or less close agreement with special forms sent out each year to States Members of the League of Nations. The full text of the form of balance of payments is reproduced on pages 8–9 of the volume covering the year 1938.

An additional volume covering the years 1939–1945, appeared in 1948 under United Nations imprint:

[82]Also published in 193 *Treaty Series*, p. 59–77, bilingual. Signed at Geneva, February 20, 1935; in force since December 6, 1938.

[83]Also published in 155 *Treaty Series*, p.349–351. In force since January 16,1935. For the background of this whaling agreement, see L. Larry Leonard, *International Regulation of Fisheries* (Washington, 1944), p.98–109. For the Whaling Agreement of June 8, 1937, concluded independent of the League of Nations, see *ibid.*, p.102. Text in 190 *Treaty Series*, p.79–93, bilingual. For the 1944 Whaling Protocol, see *ibid.*, especially p.105. For a list of multilateral agreements, see also Stefan A. Riesenfeld, *Protection of Coastal Fisheries under International Law* (Washington,1942), p.277.

[84]Prior to 1933 similar surveys appeared: from 1924 to 1926 as Vol. I of *Memorandum on Balance of Payments and Foreign Trade Balances* covering the years 1910–1923, 1910–1924, 1911–1925, respectively; from 1927 to 1928, as Vol. I of *Memorandum on International Trade and Balances of Payments*, covering the years 1912–1926, 1913–1927, respectively; from 1929 to 1930 as Vol. II of *Memorandum on International Trade and Balances of Payments*, covering the years 1926–1928, 1927–1929, respectively —the sales number of these two volumes is (1929.II.51¹¹) and (1930.II.54¹¹), but the date of publication is given as Geneva, 1930 and Geneva, 1931 respectively; in 1932 as Vol. II of *Memorandum on Trade and Balances on Payments, 1930* covering the year 1930 (including an Analysis of Capital Movements in 1931).

Balances of Payments, 1939–1945. Geneva, 1948. 207 p. (United Nations Publications: Sales No. 1947.II.1.)

The titles and publications numbers of the balance-of-payments reviews issued by the League of Nations up to and including 1938 are listed on p. 6 of this publication.

It should be noted that, beginning with 1947, the International Monetary Fund has begun the collection and publication of information on balances of payments. The first balance of payments yearbook issued on behalf of the Fund is entitled: *Balance of Payments Yearbook; Covering 1938, 1946 and 1947, and, for Some Countries, Preliminary Statistics for 1948* (Washington, 1949), 383 p.

Money and Banking

First Issue: Money and Banking, 1935/36. Volume I: Monetary Review. Geneva, 1936. 59 p. (1936.II.A.7.[1]). Volume II: Commercial Banks. Geneva, 1936. 213 p. (1936.II.A.7.[11])
Last Issue: Money and Banking, 1942/44. Geneva, 1945. 221 p. (1945.II.A.1.)

Part I: International Summaries of Essential Data on Currency, Banking and Interest Rates. Part II: Central and Commercial Banks: Balance-Sheet Position and Profit-and-Loss Accounts.

The *Money and Banking* series was published in continuation of the memoranda on *Commercial Banks*,[85] issued in 1931, 1934, and 1935. This series appeared in two issues, each having two parts.[86] The first issue contains a general review of monetary developments. The issue covering 1942–1944 includes in Part I international summaries of currency composition and movements, central and commercial bank assets, recorded central gold reserves in millions of United States dollars, value of world gold production, cash ratios of commercial banks, indices of bank clearings, interest rates and value of currencies in United States cents. Part II consists of individual balance sheets of central banks and combined balance sheets and profit-and-loss accounts of commercial banks. The commercial bank statistics are presented on a uniform basis in accordance with a schedule elaborated by the League of Nations.

Production and Prices[87]

First Volume: World Production and Prices, 1925–1932. Geneva, 1933. 155 p. (1933.II.A.12.)

[85]See above, p. 238.

[86]From 1936 to 1939 inclusively (covering the years 1935–1939), the *Money and Banking* series appeared in two volumes. In 1940 (covering 1939–1940), there appeared only Vol. I, *Monetary Review* (1940.II.A.2.I.). See the Preface to this document by Mr. A. Loveday. In 1942 and 1945 *Money and Banking* appeared in one volume.
[87]Similar surveys appeared from 1926 to 1932 under the title *Memorandum on Production and Trade*, and in 1932 under the title *Review of World Production, 1925-1931*.

Last Volume: World Production and Prices, 1938/39. Geneva, 1939. 113 p. (1939.II.A.17.)

This annual survey is based on the world as a basic unit of computation and not on the individual states. The world is divided into continental or empire groups subdivided into their original component parts, namely, the state or the statistical area. The survey contains an analysis of the development of production during the year, with particular reference to cyclical and structural fluctuations.

STATISTICS

International Statistical Yearbook

First Volume: International Statistical Yearbook, 1926. Geneva, 1927. 184 p., bilingual. (1927.II.42.)

Last Volume: International Statistical Yearbook, 1929. Geneva, 1930. 262 p., bilingual. (1930.II.10.)

Statistical Yearbook of the League of Nations

First Volume: Statistical Yearbook of the League of Nations, 1930/31. Geneva, 1931. 292 p., bilingual. (1931.II.A.16.)

Last Volume: Statistical Yearbook of the League of Nations, 1942/44 (Seventeenth Issue).[88] Geneva, 1945. 315 p. (1945.II.A.5.)

The object of this yearbook is to give an international synopsis of available statistics relating to the most important economic, financial, demographic, and social phenomena. In all cases an attempt has been made to cover as many countries as possible and to render the statistical series comparable over the whole of a given period.

Monthly Bulletin of Statistics

Beginning in 1919, the *Bulletin* was published by the British Department of the Supreme Economic Council. It was compiled for the Council by the Statistical Department of the Board of Trade "in order to bring together such published statistics as have a bearing on the economic conditions prevailing in as many of the leading countries of the world as possible before, during and since the war with a view to afford some measure of their progress towards more normal conditions" (Introduction, Volume I, Number 1).

With Volume I, Number 3, preparation of the *Bulletin* was supervised by the Inter-Allied Committee, composed of American, British, French, and Italian representatives appointed by the Supreme Economic Council. Editions in English, French, and Italian were issued.

When the Supreme Economic Council ceased to exist in 1921, the *Bulletin* was transferred to the League of Nations, but for a short

[88]The preceding volume, *1941/42*, includes *Addendum 1942/43.*

time was still prepared under the supervision of the Inter-Allied Committee in London, on behalf of the League. Finally, with Volume II, Number 7 (July, 1921), it became the full responsibility of the League.[89] From then on it has been bilingual.

Simultaneously with the usual Geneva edition an edition was published from January, 1943, through September, 1945, at Princeton, New Jersey, for countries which could not receive copies from Geneva during the war. Of necessity, the contents of the two editions were not the same. When postal contact between Switzerland and overseas countries was made again, the Princeton edition was discontinued.

The League published the *Bulletin* at Geneva through July, 1946 (Volume XXVII, Number 7). With Number 8 (August, 1946), the United Nations took it over and continued to issue it from Geneva through December, 1946, after which publication was transferred to New York. It is prepared by the Statistical Office of the United Nations "to present in summary form statistics showing changing economic and social conditions in different countries," as the Introduction to the first New York issue states.[90]

TRADE

International Trade Statistics

First Volume: International Trade Statistics, 1933.[91] Geneva, 1934. 366 p., bilingual. (1934.II.A.20.)

[89]See the following passage from the June, 1921 issue (Vol. II, No. 6) of the *Monthly Bulletin of Statistics*, Introduction, p. iii: "It was announced in the early number of the Bulletin that it was in contemplation to place the responsibility for its compilation and issue in the hands of the League of Nations in due course. The Supreme Economic Council having now ceased to exist, it has been arranged to carry out the intention there announced and the whole of the work in connection with the preparation and publication of future issues of the Bulletin will be undertaken by the League of Nations."
[90]See also League Catalogue, p.48; United Nations, Department of Public Information, *Publications; 1945-48*, p. 54-55.
[91]Prior to 1933 similar surveys appeared: from 1924 to 1926 as Vol. II of the *Memorandum on Balance of Payments and Foreign Trade Balances* covering the years 1910–1923, 1910–1924, 1911–1925, respectively—the sales number of the 1926 volume is (1926.II.51[II]), but the date of publication is given as Geneva, 1927; from 1927 to 1928 as *Memorandum on International Trade and Balances of Payments*, covering the years 1912–1926, 1913–1927—the sales number of these two volumes is (1927.II.68[II]) and (1928.II.53[II]), but the date of publication is given as Geneva, 1928 and Geneva, 1929 respectively; from 1929 to 1930 as Vol. III of the *Memorandum on International Trade and Balances of Payments*, covering the years 1926–1928, 1927–1929, respectively—the sales number of these two volumes is (1929.II.51[III]) and (1930.II.54[III]), but the date of publication is given as Geneva, 1930 and Geneva, 1931 respectively; in 1932 as Vol. III of *Memorandum on Trade and Balances of Payments, 1930* covering the year 1930 (including provisional summary figures for 1931).

Last Volume: International Trade Statistics, 1938. Geneva, 1939. 345 p., bilingual. (1939.II.A.21.)

This is an international summary of trade statistics, containing detailed trade tables covering about 67 countries.[92]

World Trade

First Volume: Review of World Trade, 1932.[93] Geneva, 1933. 64 p. (1933.II.A.10.)

Last Volume: Review of World Trade, 1938. Geneva, 1939. 85 p. (1939.II.A.11.)

In contrast to the *International Trade Statistics*, where attention is focused primarily on country by country surveys, the *Review of World Trade*, like *World Production and Prices*, is based on the world as a basic unit, divided into continental or empire groups and subdivided into states and other statistical areas.[94]

Trade in Raw Materials and Foodstuff

First Volume: International Trade in Certain Raw Materials and Foodstuffs by Countries of Origin and Consumption, 1935. Geneva, 1936. 146 p., bilingual. (1936.II.A.26.)

Last Volume: Raw Materials and Foodstuffs. Production by Countries, 1935 and 1938. Geneva, 1939. 75 p., bilingual. (1939.II.A.24.)

The purpose of this reference book is to show the production of all the more important raw materials and foodstuffs country by country.

WORLD ECONOMIC SURVEY

First Volume: World Economic Survey, 1931–1932. Geneva, 1932. 327 p. (1932.II.A.18.)

Last Volume: World Economic Survey: Eleventh Year, 1942/44 Geneva, 1945. 292 p. (1945.II.A.4.)

The *World Economic Survey* is "intended to register from a contemporary standpoint, and within the limits set by available material, the actual trends of economic development within a brief period. The emphasis throughout is upon generalized world trends, and the aim is objective exposition rather than explanation or interpretation."[95]

[92]For tables showing imports and exports groups according to the "Minimum List" classification drawn up by the League Committee of Statistical Experts, see especially the Preface of Mr. A. Loveday to Document (1939.II.A.21.).

[93]For the distribution of crude products from their source throughout the world, see *International Trade in Certain Raw Materials and Foodstuffs by Countries of Origin and Consumption.*

[94]See International Trade Relations, above, p. 257.

[95]*World Economic Survey, 1931-1932*, p.10-11.

VI. COMMUNICATIONS AND TRANSIT

1. INTRODUCTORY NOTE

THE PURPOSE of the Organization for Communications and Transit, which was constituted and exercised its functions in virtue of resolutions adopted by the Assembly of the League of Nations, was to facilitate international co-operation in the field of communications and transit and also in the fields of public works and electric power in so far as they were related to communications and transit. In particular, the Organization was to help the Council and the Assembly to accomplish the work entrusted to the League by the Covenant (Article 23 (e)) and by treaties concerning communications and transit.[1]

The work of the Organization for Communications and Transit was to be carried out by:[2] (1) a "Committee for Communications and Transit" of an advisory and technical character; (2) permanent or temporary committees; (3) a permanent secretariat provided by the Secretary-General of the League;[3] (4) conferences, general or limited, convened with a view to the conclusion or revision of international conventions on communications and transit, public works and electric power related to communications and transit.

A list of documents covering the general and special (limited) conferences held since 1920 follows. The major conventions adopted by these conferences are listed under a separate heading.

Under Article 10 of the Statute, permanent committees were to be set up "for continuous consideration of groups of related questions." The following permanent committees were provided: (a) Committee on Air Navigation; (b) Committee on Electric Power; (c) Committee on Transport by Rail; (d) Committee on Inland Navigation; (e)

---

[1]See Art. 1 of the *Statute of the Organisation for Communications and Transit. Adopted by the Council of the League of Nations on January 29th, 1938.*
[2]See Art. 3, *ibid.*
[3]For the Communications and Transit Section of the Secretariat, see Egon F. Ranshofen-Wertheimer, *The International Secretariat* (Washington, 1945), p.117–120. He writes, p. 118: "Administratively, the Transit and Communications Section, like all other sections, was subject to the authority of the Secretary-General. But it differed from practically all the other services of the Secretariat in that it received its instructions on technical matters directly from the Communications and Transit Organization, the only technical organization of the League with a written constitution and a semiautonomous status."

Committee on Maritime Ports and Navigation; (f) Committee on Road Traffic; (g) Legal Committee.

2. STATUTE OF THE ORGANIZATION

Statute of the Organisation for Communications and Transit. Geneva, 1938. 30 p. [C.95.M.48.1938.VIII.] (1938.VIII.1.)

Contains Statute of the Organization for Communications and Transit, Adopted by the Council of the League of Nations on January 29th,1938, p.5–18; Rules of Procedure for General and Limited Conferences on Communications and Transit, p.19-23. This Statute took the place of the Statute drawn up by the First General Conference on Communications and Transit[4] held at Barcelona in 1921, which, with certain minor amendments introduced by the Third General Conference on Communications and Transit in 1927[5], governed the Organization until 1938.

3. ADVISORY AND TECHNICAL COMMITTEE FOR COMMUNICATIONS AND TRANSIT

RULES OF PROCEDURE

"Rules of Procedure of the Committee for Communications and Transit," in *Records of the Work of the Twenty-first Session, Held at Geneva from August 1st to 4th, 1938*, p. 90–91. [C.266.M.159.1938. VIII.] <C.C.T./21st. Session/P.V.> (1938.VIII.4.)

MINUTES OF SESSIONS

First Recorded Session:[6] Advisory and Technical Committee for Communications and Transit. Procès-Verbal of the First Session, Held at Geneva, July 25–28th, 1921. Geneva, 1921. 35 p.+35 p., bilingual. [C.358.M.254.1921.VIII.]

Last Recorded Session: Committee for Communications and Transit.

[4]For the 1921 Rules, see Conférence de Barcelone, *Comptes Rendus et Textes Relatifs au Règlement d'Organisation des Conférences Générales et de la Commission Consultative et Technique des Communications et du Transit et au Règlement Intérieur des Conférences Générales des Communications et du Transit*, Geneva, 1923, p. 90–95; French text only [C.662.M.265.1923.VIII.[. These are also in Manley O. Hudson, *International Legislation* (7 vols., Washington, 1931–1941), I, 617–625, bilingual.

[5]For "Statute for the Organisation for Communications and Transit, Adopted by the Third General Conference on Communications and Transit at Geneva on September 2nd, 1927," see Document [A.52.1927.VIII.] <3rd C.G.C.T.35.> (1927.VIII.9.). This is also in Hudson, *International Legislation*, III, 2106-2117, bilingual.

[6]See also *First Report of the Advisory and Technical Committee for Communications and Transit on the Work of the Organisation for Communications and Transit between the Second and Third Assembly Presented to the Council, to Be Submitted to the Assembly* [C.533.M.320.1922.VIII.], and Document [A.9.1921.], p. 54.

Report to the Council on the Work of the Twenty-second Session, Held at Geneva from June 6th to 9th, 1939. Geneva, 1939. 20 p. [C.196.M.125.1939.VIII.] (1939.VIII.1.)

4. CONFERENCES

GENERAL CONFERENCES

Rules of Procedure

Rules for the Organisation of General Conferences on Communications and Transit, and of the Advisory and Technical Committee. No date. 16 p., bilingual; mimeographed. <C.T.81(h).>[7]
Rules of Procedure for General Conferences on Communications and Transit. <C.T.40.(c).>[8]

First General Conference, Barcelona, 1921

PREPARATORY DOCUMENTS

First General Conference on Freedom of Communications and Transit. Preparatory Documents. No date. 153 p., bilingual. [20/31/58.]

PROCEEDINGS

Conférence de Barcelone. Comptes Rendus et Textes Relatifs au Règlement d'Organisation des Conférences Générales et de la Commission Consultative et Technique des Communications et du Transit et au Règlement Intérieur des Conférences Générales des Communications et du Transit. Genève, 1923. 95 p.; French text only. [C.662.M.265.1923.VIII.]
Barcelona Conference. Verbatim Records and Texts of the Recommendations Relative to the International Regime of Railways and of the Recommendations Relative to Ports Placed under International Regime. Geneva, 1921. 244 p.
Barcelona Conference. Verbatim Reports and Texts Relating to the Convention on Freedom of Transit (March-April, 1921). Geneva, 1921. 313 p.
Barcelona Conference. Verbatim Records and Texts Relating to the Convention on the Regime of Navigable Waterways of International Concern and to the Declaration Recognising the Right to a Flag of States Having No Sea-Coast (March-April, 1921). Geneva, 1921. 460 p.

[7]Also in General Conference on Freedom of Communications and Transit, Barcelona, March 10th to April 20th,1921, *Official Instruments Approved by the Conference*, p.2-6. [C.15.M.10.1921.VIII.]
[8]Also in *ibid.*, p.7-10.

Final Act of the General Conference on Communications and Transit. Text Adopted and Signed 19 avril 1921.[9] 25 p., bilingual; mimeographed. <C.T.198.C.>. Additional Protocol, 26 avril 1921. <C.T.209.d.>

General Conference on Communications and Transit. Held at Barcelona from March 10th to April 20th, 1921. Report Presented to the Council by M. G. Hanotaux, President of the Conference. Geneva, 1921. 6 p.+6 p., bilingual. [C.234.M.172.1921.VIII.]

OFFICIAL INSTRUMENTS APPROVED BY THE CONFERENCE

General Conference on Freedom of Communications and Transit. Barcelona, March 10th to April 20th, 1921. Official Instruments Approved by the Conference. No date. 43 p.+43 p., bilingual. [C.15.M.10.1921.VIII.][10]

Contains: 1. Rules for the Organisation of General Conferences on Communications and Transit, and of the Advisory and Technical Committee. 2. Rules of Procedure for General Conferences on Communications and Transit. 3. Convention and Statute on Freedom of Transit. 4. Convention and Statute on the Regime of Navigable Waterways of International Concern. 5. Additional Protocol to the Regime of Navigable Waterways of International Concern. 6. Declaration Recognizing the Right to a Flag of States Having No Sea-Coast. 7. Recommendations Relative to the International Regime of Railways. 8. Recommendations Relative to Ports Subject to an International Regime. 9. Final Act.

Second General Conference, Geneva, 1923

PREPARATORY DOCUMENTS

Second General Conference on Communications and Transit. Geneva, November 15th to December 9th, 1923. Preparatory Documents. I: Railways. Geneva, 1925. 111 p. [C.376.M.169.1923. VIII.] <C.G.C.T.1.>. II: Maritime Ports. Geneva, 1922. 100 p. [C.377.M.170.1923.VIII.] <C.G.C.T.2.>. III: Electric Questions. Geneva, 1925. 13 p. [C.378.M.171.1923.VIII.] <C.G.T.3.>

PROCEEDINGS

Records and Texts Relating to the General Discussions of the Conference. Geneva, 1924. 49 p. [C.27.M.13.1924.VIII.]
Records and Texts Relating to the Convention and Statute on the

[9]Also in *ibid.*, p.36.
[10]See also Barcelona Conference, *Introduction and Complete Text of Conventions and Recommendations.* No date. 80 p. The "Convention and Statute on Freedom of Transit," Barcelona, April 20, 1921, came into force on October 31, 1922; also in 7 *Treaty Series*, p. 11–13, bilingual. The "Convention and Statute on the Regime of Navigable Waterways of International Concern," Barcelona, April 20, 1921, came into force on October 31, 1922; also in 7 *Treaty Series*, p. 35–63, bilingual. The "Additional Protocol to the Convention on the Regime of Navigable Waterways of International Concern," Barcelona, April 20, 1921, came into force on October 8, 1921; also in 7 *Treaty Series*, p. 65–71, bilingual.

International Regime of Railways. Geneva, 1924. 95 p. [C.28. M.14.1924.VIII.]

Records and Texts Relating to the Convention and Statute on the International Regime of Maritime Ports. Geneva, 1924. 103 p. [C.29.M.15.1924.VIII.]

OFFICIAL INSTRUMENTS APPROVED BY THE CONFERENCE

Second General Conference on Communications and Transit. Geneva, November 15th to December 9th, 1923. Official Instruments Approved by the Conference. Geneva, 1923. 55 p.+55 p., bilingual. [C.823.M.312.VIII.1923.] <C.G.C.T.36.>

Contains: 1. Convention and Statute on the International Regime of Railways and Protocol of Signature. 2. Convention and Statute on the International Regime of Maritime Ports and Protocol of Signature. 3. Convention Relating to the Transmission in Transit of Electric Power and Protocol of Signature. 4. Convention Relating to the Development of Hydraulic Power Affecting More Than One State and Protocol of Signature. 5. Final Act of the Conference.[11]

Third General Conference, Geneva, 1927

PREPARATORY DOCUMENTS

Third General Conference on Communications and Transit. Preparatory Documents . . . Geneva, 1927. Volume I: General Method of Working of the Organisation. 47 p. <3rd.C.G.C.T.1.(Vol.I.)> (1927.VIII.5/I.). Volume II: Identity Documents for Persons without Nationality. 20 p. <3rd.C.G.C.T.1.(Vol.II).> (1927. VIII.5/II.)

PROCEEDINGS

Third General Conference on Communications and Transit. Geneva, August 23rd to September 2nd, 1927. Volume I: Records and Texts Relating to the General Discussion of the Conference. Geneva, 1927. 89 p. [C.558.M.200.1927.VIII.] (1927.VIII.15.¹). Volume II: Records and Texts Relating to the Collection and Exchange of General Information on Communications and Transit. Geneva, 1927. 55 p. [C.558(a).M.200(a).1927.VIII.] (1927.VIII.

[11]The above documents, with the exception of the Final Act, are also published separately in the *Treaty Series*. The "Convention and Statute on the International Regime of Railways," Geneva, December 9, 1923, came into force on March 23, 1926; also in 47 *Treaty Series*, p. 55-90, bilingual. The "Convention and Statute on the International Regime of Maritime Ports," Geneva, December 9, 1923, came into force on July 26, 1926; also in 58 *Treaty Series*, p. 285-313, bilingual. The "Convention Relating to the Transmission in Transit of Electric Power," Geneva, December 9, 1923, came into force on July 26, 1926; also in 58 *Treaty Series*, p. 315-329, bilingual. The "Convention Relating to the Development of Hydraulic Power Affecting More than One State," Geneva, December 9, 1923, came into force on June 30, 1925; also in 36 *Treaty Series*, p. 75-89, bilingual.

15/[11].). Volume III: Records and Texts Relating to Identity and Travelling Documents for Persons without Nationality or of Doubtful Nationality. Geneva, 1927. 62 p. [C.558(b).M.200(b). 1927.VIII.] (1927.VIII.15.[111]). Volume IV: Records and Texts Relating to the Statute of the Organisation for Communications and Transit and the Rules of Procedure for General Conferences. Geneva, 1927. 67 p. [C.558(c).M.200(c).1927.VIII.] (1927.VIII. 15.[IV])

Extracts from the Acts of the Third General Conference on Communications and Transit. Held at Geneva, August 23rd-September 2nd, 1927. Geneva, 1927. 40 p. [A.52.1927.VIII.] <3rd.C.G. C.T.35.> (1927.VIII.9.)

Contains: Agenda and Results of the Conference, p.11-40.

INDEX

Index to the Documents Published by the Organisation for Communications and Transit between the First and Third General Conferences, 1921–1927. Geneva, 1929. 84 p. [C.356.M.130.1929. VIII.] (1929.VIII.15.)

Fourth General Conference, Geneva, 1931

PREPARATORY DOCUMENTS

Volume I: Calendar Reform. Geneva, 1931. 28 p. <4th.C.G.C.T.1.> (1931.VIII.12.[1]). Supplement to Volume I: Calendar Reform: Proposal by the National Committee of the United States of America Relating to: 1. The Improvement of the Leap-year Rule; 2. The Adjustment of the Date of the Vernal Equinox. Geneva, 1931. 8 p. <4th.C.G.C.T.1.Vol.I.Supplement.> (1938.VIII.12/I Supplement). Volume II: 1. Report by the Secretary-General of the League of Nations on Action Taken on the Decisions of Previous Conferences. 2. Memorandum on the Principal Questions Dealt with by the Advisory and Technical Committee for Communications and Transit since the Third General Conference. 3. Grave Occurrences of a General Character Affecting Routes of Communication. Geneva, 1931. 20 p. <4th.C.G.C.T.1.> (1931. VIII.12.[11])

PROCEEDINGS

Records and Texts Relating to the Fourth General Conference on Communications and Transit. Held at Geneva from 12th to 24th October, 1931. Volume I: 1. Minutes of the First Plenary Meeting of the Conference. 2. Minutes of the Plenary Committee for the Examination of the Expediency from an Economic and Social Standpoint of Fixing Movable Feasts and of Simplifying the

Gregorian Calendar. 3. Minutes of the Second and Third Plenary
Meetings of the Conference. Annexes. Geneva, 1931. 71 p. [C.
977.M.542.1931.VIII.]   <4th.C.G.C.T./P.V.1–3.>   <4th.C.G.C.
T./Com.Cal.P.V.> (1931.VIII.24.¹). Volume II: Minutes of the
Fourth to the Thirteenth Plenary Meetings of the Conference.
Annexes. Geneva, 1931. 75 p. [C.977.M.542.1931.VIII.Vol.II.]
(1931.VIII.24.¹¹)

OFFICIAL INSTRUMENTS APPROVED BY THE CONFERENCE

Fourth General Conference on Communications and Transit. Geneva, October 12th to 24th, 1931. Official Instruments Approved
by the Conference. Geneva, 1931. 16 p.+16 p., bilingual. [C.785.
M.380.1931.VIII.] (1931.VIII.19.)

Contains: Final Act; Recommendation Concerning Measures to Be Taken in Cases
of Serious Interruption of Transit Routes; Act Regarding the Economic and Social
Aspects of Fixing Movable Feasts; Resolution Concerning the Economic and Social
Aspects of the Simplification of the Gregorian Calendar.

5. SPECIAL CONFERENCES

Buoyage and Lighting of Coasts (1930)

Records and Texts of the Conference for the Unification of Buoyage
and Lighting of Coasts. Held at Lisbon, October 6th to 23rd, 1930.
Geneva, 1931. 106 p. [C.163.M.58.1931.VIII.] (1931.VIII.1.)
Conference for the Unification of Buoyage and the Lighting of Coasts.
(Lisbon, October 6th–23rd, 1930). Geneva, 1930. 23 p. [C.634.M.
253.1930.VIII.] (1930.VIII.13.)

Contains: 1. Agreement Concerning Maritime Signals. 2. Agreement Concerning
Manned Lightships not on Their Stations. 3. Recommendations on Lighthouse
Characteristics and Radio-Beacons. 4. Final Act of the Conference.
The "Agreement Concerning Maritime Signals," came into force on November 22,
1931; also in 125 *Treaty Series*, p. 95–111. The "Agreement Concerning Manned
Lightships Not on Their Stations" came into force on January 21, 1931; also in
112 *Treaty Series*, p. 21–28.

Cards for Emigrants in Transit (1929)

European Conference on Cards for Emigrants in Transit. Held at
Geneva, June 10th to 14th, 1929. Records and Texts. Geneva, 1929.
56 p. [C.326.M.112.1929.VIII.] (1929.VIII.12.).

Annex 4: Agreement Concerning the Preparation of a Transit Card for Emigrants,
Adopted by the Conference on June 14th, 1929. The Agreement is in force since
September 12, 1929. Also in 94 *Treaty Series*, p. 277–285.

Measurement of Inland Vessels (1925)

European Conference on the Measurement of Vessels Employed in
Inland Navigation. Held in Paris, November 20th to 27th, 1925.

Minutes of the Plenary Meetings of the Conference and of the Meetings of the Technical Committee. Geneva, 1926. 79 p. [C. 107.M.50.1926.VIII.] (1926.VIII.1.)

The "Convention Regarding the Measurement of Vessels employed in Inland Navigation" came into force on October 1, 1927. Also in 67 *Treaty Series*, p. 63–89.

Passport Conference (1926)

Passport Conference held at Geneva from May 12th to 18th, 1926. Minutes of the Plenary Meetings of the Conference. Geneva, 1926. 169 p. [C.423.M.156.1926.VIII.] (1926.VIII.4.)

Final Act of the Conference, Signed on Tuesday, May 18th, 1926. Geneva, 1926. 12 p. [C.320.M.119.1926.VIII.] (1926.VIII.2.).

For the First Passport Conference (Paris 15th–21st, 1920) see Document [C.641. M.230.1925.VIII.].

River Law (1930)

Organisations des Communications et du Transit. Conférence pour l'Unification du Droit Fluvial, Genève, du 17 novembre au 9 décembre 1930. Comptes Rendus et Textes. (French only). Geneva, 1931. 257 p. <Conf.U.D.F./P.V.1930, Revises> (1931. VIII.13.)

See also Documents (1931.VIII.2.), (1931.VIII.3.), (1931.VIII.4.), (1931.VIII.5.).

European Conference on Road Traffic (1931)

Records and Texts of the European Conference on Road Traffic. Held at Geneva, March 16th to 30th, 1931. Geneva, 1931. 164 p. [C.438.M.185.1931.VIII.] (1931.VIII.15.).

Agreement between Customs Authorities in Order to Facilitate the Procedure in the Case of Undischarged or Lost Triptychs. Geneva, 1931. 12 p. [C.233.M.101.1931.VIII.] (1931.VIII.9.).

The "Convention Concerning the Unification of Road Signals" came into force on July 16, 1934; also in 150 *Treaty Series*, p. 247–268. The "Convention on the Taxation of Foreign Motor-Vehicles" came into force on May 9, 1933; also in 138 *Treaty Series*, p. 149–177. The "Agreement between Customs Authorities in Order to Facilitate the Procedure in the Case of Undischarged or Lost Triptychs" came into force on June 26, 1931; also in 119 *Treaty Series*, p. 47–51.

6. SPECIAL ENQUIRIES

AIR NAVIGATION[12]

Enquiries into the Economic, Administrative and Legal Situation of International Air Navigation. Geneva, 1930. 207 p. [C.339.M. 139.1930.VIII.] <R.R.C.T.3.> (1930.VIII.6.)

[12]See also Air Transport Co-operation Committee, *Minutes of the first Session. Held at Geneva from July 8th to 12th,1930.* Geneva,1930. 51 p. <C.C.T./A.C. 1st Session/P.V.

Study Concerning the Present Situation in Regard to Publicity of Civil Aviation and Collection of Provisions in Force Concerning the Exchange or Publication of Information Relating to Civil Aviation. Geneva, 1932. 24 p. [C.95.M.47.1932.VIII.] <Conf.D. 53.> (1932.VIII.1.)

Economics of Air Transport in Europe. Report Submitted to the Sub-Committee by M. Henri Bouché, Editor of L'Aéronautique. Final ed., Geneva, 1935. 73 p. [C.97.M.44.1935.VIII.] (1935. VIII.1.)

HYDRAULIC AND ROAD QUESTIONS IN CHINA

Co-operation between the Organisation for Communications and Transit of the League of Nations and the National Government of China. Report by the Committee of Experts on Hydraulic and Road Questions in China. Geneva, 1936. 213 p. [C.91.M.34.1936. VIII.] (1936.VIII.4.)

COMPETITION BETWEEN RAILWAYS AND WATERWAYS

Report of the Special Committee on Competition between Railways and Waterways Submitted to the Advisory and Technical Committee for Communications and Transit. Geneva, 1929. 197 p. [C.127.M.43.1929.VIII.] <R.R.C.T.1.> (1929.VIII.3.)

Co-ordination of Transport. Results of an Enquiry Addressed to Governments. Geneva, 1938. 348 p. [C.347.M.208.1938.VIII.] (1938.VIII.6.)

This enquiry was based on the Circular Letter of the Secretary-General [C.L. 146. 1936.VIII.] and the Questionnaire [C.L.146.1936.VIII.].

Co-ordination of Transport. Results of an Enquiry Addressed to Governments. Addendum. Geneva, 1939. 57 p. [C.347.M.208. 1938.VIII.Addendum.] (1939.VIII.5.)

List of Multilateral Conventions, Agreements, etc. Relating to Communications Questions. Geneva, 1945. 38 p. [C.53.M.53.1945.VIII.] (1945.VIII.1.)

CUSTOMS EXEMPTION OF LIQUID FUEL

Comparative Study of the Laws in the Various European Countries Governing the Question of Customs Exemption for Liquid Fuel Used by Motor Vehicles in Traffic by Land, River, Sea and Air. Geneva, 1932. 19 p. [C.805.M.373.1932.VIII.] (1932.VIII.6.)

(Revised).> (1930.VIII.14.). Report of the Air Transport Co-operation Committee on Its Second Session Held at Geneva, May 9th to 12th,1932. [C.467.M.237.1932.VIII.] <Conf.D./ C.A. 15.> (1932.VIII.3.)

FRONTIER SECTIONS OF RAILWAY LINES

Juridical and Administrative Systems in Force on the Frontier Sections of Railway Lines and at Junction Stations. Geneva, 1935. 160 p. [C.144.M.75.1935.VIII.] (1935.VIII.2.)

INLAND NAVIGATION IN THE VARIOUS COUNTRIES OF AMERICA

Study of the International Régime of Inland Navigation in the Various Countries of America. Geneva, 1934. 12 p., mimeographed. [C.101.M.36.1934.VIII.] (1934.VIII.4.)

MERCHANT SHIPPING CRISIS

Notes by the Economic Relations Section and the Communications and Transit Section on the Merchant Shipping Crisis. Geneva, 1934. 35 p. [C.99.M.34.1934.VIII.] <R.R.C.T./4(1).> (1934. VIII.3.)

TONNAGE MEASUREMENT

Reports of the Technical Committee

Technical Committee on Maritime Tonnage Measurement. Report on the Differences in the Existing Rules for Tonnage Measurement and in the Application Thereof and on the Establishment of a Uniform Method of Tonnage Measurement. Geneva, 1926. 91 p. [C.138.M.31.1928.VIII.] (1928.VIII.2.)

Supplementary Report of the Technical Committee on Maritime Tonnage Measurement. Geneva, 1931. 8 p. [C.719.M.324.1931. VIII.] (1931.VIII.18.)

Maritime Tonnage Measurement. Report to the Advisory and Technical Committee on Communications and Transit by the Chairman and the Rapporteur of the Technical Committee for Maritime Tonnage Measurement on the Replies Received from the Governments to the Circular Letter Forwarding the Results of the Technical Committee's Work. Geneva, 1934. 22 p. [C.308.M.135.1934. VIII.] <C.4.M.4.1936.VIII.> (1936.VIII.1.)

See also the 29-page Annex to this Document. [C.308.M.135.1934.VIII.] [C.4.M.4. 1936.VIII. Annex I.] (1936.VIII.2.)

Draft Regulations

Draft Regulations for Tonnage Measurement of Ships. Geneva, of Ships. Geneva, 1931. 59 p., bilingual. [C.176(a).M.65(a).1931. VIII.] (1931.VIII.20.)

Figures Annexed to the Draft Regulations for Tonnage Measurement of Ships. Geneva, 1931. 59 p., bilingual. [C.176(a).M.65(a). 1931.VIII.] (1931.VIII.20.)

International Regulations for Tonnage Measurement of Ships. Geneva, 1939. 98 p. [C.108.M.63.1939.VIII.] (1939.VIII.2.)

Figures Annexed to the International Regulations for Tonnage Measurement of Ships. Geneva, 1939. 56 p. [C.108(a).M.63(a). 1939.VIII.] (1939.VIII.3.)

Report of the Drafting Committee of the Technical Committee for Maritime Tonnage Measurement. Geneva, 1939. 7 p. [C.219.M. 147.1939.VIII.] <C.C.T./J.M./22(1).> (1939.VIII.4.)

Revision of the Draft Regulations provided in Document [C.176.M.65.1931.VIII.].

PASSPORTS

Passport System. Replies from Governments to the Enquiry on the Application of the Recommendations of the Passport Conference of 1926. Geneva, 1937. 67 p. [C.356.M.241.1937.VIII.] <C.C.T. 652(1).> (1937.VIII.4.)

Three addenda were issued under the same general classmark.

Facilities to Be Granted to Broadcasting Reporters. Geneva, 1940. 1 p., mimeographed. <C.L.12.1940.VIII.>

PUBLIC WORKS

Circular Concerning Programmes of Important Public Works. Geneva, 1931. 4 p. [C.736.M.341.1931.VIII.] (1931.VIII.16.)

Enquiry on National Public Works. Geneva, 1934. 281 p. [C.482.M. 209.1934.VIII.] (1934.VIII.8.)

Enquiry on National Public Works. Addendum. Geneva, 1935. 226 p. [C.482.M.209.1933.VIII.Addendum.] (1935.VIII.3.)

Documentary Material Collected Regarding National Public Works. 1: Report of Experts. 2: Preliminary Statement Prepared by the Secretariat. Geneva, 1936. 48 p. [C.276.M.166.1936.VIII.] (1936. VIII.8.)

REFORM OF THE CALENDAR

Report on the Reform of the Calendar Submitted to the Advisory and Technical Committee for Communications and Transit of the League of Nations by the Special Committee of Enquiry into the Reform of the Calendar. Geneva, 1926. 163 p. [A.33.1926.VIII.] (1926.VIII.6.)

Special Committee of Enquiry into the Reform of the Calendar.

Classification and Summary of Proposals for Calendar Reform Received before July 1st, 1926. Geneva, 1927. 58 p. [C.167.M.49.1927.VIII.] [Annex III to Document A.33.1926.VIII.6.] (1927.VIII.8.)

Stabilisation of Movable Feasts. Summary of Replies from Religious Authorities to the Letter from the Secretary-General of the League of Nations Communicating the Act Regarding the Economic and Social Aspects of Fixing Movable Feasts. Geneva, 1934. 8 p. [C.335.M.154.1934.VIII.] (1934.VIII.5.)

RHINE AND DANUBE NAVIGATION

Report on Rhine Navigation Submitted to the Advisory and Technical Committee for Communications and Transit of the League of Nations by Walker D. Hines (with the Aid of Major Brehon Somervell). Geneva, 1925. 12 p. [C.444.M.164.1925.VIII.]

Report on Danube Navigation Submitted to the Advisory and Technical Committee for Communications and Transit of the League of Nations by Walker D. Hines (with the Aid of Major Brehon Somervell). Geneva, 1925. 187 p. [C.444(a).M.164(a).1925.VIII.]

ROAD TRAFFIC

Road Signalling. Recommendations and Prescriptive Rules Adopted by the European Conference on Road Traffic and the Permanent Committee on Road Traffic. (Text revised in 1933.). Geneva, 1933. 20 p. [C.671.M.321.1933.VIII.] (1934.VIII.1.)

Committee for the Unification of Statistics Relating to Road Traffic Accidents. Report on the First and Second Sessions of the Committee. Geneva, 1937. 18 p. [C.276.M.179.1937.VIII.] <C.C.T./C.R./U.S.17(1).> (1937.VIII.3.)

Statistics Relating to Road Accidents. Memorandum by the Secretariat Based on Information Received from Governments in Reply to Circular Letter No. 76, Dated May 4th, 1934. Geneva, 1937. 38 p. [C.276.M.179.1937.VIII.Annex I.] <C.C.T./C.R./U.S.17(1). C.C.T./C.R./92.>

SIGNALS AT LEVEL CROSSINGS

Signals at Level Crossings. Report of the Special Committee of Experts Presented to the Council by the Committee for Communications and Transit. Geneva, 1938. 10 p. [C.370.M.221.1938.VIII.] (1938.VIII.5.)

Traffic between the Mediterranean Ports and America

Memorandum on the Traffic between the Mediterranean Ports and America Prepared by the Secretariat of the Communications and Transit Committee. Geneva, 1929. 23 p. <R.R.C.T.2.> (1929. VIII.13.)

Restoration of Transport after the War of 1914–1918

Transport Problems Which Arose from the War of 1914–1918 and the Work of Restoration Undertaken in This Field by the League of Nations. Geneva, 1944. 41 p., mimeographed. [C.29.M.29.1944. VIII.]

Transport Situation

General Transport Situation in 1921. Statements Submitted by the States Which Took Part in the First General Conference on Communications and Transit, Held at Barcelona in March-April, 1921. With an Introduction by Professor Tajani. Geneva, 1922. 2 volumes.

Restoration of the Means of Communication in Europe. Documents on the Application of the Transport Resolutions Adopted by the Genoa Conference. Geneva, 1923. 44 p. [A.64.1923.VIII.]

Unification of Transport Statistics

Report on the Unification of Transport Statistics. Draft International Convention on Transport Statistics Together With Regulations Relating Respectively to Maritime Navigation, Railways and Inland Navigation. Geneva, 1932. 71 p. [C.L.98.1932.VIII.Annex.] (1931.VIII.21.)

Apercu mensuel des Evenements importants dans le Domaine des Transports

First issue: Transports. Apercu Mensuel des Evenements Importants. Septembre 1939. Communications en General et Transports en Transit. 9p., mimeographed. French text only. (Publication date: Septembre 1939).

Last issue: Apercu Mensuel des Evenements Importants dans le Domains des Transports. 34p., mimeographed. French text only. (Publication date: Le 31 juillet, 1946).

Continued by United Nations Department of Economic Affairs, Division of Transport and Communications, as Monthly Summary of Important Events in the Field of Transport and Communications. Vol. I, Nos. 1 and 2 (August and September, 1946). 32p.

VII. LEGAL QUESTIONS

1. INTRODUCTORY NOTE

IT IS DIFFICULT to define the exact scope of the League's activities in the legal field, but it is obvious that the League publications originating in the Legal Section, marked with the Roman numeral V, constitute only a small cross section of the legally relevant material prepared or published by the League. Moreover, since the Hague Codification Conference in 1930, whose *Proceedings* were issued on behalf of the Legal Section, was not too successful, the impression is widespread that the work of the League in this field was altogether a failure. It should be recalled, however, that the great majority of international conventions concluded under the auspices of the League were credited to other sections, for instance, the Convention Providing for a Uniform Law for Bills of Exchange and Promissory Notes, June 7, 1930, appeared on behalf of the Economic Section.

Furthermore, there was no standing committee of the League in charge of legal questions. However, the work of the First Committee of the Assembly, concerned with constitutional and legal questions, should by no means be overlooked.[1]

The two major objects of the Legal Section were (1) to promote the codification of "public" international law; (2) to supervise and to encourage the registration and ratification of agreements and conventions concluded under the auspices of the League of Nations. The Hague Codification Conference (1930) dealt with three major subjects: nationality, territorial waters, responsibility of states.[2] No agreement was reached on the issues of territorial waters and responsibility of states. However, four protocols dealing with questions of nationality and statelessness were adopted, and three of them became operative in 1937.[3]

[1]See Margaret E. Burton, *The Assembly of the League of Nations* (Chicago,1941), p.137, 159; and Marcel Henri Prévost, *Les Commissions de l'Assemblée de la Société des Nations* (Paris,1936), p.17.
[2]See J. Gustave Guerrero, *La Codification du Droit International: La Première Conférence (La Haye, 13 mars–12 avril 1930)* (Paris, 1930), and the following United Nations Documents: *Historical Survey of Development of International Law and Its Codification by International Conferences: Memorandum Prepared by the Secretariat*; A/AC./10/5, 29 April 1947 (see especially p. 27–90 on League activities concerning progressive development and codification of international law), and *Bibliography on the Codification*

The work concerned with the registration, ratification, and publication of international conventions was carried on under the authority of Article 18 of the Covenant and subsequent Assembly and Council Resolutions. Article 18, originally designed to preclude secret diplomacy altogether, was subject to varying interpretations.[4] It covered in principle "every treaty or international engagement entered into hereafter by any Member of the League." In any case, it furnished the legal basis for one of the most important League publications, the *Treaty Series*.

Agreements and conventions concluded under the auspices of the League of Nations deserve special consideration; they are of two categories: agreements and conventions drawn up by the organs of the League themselves, and agreements and conventions drawn up by diplomatic conferences convened by the organs of the League of Nations.[5] The great majority of these conventions were worked out under the second procedure.[6]

Since 1927, 21 periodical lists of ratifications of agreements and conventions concluded under the auspices of the League were issued in order to facilitate and expedite the ratification of agreements and conventions sponsored by the League.[7]

In addition to its more ambitious activities, the Legal Section of the Secretariat furnished continuously legal aid and advice to the Assembly, the Council, and the Secretary-General.[8]

2. CODIFICATION OF INTERNATIONAL LAW[9]

QUESTIONNAIRES ON SUBJECTS WHICH APPEAR RIPE FOR INTERNATIONAL REGULATION

No. 1: Nationality. Geneva, February 9, 1926. 21 p. [C.43.M.18.1926.V.] <C.P.D.I.53.> (1926.V.1.)

---

of International Law, A/AC.10/6, 2 May 1947. For the text of the Code of Private International Law (Bustamante Code), see 86 *Treaty Series*, p. 254–396; 437 articles are included, with the text in English and Spanish. See also the studies on these subjects carried on by *Research in International Law under the Auspices of the Harvard Law School*, Special Supplement to *American Journal of International Law*, XXIII (1929). See also Linden A. Mander, *Foundations of Modern World Society* (Stanford, 1941), p.616–620.

[3]See below, p.276.

[4]See Jean Ray, *Commentaire du Pacte de la Société des Nations* (Paris,1930), p.545–567; Otto Göppert, *Der Völkerbund* (Stuttgart,1938), p.46–55.

[5]See "Work of the League of Nations in the Matter of International Conventions," *Official Journal*, Special Supplement No. 193, p. 16. See also below, Appendix One, Section IX.

[6]See *ibid*.

[7]See below, p. 278–279.

[8]See Egon F. Ranshofen-Wertheimer, *The International Secretariat* (Washington, 1945), p. 104.

[9]On Codification of International Law, see also the report by Politis [A.105.1927.V.]

No. 2: Territorial Waters. Geneva, February 9, 1926. 50 p. [C.44.M. 21.1926.V.] <C.P.D.I.54.> (1926.V.10.)

No. 3: Diplomatic Privileges and Immunities. Geneva, February 9, 1926. 16 p. [C.45.M.22.1926.V.] <C.P.D.I.55.> (1926.V.2.)

No. 4: Responsibility of States for Damage Done in Their Territories to the Person or Property of Foreigners. Geneva, February 9, 1926. 16 p. [C.46.M.23.1926.V.] <C.P.D.I.56.> (1926.V.3.)

No. 5: Procedure of International Conferences and Procedure for the Conclusion and Drafting of Treaties. Geneva, February 9, 1926. 12 p. [C.47.M.24.1926.V.] <C.P.D.I.57.> (1926.V.4.)

No. 6: Piracy. Geneva, February 9, 1926. 5 p. [C.48.M.25.1926.V.] <C.P.D.I.58.> (1926.V.5.)

No. 7: Exploitation of the Products of the Sea. Geneva, February 9, 1926. 7 p. [C.49.M.26.1926.V.] <C.P.D.I.59.> (1926.V.6.)

No. 8: Communications of Judicial and Extra-Judicial Acts in Penal Matters and Letters Rogatory in Penal Matters. Geneva, April 27, 1927. 33 p. [C.201.M.75.1927.V.] <C.P.D.I.99(2).> (1927.V.6.)

No. 9: Legal Position and Function of Consuls. Geneva, April 27, 1927. 4 p. [C.202.M.76.1927.V.] <C.P.D.I.100(2).> (1927.V.7.)

No. 10: Revision of the Classification of Diplomatic Agents. Geneva, April 27, 1927. 4 p. [C.203.M.77.1927.V.] <C.P.D.I.101(2).> (1927.V.8.)

No. 11: Competence of the Courts in Regard to Foreign States. Geneva, April 27, 1927. 9 p. [C.204.M.78.1927.V.] <C.P.D.I. 102(2).> (1927.V.9.)

No. 12: Domicile. Geneva, June 27, 1927. 20 p. [C.343.M.101. 1928.V.] <C.P.D.I.119(1).> (1928.V.3.)

Nos. 1 through 7 were included in:

Report to the Council of the League of Nations on the Questions Which Appear Ripe for International Regulation (Questionnaires Nos. 1 to 7). Adopted by the Committee at Its Third Session, Held in March-April, 1927. Geneva, 1927. 282 p. [C.196.M.70.1927.V.] <C.P.D.I.95(2).> (1927.V.1.)

Contains: Assembly Resolution of September 22nd,1924. Composition of the Committee of Experts Appointed by the Council. Report on the Questions which Appear Ripe for International Regulation. Annex I. Questionnaires Adopted by the Committee at Its Second Session, Held in January,1926. Annex II. Replies by Governments to Questionnaires Received after the Committee's Session. Annex III. Analyses of Replies Received from Governments to Questionnaires Submitted by Members of the Committee.

(1927.V.21.); *Rapport du Comité de Trois Juristes designé par le Conseil le 14 décembre 1928* [A.12.1929.V.] [C.171.(1).1929.V.] (1929.V.6.); and the report by Giannini [A.82. 1930.V.] (1930.V.24.). See also *Survey of International Law in Relation to the Work of Codification of the International Law Commission,* United Nations Document [A/CN. 4/1/Rev.1] (1948.V.1(1)), February 10, 1949; James T. Shotwell and Marina Salvin, *Lessons on Security and Disarmament from the History of the League of Nations* (New York, 1949).

3. HAGUE CODIFICATION CONFERENCE, 1930

ACTS OF THE CONFERENCE

Acts of the Conference for the Codification of International Law. Held at The Hague from March 13th to April 12th, 1930. Volume I: Plenary Meetings. Geneva, 1930. 178 p. [C.351.M.145.1930.V.] (1930.V.14.). Volume II: Minutes of the First Committee. Nationality. Geneva, 1930. 321 p. [C.351 (a).M.145(a).1930.V.] (1930. V.15.). Volume III: Minutes of the Second Committee. Territorial Waters. Geneva, 1930. 221 p. [C.351 (b).M.145(b).1930.V.] (1930. V.16.). Volume IV: Minutes of the Third Committee. Responsibility of States for Damage Caused in Their Territory to the Person or Property of Foreigners. Geneva, 1930. 238 p. [C.351(c).M.145 (c).1930.V.] (1930.V.17.)

Final Act. Geneva, 1930. 26 p., in part bilingual. [C.228.M.115. 1930.V.] <Conf.C.D.I.29.> (1930.V.7.)

BASES OF DISCUSSION: NATIONALITY

Bases of Discussion Drawn up for the Conference by the Preparatory Committee. Volume I: Nationality. Geneva, 1929. 211 p.+211 p. [C.73.M.38.1929.V.] (1929.V.1.)[10]

BASES OF DISCUSSION: TERRITORIAL WATERS

Bases of Discussion Drawn up for the Conference by the Preparatory Committee. Volume II: Territorial Waters.[11] Geneva, 1929. 194 p. +194 p., bilingual. [C.74.M.39.1929.V.] (1929.V.2.)

BASES OF DISCUSSION: RESPONSIBILITY OF STATES

Bases of Discussion Drawn up for the Conference by the Preparatory Committee. Volume III: Responsibility of States for Damage Caused in Their Territory to the Person or Property of Foreigners.[12]

---

[10]See also supplements to Volume I, published under the classmarks [C. 73(a).M.38 (a). 1929.V], [C.73 (b).M.38(b). 1929.V.], [C.73 (c).M.38 (c).1929.V.], and *Report of the First Committee (Nationality). Rapporteur: His Excellency M. J. Gustavo Guerrero*, Geneva, 1930. 12p.+12p., bilingual. [C.229.M.116.1930.V.] <Conf.C.D.21.(I)> (1930.V.8.).

[11]See also supplements to Volume II, published under the classmarks [C.74 (a).M. 39 (a).1929.V.], [C.74 (b).M.39 (b).1929.V.], [C. 74 (b). M. 39(b). 1929. V. Erratum.]. See also *Report of the Second Commission (Territorial Sea). Rapporteur: M. François (Netherlands)*. Geneva, 1930. 18p.+18p., bilingual. [C.230.M.117.1930.V.] <Conf. C.D.I.19(2)> (1930.V.9.)

[12]See also supplements to Volume III, published under the classmarks [C. 75 (a).M. 69(a).1929.V.], [C. 75.M.69.1929.V.Erratum.].

Geneva, 1929. 253 p.+253 p., bilingual. [C.75.M.69.1929.V.] (1929.V.3.)

CONVENTIONS AND PROTOCOLS[13]

Conflict of Nationality Laws

Convention on Certain Questions Relating to the Conflict of Nationality Laws.[14] Geneva, 1930. 14 p., in part bilingual. [C.24.M.13. 1931.V.]

Double Nationality and Military Obligations

Protocol Relating to Military Obligations in Certain Cases of Double Nationality.[15] Geneva, 1930. 9 p., in part bilingual. [C.25.M.14. 1931.V.]

Statelessness

Protocol Relating to a Certain Case of Statelessness.[16] Geneva, 1930. 9 p., in part bilingual. [C.26.M.15.1931.V.]

Special Protocol Concerning Statelessness.[17] Geneva, 1930. 7 p., in part bilingual [C.27.M.16.1931.V.]

The above instruments were drawn up as a result of the Hague Codification Conference of 1930.

4. NATIONALITY AND LEGAL STATUS OF WOMEN

Nationality of Women. Report by the Secretary-General. Geneva, 1931. 14 p. [A.19.1931.V.] (1931.V.7.)

Nationality of Women. Observations Submitted by Governments. Geneva, 1932. 11 p. [A.15.1932.V.] (1932.V.2.)

Nationality of Women. Observations Submitted by Governments. Second series, Geneva, 1932. 3 p. [A.15 (a).1932.V.] (1932.V.4.)

Nationality of Women. Report of the Secretary-General on the Information Obtained in Execution of the Resolutions of the Assembly and the Council. Geneva, 1934. 7 p., mimeographed. [C. 342.M.158.1934.V.] (1934.V.2.)

Nationality of Women. Convention on the Nationality of Women Concluded on December 26th, 1933, at the Seventh International

---

[13]See also Convention on the Nationality of Women [A. 7. V. 1935]. (1935.V.1.)

[14]Signed at The Hague, April 12, 1930. In force since July 1, 1937. Text also in 179 Treaty Series, p.89–113, bilingual.

[15]Signed at The Hague, April 12, 1930. In force since May 25, 1937. Text also in 178 Treaty Series, p.227–238, bilingual.

[16]Signed at The Hague, April 12, 1930. In force since July 1, 1937. Text also in 179 Treaty Series, p. 115-126, bilingual.

[17]Not in force. See Official Journal, Special Supplement No.193, p. 61 (1944.V.2.)

Conference of American States at Montevideo. Geneva, 1935. 2 p. [A.7.1935.V.] (1935.V.1.)

Nationality and Status of Women. Statements Presented by International Women's Organisations. Geneva, 1935. 49 p. [A.19.1935. V.] (1935.V.5.)

Nationality and Status of Women. Statements Presented by International Women's Organisations. Supplement. Geneva, 1935. 3 p. [A.19(a).1935.V.] (1935.V.7.) Supplement No. 2. Geneva, 1935. 2 p. [A.19(b).1935.V.] (1935.V.8.)

Status of Women. Communications from Governments and Women's International Organisations. Geneva, 1936. 32 p. [A.33.1936.V.] (1936.V.8.)

Status of Women. Communications Received from Governments and Women's International Organisations. Geneva, 1938. 5 p. [C.84. M.38.1938.V.] (1938.V.1.)

Committee for the Study of the Legal Status of Women. Report on the Progress of the Enquiry (Adopted on January 10th, 1939). Geneva, 1939. 2 p. [C.59.M.21.1939.V.] <C.S.F.25 (1).> (1939. V.I.)

Legal Status of Women. A Survey of Comparative Law (Fourth Provisional Edition). Rome, August, 1942. [U.D.P.–1942. Studies No.XXI: Legal Status of Women Doc. 2.] 186 p.; typewritten.

Contains: Capacity: The Capacity of Women-General; B.Rules Relating to Capacity Applicable to Certain Specified Cases. The Law as Applied to the Family: A.Marriage; B.Personal Relations of Husband and Wife (during Marriage and after Dissolution of Marriage); C.Relation between Husband and Wife with Regard to Property (during Marriage and after Dissolution of Marriage by Divorce or Judicial Separation); D.Relations between Parents and Children (during Marriage and after Dissolution of Marriage); E.The Right of Adoption in so far as It Concerns the Wife; F.Consequences of Husband's Absence; G.Illegitimate Unions. Right of Succession and Donation "Mortis Causa" (Rules Especially Applicable to Women). Legal Situation of Widows. This is an important study, which is available only in a limited number of copies; it will no doubt furnish the basis for similar investigations in the field.

5. RATIFICATION OF INTERNATIONAL CONVENTIONS CONCLUDED UNDER THE AUSPICES OF THE LEAGUE OF NATIONS[18]

GENERAL

Accessions to International Agreements Given Subject to Ratification. Geneva, 1927. 2 p. [A.12.1927.V.] (1927.V.13.)

[18]On registration of treaties by the United States, see Registration of Treaties by the United States of America under the Provisions of Paragraph 13 of the Memorandum Approved by the Council on May 19th, 1920. Geneva, March,1934. 2p., mimeographed. [C.L. 32. 1934. V.]

Admissibility of Reservations to General Conventions. Geneva, 1927.
3 p. [C.357.M.130.1927.V.] (1927.V.16.)
Ratification of Agreements and Conventions Concluded under the
Auspices of the League of Nations. Geneva, 1927. 22 p. [C.32.
1927.V.]

See the following note by the Secretary-General: "In accordance with the instructions contained in the report adopted by the Council of the League of Nations
during the Forty-third Session on December 6th,1926, the Secretary-General has the
honor to submit herewith to the Members of the Council a list in chronological order
of the international agreements which have been concluded under the auspices of
the League. The list shows the States which have become parties to these agreements
by ratification or accession, the States which have signed but have not yet ratified
them, and, finally, the States which have neither signed nor acceded, although they
took part in the conferences at which the agreements were drawn up or have been
invited to become parties thereto."

Report of the Committee Appointed to Consider the Question of
Ratification and Signature of Conventions Concluded under the
Auspices of the League of Nations. Geneva, 1930. 10 p. [A.10.
1930.V.] (1930.V.11.)

OFFICIAL LISTS OF RATIFICATIONS

First List: [C.32.1927.V.], March 8, 1927.
Discussed in the Council on March 8, 1927.[19]
Second List: [C.379.1927.V.], September 3, 1927.
Discussed in the Council on September 3, 1927.[20]
Third List: [C.36.1928.V.], March 6, 1928.
Discussed in the Council on March 6, 1928.[21]
Fourth List: [C.393.1928.V.Annex], August 30, 1928.
Discussed in the Council on September 1, 1928.[22]
Fifth List: [C.45.1929.V.], March 4, 1929.
Discussed in the Council on March 4, 1929.[23]
Sixth List: [C.339.1929.V.], August 30, 1929.
Discussed in the Council on August 30, 1929.[24]
Seventh List: [C.4.1930.V.], January 13, 1930.
Discussed in the Council on January 13, 1930.[25]
Eighth List: [C.4(1).1930.V.], April 25, 1930.
Discussed in the Council on May 13, 1930.[26]

[19]Document and discussion in *Official Journal*, April, 1927, p. 453-474, 373-374.
Prior to 1927, *i.e.*, before the issue of the First List in this series, other lists had been
published: [A.10(a).1923.Annex], September 1,1923; [A.8(a).1924.Annex], September 1,
1924; [A.7(a). 1925.Annex], September 7,1925; [A.6(a).1926.Annex], August 31,1926.
[20]Document and discussion in *Official Journal*, October, 1927, p. 1225-1248, 1113-1114.
[21]Document and discussion in *Official Journal*, April, 1928, p. 515-539, 380-383.
[22]Document and discussion in *Official Journal*, October, 1928, p. 1532-1571, 1448.
[23]Document and discussion in *Official Journal*, April, 1929, p. 585-628, 510-511.
[24]Document and discussion in *Official Journal*, November, 1929, p. 1480-1535, 1449.
[25]Document and discussion in *Official Journal*, February, 1930, p. 193-250, 66-67.
[26]Document and discussion in *Official Journal*, June, 1930, p. 607-669, 516.

Ninth List: [A.6(a).1930.Annex], September 9, 1930.[27]

Tenth List: [C.9.1931.V.], January 15, 1931.[28]

Eleventh List: [C.9(1).1931.V.], May 12, 1931.

Discussed in the Council on May 21, 1931.[29]

Twelfth List: [A.6(a).1931.V.Annex], September 3, 1931.[30]

Thirteenth List: [A.6(a).1932.V.Annex], September 14, 1932.[31]

Fourteenth List: [A.6(a).1933.V.Annex], September 15, 1933.[32]

Fifteenth List: [A.6(a).1934.V.Annex], September 1, 1934.[33]

Sixteenth List: [A.6(a).1935.V.Annex], August 28, 1935.[34]

Seventeenth List: [A.6(a).1936.Annex I.(V).], September 10, 1936.[35]

Eighteenth List: [A.6(a).1937.Annex I.V.], August 31, 1937.[36]

Nineteenth List: [A.6(a).1938.Annex I.V.], September 1, 1938.[37]

Twentieth List: [A.6.1939.Annex I.V.], August 28, 1939.[38]

Last Official Lists: Work of the League of Nations in the Matter of International Conventions. Signatures, Ratifications and Accessions in Respect of Agreements and Conventions Concluded under the Auspices of the League of Nations [C.25.M.25.1943.V.Annex] (1944.V.2.).[39] *Official Journal,* Special Supplement No. 193, Geneva, 1944, and Special Supplement No. 195.

DIAGRAMS AND GRAPHS

Tables, Diagrams and Graphs, Showing the State of Signatures, Ratifications and Accessions in Agreements and Conventions Concluded under the Auspices of the League of Nations up to September 1st, 1930. No date. Unpaged. [A.20.1930.V.] (1930.V.18.)

Tables, Diagrams and Graphs, Showing the State of Signatures, Ratifications and Accessions in Agreements and Conventions Concluded under the Auspices of the League of Nations up to September 1st, 1931. No date. Unpaged. [A.26.1931.V.] (1931.V.9.)

---

[27] In *Official Journal,* December, 1930, p. 1689–1778.
[28] In *Official Journal,* Special Supplement No. 84, p. 395–488.
[29] Document and discussion in *Official Journal,* July, 1931, p. 1323–1422, 1113–1116.
[30] In *Official Journal,* January, 1932, p. 7–130.
[31] In *Official Journal,* January, 1933, p. 5–116.
[32] This document was not reproduced in the *Official Journal.*
[33] In *Official Journal,* Special Supplement No. 122, 125 p.
[34] In *Official Journal,* Special Supplement No. 136, 122 p.
[35] In *Official Journal,* Special Supplement No. 152, 131 p.
[36] In *Official Journal,* Special Supplement No. 167, 133 p.
[37] In *Official Journal,* Special Supplement No. 181, 139 p.
[38] In *Official Journal,* Special Supplement No. 192, 144 p.
[39] Published *as Annex to the Report on the Work of the League for the Year 1942–1943.*

6. CRIMINAL LAW

UNIFICATION OF CRIMINAL LAW

Gradual Unification of Criminal Law and Co-operation of States in the Prevention and Suppression of Crime. Geneva, 1933. 11 p. [A.7.1933.V.] (1933.V.3.)

Gradual Unification of Criminal Law and Co-operation of States in the Prevention and Suppression of Crimes. Geneva, 1933. 2 p. [A.7 (a).1933.V.] (1933.V.7.)

Gradual Unification of Criminal Law and Co-operation of States in the Prevention and Suppression of Crimes. Geneva, 1933. 2 p. [A.7(b).1933.V.] (1933.V.8.)

REPRESSION OF TERRORISM

Committee Reports and Government Observations

Committee for the International Repression of Terrorism. Report to the Council Adopted by the Committee on January 15th, 1936. Report Adopted by the Council on January 23rd, 1936. Geneva, 1936. 16 p. [A.7.1936.V.] <C.36(1).1936.V.> (1936.V.2.)

International Repression of Terrorism. Report Submitted by the First Committee to the Assembly. Rapporteur: His Excellency, Professor V. V. Pella (Roumania). Geneva, 1936. 2 p. [A.72.1936. V.]

Committee for the International Repression of Terrorism. Report Adopted by the Committee on April 26th, 1937. Geneva, 1937. 13 p. [C.222.M.162.1937.V.] (1937.V.1.)

International Repression of Terrorism. Draft Convention for the Prevention and Punishment of Terrorism, Draft Convention for the Creation of an International Criminal Court. Observations by Governments. Series I: Geneva, 1936. 12 p. [A.24.1936.V.] (1936. V.6.). Series II: Geneva, 1936. 3 p. [A.24(a).1936.V.] (1936.V.7.). Series III: Geneva, 1938. 9 p. [A.24(b).1936.V.] (1938.V.2.)

International Conference on the Repression of Terrorism, 1937

Proceedings of the International Conference on the Repression of Terrorism. Geneva, 1938. 218 p. [C.94.M.47.1938.V.] (1938.V.3.)

Contains: Part I. Official Instruments of the Conference: 1. Convention for the Prevention and Punishment of Terrorism,[40] p.5–17, bilingual. 2. Convention for the Creation of an International Criminal Court, p.18–33, bilingual.[41] Part II. Proceedings of the Conference, p.39–204. Part III. List of References to Preparatory Documents Not Reproduced in the Present Volume.

[40]Also published as a separate document.

International Conference on the Repression of Terrorism (Geneva, November 1st to 16th, 1937). Final Act. No date. 10 p., in part bilingual. [C.548.M.385.1937.V.]

CONVENTIONS

Convention for the Prevention and Punishment of Terrorism (Geneva, November 16th, 1937). No date. 12 p., in part bilingual. [C.M.546(1).M.383(1).1937.V.] (1937.V.10.)

Convention for the Creation of an International Criminal Court (Geneva, November 16th, 1937). No date. 11 p., in part bilingual. [C.547(1).M.384(1).1937.V.] (1937.V.11.)

7. UNIFICATION OF PRIVATE LAW

The International Institute for the Unification of Private Law was set up by virtue of the Council Resolution of March 15, 1926,[41] and a letter from the Italian government to the President of the Council dated March 31, 1926.[42] The Institute was opened in Rome on May 30, 1928, but 1929 is generally considered the actual starting point of the Institute's work.[43] By letter of December 27, 1937, the Italian Minister of Foreign Affairs, Count Ciano, informed the League that the Italian government had decided to denounce, effective April 20, 1940, its note of March 31, 1926, regarding the foundation and maintenance of the International Institute for the Unification of Private Law at Rome.[44] Subsequently, however, the Italian Government declared that the Institute would continue to exist as an autonomous organization. The League of Nations on its part acknowledged that the Library remained the property of the Institute. In 1939 the Governing Body of the Institute proposed to the Italian Government that the Institute be reorganized on a new basis as a public international union. The Governing Body prepared a new Statute, whose text was approved at a meeting held in Florence in May 1939. The Italian Government accepted the proposal and invited States members of the League and non-members of the League to adhere to the new Statute. On April 21, 1940 the new Statute dated March 15, 1940 entered into force. As of 1948, thirty Governments adhered to the Statute.

The main organs of the Institute were (1) the Governing Body;

[41]See *Official Journal*, April,1926, p.506, 577–578. [C.156 (3). 1926.V.]
[42]Text in *Official Journal*, June,1926, p.812–813. [C.262.M.101.1926.V.]
[43]See the 1929 Report on the work of the Institute, Document [C.421.M.188.1930.V.],p.1.
[44]See *Official Journal*, January,1938, p.15.

(2) the Standing Committee, composed of a limited number of the members of the Governing Body;[45] (3) and the Secretariat.

The object of the Institute was "to study methods for the assimilation and co-ordination of private law as between States or groups of States, and to prepare for a gradual adoption by the various States of uniform private law legislation. This work shall be done under the direction of the League of Nations in connection with, and with due regard for, the work of the Committee on Intellectual Co-operation, the International Labour Office and the technical organisations of the League."[46]

STATUTES AND INTERNAL REGULATIONS

Statutes of the Institute, Approved by the Council on March 15th, 1926. In International Institute for the Unification of Private Law: Offer of the Italian Government, Geneva, 1926, p. 3–4. [C.156 (3). 1926.V.][47]

International Institute for the Unification of Private Law. Communication to the Assembly, under Article 14 of the Statute of the Institute, of the Text Approved by the Council of the Regulations for the Administration and Internal Working of the Institute. Geneva, 1928. 4 p. [A.69.1928.V.][48]

REPORTS ON THE ACTIVITIES OF THE INSTITUTE

Rapport sur l'activité de l'Institut International de Rome pour l'Unification du Droit Privé pendant l'année 1931. Rome, no date. 7 p. [U.D.P.-Rapp.1931-IV.S.d.N.-C.D.-Italie.]

Rapport sur l'activité de l'Institut International de Rome pour l'Unification du Droit Privé pendant l'année 1932. Rome, no date. 9 p. [U.D.P.-Rapport 1932.-S.d.N.-C.D.-Italie.]

Rapport sur l'activité de l'Institut International de Rome pour l'Unification du Droit Privé pendant l'année 1933. Rome, no date. 9 p. [S.d.N.-U.D.P.-Rapport 1933-Italie.]

Rapport sur l'activité de l'Institut 1934–1935. Approuvé par le Conseil de Direction de l'Institut le 30 septembre 1935. Rome, Tipografia del Senato. A. XIV.[49] 18 p. [S.d.N.-U.D.P.-Rapport 1934–1935-Italie.]

[45]See Art.5 of the 1926 Statute of the Institute.
[46]See Art. 2, *ibid.*
[47]Also in *Official Journal*, April,1926, p.579–580. Art.4 of the Statute was amended at the Council Meeting of March 12, 1927, and the number of the members of the Governing Body increased to a maximum of 14, exclusive of the president; see *Official Journal*, April,1927,p.420.
[48]Also in *Official Journal*, October,1928, p.1752–1754.
[49]A. XIV., *i.e.*, the fourteenth year of the Fascist regime of Benito Mussolini, 1936.

Rapport sur l'activité de l'Institut International de Rome pour l'Unification du Droit Privé, 1935–1936. Rome, no date. 12 p. [S.d.N.-U.D.P.-Rapport 1935–1936-Italie.]

Rapport sur l'activité de l'Institut International de Rome pour l'Unification du Droit Privé, 1936–1937. Rome, no date. [S.d.N.-U.D.P.-Rapport 1936–1937-Italie.]

Rapport sur l'activité de l'Institut International de Rome pour l'Unification du Droit Privé, 1937–1938 et 1938–1939.[50] Rome, no date. Imprimerie du Sénat. 29 p. [S.d.N.-U.D.P.-Rapport 1937–1938 et 1938–1939-Italie.]

STUDIES AND PROPOSALS

Performance of Aliments Abroad

Obligations alimentaires[51] entre les membres de la famille légitime. Premier Partie. Obligations alimentaires entre epoux (Allemagne, Angleterre, France, Italie, Suède, Suisse). Rome, 1938. 437 p., mimeographed. [S.d.N.-U.D.P.1938.Etudes II.: Dettes Alimentaires-Doc.12.]

Comité pour l'Exécution à l'Etranger des Obligations Alimentaires. Avant-Projet de Convention adopté par le Comité lors de sa Deuxième Session, tenue à S. Margherita de 24 au 27 octobre 1938. Rome, 1938. 7 p., mimeographed. [S.d.N.-U.D.P.-1938-Etudes I.: Dettes Alimentaires.]

De l'exécution à l'étranger des obligations alimentaires. Rome, 1937. 203 p., mimeographed. [S.d.N.-U.D.P.1937-Etudes II.: Dettes Alimentaires-Doc.5.]

L'Exécution à l'étranger des obligations alimentaires. Rome, 1938. 312 p. [S.d.N.-U.D.P.1938.Etudes II.: Dettes Alimentaires-Doc. 13.]

Arbitration

Rapport sur l'arbitrage conventionnel en droit privé: Etude de droit

[50]Approuvé par le Conseil de Direction de L'Institut le 30 mai 1939. The following reports appeared in the *Official Journal*: "Report on the Work of the Rome International Institute for the Unification of Private Law during the Year 1929," *Official Journal*, December,1930, p.1835–1840. [C.421.M.188.1930.V.]; "Report by the Acting Secretary-General of the Rome International Institute for the Unification of Private Law on the Work of the Institute in the Field of Intellectual Rights," *Official Journal*, December, 1937, p.1057–1060; "Report by the Acting Secretary-General of the Rome International Institute for the Unification of Private Law on the Work of the Institute in the Field of Intellectual Rights," *Official Journal*, November,1938, p.941.

[51]The following definition of the subject of this study appears on p.x: "Nous entendons par obligation alimentaire, dans le présent rapport, toute obligation en vertu de laquelle un membre de famille est tenu à fournir effectivement des aliments à un autre membre de famille."

comparé par René David. Rome, 1932. 289 p. [U.D.P.Etudes III. S.d.N.1932-C.D.1932.]

Artistic and Literary Rights

Remarks on the Bern and Havana Conventions for the Protection of Literary and Artistic Works. No date. 19 p., mimeographed. [U.D.P.Etudes S.d.N.1930.C.D.1930.]

Droit des artistes exécutants. Compte-Rendu sur l'état actuel de la question de la protection internationale du droit des artistes exécutants et sur la méthode à suivre pour arriver à une solution de cette question. Rome, 1935. 22 p., mimeographed. [S.d.N.-U.D.P. 1935-Etudes IX. Droits Intellectuelles: Executants-Doc.2.]

"L'Auteur de l'oeuvre cinématographique." *Le Droit d'auteur*, XLV (le 15 février, 1936), 18–19.[52]

Avant-Projets de conventions connexées à la Convention de Berne pour la Protection des Oeuvres Littéraires et Artistiques. Rome, 1941. 33 p. [U.D.P.1940-Etudes:V.Droits Intellectuels-Doc.23.]

Contains: Avant-Projet de Convention assurant la protection des artistes-interprètes et des artistes-executants, aussi que des producteurs de disques phonographiques et d'instruments similaires, p.25–28; Avant-Projet de Convention assurant la protection des radio émissions, p.28–29; Avant-Projet de Convention assurant la protection des informations de presse, p.29–31; Avant-Projet de Convention assurant aux auteurs d'oeuvres d'art "Un Droit de Suite" sur le prix de revente de leurs oeuvres, p.31–33.

Automobilists: Compulsory Insurance and Civil Responsibility

Assurance obligatoire des automobilistes: Etudes préliminaires. Rome, 1936. 200 p., mimeographed. [S.d.N.-U.D.P.1936-Etudes XVII.Responsabilité Automobilistes-Doc.8.]

Responsabilité civile des automobilistes: Etudes préliminaires. Rome, 1935. 166 p., mimeographed. [S.d.N.-U.D.P.1935-Etudes XVII.Responsabilité Automobilistes-Doc.1.]

Unification internationale en matière de responsabilité civile et d'assurance obligatoire des automobilistes: Avant-Projets et rapports. Rome, 1940. 68 p. [U.D.P.1940-Etudes XVII-Responsabilité et Assurance Automobilistes-Doc.31.]

Contracts

De la formation des contrats entre absents: Etude préliminaire. Rome, 1935. 155 p., mimeographed. [S.d.N.-U.D.P.1935-Etude XVI.Contrats entre Absents-Doc.1.]

[52]See footnote, p. 18: "Nous reproduisons ici un exposé de l'Institut international de Rome pour l'unification du droit privé, qui est à l'origine d'une proposition que le Gouvernment italien a décidé de presenter à la Conférence de Bruxelles. Cette proposition est destinée à compléter l'article 14 de la Convention de Berne revisée en dernier lieu à Rome le 2 juin 1928."

Des contrats conclus par représentation: Etude préliminaire. Rome, 1936. 233 p., mimeographed. [S.d.N.-U.D.P.1936-Etude XIX.Contrat par Représentation-Doc.1.]

Innkeepers' Liability

Draft Uniform Law Respecting the Liability of Innkeepers. Rome, 1935. 26 p. [L.O.N.1935-U.P.L.-Draft II.]

Reinsurance

Contrats de réassurance. Etude préliminaire. Etablie par les soins de la Société "Le Assicurazioni d'Italia" sous la direction de M. Luigi Amoroso de l'Université de Rome. Rome, 1935. 110 p., mimeographed. [S.d.N.-U.D.P.1935-Etudes XIII-Assurances-Doc. 3(1).]

Le Contrat de réassurance. Etude de droit comparé par Bruno De Mori. Rome, 1936. 194 p. [S.d.N.-U.D.P.1935-Etudes-XIII-Assurances-Doc.5.]

Sales

Draft of an International Law of the Sale of Goods. Rome, 1935. 120 p. [L.O.N.1935-U.P.L.-Draft I.]

General Survey of Studies and Proposals

Unification of Law: A General Survey of Work for the Unification of Private Law. (Drafts and Conventions.) Rome, 1948. 821 p.

8. VARIOUS DOCUMENTS AND REPORTS

COMPETENCE OF STATES OUTSIDE THEIR TERRITORY

Criminal Competence of States in Respect of Offenses Committed outside Their Territory. Report Adopted by the Committee at Its Second Session, Held in January, 1926. Geneva, 1926. 5 p. [C.50. M.27.1926.V.] <C.P.D.I.60.> (1926.V.7.)

EXTRADITION

Committee of Experts for the Progressive Codification of International Law. Report on Extradition Adopted by the Committee at Its Second Session, Held in January 1926. Geneva, 1926. 6 p. [C.51.M.28.1926.V.] <C.P.D.I.61.> (1926.V.8.)

GOVERNMENT SHIPS EMPLOYED IN COMMERCE

Committee of Experts for the Progressive Codification of International Law. Report to the Council of the League of Nations Adopted by the Committee at Its Second Session, Held in January, 1926. Legal Status of Government Ships Employed in Commerce. Geneva, 1926. 10 p. [C.52.M.29.1926.V.] <C.P.D.I.62.> (1926. V.9.)

LEGAL AID FOR THE POOR

Legal Aid for the Poor. No date. 472 p. (1927.V.27.)

Contains: Part I. Laws, Regulations and Treaty Provisions Regulating Legal Aid in Certain Countries. Part II. List of Agencies for Legal Aid Established in Certain Countries. Part III. List of Authorities or Persons Appointed in Certain Countries to Answer Enquiries from Abroad.

THE MOST-FAVORED-NATION CLAUSE

Committee of Experts for the Progressive Codification of International Law. The Most Favored Nation Clause. Report Adopted by the Committee at Its Third Session, Held in March, 1927. Geneva, 1927. 15 p. [C.205.M.79.1927.V.] <C.P.D.I.97 (1).> (1927.V.10.)

NATIONALITY OF COMMERCIAL CORPORATIONS

Committee of Experts for the Progressive Codification of International Law. Report to the Council of the League of Nations Adopted by the Committee at Its Third Session, Held in March-April, 1927. Nationality of Commercial Corporations and Their Diplomatic Protection. Geneva, 1927. 24 p. [C.207.M.81.1927. V.] <C.D.P.I.98 (1).> (1927.V.12.)

9. REGISTRATION AND PUBLICATION OF TREATIES AND INTERNATIONAL ENGAGEMENTS

Article 18 of the Covenant of the League of Nations provided: "Every treaty or international engagement entered into hereafter by any Member of the League shall be forthwith registered with the Secretariat and shall as soon as possible be published by it. No such treaty or international engagement shall be binding until so registered."[53] This article can be directly traced to Point One of Wilson's Fourteen Points: "Open covenants of peace, openly arrived at." Accordingly, the *Treaty Series* was more than a collection of treaties[54] —it was a means of realizing the principle of open diplomacy.

[53]For the interpretation and partial abrogation of Article 18 in the practice of the League, see Jean Ray, *Commentaire du Pacte de la Société des Nations* (Paris, 1930), p. 545–558; and Otto Göppert, *Der Völkerbund* (Stuttgart, 1938), p. 47–55.
[54]For a survey of treaty collections, see Denys P. Myers, *Manual of Collections of Treaties and of Collections Relating to Treaties* (Cambridge, Mass., 1922), *passim.*

The same principle reappears in Article 102 of the Charter of the United Nations: "Every treaty and every international agreement entered into by any member of the United Nations after the present Charter comes into force shall as soon as possible be registered with the Secretariat and published by it. 2. No party to any such treaty or international agreement which has not been registered in accordance with the provisions of paragraph 1 of this Article may invoke that treaty or agreement before any organ of the United Nations."[55]

A memorandum approved by the Council of the League of Nations on May 19, 1920,[56] extended the principle of registration and publication to international engagements entered into by nonmember states. It provided specifically:

"12. It should be noted that by the provisions of Article 18 not only treaties between members of the League of Nations have to be registered, but also Treaties or Engagements entered into by a Member of the League with a State which has not yet been admitted into the League.

"13. In connection with this last point, it has been suggested that the system of Registration of Treaties by the Secretariat of the League of Nations should from the beginning be so extended as to admit registration of Treaties, etc., made by and between States or Communities that have not yet been admitted as Members of the League of Nations. This would serve to complete the Registration of Treaties and the public collection of Treaties which will be formed by the Treaty Part of the League of Nations Journal [sic]. The Secretary-General therefore proposes, although the Registration will be for this part absolutely voluntary, to accept applications for Registration of Treaties, etc., even if none of the parties is at the time a Member of the League of Nations."[57]

From 1920 to 1946, 205 volumes of the *Treaty Series*, including 4,834 registered instruments, were published.[58]

[55]On the drafting of this provision, see Henry Reiff, "Work of United Nations Legal Committees," *Department of State Bulletin*, XV (July 7, 1946), 10–11.

[56]See 1 *Treaty Series*, p. 7–13.

[57]See *ibid.*, p. 13. See also the following articles by Manley O. Hudson in the *American Journal of International Law:* "Registration of United States Treaties at Geneva," XXVIII (April, 1934), 342–345; "Legal Effect of Unregistered Treaties in Practice, under Article 18 of the Covenant," XXVIII (July, 1934), 546–552; "Registration of Treaties by the Pan American Union." XXXVIII (January, 1944), 98–99.

[58]The *Note by the Secretariat and Regulations to Give Effect to Article 102 of the Charter of the United Nations, Adopted by the General Assembly on 14 December 1946* established the continuity of the United Nations *Treaty Series* with the League of Nations *Treaty Series*. The note reads in part:

"A little less than thirty years ago a fortunate and important innovation was introduced in international law: the obligation of registering and publishing treaties and international agreements. The international engagements which constitute the laws of nations were thus made subject to the sanction of publicity and to the control of public opinion.

TREATY SERIES

First Volume: League of Nations. Treaty Series. Publication of Treaties
and International Engagements Registered with the Secretariat
of the League. Vol. I, No. 1 (September, 1920). 73 p.
Last Volume: League of Nations. Treaty Series. Treaties and Inter-

---

"This new rule, which arises from the wish to eliminate the distrust created by all
secret diplomacy and which forms a definite advance in international relations, was
originally adopted by the Covenant of the League of Nations.

"It has now been made a part of the Charter of the United Nations, Article 102. . . .

"At its meeting on 14 December 1946, the General Assembly of the United Nations
adopted Regulations to give effect to Article 102 of the Charter. The desirability of
avoiding any breach of continuity in a system which has functioned efficiently for
many years and the opportunity of extending the scope of this system have been
taken into account. These Regulations therefore provide that the publication of
treaties and international agreements by the Secretariat will not be confined to those
defined by Articles 102 of the Charter.

"Article 10 of these Regulations stipulates to this effect that:

"The Secretariat shall file and record treaties and international agreements, other
than those subject to registration under Article 1 of these regulations, if they fall in
the following categories:

"(a) Treaties or international agreements entered into by the United Nations or
by one or more of the specialized agencies;

"(b) Treaties or international agreements transmitted by a Member of the United
Nations which were entered into before the coming into force of the Charter, but
which were not included in the treaty series of the League of Nations;

"(c) Treaties or international agreements transmitted by a party not a Member of
the United Nations which were entered into before or after the coming into force of
the Charter which were not included in the treaty series of the League of Nations,
provided, however, that this paragraph shall be applied with full regard to the provisions of the Resolution of the General Assembly of 10 February 1946 set forth in
the Annex to these Regulations. . . .

"The Regulations also provide for the registration or the filing and recording and
the publication of any subsequent action which effects a change in the Parties to a
treaty or agreement, or the terms, scope, or application thereof. Subsequent action
mainly signifies ratifications, later accessions, extensions, notices of denunciation, etc.

"The two annexes A and B to the volumes of the United Nations treaty series are
devoted respectively to the publication of additional information relating to an agreement or treaty which has been registered, or which has been filed and recorded.

"Furthermore, in accordance with a decision of the General Assembly of the United
Nations of 12 February 1946 and with a decision of the League of Nations Assembly
of 18 April 1946, the United Nations has assumed the custody of the originals of
treaties, conventions, agreements and other international instruments formerly entrusted to the League of Nations, and of certain functions of the Secretariat in connection therewith.

"The Secretariat of the United Nations has therefore had to record in the registers
of the League of Nations the subsequent action affecting the above agreements and
conventions.

"The additional information will be published in Annex C of the volumes of the
present series."

For the text of the note and the regulations, see United Nations, *Treaty Series*,
Vol. I (1946–1947), p. xiii–xxxi.

national Engagements Registered with the Secretariat of the League of Nations. Vol. CCV (Final) and Annex LII (1944–1946). 220 p. Each text is reproduced in the then original language, French and English translations are rendered if either language is not used as an original language.

The first volume of the *Treaty Series* of the United Nations appeared in 1947: *United Nations, Treaty Series; Treaties and International Agreements Registered or Filed and Recorded with the Secretariat of the United Nations Volume I* (1946–1947). 269 p.

Part I (p. 3–93) contains Treaties and International Agreements Registered with the United Nations, Part II (p. 94–259). In addition, there are three Annexes: Annex A: Ratifications, accessions, etc., to treaties and international agreements registered with the Secretariat of the United Nations. p. viii. Annex B: Ratifications, accessions, etc., to treaties and international agreements filed and recorded with the Secretariat of the United Nations. p. x. Annex C: Ratifications, accessions, etc., to treaties and international agreements registered with the Secretariat of the League of Nations. p. x.

This volume includes a Note by the Secretariat and Regulations to give effect to Article 102 of the Charter of the United Nations adopted by the General Assembly on December 14, 1946.

A distinction is made in the Regulations between treaties and international agreements which are subject to registration under Article 1 of the Regulations, and those treaties or international agreements that shall be "filed and recorded" in accordance with Article 10 of the Regulations.

The United Nations invited the Governments of Members to transmit to the Secretariat for filing and publication, treaties and international agreements not included in the Treaty Series of the League of Nations and entered into in recent years before the date of the entry into force of the Charter.

The United Nations declared it desirable that arrangements be made for the publication of any treaties or international agreements which non-member States may voluntarily transmit and which have not been included in the Treaty Series of the League of Nations.

See also *Registration and Publication of Treaties and International Agreements: Report of the Sixth Committee.* Rapporteur: J. Spiropoulos (Greece) (United Nations Document A/698, October 29, 1948).

GENERAL INDEX TO THE TREATY SERIES

First Volume: League of Nations Treaty Series. Publication of Treaties and International Engagements Registered with the Secretariat of the League of Nations. General Index (1920–1926). No. 1. 864 p.
Last Volume: League of Nations. Treaty Series. Treaties and Inter-

national Engagements Registered with the Secretariat of the League of Nations. General Index (1939–1946). No. 9 (Vols. CXCIV–CCV), Treaties Nos. 4501–4834. 496 p.

The contents of these General Indices are subdivided throughout as follows: 1. Chronological Index of Treaties; 2. General International Agreements (Chronological Order); Alphabetical Index (Countries and Subjects).

CHECKLISTS

Beginning with October, 1921, the Secretariat issued checklists of registered treaties prior to the publication of the pertinent instruments.

First List: League of Nations. Registration of Treaties. No date, no official number. 12 p., bilingual.

Last List: League of Nations. Registration of Treaties. No. 248, January 1st–July 31st, 1946. Final List. 7 p., bilingual; mimeographed.

VIII. REDUCTION AND LIMITATION OF ARMAMENTS

1. INTRODUCTORY NOTE

THE COVENANT declared as one of its prime objectives "the reduction of national armaments to the lowest point consistent with national safety and the enforcement by common action of international obligations." (Article 8).[1]

A "permanent Commission" was provided for in the Covenant "to advise the Council on the execution of the provisions of Articles 1 and 8 and on military, naval and air questions generally." (Article 9). Accordingly, the Permanent Advisory Commission for Military, Naval, and Air Questions was instituted by Council Resolution of May 19, 1920.[2] The Commission was composed of a military, a naval, and an air representative appointed by each state represented at the Council. Unfortunately, but significantly, the "permanent Commission" designed to bring about mutual agreement on the reduction and limitation of national armaments met for the last time in September, 1932.[3]

A Temporary Mixed Commission for the Reduction of Armaments was set up by Council Resolution of February 25, 1921,[4] to consider the disarmament problem not only from the military, but also from the social, economic, and political viewpoints. The Commission was active until about September, 1924.

"To prepare for a Conference on the reduction and limitation of armaments," a Preparatory Commission for the Disarmament Con-

---

[1]For the genesis of Art.8, see David Hunter Miller, *The Drafting of the Covenant* (2 vols., New York,1928), *passim;* see also the fourth of President Wilson's Fourteen Points.
[2]See Council Minutes, 5th Sess., p.45, 206–216; text of Council Resolution of May 19, 1920, *ibid.*, p.212-215. For the revised Rules of Procedure, approved by the Council on June 14,1924, see *Official Journal*, July,1924, p.913, 983–986, Document <C.P.C.48 (1).1924.>.
[3]See *Essential Facts about the League of Nations* (10th ed., revised, Geneva,1939), p.142. On the general question of disarmament,see Laura Puffer Morgan, "Disarmament," in Harriet E. Davis, ed., *Pioneers in World Order,* (New York,1944), p.42–64, and Linden A. Mander, *Foundations of Modern World Society* (Stanford,1941), p.768–797.
[4]See Council Minutes, 12th Sess., p.103-108, especially p.107-108. For the succession of this Commission by the Coordination Committee, see Marie J. Carroll, *Key to League of Nations Documents Placed on Public Sale, 1920-1929* (Boston,1930), p.295.

ference was established by Council Resolution of December 12, 1925.[5]
The Preparatory Commission was dissolved on December 9, 1930.[6]

Numerous subcommittees of a temporary nature were established
to cope with the disarmament problem.[7]

On February 2, 1932, the Conference for the Reduction and Limitation of Armaments met.[8] Although the beginning of the Conference
can be clearly ascertained, League historians disagree on when or
whether the Disarmament Conference was ever adjourned.

The League studied the problem of the reduction and limitation
of armaments from many angles. In particular, the ways and means
of extending the League's system of war prevention were explored
time and again.[9] Numerous theories of and proposals for war prevention were advanced. Yet, unfortunately, no general agreement
was reached, either on the theory or on the practice of war prevention.[10]

2. PRIVATE MANUFACTURE OF ARMS, AMMUNITION, AND IMPLEMENTS OF WAR

REPORTS AND OTHER DOCUMENTS

Report of the Temporary Mixed Commission for the Reduction of
Armaments. Summary. Geneva, 1924. 31 p. [A.16.1924.IX.]

For private manufacture of arms, see especially p. 20–23.

Supervision of the Private Manufacture of Arms and Ammunition
and of Implements of War. Geneva, 1926. 10 p. [A.47.1926.IX.]
(1926.IX.8.)

[5]See *Official Journal*, February,1926, p.164–170.
[6]For a historical survey of the work of the Preparatory Commission, see *Official Journal*,
February 1931, p. 312–317.
[7]For information on this very complex subject, consult Carroll, *Key to League of Nations Documents . . . 1920–1929*, p. 293–302; and the supplements for the years 1930–
1931 (2 vols., Boston, 1931–1933), Vol. I, p. 51–52, Vol. II, p. 61; 1932–1933 (Boston,
1935), p. 77–81; 1934–1936 (New York, 1938), p. 132–138. See also Ottlik, *passim*.
[8]See *Essential Facts*, p.146. For the Disarmanent Conference, see Carl Loosli-Usteri,
*Geschichte der Konferenz für die Herabsetzung und Begrenzung der Rüstungen, 1932–1934;
Ein Politischer Weltspiegel* (Zürich,1940), and Denys P. Myers, *World Disarmament:
Its Problems and Prospects* (Boston, 1932).
[9]See Maurice Bourquin, ed., *Collective Security; a Record of the Seventh and Eighth
International Studies Conference, Paris 1934-London 1935* (Paris, 1936); Maksim M.
Litvinoff, *Against Aggression* (New York, 1939); Clyde Eagleton, "The Attempt to
Define Aggression," in *International Conciliation*, No. 264, November, 1930; "Draft
Convention Concerning Rights and Duties of States in Case of Aggression," in *Re-
search in International Law under the Auspices of the Harvard Law School*, Special
Supplement to the *American Journal of International Law*, Vol. XXXIII (1939).
[10]See James T. Shotwell, "Security," in Davis, ed., *Pioneers in World Order*, p. 26–41.

Supervision of the Private Manufacture of Arms and Ammunition and of Implements of War. Report of the Third Committee. Submitted by H. E. M. Guerro (Salvador). Geneva, 1926. 2 p. [A.73. 1926.IX.] (1926.IX.9.)

Supervision of the Private Manufacture and Publicity of the Manufacture of Arms and Ammunition and of Implements of War. Report by the Third Committee to the Assembly. Rapporteur: M. Sandler (Sweden). Geneva, 1929.1 p.+ 1 p., bilingual. [A.87.1929.IX.] (1929.IX.10.)

National Supervision of the Manufacture of and Trade in Arms. Action Taken on the Resolution Adopted by the Assembly of the League of Nations on September 30th, 1937. Geneva, 1938. 30 p. <Conf.D.183.> (1938.IX.2.)[11]

National Control of the Manufacture of and Trade in Arms. Information as to Present Position Collected by the Secretariat in Accordance with the Resolution Adopted on May 31st, 1937, by the Bureau of the Conference. Geneva, 1938. 241 p. <Conf.D.184.> (1938.IX.1.)

DRAFT CONVENTION ON THE PRIVATE MANUFACTURE OF ARMS, AMMUNITION, AND IMPLEMENTS OF WAR

Special Commission for the Preparation of a Draft Convention with Regard to the Supervision of the Private Manufacture and Publicity of the Manufacture of Arms and Ammunition and of Implements of War. Geneva, 1929. 8 p. [C.393.1929.IX.] <C.F.A./39. (1).> (1929.IX.4.)

Supervision of the Private Manufacture and Publicity of the Manufacture of Arms and Ammunition and of Implements of War. Geneva, 1929. 48 p. [A.30.1929.IX.] (1929.IX.5.)

For Draft Convention[12] with Regard to the Supervision of the Private Manufacture and Publicity of the Manufacture of Arms and Ammunition and of Implements of War, Submitted to the Council by the Special Commission, see p.6–9.

3. INTERNATIONAL TRADE IN ARMS

CONFERENCE

Proceedings of the Conference for the Supervision of the International Trade in Arms and Ammunition and in Implements of War.

[11]See also <Conf.D.183(a).>, <Conf.D.183(c).>.
[12]On the Draft Convention of 1929, see Myers, *World Disarmament*, p.63–68.

Held at Geneva, May 4th to June 17th, 1925.[13] Geneva, 1925. 799 p. [A.13.1925.IX.]

Contains: Convention for the Supervision of the International Trade in Arms and Ammunition and in Implements of War, p.29–67; Protocol for the Prohibition of the Use in War of Asphyxiating, Poisonous or Other Gases and of Bacteriological Methods of Warfare,[14] p.75–84; Protocol of Signature, p.85–92; Final Act, p.93–116.

STATISTICAL INFORMATION

Statistical Information on the Trade in Arms, Ammunition and Material of War. Geneva, 1924. 89 p., bilingual. [A.30.1924.IX.]

Statistical Yearbook of the Trade in Arms and Ammunition. Geneva, 1938. 340 p. [C.263.M.156.1938.IX.] (1938.IX.4.)

The main purpose of this annual survey was to give all possible information on the international trade in the various arms, ammunition, and implements intended for use in war or capable of being used. In all, 14 volumes were published in this series from 1924 to 1938.[15]

4. ARBITRATION, SECURITY, AND RELATED QUESTIONS

ARBITRATION, SECURITY, AND REDUCTION OF ARMAMENTS

General Report Submitted to the Fifth Assembly on Behalf of the First and Third Committees by M. Politis (Greece), Rapporteur for the First Committee, and Mr. Benes (Czechoslovakia), Rapporteur for the Third Committee. Geneva, 1924. 20 p. [A.135. 1924.]

Contains: 1. Introduction: Historical Summary. II. Analysis of the Scheme: 1. Work of the First Committee; 2. Work of the Third Committee. III. Conclusion. See also Document [A.135(1).1924.IX.].

Extracts from the Debates of the Fifth Assembly Including Those of the First and Third Committees. Reports and Resolutions Adopted by the Assembly and the Council. Geneva, 1924. 373 p. [C.708. 1924.IX.] <C.C.O.1.>

Arbitration and Security. Systematic Survey of the Arbitration Conventions and Treaties of Mutual Security Deposited with the

---

[13]See also Index to the Proceedings of the Conference for the Supervision of the International Trade in Arms and Ammunition and in Implements of War (Geneva, May 4th to June 17th,1925). No date. 28p. [C.362.M.135.1927.IX.]

[14]Also in 94 Treaty Series, p. 65–74.

[15]The information of the Statistical Yearbook of the Trade in Arms and Ammunition is, "however, confined to private commerce and includes neither sales of military and naval materials to states nor any information respecting either quantities or qualities actually manufactured." See Myers, World Disarmament, p.64.

League of Nations. Lausanne, 1926. 200 p. [C.34.M.74.1926.V.] (1926.V.14.)

Preparatory Commission for the Disarmament Conference. Committee on Arbitration and Security. Geneva, 1928. 60 p. <C.A.S. 10.> (1928.IX.3.)

Contains: 1. Introduction to the Three Memoranda on Arbitration, Security and the Articles of the Covenant, Submitted by the Chairman of the Committee in Agreement with the Rapporteurs. 2. Memorandum on Arbitration and Conciliation, Submitted by M. Holsti, Rapporteur. 3. Memorandum on Security Questions, Submitted by M. Politis, Rapporteur. 4. Memorandum on Articles 10, 11, and 16 of the Covenant, Submitted by M. Rutgers, Rapporteur. 5. Annexes.

Preparatory Commission for the Disarmament Conference. Committee on Arbitration and Security. Report of the Committee on Arbitration and Security on the Work of Its Third Session. Held at Geneva from June 27th to July 4th, 1928. Geneva, 1928. 85 p. [C.342.M.100.1928.IX.] <C.P.D.123.> <C.A.S.75.> (1928.IX.9.)

General Information

Reduction of Armaments. Debate in the Fifth Assembly, September 4th to 6th, 1924. (Pamphlet prepared by the Information Section). Geneva, 1924. 124 p.

Arbitration, Security and Reduction of Armaments. Documents and Proceedings of the Fifth Assembly. September, 1924. (Prepared by the Information Section). Geneva, 1924. 192 p.

The Reduction of Armaments and the Organisation of Peace. Revised edition. Geneva, 1928. 166 p.

Annotated Bibliography on Disarmament and Military Questions. Geneva, 1931. 163 p.

GENEVA PROTOCOL, 1924

Protocol for the Pacific Settlement of International Disputes. Adopted by the Fifth Assembly of the League of Nations on October 2nd, 1924. No date. 10 p., in part bilingual. [C.606.M.211.1924.IX.] [A.25.1925.IX.]

The "Geneva Protocol," though never ratified, perhaps provides for the most refined procedure for the peaceful settlement of international disputes ever devised by an international conference.[16]

LOCARNO CONVENTIONS, 1925

Treaty of Mutual Guarantee, Done at Locarno, October 16, 1925, Final Protocol of the Locarno Conference of the Same Date and

[16]See Shotwell, in Davis, ed., *Pioneers in World Order*, p.34–46, and David Hunter Miller, *The Geneva Protocol* (New York, 1925), *passim.*

Collective Note to Germany Dated London, December 1, 1925, Regarding Article 16 of the Covenant of the League of Nations. 54 *Treaty Series*, p. 289–301, bilingual.[17]

FINANCIAL ASSISTANCE TO STATES VICTIMS OF AGGRESSION

Financial Assistance to States Victims of Aggression. Geneva, 1927. 10 p. [A.57.1927.IX.] (1927.IX.8.)

Financial Assistance to States Victims of Aggression. Geneva, 1927. 9 p. <C.P.D.94.> (1927.IX.16.)

Financial Assistance to States Victims of Aggression. Geneva, 1928. 9 p. <C.P.D.133.> <F.586.> (1928.IX.14.)[18]

Convention

Convention on Financial Assistance. Geneva, October 2nd, 1930. Geneva, 1932. 20 p., in part bilingual. [C.611(1).M.237(1).1930. IX.][19]

KELLOGG-BRIAND PACT, 1928

General Treaty for Renunciation of War as an Instrument of National Policy. Signed at Paris, August 27, 1928. 94 *Treaty Series*, p. 57–64, bilingual.[20]

GENERAL ACT, 1928

Pacific Settlement of International Disputes, Non-Aggression and Mutual Assistance. Geneva, 1928. 46 p. [C.536.M.163.1928.IX.] (1928.IX.13.)

Contains: A. Report of the Third Committee to the Assembly. B. Pacific Settlement of International Disputes: 1. Resolution Adopted by the Assembly on September 26th, 1928, on the Submission and Recommendation of a General Act and of Three Model Bilateral Conventions in Regard to Conciliation, Arbitration, and Judicial Settlement; 2. Resolution Adopted by the Assembly on September 26th, 1928, Concerning the Good Offices of the Council; 3. Introductory Note to the General Act and the Model Bilateral Conventions for the Pacific Settlement of International

[17]Entered into force on September 14,1926. For Arbitration Treaties between Germany on the one hand and Belgium, France, Poland, and Czechoslovakia on the other, see p. 303,315,327,341. For Treaties of Mutual Guarantee between France on the one hand and Poland and Czechoslovakia on the other, see p. 353,359.

[18]See League Catalogue <C.P.D.133.1928.IX.>.

[19]See also Document [C.611.M.237.1930.IX.] (1930.IX.7.).

[20]According to Article III the Treaty would take effect among the signatories as soon as all their several instruments were deposited at Washington. On July 25,1929, all signatories had deposited their instruments of ratification.

Disputes; 4. General Act. 5. Model Bilateral Conventions for Conciliation, Arbitration and Judicial Settlement. C. Non-Aggression and Mutual Assistance: 1. Resolution Adopted by the Assembly on September 26th, 1928, on the Submission and Recommendation of Model Treaties of Non-Aggression and Mutual Assistance; 2. Resolution Adopted by the Assembly on September 26th, 1928, Concerning the Good Offices of the Council; 3. Introductory Note to the Model Collective Treaty of Mutual Assistance and Collective and Bilateral Treaties of Non-Aggression, Drawn up by the Committee on Arbitration and Security; 4. Model Collective Treaty of Mutual Assistance and Collective and Bilateral Treaties of Non-Aggression.

Pacific Settlement of International Disputes. General Act. Geneva, 1928. 7 p.+7 p., bilingual. [C.537.M.164.1928.IX.][21]

Non-Aggression and Mutual Assistance. Geneva, 1928. 16 p.+16 p., bilingual. [C.538.M.165.1928.IX.]

Contains: 1. Model Collective Treaty of Mutual Assistance. 2. Model Collective Treaty of Non-Aggression. 3. Model Bilateral Treaty of Non-Aggression.

Pacific Settlement of International Disputes. Model Bilateral Conventions for Conciliation, Arbitration and Judicial Settlement. Geneva, 1928. 13 p.+13 p., bilingual. [C.539.M.166.1928.IX.]

DEFINITION OF AGGRESSION

Report of the Committee on Security Questions. Rapporteur: M. N. Politis. Geneva, May 24th, 1933. <Conf.D./C.G.108.>. In Conference for the Reduction and Limitation of Armaments. Conference Documents, Vol. II., p. 679–690. (1935.IX.4.)

Includes: Act Relating to the Definition of Aggressor, Annex I, p.683.[22] Protocol Annexes to Article 2 of the Act Relating to the Definition of the Aggressor, Annex II p.684. Act Relating to the Establishment of Facts ConstitutingAggression, Annex III, p.684–685. European Security Pact, p.685. Draft Convention Submitted by the United Kingdom Delegation <Conf. D.157>, p.688–690.

5. CONFERENCE FOR THE REDUCTION AND LIMITATION OF ARMAMENTS

DOCUMENTS OF THE PREPARATORY COMMISSION[23]

Series I: Documents of the Preparatory Commission for the Disarmament Conference Entrusted with the Preparation for the Con-

[21]Also published in 93 *Treaty Series*, p. 343–363. Entered into force on August 16,1929.
[22]For the "Convention for the Definition of Aggression," signed at London, July 3, 1933, in 147 *Treaty Series*, p.67–77, bilingual, see also "Convention for the Definition of Aggression," signed at London, July 4,1933, in 148 *Treaty Series*, p.211–219, bilingual.
[23]See also Preparatory Commission for the Disarmament Conference, *Report of Sub-Commission A* (*Military, Naval and Air*). Geneva, 1926. 176 p. [C.739.M.278.1926. IX.]; *Sub-Commission B. Report No.I*: Geneva, 1926. 35 p.[C.738.M.277.1926.IX.]. *Report No. II*: Geneva, 1927. 39 p. <C.P.D.39.> <C.P.D./C."B"13.> (1927.IX. 3.). *Report No. III*: Geneva, 1927. 39 p. <C.P.D.40.> <C.P.D./C."B"/14.> (1927.IX.4.)

ference for the Reduction and Limitation of Armaments, Geneva, 1925. 50 p. <C.P.D.I.> (C.9.M.5.1926.IX.)

Series II: Documents of the Preparatory Commission . . . Geneva, 1926. 130 p. [C.425.M.158.1926.IX.] <C.P.D.1.(a).> (1926.IX.7.)

Series III: Documents of the Preparatory Commission . . . Geneva, 1927. 110 p. [C.740.M.279.1926.IX.] <C.P.D.1(b).> (1927.IX.2.)

Series IV: Minutes of the Third Session of the Preparatory Commission for the Disarmament Conference. Held at Geneva from March 21st to April 26th, 1927. Geneva, 1927. 419 p. [C.310.M.109.1927. IX.] <C.P.D.1.(c).> (1927.IX.5.)

Series V: Minutes of the Fourth Session of the Preparatory Commission for the Disarmament Conference and of the First Session of the Committee on Arbitration and Security. Geneva, 1928. 56 p. [C.667.M.225.1927.IX.] <C.P.D.1.(d).> (1928.IX.2.)

Series VI: Minutes of the Second Session of the Committee on Arbitration and Security and of the Fifth Session of the Preparatory Commission for the Disarmament Conference. Geneva, 1928. 356 p. [C.165.M.50.1928.IX.] <C.P.D.1.(e).> (1928.IX.6.)

Series VII: Minutes of the Third Session of the Committee on Arbitration and Security. Geneva, 1928. 131 p. [C.358.M.112.1928. IX.] <C.P.D.1.(f).> (1928.IX.8.)

Series VIII: Minutes of the Sixth Session (First Part) of the Preparatory Commission for the Disarmament Conference. Geneva, 1929. 244p. [C.195.M.74.1929.IX.] <C.P.D.1.(g).> (1929.IX.3.)

Series IX: Minutes of the Fourth Session of the Committee on Arbitration and Security. Geneva, 1930. 222 p. [C.357.M.149.1930. IX.] <C.P.D.1.(h).> (1930.IX.3.)

Series X: Minutes of the Sixth Session (Second Part) of the Preparatory Commission for the Disarmament Conference. Geneva, 1931. 620 p. [C.4.M.4.1931.IX.] <C.P.D.1.(i).> (1931.IX.1.)

Series XI: Documents of the Preparatory Commission for the Disarmament Conference Entrusted with the Preparation for the Conference for the Reduction and Limitation of Armaments. Geneva, 1931. 99 p. [C.428.M.178.1931.IX.] <C.P.D.1(j).> (1931.IX.5.)

Part I: Index Containing a Detailed Analysis of the Documents of the Preparatory Commission for the Disarmament Conference and Its Sub-Commissions with the Exception of the Documents of the Committee on Arbitration and Security. Part II: Index or Brief Analysis of the Documents of the Committee on Arbitration and Security.

PROCEEDINGS OF THE CONFERENCE

Series A: Volume I: Verbatim Records of Plenary Meetings. February 2nd-July 23rd, 1932. Geneva, 1932. 201 p. (1932.IX.60.)

Series B: Volume I: Minutes of the General Commission. February 9th-July 23rd, 1932. Geneva, 1932. p. 1–206. (1932.IX.64.)

Series B: Volume II: Minutes of the General Commission. December 14th, 1932-June 29th, 1933. Geneva, 1933. p. 207–643. (1933.IX. 10.)

Series B: Volume III: Minutes of the General Commission. October 16th, 1933–June 11th, 1934. Geneva, 1936. p. 645–694. (1936. IX.1.)

Series C: Volume I: Minutes of the Bureau. September 21st, 1932–June 27th, 1933.[24] Geneva, 1935. 178 p. (1935.IX.2.)

Series C: Volume II: Minutes of the Bureau. October 9th, 1933–November 20th, 1934. Geneva, 1936. p. 179–256. 255 p. (1936. IX.2.)

Series D: Volume I: Minutes of the Land Commission. February 27th-June 6th, 1932. Geneva, 1935. 128 p. (1935.IX.9.)

Series D: Volume 2: Minutes of the Naval Commission. February 27th-July 20th, 1932. Geneva, 1937. 149 p. (1937.IX.1.)

Series D: Volume 3: Minutes of the Air Commission. February 27th-June 24th, 1932. Geneva, 1936. 316 p. (1936.IX.7.)

Series D: Volume 4: Minutes of the National Defense Expenditure Commission. February 27th, 1932–June 3rd, 1933. Geneva, 1935. 106 p. (1935.IX.8.)

Series D: Volume 5: Minutes of the Political Commission. February 27, 1932–March 10, 1933. Geneva, 1936. 62 p. (1936.IX.8.)

REPORT ON THE WORK OF THE CONFERENCE

Preliminary Report on the Work of the Conference. Prepared by the President, Mr. Arthur Henderson. Geneva, 1936. 206 p. <Conf. D.171.(1).> (1936.IX.3.)

Mr. Henderson "hoped that this statement would be received as a sincere attempt to present an impartial survey of the great mass of material lying scattered through the long succession of documents distributed to the conference, and that it would be regarded not only as a progress report to the conference but as an instrument of work and a guide to its proceedings and documentation."

CONFERENCE DOCUMENTS

Conference Documents: Volume I: Geneva, 1932. p. 1–282. (1932. IX.63.). Volume II: Geneva, 1934. p. 283–736. (1935.IX.4.). Volume III: Geneva, 1936. p. 737–938. (1936.IX.4.)

These volumes include documents that are considered useful for understanding of the Conference Records Series A-C.[25] The individual documents in the series are for the most part referred to under their conference symbols, e.g., <Conf.D.44(1) >. Some of the documents included in these volumes are listed below.

[24]For the functions of Bureau of the Disarmament Conference: see p. iii.
[25]See also <Conf.D.102.>, "Co-ordinating Table of the Draft Convention and of the Propositions Referred to the General Commission," in Vol. I, p. 148–175.

General Resolutions and Draft Convention

<Conf.D.136 (I).> Resolution Adopted by the General Commission on July 22nd, 1932. Volume I, p. 268–271. Also as separate document (1932.IX.51.).

<Conf.D.163 (I).>. Draft Convention. Provisional Text Prepared in the Light of the Modifications Adopted in the First Reading and of the Amendments Presented by the Delegations. Text Dated September 22nd, 1933. Volume II, p. 600–654.

Manufacture of and Trade in Arms

<Conf.D.167.>. Draft Articles for the Regulation and Control of the Manufacture of and Trade in Arms and the Establishment of a Permanent Disarmament Commission. Proposal Submitted by the Delegation of the United States of America. Geneva, November 20th, 1934. Volume III, p. 776–783.

Moral Disarmament

[C.602.M.240.1931.IX.] <Conf.D.16.>. Moral Disarmament. Memorandum from the Polish Government. Geneva, September 23rd, 1931. Volume I, p. 66–70.

<Conf.D.98.>. Moral Disarmament. Documentary Material Forwarded by the International Organisation on Intellectual Cooperation. Geneva, February 24th, 1932. Volume I, p. 83–92. Also as separate document (1932.IX.24.).

<Conf.D.138.>. Moral Disarmament. Report by the Committee on Moral Disarmament. Geneva, July 25th, 1932. Volume I, p. 271–273. Also as separate document (1932.IX.52.).

Narcotics Control and Disarmament Control

<Conf.D.159.>. Analogies between the Problem of the Traffic in Narcotic Drugs and That of the Trade in and Manufacture of Arms. Geneva, May 4th, 1933. Volume I, p. 494–502.

6. DOCUMENTS RELATED TO VARIOUS QUESTIONS

ARMAMENTS TRUCE

Armaments Truce.[26] Geneva, 1931. 20 p. [C.919.M.484.1931.IX.] <Conf.D.35.> (1931.IX.40.)

Contains: I. Report of the Third Committee, Adopted by the Twelfth Assembly on September 29th,1931. II. Report by the Spanish Representative, Adopted by the

[26]See also *Armaments Truce: Information on the Position of Armaments in Various Countries. Report of the Third Committee to the Assembly. Rapporteur: M. de Madariaga.* Geneva, 1931. 3p. [A.93.1931.IX.]; and Document [C.639.(1).1931.IX.], *Official Journal,* December,1931, p.2304–2305.

Council on September 30th,1931. III. Letter from the Secretary-General, Dated October 2nd, 1931, to All the States Invited to the Disarmament Conference. IV. Replies from Fifty-four Governments to the Letter from the Secretary-General, Dated October 2nd,1931. V. Letter from the Secretary-General, Dated November 14th,1931, to All States Invited to the Disarmament Conference.

Armaments Truce (Renewal).[27] Geneva, 1932. 10 p. <Conf.D.144.> (1932.IX.57.)

Contains: Letter Dated August 4th,1932, from the President of the Conference for the Reduction and Limitation of Armaments to All the States Invited to the Conference. Replies from Governments.

MEANS OF PREVENTING WAR

General Convention to Improve the Means of Preventing War[28] (Geneva, September 26, 1931.). Geneva, 1932. 9 p., in part bilingual. [C.658 (1).M.269 (1).1931.IX.] (1932.IX.17.)

"The high contracting Parties undertake in the event of a dispute arising between them and being brought before the Council of the League of Nations, to accept and apply the conservatory measures of a non-military nature relating to the substance of the dispute which the Council may recommend with a view to preventing the aggravation of the dispute."

NATIONAL DEFENSE EXPENDITURE

Limitation of National Expenditure on Armaments.[29] Geneva, 1924. 7 p. [A.40.1924.IX.]

Contains: Action Taken by the Council and the Commissions of the League on the Resolutions Adopted by the Fourth Assembly. Replies from the Governments (in chronological order).

Limitation of National Expenditure on Armaments. Reply from the Japanese Government. Geneva, 1924. 2 p., bilingual. [A.40 (a). 1924.IX.]

Limitation of National Expenditure on Armaments. Reply from the Danish Government. Geneva, 1924. 2 p., bilingual. [A.40 (b). 1924.IX.]

Limitation of National Expenditure on Armaments. Reply from the Swedish Government. Geneva, 1924. 1 p., bilingual. [A.40 (c). 1924.IX.]

Publicity of National Defence Expenditure. Draft Convention, Prepared by the Technical Committee of the National Defence Expenditure Commission. Geneva, 1934. 86 p. <Conf.D./C.G. 160(1).> <Conf.D./C.D./C.T.239(1).>

[27] See also Addendum to <Conf.D.144.> (1932.IX.57.), and the Second Addendum (1932.IX.57.2.Add.).
[28] Not in force.
[29] See also Official Journal, September,1924, p.1179–1184.

NAVAL DISARMAMENT

Report of the Naval Sub-Commission of the Permanent Advisory Commission on the Extension of the Washington Naval Treaty to the Non-Signatory Powers Members of the League of Nations. Geneva, 1922. 7 p.+7 p., bilingual. [C.477.1922.IX.]

Draft Convention for the Extension of the Washington Naval Treaty to the Non-Signatory Powers Members of the League of Nations. Geneva, 1922. 7 p.+7 p., bilingual. [C.477 (a).1922.IX.]

Extension to Non-Signatory States of the Principles of the Treaty of Washington for the Limitation of Naval Armaments. Report to the Council. Geneva, 1924. 16 p. <C.P.C./S.C.N.31.1924.> (C. 76.1924.IX.)

Proceedings of the Second Session Held at the Palazzo della Prefettura, from February 14th to 25th, 1924. Geneva, 1924. 124 p. [C.76.1924.IX.] <C.P.S./S.C.N.31.1924.>

ORGANIZATION OF PEACE

Collaboration of Women in the Organisation of Peace. Geneva, 1932. 3 p. <Conf.D.75.> (1932.IX.19.)

Co-operation of the Press in the Organisation of Peace. Geneva, 1932. 40 p. <Conf.D.143.> (1932.IX.56.)

RIGHT OF INVESTIGATION

Organisation with a View to the Exercise of the Right of Investigation in the Four States Subjected to Investigation by the Treaties of Versailles, St. Germain, Trianon and Neuilly (Adopted by the Council on September 27, 1924).[30] Geneva, 1924. 3 p. [C.541(1). 189(1).1924.IX.]

Rules Adopted by the Council for the Exercise of the Right of Investigation Provided for by the Treaties of Versailles, Saint Germain, Trianon and Neuilly. Geneva, 1926. 8 p. [C.729.1926.IX.] <C.P.C.211.> (1926.IX.17.)

Includes: Part I. Organization of the Right of Investigation. Part II. Ways and Means of Assuring to Commissions of Investigation Free and Complete Execution of the Duties Entrusted to Them. Part III. Explanations with Regard to the Rules Contained in Parts I and II.

7. *ARMAMENTS YEARBOOK*

First Volume: Armaments Year-Book. Geneva, 1924. 844 p. [A.37. 1924.IX.]

[30] Also published in *Official Journal*, October, 1924, p.1592–1595.

Last Volume: Armaments Year-Book, 1939/40. Geneva, 1940. 396 p. [C.228.M.155.1939.IX.] (1940.IX.1.)

The Council of the League of Nations in July, 1923, decided that an *Armaments Year-Book* should be published by the Secretariat, "it being clearly understood that the information would be drawn solely from official and public documents, and that it correspond to the terms of the last paragraph of Article 8 of the Covenant." The *Year-book* contains information on military forces (land, sea, and air), budget expenditure on national defense, and industries capable of being used for war purposes.

IX. POLITICAL QUESTIONS

1. INTRODUCTORY NOTE

THE POLITICAL activities of the League are mainly reflected in its records concerning international "disputes" and "incidents."

An objective and fair appraisal of the League's action to maintain or restore peaceful international relations is more difficult than may seem at first sight. More or less blind adherents of the League are inclined to overestimate the League's success as an instrument of settling international disputes, while opponents of the League tend to ignore altogether the League's political action, even when it was successful. Both attitudes are unrealistic.

No historian of Latin American affairs, for instance, can afford to overlook the League action in reference to the Leticia incident (see below, p. 316. On the other hand, all too eager advocates of the League are inclined to claim that the majority of all international "disputes" and "incidents" that have ever been discussed by the League have been settled successfully through League action.

There is also disagreement concerning the number of "cases" the League considered formally, for the purpose of pacific settlement. The Information Section of the League listed 43 issues under the heading "Political Questions Dealt with by the League of Nations," in the tenth edition of *Essential Facts about the League of Nations* (1939). The appeal of the Finnish government in December, 1939, is not included in this list.

Twenty-four out of these 44 political incidents and disputes will be taken up in this chapter. However, in view of the great number of League documents on political issues—most of them carry the document symbol "VII"—the bibliographical system used throughout the greater part of this book has been abandoned in favor of concise statements of facts, issues, or procedures, accompanied by footnotes that indicate the major documents related to these questions.

For more complete reference the reader is advised to consult th *Official Journal* and its Special Supplements. The Index to the *Jour nal* as well as the "Numerical List of Documents Published in th Official Journal of . . .," which appeared from 1929 to 1939 as par of the Index, are the most useful tools for identifying pertinent docu ments and the place where they can be located among the League documents. It should be recalled, however, that these indices do not furnish a complete list of all relevant documentary material. They do not include, for instance, those Assembly documents published as separate documents that are not reproduced in the *Official Journal*, nor do they cover the confidential mimeographed material that was made available only to the recipients of the States Members Service. In addition, there are a considerable number of documents deposited in the archives of the League that were never published or circulated to its members.

Beyond this introductory note, this chapter has been arranged under three headings:

2. Political Questions Dealt with by the League of Nations
3. Political Questions of Special Interest
4. Various Questions

The first two headings cover 26 issues; under the third is a list of those political questions that are discussed in *Essential Facts about the League of Nations*, but are not mentioned under the first two headings.

It may seem arbitrary to have singled out the dispute between Bolivia and Paraguay, the dispute between Italy and Ethiopia, and the Sino-Japanese disputes of 1931-1933 and 1937-1945 as political questions of special interest. Yet the procedural aspects of these disputes are still of interest, notwithstanding the fact that the League obviously failed to settle them. Actually, the dispute between Bolivia and Paraguay over Chaco was settled in 1938 independently of the League; Italy's conquest of Ethiopia was subsequently nullified in the course of World War II; and the Sino-Japanese dispute was presumably terminated through the unconditional surrender of Japan to the United Nations on September 2, 1945.

Yet, the Chaco and Italo-Ethiopian wars occasioned the first attempts by groups of states to apply concerted economic measures with the intention of preventing or shortening war. Thus, whoever favors "economic sanctions" as a means of war prevention should carefully study the League's record in these disputes. Moreover, the League documents on the Sino-Japanese disputes contain, at least in part, unique source material on this tragic chapter of modern history.

It should be noted that not all the disputes "dealt with" by the League, even if successfully settled, were settled by the League proper. There were several questions that were settled directly by the parties concerned. The issue here, in each individual instance, is whether the parties would have settled the dispute irrespective of the League or whether the League was at least indirectly responsible for the settlement. In other instances, the League acted only as an intermediary between the parties and other international organs. For example, the Jaworzina Question (see below, p. 311) was brought before the Council by the President of the Conference of Ambassadors. Thereupon the Council requested an advisory opinion from the Permanent Court of International Justice. The Court addressed its advisory opinion to the Council, and the Conference of Ambassadors passed a resolution in accordance with the advisory opinion.

In this connection the question may be raised whether settlement by recourse to an advisory opinion of the Permanent Court of International Justice can be considered as a settlement by the League. Such a conclusion could be justified on the ground that advisory opinions had to be requested by the Council or the Assembly, and to be binding they had, in turn, to be adopted by the Council or the Assembly. A complete list of all Advisory Opinions rendered by the Permanent Court of International Justice is to be found on p. 391.

A further note: the statement that a "dispute" or "incident" has been settled does not always imply that it has thereby been settled once and for all. It may simply mean that a particular phase of a dispute was officially declared "settled" by the parties or the League.

2. POLITICAL QUESTIONS DEALT WITH BY THE LEAGUE OF NATIONS

(1)[1] EUPEN AND MALMÉDY, 1920–1922

The sovereignty over the territory comprising the whole of the *Kreise* of Eupen and Malmédy was under Article 34 of the Treaty of Versailles to be determined by "public expression of opinion."[2] The result of this expression of opinion was to be communicated to the League of Nations by the Belgian government, which pledged itself to accept the decision of the League. On September 20, 1920,

[1] The numbers in parentheses correspond to the numbering of "Political Questions Dealt with by the League of Nations," in *Essential Facts about the League of Nations* (10th ed., revised, Geneva, 1939), p.161-199. Myers includes in the 76 questions which he discusses in the second edition of his *Handbook*, 18 cases which "were in the single category concerning railroads in succession states . . ." See Denys P. Myers, *Handbook of the League of Nations* (Boston, 1935), p. 297; see also p. 293-364, covering cases brought before the League from 1920 to July 1, 1935.

[2] See Sarah Wambaugh, *Plebiscites since the World War* (2 vols., Washington, 1933), I, 518: "The consultation held in Eupen and Malmédy during the first six months of 1920, under Article 34 of the Treaty of Versailles, was not in any sense a plebiscite, and even the term 'public expression of opinion' by which it was described in the treaty was a misnomer for what was actually afforded was merely an opportunity to protest against a cession already made."

the Council of the League of Nations resolved that the cession of the districts to Belgium was effective and valid.[3] Germany protested against the decision of the Council on the ground that it was incompatible with the Treaty of Versailles.[4] By a letter approved by the Council on February 22, 1921, the German Minister of Foreign Affairs was informed that the Council considered the question finally settled.[5]

(3) QUESTION OF THE ÅLAND ISLANDS, 1920–1921

The dispute between Sweden and Finland regarding the Aland Islands centered on the questions (1) whether a plebiscite should be held among the inhabitants of the Islands with a view to incorporating the Islands into Sweden or to maintain them as an integral part of Finnish territory; (2) whether previous collective requests by inhabitants of the Islands should be considered equivalent to a plebiscite.[6] The dispute was submitted to the Council by the British government under Article 11 of the Covenant.[7] The Finnish government was averse to the idea of the plebiscite on various grounds.[8] On June 24, 1921, the Council resolved that "the sovereignty of the Åland Islands is recognized to belong to Finland," but that "the interests of the world, the future of cordial relations between Finland and Sweden, the prosperity and happiness of the Islands themselves cannot be ensured unless (a) certain further guarantees are given for the protection of the Islanders; and unless (b) arrangements are concluded for the non-fortification and neutralization of the Archipelago."[9] In accordance with this resolution a new convention on the neutralization and nonfortification of the Åland Islands was signed at Geneva on October 20, 1921.[10]

[3]Council Minutes, 9th Sess., p.50–57.
[4]Council Minutes, 11th Sess., p.17.
[5]Council Minutes, 12th Sess., p.7,58.
[6]For the background of the dispute, see Wambaugh, *Plebiscites since the World War*, I, 515–518. See also "The Åland Islands Question," *Official Journal*, Special Supplement No.1, August,1920, 67p.+67p.; and "Report of the International Committee of Jurists Entrusted by the Council of the League of Nations with the Task of Giving an Advisory Opinion upon the Legal Aspects of the Åland Islands Question," *Official Journal*, Special Supplement No.3, October,1920.
[7]*Official Journal*, July–August, 1920,p.247f.
[8]See especially *Official Journal*, Special Supplement No.1, p.4–5.
[9]Council Minutes,13th Sess., p.41–42.
[10]Text in 9 *Treaty Series*, p. 211–221, bilingual; official text in French in force since April 6, 1922.

(9). THE UPPER SILESIAN QUESTION, 1921
(FRONTIER BETWEEN GERMANY AND POLAND)

The Supreme Council resolved on August 12, 1921, before taking a decision on the demarcation of the frontier between Germany and Poland in Upper Silesia as authorized by Article 88 of the Treaty of Versailles, to submit to the Council the difficulties involved in the delimitation of this frontier and to ask the Council to recommend a frontier line.[11] This procedure was initiated under Article 11, Paragraph 2, of the Covenant. No workable solution had been reached, either by the parties most directly concerned, that is, Germany and Poland, or by the Committee of Experts established for this purpose.[12] Both governments agreed in advance to accept the decision of the Council on this matter. On October 12, 1921, the Council recommended a definite frontier line,[13] and the Conference of Ambassadors adopted the Council's recommendation on October 20, 1921.[14] In addition, as suggested by the Council, the Geneva Convention of May 15, 1922,[15] was concluded.

(10). EASTERN CARELIA, 1922–1923 (FINLAND
AND SOVIET RUSSIA)

The dispute between Finland and the Union of Soviet Socialist Republics concerning the situation in Eastern Carelia was never

[11]The text of the Supreme Council's (British Empire, France, Italy, and Japan) request is in *Official Journal*, November,1921, p.982.
[12]For the conflicting views of the British, French, and Italian delegations, see especially "Report of the Committee of Experts Appointed to Study the Frontier to Be Laid down between Germany and Poland in Upper Silesia as the Result of the Plebiscite" (with map), in Georges Kaeckenbeeck, *The International Experiment of Upper Silesia* (New York, 1942), p.552–557.
[13]See "Recommendation of the Council of the League Forwarded to the Supreme Council of the Principal Allied Powers on October 12, 1921," in *Minutes of the Extraordinary Session of the Council of the League of Nations, Held at Geneva from August 29th to October 12th, 1921, to Consider the Question of Upper Silesia*, p.16–24, especially p.19.
[14]For the "Decision of the Conference of Ambassadors," see *Official Journal*, December 1921, p.1226–1232. This decision was dated October 20, 1921. For the plebiscite in Upper Silesia which was held on March 20, 1921, see Wambaugh, *Plebiscites since the World War*, I, p. 206–270, especially p. 249.
[15]The text of the Convention between Germany and Poland Relating to Upper Silesia, signed at Geneva, May 15, 1922, was not published in the *Treaty Series*. See 9 *Treaty Series*, p.466. The original text, French only, is reproduced in Kaeckenbeeck, *The International Experiment of Upper Silesia*, p.567–822, including a translation into English of the first 158 articles. This convention is very elaborate, covering 606 articles. The original document was published under the title *Convention Germano-Polonaise relative à la Haute Silésie faite à Genève le 15 mai 1922*. No date. 309 p. See also *Protection of Minorities in Upper Silesia. Note by the Secretary-General, and Resolution Adopted by the Council, May 16, 1922*. Geneva, 1922. 2p., mimeographed. [C.266.M.

settled by League action.[16] It is noteworthy primarily from the procedural viewpoint, especially as regards the question whether the Permanent Court of International Justice is entitled to give an advisory opinion concerning a nonmember in the absence of any special agreement that would confer the required jurisdiction upon the Court. The Court found "it impossible to give its opinion on a dispute of this kind."[17] On September 27, 1923, the Council noted "the opinion of the Court."[18]

(11). THE AUSTRO-HUNGARIAN FRONTIER, 1921–1922 (BURGENLAND)

Under the Protocol of Venice (October 13, 1921)[19] regarding the settlement of the question of Western Hungary, Austria agreed to accept as far as possible the decisions of an inter-Allied commission for the delimitation of the frontier between Austria and Hungary. Austria declared that if she found it necessary to appeal to the Council against the decisions of the Commission, she would "accept the decision recommended by the Council of the League of Nations."[20] It should be added that a plebiscite concerning the status of Sopron and the surrounding territory was provided for in the Protocol of Venice.[21] On September 19, 1922, [22] the Council issued a decision which actually had the character of a directive to the Commission for the delimitation of frontiers. This decision was carried out under the supervision of the Conference of Ambassadors.[23]

(14). FRONTIER BETWEEN HUNGARY AND CZECHO-SLOVAKIA IN THE SALGO-TARJAN REGION, 1922–1923

By mutual agreement between Hungary and Czechoslovakia, the Council of the League of Nations was authorized to act as an arbi-

167.1922.I.]. See also the circular letter of the Secretary-General [June 9, 1922], forwarding the text of the convention. [C.396.M.243.1922.]

[16]For a brief summary of the League procedure in this case, see Manley O. Hudson, *World Court Reports*, Vol. I., p.190. See also "Finland and Union of Soviet Socialist Republics: Exchange of Notes Appointing Frontier Commissioners on the Carelian Isthmus," 82 *Treaty Series*, p.63–69.

[17]See Permanent Court of International Justice, Series B, No. 5. For a considerable list of pertinent League documents, see *ibid.*, p.10–11, and P.C.I.J., Series C, No. 3.

[18]*Official Journal*, November 1923, p. 1337. See also Assembly Resolution of September 24, 1923, *Official Journal*, Special Supplement No. 11, p. 29.

[19]Text in 9 *Treaty Series*, p.202–209, bilingual; French text official.

[20]*Ibid*. See Also *Official Journal*, November, 1922, p.1315–1339.

[21]For the plebiscite in Sopron (December 14–16, 1921), see Wambaugh, *Plebiscites since the World War*, I, 292, 271–297.

[22]See Document [C.659.M.392.1922.VII.], *Official Journal*, November,1922, p.1338–1339.

[23]See also Gerhard P. Pink, "The Conference of Ambassadors (Paris 1920–1931)," in Geneva Research Center, *Geneva Studies*, Vol.XII, Nos. 4–5 (1942), p.80–87.

trator in reference to the demand of Hungary for a "rectification" of the Czechoslovak-Hungarian border in the Salgo-Tarjan coal district.[24]

On April 23, 1923, the Council announced its award in the presence of the representatives of Czechoslovakia and Hungary.[25]

(15). Conflict over Nationality Decrees in Tunis and Morocco, 1922–1923 (France and the United Kingdom)

In this case the point at issue was whether a change in the French nationality decrees issued in Tunis and Morocco (French Zone) on November 8, 1921, and their application to British subjects was or was not solely a matter of domestic jurisdiction to be settled by France at will. After Britain had placed the question on the agenda of the Council on August 11, 1922,[26] the Permanent Court of International Justice was asked for an advisory opinion, which was delivered on February 7, 1923.[27] The Court held that the question was one of international concern. The Council adopted the opinion of the Court. Subsequently the dispute was settled directly by mutual agreement between Britain and France.[28]

(16). Expropriation by the Roumanian Government of the Landed Properties of the Hungarian Optants, 1923–1930

This dispute was submitted to the Council time and again, either by the Hungarian or the Roumanian government, under Article 11, Paragraph 2, Article 13, Paragraph 3, and Article 14 of the Covenant as well as under Article 239 of the Treaty of Trianon. The main issue in their dispute was whether certain measures taken by the Roumanian government in the course of the Roumanian land reform were compatible with Roumania's treaty obligations—in particular with Article 63 of the Treaty of Trianon and with Article 3 of the Treaty of December 9, 1919, between the Principal Allied and Associated Powers and Roumania. Under these provisions persons who opted for Hungarian nationality were entitled to retain their immovable prop-

[24] See Official Journal, March, 1923, p.209, 282–293.
[25] See Official Journal, June, 1923, p.601–602.
[26] See Official Journal, November, 1922, p.1206–1207.
[27] P.C.I.J., Series B, No. 4.
[28] "Exchange of Notes between the British and French Governments Relative to Certain Nationality Decrees Promulgated in Tunis and Morocco (French Zone) on November 8, 1921. London, May 24, 1923." 18 Treaty Series, p.305–309, bilingual.

erty.[29] For seven years the Council attempted to settle the dispute, but without success. Following the conclusion of the Agreements Relating to the Obligations Resulting from the Treaty of Trianon, signed in Paris, April 28, 1930,[30] the question was withdrawn from the agenda of the Council on May 12, 1930, on the motion of the Hungarian delegate and with the support of the Roumanian representative.[31]

(17). QUESTION OF THE POLISH-CZECHOSLOVAK FRONTIER (THE JAWORZINA QUESTION), 1923-1924

The question was brought before the Council under Article 11, Paragraph 2, of the Covenant on September 20, 1923, by virtue of a letter of August 18, 1923, from the President of the Conference of Ambassadors to the Secretary-General of the League.[32] The controversy centered primarily on the question of whether the Delimitation Commission designed to fix the boundary between Czechoslovakia and Poland in the Jaworzina District was authorized to deviate from a decision of the Conference of Ambassadors. The Council requested the opinion of the Permanent Court of International Justice. The Court delivered its opinion on December 6, 1923,[33] and declared the decision of the Conference of Ambassadors of July 28, 1920, subject to the modifications provided for under Paragraph 3 of Article II of the same decision, as binding. On the basis of this advisory opinion the Council recommended by its resolution of March 12, 1924,[34] a new boundary which was accepted by the Conference of Ambassadors as well as by the parties concerned.[35]

(18). DISPUTE BETWEEN GREECE AND ITALY (THE CORFU INCIDENT), 1923

On August 27, 1923, General Tellini and three other Italians engaged in delimitating the Albanian boundaries were assassinated on

[29]For the first phases of the dispute, see *Official Journal*, 1923, especially June,1923, p.604-611.
[30]Text in 121 *Treaty Series*, p.69-151.
[31]See Item: "2596. Report of the Hungarian Government under Article 239 of the Treaty of Trianon and Article 13, Paragraph 4 and Article 14 of the Covenant of the League of Nations," *Official Journal*, June,1930, p.498.
[32]See *Official Journal*, November,1923, p.1472.
[33]See P.C.I.J., Series B, No. 8.
[34]Text of the Council Resolution in *Official Journal*, April,1924, p. 520-521; see also p.627-629.
[35]See "Resolution Adopted by the Conference of Ambassadors in Pursuance of the Resolution Adopted by the Council of the League on March 12th,1924," *Official Journal*, June,1924, p.828.

Greek soil near Janina. On August 28 and 29 Italy addressed several demands to Greece, and on August 31, after having received a reply from the Greek government which it considered unsatisfactory, the Italian government ordered the bombardment and occupation of Corfu. Greece appealed to the Council under Articles 12 and 15 of the Covenant.[36] The Italian government declared that "any discussion or any step taken by the League of Nations would be out of place owing to its clear incompetence,"[37] but recognized the jurisdiction of the Conference of Ambassadors to settle this matter. On September 17, 1923, the President of the Council notified the Council that the Conference of Ambassadors had settled the dispute.[38]

(19). THE STATUS OF THE MEMEL, 1923–1924

The question of the legal status of the Memel Territory arose because Lithuania protested in part against the decision of the Conference of Ambassadors of February 16, 1923.[39] In particular, the Draft Convention worked out by a special commission under the chairmanship of Mr. Jules Laroche[40] appeared not acceptable to the Lithuanian government.[41] The Conference of Ambassadors appealed to the Council [42] under Article 11, Paragraph 2, of the Covenant. A League commission under the chairmanship of Mr. Norman Davis completed a new Draft Convention, and the Council on March 14, 1924, recommended to the British Empire, France, Italy, and Japan that they accept the Convention[43] to which the Lithuanian government had already agreed. The Convention as proposed by the League was signed on May 8, 1924, and entered into force on August 25, 1925.[44]

(20). FRONTIER BETWEEN TURKEY AND IRAQ, (THE MOSUL AFFAIR), 1924–1925

This was a boundary dispute revolving around the interpretation

[36]See *Official Journal*, November,1923, p.1283–1285.
[37]*Ibid.*, p.1287.
[38]The note of the Conference of Ambassadors is dated September 13, 1923. See *ibid.*, p.1305–1310. On this incident see also Pink, in *Geneva Studies*, XII, p.207–246. See also the "Report of the Special Commission of Jurists" on certain questions arising out of the interpretation of the Covenant, *Official Journal*, April, 1924, p. 523–527, especially p. 524.
[39]For text of the decision, see *Official Journal*, January,1924, p.122–123.
[40]For the text of the "Draft Convention and Protocol Concerning the Transfer to Lithuania of the Rights of Sovereignty over the Memel Territory," see *ibid.*, p.133–140.
[41]See the "Letter of M. Galvanauskas to the President of the Conference of Ambassadors," *ibid.*, p.141–142.
[42]See *ibid.*, p.122.
[43]Text of the "Convention concerning the Territory of Memel," signed at Paris, May 8, 1924, 29 *Treaty Series*, p.85–115, bilingual.
[44]See 39 *Treaty Series*, p.200, bilingual.

of Article 3, Paragraph 2, of the Treaty of Lausanne[45] concerning the frontier between Iraq and Turkey. According to this treaty provision, Great Britain, as mandatory for Iraq, and Turkey should by mutual agreement determine the border within nine months. In case no agreement was reached between the two governments within the time mentioned, the dispute was to be referred to the Council of the League of Nations. On August 6, 1924, the British government asked that the question be placed on the agenda of the next Council meeting.[46] On September 19, 1925, the Council requested the Permanent Court of International Justice to give an advisory opinion,[47] with particular emphasis on questions of Council procedure.[48] The Court was of the opinion "(1) that the decision to be taken by the Council of the League of Nations in virtue of Article 3, paragraph 2, of the Treaty of Lausanne, will be binding on the Parties and will constitute a definitive determination of the frontier between Turkey and Iraqu; (2) that the decision to be taken must be taken by a unanimous vote, the representatives of the Parties taking part in the voting, but their votes not being counted in ascertaining whether there is unanimity."[49] On December 16, 1925, the Council delimitated the frontier by resolution.[50] On March 11, 1926, the settlement of the issue was declared definitive.[51]

(22). Incident on the Greco-Bulgarian Frontier, 1925

On October 22, 1925, Bulgaria appealed to the Council under Articles 10 and 11 of the Covenant.[52] The reason for the appeal was a border incident which had led to the invasion of Bulgarian territory by Greek troops. The Council met in extraordinary session[53] and suggested on October 26 that the Bulgarian and Greek governments

[45]For text of the Treaty of Peace, signed at Lausanne, July 24, 1923, see 28 *Treaty Series*, p.11–113, bilingual. French text official.

[46]*Official Journal*, 1924, p. 1291–1292.

[47]See P.C.I.J., Series B, No. 12.

[48]The Council Resolution of September 19, 1925, raised the following questions: "1) What is the character of the decision to be taken by the Council in virtue of Article 3, paragraph 2, of the Treaty of Lausanne—is it an arbitral award, a recommendation or a simple mediation? 2) Must the decision be unanimous or may it be taken by a majority? May the representatives of the interested parties take part in the vote?" *Ibid.*, p.6–7.

[49]*Ibid.*, p.33.

[50]*Official Journal*, February,1926, p.187–193.

[51]See "Entry into Force of the Council's Decision of September 16th, 1925, Fixing the Frontier between Turkey and Iraque," *Official Journal*, April,1926, p.502–503.

[52]See *Official Journal*, November,1925, p.1699.

[53]Council Minutes, 36th (Extraordinary) Sess., *Official Journal*, November,1925, p.1695–1720.

withdraw their troops within sixty hours.[54] A commission was appointed by the Council to carry out a full enquiry into the incidents on the Greco-Bulgarian frontier, to ascertain the facts that led to the Council's intervention, and to establish the responsibility.[55] On December 14, 1925, the Council settled the incident in accordance with the recommendations of the Commission of Enquiry.[56]

(24). ALBANIAN MINORITIES IN GREECE, 1924–1926

This dispute between Greece and Albania arose in connection with the exchange of Greek and Turkish populations. Some time after the signature of the Convention of Lausanne of January 30, 1923,[57] the Greek authorities announced in the various towns of Epirus that the Moslems must leave Greece and proceed to Asia, without specifying that Moslems of Albania were excluded from this measure. The main purpose of the appeal of the Albanian government to the Council was to prevent Moslems of Albanian origin being subject to forced emigration from Greece in the same way as Moslems of Turkish origin.[58] Since the Greeks adopted in principle a conciliatory attitude, the Albanian demand was recognized as just, though its application was not without difficulties. On September 16, 1926, the President of the Council declared: "It appears that the mandate entrusted by the Council on December 11th, 1924, to the Council's mandatories for the protection of the Moslem minority of Albanian origin in Greece is now drawing to a close."[59]

There was a procedural as well as a substantive question involved, namely, whether Albania's appeal was rightly based on Article 11, Paragraph 2, of the Covenant. On September 30, 1924, the Council resolved to treat the matter "as a question of the application of the Greek Treaty for the Protection of Minorities."[60]

(29). SETTLEMENT OF THE ASSYRIANS OF IRAQ, 1932–1937

The Assyrians of Iraq had been restive for several years and wanted to emigrate as a group. Their aspirations could not be ful-

[54] Ibid., p.1699.
[55] Ibid., p. 1711–1713.
[56] See Official Journal, February,1926, p.172–177, for the "Report of the Commission of Enquiry into the Incident on the Frontier between Bulgaria and Greece." See also ibid., p.196–209.
[57] See "Convention Concerning the Exchange of Greek and Turkish Populations, and Protocol, Signed at Lausanne, January 30,1923," 32 Treaty Series, p.75–87.
[58] See Official Journal, February,1924, p.364–368. For a similar appeal submitted by Albania on May 9,1928, see ibid., July,1928, p.942–944.
[59] Official Journal, April, 1926, p.510–511.
[60] Official Journal, October, 1924, p.1367. On this issue see also Stephen P. Ladas, The Exchange of Minorities: Bulgaria, Greece and Turkey (New York, 1932), p.387–391.

filled, except for the settlement of a considerable number of them in Syria. After several clashes in Iraq, especially after the deplorable events of July and August, 1933, a group of 550 persons took refuge in Syria;[61] by 1937 the Assyrian settlers in Syria totaled about 8,800 persons.[62] From 1933 the attempts of the League to solve the question were undertaken with a view to aiding the Assyrians in Syria and to finding additional places where the Assyrian inhabitants of Iraq could go. The latter question could not be solved, since no country was willing to admit Assyrian immigrants as a group. In the words of Viscount Cranborne, the inability of the Special Council Committee "to find a radical solution of the whole problem was due not to any fault on its part, but rather to the fact that the political and economic conditions of the modern world had placed almost insuperable obstacles in the way of the accomplishment of the Committee's task —namely the mass migration of a whole community."[63] In the circumstances the Council adopted a resolution on September 29, 1937,[64] which provided that the Khabur Settlement in Syria[65] should be put on a fully self-supporting basis, while the "Assyrian community in Iraqu will now resume its position as an ordinary national minority," which would enjoy the benefits of the Declaration on the Protection of Minorities, signed by the Iraqui government at the time of its admission to the League of Nations and approved by the Council on May 19, 1932.[66]

(30). DISPUTE BETWEEN THE UNITED KINGDOM AND IRAN WITH REGARD TO THE ANGLO-PERSIAN OIL COMPANY, 1932–1933

By letter of December 14, 1932, the government of the United Kingdom submitted to the Council, under Article 15 of the Covenant, the question of the Persian government's intention of canceling the concession held by the Anglo-Persian Oil Company.[67] At the Council meeting of October 12, 1933, the dispute was declared completely settled,[68] since a new concession had been signed by the Company and the Imperial Government of Persia.[69]

[61]For the situation up to 1935, see Information Section, *The Settlement of the Assyrians: A Work of Humanity and Appeasement*, No.5 of *League of Nations Questions* (Geneva, 1935), especially p.16,19.
[62]See *Official Journal*, December,1937, p.1176.
[63]*Ibid.*, p.927.
[64]*Ibid.*, p.928–929.
[65]For a report on the Khabur Settlement in 1937, see *ibid.*, p.1174–1196.
[66]See *Official Journal*, July,1932, p.1212 and 1347.
[67]See *Official Journal*, December,1932, p.2296–2308, especially Document [C.836.M 388.1932.VII.] on p.2297.
[68]See *Official Journal*, December,1933, p. 1606.
[69]For the text of the "Agreement between the Imperial Government of Persia and the Anglo-Persian Oil Company Limited, Made at Teheran on April 29th, 1933," see *ibid.*, p.1653–1660; this agreement came into force on May 29, 1933.

(31). Conflict between Colombia and Perú,
1932–1934 (Leticia)

On the night of August 31–September 1, 1932, the village of
Leticia was attacked by a group of Peruvians, who had crossed the
Amazon, captured the Colombian authorities, imprisoned them, seized
all the administration material, and replaced the Colombian flag by
the Peruvian flag. They also declared that the Colombian territory
of Leticia had once more become part of Peru.[70] The Council took
up the matter at its meetings of January 24 and 26, 1933. By letter
of February 17, 1933,[71] the Colombian government appealed to the
Council under Article 15 of the Covenant.[72] On May 25, 1933, the
representatives of the governments of Colombia and Peru accepted
the recommendation of the Council for a settlement of the dispute.[73]
Accordingly, the Peruvian forces were to be withdrawn from the
territory of Leticia, and a special commission, appointed by the
Council, was instituted to administer the territory in the name of
the government of Colombia.[74] The Commission functioned from
June 23, 1933 to June 19, 1934, the day the territory was handed
over to Colombia.[75] As early as May 19, the Council declared that
"the traditional bonds of friendship between two sister nations"
had been restored.[76]

(33). Dispute between Hungary and Yugoslavia Arising out of the Assassination
of the King of Yugoslavia, 1934–1935

The Yugoslav government appealed to the Council under Article
11, Paragraph 2, of the Covenant[77] and called attention to a situation which seriously compromised relations between Yugoslavia and
Hungary and which threatened to disturb peace and good under-

[70]See Official Journal, April,1933, p.533.
[71]See Document [C.139.M.63.1933.VII.], ibid., p.562–563.
[72]See also Document [C.147.M.70.1933.VII.], ibid., p. 563.
[73]See Official Journal, July,1933, p.944–946.
[74]Ibid., p.945; see also p.1107–1111. On the question of the flag of the Commission, see
ibid., p.1110–1111.
[75]Official Journal, July,1934, p.944.
[76]Ibid., p.874. For the pertinent "Text of the Agreement of Rio de Janeiro between
Colombia and Peru, Comprising a Protocol of Peace, Friendship and Co-operation, and
an Additional Act," signed at Rio de Janeiro, May 24, 1934, see ibid., p.933–938.
Exchange of ratification took place on September 27, 1935. See also Dana Gardner
Munro, The Latin American Republics (New York, 1942,) p.341–342.
[77]Official Journal, December,1934, p.1765.

standing among nations. Specifically the Yugoslav government stated that the assassination of King Alexander of Yugoslavia and French Foreign Minister Louis Barthou[78] at Marseilles was organized and executed with the participation of certain Yugoslav terrorist elements which had taken refuge in Hungary and that Hungarian authorities had aided and abetted the terrorist activities of these elements.[79] On January 12, 1935, the Hungarian government handed a memorandum concerning the Marseilles outrage to the Council[80] which contained the result of its enquiry on terrorist activities on Hungarian soil. At the Council meeting of May 25, 1935, Mr. Anthony Eden, in the capacity of rapporteur, declared "I am confident that I can rely upon the goodwill of the Hungarian Government and the spirit of conciliation of the Yugoslav Government to make it now possible for the question before us to be thus disposed of." Accordingly, the Council declared the examination of this question closed.[81]

(36). FRONTIER BETWEEN IRAN AND IRAQ, 1934-1937

On November 29, 1934, "persistent disregard and violation of the Iraqui-Persian boundary by official agents of the Imperial Persian Government" was charged by the Iraqui government in its appeal to the Council under Article 11, Paragraph 2, of the Covenant.[82] In the course of the dispute the Council recommended to the parties concerned settlement by direct conversations.[83] On August 27, 1937, the Iraqui government informed the Secretary-General "that the negotiations between Iraqu and Iran regarding the frontier difference having fortunately resulted in an agreement between the two parties, the existing dispute concerning the boundary has been settled."[84] After having received a corresponding letter from the government of Iran, the Council agreed to withdraw the item from its agenda.[85]

[78]This criminal act occurred on October 9,1934. See Louis Adamic, *My Native Land* (New York,1943).
[79]See *Official Journal*, December,1934, p.1766.
[80]See Document [C.48.M.21.1935.VII.] (1935.VII.2.), *Official Journal*, February,1935, p.277-291, especially p.291.
[81]*Official Journal*, June,1935, p.650.
[82]See *Official Journal*, February,1935, p.196-242, especially p.196.
[83]See *Official Journal*, June,1935, p.651-652, and November,1935, p.1204. See letter from the Minister of Foreign Affairs of Iran, B. Kazemi, of September 25, 1935: "The favourable development of the negotiations at the present time makes it unnecessary to bring the matter before the Council at its present session."
[84]*Official Journal*, December,1937, p.949.
[85]*Ibid.*, p.884.

3. POLITICAL QUESTIONS OF SPECIAL INTEREST

(25). DISPUTE BETWEEN BOLIVIA AND PARAGUAY, 1928–1938

The territory of the Chaco-Boreal has an extent of close to 150,000 square miles. The Bolivians believed this area to be potentially rich in crude oil, and as early as 1928 they had attacked Paraguayan soil. From 1932 to 1935 the Bolivian and Paraguayan armies again fought ·in the Chaco region.[86]

Neither of the parties brought the dispute before the League of Nations after fighting had been resumed in 1932. For a long time efforts were made to settle the dispute by negotiations conducted by American states. To avoid a duplication of jurisdiction the Council deemed it advisable to follow the developments through a committee of three[87] of its members, (Irish Free State, Spain, and Guatemala). On March 8, 1933, the three states represented on the Committee submitted the case to the Council under Article 11 of the Covenant.[88] On May 20, 1933, the Council adopted a report and suggested: "(1) The cessation of hostilities and the withdrawal by Paraguay of the declaration of a State of war with Bolivia; (2) the establishment of an agreement for submission of the dispute to arbitration."[89] In the fall of 1933 a League of Nations Commission went to South America to bring about a settlement of the dispute. The Commission had apparently to work under several handicaps,[90] and its Report of May 9, 1934, although noteworthy in many respects, was inconclusive.

By letter of May 31, 1934, the Bolivian government appealed to the Council to settle the dispute in accordance with Article 15 of the Covenant.[91] On June 9 the Bolivian government requested that the dispute be referred to the Assembly under Article 15, Paragraph 9, of the Covenant.[92] On February 23, 1935, Paraguay informed the

[86]For the early phases of the dispute, see, *e.g.*, *Official Journal*, February,1929, p.264–274; and especially the letter from the Bolivian Government to the Secretary-General (September 12,1929), confirming the acceptance of the proposals of conciliation made by the Commission of Enquiry of Washington *Official Journal*, December,1929, p.1837. See also Munro, *op. cit.*, p.266f. The Commission "was able to bring about a satisfactory settlement of the Vanguardia incident. It failed, however, to persuade Paraguay and Bolivia to take any steps toward a solution of the boundary question itself."

[87]On the work of the Committee, see *Report of the Chaco Commission*. Geneva, 1934. 58 p. [C.154.M.64.1934.VII.] (1934.VII.1.)

[88]See Document [C.171.M.85.1933.VII.]. 1p., mimeographed.

[89]*Report of the Chaco Commission*, p.5.

[90]See, *e.g.*, the following statement, on p.57: "If the parties can feel that, even after the failure of the various efforts that have been made during the last two years, the League of Nations is not the final authority, but they can still contemplate the possibility of intervention from some other quarter, the cause of peace will be gravely jeopardized."

[91]See *Official Journal*, July, 1934, p. 846.

League of its intention to withdraw.[93] In May and June, 1935, representatives of Argentina, Brazil, Chile, Peru, the United States, and Uruguay met in Buenos Aires as mediators in the Chaco dispute.[94] On June 12, 1935, the belligerents signed a protocol for the cessation of hostilities,[95] and other purposes. Under the Protocol the President of Argentina convoked the Chaco Peace Conference, which held its first session in Buenos Aires on July 1, 1935. The dispute was finally settled by the Treaty of Peace of July 21, 1938[96] and by the arbitral award of the Presidents of the six mediating republics of October 10, 1938.[97]

Documents

1934 *Official Journal* Special Supplement No. 124	Dispute between Bolivia and Paraguay. Appeal of the Bolivian Government under Article 15 of the Covenant. Geneva, 1934.
Official Journal Special Supplement No. 132.	Dispute between Bolivia and Paraguay. Part I: Records of the Special Session of the Assembly . . . Part II: Documents. Geneva, 1934.
1935 *Official Journal* Special Supplement No. 133.	Dispute between Bolivia and Paraguay. Appeal of the Bolivian Government under Article 15 of the Covenant. Documentation . . . Geneva, 1935.
Official Journal Special Supplement No. 134.	Dispute between Bolivia and Paraguay. Appeal of the Bolivian Government under Article 15 of the Covenant. Geneva, 1935.
Official Journal Special Supplement No. 135.	Dispute between Bolivia and Paraguay. Part I: Records of the Special Session of the Assembly . . . Part II: Documentation . . . Geneva, 1935.

---

[92]For Assembly Resolutions of September 27, 1934, see *Official Journal*, Special Supplement No.124, p.88.

[93]*Official Journal*, March,1935, p.451.

[94]*Official Journal*, July,1935, p.900.

[95]Text in *ibid.*, p.901-903.

[96]For the work of the Peace Conference, see the *Report by the United States Delegation to the Chaco Peace Conference, Buenos Aires, 1935-1939. Rapporteur: Mr. Spruille Braden.* (Washington, 1940). See also the telegram by the Argentine Minister of Foreign Affairs (Cantilo), July 21,1938, to the Secretary-General: "I have the honour to inform you that the Ministers of Foreign Affairs of Bolivia and Paraguay, who have come to Buenos Aires at the invitation of the peace Conference have this day signed a Treaty of peace and friendship and on frontier questions which brings the Chaco dispute to an end." Document [C.245.M.144.1938.VII.], *Official Journal*, August-September,1938, p.662. For text of the Peace Treaty, see Document [C.274.M.165.1938.VII.], *ibid.*, p.662-664.

[97]For text of the award, see the *Report by the United States Delegation*, *op.cit.*, p.172. For a map of the final territorial settlement, see also *Essential Facts*, p.173.

(28). SINO-JAPANESE CONFLICT, 1931–1933
(QUESTION OF MANCHURIA)

On September 21, 1931, the Chinese government appealed to the Council under Article 11 of the Covenant. It pointed to the fact that "beginning from ten o'clock of the night of September 18th regular troops of Japanese soldiers, without provocation of any kind, opened rifle and artillery fire upon Chinese soldiers at or near the city of Mukden, bombarded the arsenal and barracks . . . and later took military occupation of the cities of Mukden and Antung and other places, and of public buildings therein, and are now in such occupation."[98] The Chinese government considered the situation one which called for action under the terms of Article 11. On January 29, 1932, China requested "the application (not in derogation of the measures taken, or which may be taken by the League in the exercise of its functions under Article 11, but in addition thereto) both of Article 10 and of Article 15 of the Covenant" to the dispute.[99] By Council Resolution of February 19, 1932, the dispute was referred to the Assembly.[100] On February 24, 1933, the extraordinary session of the Assembly adopted a report[101] containing a statement of the facts of the dispute and the recommendations which were deemed just and proper in regard thereto. Forty-two member states voted for the report; Siam (Thailand) abstained from voting. China voted for the report, Japan against it.[102] On March 27, 1933, Japan notified the League of its intention of withdrawal.[103] Japan's political control of Manchuria— it sponsored since February 18, 1932, the "independent" state of Manchukuo, including the three provinces of Fengtien, Kirin and Heilungkiang, together with Jehol—was terminated by the Treaty of Friendship and Alliance between the Republic of China and the U. S. S. R., signed at Moscow on August 14, 1945.[104]

Documents

1931 *Official Journal*   Records of the Twelfth Ordinary Ses-
     Special Supplement   sion of the Assembly. Plenary Meet-
     No. 93.   ings. Text of the Debates. Geneva,
                                 1931.

[98]See *Official Journal*, November,1931, p.2453–2454.
[99]*Official Journal*, March,1932, p.373.
[100]*Ibid.*, p.371. See also Document [A.(Extr.)1.1932.VII.] (1932.VII.3.), and "Letter Dated February 12, 1932, from the Chinese Representative to the Secretary-General, Requesting That the Dispute be Transferred to the Assembly," *ibid.*, p.386.
[101]See Document [A.(Extr.)22.1933.VII.] (1933.VII.2.).
[102]*Official Journal*, March, 1933.
[103]*Official Journal*, May,1933. p.657
[104]See *Department of State Bulletin*, February 10,1946, p.201–208.

1932	*Official Journal* Special Supplement No. 101.	Records of the Special Session of the Assembly Convened in Virtue of Article 15 of the Covenant at the Request of the Chinese Government. Volume I. Geneva, 1932.
	Official Journal Special Supplement No. 102.	Records of the Special Session of the Assembly Convened in Virtue of Article 15 of the Covenant at the Request of the Chinese Government. Volume II. Geneva, 1932.
	[A.(Extr.)1. 1932.VII.]	Appeal from the Chinese Government under Article 15 of the Covenant. Statement Communicated by the Chinese Delegation in Conformity with Article 15, Paragraph 2.
	[A.(Extr.)3. 1932.VII.]	Reports of the Committee of Enquiry Set up at Shanghai under Article 15, Paragraph 1 of the Covenant.
	[C.663.M.320. 1932.VII.]	Appeal by the Chinese Government. Report of the Commission of Enquiry (Lytton).
	[C.663.M.320. 1932.VII. Annexes.]	Appeal by the Chinese Government. Supplementary Documents to the Report of the Commission of Enquiry (Lytton). Geneva.
1933	*Official Journal* Special Supplement No. 111.	Records of the Special Session of the Assembly Convened in Virtue of Article 15 of the Covenant at the Request of the Chinese Government. Volume III. Geneva, 1933.
	Official Journal Special Supplement No. 112.	Records of the Special Session of the Assembly Convened in Virtue of the Article 15 of the Covenant at the Request of the Chinese Government Volume IV. Geneva, 1933.
	Official Journal Special Supplement No. 113.	Records of the Special Session of the Assembly Convened in Virtue of Article 15 of the Covenant at the Request of the Chinese Government. Volume V: Documentation. Geneva, 1933.
	[A.(Extr.)22. 1933.VII.]	Appeal of the Chinese Government. Draft of the Report Provided for in Article 15, Paragraph 4 of the Covenant.

[A.(Extr.)22.(a).   Appeal of the Chinese Government.
1933.VII.]   Draft of the Report Provided for in
                                  Article 15, Paragraph 4 of the Cove-
                                  nant. Addendum.

(35). THE ITALO-ETHIOPIAN DISPUTE, 1935–1936

The dispute between Italy and Ethiopia was formally brought to the attention of the Council for the first time on January 15, 1935, under Article 11, Paragraph 2, of the Covenant.[105] The Ethiopian government demanded on March 17 "full investigation and consideration as provided in Article 15, pending the arbitration of the Wal-Wal incident of December 5, 1934."[106] Several months of discussion passed by during which the Council adopted several resolutions.[107] On September 3, 1935, the decision[108] of the Italo-Ethiopian Commission of Conciliation and Arbitration was released; it held in substance that neither the Italian nor the Ethiopian government was responsible for the Wal-Wal incident, which was rather "due to an unfortunate chain of circumstances,"[109] or the incidents that occurred from December 6, 1934 to May 25, 1935. Nevertheless Italy invaded Ethiopia on October 3, 1935.[110] Five days after the opening of hostilities, on October 7, the Council declared the existence of a state of "war begun in disregard of the obligations of Article 12 of the Covenant."[111] Furthermore, economic measures under Article 16 were approved by all League members, except Albania, Austria, and Hungary, who pointed to their special economic and political relations with Italy. On October 10 a Co-ordination Committee met and appointed a Committee of Eighteen, which from October 11–19 drafted five proposals regarding arms embargo as well as special financial and economic measures.[112] Italian forces entered Addis Ababa, capital of Ethiopia, on May 5. Thereupon the Italian government annexed

[105]See letter from the Abyssinian government to the Secretary-General, dated January 15, 1935, in *Official Journal*, February, 1935, p.252-258.
[106]See footnote 108 below.
[107]See especially Council Resolution of May 25, 1935, *Official Journal*, June,1935, p.640, and Council Resolutions of August 3, 1935, *Official Journal*, August,1935, p.967–968.
[108]*Official Journal*, November,1935, p.1350–1355.
[109]*Ibid.*, p.1354.
[110]For the Italian viewpoint prior to the invasion of Ethiopia, see especially *Memorandum by the Italian Government on the Situation in Ethiopia. I: Report*. Geneva, 1935. 63p. [C.340.M.171.1935.VII.] (1935.VII.11). *II: Documents*. Geneva, 1935. 161 p. [C.340.6(a).M.171.(a).1935.VII.] (1935.VII.13). *Annex to Vol.II*. 22p. [C.340.(b). M.171(b).1935.VII.] (1935.VII.14.).
[111]*Official Journal*, November,1935, p.1226.
[112]For the text of those proposals, see *Official Journal* Special Supplement No.145.

Ethiopia by decree-law of May 9 and conferred upon the Italian King the title of Emperor of Ethiopia.[113]

Shortly before the Council Session of May 12, the Italian representative, Baron Aloisi, informed the Secretary-General of the League that he had received orders from his government to leave Geneva with the Italian delegation.[114] The representative of Ethiopia, Mr. Wolde Maryam, declared at the Council table: "[Ethiopia] requests the Council vigorously to condemn the new act of violence of the Italian Government and its claim to suppress by force a State Member of the League of Nations. The Ethiopian delegation asks that all the provisions of Article 16 of the Covenant should at last be enforced, so that all States, weak or powerful, which are threatened by the ambition and covetousness of an unscrupulous Government, may be reassured. The moment is a tragic one for the League of Nations. On the resolution that the Council takes to-day depends the future and the very existence of the League of Nations."[115] On July 6, 1936, the Co-ordination Committee proposed with regard to the dispute between Ethiopia and Italy that "the Governments of the Members of the League should abrogate on July 15, 1936 the restrictive measures taken by them in conformity with its proposals I(a), II, II(a), III, IV, and IV(b)."[116] The resolution was adopted.

Documents

1935	*Official Journal* Vol.XVI, No. 11.	Council Committee of Six. Report Adopted by the Council on October 7, 1935.
	Official Journal Special Supplement No. 138.	Records of the 16th Ordinary Session of the Assembly. Plenary Meetings Text of the Debates. Geneva, 1935.
	Official Journal Special Supplement No. 145.	Dispute between Ethiopia and Italy Co-ordination of Measures under Article 16 of the Covenant. Geneva, 1935.
1936	*Official Journal* Special Supplement No. 146.	Dispute between Ethiopia and Italy. Co-ordination of Measures under Article 16 of the Covenant. Geneva, 1936.

[113]Extracts from the Decree Law XIV, No.1019 in *Documents on International Affairs*, *1935*, Vol. II, ed. by Stephen Heald (London, 1935), p.474–477. Original text in *Gazetta Ufficiale* of the Kingdom of Italy, June 13, 1936, XIV, No. 136. The Emperor Haile Selassie, who was driven into exile May 2,1936, returned to his throne in Addis Ababa on May 5, 1941.
[114]*Official Journal*, June,1936, p.539.
[115]*Ibid.*, p.540. See *ibid.*, for Council Resolutions of the same date.
[116]*Official Journal*, Special Supplement No.149. For the nature of these measures, see Documents of the Co-ordination Committee, 40, 46, 89, 97, 100 and 106(1).

Official Journal Special Supplement No. 147.	Dispute between Ethiopia and Italy. Co-ordination of Measures under Article 16 of the Covenant. Geneva, 1936.
Official Journal Special Supplement No. 148.	Dispute between Ethiopia and Italy. Co-ordination of Measures under Article 16 of the Covenant. Geneva, 1936.
Official Journal Special Supplement No. 149.	Dispute between Ethiopia and Italy. Co-ordination of Measures under Article 16 of the Covenant. Geneva, 1936.
Official Journal Special Supplement No. 150.	Dispute between Ethiopia and Italy. Co-ordination of Measures under Article 16 of the Covenant. Geneva, 1936.
1937 *Official Journal* Special Supplement No. 164.	Dispute between Ethiopia and Italy. Co-ordination of Measures under Article 16 of the Covenant. General Index to Special Supplements Nos. 145–150. Geneva, 1937.
1935 [A.6.1935.]	Report on the Work of the League since the 15th Session of the Assembly. Part I. (Also numbered as *Official Journal*, Special Supplement No. 136).
[A.6.(a).1935.]	Report on the Work of the League since the 15th Session of the Assembly. Part II.
1936 [A.6.1936.]	Report on the Work of the League, 1935–1936. Part I.
[A.6.(a).1936.]	Report on the Work of the League, 1935–1936. Part II.
[A.6.(a).1936. Annex II.]	Annex to the Report on the Work of the League, 1935–1936. Part II: Note by the Secretary-General on the Economic Situation.

(43). SINO-JAPANESE CONFLICT, 1937–1945

On September 12, 1937, China invoked the application of Articles 10, 11, and 17 of the Covenant and appealed to the Council to advise upon such means and take such action as would be appropriate and necessary in the face of Japanese aggression.[117] The beginning of

[117]*Official Journal*, December,1937, p.1100.

hostilities at Lukouchiao on the evening of July 7 are graphically described in the Chinese communication of August 30.[118] On September 16 the Council resolved to refer the matter to the Advisory Committee on the Sino-Japanese conflict.[119] The Advisory Committee investigated the situation and summarized its findings in three reports.[120]

The recommendations of the Committee to convoke a meeting of the Members of the League which were parties to the Nine-Power Treaty signed at Washington on February 6, 1922,[121] to lend moral support to China,[122] were reaffirmed by the Assembly in its resolution of October 6, 1937. On September 30, 1938, the representative of Sweden supported the finding of these reports and called attention to the circumstances that "the provisions of Article 16 are applicable in present conditions and the members of the League are entitled, not only to act as before on the basis of the said finding, but also to adopt individually the measures provided for in Article 16."[123] Furthermore, on September 11, 1938, the Chinese delegate, Wellington Koo, requested "the Council to give immediate effect to Article 17 of the Covenant, which the Council has hitherto failed to apply but which, in the opinion of the Chinese Government, provides the most relevant procedure for effective action by the League in the present case."[124] However, the Japanese government declined by telegram of September 22, 1938, to discuss the matter with the League.[125]

Documents

1937 *Official Journal* Special Supplement No. 177.	Sino-Japanese Conflict. Appeal by the Chinese Government. Containing Also League Documents: [A.78.1937. VII.], [A.79.1937.VII.], [A.80.1937. VII.], [A.81.1937.VII.]. Geneva, 1937.
1938 *Official Journal* Special Supplement No. 183.	Records of the Nineteenth Ordinary Session of the Assembly. Plenary Meetings. Geneva, 1938.
Official Journal Vol. 19, May-June 1938, p. 306-308, 378-380.	Appeal by the Chinese Government.

[118]See *Official Journal*, August-September,1937, p.653-655.
[119]*Official Journal*, December,1937, p.906.
[120]These reports—Documents [A.78.1937.VII.], [A.79.1937.VII.], [A.80.1937.VII.]—are also in *Official Journal*, Special Supplement No. 177, p.35-44.
[121]See Hudson, *International Legislation*, I. p. 823-828.
[122]See Document [A.79.1937.VII.].
[123]*Official Journal*, November, 1938, p. 879-880. See, however, Sweden's proviso, *ibid.*, p. 880.
[124]*Official Journal*, November,1938, p.988.
[125]*Ibid.*

Official Journal   Appeal by the Chinese Government;
Vol. 19, November 1938,   includes cable by the Tokyo Gov-
p. 988.   ernment refusing the invitation by
                        virtue of Article 17 of the Covenant.

APPEAL OF THE FINNISH GOVERNMENT

By letter of December 3, 1939, the Finnish government called for
summoning a meeting of the Council and the Assembly with reference
to Articles 11 and 15 of the Covenant. Finland complained about the
unexpected attack on the morning of November 30, 1939, by forces
of the Union of Soviet Socialist Republics.[126] On December 5, the
Secretary-General received a telegram from the government of the
Union of Soviet Socialist Republics which read in part as follows:
"The U.S.S.R. is not at war with Finland and does not threaten the
Finnish nation with war. Consequently, reference to Article 11, paragraph 1, is unjustified. Soviet Union maintains peaceful relations with
the Democratic Republic of Finland, whose Government signed with
the U.S.S.R. on December 2nd a Pact of Assistance and Friendship.
This Pact settled all the questions which the Soviet Government had
fruitlessly discussed with delegates of the former Finnish Government
now divested of its power. . . . In these circumstances, appeal of M.
Rodolphe Holsti to the League cannot justify convocation of the
Council and the Assembly, especially as the persons on whose behalf
M. Rodolphe Holsti has approached the League cannot be regarded
as mandatories of the Finnish people."[127] Despite the protest of Soviet
Russia the Council as well as the Assembly were convoked. The
Council took up the issue for the first time at its meeting of December 9, while the Assembly began considering the appeal on December
11. An attempt at mediation, undertaken by a Special Committee,
proved futile. On December 14 at 10 A.M. the Assembly adopted a
resolution declaring that "by the aggression which it has committed
against Finland, the Union of Soviet Socialist Republics has failed to
observe not only its special political agreements with Finland but also
Article 12 of the Covenant of the League of Nations and the Pact of
Paris. . ."[128] Simultaneously, the Assembly declared that the U.S.S.R.
"has by its own action placed itself outside the Covenant,"[129] and
suggested that the U.S.S.R. be excluded from the League by virtue
of Article 16. Accordingly, the Council, meeting in the afternoon of
the same day, resolved that "In virtue of Article 16, Paragraph 4 of
the Covenant, [the Council] finds, that, by its act, the U.S.S.R. has

[126]*Official Journal*, November-December,1939, p.509.
[127]*Ibid.*, p.512.
[128]*Ibid.*, p.540.
[129]*Ibid.*, p.541.

placed itself outside the League of Nations. It follows that the U.S.S.R. is no longer a Member of the League."[130] Whether the Council and Assembly procedure applied in this case was warranted by the Covenant has been a controversial issue.[131]

4. VARIOUS QUESTIONS

LIST OF OTHER POLITICAL QUESTIONS DEALT WITH BY THE LEAGUE OF NATIONS[132]

(2).[133] Conflict between Persia and Soviet Russia (the Enzeli Affair), p. 162.

(4). Conflict between Lithuania and Poland, p. 162.

(5). The Tacna-Arica Dispute (Bolivia, Peru and Chile), p. 163.

(6). Dispute between Panama and Costa Rica, 1921. p. 163.

(7). Delimitation and Alleged Violations of the Albanian Frontier (Albania, Yugoslavia and Greece), p. 164.

(8). Liquidation of Estates of the Former Austro-Hungarian Monarchy in Yugoslavia, 1921, p. 164.

(12). Incursions of Armed Bands into the Frontier Districts of the States Bordering upon Bulgaria (Bulgaria, Roumania, Yugoslavia and Greece), p. 166.

(13). Frontiers between Hungary and Yugoslavia, p. 167.

(21). Expulsion of the Oecumenical Patriarch from Constantinople, p. 170.

(23). Delimitation of the Frontier between Greece and Turkey (Maritza), p. 171.

(26). Assistance Furnished to the Liberian Government, p. 175.

(27). Question of Finnish Vessels Employed by the United Kingdom during the War, p. 176.

(32). Incidents on the Hungarian-Yugoslav Frontier, p. 182.

(34). Rearmament of Germany, p. 183.

(37). Delimitation of the Frontier between Burma and China, p. 189.

(38). The Saar Territory,[134] p. 190.

(39). Relations of the Union of Soviet Socialist Republics with Uruguay, p. 191.

[130] *Ibid.*, p.506.
[131] See Leo Gross, "Was the Soviet Union Expelled from the League of Nations?" *American Journal of International Law*, XXXIX (January,1945), 35-44, especially 39,43.
[132] This list has been drawn up in accordance with the related chapter—Political Questions Dealt with by the League of Nations—in Information Section, *Essential Facts about the League of Nations* (10th ed., revised, Geneva, 1939). The page numbers given are those in *Essential Facts*.
[133] The numbers in parentheses correspond to the numbers in *Essential Facts*.
[134] For the Saar Territory, see above, p. 143-147.

(40). Treaty of Locarno, p. 191.
(41). Request by the Government of Iraq, p. 193.
(42). Appeal by the Spanish Government, p. 194.

COMMISSION OF ENQUIRY FOR EUROPEAN UNION

The Commission of Enquiry for European Union was established to bring about within the framework of the League of Nations "close co-operation between the Governments of Europe in every field of international activity,"[135] and to carry on the enquiry undertaken on the basis of the French Memorandum of May 17, 1930.[136]

The government of each European State Member of the League of Nations could be represented by a delegate or by a deputy delegate.[137]

The Commission met for the first time on September 23, 1930. Its mandate was renewed by the Assembly each year, for the last time on September 23, 1938.[138]

At the first Session instead of the name "Commission of European Union" the "Commission of Enquiry for European Union" was decided upon, thus emphasizing study rather than action.

Organization and Procedure of the Commission

Report by M. Motta on the Constitution, Organization and Procedure of the Commission of Enquiry for European Union. Geneva, 1931. 2 p. [C.204.M.82.1931.VII.] <C.E.U.E.167.> <C.E.U.E./ C.O./5(1).> (1931.VII.2.)

Basic Documents

Documents Relating to the Organisation of a System of European Federal Union. Geneva, 1930. 77 p. [A.46.1930.VII.] (1930.VII.4.)

Contains: I.Communication Distributed to the Press. II. Memorandum by the French Government (May 1st,1930). III. Replies to the French Government's Mem-

---

[135]For the political steps preceding the establishment of the Commission, see Richard N, Coudenhove-Kalergi, *Crusade for Pan-Europe* (New York,1943), p.125f., and Ray. *Commentaire*, 1er Supplément au Commentaire du Pacte, p.27–34. The Commission was set up under Assembly Resolution of September 17, 1930. *Official Journal*, Special Supplement, No. 83, October, 1930, p.50.

[136]This is cited as of May 1 as well as of May 17,1930, though the latter date is more generally accepted. See Coudenhove-Kalergi, *Crusade for Pan-Europe*, p.133,135.

[137]See *Committees of the League of Nations*, p.13. [C.287.M.125.1934]. The Commission included at times 28 Continental States Members, namely, Albania, Austria, Belgium, United Kingdom, Bulgaria, Czechoslovakia, Denmark, Estonia, Finland, France, Germany, Greece, Hungary, Irish Free State, Italy, Latvia, Lithuania, Luxemburg, Netherlands, Norway, Poland, Portugal, Roumania, Spain, Sweden, Switzerland, Turkey, Yugoslavia. The Commission also invited Iceland, the U.S.S.R., and the Free City of Danzig.

[138]See Assembly Resolution of September 23,1938, in *Official Journal*, Special Supplement No.182, October,1938,p.37.

orandum. IV. Reports by the French Government on the Results of the Enquiry, September 8th,1930.

Report by the Secretary-General on Certain Technical Questions Which Have Been Dealt with by the League of Nations. Geneva, 1930. 22 p. [C.693.M.290.1930.VII.] <C.E.U.E.2.> (1930.VII.6.)

Report by the Secretary-General to the Assembly on the Work of the Commission of Enquiry for European Union. Geneva, 1931. 21 p. [A.17.1931.VII.] (1931.VII.9.)

Includes a summary of the work of the Commission.

Report of the Secretary-General to the Assembly on the Work of the Commission of Enquiry for European Union. Geneva, 1932. 3 p. [A.16.1932.VII.] (1932.VII.8.)

Minutes

First Session: Minutes of the First Session, Held at Geneva on Tuesday, September 23rd, 1930. Geneva, 1930. 2 p. [C.565.M.225. 1930.VII.] <C.E.U.E./1st Session/P.V.1.> (1930.VII.5.)

Last Session: Minutes of the Seventh Session of the Commission, Held at Geneva on Friday, October 1st, 1937. Geneva, 1937. 4 p. [C.532.M.370.1937.VII.] <C.E.U.E./7th Session/P.V.1.> (1937. VII.3.)

For the intermediary sessions, see the following:

Second Session: Geneva, January 16–21, 1931. [C.144.M.45.1931. VII.] <C.E.U.E./2nd Session/P.V.> (1931.VII.1.)

Third Session: Geneva, May 15–21, 1931. [C.395.M.158.1931.VII.] <C.E.U.E./3rd Session/P.V.> (1931.VII.7.)

Fourth Session: Geneva, September 3–5, 1931. [C.681.M.287.1931. VII.] <C.E.U.E./4th Session/P.V.> (1931.VII.15.)

Fifth Session: Geneva, September 26, 1931. [C.685.M.291.1931.VII.] <C.E.U.E./5th Session/P.V.1.> (1931.VII.16.)

Sixth Session: Geneva, September 30–October 1, 1932. [C.724.M. 342.1932.VII.] <C.E.U.E./6th Session/P.V.> (1932.VII.13.)

Various Documents

DISPOSAL OF CEREAL STOCKS

Disposal of 1930 Cereal Stocks. Communications from the Governments of Great Britain and Czechoslovakia. Geneva, 1931. 1 p.+ 1 p., bilingual. [C.296.M.138.1931.VII.] <C.E.U.E.25.> (1931. VII.5.)

Committee to Study the Problem of the Export of Future Harvest Surpluses of Cereals (Second Session—June 25th to 27th). Report. Geneva, 1931. 3 p. [C.430.M.179.1931.VII.] (1931.VII.10.)

ECONOMIC DEPRESSION

Economic Depression. Geneva, 1931. 16 p. [C.284.M.134.1931.VII.] <C.E.U.E.24.> (1931.VII.4.)

Resolutions on Economic Questions. Geneva, 1931. 4 p. [C.395.M.
158.1931.VII. (Extract).]

ECONOMIC NON-AGGRESSION

Report by the Special Committee to Examine the Draft Pact of
Economic Non-Aggression.[139] Geneva, 1931. 3 p. [C.807.M.398.
1931.VII.] <C.E.U.E.56.> (1931.VII.17.)

Special Committee to Consider A Pact of Economic Non-Aggression.
Minutes of Session, Held at Geneva from November 2nd to 5th,
1931. Geneva, 1931. 27 p. [C.910.M.478.1931.VII.] <C.E.U.E./
N.A./P.V.> (1931.VII.18.)

STRESA CONFERENCE (1932)

Report by the Stresa Conference for the Economic Restoration of
Central and Eastern Europe. Submitted to the Commission of Enquiry for European Union. Geneva, 1932. 40 p. [C.666.M.321.
1932.VII.] <C.E.U.E.77.> (1932.VII.11.)[140]

UNEMPLOYMENT

Unemployment. Geneva, 1931. 20 p. [C.275.M.127.1931.VII.] <C.
E.U.E.23.> (1931.VII.3.)

Contains: Proposals of the International Labour Office for Practical Action in Connection with Unemployment in Europe for Submission to the Commission of Enquiry for European Union, May,1931.

Unemployment Committee. Geneva, 1931. 2 p. [C.437.M.184.1931.
VII.] <C.E.U.E.43.> (1931.VII.11.)

STRAITS COMMISSION

Legal Structure and Functions

The Straits Commission was established by virtue of and in accordance with Articles 10–16 of the Convention on the Régime of
the Straits, signed at Lausanne, July 24, 1923.[141] The term "Straits,"
as used in this context, comprises the Strait of the Dardanelles, the
Sea of Marmara, and the Bosporus.

"The Commission shall be composed of a representative of Turkey
who shall be the President and representatives of France, Great
Britain, Italy, Japan, Bulgaria, Greece, Romania, Russia and the
Serb-Croat-Slovene State, in so far as these Powers are signatories

[139]See also the Draft Protocol communicated to the members of the Commission of
Enquiry for European Union at the request of the delegation of the Union of Soviet
Socialist Republics: [C.354.M.153.1931.VII.] <C.E.U.E.34.>, mimeographed.
[140]See also Documents [C.707(1).M.341(1).1932.VII.] and [C.703.M.339.1932.VII],
Official Journal, December, 1932, p. 1932–1933, 2036–2037.
[141]Text in 28 Treaty Series, p.115–137, bilingual.

of the present convention, each of these Powers being entitled to representation as from its ratification of the said Convention."[142]

The individual members of the Commission acted on behalf of their governments. The salaries of these representatives were, in principle, paid by their respective governments.

The Commission had two main functions: (1) to see that the provisions of the Straits Convention of 1923 relating to the passage of warships and military aircraft were carried out;[143] (2) to furnish annual reports to the League "giving an account of its activities, and rendering all information which may be useful in the interests of commerce and navigation."[144]

The Commission held its first meeting on October 25, 1924. It discontinued its activities as of August 15, 1936,[145] in accordance with Article 24 of the Convention Relating to the Régime of the Straits, signed at Montreux, July 20, 1936,[146] and thereupon the functions of the Straits Commission were transferred to the Turkish government.[147]

Rules of Procedure

Rules of Procedure of the Commission. Report to the League by the Straits Commission for the Year 1925, p. 23–25. [C.265.1926.VII.]

Annual Reports by the Straits Commission to the League

First Report: Report to the League by the Straits Commission for the Year 1925. Geneva, 1926. 26 p. [C.265.1926.VII.]

Last Report: Rapport de la Commission des Détroits à la Société des Nations. Année 1935. Istanbul, 1936. 122 p.[148]

Since there was only a limited number of copies of the reports for the years 1927 and 1928, only one copy was distributed to each state.

1928: Rapport de la Commission des Détroits à la Société des Nations. Année 1928. Constantinople, 1929. 89 p.

1929: Rapport de la Commission des Détroits à la Société des Nations. Année 1929. Constantinople, 1930. 87 p.

[142]See Art. 12, *ibid.*
[143]See 2, 3, and 4 of the Annex to Art.2, *ibid.*, p.123–127.
[144]See *ibid.*, p.133.
[145]See Document [C. 371.M.244.1926.VII.], in *Official Journal*, August-September, 1936, p. 933.
[146]Text in 173 *Treaty Series*, p. 213–241, bilingual.
[147]For comparative appraisal of the Lausanne and the Montreux Conventions, see James T. Shotwell and Francis Deák, *Turkey at the Straits: A Short History* (New York, 1940), p.124–127. See also *Powers and Duties Attributed to the League of Nations by International Treaties*, p.41–42. [C.3.M.3.1944.V.] (1944.V.1.)
[148]French text only. The reports covering the years 1928–1935(inclusive) were not published as League documents proper; but they were distributed to the States Members of the League by the Secretary-General. See *e.g.*, Document [C.164.M.65.1929.], mimeographed.

1930: Rapport de la Commission des Détroits à la Société des Nations. Année 1930. Stanboul, 1931. 92 p.

1931: Rapport de la Commission des Détroits à la Société des Nations. Année 1931. Istanbul, 1932. 102 p.

1932: Rapport de la Commission des Détroits à la Société des Nations. Année 1932. Istanbul, 1933. 100 p.

1933: Rapport de la Commission des Détroits à la Société des Nations. Année 1933. Istanbul, 1934. 116 p.

1934: Rapport de la Commission des Détroits à la Société des Nations. Année 1934. Istanbul, 1935. 120 p.

1935: Rapport de la Commission des Détroits à la Société des Nations. Année 1935. Istanbul, 1936. 122 p.

In 1938 the Turkish government issued its first annual report: République turque. Ministère des Affaires Etrangères. Rapport annuel sur le mouvement des navires à travers les Détroits et des aèronefs civils entre la Méditerranée et la Mer Noire. Première année, janvier 1938. Ankara, 1938. 93 p.

Last Published Report: République turque. Ministère des Affaires Etrangères. Rapport annuel sur le mouvement des navires à travers les Détroits et des aèronefs civils entre la Méditerranée et la Mer Noire. Quatrième année, janvier 1941. Ankara, 1941. 31 p.

On March 10, 1942, the Acting Secretary-General of the League communicated to the Council and the members of the League the following note:[149]

(*Translation*)   Ankara, February 3rd, 1942

To the Acting Secretary-General:

I have the Honour to inform you that the Report for the year 1941 on the movement of vessels through the Straits, provided for in Article 24 of the Montreux Convention, has been prepared.

In view of present circumstances, however, the Government of the Turkish Republic intends to postpone publication thereof.

For the Minister:
Aciklin,[150]
Deputy Secretary-General

[149]Document [C.23.M.23.1942.VII.].
[150]See also Document [C.5.M.5.1943.VII.], mimeographed.

X. INTELLECTUAL CO-OPERATION

1. INTRODUCTORY NOTE

THE ACTIVITIES of the League in the field of intellectual co-operation are reflected in two sets of publications. There are, on the one hand, several publications bearing on intellectual co-operation issued by the League proper, and, on the other hand, a considerable number of publications issued by the Institute of Intellectual Co-operation[1] in Paris. The publications of the Institute are, in principle, excluded from this bibliographical guide,[2] while the major publications by the League are listed below.

The League's work on intellectual co-operation was for the most part carried out through the following agencies: (1) the International Committee on Intellectual Co-operation;[3] (2) the Institute of Intellectual Co-operation, controlled by the Governing Body, the Director's Committee, and the Director of the Institute;[4] (3) the National Committees on Intellectual Co-operation, designed to act as a link

[1]On the Institute see Gilbert Murray, "Intellectual Co-operation," *The Annals of the American Academy of Political and Social Science*, CCXXXV (September,1944), 1–9; Malcolm W. Davis, "The League of Minds," in Harriet E. Davis, ed., *Pioneers in World Order* (New York,1944), p.240–249; Henri Bonnet, "Intellectual Co-operation," in *World Organization: A Balance Sheet of the First Great Experiment* (Washington,1942), p.191. For the related activities of the Secretariat in this field, see Egon F. Ranshofen-Wertheimer, *The International Secretariat* (Washington,1945), p.130–133. The Intellectual Co-operation Section of the Secretariat served as the administrative secretariat of the International Committee in its relation with the Council and the Assembly and for official communications with governments. It was also the channel of communication with the Institute of Intellectual Co-operation, the Educational Cinematographic Institute, the Secretariat of the Advisory Committee on the Teaching of the Principles and Facts of Intellectual Co-operation, and the Permanent Committee on Arts and Letters. See *Essential Facts about the League of Nations* (10th ed., revised, Geneva,1939), p.266.
[2]For bibliographical information on the publications of the Institute, see International Institute of Intellectual Cooperation, *Publications*, 11p., mimeographed; published by Columbia University Press.
[3]See Assembly Resolution of September 21,1921, *Official Journal*, Special Supplement No.6, October,1921, p.34. For Rules of Procedure of the Committee, see Document [C.711.M.423.1922.XII.]. In addition to the International Committee on Intellectual Co-operation and the Executive Committee there were 14 Committees of Experts; for a list of these, see *The Committees of the League of Nations*, p. 71. [C.99.M.99.1945.V.]
[4]See Art. 4 of the 1931 Rules and Regulations in Document, [A.24.1931.XII.], p.9.

between the International Committee and intellectual life in the different countries.[5]

The International Committee on Intellectual Co-operation was composed of 18 members appointed in an individual capacity for three years by the Council of the League of Nations. In 1930, by Council Resolution of September 9, 1930 (*Official Journal*, November, 1930, p. 1304–1306), an Executive Committee of the International Committee was set up to supervise the whole organization and to see that the decisions of the Committee were carried out between its meetings. The Executive Committee was composed of eight members, five were chosen from among the members of the Committee (including the Chairman) and three were chosen from outside the Committee; the latter acted only in an advisory capacity. Under Article 5 of the Organic Statute of the Institute of Intellectual Co-operation, the International Committee on Intellectual Co-operation constituted the Governing Body of the Institute.

In 1928 there was initiated the International Studies Conference; this Conference was declared to be an autonomous and "independent" organization in 1934.[6]

On the work of the International Institute for Intellectual Co-operation in general see the Institute's publication:

L'Institut International de Coopération Intellectuelle. 1925–1946. Paris, 1946. 599 p.

A comprehensive survey on the work of the Institute. Contains a bibliography of the publications of the Institute on p. 583–599.

2. BASIC TEXTS

COMMITTEE ON INTELLECTUAL CO-OPERATION

Assembly Resolution of September 21, 1921. *Official Journal*, Special Supplement No. 6, October, 1921, p. 34.
Nomination of a Committee on Intellectual Co-operation. Report

[5]On national committees, see especially International Committee on Intellectual Co-operation, *Report by the Committee on the Work of Its Twelfth Plenary Session*, p.31. [A.21.1930.XII.] (1930.XII.A.3.). For a list of the 44 national committees in existence in 1939, see *Essential Facts*, p.267.
[6]See International Institute of Intellectual Co-operation, *The International Studies Conference: Origins, Functions, Organization* (Paris,1937), p.29. For a list of the sessions and meetings of the International Studies Conference, 1928–1937, see *ibid.*, p.51–54. The following publications of the Conference are of particular interest: *The State and Economic Life*, Vol. I, 1932, 168p.; Vol. II, 1934, 422p. *Collective Security*, 1936, 514p. *Peaceful Change; Procedures, Population, Raw Materials, Colonies. Proceedings of the Tenth International Studies Conference.* Paris, June 28–July 3, 1937. Paris, 1938. 685 p. *Peaceful Change. Population and Peace; a Survey of International Opinion on Claims*

Presented by M. Léon Bourgeois and Adopted by the Council on May 15th, 1922. [C.312.M.155.1922.XII.][7]

Rules of Procedure of the International Committee on Intellectual Co-operation, Adopted by the Committee. *Official Journal*, December, 1937, p. 1067–1068.[8]

INSTITUTE OF INTELLECTUAL CO-OPERATION

Letter from the French Government to the President of the Council of the League of Nations, Dated December 8th, 1924. *Official Journal*, February, 1925, p. 285–286.[9]

Organic Statute of the Institute. *Official Journal*, February, 1925, p. 286–287.

International Act Concerning Intellectual[10] Co-operation. No date. 39 p., bilingual.

3. INTERNATIONAL COMMITTEE ON INTELLECTUAL CO-OPERATION

MINUTES OF SESSIONS

First Session: Minutes of the First Session. Geneva, August 1st–5th, 1922. Geneva, 1922. 50 p. [C.711.M.423.1922.XII.]

Last Recorded Session: Minutes of the Thirteenth Session, Held at Geneva, from Monday, July 20th, to Saturday, July 25th, 1931. 106 p. [C.471.M.201.1931.XII.] <C.I.C.I./13th Session/P.V.> (1931.XII.A.3.)

No minutes for the Fourteenth and subsequent sessions were published. For the intermediate sessions, see the following:

Second Session: Geneva, July 26–August 2, 1923. [C.570.M.224. 1923.XII.]

Third Session: Paris, December 5–8, 1923. [C.3.M.3.1924.XII.]

Fourth Session: Geneva, July 25–29, 1924. [A.20.1924.XII.]

---

[7] *Relief from Population Pressure*. Paris, 1939. 373 p. (On spine: Vol. II.) *Le Contrôle s changes*, 2 vols. (Paris, 1947). Tome I: *Rapport général*, by A. Piatier; Tome II: *apports nationaux: Allemagne, Amérique latine, Argentine et Bulgarie*.

[8] Also in *Official Journal*, June,1922, p.679–680; see also *ibid.*, p.535–536. For the pernent Council Resolution of January 14,1922, see *Official Journal*, February,1922, 111, 174–175.

[9] Document [C.327.M.220.1937.XII.Appendix 12.]; see also *Official Journal*, December, 37, p.925. For 1922 Rules of Procedure, see *Minutes of the First Session of the Internanal Committee on Intellectual Co-operation*, p.40. [C.711.M.423.1922.XII.]

[10] See also the original Document [C.825(1)M.280.1924.XII.], mimeographed.
Signed in Paris, December 3,1938. Also published as part of "International Act Conrning Intellectual Co-operation, Signed at Paris on December 3rd, 1938" [C.514.1938], icial Journal, February,1939, p.174–187. The Act entered in force on January 31,1940.

Fifth Session: Paris, May 11–14, 1925. [C.286.M.104.1925.XII.]
Sixth Session: Geneva, July 27–30, 1925. [C.445.M.165.1925.XII.]
Seventh Session: Paris, January 14–18, 1926. [C.87.M.43.1926.XII.]
  C.I.C.I./7th Session/P.V.> (1926.XII.A.2.)
Eighth Session: Geneva, July 26–29, 1926. [C.462.M.181.1926.XII.]
  <C.I.C.I./8th Session/P.V.> (1926.XII.A.8.)
Ninth Session: Geneva, July 20–26, 1927. [C.424.M.157.1927.XII.]
  <C.I.C.I./9th Session/P.V.>
Tenth Session: Geneva, July 25–30, 1928. [C.533.M.160.1928.XII.]
  (1928.XII.A.7.)
Eleventh Session: Geneva, July 22–26, 1929. [C.342.M.121.1929.
  XII.] (1929.XII.A.3.)
Twelfth Session: Geneva, July 23–29, 1930. [C.428.M.192.1930.XII.
  <C.I.C.I./12th Session/P.V.> (1930.XII.A.2.)

Indices to Minutes of Sessions

Index to the Minutes of the Meetings of the Committee on Intel
  lectual Co-operation. Sessions I–IV: Geneva, 1925. 24 p. [C.290.M
  105.1925.XII.]. Sessions V–VII: Geneva, 1926. 9 p. [C.431.M.163
  1926.XII.] (1926.XII.A.4.). Sessions VIII–XII: Geneva, 1926
  1930. 28 p. [C.652.M.268.1930.XII.] (1931.XII.A.1.)

REPORTS TO THE COUNCIL ON THE WORK OF
THE COMMITTEE

First Report: Committee on Intellectual Co-operation. First Sessio
  Held at Geneva from August 1st to 5th, 1922. Report of the Com
  mittee Approved by the Council on September 13th, 1922. Geneva
  1922. 9 p.+9 p., bilingual. [A.61.1922.XII.] [C.559.1922.XII.]
Last Report: International Committee on Intellectual Co-operatior
  Report by Professor G. de Reynold (Rapporteur) on the Work o
  the Twenty-first Plenary Session of the Committee (Geneva, Jul
  17th–22nd, 1939). Geneva, 1939. 48 p. [C.231.M.153.1939.XII
  (1939.XII.A.2.)
For the intermediate sessions, see the following:
Second Session: Geneva, July 26–August 2, 1923. [A.31.1923.XII.]
Third Session: Paris, December 5–8, 1923 and Fourth Session: G
  neva, July 25–29, 1924. [A.31.1924.XII.]
Fifth Session: Paris, May 11–14, 1925. [C.288.1925.XII.]
Sixth Session: Geneva, July 27–30, 1925. [A.24.1925.XII.]
Seventh Session: Paris, January 14–18, 1926. [C.77.1926.XII.] (192
  XII.A.1.)
Eighth Session: Geneva, July 26–29, 1926. [A.28.1926.XII.] (192
  XII.A.7.)

Ninth Session: Geneva, July 20–26, 1927. [A.35.1927.XII.] (1927. XII.A.4.)

Tenth Session: Geneva, July 25–30, 1928. [A.28.1928.XII.] (1928. XII.A.2.)

Eleventh Session: Geneva, July 22–26, 1929. [A.20.1929.XII.] (1929. XII.A.1.)

Twelfth Session: Geneva, July 23–29, 1930. [A.21.1930.XII.] (1929. XII.A.3.)

Thirteenth Session: Geneva, July 20–25, 1931. [A.23.1931.XII.] (1931.XII.A.4.)

Fourteenth Session: Geneva, July 18–23, 1932. [A.11.1932.XII.] (1932.XII.A.1.)

Fifteenth Session: Geneva, July 17–22, 1933. [A.14.1933.XII.] (1933. XII.A.1.)

Sixteenth Session: Geneva, July 16–21, 1934. [C.339.M.156.1934. XII.] (1934.XII.A.2.)

Seventeenth Session: Geneva, July 15–20, 1935. [C.290.M.154.1935. XII.] (1935.XII.A.2.)

Eighteenth Session: Geneva, July 13–18, 1936. [C.328.M.205.1936. XII.] (1936.XII.A.2.)

Nineteenth Session: Paris, July 12–17, 1937. [C.327.M.220.1937. XII.] (1937.XII.A.2.)

Twentieth Session: Geneva, July 11–16, 1938. [C.253.M.150.1938. XII.] (1938.XII.A.4.)[11]

4. REPORTS OF THE GOVERNING BODY OF THE INTERNATIONAL INSTITUTE OF INTELLECTUAL CO-OPERATION

In accordance with Article 14 of the Organic Statute of the International Institute of Intellectual Co-operation the Governing Body of the Institute reported annually to the Council of the League of Nations and to the government of the French Republic.

First Report: International Committee on Intellectual Co-operation. First Report: Governing Body of the International Institute of Intellectual Co-operation. Report on the Work of the International Institute of Intellectual Co-operation. Geneva, 1926. 2 p. [A.27. 1926.XII.] (1926.XII.A.6.)

Last Report: Intellectual Co-operation Organisation. Report of the Governing Body of the International Institute of Intellectual Co-operation. Geneva, 1939. 10 p. [C.224.M.152.1939.XII.] (1939. XII.A.1.)

[11]*Report by Professor G. de Reynold (Rapporteur) on the Work of the Twentieth Plenary Session of the Committee.*

For the intermediate reports, 1927–1938, see the following:
1927: [A.31.1927.XII.] (1927.XII.A.2.)
1928: [A.29.1928.XII.]
1929: [A.24.1929.XII.]
1930: [A.27.1930.XII.] (1930.XII.A.4.)
1931: [A.24.1931.XII.] (1931.XII.A.5.)
1932: [A.19.1932.XII.]
1933: [A.12.1933.XII.]
1934: [C.338.M.155.1934.XII.] (1934.XII.A.1.)
1935: [C.278.M.145.1935.XII.] (1935.XII.A.1.)
1936: [C.318.M.199.1936.XII.] (1936.XII.A.1.)
1937: [C.326.M.219.1937.XII.] (1937.XII.A.1.)
1938: [C.247.M.145.1938.XII.] (1938.XII.A.3.)

5. LEAGUE OF NATIONS TEACHING

INDIVIDUAL DOCUMENTS

How to Make the League of Nations Known and to Develop the Spirit of International Co-operation. Recommendations by the Sub-committee of Experts, International Committee on Intellectual Co-operation, League of Nations. Geneva, 1927. 82 p. [C. 515.M.174.1927.XII.] <C.I.C.I.190.> (1927.XII.A.9.)[12]

The Aims and Organisation of the League of Nations. Revised Edition.[13] Published for the Use of Teachers by the Secretariat of the League of Nations. Geneva, 1930. 90 p. (1928.XII.A.6.)

Sub-committee of Experts for the Instruction of Youth in the Aims of the League. Report on the Third Session Held at Geneva from July 3rd to 5th, 1930. Geneva, 1930. 32 p. <C.I.C.I./E.J./48.>[14]

BULLETIN OF LEAGUE OF NATIONS TEACHING

First Issue: Bulletin of League of Nations Teaching. No. 1, Geneva, December, 1934. 161 p.

Last Issue: Bulletin of League of Nations Teaching: The Teaching of the Principle and Facts of International Co-operation. No. 5, Geneva, December, 1938. 235 p.

The *Bulletin* appeared once a year; from 1929 to 1933 (inclusive) a

[12]There is also an abbreviated 34p. ed. of this document: [C.515.M.174.1927.XII.] <C.I.C.I.190.(Extract).> (1927.XII.A.9(Extract).).
[13]First ed., Geneva, 1929. (1928.XII.A.6.).
[14]See also the following Assembly Documents: [A.10.1925.XII.], [A.10(a).1925.XII.], [A.26(1).1926.], [A.26.1927.XII.], [A.23.1931.XII.], [A.11.1932.XII.].

serial publication, dedicated to similar objectives, appeared under the title *Educational Survey*.[15]

6. BULLETIN OF THE INTERNATIONAL UNIVERSITY INFORMATION OFFICE

Committee on Intellectual Co-operation. Bulletin of the International University Information Office. 1st year, 1924, 4 numbers. 2nd year, 1925, 6 numbers.

3d year, No. 1 (1926) through 4th year, No. 2 (1928) published by the International Institute of Intellectual Co-operation, with the title *Bulletin for University Relations*. Absorbed in January, 1929, by *La Coopération intellectuelle* (Première Année, No. 1, January 15, 1929).

7. PRESS

CONFERENCE OF PRESS EXPERTS, GENEVA, 1927

Preparatory Work

Documents Relating to the Preparation of the Press Experts Committee (Resolution of the Sixth Assembly, 1925). Geneva, June 29, 1926. 15 p. [C.399.M.140.1926.] <C.E.P.I.> (General.1926.5.)

Conference of Press Experts (Geneva, August 24, 1927). Preparatory Documents. Geneva, May 11, 1927. 31 p. [C.231.M.93.1927.] <Conf.E.P.I.> (General.1927.1.)

Conference of Press Experts, Geneva, August 24, 1927. Protection of Press Information. Geneva, July 8, 1927. 28 p. [C.352.M.126.1927.] <Conf.E.P.2.> General.1927.5.)

Conference

Conference of Press Experts, Geneva, August 1927. Final Report. Geneva, October 25, 1927. 32 p. <Conf.E.P.13.> (General.1927. 15.)

Conference of Press Experts, Held in Geneva, August 24–29, 1927. Final Resolutions and Various Other Documents. Geneva, September 2, 1927. 24 p. [A.43.1927.] (General.1927.8.)

Conference of Press Experts. Report Presented to the Assembly by the Sixth Committee. Geneva, September 19, 1927. 2 p. [A.77.1927.] (General.1927.9.)

Conference of Press Experts. Resolution Adopted by the Assembly on September 22, 1927, on the Proposal of the Sixth Committee.

[15]See League Catalogue, p.255.

Geneva, September 22, 1927. 1 p. [A.102.1927.] (General.1927.10.)
See also the following League documents: [A.114.1925.VII.], [A.31.
1932.], [C.348.M.161.1934.VIII.], [A.138.1935.].
For reports on the Conferences of Governmental Press Bureaux
and Representatives of the Press held in Copenhagen (1932) and
Madrid (1933), see: "Collaboration of the Press in the Organisation
of Peace" [C.96.1932.], *Official Journal*, March, 1932, p. 789–797, and
November, 1932, p. 1736–1737 (Copenhagen); and *Official Journal*,
February, 1934, p. 131–133 (Madrid). See also the Assembly Resolution of September 26, 1934, *Official Journal*, November, 1934, p.1473–
1474.

EUROPEAN CONFERENCE ON THE TRANSPORT OF NEWSPAPERS AND PERIODICALS, GENEVA, 1929[16]

European Conference on Transport of Newspapers. Preparatory
Documents. Geneva, 1929. 8 p. <C.E.T.J.1.> (1929.VIII.11.)
European Conference on the Transport of Newspapers and Periodi-
cals. Final Act. Geneva, 1929. 8 p., in part double-paged. [C.557.
M.208.1929.VIII.] <C.E.T.J.17.> (1929.VIII.16.)
European Conference on the Transport of Newspapers and Periodi-
cals, Held in Geneva, November 25th to 29th, 1929. Records and
Texts. Geneva, 1930. 60 p. [C.115.M.36.1930.VIII.] (1930.VIII.1.)

8. USE OF BROADCASTING IN THE CAUSE OF PEACE

CONFERENCE, GENEVA, SEPTEMBER 17–23, 1936

Inter-Governmental Conference for the Conclusion of an Interna-
tional Convention Concerning the Use of Broadcasting in the
Cause of Peace. Final Act. Geneva, 1936. 12 p., in part bilingual.
[C.399.(a).M.252.(a).1936.XII.] (1936.XII.B.11.)

CONVENTION

International Convention[17] Concerning the Use of Broadcasting in
the Cause of Peace. Geneva, September 23, 1936. 10 p., in part
bilingual. Geneva, 1936. [C.399.M.252.1936.XII.] (1936.XII.B.10.)

[16]See also Document [C.143(a).M.55(a).1929.] <C.C.T.395(1).(a).>.
[17]Signed at Geneva on September 23, 1936; in force since April 2, 1938. Text also in
186 *Treaty Series*, p. 301–317, bilingual.

ASSEMBLY DOCUMENTS

Modern Means of Spreading Information Utilized in the Cause of Peace. Report Submitted by the Sixth Committee to the Assembly. Rapporteur: M. H. Frisch, Denmark. Geneva, 1937. 3 p. (A.68. 1937.XII.)

Modern Means of Spreading Information Utilized in the Cause of Peace. Report by the Seventh Committee to the Assembly. Rapporteur: M. Hartvig Frisch (Denmark). Geneva, 1938. 2 p. (A. 57.1938.)[18]

Modern Means of Spreading Information Utilized in the Cause of Peace. Report by M. de Reynold, on Behalf of the International Committee on Intellectual Co-operation. Geneva, 1938. 6 p. [A. 19.1938.XII.] (1938.XII.A.2.)

9. INTERNATIONAL EDUCATIONAL CINEMATO-GRAPHIC INSTITUTE

INTRODUCTORY NOTE

The legal basis of the Institute is to be found in Article 3[19] of the General and Administrative Regulations of the International Educational Cinematographic Institute[20] and, after 1931, in the Organic Statute of the International Educational Cinematographic Institute. These were approved by the Council of the League of Nations on August 30, 1928, and amended by the Council on September 26, 1928, September 19, 1929, and January 19, 1931.[21]

[18]See also the following publications of the International Institute of Intellectual Co-operation: *Broadcasting and Peace: Studies and Projects in the Matter of International Agreements* (Paris, 1933), 231 p.; *The Educational Role of Broadcasting*, by F.W. Beidler-Wagner, Henri Bonnet, Kristine Bonnevie, and others (Paris, 1935), 289 p.; *School Broadcasting* (Paris,1933), 210 p.

[19]Art. 3 reads as follows: "The guiding principles and the programme of the International Educational Cinematographic Institute are defined: (a) By the resolution of the Assembly of the League of Nations dated September 20th,1927; (b) By the resolution of the Council of the League of Nations dated September 28th, 1927; (c) By the letter dated January 7th, 1928, from M. Mussolini, Prime Minister of Italy, to the President of the Council of the League of Nations; (d) By the resolution of the Council of the League of Nations dated March 7th, 1928; (e) By the Organic Statute approved by the Council of the League of Nations on August 30th,1928; (f) By the report of the Italian representative on the Council of the League of Nations and the conclusions adopted in this connection on September 26th,1928; (g) By the letter from the Italian Government dated October 13th,1928." For the text of the Art. and the above enumerated documents, see Extract No. 45 from the *Official Journal*, January, 1929. [C.573.rev.1928.XII.] See also *Official Journal*, January 1929, p. 157-170.

[20]See Extract No. 45 from the *Official Journal*, January,1929, p.5-10.

[21]Text in Document [C.694.M.291.1930.XII.] (1931.XII.A.2.), p. 21-22.

The main organs of the Institute were the Governing Body, the Permanent Executive Committee, and the Director.[22] There was also a Technical and Advisory Committee.[23] Financial and staff regulations had to be submitted to the Council of the League of Nations for approval.

On the whole, the work of the International Educational Cinematographic Institute was carried on under the direction of the Council of the League of Nations, which was advised in this respect by the International Committee on Intellectual Co-operation. The program of the Institute took due consideration of the powers of related League agencies, such as the International Institute of Intellectual Co-operation, the International Labor Organization,[24] and the Child Welfare Committee.

The purpose of the Institute was to encourage the production, distribution, and exchange between the various countries of educational films concerning instruction, art, industry, agriculture, commerce, health, social education, etc. by any means which the Governing Body considered necessary.[25]

The International Educational Cinematographic Institute was juridically distinct from the League of Nations. It was created by Italy through agreements concluded between the League of Nations and the Italian government. The League reserved substantial rights of supervision and direction.

The Institute was formally opened on November 5, 1928.[26] It terminated its activities as of December 31, 1937.[27] By Article I of the Procès-Verbal, signed at Geneva on September 12, 1938, the signatories agreed that the functions given to the International Cinematographic Institute by Articles IV, V, VI, VII, IX, XII, and XIII of the Convention for Facilitating the International Circulation of Films of an Educational Character of October 11, 1933, would henceforth be performed by the International Committee on Intellectual Co-operation.[28]

[22]See Art. 4 of the Organic Statute.
[23]*Report to the Council of the League of Nations on the Seventh Session of the Governing Body of the Institute*, p. 2. [C.350.M.163.1934.XII.] (1934.XII.B.1.)
[24]Art.10 of the Organic Statute; see especially the "Agreement between the International Labour Bureau and the International Cinematographic Institute," *International Review of Educational Cinematograph*, I (1929), 331–334.
[25]Art. 2 of the Organic Statute.
[26]See Louis Dop, "The Role and the Purpose of the International Educational Cinematographic Institute," *International Review of Educational Cinematograph*, I (1929), 19. [*sic*]
[27]See "Letter dated December 18th,1937, from the President of the International Educational Cinematographic Institute to the Secretary-General," and the accompanying note by Count Ciano, *Official Journal*, January,1938, p.14. [C.21.M.9.1938.XII.]
[28]See Document [C.302.M.177.1938.XII.] (1938.XII.A.5), cited below, p. 344.

BASIC DOCUMENTS

Organic Statute of the International Educational Cinematographic Institute, Approved by the Council of the League of Nations, August 30th, 1928. In Report to the Council on the First Session of the Governing Body of the Institute, Held at Rome from November 5th to 9th, 1928. Extract No. 45 from the *Official Journal*, January, 1929, p. 12–13. [C.573.(revised).1928.XII.]

General and Administrative Regulations of the International Educational Cinematographic Institute. In Report to the Council on the First Session . . . Extract No. 45 from the *Official Journal*, January, 1929, p. 5–10.

Financial Regulations of the Institute. In Report to the Council on the First Session . . . Extract No. 45 from the *Official Journal*, January, 1929, p. 15–17.

ANNUAL REPORTS

Annual reports on the work of the Institute were sent to the Council of the League of Nations and to the Italian government in accordance with Article 18 of its Organic Statute.

First Report: Report to the Council on the First Session of the Governing Body of the Institute, Held at Rome from November 5th to 9th, 1928. 18 p. In Extract No. 45 from the *Official Journal*, January, 1929. [C.573. (revised).1928.XII.]

Last Report: Report to the Council of the League of Nations on the Seventh Session of the Governing Body of the Institute Held at Stresa on June 25th, 1934. Geneva, 1934. 11 p. [C.350.M.163. 1934.XII.] (1934.XII.B.1.)

The intermediate reports have the following document numbers: Second Session, Rome, October 2–4, 1929, [C.3.M.1.1930.XII.]; Third Session, Rome, October 8–10, 1930, [C.694.M.291.1930.XII.] (1931.XII.A.2.); Fourth Session, Rome, October 13–14, 1931, [C. 922.M.487.1931.XII.] (1931.XII.A.6.); Fifth Session, Rome, October 26–27, 1932, [C.33.M.12.1933.XII.]; Sixth Session, Rome, November 29–30, 1933, [C.8.M.6.1934.XII.].

CONFERENCE FOR FACILITATING THE INTERNATIONAL CIRCULATION OF FILMS OF AN EDUCATIONAL CHARACTER, 1933, 1938

Final Acts

Conference for Facilitating the International Circulation of Films of an Educational Character (Geneva, October 5th–11th, 1933).

Final Act. Geneva, 1933. 10 p., bilingual. [C.589.M.275.1933.XII.] (1933.XII.B.2.)

Conference on the Application of the Convention for Facilitating the International Circulation of Films of an Educational Character (Geneva, September 10th–12th, 1938). Final Act. No date. 6 p., bilingual. [C.303.M.178.1938.XII.] (1938.XII.A.6.) Also in *Official Journal*, Special Supplement No. 183, p. 115–123.

Convention

Convention for Facilitating the International Circulation of Films of an Educational Character.[29] Geneva, 1933. 10 p., bilingual. [C.588.M.274.1933.XII.] (1933.XII.B.1.)

Procès-Verbal Concerning the Application of Articles IV, V, VI, VII, IX, XII and XIII of the Convention of October 11th, 1933, Facilitating the International Circulation of Films of an Educational Character (Geneva, September 12th, 1938). No date. 3 p., bilingual. [C.302.M.177.1938.XII.] (1938.XII.A.5.) Also in *Official Journal*, Special Supplement No. 183, p. 111–114.

Review

From 1929 to 1934 the Institute published the *International Review of Educational Cinematography*.
First Issue: Rome, July, 1929. 116 p.
Last Issue: Rome, December, 1934. 839 p.
Volumes I–VI (inclusive) appeared from 1929–1934. Volume VII (1935) appeared as *Intercine: International Institute of Educational Cinematography. League of Nations*. Both the *Review* and the *Intercine* were published monthly in five editions: English, French, Italian, Spanish, and German.

10. TEACHING OF HISTORY

Declaration Regarding the Teaching of History (Revision of School Text-Books). Opened for Signature at Geneva, October 2nd, 1937. In 182 *Treaty Series*, p. 263–266, bilingual.[30]

11. INTERNATIONAL ORGANIZATIONS

HANDBOOK OF INTERNATIONAL ORGANIZATIONS

First Edition: Handbook of International Organisations (Associations, Bureaux, Committees, etc.). Geneva, 1921. 167 p.

[29] In force since October 11, 1933.
[30] In force since November 24, 1937.

Last Edition:[31] League of Nations Handbook of International Organisations (Associations, Bureaux, Committees, etc.). Geneva, 1938. 491 p.

The League's aim in publishing the *Handbook of International Organisations* was to provide a source of information for all who were interested, whether theoretically or practically, in the international movement. Organizations are classified in the *Handbook* according to the subjects with which they deal. There are three indices to facilitate reference. The League's own organizations are, in general, not mentioned.

QUARTERLY BULLETIN OF INFORMATION ON THE WORK OF INTERNATIONAL ORGANIZATIONS

First Issue: Bulletin trimestriel de renseignments sur l'oeuvre des organisations internationales publié par la Section des Bureaux Internationaux.[32] No. 1, October, 1922. 30 p.

Last Issue: Bulletin of Information on the Work of International Organisations Compiled by the Section of International Bureaux. Vol. X,[33] No. 2, December, 1938, p. 77–154.[34]

The *Bulletin* gives a summary of the discussions at the meetings of over 400 international organizations established either under general conventions concluded between governments or by private initiative. It also contains reports of major international congresses or conferences, together with the texts of the most important resolutions; the dates and places of forthcoming meetings are also given. From 1922 to 1931 (inclusive) the *Bulletin* appeared as a quarterly. In 1932 its title was changed to *Bulletin of Information on the Work of International Organisations Compiled by the Section of International Bureaux.*

12. VARIOUS PUBLICATIONS

INDEX BIBLIOGRAPHICUS

Godet, Marcel. Index Bibliographicus: International Catalogue of Sources of Current Bibliographical Information (Periodicals and Institutions). Geneva, 1925. 233 p.

Godet, Marcel & Vorstius, Joris. Index bibliographicus: Catalogue

[31]See also the 1923,1925,1926,1929, and 1936 editions.
[32]For the most part in French only.
[33]See also Supplement to Vol.X, 18p.
[34]Beginning with No.2, January,1923, there appeared an English and a French edition of the *Bulletin.*

international des bibliographies courantes. 2d ed., Berlin et Leipzig, 1931. 420 p.

ENQUIRY INTO THE CONDITIONS OF INTELLECTUAL WORK

In all 41 brochures appeared in this series, which dealt partly with general questions, partly with the conditions of intellectual life in individual countries. A complete list may be found in *League Catalogue*, p. 259–261, as well as on the covers of Brochure No. 41, entitled "Science in the United States."

LEARNING AND LEADERSHIP

Zimmern, Alfred. Learning and Leadership: A Study of the Needs and Possibilities of International Intellectual Co-operation. Geneva, 1927. 121 p. [C.I.C.I.188.] (1927.XII.A.1.)

13. SERIAL PUBLICATIONS OF THE INTERNATIONAL INSTITUTE OF INTELLECTUAL CO-OPERATION

LA COOPÉRATION INTELLECTUELLE, 1929–1930

First Issue: La coopération intellectuelle. Revue mensuelle. 1re Année, No. 1. Paris, 15 janvier 1929. 64 p.
Last Issue: La coopération intellectuelle. Revue mensuelle. 2e Année, No. 24. Paris, 15 decembre 1930. p. 619–681.
This was a monthly publication.

BULLETIN DE LA COOPÉRATION INTELLECTUELLE, 1931–1945

First Issue: Société des Nations. Bulletin de la Coopération intellectuelle [No.] 1. Institut International de Coopération intellectuelle, Paris, janvier 1931. 47 p.
Last Issue: Société des Nations. Coopération intellectuelle [No.] 95–96. La Conférence de Santiago du Chili. Paris [decembre 1938.] p. 575–681.

Special Issues

La Coopération intellectuelle internationale. Numéro spéciale (octobre–novembre, 1945). 132 p.
La Coopération intellectuelle internationale. Numéro spéciale. [No.] 1–2: U.N.E.S.C.O. (janvier–mars 1946). 102 p.
La Coopération intellectuelle internationale. Numéro spéciale. [No.] 3–4 (avril–juin 1946). 159 p.
The April–June, 1946 issue was the last. All these special issues were

published on behalf of the Institut International de Coopération Intellectuelle.

MOUSEION, 1927–1940

First Issue: Mouseion. Bulletin de l'Office International des Musées. Institut de Coopération Intellectuelle de la Société des Nations. [No.] 1, avril 1927. 86 p.
Last Regular Issue: Mouseion. XIVe Année, Vol. 49–50. Numéros 1–11, 1940. 228 p. 2 p.[35]

Mouseion appeared at first three times a year; from 1931 to 1939 it was a quarterly. From March, 1932 to June, 1940, there appeared monthly supplements. The first 14 fascicules (March, 1932–April, 1933) were published in mimeographed form.

An index covering the 100 fascicules published from March, 1932 through May–June, 1940, is entitled: *Index des Fascicules 1 à 100: Index alphabétique des matières et index alphabétique des noms d'auteurs.* [No date]. 312 p. This index is a convenient guide through this series; see especially pages 7 and 8 for the numbering of the fascicules and the introductory note on changes of the title of the series. Eight additional supplements (Nos. 101 to 108) appeared from June, 1940 to the end of 1946. In 1948 the United Nations Educational, Scientific and Cultural Organization began publication in Paris of the quarterly, *Museum,* termed the successor to *Mouseion.* Volume I, No. 1–2, 1948.

[35]See also *Index des volumes 1 à 50. Index alphabétique des matières et index alphabétique des noms d'auteurs.* 196 p.+1 p.

Part Five

THE INTERNATIONAL LABOR ORGANIZATION AND THE PERMANENT COURT OF INTERNATIONAL JUSTICE

Part Five

THE INTERNATIONAL LABOR
ORGANIZATION AND THE
PERMANENT COURT OF
INTERNATIONAL JUSTICE

I. THE INTERNATIONAL LABOR ORGANIZATION

1. INTRODUCTORY NOTE

THE INTERNATIONAL LABOR ORGANIZATION, frequently styled an "autonomous" body within the League system, closely co-operated with the League of Nations from the outset. The Covenant of the League did not specifically mention the International Labor Organization; it merely stated in rather general terms: "Subject to and in accordance with the provisions of international conventions existing or hereafter to be agreed upon, the Members of the League: (a) will endeavour to secure and maintain fair and humane conditions of labour for men, women and children, both in their own countries and in all countries to which their commercial and industrial relations extend, and for that purpose will establish and maintain the necessary international organisations" (Article 23 (a)).

By contrast, the "Constitution" of the International Labor Organization provided in Article 6 (Article 392 of the Treaty of Versailles):[1] "The International Labour Office shall be established at the seat of the League of Nations as part of the organisation of the League." Under Article 12(398).[2] the International Labor Office was "entitled to the assistance of the Secretary-General of the League of Nations in any matter in which it can be given."

The reference to the "International Labour Office" in Article 12 is obviously misleading, for not only the Secretariat of the Organization, that is, the International Labor Office, but also the Governing Body and the International Labor Conference were entitled to the assistance of the Secretary-General of the League, who, for example, communicated to the members of the Organization certified copies of International Labor Conventions in accordance with Article 19(405) of the Constitution. It is noteworthy that the Constitution originally referred only to "a permanent organisation . . . for the promotion of

---

[1]Arts. 387–427, constituting Part XIII of the Treaty of Versailles, contained the organic law of the International Labor Organization, generally referred to as the "Constitution" or "Statute." For the separate publication of the Statute, see below, p. 356–357.
[2]The figures in parentheses here and in succeeding references to articles of the Statute indicate their numbering in Part XIII of the Treaty of Versailles.

the objects set forth in the Preamble . . ." [Article 1(387)] which was to be composed of a General Conference of Representatives of the Members and an International Labour Office controlled by the Governing Body [Article 2(388)]. The Governing Body consisted of twenty-four persons, twelve representing governments, six representing employers, and six representing workers [Article 7(393)]. Of the twelve persons representing governments, eight were to be nominated by the members which were of chief industrial importance. The Council of the League was authorized to decide any question as to which were the members of chief industrial importance.[3] On November 2, 1922, an amendment was adopted to reorganize the Governing Body so that it would include sixteen members representing governments, eight representing employers, and eight representing workers. This amendment came into force on June 4, 1934. Article 7, Paragraph 1 of the Constitution of the International Labor Organization, adopted in Montreal, October 9, 1946, provides for the same composition in the Governing Body.

For the most part the terms "International Labour Organisation" and "International Labour Office" have frequently been used as if they were interchangeable; the ambiguous abbreviation "I.L.O.," which actually stands for International Labor Organization, adds to the resulting confusion.

The expenses of the International Labor Organization, except the traveling and subsistence expenses of delegates and advisers who attended the meetings of the International Labor Conference and of the Governing Body, were paid to the Director by the Secretary-General of the League of Nations out of the general funds of the League [Article 13(399)].[4] Actually, however the budget of the Organization was larger than the allocations for it contained in the League budget. This discrepancy was due to the fact that the Organization budget included contributions from both members and nonmembers of the League.

[3]Under the new Constitution of the International Labor Organization, adopted in Montreal on October 9, 1946, the Governing Body or the International Labor Conference are authorized to decide this question. Art. 7 (393), Par. 3 of the new Constitution reads: "The Governing Body shall as occasion requires determine which are the Members of the Organisation of chief industrial importance and shall make rules to ensure that all questions relating to the selection of the Members of chief industrial importance are considered by an impartial committee before being decided by the Governing Body. Any appeal made by a Member from the declaration of the Governing Body as to which are the Members of chief industrial importance shall be decided by the Conference, but an appeal to the Conference shall not suspend the application of the declaration until such time as the Conference decides the appeal."

[4]On the financial relations between the League and the International Labor Organization, see International Labor Conference, *Twenty-ninth Session, Montreal, 1946* (Montreal, 1946), p. 77–82. For budget figures of the Organization covering the years 1920 to 1946, see Appendix One, Section XIII, p. 532.

At its Twenty-seventh Session (Paris, 1945), the International Labor Conference authorized the Organization to make such financial and budgetary arrangements with the United Nations as appeared appropriate, but, in principle, the expenses of the International Labor Organization are now borne by its members, and not by the United Nations. Whereas under the League system the budget of the Organization formed part of the League budget, under the new Constitution there will be a separate budget for the Organization, although contributions from the United Nations are not excluded.[5]

The purpose of the International Labor Organization is the advancement of humane labor conditions everywhere in the world; for, in the words of the Preamble of the Statute of the Organization, "peace can be established only, if it is based on social justice."

Two aspects of the activities of the Organization have attracted wide attention: the composition of the International Labor Conference and the pioneering work of the Organization in the field of International Labor Conventions and Recommendations. The "General Conference of Representatives of the Members" [Article 3(389)], in short, the "International Labour Conference"—this title appears on the official proceedings of the Conference—is composed of four representatives from each member: two delegates representing governments, one representing employers, and one representing workers.[6] The principle of tripartite representation, including government, business, and labor, constituted a new and, on the whole, successful device in international conference procedure.

One of the main functions of the International Labor Conference is the drafting of International Labor Conventions and Recommendations.[7] Draft Conventions or Recommendations may be adopted by a majority of two thirds of the votes cast by the delegates present. Draft Conventions to be binding require subsequent ratification[8] by the appropriate organ of the member state. A Recommendation is merely "submitted to the Members for consideration with a view to effect being given to it by national legislation or otherwise."[9] Up to and inclusive of the 1946 Montreal Conference, 80 Draft Conventions and 80 Recommendations were adopted by the 29 International Labor Conferences, held from 1919 to 1946. The Thirtieth International Labor Conference (Geneva, 1947) adopted the Conventions Nos. 81–86 and the Recommendations Nos. 81–82.

[5] See Art. 13 (399) as amended in 1945 and 1946.
[6] For advisers from nonmetropolitan territories, see Art. 3, Par. 3 as amended in 1946.
[7] See Art. 19 (405). Art. 19 was thoroughly revised in 1946, particularly in regard to Recommendations; see especially Par. 1 and Pars. 6 and 7 as amended.
[8] See Art. 19, Par. 1 as amended. On adoption and ratification of International Labor Conventions, see Francis O. Wilcox, *The Ratification of International Conventions* (London, 1935), p. 161–204.
[9] See Art. 19.

In addition to the International Labor Conference proper, other international conferences are held under the auspices of the Organization: (1) regional conferences, such as the labor conferences of the American states which are members of the International Labor Organization; (2) World Industrial Committee Conferences, such as the 1946 conferences of the Coal Mines, Inland Transport, Iron and Steel, and Metal Trades Industrial Committees;[10] (3) committee meetings of various committees related to the Organization, such as the Permanent Migration Committee.

The International Labor Organization sends missions abroad[11] to investigate labor problems in various countries or to advise governments on special technical problems related to labor and economic policy.

Moreover it functions as a clearinghouse for information on labor matters.[12] Its publications activities are particularly noteworthy. In addition to the publications listed below, numerous monographs[13] on many aspects of labor, social, and economic questions have been published by the Organization. In certain instances material prepared by the International Labor Organization was published under the auspices of the League of Nations, for instance, some of the documentation on the World Economic Conference in 1927 and on the European Conference on Rural Life, which was to have been held in 1939. For further information, see the catalogues published by the Organization.[14]

2. MISCELLANEOUS LEAGUE DOCUMENTS CONCERNING THE INTERNATIONAL LABOR ORGANIZATION

Permanent Labour Organisation. Resolution Adopted by the Council of the League of Nations, Meeting in Rome on 19th May, 1920. No date. 1 p., bilingual. [20/41/14]

[10]On World Industrial Committee Conferences, see Ervin Hexner, "World Industrial Committees," *The Southern Economic Journal,* XII (April, 1946), 348–356, and International Labor Conference, *Twenty-ninth Session, Montreal, 1946: Director's Report* (Montreal, 1946), p. 99–100.
[11]International Labor Conference, *Twenty-ninth Session, Montreal, 1946: Director's Report,* p. 90–93.
[12]*Ibid.,* p. 101–103.
[13]See, *e.g., International Commodity Control Agreements.* Montreal, 1943. 221 p. *Constitutional Provisions Concerning Social and Economic Policy.* Montreal, 1944. 755 p.
[14]Especially *Abridged Catalogue of Publications of the International Labour Office (Twenty-sixth Edition).* Geneva, 1940, 52 p. *Recent Publications of the International Labour Office, December, 1943.* Montreal, no date. 39 p. *Recent Publications of the International Labour Office, January, 1946.* Montreal, no date. 52 p. *Recent Publications, 1946–47.* Geneva, 1947. 9. p.

Approves the action taken by the Secretary-General in connection with the first annual meeting of the International Labor Conference, held at Washington in October and November, 1919.

Permanent Labour Organisation. Memorandum Adopted by the Council of the League of Nations, Meeting in Rome, on 19th May, 1920. No date. 5 p., bilingual. [20/41/15][15]

Contains report by the Secretary-General on the International Labor Conference (Washington, 1919).

League of Nations. Transfer of the International Labour Office to Geneva. London, June 26, 1920. 2 p., bilingual. [20/4/117] and [15/4912/2858]

Refers to decision by the Administrative Council of the International Labor Office of June 8, 1920, to transfer its offices to Geneva, pending a definite decision of the League of Nations.

League of Nations. Accommodation for the International Labour Office: Extract from the Report of the Finance Committee, Approved by the Governing Body, and Memorandum Submitted by the Director. Geneva, June 1, 1922. 26 p., bilingual. [C.336.M.187.1922.I.]

League of Nations. Report of the Committee Appointed to Consider the Criteria to Be Adopted in the Selection of the Eight States of Chief Industrial Importance. Geneva, May 31, 1922. 34 p.+ 34 p., bilingual. [C.410.M.316.1922.V.]

League of Nations. Question as to Which Are the Eight Members of the International Labour Organisation of Chief Industrial Importance: First Report by the Representative of Japan; Second Report and Resolution Adopted by the Council on September 30th, 1922. Geneva, October 3, 1922. 8 p.+8 p., bilingual. [C.643(1). M.400.1922.]

3. CONSTITUTION AND RULES OF THE INTERNATIONAL LABOR ORGANIZATION

Originally, Part XIII of the Treaty of Peace with Germany, signed at Versailles on June 28, 1919, constituted the organic law of the International Labor Organization. Identical provisions were incorporated into the corresponding sections of the peace treaties with Austria (St. Germain, September 10, 1919), Hungary (Trianon, June 4, 1920), Bulgaria (Neuilly, November 27, 1919). Accordingly, the authentic text of the original Constitution of the International Labor Organization is to be found in Articles 387–427 of the Treaty of Versailles. Later the Constitution was numbered independently of the Treaty clauses, including 41 articles.

[15]Also numbered [16/4430/1892] and Council Document 27 [16/2747/1892].

On November 5, 1945, the Twenty-seventh Session of the International Labor Conference adopted the "Instrument for the Amendment of the Constitution of the International Labour Organisation," which for the first time contains the revised text of the Preamble referring expressly to the "Constitution of the International Labour Organisation." Under Article 5 of the Instrument the Director is obligated to communicate to each of the members of the Organization a certified copy of the Instrument, which came into force on September 26, 1946.

In the course of the Twenty-ninth Session (1946) of the International Labor Conference additional changes were adopted. The new Constitution will come into force "when ratified or accepted by two-thirds of the Members of the Organisation including five of the eight members which are represented on the Governing Body as members of chief industrial importance" (Art. 36 of the Constitution as adopted by the Conference). This amendment clause emphasizes the relative independence of the International Labor Organisation as compared with its status in relation to the League of Nations, since the original amendment procedure required "two-thirds of the votes cast by the Delegates present" and ratification "by the States whose representatives compose the Council of the League of Nations and by three fourths of the members" [Article 36(422)].

A selected list of documents pertaining to the Constitution of the International Labor Organization follows.

International Labour Organisation. Constitution and Rules.[16] Montreal, 1946. 114 p., bilingual.

Includes: The Constitution of the International Labour Organisation, p. 5–21; Resolutions Adopted by the Commission on International Labour Legislation of the Peace Conference (Paris, 1919), p. 22; Instrument for the Amendment of the Constitution of the International Labour Organisation, p. 23–26; The Declaration of Philadelphia, p. 27–29; Standing Orders of the International Labour Conference, p. 33–68; Standing Orders of the Governing Body, p. 71–80.

International Labour Conference. Instrument for the Amendment of the Constitution of the International Labour Organisation. Adopted by the Conference at Its Twenty-seventh Session. Paris, 5 November, 1945[17] (Authentic Text). No date. 7 p., bilingual.

A first attempt to adjust the Constitution of the International Labor Organization to the United Nations Charter.

International Labour Conference. The Constitution of the International Labour Organisation Instrument of Amendment, 1946. The

---

[16]The authentic English and French texts of the original Statute of the International Labor Organization are, of course, to be found in every complete edition of the Treaty of Versailles, Part XIII.

[17]Also in *Official Bulletin*, Vol. 28 (December 15, 1946), p. 1–4.

Final Articles Revision Convention, 1946. Adopted by the Conference at Its Twenty-ninth Session. Montreal, 9 October, 1946 (Authentic Texts). 63 p., bilingual.

Synoptic print of the text in force on October 9, 1946, and amended text in English and French, together with the 1946 Instrument of Amendment. English text also in *Official Bulletin*, Vol. 29, No. 4 (November 15, 1946), p. 203–253. Bilingual edition also in *International Labour Conference, Twenty-ninth Session, Montreal, 1946. Record of Proceedings*, Montreal, 1948, p. 544–596. The new Constitution of the I.L.O. entered into force on April 20, 1948.

4. SEPARATION OF THE INTERNATIONAL LABOR ORGANIZATION FROM THE LEAGUE OF NATIONS

International Labour Conference. Twenty-ninth Session, Montreal, 1946. Constitutional Questions. Part I: Reports of the Conference Delegation on Constitutional Questions. Second Item on the Agenda. Montreal, International Labour Office, 1946. 197 p.
International Labour Office. Official Bulletin. Vol. XXIX, No. 1 (31 August 1946). 70 p.

Contains: Memorandum Submitted by the Acting Director of the International Labour Office to the 97th Session of the Supervisory Commission of the League of Nations, p. 1; Memorandum Submitted to the United Nations Committee on League Assets by the Supervisory Commission of the League of Nations: The Interests of the I.L.O. in the Assembly Hall and Library of the League of Nations, p. 7; Report of the Committee Set up by the Preparatory Commission of the United Nations to Discuss and Establish with the Supervisory Commission of the League of Nations a Common Plan for the Transfer of the Assets of the League of Nations, p. 10; Resolution of the General Assembly of the United Nations Approving the Report of the League of Nations Committee and the Common Plan for the Transfer of the Assets of the League, p. 17; Report of the Supervisory Commission of the League of Nations on Discussions with the Representatives of the United Nations on Questions of the Transfer of the League of Nations Assets, p. 18; General Report of the Finance Committee to the Twenty-first Ordinary Session of the Assembly of the League of Nations, p. 23; Agreement Concerning the Execution of the Transfer to the United Nations of Certain Assets of the League of Nations (Extracts), p. 36; Judgments Pronounced by the Administrative Tribunal Concerning Certain Officials of the International Labour Office Discharged in Application of the Emergency Measures Adopted by the Assembly in 1939 (Note Submitted to the Governing Body of the International Labour Office at Its 98th Session), p. 37. Appendix: Text of the Judgment Given in the Case of: Zoppino *versus* International Labour Office, p. 42; Agreement Concerning the Legal Status of the International Labour Organisation in Switzerland after the Dissolution of the League of Nations, p. 47; Entry into Force of the Agreement Concerning the Legal Status of the International Labour Organisation in Switzerland, p. 63; Letters Exchanged between the Acting Director of the International Labour Office and the Head of the Federal Political Department, p. 63; Agreement between the League of Nations and the International Labour Organisation Concerning the Transfer of Certain Properties, p. 65; Conveyance of Certain Properties from the League of Nations to the International Labour Organisation, p. 67; Procès-Verbal Concerning the Transfer of Documents Relating to International Labour Conventions, p. 70.

5. AGREEMENT WITH THE UNITED NATIONS

In accordance with Articles 57 and 63 of the United Nations Charter an agreement between the United Nations and the International Labor Organization was made on May 30, 1946, in New York City. It was subsequently approved by the General Assembly of the United Nations and the Twenty-ninth Session of the International Labor Conference.

Draft Agreement between the United Nations and the International Labour Organisation. United Nations Document A/72, September 30, 1946, bilingual. 8 p.

(Also in *Official Bulletin*, Vol. 29, No. 6, December 20, 1946.)

6. STAFF REGULATIONS

International Labour Office. Staff Regulations. Geneva, 1923. 46 p.

International Labour Office. Staff Regulations (Reprinted from the Geneva Edition of December, 1939). Montreal, 1944. 72 p.

7. BUDGET

International Labour Organisation. Budget for the Twenty-third Financial Period, 1941. Montreal, 1941. 11 p.

International Labour Organisation. Budget for the Twenty-fourth Financial Period, 1942. Montreal, 1941. 12 p.

International Labour Organisation. Budget for the Twenty-fifth Financial Period (1943). Montreal, 1943. 19 p.

International Labour Organisation. Budget for the Twenty-sixth Financial Period (1944). Montreal, 1943. 15 p.

International Labour Organisation. Budget for the Twenty-seventh Financial Period (1945). Montreal, 1944. 15 p.

International Labour Organisation. Budget for the Twenty-eighth Financial Period (1946). Montreal, 1946. 14 p.

International Labour Organisation. Budget for the Twenty-ninth Financial Period (1947). Montreal, 1946. 21 p.

International Labour Organisation. Budget for the Thirtieth Financial Period (1948). Geneva, 1947. 19 p.

8. PROCEEDINGS OF INTERNATIONAL LABOR CONFERENCES

GENERAL CONFERENCES

League of Nations. International Labour Conference. First Annual

Meeting, October 29, 1919–November 29, 1919. Washington, Government Printing Office, 1920. 300 p.

League of Nations. International Labour Conference. Second Session, Genoa, 15th June–10th July, 1920. Geneva, International Labour Office, 1920. xlii+699 p., bilingual.

League of Nations. International Labour Conference. Third Session, Geneva, 1921. Geneva, International Labour Office, 1921. 2 volumes, bilingual: Volume I, lxxiv+597 p.; Volume II, p. 601–1306.

League of Nations. International Labour Conference. Fourth Session, Geneva, 1922. Geneva, International Labour Office, 1922. 2 volumes, bilingual: Volume I, lviii+1–615 p.; Volume II, p. 621–1166.

League of Nations. International Labour Conference. Fifth Session, Geneva, 22–29 October, 1923. Geneva, International Labour Office, 1923. liv+494 p., bilingual.

League of Nations. International Labour Conference. Sixth Session, Geneva, 1924. Geneva, International Labour Office, 1924. 2 volumes, bilingual: Volume I, lxi+1–498 p.; Volume II, p. 503–1215.

League of Nations. International Labour Conference. Seventh Session, Geneva, 1925. Geneva, International Labour Office, 1925. 2 volumes, bilingual: Volume I, lxxxix+1–577 p.; Volume II, p. 583–1450.

League of Nations. International Labour Conference. Eighth Session, Geneva, 1926. Geneva, International Labour Office, 1926. 2 volumes, bilingual: Volume I, lxvi+480 p.; Volume II, p. 1–769.

League of Nations. International Labour Conference. Ninth Session, Geneva, 1926. Geneva, International Labour Office, 1926. lxvii+692 p., bilingual.

League of Nations. International Labour Conference. Tenth Session, Geneva, 1927. Geneva, International Labour Office, 1927. 2 volumes: Volume I, lxxix+745 p., bilingual; Volume II: Report of the Director Presented to the Conference. 420 p. (English Edition).

League of Nations. International Labour Conference. Eleventh Session, Geneva, 1928. Geneva, International Labour Office, 1928. 2 volumes: Volume I, lxxix+773 p., bilingual; Volume II, Report of the Director Presented to the Conference. 468 p. (English Edition)

League of Nations. International Labour Conference. Twelfth Session, Geneva, 1929. Geneva, International Labour Office, 1929. 2 volumes: Volume I, xxvii+644 p., bilingual (First and Second Parts); Volume I, p. 647–1149, bilingual (Third Part); Volume II, Report of the Director Presented to the Conference. 534 p. (English Edition).

League of Nations. International Labour Conference. Thirteenth Session, Geneva, 1929. Geneva, International Labour Office, 1929. xlvii+467 p., bilingual.

League of Nations. International Labour Conference. Fourteenth Session, Geneva, 1930. Geneva, International Labour Office, 1930. 2 volumes: Volume I, lxiii+531 p., bilingual (First and Second Parts); Volume I, p. 535–946, bilingual (Third Part); Volume II: Report of the Director Presented to the Conference. 626 p. (English Edition).

League of Nations. International Labour Conference. Fifteenth Session, Geneva, 1931. Geneva, International Labour Office, 1931. 2 volumes: Volume I, lxii+494 p., bilingual (First and Second Parts); Volume I, p. 497–802, bilingual (Third Part); Volume II: Report of the Director Presented to the Conference. 493 p. (English Edition).

League of Nations. International Labour Conference. Sixteenth Session, Geneva, 1932. Record of Proceedings. Geneva, International Labour Office, 1932. lxiii+1003 p., bilingual.

League of Nations. International Labour Conference. Seventeenth Session, Geneva, 1933. Record of Proceedings. Geneva, International Labour Office, 1933. xxxi+780 p., bilingual.

League of Nations. International Labour Conference. Eighteenth Session, Geneva, 1934. Record of Proceedings. Geneva, International Labour Office, 1934. xxx+707 p., bilingual.

International Labour Conference.[18] Nineteenth Session, Geneva, 1935. Record of Proceedings. Geneva, International Labour Office, 1935. xxxv+1015 p.

International Labour Conference. Twentieth Session, Geneva, 1936. Record of Proceedings. Geneva, International Labour Office, 1936. xxxiii+797 p.

International Labour Conference. Twenty-first Session and Twenty-second Session, Geneva, 1936. Record of Proceedings. Geneva, International Labour Office, 1937. x+416 p., bilingual.

International Labour Conference. Twenty-third Session, Geneva, 1937. Record of Proceedings. Geneva, International Labour Office, 1937. xxxiii+881 p., bilingual.

International Labour Conference. Twenty-fourth Session, Geneva, 1938. Record of Proceedings. Geneva, International Labour Office, 1938. xxxii+712 p., bilingual.

International Labour Conference. Twenty-fifth Session, Geneva, 1939. Record of Proceedings. Geneva, International Labour Office, 1939. xxx+670 p., bilingual.

International Labour Conference. Twenty-sixth Session, Philadelphia, 1944. Record of Proceedings. Montreal, International Labour Office, 1944. xxxiv+647 p. English text only.

[18]This was the first issue which did not carry the imprint "League of Nations."

Recommendations and Declarations, p. 542–623, bilingual.

International Labour Conference. Twenty-seventh Session, Paris, 1945. Record of Proceedings. Geneva, International Labour Office, 1946. xxxiii+507 p. English text only.

Instrument of Amendment and Recommendation Adopted by the Conference, p. 470–485, bilingual.

International Labour Conference. Twenty-eighth Session, Seattle, 1946. Record of Proceedings. Montreal, International Labour Office, 1946. xxviii+411 p. English text only.

International Labour Conference. Twenty-ninth Session, Montreal, 1946. Record of Proceedings, Montreal International Labour Office, 1948. xxxvii+648 p.

REGIONAL CONFERENCES—LATIN AMERICA

Labour Conference of the American States Which Are Members of the International Labour Organisation, Santiago (Chile). Record of Proceedings. Geneva, International Labour Office, 1936. viii+319 p.

Second Labour Conference of the American States Which Are Members of the International Labour Organisation, Havana (Cuba), 21 November–2 December, 1939. Record of Proceedings. Montreal, International Labour Office, 1941. ix+284 p.

Third Labour Conference of the American States Which Are Members of the International Labour Organisation, Mexico, April, 1946. Record of Proceedings. Montreal, International Labour Office, 1946. xx+308 p.

NEW YORK AND WASHINGTON CONFERENCE, 1941

Conference of the International Labour Organisation, 1941. New York and Washington, D. C. Record of Proceedings. Montreal, International Labour Office, 1941. xviii+201 p.

9. REPORTS TO THE INTERNATIONAL LABOR CONFERENCE

REPORTS OF THE DIRECTOR

For the first fourteen sessions of the International Labour Conference the Director's Report to the Conference appeared either as separate volumes of the Proceedings of the International Labour Conference, e.g., "International Labour Conference. Tenth Session,

Geneva, 1927. Vol. II: Report of the Director Presented to the Conference. 420 p. (English Edition)," or as subsections of individual volumes. It should be noted that in the preceding cumulative list of International Labour Conference Proceedings, Director's Reports are expressly listed only where they appeared as special volumes of the Conference Proceedings, as for instance, in the above reference to the 1927 Report. No reference is made when such a Report appeared as a subsection of a more inclusive volume. Beginning with the Fifteenth Session of the International Labour Conference (1931) the form and content of the Director's Report underwent certain changes. In 1931 the International Labour Office decided "to divide the old Report into two separate documents. One part, under the title 'Annual Review' was designed to furnish a general survey," whereas the second part was designed to review "the more urgent problems with which the organization is faced, the outlook for the future, and the general policy of the Organization." (See *International Labour Conference Fifteenth Session, Geneva, 1931. Report of the Director. First Part, p. 1*). Beginning with the *Seventeenth Session* (1933) the legal-size format for the annual review was abandoned, and the Reports appeared henceforth in convenient pamphlet form. No Director's Report was issued for the 22nd Session (1936). No complete listing of the Director's Reports has been attempted here. For additional information see: *International Labour Office. Abridged Catalogue of Publications of the International Labour Office* (27th ed.), Geneva, 1948, p. 9–34.

International Labour Office. The I.L.O. and Reconstruction: Report by the Acting Director of the International Labour Office to the Conference of the International Labour Organisation, New York, 1941. Montreal, International Labour Office, 1941. 112 p.

International Labour Conference. Twenty-sixth Session. Director's Report. Seventh Item on the Agenda. Montreal, 1944. 91 p.

International Labour Conference. Twenty-seventh Session, Paris, 1945. Director's Report. First Item on the Agenda. Montreal, International Labour Office, 1945. 163 p.

International Labour Conference. Twenty-eighth Session, 1946. Director's Report. First Item on the Agenda. Montreal, International Labour Office, 1946. 59 p.

International Labour Conference. Twenty-ninth Session, Montreal, 1946. Director's Report. First Item on the Agenda. Montreal, International Labour Office, 1946. 113 p.

International Labour Conference. Thirtieth Session, Geneva, 1947. Report of the Director-General. First Item on the Agenda. Report I. Geneva, International Labour Office, 1947. 120 p.

SUMMARY OF ANNUAL REPORTS UNDER ARTICLE 22
OF THE CONSTITUTION (ARTICLE 408 OF THE
TREATY OF VERSAILLES)[19]

League of Nations. International Labour Conference. Sixteenth Session, Geneva, 1932. Summary of Annual Reports under Article 408. Geneva, International Labour Office, 1932. 402 p.

International Labour Conference. Seventeenth Session, Geneva, 1933.[20] 505 p.

International Labour Conference. Eighteenth Session, Geneva, 1934. Summary of Annual Reports under Article 408. Geneva, International Labour Office, 1934. 233 p.

International Labour Conference. Nineteenth Session, Geneva, 1935. Summary of Annual Reports under Article 408. Geneva, International Labour Office, 1935. 290 p.

International Labour Conference. Twentieth Session, Geneva, 1936. Summary of Annual Reports under Article 22 of the Constitution of the International Labour Organisation. Geneva, International Labour Office, 1936. 394 p.

International Labour Conference. Twenty-third Session, Geneva, 1937. Summary of Annual Reports under Article 22 of the Constitution of the International Labour Organisation. Geneva, International Labour Office, 1937. 462p.

International Labour Conference. Twenty-fourth Session, Geneva, 1938. Summary of Annual Reports under Article 22 of the Constitution of the International Labour Organisation. Geneva, International Labour Office, 1938. 283 p.

International Labour Conference. Twenty-fifth Session, Geneva, 1939. Summary of Annual Reports under Article 22 of the Constitution of the International Labour Organisation. Geneva, International Labour Office, 1939. 372 p.

See also Appendix: Report of the Committee of Experts on the Application of Conventions. Geneva, 1939. 23 p.

[19]Article 22 reads in part: "Each of the Members agrees to make an annual report to the International Labour Office on the measures which it has taken to give effect to the provisions of conventions to which it is a party." These reports are to be made in such form and are to contain such particulars as the Governing Body may request and the Director is required to lay a summary of them before the Conference. Until 1931 inclusive this summary appeared as a part of the Director's report; since 1932 it has been a separate document. On this point, see *International Labour Code, 1939* (Montreal, 1939), p. xix–xx.

[20]The 1933 Summary constitutes a basic volume for the five years 1934–1938, and the Summary submitted to the Conference in each of these years contains, in principle, only such information as is supplementary to that contained in the 1933 volume.

International Labour Conference. Twenty-seventh Session, Paris, 1945. Reports on the Application of Conventions (Article 22 of the Constitution). Montreal, International Labour Office, 1945. 72 p.+1 p.

See also Appendix: Report of the Committee of Experts on the Application of Conventions. Montreal, 1945. 6 p.

International Labour Conference. Twenty-ninth Session, Montreal, 1946. Reports on the Application of Conventions (Article 22 of the Constitution). Montreal, International Labour Office, 1946. 121 p.[21]

International Labour Conference. Reports on the Application of Conventions (Article 22 of the Constitution). Geneva, International Labour Office, 1947. 138. p.

Contains: Appendix, 29 p.

Other Reports to the International Labor Conference

Several types of reports have been published in connection with the "General Conference of Representatives of the Members": (1) Reports of the Director; (2) Summary of Annual Reports under Article 22; (3) Special Reports on the Working of Conventions. The Special Reports are presented to the International Labor Conference by the Governing Body at irregular intervals, usually at the expiration of ten years from the date on which a convention came into force.

Since the First Session of the Conference in 1919, various procedures have been employed in the formal discussion of proposals for the adoption of International Labor Conventions and Recommendations. Since 1932 the normal procedure has been to discuss each item on the agenda twice. Thus, the Office has submitted to the Conference two main reports, customarily referred to as the *Grey* Report and the *Blue* Report, with an intervening subsidiary report designated as the *Red* Report (Questionnaire). The International Labor Office explains the nature of these reports as follows: "On each item of the Agenda of the International Labour Conference the Office submits to the Conference a preliminary report setting out the law and practice on the subject in a number of countries. This is followed by detailed conclusions serving as an introduction to a draft list of points on which the Conference may instruct the Office to consult Governments, with a view to a second discussion of the question at the next

[21]See also the Supplement to this, 42 p.+2 p., and Appendix. Report of the Committee of Experts on the Application of Conventions, 10 p.

Session. These reports have grey covers and are referred to as *Grey* Reports. . . .[22] Immediately after the Session to which the *Grey* Report is submitted and at which the first discussion takes place the Office prepares and issues to Governments a *Red* Report (Questionnaire). This contains the text of the Report of the Conference Committee to which the *Grey* Report was referred for examination, and concludes with the Questionnaire proper, which is based on the list of points adopted by the Conference Committee and approved by the Conference.[23] For the second discussion at the next Session of the Conference the Office prepares a *Blue* Report, giving the replies of Governments to the above-mentioned *Red* Report (Questionnaire), and containing a proposed text of a Draft Convention or Recommendation; this is submitted to the Conference with a view to final decision on the question."[24] *Blue* Reports issued prior to 1932 do not exactly conform to this description, but in principle serve the same purpose as the more recent *Blue* Reports.

10. INTERNATIONAL LABOR CONVENTIONS

Article 19 (405), Paragraph 4 of the Constitution of the International Labor Organization provides: "A copy of the recommendation or draft convention shall be authenticated by the signature of the President of the Conference and of the Director and shall be deposited with the Secretary-General of the League of Nations. The Secretary-General will communicate a certified copy of the recommendation or draft convention to each of the Members." Article 20 (406) provides: "Any convention so ratified shall be registered by the Secretary-General of the League of Nations, but shall only be binding upon the members which ratify it."[25] It should be noted that International Labor Conventions were registered but not published in the *Treaty Series of the League of Nations*. A List of Conventions in Chronological Order with explanatory particulars is to be found in

[22]See *Abridged Catalogue of Publications of the International Labour Office* (*Twenty-sixth Edition*) (Geneva, 1940), p. 8.
[23]*Ibid.*, p. 9.
[24]*Ibid.*
[25]Art. 21(407) as amended in Montreal, October 9, 1946, reads: "1. If any Convention coming before the Conference for final consideration fails to secure the support of two thirds of the votes cast by the delegates present, it shall nevertheless be within the right of any of the Members of the Organisation to agree to such Convention among themselves. 2. Any Convention so agreed to shall be communicated by the Governments concerned to the *Director-General of the International Labour Office and to the Secretary-General of the United Nations for registration in accordance with the provisions of Article 102 of the Charter of the United Nations*." (Italics added.)

Official Journal, Special Supplement No. 195 [C.87.M.87.1946.V.] (1946.V.1.), p. 25–47.[26]

CERTIFIED COPIES

League of Nations. International Labour Conference. Draft Conventions and Recommendations Adopted by the Conference at Its First Annual Meeting, 29 October–29 November, 1919 (Authentic Texts). No date. 38 p., bilingual. [20/31/6]

League of Nations. International Labour Conference. Draft Conventions and Recommendations Adopted by the Conference during Its Second Meeting, 15 June–10 July, 1920 (Authentic Texts). No date. 19 p., bilingual. [20/31/51]

League of Nations. International Labour Conference. Draft Conventions and Recommendations Adopted by the Conference at Its Third Session, 25 October–19 November, 1921 (Authentic Texts). No date. 42 p., bilingual. No official number.

League of Nations. International Labour Conference. Recommendation Adopted by the Conference at Its Fourth Session, 18 October–3 November 1922 (Authentic Text). No date. 7 p., bilingual. No official number.

League of Nations. International Labour Conference. Amendment to Article 393 of the Treaty of Versailles and to the Corresponding Articles of the Other Treaties of Peace Adopted by the Conference at Its Fourth Session, 18 October–3 November, 1922 (Authentic Text). No date. 4 p., bilingual. No official number.

League of Nations. International Labour Conference. Recommendation Adopted by the Conference at Its Fifth Session, 22–29 October, 1923 (Authentic Text). No date. 14 p., bilingual. No official number.

League of Nations. International Labour Conference. Recommendation Adopted by the Conference at Its Sixth Session, 16 June–5 July, 1924 (Authentic Text). No date. 7 p., bilingual. No official number.

League of Nations. International Labour Conference. Draft Conventions and Recommendations Adopted by the Conference at Its Seventh Session, 19 May–10 June, 1925 (Authentic Texts). No date. 38 p., bilingual. No official number.

League of Nations. International Labour Conference. Draft Convention and Recommendation Adopted by the Conference at Its Eighth Session, 26 May–5 June, 1926 (Authentic Texts). No date. 13 p., bilingual. No official number.

[26]See also *ibid.*, p. 22–24, and Conley H. Dillon, *International Labor Conventions: Their Interpretation and Revision* (Chapel Hill, 1942), *passim.*

League of Nations. International Labour Conference. Draft Conventions and Recommendations Adopted by the Conference at Its Ninth Session, 7–24 June, 1926 (Authentic Texts). No date. 31 p., bilingual. No official number.

League of Nations. International Labour Conference. Draft Conventions and Recommendation Adopted by the Conference at Its Tenth Session, 25 May–16 June, 1927 (Authentic Texts). No date. 24 p., bilingual. No official number.

League of Nations. International Labour Conference. Draft Convention and Recommendation Adopted by the Conference at Its Eleventh Session, 30 May–16 June, 1928 (Authentic Texts). No date. 17 p., bilingual. No official number.

League of Nations. International Labour Conference. Draft Conventions and Recommendations Adopted by the Conference at Its Twelfth Session, 30 May–June 21, 1929 (Authentic Texts). No date. 41 p., bilingual. No official number.

League of Nations. International Labour Conference. Draft Conventions and Recommendations Adopted by the Conference at Its Fourteenth Session, 10–28 June, 1930 (Authentic Texts). No date. 45 p., bilingual. No official number.

League of Nations. International Labour Conference. Draft Convention Adopted by the Conference at Its Fifteenth Session, 28 May–18 June, 1931 (Authentic Texts) [sic.]. No date. 10 p., bilingual. No official number.

League of Nations. International Labour Conference. Draft Conventions and Recommendations Adopted by the Conference at Its Sixteenth Session, 12–30 April, 1932 (Authentic Texts). No date. 33 p., bilingual. No official number.

League of Nations. International Labour Conference. Draft Conventions and Recommendations Adopted by the Conference at Its Seventeenth Session, 8–30 June, 1933 (Authentic Texts). No date. 88 p., bilingual. No official number.

League of Nations. International Labour Conference. Draft Conventions and Recommendation Adopted by the Conference at Its Eighteenth Session, 4–23 June, 1934 (Authentic Texts). No date. 30 p., bilingual. No official number.

League of Nations. International Labour Conference. Draft Conventions and Recommendation Adopted by the Conference at Its Nineteenth Session, 4–25 June, 1935 (Authentic Texts). No date. 46 p., bilingual. No official number.

League of Nations. International Labour Conference. Draft Conventions and Recommendations Adopted by the Conference at Its Twentieth Session, 4–24 June, 1936 (Authentic Texts). No date. 33 p., bilingual. No official number.

League of Nations. International Labour Conference. Draft Conventions and Recommendations Adopted by the Conference at Its Twenty-first Session, 6–24 October, 1936. (Authentic Texts). No date. 52 p., bilingual. No official number.

League of Nations. International Labour Conference. Draft Convention Adopted by the Conference at Its Twenty-second Session, 22–24 October, 1936 (Authentic Text). No date. 8 p., bilingual. No official number.

League of Nations. International Labour Conference. Draft Conventions and Recommendations Adopted by the Conference at Its Twenty-third Session, 3–23 June, 1937 (Authentic Texts). No date. 84 p., bilingual. No official number.

League of Nations. International Labour Conference. Draft Convention Adopted by the Conference at Its Twenty-fourth Session. 2–22 June, 1938 (Authentic Text). No date. 15 p., bilingual. No official number.

League of Nations. International Labour Conference. Draft Conventions and Recommendations Adopted by the Conference at Its Twenty-fifth Session, 8–28 June, 1939 (Authentic Texts). No date. 74 p., bilingual. No official number.

This bibliographer has had no access to the certified copies of the International Labour Conventions and Recommendations adopted after June 1939. Itemized lists of all International Labour Conventions and Recommendations adopted from 1919 inclusive are given below.

LIST OF INTERNATIONAL LABOR CONVENTIONS AND RECOMMENDATIONS, 1919–1947

The International Labor Office has published the texts of International Labor Conventions and Recommendations in the Proceedings of the International Labor Conference, the *Official Bulletin*, and other of its publications. All Conventions and Recommendations which had been adopted in the course of the 23 sessions held from 1919–1937 were published by the Conference in 1937 in one volume: *Conventions and Recommendations, 1919–1937.*[27] Geneva, International Labour Office, 1937. 492 p.

Conventions and Recommendations are usually listed according to their numbers or short titles. The numbers and short titles have no official character, but both have been widely used within and without the International Labor Office. In the following list the short

[27]A footnote to each convention gives the date on which it came into force and the names of the states which had ratified the Convention by September 1, 1937. For later ratification of International Labor Conventions, see *Official Journal*, Special Supplement No. 195, p. 21–37, which contains the status of ratifications as of July 31, 1946. No convention came into force between July 10, 1944, and July 31, 1946.

title of each Convention and Recommendation is given in brackets after the official title. Conventions No. 1–62 are in *Conventions and Recommendations, 1919–1937,* and the page references are to that volume.

Conventions

Convention [No. 1] Limiting the Hours of Work in Industrial Undertakings to Eight in the Day and Forty-eight in the Week [Hours of Work (Industry)], p. 9–16.

Convention [No. 2] Concerning Unemployment [Unemployment], p. 16–19.

Convention No. 3 Concerning the Employment of Women before and after Childbirth [Childbirth (Employment before and after)], p. 21–24.

Convention No. 4 Concerning Employment of Women during the Night [Night Work (Women)], p. 24–47.

Convention No. 5 Fixing the Minimum Age for Admission of Children to Industrial Employment [Minimum Age (Industry)], p. 30–33.

Convention No. 6 Concerning the Night Work of Young Persons Employed in Industry [Night Work (Young Persons)], p. 33–37.

Convention No. 7 Fixing the Minimum Age for Admission of Children to Employment at Sea [Minimum Age (Sea)], p. 42–44.

Convention No. 8 Concerning Unemployment Indemnity in Case of Loss or Foundering of the Ship [Unemployment Indemnity (Shipwreck)], p. 45–47.

Convention No. 9 for Establishing Facilities for Finding Employment for Seamen [Placing of Seamen], p. 48–51.

Convention No. 10 Concerning the Age for Admission of Children to Employment in Agriculture [Minimum Age (Agriculture)], p. 54–56.

Convention No. 11 Concerning the Rights of Association and Combination of Agricultural Workers [Right of Association (Agriculture)], p. 59–61.

Convention No. 12 Concerning Workmen's Compensation in Agriculture [Workmen's Compensation (Agriculture)], p. 61–63.

Convention No. 13 Concerning the Use of White Lead in Painting [White Lead (Painting)], p. 64–67.

Convention No. 14 Concerning the Application of the Weekly Rest in Industrial Undertakings [Weekly Rest (Industry)], p. 67–71.

Convention No. 15 Fixing the Minimum Age for Admission of Young Persons to Employment as Trimmers or Stokers [Minimum Age (Trimmers and Stokers)], p. 72–75.

Convention No. 16 Concerning the Compulsory Medical Examina-

(21 August, 1939). The page references are to those respective volumes.

Draft Convention No. 63 Concerning Statistics of Wages and Hours of Work in the Principal Manufacturing Industries, Including Building and Construction, and in Agriculture [Convention Concerning Statistics of Wages and Hours of Work, 1938], p. 75–84.

Draft Convention [No. 64] Concerning the Regulation of Written Contracts of Employment of Indigenous Workers [Contracts of Employment (Indigenous Workers) Convention, 1939], p. 48–60.

Draft Convention [No. 65] Concerning Penal Sanctions for Breaches of Contracts of Employment by Indigenous Workers [Penal Sanctions (Indigenous Workers) Convention, 1939], p. 60–63.

Draft Convention [No. 66] Concerning the Recruitment, Placing and Conditions of Labour of Migrants for Employment [Migration for Employment Convention, 1939], p. 68–73.

Draft Convention [No. 67] Concerning the Regulation of Hours of Work and Rest Periods in Road Transport [Hours of Work and Rest Periods (Road Transport) Convention, 1939], p. 80–89.

The texts of Conventions No. 68–76 are in International Labor Conference, *Twenty-eighth Session. Seattle, 1946. Record of Proceedings*. Montreal, International Labour Office, 1946. 411 p. The page references are to that volume. See also *Official Bulletin*, Vol. XXIX, No. 3. (September 20, 1946), p. 115–194.

Convention [No. 68] Concerning Food and Catering for Crews on Board Ship [Food and Catering (Ships' Crews)], p. 333–338.

Convention No. 69 Concerning the Certification of Ships' Cooks [Certification of Ships' Cooks], p. 338–441.

Convention No. 70 Concerning Social Security for Seafarers [Social Security (Seafarers)], p. 341–347.

Convention No. 71 Concerning Seafarers' Pensions [Seafarers' Pensions], p. 349–353.

Convention No. 72 Concerning Vacation Holidays with Pay for Seafarers [Paid Vacations (Seafarers)], p. 353–358.

Convention No. 73 Concerning the Medical Examination of Seafarers [Medical Examination (Seafarers)], p. 358–362.

Convention No. 74 Concerning the Certification of Able Seamen [Certification of Able Seamen)], p. 362–365.

Convention No. 75 Concerning Crew Accommodation on Board Ship [Accommodation of Crews], p. 367–381.

Convention No. 76 Concerning Wages, Hours of Work on Board Ship and Manning [Wages, Hours of Work and Manning (Sea)], p. 382–394.

The texts of Conventions No. 77–80 are in International Labor Conference, *Conventions and Recommendations Adopted by the Conference at*

*Its Twenty-ninth Session, Montreal, 19 September–9 October, 1946.
Authentic Texts.* 35 p., bilingual. Page references are to that volume.
See also *Official Bulletin* Vol. XXIX No. 4 (November 15, 1946).
Convention No. 77 Concerning Medical Examination for Fitness for
  Employment in Industry for Children and Young Persons [Medical
  Examination of Young Persons (Industry)], p. 5–11.
Convention No. 78 Concerning Medical Examination of Children
  and Young Persons for Fitness for Employment in Non-industrial
  Occupations [Medical Examination of Young Persons (Non-indus-
  trial Occupations], p. 12–17.
Convention No. 79 Concerning the Restriction of Night Work of
  Children and Young Persons in Non-industrial Occupations
  [Night Work of Young Persons (Non-industrial Occupations)],
  p. 24–30.
Convention [No. 80] for the Partial Revision of the Conventions
  Adopted by the General Conference of the International Labour
  Organisation at Its First Twenty-eight Sessions for the Purpose of
  Making Provision for the Future Discharge of Certain Functions
  Entrusted by the Said Conventions to the Secretary-General of
  the League of Nations and Introducing Therein Certain Further
  Amendments Consequential upon the Dissolution of the League of
  Nations and the Amendment of the Constitution of the Interna-
  tional Labour Organisation (Final Articles Revision), p. 59–63.
The texts of Conventions No. 81 to 86 are in the *Official Bulletin*,
Vol. XXX, No. 1 (31 July 1947). Page references are to that volume.
Convention No. 81 Concerning Labour Inspection in Industry and
  Commerce, p. 1–12.
Convention No. 82 Concerning Social Policies in Non-metropolitan
  Territories, p. 17–28.
Convention No. 83 Concerning the Application of International
  Labour Standards to Non-metropolitan Territories, p. 28–47.
Convention No. 84 Concerning the Right of Association and the
  Settlement of Labour Disputes in Non-metropolitan Territories,
  p. 47–52.
Convention No. 85 Concerning Labour Inspection in Non-metropoli-
  tan Territories, p. 53–58.
Convention No. 86 Concerning the Maximum Length of Contracts
  of Employment of Indigenous Workers, p. 58–64.

Recommendations

  Recommendations No. 1–56 are in International Labor Conference, *Conventions and Recommendations, 1919–1937.* The page references are to that volume.
Recommendation No. 1 Concerning Unemployment [Unemploy-
  ment], p. 19–20.

Recommendation No. 2 Concerning Reciprocity of Treatment of Foreign Workers [Reciprocity of Treatment], p. 20.

Recommendation No. 3 Concerning the Prevention of Anthrax [Anthrax Prevention], p. 27–28.

Recommendation No. 4 Concerning the Protection of Women and Children against Lead Poisoning [Lead Poisoning (Women & Children)], p. 28–29.

Recommendation No. 5 Concerning the Establishment of Government Health Services [Labour Inspection (Health Services)], p. 29–30.

Recommendation No. 6 Concerning the Application of the Berne Convention of 1906, on the Prohibition of the Use of White Phosphorus in the Manufacture of Matches [White Phosphorus], p. 37–38.

Recommendation No. 7 Concerning the Limitation of Hours of Work in the Fishing Industry [Hours of Work (Fishing)], p. 39.

Recommendation No. 8 Concerning the Limitation of Hours of Work in Inland Navigation [Hours of Work (Inland Navigation)], p. 40–41.

Recommendation No. 9 Concerning the Establishment of National Seamen's Codes [National Seamen's Codes], p. 41–42.

Recommendation No. 10 Concerning Unemployment Insurance for Seamen [Unemployment Insurance (Seamen)], p. 44–45.

Recommendation No. 11 Concerning the Prevention of Unemployment in Agriculture [Unemployment (Agriculture)], p. 52–53.

Recommendation No. 12 Concerning the Protection, before and after Childbirth, of Women Wage-earners in Agriculture [Childbirth (Agriculture)], p. 53–54.

Recommendation No. 13 Concerning Night Work of Women in Agriculture [Night Work of Women (Agriculture)], p. 54.

Recommendation No. 14 Concerning Night Work of Children and Young Persons in Agriculture [Night Work of Children and Young Persons (Agriculture)], p. 57.

Recommendation No. 15 Concerning the Development of Technical Agricultural Education [Vocational Education (Agriculture)], p. 57–58.

Recommendation No. 16 Concerning Living-in Conditions of Agricultural Workers [Living-in Conditions (Agriculture)], p. 58–59.

Recommendation No. 17 Concerning Social Insurance in Agriculture [Social Insurance (Agriculture)], p. 63–64.

Recommendation No. 18 Concerning the Application of the Weekly Rest in Commercial Establishments [Weekly Rest (Commerce)], p. 71–72.

Recommendation No. 19 Concerning Communications to the International Labour Office of Statistical and Other Information Regarding Emigration, Immigration and the Repatriation and Transit of Emigrants [Migration Statistics], p. 78–79.

Recommendation No. 20 Concerning the General Principles for the Organisation of Systems of Inspection to Secure the Enforcement of the Laws and Regulations for the Protection of the Workers [Labour Inspection], p. 80–87.

Recommendation No. 21 Concerning the Development of Facilities for the Utilisation of Workers' Spare Time [Utilization of Spare Time], p. 88–92.

Recommendation No. 22 Concerning the Minimum Scale of Workmen's Compensation [Workmen's Compensation (Minimum Scale)], p. 97–98.

Recommendation No. 23 Concerning Jurisdiction in Disputes on Workmen's Compensation [Workmen's Compensation (Jurisdiction)], p. 98–100.

Recommendation No. 24 Concerning Workmen's Compensation for Occupational Diseases [Workmen's Compensation (Occupational Diseases)], p. 103–104.

Recommendation No. 25 Concerning Equality of Treatment for National and Foreign Workers as Regards Workmen's Compensation for Accidents [Equality of Treatment (Accident Compensation)], p. 107–108.

Recommendation No. 26 Concerning the Protection of Emigrant Women and Girls on Board Ship [Migration (Protection of Females at Sea)], p. 115–116.

Recommendation No. 27 Concerning the Repatriation of Masters and Apprentices [Repatriation (Ship Masters and Apprentices)], p. 127.

Recommendation No. 28 Concerning the General Principles for the Inspection of the Conditions of Work of Seamen [Labour Inspection (Seamen)], p. 127–133.

Recommendation No. 29 Concerning the General Principles of Sickness Insurance [Sickness Insurance], p. 144–148.

Recommendation No. 30 Concerning the Application of Minimum Wage-fixing Machinery [Minimum Wage-fixing Machinery], p. 152–155.

Recommendation No. 31 Concerning the Prevention of Industrial Accidents [Prevention of Industrial Accidents], p. 156–162.

Recommendation No. 32 Concerning Responsibility for the Protection of Power-driven Machinery [Power-driven Machinery], p. 165–166.

Recommendation No. 33 Concerning Reciprocity as Regards the Protection against Accidents of Workers Employed in Loading or Unloading Ships [Protection against Accidents (Dockers) Reciprocity], p. 177.

Recommendation No. 34 Concerning the Consultation of Workers' and Employers' Organisations in the Drawing up of Regulations Dealing with the Safety of Workers Employed in Loading or Unloading Ships [Protection against Accidents (Dockers) Consultation of Organisations], p. 178.

Recommendation No. 35 Concerning Indirect Compulsion to Labour [Forced Labour (Indirect Compulsion)], p. 190–191.

Recommendation No. 36 Concerning the Regulation of Forced or Compulsory Labour [Forced Labour (Regulation)], p. 191–193.

Recommendation No. 37 Concerning the Regulation of Hours of Work in Hotels, Restaurants and Similar Establishments [Hours of Work (Hotels, etc.)], p. 199–200.

Recommendation No. 38 Concerning the Regulation of Hours of Work in Theatres and Other Places of Public Amusement [Hours of Work (Theatres, etc.)], p. 200–201.

Recommendation No. 39 Concerning the Regulation of Hours of Work in Establishments for the Treatment or the Care of the Sick, Infirm, Destitute or Mentally Unfit [Hours of Work (Hospitals, etc.)], p. 201–202.

Recommendation No. 40 for Expediting Reciprocity as Provided for in the Convention Adopted in 1932, Concerning the Protection against Accidents of Workers Employed in Loading or Unloading Ships [Protection against Accidents (Dockers) Reciprocity], p. 222–223.

Recommendation No. 41 Concerning the Age for Admission of Children to Non-industrial Employment [Minimum Age (Non-industrial Employment)], p. 229–232.

Recommendation No. 42 Concerning Employment Agencies [Employment Agencies], p. 237–238.

Recommendation No. 43 Concerning the General Principles of Invalidity, Old-age and Widows' and Orphans' Insurance [Invalidity, Old-age and Survivors' Insurance], p. 295–302.

Recommendation No. 44 Concerning Unemployment Insurance and Various Forms of Relief for the Unemployed [Unemployment Provision], p. 320–323.

Recommendation No. 45 Concerning Unemployment among Young Persons [Unemployment (Young Persons)], p. 349–356.

Recommendation No. 46 Concerning the Progressive Elimination of Recruiting [Elimination of Recruiting], p. 367–368.

Recommendation No. 47 Concerning Annual Holidays with Pay [Holidays with Pay], p. 378–379.

Recommendation No. 48 Concerning the Promotion of Seamen's Welfare in Ports [Seamen's Welfare in Ports], p. 380–384.

Recommendation No. 49 Concerning Hours of Work on Board Ship and Manning [Hours of Work and Manning (Sea)], p. 417–418.

Recommendation No. 66 Concerning Rest Periods of Professional Drivers of Private Vehicles [Rest Periods (Private Chauffeurs) Recommendation, 1939], p. 92.

The texts of Recommendations No. 67–73 are in the *Official Bulletin*, Vol. XXVI No. 1 (June 1, 1944). The page references are to that volume.

Recommendation No. 67 Concerning Income Security [Income Security], p. 4–25.

Recommendation No. 68 Concerning Income Security and Medical Care for Persons Discharged from the Armed Forces and Assimilated Services and from War Employment [Social Security (Armed Forces)], p. 26–28.

Recommendation No. 69 Concerning Medical Care [Medical Care], p. 29–45.

Recommendation No. 70 Concerning Minimum Standards of Social Policy in Dependent Areas [Social Policy in Dependent Territories], p. 45–61.

Recommendation No. 71 Concerning Employment Organisation in the Transition from War to Peace [Employment (Transition from War to Peace)], p. 61–73.

Recommendation No. 72 Concerning the Employment Service [Employment Service], p. 74–75.

Recommendation No. 73 Concerning the National Planning of Public Works [Public Works (National Planning)], p. 75–77.

Recommendation No. 74 Concerning Minimum Standards of Social Policy in Dependent Territories (Supplementary Provisions) (Adopted on 5 November 1945). In *Official Bulletin*, Vol. XXVIII (December 15, 1945), p. 4–16.

The texts of Recommendations No. 75–78 are in International Labor Conference, *Twenty-eighth Session, Seattle, 1946, Record of Proceedings*. Montreal, International Labor Office, 1946. 411 p. The page references are to that volume. See also *Official Bulletin*, Vol. XXIX, No. 3 (September 20, 1946), p. 115–194.

Recommendation No. 75 Concerning Agreements Relating to the Social Security of Seafarers, p. 347–348.

Recommendation No. 76 Concerning Medical Care for Seafarers' Dependants, p. 348–349.

Recommendation No. 77 Concerning the Organisation of Training for Sea Service, p. 365–367.

Recommendation No. 78 Concerning the Provision to Crews by Shipowners of Bedding, Mess Utensils and Other Articles, p. 381–382.

Recommendations No. 79–80 are in International Labor Conference, *Conventions and Recommendations Adopted by the Conference at Its Twenty-ninth Session, Montreal, 19 September–9 October, 1946*. 35 p., bilingual.

Recommendation No. 79 Concerning the Medical Examination for Fitness for Employment of Children and Young Persons, p. 18–23.
Recommendation No. 80 Concerning the Restriction of Night Work of Children and Young Persons in Non-industrial Occupations, p. 24–30.
The texts of Recommendations No. 81–82 are in the *Official Bulletin*, Vol. XXX, No. 1 (31 July 1947). The page references are to that volume.
Recommendation No. 81 Concerning Labour Inspection in Industry and Commerce, p. 12–15.
Recommendation No. 82 Concerning Labour Inspection in Mining and Transport Undertakings, p. 16.

INTERNATIONAL LABOR CODE

International Labour Office. The International Labour Code, 1939.[28] A Systematic Arrangement of the Conventions and Recommendations Adopted by the International Labour Conference, 1919–1939, with Appendices Embodying Other Standards of Social Policy Framed by the International Labour Organisation, 1919–1939. Montreal, 1941. 920 p.

An attempt to codify in 924 articles the essential provisions of the International Labor Conventions and Recommendations adopted from 1919 through 1939. Contains extensive annotation and bibliographical references. The Code consists of 13 books dealing with Employment and Unemployment; General Conditions of Employment (wages, hours of work, weekly rest periods, holidays with pay); Employment of Children and Young Persons; Employment of Women; Industrial Health, Safety and Welfare; Social Insurance; Industrial Relations; Administration of Social Legislation; Conditions of Work of Seamen; Standards of Colonial Labour Policy; Migration; and Statistics. The Appendices include: Selected Resolutions Embodying Standards of Social and Economic Policy Adopted by the International Labour Conference; Selected Standards Approved by Technical Advisory Bodies; Reports of Special Conferences; Asiatic Regional Supplement; American Regional Supplement; Labour Clauses of League of Nations Instruments.

11. MINUTES OF THE SESSIONS OF THE GOVERNING BODY

From 1919 to 1946, 100 sessions of the Governing Body of the International Labor Organization were held. Its proceedings are recorded in the *Minutes of the Sessions of the Governing Body*.
First Volume: Minutes of the First Session of the Governing Body of the International Labour Office. Washington, November, 1919. International Labour Office, 1920. 11 p. (Confidential).

[28]A significant corollary to the Code is International Labor Office, *Constitutional Provisions Concerning Social and Economic Policy: An International Collection of Texts Covering 450 Countries and Other Governmental Units*. Montreal, 1944. 755 p.

12. MAJOR PUBLICATIONS ON OCCUPATION AND HEALTH

Major Publications

Occupation and Health. Encyclopedia of Hygiene, Pathology and Social Welfare. Volume I, A-H, Geneva, 1930. 999 p. Volume II, I-Z, Geneva, 1934. 1310 p.[29]
Industrial Environment and Health. Practical Methods of Investigation. Geneva, International Labour Office, 1936. 336 p.

Bibliography of Industrial Hygiene

First Issue: Bibliography of Industrial Hygiene. Volume I, Number 1, March, 1923. 47 p.
Latest Issue: Bibliography of Industrial Hygiene. Volume XV, 1945. Geneva, 1945. 147 p.

13. SERIAL PUBLICATIONS

International Labour Review

First Volume: International Labour Office. International Labour Review. Volume I, Number 1 (January, 1921). 149 p.

Fifty-six volumes to December 1947, inclusive. Published monthly. Includes articles, book reviews, statistical and other information related to the work of the Organization.[30]

International Labour Office. International Labour Review. Index, Volumes I–XX (1921–1929). Geneva, 1930. 64 p.
International Labour Office. International Labour Review. Index, Volumes XXI–XXX (1930–1934). Geneva, 1935. 34 p.
After 1934 no cumulative index was issued in pamphlet form. Indices appear twice a year in the June and December issue, covering the preceding six months period.

[29]The following Supplements were issued: No. 1–4, Geneva, 1938–1940; No. 5, Montreal, 1941; Special Supplement, *Industrial Health in Wartime*, Montreal, 1944, 39 p.
[30]The *International Labour Review* is issued in accordance with Art. 10(396), Par. 4 of the Constitution of the International Labor Organization, which reads: The International Labour Office "will edit and publish in French and English, and in such other languages as the Governing Body may think desirable, a periodical paper dealing with problems of industry and employment of international interest." Art. 10, Par. 4 as amended in 1946 reads: "edit and issue, in such languages as the Governing Body may think desirable, publications dealing with problems of industry and employment of international interest." (See Art. 10(2) (d) of the 1946 Constitution.)

Official Bulletin

First Volume: International Labour Office. Official Bulletin. Volume I[31] (April 1919–August 1920). Geneva, 1923, 587 p.

Particularly valuable as a source of documents relating to the work of the Organization. It appears at irregular intervals. Thirty volumes up to the end of 1947.

The I.L.O. Yearbook

First Volume: International Labour Office. Annual Review. 1930. Geneva, 1930. 505 p.

Last Volume: The I.L.O. Yearbook, 1939–1940. Tenth Year of Issue. Geneva, 1940. 345 p.

The title varies. Beginning with the second issue the title reads: "International Labour Office: The I.L.O. Yearbook, 1931. Second Year of Issue. Geneva, 1932." Ten volumes were issued up to 1940, when it was discontinued. The 1934–1935 volume is in two parts. All issues follow the same pattern. The first chapter summarizes the activities of the Organization during the period under review. Ten chapters survey developments of the year throughout the world under the following headings: Industrial Organisations and Social Movements; Economic Developments; Conditions of Work; Social Insurance; Remuneration of Labour; Employment and Unemployment; Migration; Labour Law; Living Conditions; Special Problems of Certain Categories of Workers.

Yearbook of Labour Statistics

First Volume: International Labour Office. Yearbook of Labour Statistics, 1935–36. First Year of Issue. Geneva, 1936. 227 p.

Latest Volume: International Labour Office. Yearbook of Labour Statistics, 1945/46. Ninth Issue. Montreal, 1947. 284 p., trilingual (English, French, and Spanish).

The *Yearbook* contains: I. Total and Gainfully Occupied Population; II. Employment and Unemployment; III. Hours of Work; IV. Wages; V. Cost of Living and Retail Prices; VI. Family Living Studies; VII. Migration; VIII. Industrial Accidents; IX. Industrial Disputes.[32] The statistical material together with explanatory notes is listed in 31 tables. The figures in the *Yearbook*, with a few exceptions, were taken from official publications or were communicated to

[31]For a deliberate irregularity in the numbering, see Vol. II, No. 1 (8 September 1920).
[32]Previous issues of the *Yearbook* contained information on additional subject matters. Appendices 1–4 of the *Yearbook, 1943–1944* were supplied by the Economic, Financial and Transit Department of the League of Nations: 1. Production; 2. Index Numbers of Wholesale Prices; 3. Values of Currencies as Percentages of Their Gold Parity in 1929; 4. Exchange Rates.

the Office by governments. In the majority of cases, the tables were submitted before publication to the statistical services of the different countries. Several of the tables given in the *Yearbook* are brought up to date from time to time in the *International Labour Review*, namely, those relating to the general level of employment, actual hours worked, wages, and the cost of living.

LEGISLATIVE SERIES

The *Legislative Series*, published in English and French, includes reprints and translations of the major legal provisions concerning labor adopted by various countries. The texts of the laws and regulations formerly appeared monthly in pamphlet form. The various pamphlets were subsequently reprinted in annual volumes. Altogether 17 volumes were published in this series, covering the years 1919–1936.[33] In December, 1936, the volume edition was discontinued. More recently the *Legislative Series* appeared as a quarterly; see, for instance, the July-September, 1946 issue which is devoted primarily to Belgian and French legislation concerning social security; it includes the French Native Labor Code. Since January, 1948, the *Legislative Series* has appeared every two weeks.

INDUSTRIAL AND LABOUR INFORMATION, 1922–1940

First Volume: Industrial and Labour Information. Vol. I, No. 1 (6 January–March 1922). 44 p.
Latest Volume: Industrial and Labour Information, Vol. LXXIV (April–June 1940), p. 236.
This publication contains information on industry and labor based on official and unofficial sources. Since 1940 *Industrial and Labour Information* has been incorporated in the *International Labour Review*.

INDUSTRIAL SAFETY SURVEY

First Volume: Industrial Safety Survey. Vol. I, 1925. Geneva, no date. 152 p.
Latest Volume: Industrial Safety Survey. Vol. XXII, 1946. Montreal, 160 p.
This quarterly publication is being continued.

[33]For a complete list of these annual volumes, see *Abridged Catalogue of Publications of the International Labour Office*, p. 7. The *Legislative Series* for the year 1919 was issued also in book form as the *Bulletin of the International Labour Office of Basle*, Vol. XIV.

INTERNATIONAL SURVEY OF LEGAL DECISIONS
ON LABOR LAW

First Volume: International Labour Office. International Survey of Legal Decisions on Labour Law, 1925. Geneva, 1926. 267 p.

Last Volume: International Labour Office. International Survey of Legal Decisions on Labour Law 1937–38. Thirteenth Year. Geneva, 1939. 297 p.

The *Survey* was designed to supplement the *Legislative Series* by surveying the application and interpretation of labor law in selected countries. The first two volumes cover Germany, England, France, and Italy; subsequently, United States practice was included. After the publication of the volume dated 1937–38, the *Survey* was discontinued.

14. STUDIES AND REPORTS

OLD SERIES

Under the heading "Studies and Reports," several serial publications of the International Labor Organization, covering a great variety of subjects, appeared since 1920. The individual publications in this category vary considerably in size. They range from 10-page pamphlets to 700-page monographs. A list of the series headings may serve to indicate the scope of these publications. For a complete list of "Studies and Reports" for the years 1920–1940, see *Abridged Catalogue of Publications of the International Labour Office* (*Twenty-sixth Edition*) (Geneva, 1940), p. 30–41.

Series A. Industrial Relations
Series B. Economic Conditions
Series C. Employment and Unemployment
Series D. Wages and Hours of Work
Series E. The Disabled
Series F. Industrial Hygiene
Series F (Second Series). Safety
Series G. Housing and Welfare
Series H. Co-operation
Series I. Employment of Women and Children
Series J. Education
Series K. Agriculture
Series L. Professional Workers
Series M. Social Insurance
Series N. Statistics
Series O. Migration
Series P. Seamen

NEW SERIES

The War and Women's Employment: The Experience of the United Kingdom and the United States. *Studies and Reports. New Series No. 1*. Montreal, International Labour Office, 1946. 287 p.

Wartime Labour Conditions and Reconstruction Planning in India. *Studies and Reports. New Series No. 2*. Montreal, International Labour Office, 1946. 113 p.

Public Investment and Full Employment. *Studies and Reports. New Series No. 3*. Montreal, International Labour Office, 1946. 348 p.

Nutrition in Industry. *Studies and Reports. New Series No. 4*. Montreal, International Labour Office, 1946. 177 p.

The Chilean Development Corporation, by Herman Finer. *Studies and Reports. New Series No. 5*. Montreal, International Labour Office, 1947. 83 p.

Labour-Management Co-operation in United States War Production. *Studies and Reports. New Series No. 6*. Geneva, International Labour Office, 1948. 405 p.

Employment, Unemployment and Labour Force Statistics: A Study of Methods. *Studies and Reports. New Series. No 7 (Part 1)*. Geneva, International Labour Office, 1948. 130 p.

Cost-of-Living Statistics. *Studies and Reports. New Series No. 7 (Part 2)*. Geneva, International Labour Office, 1948. 56 p.

Methods of Statistics of Industrial Injuries. *Studies and Reports. New Series No. 7 (Part 3)*. Geneva, International Labour Office, 1947. 32 p.

II. THE PERMANENT COURT OF INTERNATIONAL JUSTICE

1. INTRODUCTORY NOTE

THE COUNCIL of the League of Nations, in accordance with Article 14 of the Covenant, had the Draft Statute of the Permanent Court of International Justice prepared by an Advisory Committee of Jurists.[1] On December 23, 1920, the Assembly unanimously passed a resolution[2] approving the Draft Statute, which came into force on September 1, 1921, through ratification by the majority of the members of the League.

The seat of the Court was established at The Hague (Article 22 of the Statute). The judges of the Court were, in general, elected by the Assembly and by the Council from a list of persons nominated by the national groups in the Permanent Court of Arbitration (Article 4, Paragraph 1 of the Statute).[3]

The budget of the Court formed an integral part of the budget of the League.[4]

The cases taken up by the Court may be classified under two major headings: "Contentious Procedure" and "Advisory Opinions."

The Permanent Court of International Justice constituted a legal entity[5] composed of 15 independent judges, elected, regardless of their nationality from among persons of high moral character, who possessed the qualifications required in their respective countries for appointment to the highest judicial offices or were jurists of recognised competence in international law[6] (Article 2). The bench was to repre-

[1] See below, p. 388. On the genesis of the Court, see also Philip C. Jessup, *Elihu Root* (2 vols., New York, 1938), II, 418–444.
[2] For the text of this resolution, see *Official Journal*, Special Supplement, January, 1921, p. 23.
[3] For election procedure concerning "Members of the League of Nations not represented in the Permanent Court of Arbitration," see Art. 4, Par. 2 of the Statute.
[4] See below, p. 532.
[5] The English version of Art. 2 somewhat distorted the meaning of the original French version. The French of Art. 2 is: "La Cour Permanente de Justice Internationale est un corps de magistrats indépendants . . ."; the English version reads: "The Permanent Court of International Justice shall be composed of a body of independent judges . . ." The same discrepancy between the French and English texts is to be found in Art. 2 of the Statute of the International Court of Justice, which forms an integral part of the United Nations Charter.
[6] For a list of the judges, deputy-judges, and registrars of the Court, see Manley O.

sent the main forms of civilization and the principal legal systems of the world (Article 9). The members were elected for nine years.

The Court rendered altogether 32 judgments and 27 advisory opinions. Eleven of the contentious cases were submitted by virtue of special agreements (*compromis*). Twenty-six cases were submitted by virtue of the compulsory jurisdiction of the Court in accordance with Article 36, Paragraph 2 of the Statute or corresponding provisions in international treaties.

The Court based its findings and decisions on general or particular international conventions, on international customs, and on the general principles of law recognized by civilized nations (Article 38).

Many states accepted the compulsory jurisdiction of the Permanent Court of International Justice by adhering to the so-called optional clause in Article 36, Paragraph 2 recognizing as compulsory *ipso facto* and without special agreement, in relation to any other member or state accepting the same obligation, the jurisdiction of the Court in all or any of the classes of legal disputes concerning: (a) the interpretation of a treaty; (b) any question of international law; (c) the existence of any fact which, if established, would constitute a breach of an international obligation; (d) the nature or extent of the reparation to be made for the breach of an international obligation.

Article 59 of the Statute provided that the decision of the Court "has no binding force except between the parties and in respect of that particular case." Nevertheless, the Court in its rulings built up an impressive set of legal principles which, though not precedents in the technical sense, wielded enormous influence in international jural relations.[7]

The documentation of the Court appeared in the following series:
Series A. Judgments and Orders. Nos. 1–24, 1922–1930.
Series B. Advisory Opinions. Nos. 1–18, 1922–1930.
Series A/B. Judgments, Orders and Advisory Opinions. Nos. 40–80, 1931–1940.

This is a combined continuation of Series A and Series B.

Series C. Acts and Documents Relating to Judgments and Advisory Opinions. Nos. 1–19, 1922–1931; Nos. 52–88, 1931–1942.

Hudson, *The Permanent Court of International Justice, 1920–1942* (New York, 1943), p. 776–777. The regular nine-year term of the judges elected in the general election of September 25, 1930, was extended beyond 1939 due to the postponement of the third general election in 1939; see Hudson, *The Permanent Court,* p. 252, 258.

[7]See "Digest of the Decisions of the Permanent Court of International Justice, 1922–1930," *Fontes Iuris Gentium*, Series A, Section I, Tomus I (Berlin, 1930), and "Digest of the Decisions of the Permanent Court of International Justice, 1931–1934," *Fontes Iuris Gentium*, Series A, Section I, Tomus III (Berlin, 1935). See also Manley O. Hudson, *World Court Reports: A Collection of the Judgments, Orders and Opinions of the Permanent Court of International Justice* (4 vols., Washington, 1939–1943).

Series D. Acts and Documents Concerning the Organisation of the Court. Nos. 1–6 (1922–1940).

Series E. Annual Reports. Nos. 1–16, 1925–1945.

Contains valuable bibliographical information on publications relating to the Court.

Series F. General Index. Nos. 1–4, 1922–1936.

Note that in the foregoing listing of the Serial Publications of the Court, dates refer to the date of publication rather than to the periods covered in the publications.

2. THE DRAFTING OF THE STATUTE

Advisory Committee of Jurists.[8] Documents Presented to the Committee Relating to Existing Plans for the Establishment of a Permanent Court of International Justice. No date. 373 p., bilingual.

Advisory Committee of Jurists.[9] Procès-Verbaux of the Proceedings of the Committee, June 16th–July 24th, 1920, with Annexes. The Hague, 1920. 779 p. Bilingual.

An indispensable source for an understanding of the Court.

Documents Concerning the Action Taken by the Council of the League of Nations under Article 14 of the Covenant and the Adoption by the Assembly of the Statute of the Permanent Court. No date. 284 p.+284 p., bilingual.

Includes Resolution Concerning the Establishment of a Permanent Court of International Justice Passed by the Assembly of the League of Nations at Geneva on December 13th, 1920,[10] p. 257; Protocol of Signature[11] with Statute for Permanent Court of International Justice, p. 258–266.

3. CONFERENCE OF SIGNATORIES, GENEVA, 1926[12]

Minutes of the Conference of States Signatories of the Protocol of Signature of the Statute of the Permanent Court of International

[8]For the term "Advisory Committee of Jurists," see Hudson, The Permanent Court, p. 116, note 16.

[9]The so-called "1920 Committee of Jurists" or the "Committee of Ten" included: Adatci (Japan), Altamira (Spain), Fernandez (Brazil), Baron Descamps (Belgium), Hagerup (Sweden), Lapradelle (France), Loder (Netherlands), Lord Phillimore (England), Ricci-Busatti (Italy), Root (U.S.A.). It should be recalled, however, that in drafting the Statute of the Permanent Court these jurists acted as private individuals and not as representatives of their respective countries. For a useful synopsis of the various proposals submitted to these jurists, see ibid., p. 51–99.

[10]For the adoption of the Draft Statute by the Assembly, see Hudson, The Permanent Court, p. 120–124. "It may be said . . . that the Statute came into force by September 1, 1921." Ibid., p. 128.

[11]For the Protocol of Signature, see ibid., p. 124–126; for the optional clause, ibid., p. 126–127.

[12]For the Conference of Signatories of 1926, see ibid., p. 220–223.

Justice. Held at Geneva from September 1st to 23rd, 1926. No date. 88 p. (1926.V.26.)

Report by M. Pilotti, Rapporteur. Presented to the Conference on September 23rd, 1926. Geneva, 1926. 4 p.+4 p., bilingual (1926.V.25.)

Final Act of the Conference. No date. 13 p., in part bilingual (1926.V.24)

4. CONFERENCE OF SIGNATORIES, GENEVA, 1929[13]

Committee of Jurists on the Statute of the Permanent Court of International Justice. Minutes of the Session Held at Geneva, March 11th–19th, 1929. Geneva, 1929. 135 p. [C.166.M.66.1929.V.] (1929.V.5.)

Committee of Jurists on the Statute of the Permanent Court of International Justice. Reports Adopted by the Committee at Its Session Held at Geneva from March 11th to 19th, 1929. Geneva, 1929. 19 p. [C.142.M.52.1929.V.] (1929.V.4.)

Revision of the Statute of the Permanent Court of International Justice. Protocol.[14] Geneva, 1929, 18 p.+18 p., bilingual. [C.492.M.156.1929.V.]

Minutes of the Conference Regarding the Revision of the Statute of the Permanent Court of International Justice and the Accession of the United States of America to the Protocol of Signature of That Statute, Held at Geneva from September 4th to 12th, 1929. Geneva, 1929. 88 p. [C.514.M.173.1929.V.] (1929.V.18.)[15]

5. STATUTE AND RULES OF THE COURT

Permanent Court of International Justice. Resolution Concerning Its Establishment Passed by the Assembly on December 13th, 1920.

[13]For the "Question of the Revision of the Statute of the Permanent Court of International Justice," see Assembly Resolution of September 20, 1928, *Official Journal*, Special Supplement No. 63, p. 11. For the work of the 1929 Committee of Jurists, see Hudson, *The Permanent Court*, p. 133–134.

[14]Contains the Protocol of September 14, 1929, plus several annexes. For the "Failure of the Revision Protocol to Enter into Force," see Hudson, *The Permanent Court*, p. 137. "In a resolution of September 27, 1935, the Assembly observed that the entry into force of the Revision Protocol 'seems no longer to encounter any difficulty,' and it requested the Council to take the necessary measures to put the Protocol into force on February 1, 1936, on condition that the States which have not already ratified have not in the meanwhile made objection to the contemplated procedure." *Ibid.*, p. 140.

[15]For the Conference of 1929, see *ibid.*, p. 224 f. See especially Hudson's analysis of the Protocol for the Accession of the United States, p. 225–234. See also the erratum sheet issued in connection with Document [C.514.M.173.1929.V.], which bears the official number [No. Officiel. C.541.M.173.1929.V.Erratum], not [C. 514....Erratum].

Protocol of Signature of the Statute Provided for by Article 14 of the Covenant, with the Text of the Statute. Resolution Concerning the Salaries of the Members Passed by the Assembly on December 18th, 1920. No date. 13 p.+13 p., bilingual. [21/31/16][16]

Publications of the Permanent Court of International Justice. Series D. No. 1. Statute of the Court. Rules of Court (as Amended on July 31st, 1926). Leyden, 1926. 82 p.+82 p., bilingual.

Publications of the Permanent Court of International Justice. Series D. Acts and Documents Concerning the Organisation of the Court. No. 1. Statute and Rules of Court and Other Constitutional Documents, Rules or Regulations (with the Modifications Effected Therein up to February 21st, 1931). Second Edition. Leyden, no date. 58 p.+58 p., bilingual.

Permanent Court of International Justice. Series D. Acts and Documents Concerning the Organisation of the Court. No. 1. Statute and Rules of Court and Other Constitutional Documents, Rules or Regulations. Third Edition (March 1936).[17] Leyden, no date. 79 p.+79 p., bilingual.

Contains: 1. Article 14 of the Covenant of the League of Nations. 2. Resolution Passed by the Assembly of the League of Nations on December 13th, 1920. 3. Protocol of Signature of the Statute (December 16th, 1920). 4. The Optional Clause Attached, Relating to the Acceptance of the Jurisdiction of the Court as Compulsory. 5. Resolution Concerning the Revision of the Statute (Tenth Assembly, September 14th, 1929). 6. Protocol Concerning the Revision of the Statute (September 14th, 1929). 7. Letter from the Secretary-General of the League of Nations to the Registrar (February 1st, 1936). 8. Statute of the Court. 9. Rules of Court Adopted on March 11th, 1936. 10. A. Resolution Concerning the Salaries of Judges (Tenth Assembly, September 14th, 1929); B. Resolution Concerning the Regulations Governing the Grant of Pensions to Members and to the Registrar of the Court (Tenth Assembly, September 14th, 1929); C. Resolution Concerning the Regulations for the Repayment of Travelling Expenses of Judges (Tenth Assembly, September 14th, 1929). 11. Indemnities Payable to Certain Judges and Technical Assessors of the Court: A. Resolution Adopted by the Assembly of the League of Nations on September 23rd, 1922; B. Rules for the Payment of Allowances and Expenses to Technical Assessors, Adopted by the Court on January 20th, 1923. 12. Salary of the Registrar of the Court: A. Extract from the Minutes of the 21st Session of the Council, 1st meeting, August 31st, 1922; B. Resolution Adopted by the Council on May 21st, 1931. 13. Diplomatic Privileges and Immunities of Judges and Officials of the Registry: 1. Letter from the President of the Court to the Minister for Foreign

[16]Also in International Intermediary Institute, *The Permanent Court of International Justice*. Leyden, 1922. 126 p., bilingual.

[17]In force since February 1, 1936. For the Rules of Court, see also Permanent Court of International Justice, Series D: Acts and Documents Concerning the Organisation of the Court, *Third Addendum to No. 2. Elaboration of the Rules of Court of March 11th, 1936*. Leyden, 1936. 1092 p., bilingual; and Permanent Court of International Justice, Series D: Acts and Documents Concerning the Organisation of the Court, *Fourth Addendum to No. 2. Elaboration of the Rules of Court of March 11th, 1936* (*Extracts from the Minutes of 1934, 1935, 1936 Arranged According to the Articles of the Rules*). No date. 428 p.; see especially the Introduction, p. v–vi, dated March, 1943, on the history of the Rules of Court.

Affairs of the Netherlands (May 22nd, 1928); 2. Letter from the Minister for Foreign Affairs of the Netherlands to the President of the Court (May 22nd, 1928); 3. General Principles; 4. Regulations for the Application of the Foregoing Principles. 14. Staff Regulations for the Registry.

6. MISCELLANEOUS DOCUMENTS

Acts Relating to the Constitution of the Permanent Court of International Justice. No date. 42 p.+42 p., in part bilingual [C.80. M.28.1936.V.] (1936.V.1.)

Contains: Resolution Concerning the Establishment of a Permanent Court of International Justice Passed by the Assembly of the League of Nations, Geneva, December 13th, 1920. Protocol of Signature of the Statute of the Permanent Court of International Justice Provided for by Article 14 of the Covenant of the League of Nations, Geneva, December 16th, 1920. Resolution Concerning the Revision of the Statute of the Permanent Court of International Justice Adopted by the League of Nations, Geneva, September 14th, 1929. Protocol Concerning the Revision of the Statute of the Permanent Court of International Justice, September 14th, 1929. Statute for the Permanent Court by Article 14 of the Covenant of the League of Nations as Amended in Accordance with the Protocol of September 14th, 1929.

Conditions of Voting Requests for Advisory Opinions from the Permanent Court of International Justice. Observations Received from Governments and from the International Labour Office. Geneva, 1937. 17 p. [C.543.M.351.1936.V.] (1936.V.9.)

Collection of Texts Governing the Jurisdiction of the Court (Fourth Edition). Series D. No. 6. Leyden, 1932. 728 p.

See also "Table in Chronological Order of Instruments in Force, or Signed Only, Governing the Court's Jurisdiction," in *Permanent Court of International Justice*, Series E, No. 16, p. 414–454.

7. LIST OF JUDGMENTS, ORDERS, AND ADVISORY OPINIONS[18]

JUDGMENTS AND ORDERS

Series A, No. 1. [Judgment No. 1.] The S. S. "Wimbledon." Leyden, 1923. 47 p.+47 p., bilingual.

Series A, No. 2. [Judgment No. 2.] The Mavrommatis Palestine Concessions. Leyden, 1924. 93 p.+93 p., bilingual.

[18]See *Note by the Registrar*, Series A/B, Fasc. No. 40, May 15th, 1931. 5 p. + 5 p., bilingual. "On February 21st, 1931, the Permanent Court of International Justice adopted a new version of Article 65 of its Rules providing that its judgments, orders and advisory opinions, which had previously been embodied in two series of publications namely: Series A.—Judgments and Orders, Series B.—Advisory Opinions, should be combined in a *single* series" (*i.e.*, Series A/B). *Ibid.*, p. 1. This document contains a list of all decisions given by the Court from 1922 to 1930, including the new numbering (Series A/B), the old numbering (Series A and Series B), and short titles of the cases.

Series A, No. 3. [Judgment No. 3.] Treaty of Neuilly, Article 179, Annex, Paragraph 4 (Interpretation). Leyden, 1924. 10 p.+10 p., bilingual.

Series A, No. 4. [Judgment No. 4.] Interpretation of Judgment No. 3. Leyden, 1925. 8 p.+8 p., bilingual.

Series A, No. 5. [Judgment No. 5.] The Mavrommatis Jerusalem Concessions. Leyden, 1925. 51 p.+51 p., bilingual.

Series A, No. 6. [Judgment No. 6.] Case Concerning Certain German Interests in Polish Upper Silesia. Leyden, 1925. 41 p.+41 p., bilingual.

Series A, No. 7 [Judgment No. 7.] Case Concerning Certain German Interests in Polish Upper Silesia (the Merits). Leyden, 1926. 97 p.+97 p., bilingual; p. 98–107, French only.

Series A, No. 8. Denunciation of the Treaty of November 2nd, 1865 between China and Belgium. [Orders of January 8th, February 15th, and June 18th, 1927.] Leyden, 1927. 15 p.+15 p., bilingual.

Series A, No. 9. [Judgment No. 8.] Case Concerning the Factory at Chorzów (Claim for Indemnity) (Jurisdiction). Leyden, 1927. 44 p.+44 p., bilingual.

Series A, No. 10. [Judgment No. 9.] The Case of the S. S. "Lotus." Leyden, 1927. 108 p.+108 p., bilingual.

Series A, No. 11. [Judgment No. 10.] Case of the Readaptation of the Mavrommatis Jerusalem Concessions (Jurisdiction). Leyden, 1927. 64 p.+64 p., bilingual.

Series A, No. 12. Case Concerning the Factory at Chorzów (Indemnities). Order Made on November 21st, 1927. Leyden, 1927. 11 p.+11 p., bilingual.

Series A, No. 13. [Judgment] No. 11. Interpretation of Judgments Nos. 7 and 8 (the Chorzów Factory). Leyden, 1927. 27 p.+27 p., bilingual.

Series A, No. 14. Denunciation of the Treaty of November 2nd, 1865 between China and Belgium. Order of February 21st, 1928. Leyden, 1928. 7 p.+7 p., bilingual.

Series A, No. 15. [Judgment] No. 12. Rights of Minorities in Upper Silesia (Minority Schools). Leyden, 1928. 88 p.+88 p., bilingual.

Series A, No. 16. Denunciation of the Treaty of November 2nd, 1865 between China and Belgium. Order of August 13th, 1928. Leyden, 1928. 7 p.+7 p., bilingual.

Series A, No. 17. [Judgment] No. 13. Case Concerning the Factory at Chorzów (Claim for Indemnity) (Merits). Leyden, 1928. 105 p.+105 p., bilingual.

Series A, Nos. 18/19. Denunciation of the Treaty of November 2nd, 1865 between China and Belgium. Case Concerning the Factory at Chorzów (Indemnities). Orders of May 25th, 1929. Leyden, 1929. 15 p.+15 p., bilingual.

Series A, Nos. 20/21. [Judgments Nos. 14 and 15.] Case Concerning the Payment of Various Serbian Loans Issued in France. Case Concerning the Payment in Gold of the Brazilian Federal Loans Issued in France. Leyden, 1929. 155 p.+155 p., bilingual.

Series A, No. 22. Case of the Free Zones of Upper Savoy and the District of Gex. Order of August 19th, 1929. Leyden, 1929. 51 p. +51 p., bilingual.

Series A, No. 23. [Judgment] No. 16. Case Relating to the Territorial Jurisdiction of the International Commission of the River Oder. Leyden, 1929. 46 p.+46 p., bilingual.

Series A, No. 24. Case of the Free Zones of Upper Savoy and the District of Gex (Second Phase). Order of December 6th, 1930. Leyden, 1930. 43 p.+43 p., bilingual.

Series A/B, Fascicule No. 46. Case of the Free Zones of Upper Savoy and the District of Gex. Judgment of June 7th, 1932. Leyden, no date. p. 96–238, bilingual.

Series A/B, Fascicule No. 47. Interpretation of the Statute of the Memel Territory (Preliminary Objection). Judgment of June 24th, 1932. Leyden, no date. p. 243–263, bilingual.

Series A/B, Fascicule No. 48. Legal Status of the South-Eastern Territory of Greenland. Orders of August 2nd and 3rd, 1932. Leyden, no date. p. 268–289, bilingual.

Series A/B, Fascicule No. 49. Interpretation of the Statute of the Memel Territory. Judgment of August 11th, 1932. Leyden, no date. p. 294–360, bilingual.

Series A/B, Fascicule No. 51. Case Concerning the Delimitation of the Territorial Waters between the Island of Castellorizo and the Coasts of Anatolia. Order of January 26th, 1933. Leyden, no date. p. 4–6, bilingual.

Series A/B, Fascicule No. 52. Case Concerning the Administration of the Prince von Pless (Preliminary Objection). Order of February 4th, 1933. Leyden, no date. p. 11–17, bilingual.

Series A/B, Fascicule No. 53. Legal Status of Eastern Greenland. Judgment of April 5th, 1933. Leyden, no date. p. 22–147, bilingual.

Series A/B, Fascicule No. 54. Case Concerning the Administration of the Prince von Pless (Interim Measures of Protection). Order of May 11th, 1933. Leyden, no date. p. 150–154, bilingual.

Series A/B, Fascicule No. 55. Legal Status of the South-Eastern Territory of Greenland. Order of May 11th, 1933. Leyden, no date. p. 157–164, bilingual.

Series A/B, Fascicule No. 56. Appeals from Certain Judgments of the Hungaro-Czechoslovak Mixed Arbitral Tribunal. Order of May 12th, 1933. Leyden, no date. p. 162–164, bilingual.

Series A/B, Fascicule No. 57. Case Concerning the Administration of the Prince von Pless (Prorogation). Order of July 4th, 1933. Leyden, no date. p. 167–170, bilingual.

Series A/B, Fascicule No. 58. Case Concerning the Polish Agrarian Reform and the German Minority (Interim Measures of Protection). Order of July 29th, 1933. Leyden, no date. p. 175–189, bilingual.

Series A/B, Fascicule No. 59. Case Concerning the Administration of the Prince of Pless. Order of December 2nd, 1933. Leyden, no date. p. 194–196, bilingual.

Series A/B, Fascicule No. 60. Case Concerning the Polish Agrarian Reform and the German Minority. Order of December 2nd, 1933. Leyden, no date. p. 201–203, bilingual.

Series A/B, Fascicule No. 61. Appeal from a Judgment of the Hungaro-Czechoslovak Mixed Arbitral Tribunal (the Peter Pázmány University v. the State of Czechoslovakia). Judgment of December 15th, 1933. Leyden, no date. p. 208–270, bilingual.

Series A/B, Fascicule No. 62. Lighthouses Case between France and Greece. Judgment of March 17th, 1934. Leyden, no date. p. 4–60, bilingual.

Series A/B, Fascicule No. 63. The Oscar Chinn Case. Judgment of December 12th, 1934. Leyden, no date. p. 65–152, bilingual.

Series A/B, Fascicule No. 66. The Pajzs, Csáky, Esterházy Case (Preliminary Objection). Order of May 23rd, 1936. Leyden, no date. p. 4–10, bilingual.

Series A/B, Fascicule No. 67. The Losinger & Co. Case (Preliminary Objection). Order of June 27th, 1936. Leyden, no date. p. 15–25, bilingual.

Series A/B, Fascicule No. 68. The Pajzs, Csáky, Esterházy Case. Judgment of December 16th, 1936. Leyden, no date. p. 30–94, bilingual.

Series A/B, Fascicule No. 69. The Losinger & Co. Case (Discontinuance). Order of December 14th, 1936. Leyden, no date. p. 99–102, bilingual.

Series A/B, Fascicule No. 70. The Diversion of Water from the Meuse. Judgment of June 28th, 1937. Leyden, no date. p. 4–89, bilingual.

Series A/B, Fascicule No. 71. Lighthouses in Crete and Samos. Judgment of October 8th, 1937. Leyden, no date. p. 94–153, bilingual.

Series A/B, Fascicule No. 72. The Borchgrave Case (Preliminary Objections). Judgment of November 6th, 1937. Leyden, no date. p. 158–175, bilingual.

Series A/B, Fascicule No. 73. The Borchgrave Case (Discontinuance). Order of April 30th, 1938. Leyden, no date. p. 4–5, bilingual.

Series A/B, Fascicule No. 74. Phosphates in Morocco (Preliminary

Objections). Judgment of June 14th, 1938. Leyden, no date. p. 10–48, bilingual.

Series A/B, Fascicule No. 75. The Panevezys-Saldutiskis Railway Case (Preliminary Objections). Order of June 30th, 1938. Leyden, no date. p. 53–57, bilingual.

Series A/B, Fascicule No. 76. The Panevezys-Saldutiskis Railway Case. Judgment of February 28th, 1939. Leyden, no date. p. 4–59, bilingual.

Series A/B, Fascicule No. 77. The Electricity Company of Sofia and Bulgaria (Preliminary Objection). Judgment of April 4th, 1939. Leyden, no date. p. 64–155, bilingual.

Series A/B, Fascicule No. 78. The "Société Commerciale de Belgique." Judgment of June 15th, 1939. Leyden, no date. p. 160–190, bilingual.

Series A/B, Fascicule No. 79. The Electricity Company of Sofia and Bulgaria (Interim Measures of Protection). Order of December 5th, 1939. Leyden, no date. p. 194–200, bilingual.

Series A/B, Fascicule No. 80. The Electricity Company of Sofia and Bulgaria. Order of February 26th, 1940. Leyden, no date. p. 4–10, bilingual.

ADVISORY OPINIONS

Series B, No. 1. Advisory Opinion Given by the Court on July 31st, 1922, upon the Following Question: "Was the Workers' Delegate for the Netherlands at the Third Session of the International Labour Conference Nominated in Accordance with the Provisions of Paragraph 3 of Article 389 of the Treaty of Versailles?" Leyden, 1922. 27 p.+27 p., bilingual.

Series B, Nos. 2 and 3. Advisory Opinion Given by the Court on August 12th, 1922, upon the Following Question: "Has the International Labour Organisation the Competence in Regard to International Regulation of the Conditions of Labour of Persons Employed in Agriculture and to Examine Proposals for the Organisation and Development of the Methods [sic] of Agricultural Production as Well as Other Questions of a Like Character[?]" Leyden, 1922. 61 p.+61 p., bilingual.

Series B, No. 4. Advisory Opinion Given by the Court on February 7th, 1923, upon the Following Question: "Is the Dispute between France and Great Britain as to the Nationality Decrees Issued in Tunis and Morocco (French Zone) on November 8th, 1921, and Their Application to British Subjects by International Law Solely a Matter of Domestic Jurisdiction or Not?" Leyden, 1923. 32 p. +32 p., bilingual.

Series B, No. 5. Advisory Opinion Given by the Court on July 23rd,

1923, upon the Following Question: "Do Articles 10 and 11 of the Treaty of Peace between Finland and Russia, Signed at Dorpat on October 14th, 1920, and the Annexed Declaration of the Russian Delegation Regarding the Autonomy of Eastern Carelia, Constitute Engagements of an International Character Which Place Russia under an Obligation to Finland as to the Carrying Out of the Provisions Contained Therein?" Leyden, 1923. 29 p. +29 p., bilingual.

Series B, No. 6. Advisory Opinion Given by the Court on September 10th, 1923, on Certain Questions Relating to Settlers of German Origin in the Territory Ceded by Germany to Poland. Leyden, 1923. 43 p.+43 p., bilingual.

Series B, No. 7. Advisory Opinion Given by the Court on September 15th, 1923, on the Question Concerning the Acquisition of Polish Nationality. Leyden, 1923. 26 p.+26 p., bilingual.

Series B, No. 8. Advisory Opinion Regarding the Delimitation of the Polish-Czechoslovakian Frontier (Question of Jaworzina), Delivered by the Court on December 6th, 1923. Leyden, 1923. 57 p.+57 p., bilingual.

Series B, No. 9. September 4th, 1924. Question of the Monastery of Saint-Naoum (Albanian Frontier). Leyden, no date. 27 p.+27 p., bilingual.

Series B, No. 10. February 21st, 1925. Exchange of Greek and Turkish Populations. Leyden, no date. 28 p.+28 p., bilingual.

Series B, No. 11. May 10th, 1925. Polish Postal Service in Danzig. Leyden, no date. 45 p.+45 p., bilingual.

Series B, No. 12. November 21st, 1925. Article 3, Paragraph 2, of the Treaty of Lausanne (Frontier between Turkey and Iraq). Leyden, no date. 35 p.+35 p., bilingual.

Series B, No. 13. July 23rd, 1926. Competence of the International Labour Organization to Regulate, Incidentally, the Personal Work of the Employer. Leyden, no date. 26 p.+26 p., bilingual.

Series B, No. 14. December 8th, 1927. Jurisdiction of the European Commission of the Danube between Galatz and Braila. Leyden, 1927. 146 p.+146 p., bilingual.

Series B, No. 15. March 3rd, 1928. Jurisdiction of the Courts of Danzig (Pecuniary Claims of Danzig Railway Officials Who Have Passed into the Polish Service, against the Polish Railways Administration). Leyden, 1928. 47 p.+47 p., bilingual.

Series B, No. 16. August 28th, 1928. Interpretation of the Greco-Turkish Agreement of December 1st, 1926 (Final Protocol, Article IV). Leyden, 1928. 29 p.+29 p., bilingual.

Series B, No. 17. July 31st, 1930. The Greco-Bulgarian "Communities." Leyden, 1930. 46 p.+46 p., bilingual.

Series B, No. 18. August 26th, 1930. Free City of Danzig and International Labour Organization. Leyden, 1930. 36 p.+36 p., bilingual.

Series A/B, Fascicule No. 40. Access to German Minority Schools in Upper Silesia. Advisory Opinion of May 15th, 1931. Leyden, no date. 32 p.+32 p., bilingual.

Series A/B, Fascicule No. 41. Customs Régime between Germany and Austria (Protocol of March 19th, 1931). Advisory Opinion of September 5th, 1931. Leyden, no date. p. 37–103, bilingual.

Series A/B, Fascicule No. 42. Railway Traffic between Lithuania and Poland (Railway Sector Landwarów-Kaisiadorys). Advisory Opinion of October 15th, 1931. Leyden, no date. p. 108–123, bilingual.

Series A/B, Fascicule No. 43. Access to, or Anchorage in, the Port of Danzig, of Polish War Vessels. Advisory Opinion of December 11th, 1931. Leyden, no date. p. 128–164, bilingual.

Series A/B, Fascicule No. 44. Treatment of Polish Nationals and Other Persons of Polish Origin or Speech in the Danzig Territory. Advisory Opinion of February 4th, 1932. Leyden, no date. p. 4–63, bilingual.

Series A/B, Fascicule No. 45. Interpretation of the Greco-Bulgarian Agreement of December 9th, 1927 (Caphandaris-Molloff Agreement). Advisory Opinion of March 8th, 1932. Leyden, no date. p. 66–91, bilingual.

Series A/B, Fascicule No. 50. Interpretation of the Convention of 1919 Concerning Employment of Women during the Night. Advisory Opinion of November 15th, 1932. Leyden, no date. p. 363–390, bilingual.

Series A/B, Fascicule No. 64. Minority Schools in Albania. Advisory Opinion of April 6th, 1935. Leyden, no date. p. 4–36, bilingual.

Series A/B, Fascicule No. 65. Consistency of Certain Danzig Legislative Decrees with the Constitution of the Free City. Advisory Opinion of December 4th, 1935. Leyden, no date. p. 41–106, bilingual.

UNOFFICIAL COLLECTIONS, GUIDES, AND MAJOR PUBLICATIONS RELATING TO LEAGUE ACTIVITIES

IN VIEW OF THE magnitude of the League's documentation and the virtually innumerable books, pamphlets, and articles on the League of Nations, the following bibliographical hints may be helpful.

. There are very few libraries in the world which have a complete collection of League documents, and there are even fewer that have League documents adequately housed, bound, and catalogued. A considerable number of libraries have, however, a complete set of the *Official Journal* and of the *Treaty Series* of the League. The reader who looks for individual League documents other than treaties, monographs, or periodicals is advised to consult first of all the *Official Journal* with the aid of the Numerical Index which covers the years 1925 to 1939. Moreover, there is a subject and author index to the *Official Journal* which covers the years 1920 to 1946. For treaties and other international engagements concluded under the auspices of the League or registered with the League, the *Treaty Series* of the League of Nations and the indices to the *Treaty Series* are the most convenient sources.

Two unofficial collections of documents contain a considerable number of League documents of major importance. The Royal Institute of International Affairs (London) published annually from 1929 to 1939: *Documents on International Affairs*, covering the years 1928 to 1938, a series which includes many League documents relating to political questions. This series, taken together with the descriptive companion volumes *Survey of International Affairs* (London, 1920–1938), constitutes an extremely valuable source for an understanding of the League's political activities. Manley O. Hudson's collection of multilateral treaties, entitled *International Legislation* (9 volumes, covering the years 1919 to 1945), published by the Carnegie Endowment for International Peace, contains *inter alia* the texts of all multilateral conventions concluded under the auspices of the League. Bibliographical and other annotations enhance the usefulness of this collection.

The League of Nations built up a body of rules of international law, partly by interpreting the rules which are germane to League law proper, partly by interpreting general rules of international law

Walter Schiffer's systematic digest of these rules in his *Repertoire of Questions of General International Law Before the League of Nations* (Geneva, 1942) is an indispensable guide to the study of these questions.

Among the non-League publications the commentaries on the League of Nations should be considered as a group in itself. There are extant only two comprehensive commentaries, covering all articles of the Covenant: the standard French work by Jean Ray, and the comparatively unknown book by Otto Göppert, *Der Völkerbund* (Stuttgart, 1938). Schücking and Wehberg, *Die Satzung des Völkerbundes* (3d, ed., Berlin, 1931) covers only the first seven articles of the Covenant. Concise but valuable annotations to the League Covenant are contained in *The Treaty of Versailles and After* (U.S. Department of State Publication 2724, Conference Series 92, Washington, 1947).

Although there is no League commentary of the type prepared by Ray, Göppert, or Schücking-Wehberg available in English, there are numerous monographs covering the League in action, for instance, Viscount Cecil, *A Great Experiment* (New York, 1941), Charles Howard-Ellis, *The Origin, Structure and Working of the League of Nations* (Boston, 1928), Felix Morley, *The Society of Nations* (Washington, 1932), Denys P. Myers, *Handbook of the League of Nations* (Boston, 1935), Herbert and Webster, *The League of Nations in Theory and Practice* (Boston, 1933), and Georg Schwarzenberger, *The League of Nations and World Order* (London, 1936). The symposia *World Organization* (Washington, 1942) and *Pioneers in World Order* (New York, 1944) include informative contributions by many former League officials. Moreover, many textbooks published in English deal extensively with the League, for instance, Clyde Eagleton, *International Government* (New York, 1948) p. 247–295; Pitman B. Potter, *An Introduction to the Study of International Organization* (5th ed., New York, 1948) p. 240–257; Oppenheim-Lauterpacht, *International Law*, Vol. I (London, 1945), p. 341–372, Georg Schwarzenberger, *International Law*, Vol. I (2d. ed., London, 1949), p. 520–544. Most textbooks on international law published since 1919 in languages other than English contain references to the League. Hans Kelsen, *Legal Technique in International Law* (Geneva, 1939) contains a critical analysis of the text of the Covenant. David Hunter Miller, *The Drafting of the Covenant* (New York, 1928) is the standard work on the genesis of the Covenant. A comprehensive history of the League of Nations by Dr. Frank Walters is being prepared under the auspices of the Royal Institute of International Affairs.

Several monographs deal with the principal organs of the League, for instance, Margaret E. Burton, *The Assembly of the League of Nations* (Chicago, 1941), Thomas P. Conwell-Evans, *The League Coun-*

cil in Action (London, 1929), and Egon F. Ranshofen-Wertheimer, *The International Secretariat* (Washington, 1945).

Numerous monographs published by the Geneva Research Centre deal with various aspects of the League's work; several of them have been cited in this *Guide*. The collection of lectures held in French at the Hague Academy of International Law from 1923 to 1939 (*Recueil des Cours*, 69 vols.) contains valuable analyses of many legal questions relating to the League.

The series "Studies in the Administration of International Law and Organization," published by the Carnegie Endowment for International Peace, includes the following studies: No. 2, *International Tribunals: Past and Future*, by Manley O. Hudson (Washington, 1944); No. 3, *The International Secretariat: A Great Experiment in International Administration*, by Egon F. Ranshofen-Wertheimer (Washington, 1945); No. 4, *A Guide to the Practice of International Conferences*, by Vladimir D. Pastuhov (Washington, 1944); No. 5, *League of Nations and National Minorities*, by P. de Azcárate (Washington, 1945); No. 6, *The Economic and Financial Organization of the League of Nations: A Survey of Twenty-five Years' Experience*, by Martin Hill (Washington, 1946); No. 7, *International Drug Control: A Study of International Administration by and through the League of Nations*, by Bertyl A. Renborg (Washington, 1947); No. 8, *Immunities and Privileges of International Officials: The Experience of the League of Nations*, by Martin Hill (Washington, 1947); No. 9, *Mandates, Dependencies and Trusteeship*, by Duncan Hall (Washington, 1948).

Many publications on the League are listed in the *Catalogue of the Palace of the Peace Library* at the Hague (Vol. I, 1916, and three supplements, 1922, 1929, 1937). In 1928 the League published a 274-page catalogue of *Books on the Work of the League of Nations Catalogued in the Library of the Secretariat*, and in 1931, a 156-page supplement to this catalogue. From 1929 to 1946 the League of Nations Library published a *Monthly List of Books Catalogued in the Library of the League of Nations*, and from 1930 to 1946, a *Monthly List of Selected Articles*. Both publications contain valuable references to the League of Nations.

The following reference tools are extremely useful, especially to librarians:

Annuaire de la Société des nations. Préparé sous la direction de Georges Ottlik. Génève.

This *Annuaire* did not appear at yearly intervals; in all, eight volumes were published, covering the years: 1920–1927, 1928, 1929, 1930, 1931, 1932–1936, 1937, 1938

Breycha-Vauthier, A. C. de. Sources of Information: A Handbook of the Publications of the League of Nations. New York, 1939.

Carroll, Marie J. Key to League of Nations Documents Placed on Public Sale. Boston and New York, 1930–1938.

Five volumes, covering the years 1920–1929, 1930, 1931, 1932–1933, 1934–1936.

League of Nations. Catalogue of Publications 1920–1935. Geneva, 1935.

Also, four supplements covering the years 1936, 1937, 1938, and 1939, respectively, and one supplement covering the years 1940–1945.

A complete listing in card form of all League documents, including documents on public sale and others, is being prepared in connection with the cataloguing project undertaken by the Woodrow Wilson Foundation in co-operation with the Library of Congress and the Rockefeller Foundation. Individual cards and sets of cards can currently be obtained from the Library of Congress, Washington, D. C.

No attempt has been made here to furnish an all-inclusive bibliography on the League. However, the bibliographies contained in the books, pamphlets, and articles cited in this *Guide* are for the most part mutually complementary, and are apt to render useful bibliographical information on all major and many special aspects of the League. The Index to this *Guide* contains references to all authors whose books, pamphlets, or articles on the League, the International Labour Organisation, or the Permanent Court of International Justice have been cited in this *Guide*.

Valuable source material relating to the League of Nations and to the transfer of its assets and functions to the United Nations is to be found in *Yearbook of the United Nations, 1946–47* (Lake Success, 1947) and *Yearbook of the United Nations, 1947–48* (Lake Success, 1949). On the specialized agencies, see *Selected Bibliography of the Specialized Agencies Related to the United Nations* (United Nations Document; Sales Number 1949.I.16., 28 p.).

Appendix One

DOCUMENTS RELATING TO
THE LEAGUE OF NATIONS

I. THE COVENANT[1] OF THE LEAGUE OF NATIONS[2]

PREAMBLE[3]

The High Contracting Parties,

In order to promote international co-operation and to achieve international peace and security
> by the acceptance of obligations not to resort to war,
> by the prescription of open, just and honourable relations between nations,
> by the firm establishment of the understandings of international law as the actual rule of conduct among Governments,
> and by the maintenance of justice and a scrupulous respect for all treaty obligations in the dealings of organised peoples with one another,

Agree to this Convenant of the League of Nations.

ARTICLE I[4]

1. The original Members of the League of Nations shall be those of the Signatories which are named in the Annex to this Convenant

[1] Text and amendments, including amendments not in force, as contained in *Essential Facts about the League of Nations* (10th ed., revised, Geneva, 1939), p. 11–31. The footnotes, with the exception of the present one, are those of *Essential Facts.*

[2] Text numbered in conformity with the resolution adopted by the seventh ordinary session of the Assembly on September 16th, 1926, and containing Article 6 as amended, in force since August 13th, 1924, Articles 12, 13, and 15 as amended, in force since September 26th, 1924, and Article 4 as amended, in force since July 29th, 1926. The texts printed in italics indicate the amendments.

[3] On September 30th, 1938, the Assembly voted the following amendment (not in force) to the Preamble:

The Preamble shall read as follows:

"In order to promote international co-operation and to achieve international peace and security
"by the acceptance of obligations not to resort to war,
"by the prescription of open, just and honourable relations between nations,
"by the firm establishment of the understandings of international law as the actual rule of conduct among Governments, and
"by the maintenance of justice and a scrupulous respect for all treaty obligations in the dealings of organised peoples with one another,
"This Covenant has been adopted for the establishment of the League of Nations."

[4] On September 30th, 1938, the Assembly voted the following amendment (not in

and also such of those other States named in the Annex as shall accede without reservation to this Convenant. Such accession shall be effected by a Declaration deposited with the Secretariat within two months of the coming into force of the Covenant. Notice thereof shall be sent to all Members of the League.

2. Any fully self-governing State, Dominion or Colony not named in the Annex may become a Member of the League if its admission is agreed to by two-thirds of the Assembly, provided that it shall give effective guarantees of its sincere intention to observe its international obligations, and shall accept such regulations as may be prescribed by the League in regard to its military, naval and air forces and armaments.

3. Any Member of the League may, after two years' notice of its intention so to do, withdraw from the League, provided that all its international obligations and all its obligations under this Covenant shall have been fulfilled at the time of its withdrawal.

ARTICLE 2

The action of the League under this Convenant shall be effected through the instrumentality of an Assembly and of a Council, with a permanent Secretariat.

ARTICLE 3

1. The Assembly shall consist of Representatives of the Members of the League.

2. The Assembly shall meet at stated intervals and from time to time as occasion may require at the Seat of the League or at such other place as may be decided upon.

3. The Assembly may deal at its meetings with any matter within the sphere of action of the League or affecting the peace of the world.

4. At meetings of the Assembly, each Member of the League shall have one vote, and may have not more than three Representatives.

---

force) to Article I:

Paragraph 1 shall be struck out.

Paragraph 2 shall become paragraph 1 and shall read as follows:

"1. Any fully self-governing State, Dominion or Colony *not being a Member of the League of Nations* may become a Member *thereof* if its admission is agreed to by two-thirds of the Assembly, provided that it shall give effective guarantees of its sincere intention to observe its international obligations, and shall accept such regulations as may be prescribed by the League in regard to its military, naval and air forces and armaments."

Paragraph 3 shall become paragraph 2.

ARTICLE 4[5]

1. The Council shall consist of Representatives of the Principal Allied and Associated Powers, together with Representatives of four other Members of the League. These four Members of the League shall be selected by the Assembly from time to time in its discretion. Until the appointment of the Representatives of the four Members of the League first selected by the Assembly, Representatives of Belgium, Brazil, Spain and Greece shall be members of the Council.

2. With the approval of the majority of the Assembly, the Council may name additional Members of the League whose Representatives shall always be Members of the Council; the Council with like approval may increase the number of Members of the League to be selected by the Assembly for representation on the Council.

2 bis. The Assembly shall fix by a two-thirds majority the rules dealing with the election of the non-permanent Members of the Council, and particularly such regulations as relate to their term of office and the conditions of re-eligibility.

3. The Council shall meet from time to time as occasion may require, and at least once a year, at the Seat of the League, or at such other place as may be decided upon.

4. The Council may deal at its meetings with any matter within the sphere of action of the League or affecting the peace of the world.

5. Any Member of the League not represented on the Council shall be invited to send a Representative to sit as a member at any meeting of the Council during the consideration of matters specially affecting the interests of that Member of the League.

6. At meetings of the Council, each Member of the League represented on the Council shall have one vote, and may have not more than one Representative.

ARTICLE 5[6]

1. Except where otherwise expressly provided in this Convenant or by the terms of the present Treaty, decisions at any meeting of the

[5]On September 30, 1938, the Assembly voted the following amendment (not in force) to Article 4:

Paragraph 1 shall read as follows:

"The Council shall consist of *Members of the League of Nations entitled to a permanent seat on the Council, and of other Members entitled to a temporary seat thereon. The latter* shall be selected by the Assembly from time to time in its discretion."

Paragraph 2 shall read as follows:

"*2. In addition to the Members of the League that have a permanent seat*, the Council may, with the approval of the majority of the Assembly, name additional Members of the League whose Representatives shall always be members of the Council; the Council with like approval may increase the number of Members of the League to be selected by the Assembly for representation on the Council."

[6]On September 30th, 1938, the Assembly voted the following amendment (not in

Assembly or of the Council, shall require the agreement of all the Members of the League represented at the meeting.

2. All matters of procedure at meetings of the Assembly or of the Council, including the appointment of Committees to investigate particular matters, shall be regulated by the Assembly or by the Council and may be decided by a majority of the Members of the League represented at the meeting.

3. The first meeting of the Assembly and the first meeting of the Council shall be summoned by the President of the United States of America.

ARTICLE 6

1. The permanent Secretariat shall be established at the Seat of the League. The Secretariat shall comprise a Secretary-General and such secretaries and staff as may be required.

2. The first Secretary-General shall be the person named in the Annex; thereafter the Secretary-General shall be appointed by the Council with the approval of the majority of the Assembly.

3. The secretaries and staff of the Secretariat shall be appointed by the Secretary-General with the approval of the Council.

4. The Secretary-General shall act in that capacity at all meetings of the Assembly and of the Council.

5. *The expenses of the League shall be borne by the Members of the League in the proportion decided by the Assembly.*

ARTICLE 7

1. The Seat of the League is established at Geneva.

2. The Council may at any time decide that the Seat of the League shall be established elsewhere.

3. All positions under or in connection with the League, including the Secretariat, shall be open equally to men and women.

4. Representatives of the Members of the League and officials of the League when engaged on the business of the League shall enjoy diplomatic privileges and immunities.

5. The buildings and other property occupied by the League or its officials or by Representatives attending its meetings shall be inviolable.

---

force) to Article 5:

Paragraph 1 shall read as follows:

"1. Except where otherwise expressly provided in this Covenant or by *agreements conferring certain powers on the League of Nations,* decisions at any meeting of the Assembly or of the Council shall require the agreement of all the Members of the League represented at the meeting."

ARTICLE 8

1. The Members of the League recognise that the maintenance of peace requires the reduction of national armaments to the lowest point consistent with national safety and the enforcement by common action of international obligations.

2. The Council, taking account of the geographical situation and circumstances of each State, shall formulate plans for such reduction for the consideration and action of the several Governments.

3. Such plans shall be subject to reconsideration and revision at least every ten years.

4. After these plans have been adopted by the several Governments, the limits of armaments therein fixed shall not be exceeded without the concurrence of the Council.

5. The Members of the League agree that the manufacture by private enterprise of munitions and implements of war is open to grave objections. The Council shall advise how the evil effects attendant upon such manufacture can be prevented, due regard being had to the necessities of those Members of the League which are not able to manufacture the munitions and implements of war necessary for their safety.

6. The Members of the League undertake to interchange full and frank information as to the scale of their armaments, their military, naval and air programmes and the condition of such of their industries as are adaptable to warlike purposes.

ARTICLE 9

A permanent Commission shall be constituted to advise the Council on the execution of the provisions of Articles 1 and 8 and on military, naval and air questions generally.

ARTICLE 10

The Members of the League undertake to respect and preserve as against external aggression the territorial integrity and existing political independence of all Members of the League. In case of any such aggression or in case of any threat or danger of such aggression, the Council shall advise upon the means by which this obligation shall be fulfilled.

ARTICLE 11

1. Any war or threat of war, whether immediately affecting any of the Members of the League or not, is hereby declared a matter of con-

cern to the whole League, and the League shall take any action that may be deemed wise and effectual to safeguard the peace of nations. In case any such emergency should arise, the Secretary-General shall, on the request of any Member of the League, forthwith summon a meeting of the Council.

2. It is also declared to be the friendly right of each Member of the League to bring to the attention of the Assembly or of the Council any circumstance whatever affecting international relations which threatens to disturb international peace or the good understanding between nations upon which peace depends.

ARTICLE 12

1. The Members of the League agree that if there should arise between them any dispute likely to lead to a rupture they will submit the matter either to arbitration *or judicial settlement* or to enquiry by the Council, and they agree in no case to resort to war until three months after the award by the arbitrators *or the judicial decision* or the report by the Council.

2. In any case under this Article the award of the arbitrators *or the judicial decision* shall be made within a reasonable time, and the report of the Council shall be made within six months after the submission of the dispute.

ARTICLE 13

1. The Members of the League agree that whenever any dispute shall arise between them which they recognise to be suitable for submission to arbitration *or judicial settlement*, and which cannot be satisfactorily settled by diplomacy, they will submit the whole subject-matter to arbitration *or judicial settlement*.

2. Disputes as to the interpretation of a treaty, as to any question of international law, as to the existence of any fact which, if established, would constitute a breach of any international obligation, or as to the extent and nature of the reparation to be made for any such breach, are declared to be among those which are generally suitable for submission to arbitration *or judicial settlement*.

3. *For the consideration of any such dispute, the court to which the case is referred shall be the Permanent Court of International Justice, established in accordance with Article 14, or any tribunal agreed on by the parties to the dispute or stipulated in any convention existing between them.*

4. The Members of the League agree that they will carry out in full good faith any award *or decision* that may be rendered, and that they will not resort to war against a Member of the League which complies therewith. In the event of any failure to carry out such an award *or*

decision, the Council shall propose what steps should be taken to give effect thereto.

ARTICLE 14

The Council shall formulate and submit to the Members of the League for adoption plans for the establishment of a Permanent Court of International Justice. The Court shall be competent to hear and determine any dispute of an international character which the parties thereto submit to it. The Court may also give an advisory opinion upon any dispute or question referred to it by the Council or by the Assembly.

ARTICLE 15

1. If there should arise between Members of the League any dispute likely to lead to a rupture, which is not submitted to arbitration *or judicial settlement* in accordance with Article 13, the Members of the League agree that they will submit the matter to the Council. Any party to the dispute may effect such submission by giving notice of the existence of the dispute to the Secretary-General, who will make all necessary arrangements for a full investigation and consideration thereof.

2. For this purpose, the parties to the dispute will communicate to the Secretary-General, as promptly as possible, statements of their case with all the relevant facts and papers, and the Council may forthwith direct the publication thereof.

3. The Council shall endeavour to effect a settlement of the dispute, and if such efforts are successful, a statement shall be made public giving such facts and explanations regarding the dispute and the terms of settlement thereof as the Council may deem appropriate.

4. If the dispute is not thus settled, the Council either unanimously or by a majority vote shall make and publish a report containing a statement of the facts of the dispute and the recommendations which are deemed just and proper in regard thereto.

5. Any Member of the League represented on the Council may make public a statement of the facts of the dispute and of its conclusion regarding the same.

6. If a report by the Council is unanimously agreed to by the members thereof other than the Representatives of one or more of the parties to the dispute, the Members of the League agree that they will not go to war with any party to the dispute which complies with the recommendations of the report.

7. If the Council fails to reach a report which is unanimously agreed to by the members thereof, other than the Representatives of one or

more of the parties to the dispute, the Members of the League reserve to themselves the right to take such action as they shall consider necessary for the maintenance of right and justice.

8. If the dispute between the parties is claimed by one of them, and is found by the Council, to arise out of a matter which by international law is solely within the domestic jurisdiction of that party, the Council shall so report, and shall make no recommendation as to its settlement.

9. The Council may in any case under this Article refer this dispute to the Assembly. The dispute shall be so referred at the request of either party to the dispute provided that such request be made within fourteen days after the submission of the dispute to the Council.

10. In any case referred to the Assembly, all the provisions of this Article and of Article 12 relating to the action and powers of the Council shall apply to the action and powers of the Assembly, provided that a report made by the Assembly, if concurred in by the Representatives of those Members of the League represented on the Council and of a majority of the other Members of the League, exclusive in each case of the Representatives of the parties to the dispute, shall have the same force as a report by the Council concurred in by all the members thereof other than the Representatives of one or more of the parties to the dispute.

ARTICLE 16

1. Should any Member of the League resort to war in disregard of its covenants under Articles 12, 13 or 15, it shall *ipso facto* be deemed to have committed an act of war against all other Members of the League, which hereby undertake immediately to subject it to the severance of all trade or financial relations, the prohibition of all intercourse between their nationals and the nationals of the covenant-breaking State, and the prevention of all financial, commercial or personal intercourse between the nationals of the covenant-breaking State and the nationals of any other State, whether a Member of the League or not.[7]

[7]*Amendments not in force.*

(a) On September 27th, 1924, the Assembly voted the following amendment, not in force, regarding the first paragraph of Article 16:

"The latter part of the first paragraph of Article 16 of the Covenant shall read as follows:

" '. . . which hereby undertake immediately to subject it to the severance of all trade or financial relations and to prohibit all intercourse at least between persons resident within their territories and persons resident within the territory of the covenant-breaking State, and, if they deem it expedient, also between their nationals and the nationals of the covenant-breaking State, and to prevent all financial, commercial or personal intercourse at least between persons resident within the territory of that State and persons resident within the territory of any other State, whether a Member of the

2. It shall be the duty of the Council in such case to recommend to the several Governments concerned what effective military, naval or air force the Members of the League shall severally contribute to the armed forces to be used to protect the covenants of the League.[8]

3. The Members of the League agree, further, that they will mutually support one another in the financial and ecomonic measures which are taken under this Article, in order to minimise the loss and inconvenience resulting from the above measures, and that they will mutually support one another in resisting any special measures aimed at one of their number by the covenant-breaking State, and that they will take the necessary steps to afford passage through their territory to the forces of any of the Members of the League which are co-operating to protect the covenants of the League.

4. Any Member of the League which has violated any covenant of the League may be declared to be no longer a Member of the League by a vote of the Council concurred in by the Representatives of all the other Members of the League represented thereon.

ARTICLE 17

1. In the event of a dispute between a Member of the League and a State which is not a member of the League, or between States not mem-

---

League or not, and, if they deem it expedient, also between the nationals of that State and the nationals of any other State whether a Member of the League or not.'"

(This amendment has obtained five ratifications and thirteen signatures.)

(*b*) On October 4th, 1921, the Assembly voted the following three amendments, not in force, to be inserted after the first paragraph of Article 16:

"1. The second paragraph of Article 16 shall read as follows:

"'It is for the Council to give an opinion whether or not a breach of the Covenant has taken place. In deliberations on this question in the Council, the votes of Members of the League alleged to have resorted to war and of Members against whom such action was directed shall not be counted.'"

(This amendment has obtained thirty-one ratifications and nine signatures.)

"2. The third paragraph of Article 16 shall read as follows:

"'The Council will notify to all Members of the League the date which it recommends for the application of the economic pressure under this article.'"

(This amendment has obtained thirty-one ratifications and nine signatures.)

"3. The fourth paragraph of Article 16 shall read as follows:

"'Nevertheless, the Council may, in the case of particular Members, postpone the coming into force of any of these measures for a specified period where it is satisfied that such a postponement will facilitate the attainment of the object of the measures referred to in the preceding paragraph, or that it is necessary in order to minimise the loss and inconvenience which will be caused to such Members.'"

(This amendment has obtained thirty ratifications and eleven signatures.)

[8]On September 21st, 1925, the Assembly voted an amendment, not in force, regarding the second paragraph of Article 16:

"The Assembly adopts the following resolution, being an amendment to Article 16

bers of the League, the State or States not members of the League shall be invited to accept the obligations of membership in the League for the purposes of such dispute, upon such conditions as the Council may deem just. If such invitation is accepted, the provisions of Articles 12 to 16 inclusive shall be applied with such modifications as may be deemed necessary by the Council.

2. Upon such invitation being given, the Council shall immediately institute an enquiry into the circumstances of the dispute and recommend such action as may seem best and most effectual in the circumstances.

3. If a State so invited shall refuse to accept the obligations of membership in the League for the purposes of such dispute, and shall resort to war against a Member of the League, the provisions of Article 16 shall be applicable as against the State taking such action.

4. If both parties to the dispute when so invited refuse to accept the obligations of membership in the League for the purposes of such dispute, the Council may take such measures and make such recommendations as will prevent hostilities and will result in the settlement of the dispute.

ARTICLE 18

Every treaty or international engagement entered into hereafter by any Member of the League shall be forthwith registered with the Secretariat and shall as soon as possible be published by it. No such treaty or international engagement shall be binding until so registered.

ARTICLE 19

The Assembly may from time to time advise the reconsideration by Members of the League of treaties which have become inapplicable and the consideration of international conditions whose continuance might endanger the peace of the world.

ARTICLE 20

1. The Members of the League severally agree that this Covenant is accepted as abrogating all obligations or understandings *inter se* which are inconsistent with the terms thereof, and solemnly undertake that they will not hereafter enter into any engagements inconsistent with the terms thereof.

2. In case any Member of the League shall, before becoming a Member of the League, have undertaken any obligations inconsistent with the terms of the Covenant, it shall be the duty of such Member to take immediate steps to procure its release from such obligations.

of the Covenant: "The words 'in such case' in the second paragraph of the original text of Article 16 of the Covenent shall be deleted."

(This amendment has obtained four ratifications and fifteen signatures.)

Article 21

Nothing in this Covenant shall be deemed to affect the validity of international engagements, such as treaties of arbitration or regional understandings like the Monroe doctrine, for securing the maintenance of peace.

Article 22

1. To those colonies and territories which as a consequence of the late war have ceased to be under the sovereignty of the States which formerly governed them and which are inhabited by peoples not yet able to stand by themselves under the strenuous conditions of the modern world, there should be applied the principle that the well-being and development of such peoples form a sacred trust of civilisation and that securities for the performance of this trust should be embodied in this Covenant.

2. The best method of giving practical effect to this principle is that the tutelage of such peoples should be entrusted to advanced nations who, by reason of their resources, their experience or their geographical position, can best undertake this responsibility, and who are willing to accept it, and that this tutelage should be exercised by them as Mandatories on behalf of the League.

3. The character of the mandate must differ according to the stage of the development of the people, the geographical situation of the territory, its economic conditions and other similar circumstances.

4. Certain communities formerly belonging to the Turkish Empire have reached a stage of development where their existence as independent nations can be provisionally recognised subject to the rendering of administrative advice and assistance by a Mandatory until such time as they are able to stand alone. The wishes of these communities must be a principal consideration in the selection of the Mandatory.

5. Other peoples, especially those of Central Africa, are at such a stage that the Mandatory must be responsible for the administration of the territory under conditions which will guarantee freedom of conscience and religion, subject only to the maintenance of public order and morals, the prohibition of abuses such as the slave trade, the arms traffic and the liquor traffic, and the prevention of the establishment of fortifications or military and naval bases and of military training of the natives for other than police purposes and the defence of territory, and will also secure equal opportunities for the trade and commerce of other Members of the League.

6. There are territories, such as South West Africa and certain of the South Pacific Islands, which, owing to the sparseness of their population, or their small size, or their remoteness from the centres of

civilisation, or their geographical contiguity to the territory of the Mandatory, and other circumstances, can be best administered under the laws of the Mandatory as integral portions of its territory, subject to the safeguards above mentioned in the interests of the indigenous populations.

7. In every case of mandate, the Mandatory shall render to the Council an annual report in reference to the territory committed to its charge.

8. The degree of authority, control or administration to be exercised by the Mandatory shall, if not previously agreed upon by the Members of the League, be explicitly defined in each case by the Council.

9. A permanent Commission shall be constituted to receive and examine the annual reports of the Mandatories and to advise the Council on all matters relating to the observance of the mandates.

ARTICLE 23

Subject to and in accordance with the provisions of international conventions existing or hereafter to be agreed upon, the Members of the League:

(a) will endeavour to secure and maintain fair and humane conditions of labour for men, women and children, both in their own countries and in all countries to which their commercial and industrial relations extend, and for that purpose will establish and maintain the necessary international organisations;

(b) undertake to secure just treatment of the native inhabitants of territories under their control;

(c) will entrust the League with the general supervision over the execution of agreements with regard to the traffic in women and children, and the traffic in opium and other dangerous drugs;

(d) will entrust the League with the general supervision of the trade in arms and ammunition with the countries in which the control of this traffic is necessary in the common interest;

(e) will make provision to secure and maintain freedom of communications and of transit and equitable treatment for the commerce of all Members of the League. In this connection, the special necessities of the regions devastated during the war of 1914–1918 shall be borne in mind;

(f) will endeavour to take steps in matters of international concern for the prevention and control of disease.

ARTICLE 24

1. There shall be placed under the direction of the League the international bureaux already established by general treaties if the parties

to such treaties consent. All such international bureaux and all commissions for the regulation of matters of international interest hereafter constituted shall be placed under the direction of the League.

2. In all matters of international interest which are regulated by general conventions but which are not placed under the control of international bureaux or commissions, the Secretariat of the League shall, subject to the consent of the Council and if desired by the parties, collect and distribute all relevant information and shall render any other assistance which may be necessary or desirable.

3. The Council may include as part of the expenses of the Secretariat the expenses of any bureau or commission which is placed under the direction of the League.

ARTICLE 25

The Members of the League agree to encourage and promote the establishment and co-operation of duly authorised voluntary national Red Cross organisations having as purposes the improvement of health, the prevention of disease and the mitigation of suffering throughout the world.

ARTICLE 26

1. Amendments to this Covenant will take effect when ratified by the Members of the League whose Representatives compose the Council and by a majority of the Members of the League whose Representatives compose the Assembly.[9]

2. No such amendments shall bind any Member of the League which signifies its dissent therefrom but in that case it shall cease to be a Member of the League.[10]

[9]*Amendments not in force.*

(*a*) On October 3rd, 1921, the Assembly voted the following amendment, not in force, to the first paragraph of Article 26:

"The first paragraph of Article 26 of the Covenant shall be replaced by the following text:

" 'Amendments to the present Covenant the text of which shall have been voted by the Assembly on a three-fourths majority, in which there shall be included the votes of all the Members of the Council represented at the meeting, will take effect when ratified by the Members of the League whose representatives composed the Council when the vote was taken and by the majority of those whose representatives form the Assembly.' "

(This amendment has obtained thirty-seven ratifications and eight signatures.)

(*b*) On October 3rd, 1921, the Assembly voted a resolution to insert the following new paragraph after paragraph 1:

"If the required number of ratifications shall not have been obtained within twenty-two months after the vote of the Assembly, the proposed amendment shall remain without effect."

(This amendment has obtained thirty-seven ratifications and seven signatures.)

[10]*Amendment not in force.*

On October 3rd, 1921, the Assembly voted the following amendment, not in force,

ANNEX TO THE COVENANT[11]

I. ORIGINAL MEMBERS OF THE LEAGUE OF NATIONS, SIGNATORIES OF THE TREATY OF PEACE

United States of America	Haiti
Belgium	Hejaz
Bolivia	Honduras
Brazil	Italy
British Empire	Japan
Canada	Liberia
Australia	Nicaragua
South Africa	Panama
New Zealand	Peru
India	Poland
China	Portugal
Cuba	Roumania
Ecuador	Serb-Croat-Slovene State
France	Siam
Greece	Czechoslovakia
Guatemala	Uruguay

States Invited to Accede to the Covenant

Argentine Republic	Persia
Chile	Salvador
Colombia	Spain
Denmark	Sweden
Netherlands	Switzerland
Norway	Venezuela
Paraguay	

II. FIRST SECRETARY-GENERAL OF THE LEAGUE OF NATIONS

The Hon. Sir James Eric Drummond, K.C.M.G., C.B.

---

regarding the second paragraph of Article 26:

"The second paragraph of the present Article 26 shall be replaced by the two following paragraphs:

" 'The Secretary-General shall inform the Members of the taking effect of an amendment.

" 'Any Member of the League which has not at that time ratified the amendment is free to notify the Secretary-General within a year of its refusal to accept it, but in that case it shall cease to be a Member of the League.' "

(This amendment has obtained thirty-seven ratifications and seven signatures.)

[11]On September 30th, 1938, the Assembly voted the following amendment (not in force) regarding the Annex:

The first part of the Annex shall be omitted.

II. RULES OF PROCEDURE OF THE ASSEMBLY. REVISED EDITION, NOVEMBER 1, 1938[1]

RULE 1.

RULE 1. SESSIONS

Ordinary

1. The Assembly shall meet in general session every year at the seat of the League of Nations, commencing on the Monday which falls in the period September 10th to September 16th inclusive.

Extraordinary

2. Sessions may also be held at such times as the Assembly at a previous meeting decides, and at such times as the Council, by a majority vote, decides.

3. If a Member of the League considers a session to be desirable, it may request the Secretary-General to summon a special session of the Assembly. The Secretary-General shall thereupon inform the other Members of the League of the request, and enquire whether they concur in it. If within a period of one month from the date of the communication of the Secretary-General, a majority of the Members concur in the request, a special session of the Assembly shall be summoned.

RULE 2. PLACE OF MEETING

The sessions of the Assembly shall be held at the seat of the League, or, in exceptional circumstances, at such other place as is designated by the Assembly or by a majority of the Council, or approved by a majority of the Members of the League.

RULE 3. SUMMONS

1. The sessions of the Assembly shall be summoned by the President of the Council, acting through the Secretary-General.

2. The summons shall be addressed to the Members of the League not less than four months before the date fixed for the opening of the session. In exceptional circumstances, however, the Council, by a majority vote, may sanction a shorter period.

[1]Document [C.144.M.92.1937.] (1937.I.). Annexes I to VI are not reprinted here. The footnotes, with the exception of the present one, are those in Document [C.144.M.92. 1937.].

3. Nothing contained in paragraph 2 of this Rule shall affect the provisions, concerning special cases, contained in the Covenant.

Rule 4. Agenda

1. The agenda shall be drawn up by the Secretary-General with the approval of the President of the Council. The complete agenda shall be circulated as nearly as possible four months before the date fixed for the opening of the session.

2. The agenda of a general session shall include:

(*a*) A report on the work of the Council since the last session of the Assembly, on the work of the Secretariat, and on the measures taken to execute the decision of the Assembly;

(*b*) All items whose inclusion has been ordered by the Assembly at a previous session;

(*c*) All items proposed by the Council;

(*d*) All items proposed by a Member of the League; and

(*e*) The Budget for the next fiscal period, and the report on the accounts of the last fiscal period.

Inclusion of Additional Items

3. Any Member of the League may, at least one month before the date fixed for the opening of the session, request the inclusion of additional items in the agenda. Such items shall be placed on a supplementary list, which shall be circulated to the Members of the League at least three weeks before the date fixed for the opening of the session. The Assembly shall decide whether items on the supplementary list shall be included in the agenda of the session.

4. The Assembly may in exceptional circumstances place additional items on the agenda; but all consideration of such items shall, unless otherwise ordered by a two-thirds majority of the Assembly, be postponed until four days after they have been placed on the agenda, and until a committee has reported upon them.

4 *a*. No proposal for the placing of a new question on the agenda of the Assembly may be signed by more than fifteen Members of the League.

5. No proposal for a modification of the allocation of expenses for the time being in force shall be inserted in the agenda, unless it has been communicated to the Members of the League at least four months before the date fixed for the opening of the session.

Rule 5. Communication of Names of Representatives. Full Powers

1. Each Member shall communicate to the Secretary-General, if possible one week before the date fixed for the opening of the session, the names of its representatives, of whom there shall be not more than three. The names of substitute-representatives may be added.

2. The full powers of the representatives shall be delivered to the Secretary-General, if possible, one week before the date fixed for the opening of the session. They shall be issued either by the Head of the State or by the Minister for Foreign Affairs.[2]

3. A Committee of nine members for the examination of the full powers shall be elected by the Assembly on the proposal of the President. The Committee shall appoint its own Chairman and Vice-Chairman. It shall report without delay.

4. Any representative to whose admission objection has been made shall sit provisionally with the same rights as other representatives, unless the Assembly decides otherwise.

RULE 6.   SUBSTITUTE REPRESENTATIVES AND SUBSTITUTES

1. In addition to the substitute-representatives mentioned in paragraph 1 of Rule 5, the representatives of a Member of the League attending the Assembly, acting together as a delegation, may appoint substitutes. Any such appointment shall be communicated in writing to the President.

2. A substitute-representative appointed by a Member of the League may take the place of a representative without nomination by the representatives.

3. A substitute-representative or substitute may take the place of a representative who is absent from a meeting of the Assembly, or is temporarily prevented from taking part in its deliberations, but, if the representative is present at the meeting, the substitute representative or substitute is only entitled to assist him.

Deputies and Technical Advisers.

4. A delegation may appoint for service on a committee a deputy or technical adviser other than those referred to in the above paragraphs of this Rule; but a deputy or adviser so appointed shall not be eligible for appointment as Chairman or Rapporteur, or for a seat in the Assembly.

RULE 7.   PRESIDENT, VICE-PRESIDENTS AND GENERAL COMMITTEE[3]

1. The General Committee of the Assembly shall consist of the President of the Assembly, eight Vice-Presidents and the Chairmen

[2] It is obvious that, in the case of countries which do not possess a Minister for Foreign Affairs, the full powers may be issued by an authority possessing similar or equivalent powers.

[3] On September 30th, 1933, the Assembly approved the following recommendation, which was made to it by the General Committee:

"When proceeding to the election of the Vice-Presidents of the Assembly, in application of Rule 7, paragraphs 1 and 4, of the Rules of Procedure, the voting-papers should not bear the names of individuals, but should be marked 'The First Delegate' of such and such a country."

of the main Committees of the Assembly, the Agenda Committee and the Committee for the examination of the full powers.

The Assembly may decide to add to the General Committee the Chairmen of other Assembly Committees and, in exceptional cases, other members.

2. The President shall be elected at the beginning of each session.

3. Until the election of the President, the President of the Council shall act as President of the Assembly.

4. The election of the Vice-Presidents shall take place at one of the early meetings of the session.

RULE 7(a).   AGENDA COMMITTEE

1. An Agenda Committee shall be set up at the beginning of each session. It shall consist of seven members, who shall be appointed by the Assembly on the nomination of the President.

2. The Committee shall elect its own Chairman and Vice-Chairman.

3. The Committee shall consider applications for the inclusion of new questions in the agenda of the Assembly, and shall report to the Assembly thereon.

4. Proposals for the mere reference to one of the main Committees of portions of the Report on the Work of the League shall be decided upon by the Assembly without previous reference to the Agenda Committee.

RULE 7(b).   NOMINATION COMMITTEE[4]

1. *At the commencement of each session, the Assembly shall appoint a committee of eleven members whose duty shall be to nominate candidates for functions which carry with them a seat on the General Committee.*

2. *The provisional President of the Assembly shall submit proposals to it regarding the composition of this Committee.*

3. *The Members of the Assembly and the Committees shall retain the right to vote for persons other than those proposed by the above-mentioned Committee.*

RULE 8.   FUNCTIONS OF PRESIDENT AND GENERAL COMMITTEE

1. The President shall announce the opening, suspension and adjournment of the meetings of the Assembly, direct the work of the Assembly, ensure the observance of the Rules of Procedure, accord the right to address the Assembly, declare the debates to be closed, put questions to the vote, and announce the result of the voting.

[4]On October 10th, 1936, the Assembly adopted as an experiment the procedure laid down in this rule, which, unless otherwise decided in the interval, is to have effect down to the termination of the ordinary session of 1939.

2. In the general direction of the work of the Assembly, in the constitution of such committees as the Assembly decides to create, in deciding on the communications to be made to the Assembly, in the framing of the agenda for each meeting, and in the determination of the order of priority for its various items, the President shall be assisted by the General Committee.

RULE 9. SECRETARIAT

1. The Secretary-General shall be responsible for the organisation of the Secretariat of the Assembly and of the secretariat of any committees set up by the Assembly.

2. The Secretary-General may be assisted or replaced at the meetings of the Assembly by a deputy or deputies. The Secretary-General, or one of his deputies, may at any time, on the invitation of the President, bring before the Assembly reports concerning any question which is being considered by the Assembly, and may be invited by the President to make verbal communications concerning any question under consideration.

RULE 10. DOCUMENTS

1. It shall be the duty of the Secretariat, *inter alia*, to receive, print, circulate and translate documents, reports and resolutions; to translate speeches made at the meetings; to draft, print and circulate the Minutes of the session; to have the custody and proper preservation of the documents in the archives of the Assembly; to publish the reports of the meetings, and, generally, to perform all other work which the Assembly thinks fit to entrust to it.

2. All documents emanating from the Assembly shall be circulated to the Governments of the Members of the League.

RULE 11. PUBLICITY OF PLENARY MEETINGS

1. The public shall be admitted to the plenary meetings of the Assembly, by cards distributed by the Secretary-General.

2. The Assembly may decide that particular meetings shall be private.

3. All decisions of the Assembly upon items on the agenda, which have been taken at a private meeting, shall be announced at a public meeting of the Assembly.

RULE 12
(Deleted.)

RULE 13. COMMUNICATIONS TO THE ASSEMBLY

At the beginning of each meeting the President shall present to the

Assembly all communications addressed to the Assembly or to the League, the importance of which appears to him to warrant such action.

RULE 14. COMMITTEES[5]

Constitution

1. The Assembly shall establish such committees as it thinks fit, for the consideration of the items on the agenda. Items of the same nature will be referred to the same committee.

Reports of Committees, particularly Reports involving Expenditure

2. The Assembly shall not decide items on the agenda in full meeting until the report of a committee upon them has been presented and circulated, unless the Assembly itself, by a two-thirds majority, determines otherwise.

Decisions involving expenditure shall be subject to the rules laid down in the Regulations for the Financial Administration of the League of Nations.[6]

Reports by a committee involving the expenditure of money must indicate whether the expenditure will constitute part of the general expenses of the League or whether it will be recovered from the Members of the League particularly concerned.

No resolution involving expenditure shall in any case be voted by the Assembly before the Finance Committee shall have expressed its opinion on the advisability of the proposed expenditure from the point of view of general budgetary resources.[7]

Membership

3. Each delegation may designate one member, and may nominate technical advisers, for each committee.

Officers

4. Each committee shall appoint its Chairman and Rapporteurs.

Sub-committees

5. Each committee may appoint sub-committees, which shall elect their own officers.

[5]On October 10th, 1936, the Assembly decided that the following rule, established as an experiment by the Assembly's resolution of October 11th, 1933, should be maintained for the session of 1937:

The President of the Council, after consulting the Chairman of the Supervisory Commission, may convene the Finance Committee for a date preceding by not more than one week the first meeting of the ordinary session of the Assembly. The Committee shall be composed of the representatives accredited for the purpose by the Members of the League. It shall appoint its Chairman, who shall thereby become a member of the General Committee of the Assembly under the terms of Rule 7 of the Rules of Procedure. The establishment of the Committee shall be reported to the Assembly at the first plenary meeting of the Assembly.

[6]See Annex III.
[7]See Annex II.

Publicity of Meetings. Minutes

6. Each committee shall meet in private unless it decides otherwise. It shall keep a register of its discussions, and Minutes, which shall be published at the earliest possible date, but not until they have been approved by the committee. They may at any time be consulted by any Member of the Assembly.

Right to speak in Committees

7. Every representative shall have the right to place before any committee any communication which he considers should be made to it, but no representative may, without special leave from the Chairman, speak at a meeting of any committee of which he is not a member.

Secretariat

8. The Secretary-General or his deputies may make to any committee or sub-committee any report or verbal communication which he or they may consider desirable.

RULE 14(*a*). PROCEDURE FOR PRESENTATION AND ADOPTION OF REPORTS OF COMMITTEES IN PLENARY SESSION

1. When the reports and resolutions submitted by the various Committees of the Assembly are brought up for adoption in plenary session, the President, in the cases indicated below, shall read the titles of the reports and put forthwith to the vote the resolutions which are proposed.

2. The procedure provided for in paragraph 1 shall only apply in cases where the Committee has unanimously declared that it does not consider a discussion of the report in plenary session to be necessary and where no delegation has subsequently asked the President to open a discussion on the report. The report must be circulated to the delegations twenty-four hours before it is brought up in plenary session.

RULE 15. PROCEDURE FOR DISCUSSIONS

1. No representative may address the Assembly without having previously obtained the permission of the President.

2. Speakers shall be called upon in the order in which they have signified their desire to speak. The Chairman and the Rapporteur of a committee may be accorded precedence for the purpose of defending or explaining the conclusions arrived at by their committee. The same principle shall apply to any Member of the Council.

3. The President may call a speaker to order if his remarks are not

relevant to the subject under discussion. If necessary, he may direct the speaker to resume his seat.

4. When a motion is under discussion, a representative may rise to a point of order, and such point of order shall be immediately decided by the President in accordance with the Rules of Proceedure.

5. The Assembly may limit the time allowed to each speaker.

RULE 16. TRANSLATION OF SPEECHES AND DOCUMENTS

1. Speeches in French shall be summarized in English, and *vice versa*, by an interpreter belonging to the secretariat.

2. A representative speaking in another language shall provide for the translation of his speech into one of these two languages.

3. All documents, resolutions and reports circulated by the President or the Secretariat shall be rendered in both French and English.

4. Any representative may have documents circulated in a language other than French or English, but the Secretariat will not be responsible for their translation or printing.

5. Any Member of the League, or any group of Members, may require that all documents and publications of the League shall be regularly translated into, and printed and circulated in, a language other than French and English, but shall in such case defray all the necessary expenses.

RULE 17. RESOLUTIONS, AMENDMENTS AND MOTIONS

1. Resolutions, amendments and motions must be introduced in writing and handed to the President. The President shall cause copies to be distributed to the representatives.

1 *a*. No resolution, amendment or motion may be signed by more than fifteen Members of the League.

2. As a general rule, no proposal shall be discussed or put to the vote at any meeting of the Assembly unless copies of it have been circulated to all representatives not later than the day preceding the meeting.

3. The President may, however, permit the discussion and consideration of amendments, or of motions as to procedure, without previous circulation of copies.

RULE 18

Previous Question or Adjournment

1. During the discussion of any question, any representative may move the previous question or the adjournment. Any such motion shall have priority in the debate. In addition to the proposer of the motion, two representatives may speak in favour of, and two against, the motion.

Division of Proposals

2. Parts of a proposal shall be voted on separately, if a representative request that the proposal be divided.

Closure

3. A representative may at any time move the closure of the debate, whether any other representative has signified his wish to speak or not. If application is made for permission to speak against the closure, it may be accorded to not more than two speakers.

4. The President shall take the sense of the Assembly on a motion for closure. If the Assembly decides in favour of the closure, the President shall declare the closure of the debate.

Procedure for voting Proposals and Amendments

5. When a number of proposals are before the Assembly, the proposal furthest removed in substance from the principal one shall be voted on first.

6. If an amendment striking out part of a proposal is moved, the Assembly shall first vote on whether the words in question shall stand part of the proposal. If the decision is in the negative, the amendment shall then be put to the vote.

7. When an amendment adds to a proposal it shall be voted on first, and if it is adopted the amended proposal shall then be voted on.

RULE 19. MAJORITY

1. Except where otherwise expressly provided in the Covenant or by the terms of a treaty, decisions of the Assembly shall be taken by a unanimous vote of the Members of the League represented at the meeting.

2. All matters of procedure at a meeting of the Assembly, including the appointment of committees to investigate particular matters, shall be decided by a majority of the Members of the League represented at the meeting.

3. All decisions taken in virtue of these Rules shall be considered as matters of procedure.

4. A majority decision requires the affirmative votes of more than half of the Members of the League represented at the meeting.

5. For the purposes of this Rule, representatives who abstain from voting shall be considered as not present.

RULE 20. "APPEL NOMINAL"

The Assembly shall vote by "Appel Nominal," except when the Members of the League represented at the meeting agree that the method of voting shall be by heads of delegations rising in their seats, and except in the cases provided for in Rule 21. The "Appel Nominal" shall be taken in one of the following manners, as the Assembly may decide:

(*a*) The name of each delegation shall be called, and one of its members shall reply "Yes," "No," or "Not voting." The result of the vote shall be recorded and announced to the Assembly; or

(*b*) The delegation of each Member of the League represented at the meeting shall be provided with two voting tickets, on which the name of the country is written, one red and one blue, the former being "Aye" the latter "No". The voting tickets shall be deposited in an urn placed near the President's platform. When all the votes have been collected the President shall declare the ballot closed, and the General Committee shall proceed to count the votes. The individual votes shall be communicated to the Assembly and the result shall be announced by the President.

RULE 21. ELECTIONS

1. All decisions relating to individuals shall be taken by a secret ballot.

2. If, when one person only is to be elected, no one person obtains at the first ballot an absolute majority of votes, an entirely new ballot shall be taken; but on this occasion the voting shall be confined to the two candidates who obtained the largest number of votes at the first ballot. If there is at this ballot an equality of votes for the two candidates, the elder candidate shall be declared elected.

3. When a number of elective places of the same nature are to be filled at one time, those persons who obtain an absolute majority at the first ballot shall be elected. If the number of persons obtaining such majority is less than the number of persons to be elected, there shall be a second ballot to fill the remaining places, the voting being restricted to the unsuccessful candidates who obtained the greatest number of votes at the first ballot, not more than double in number the places remaining to be filled. Those candidates, to the number required to be elected, who receive the greatest number of votes at the second ballot shall be declared elected.[8]

RULE 22. EQUALITY IN VOTING. SECOND VOTE

In case of equality in any voting other than that referred to in Rule 21, in which a majority is required, a second vote shall be taken in the course of the next meeting; this meeting shall be held within 48 hours

[8]For the rules concerning the election of members of the Permanent Court of International Justice, see Annex VI. Annex VI is not reprinted here.

from the date on which the first vote was taken, and it shall be expressly mentioned on the agenda that a second vote will be taken on the matter in question. Unless there is at this subsequent meeting a majority in favour of the proposal, it shall be considered as lost.

RULE 22a. ELECTION OF NON-PERMANENT MEMBERS OF THE COUNCIL

1. The Members whose representatives are to sit on the Council as non-permanent Members of that body shall be selected by the Assembly by secret ballot.
2. Where several seats are to be filled, the election shall be made by voting a list of names. Any ballot-paper containing more names than there are seats to be filled shall be null and void.
3. No Member shall be elected at the first or at the second ballot unless it has obtained at least the absolute majority of the votes. If, after two ballots, there still remain seats to filled, a third ballot shall be held upon a list consisting of the candidates which obtained most votes at the second ballot, up to a number double that of the seats still to be filled, and those Members shall be elected which obtain the greatest number of votes.
4. If two or more Members obtain the same number of votes and there is not a seat available for each, a special ballot shall be held between them; if they again obtain an equal number of votes, the President shall decide between them by drawing lots.

RULE 23. ADJOURNMENT OR SUSPENSION OF MEETINGS

1. The President may declare a meeting to be adjourned or suspended if a proposal for adjournment or suspension made by him does not meet with objection from the Assembly.
2. The President shall declare an adjournment or supension of the meeting upon a vote to this effect by the Assembly.

RULE 24. REVISION OF RESOLUTIONS

The General Committee, in cases where it deems it necessary, may revise the resolutions adopted by the Assembly, changing their form but not their substance. Any such changes shall be reported to the Assembly.

RULE 25. VERBATIM REPORTS

The verbatim report of each meeting shall be drawn up by the Secretariat and submitted to the Assembly after approval by the President.

RULE 26. CIRCULATION OF ASSEMBLY RESOLUTIONS

The resolutions adopted by the Assembly shall be circulated by the Secretary-General to the Members of the League within fifteen days after the termination of the session.

RULE 27. APPLICATION OF RULES TO COMMITTEE PROCEEDINGS

These Rules of Procedure shall apply to the proceedings of committees of the Assembly. [9]

RULE 28. ALTERATION OF RULES OF PROCEDURE

These Rules of Procedure may be altered by a decision of the Assembly; but no such alteration shall be made except upon a majority vote of the Assembly, taken after a committee has reported on the proposed alteration.

[9] As regards the adoption of decisions by committees by a majority vote, and the question of minority reports, see the report adopted by the Assembly in 1924 (Annex V). Annex V is not reprinted here.

III. RULES OF PROCEDURE
OF THE COUNCIL. ADOPTED BY THE COUNCIL
ON MAY 26TH, 1933[1]

ARTICLE I.

Ordinary sessions

1. The Council shall meet in ordinary session four times in each year —namely, on the third Monday in January, the second Monday in May, three days before the meeting of the Assembly and, for the fourth session, at a date following closely upon the appointment by the Assembly of the non-permanent members of the Council and fixed by the President of the Council.

Extraordinary sessions

2. The Council may at any time decide to meet in extraordinary session.

Date of opening

3. The Council must meet, at the request of any Member of the League of Nations (if necessary, in extraordinary session), in the circumstances referred to in Articles 11, 15 and 17 of the Covenant.

4. If not fixed by the Council, the date of the opening of an extraordinary session shall be fixed by the President, if possible after consultation with his colleagues.

5. The President of the Council, after consulting his colleagues and with the consent of the majority, may, where necessary, advance or retard the date of the opening of a session of the Council. The President may not, however, without the consent of all his colleagues, advance or retard by more than seven days the opening of an ordinary session.

6. The Secretary-General shall give notice to the members of the Council of the date at which a session is to begin, unless the session is to be held at a date provided by the present Rules or fixed by the Council.

ARTICLE II. PLACE OF MEETING

The sessions of the Council shall be held at the seat of the League of Nations, except in cases where the majority of the members of the Council consider that the Council should meet elsewhere.

[1]Document [C.197.M.106.1938.] (1938.3), including Annexes I and II. Annex I is not reprinted here.

ARTICLE III.

Agenda

1. A provisional agenda shall be drawn up by the Secretary-General and approved by the President of the Council. It shall in all cases include any questions which a Member of the League has asked the Council to consider. It shall, so far as possible, show the rapporteurs for the various questions and give references to the documents relating thereto.

2. The provisional agenda shall be sent to the members of the Council not less than three weeks before the opening of the session, except in the case of the fourth ordinary session of the year or of a session the date of which is such as to make it impossible to maintain this interval.

3. Any subsequent modification of the provisional agenda shall be communicated to the members of the Council.

"Rapporteurs"

4. At the last ordinary session of each year the Council shall draw up a list of rapporteurs for the various matters with which it is habitually called upon to deal.

5. Where rapporteurs have not been appointed by the Council, they shall be appointed by the President.

Adoption of Agenda

6. At the opening of the session, the Council shall adopt its agenda at a private meeting.

Insertion of items during session

7. The Council may, by a majority, add during a meeting new questions to its agenda. In such case, unless the Council otherwise unanimously decides, such questions shall not be discussed before the next meeting.

ARTICLE IV. PRESIDENCY OF THE COUNCIL

1. The representatives on the Council shall preside over its sessions in rotation in the alphabetical order in French of the names of the countries which they represent.

2. A President shall, in principle, enter into office at the beginning of an ordinary session and remain in office until the opening of the next ordinary session.

3. Extraordinary sessions shall be presided over by the President for the time being in office.

4. If the representative who should act as President considers that he should decline to do so during a particular session, or during the consideration of a particular matter, the Council shall arrange for another member to act as President.

ARTICLE V. TEMPORARY REPLACEMENT OF PRESIDENT

Where, during the interval between sessions of the Council, the Secretary-General, for the purposes of the application of the provisions of the present Rules or for any other purpose, has occasion to apply to the President of the Council and the President is prevented from acting, the Secretary-General shall apply to the last President, if the country which he represents continues to belong to the Council. If the last President is unable to act, the Secretary-General shall apply, subject to the same condition, to his predecessor, and, thereafter, in accordance with the same system, to earlier Presidents of the Council.

ARTICLE VI. CHANGES IN THE PRESIDENCY

1. If the person who is President ceases to represent his country on the Council, he shall be replaced by the new representative.

2. In like manner, if a former President has ceased to represent his country on the Council, the new representative shall act in his place for the purposes of Article V of the present Rules.

ARTICLE VII.

Publicity of meetings

1. Subject to the provisions of Article III, paragraph 6, and Article X of the present Rules, the meetings of the Council shall, unless the Council otherwise decides, be held in public.

Circulation of reports

2. Unless they have been previously circulated, the reports of rapporteurs and the documents to which they relate shall, so far as possible, be sent to the members of the Council not less than forty-eight hours before the opening of the meeting at which they are discussed. Where this has been done, the report will not be read, unless the rapporteur desires or another member of the Council asks that it shall be read; the rapporteurs may always give such explanations in regard to their reports as they consider desirable. The text of resolutions proposed in the reports shall be read in all cases.

ARTICLE VIII. QUORUM

The Council shall not discuss or decide upon any matter unless the majority of its members are present.

ARTICLE IX.

Unanimity

1. Except where otherwise expressly provided by the Covenant, or

by the terms of any other instrument which is to be applied, decisions at any meeting of the Council shall require the agreement of all the Members of the League represented at the meeting.

Majority decisions

2. All matters of procedure at meetings of the Council, including the appointment of committees to investigate particular matters, shall be regulated by the Council and may be decided by a majority of the Members of the League represented at the meeting.

Vote by roll call

3. Subject to the provisions of Article X of the present Rules, each member of the Council shall be called upon separately to vote, if a member of the Council so requires. In counting the votes, abstentions from voting shall be disregarded.

ARTICLE X. DECISIONS CONCERNING PERSONS

All decisions concerning persons shall be taken at a private meeting. On the demand of any member of the Council, the voting shall be by secret ballot.

ARTICLE XI.

Minutes

1. The Minutes of the meetings of the Council shall be kept by the Secretariat. They shall be published.

2. The Minutes of each meeting of the Council shall be sent as soon as possible to the members of the Council, who shall, within forty-eight hours, inform the Secretariat of any corrections which they may desire to have made in their own speeches.

3. Where the Minutes were sent to the members of the Council less than forty-eight hours before the close of the session, they shall be considered as approved if no corrections have been asked for within ten days.

Summary record

4. The Council may decide not to have published Minutes. In this case, a summary record in a single copy shall alone be made. Such record shall be kept in the Secretariat of the League of Nations, where the representatives of Governments which took part in the meeting may have corrections made in their own speeches within a period of ten days. On the expiration of this period, the record shall be considered as approved and shall be signed by the Secretary-General. Representatives of the said Governments shall at all times have the right to consult the record at the Secretariat.

Article XII.

Administrative measures adopted by corrrespondence

1. When the Council is not in session, its members may be consulted by correspondence by the Secretary-General, on instructions from the President, and may by this means adopt such measures of an administrative character as appear on grounds of urgency to be strictly necessary before the Council again meets.

Financial measures taken by President

2. Subject to confirmation by the Council at its next session, the President of the Council, at the request of the Secretary-General, may, in the interval between sessions, take financial measures of an urgent character which fall within the competence of the Council, such as the approval of transfers, charging of expenditure to the Council's vote for unforeseen expenditure, and advances from the Working Capital Fund.

Article XIII. Presence of Committee Chairmen, etc.

The chairmen and members of committees, experts and officials of the League may be admitted to give information or assistance at meetings of the Council.

Article XIV.

Amendment of Rules

1. Subject to the provisions of the Covenant, the present Rules may be amended by a three-fourths majority, subject to the proposal for amendment of the Rules having been first placed on the agenda.

Departure from Rules

2. Subject to the same restriction, a departure from the provisions of the present Rules may be sanctioned, by the same majority, without its being necessary for a proposal to that effect to be first placed on the agenda.

ANNEX II. REPORT OF THE COMMITTEE ON COUNCIL PROCEDURE

I. Introductory Note

The Committee appointed by the Council on May 27th, 1937 (ninety-seventh session), to consider certain points in connection with Council procedure was composed as follows:

United Kingdom: Mr. R. C. S. Stevenson;
Chile: His Excellency M. F. García-Oldini;
China: His Excellency Dr. Hoo Chi-tsai;

France: M. Lagarde;

Poland: His Excellency M. Tytus Komarnicki.

M. Komarnicki was appointed Rapporteur.

The Committee was of opinion that it would be a mistake to attempt to regulate the procedure of the Council in too great detail. Nevertheless, it considered that experience had shown that a number of points not covered by the Rules of Procedure might with advantage be clarified. Moreover, it thought that it might be convenient if, on one or two points, the procedure of the Council, as established by custom, were expressly stated.

The Committee therefore submits the following points for the consideration of the Council.

The Committee does not consider it necessary, at all events at the present stage, to amend or supplement the Rules of Procedure.

Certain resolutions on procedure already adopted by the Council but not included in its Rules of Procedure, and on which the Committee has no suggestions to make, are annexed for convenience to the present report.

II. Recommendations of the Committee

1. *Secret Meetings*

(*a*) It is desirable to limit as far as possible the number of persons attending secret meetings. It is therefore recommended that each member of the Council be normally accompanied by not more than one assistant. If, for exceptional reasons, a member of the Council wishes to be accompanied by more than one assistant, he should so inform the President beforehand. In no case should the number of assistants exceed three.

The same considerations apply to the number of persons who may accompany the Secretary-General (apart from technical staff).

(*b*) It is desirable that, where circumstances permit, the Council should issue a *communiqué*. The preparation of such *communiqué* might normally be left to the President and the Secretary-General.

As regards information of a confidential nature, of importance to permanent delegates or other representatives of the Members of the League duly authorised by their respective Governments to follow the Council's proceedings, the latter might empower the President or the Secretary-General to furnish such information with due regard both for the interests of the League and for the legitimate desire of these representatives to be kept duly informed of the general course of the Council's proceedings.

Except in so far as the issue of information is authorised by the Council itself, no person present has the right to divulge what passed at the meeting.

2. *Private Meetings*

(*a*) With a view to avoiding overcrowding in the room assigned to the Council for its private meetings, it is recommended that each member of the Council be normally accompanied by not more than three assistants. If, for exceptional reasons, a member of the Council wishes to be accompanied by more than three assistants, he should so inform the President beforehand. In no case should the number of assistants exceed five.

The representatives of Members of the League not represented on the Council may also attend private meetings. In view of the limited accommodation available, however, it is desirable that, as far as possible, each Member should be represented by one person only.

The Secretary-General shall limit as far as possible the number of officials attending private meetings.

The Committee considers that a reasonable allocation of the seating accommodation available at private meetings would be as follows:

For each Council delegation	2 seats.
For representatives of Members of the League not represented on the Council	15 seats.
For members of the Secretariat (other than technical staff)	5 seats.

(*b*) It is recommended that the President should open the private meeting not later than five minutes after the time announced.

3. *Adoption of Agenda*

It is recommended that the following procedure, which corresponds to the practice generally adopted hitherto, should be followed, unless the Council, in a given case, should decide otherwise:

At the private meeting at which it adopts the agenda, whether of the session or of the meeting, the Council sits in its ordinary composition. Nevertheless, if the representative of a Member of the League entitled to send a representative to the Council for the discussion of the substance of an item asks permission to present any observations to the Council in regard to the inclusion of that item on the agenda, that representative is invited to the Council table. Similarly, if any discussion in regard to the inclusion of the item otherwise arises, the representative of such Member of the League, if present in the room, is invited to the Council table.

4. *Voting*

It is recommended that the following procedure, which corresponds to the practice generally adopted hitherto, should be followed, unless the Council, in a given case, should decide otherwise:

When a vote by roll-call is required under Article IX, paragraph 3, of the Rules of Procedure, it shall be taken in French alphabetical order of the Members of the League represented at the meeting, the President voting last. In cases in which the vote concerns a dispute, the representatives of the parties to the dispute shall vote after the other members of the Council and the President. The vote of the parties shall also be taken in French alphabetical order.

5. *Distribution of the Text of Speeches*

In deference to the dignity of Council meetings, it is recommended that those delegations desirous of communicating the text of a speech to the Press should wait, before doing so, until the speaker in question has finished speaking.

6. *Presidency of the Council*

In order to expedite the operation of the system of rotation, it is recommended that the practice followed hitherto, by which the two autumn sessions of the Council are presided over by the same President, should be discontinued, and that a new President should take office for each of the four regular sessions of the Council.

7. *Deputations*

The President of the Council cannot speak in the name of the Council unless he has been specially requested to do so by the latter, and therefore should not, in that capacity, receive deputations. Any statement made to him should therefore be received by him in his capacity as a member of the Council only.

8. *Reports of Technical Committees*

In order to avoid to some extent the inconvenience resulting from members of the Council being asked to discuss reports of technical Committees distributed during or immediately before the Council session, it is recommended that the following practice be observed:

When the report of a standing technical Committee has not been distributed to the Council at least one week before the date fixed for the opening of the session, the relevant question shall be excluded from the revised agenda which is distributed by the Secretariat just before the session. Members of the Council shall nevertheless retain their right, under Article III, paragraph 7, of the Rules of Procedure, to propose to the Council that the discussion of a particular report should be added to the agenda in the course of the session.

9. *Presence of Representatives of League Committees at the Council Table*

It is generally unnecessary for the chairman or other representatives of League Committees to come to the Council table for the discussion of their Committees' reports. Nevertheless, it is open to the Rapporteur for the particular question on the agenda to ask the Secretary-General to arrange for the representation of the Committee, should special circumstances appear to the Rapporteur to warrant such action.

10. *Occasional Speeches*

Occasional speeches, such as speeches of condolence or congratulation, are normally made by the President on behalf of the Council as a whole, so that any member of the Council may refrain from speaking without any discourtesy being imputed to him. Members of the Council other than the President are nevertheless at liberty to speak on such occasions, but it is recommended that so far as possible they should make their intention of speaking known at the private meeting preceding the public meeting in question.

IV. SECRETARIAT OF THE LEAGUE OF NATIONS: STAFF REGULATIONS[1]

DUTIES AND OBLIGATIONS OF OFFICIALS

ARTICLE 1

1. The officials of the Secretariat of the League of Nations are exclusively international officials and their duties are not national, but international. By accepting appointment, they pledge themselves to discharge their functions and to regulate their conduct with the interests of the League alone in view. They are subject to the authority of the Secretary-General, and are responsible to him in the exercise of their functions, as provided in these Regulations. They may not seek or receive instructions from any Government or other authority external to the Secretariat of the League of Nations.

2. No official of the Secretariat may, during the term of his appointment, accept from any Government any honour or decoration except for services rendered before appointment.

3. The diplomatic privileges and immunities attaching to officials of the League of Nations under Article 7 of the Covenant are conferred upon them in the interest of their duties. They furnish no excuse to the officials who enjoy them for non-performance of their private obligations or failure to observe laws and police regulations. Officials of the Secretariat invoking these privileges and immunities must report to the Secretary-General, with whom it rests to decide whether they shall be waived.

ARTICLE 2

On assuming office, the Secretary-General of the League of Nations shall make and sign the following declaration before the Council in public session:

"I solemnly undertake to exercise in all loyalty, discretion and conscience the functions that have been entrusted to me as Secretary-General of the League of Nations, to discharge my functions and to regulate my conduct with the interests of the League alone in view and not to seek or receive instructions from any Government or other authority external to the League of Nations."

[1]Reprinted from the "Edition issued in September 1945 and incorporating amendments in force on the date of issue." The footnotes, with the exception of the present one, are from the September, 1945 edition.

ARTICLE 3

1. On assuming office, officials of the Secretariat shall make and sign the following declaration:

"I solemnly undertake to exercise in all loyalty, discretion and conscience the functions that have been entrusted to me as an official of the Secretariat of the League of Nations, to discharge my functions and to regulate my conduct with the interests of the League alone in view and not to seek or receive instructions from any Government or other authority external to the Secretariat of the League of Nations."

2. The declaration shall be made and signed:

(a) In the case of officials of the rank of Director and above, before the Council in public session;

(b) In the case of other officials of the First Division, before the Committee on Appointments and Promotion;

(c) In the case of officials of the Second and Third Divisions, before the Sub-Committee on Appointments and Promotion.

3. This Article shall not apply to temporary officials engaged for less than one year.

ARTICLE 4

1. No official may accept or hold or engage in any office or occupation which, in the opinion of the Secretary-General, is incompatible with the proper discharge of his duties in the Secretariat.

2. No official of the Secretariat may, while he holds that position, be a candidate for office of a political character in his own country.

ARTICLE 5

1. Officials are required to exercise the utmost discretion in regard to all matters of official business.

2. No official of the Secretariat may, during the term of his appointment, publish or cause to be published or assist in the publication of any book, pamphlet, article, letter or other document, or deliver any lecture or speech, dealing with the activities of the League of Nations, the International Labour Organisation or the Permanent Court of International Justice, or communicate to any person any unpublished information known to him by reason of his official position, except in the course of his duty or by authorisation of the Secretary-General.

3. It is the duty of officials to avoid any action, and in particular any kind of public pronouncement, which may affect their position as international officials either in their own countries or elsewhere.

4. For detailed rules as to the application of the principles of the

present Article officials are referred to Annex IV of the present Regulations.

ARTICLE 6

Officials are assigned their duties by the Secretary-General or by the heads of their respective services acting by his authority. Subject to the terms of his appointment an official may be required to work in any service of the Secretariat, but in appointing an official to any service or duty, his technical qualifications shall receive consideration.

ARTICLE 7

1. The hours of attendance at the offices of the Secretariat and the rules regarding compensation for overtime will be fixed by the Secretary-General from time to time to meet the needs of the service in accordance with the following principles:

(*a*) The whole time of officials is, in principle, at the disposal of the Secretary-General.

(*b*) The normal period of attendance at the office shall be seven hours on each ordinary working-day (not including intervals for meals) and three and a half hours on Saturday.

(*c*) Attendance on Sunday and on the public holidays enumerated in Article 42 shall only be required in cases of proved urgency and in the case of officials employed to guard and keep open the premises of the Secretariat.

(*d*) The Secretary-General may allow compensation for overtime on the conditions determined by him.

2. Officials not ordinarily entitled to compensation for overtime who are expressly required to attend the office on Sunday, or on one of the public holidays enumerated in Article 42, shall be entitled to one half-day's leave if required to attend in the morning or afternoon only and to a whole day's leave if required to attend both in the morning and in the afternoon. Such leave must be taken as soon as the requirements of the service permit.

3. Attendance books may be kept at each office of the Secretariat for the purpose of recording the times of arrival and departure of officials employed therein.

4. The regulations as to hours of attendance, attendance books and overtime contained in Annex II shall apply pending any further or contrary decision by the Secretary-General.

ORGANISATION OF THE STAFF AND SCALES OF SALARY

ARTICLE 8

1. The staff of the Secretariat is organised in three Divisions, as shown in Annex I, according to the nature of the official's duties.

2. Officials of the Secretariat will be appointed on or within the scales of salary set out in Annex I and for the following periods, subject to the provisions of the present Regulations:

(a) *Principal Officers:*[2]

Secretary-General: 10 years;
Deputy-Secretaries-General: 8 years;
Under-Secretaries-General and Legal Adviser: 7 years;
Directors: 7 years.

(b) *Other Officials:*

Without limit of time, subject to the age-limit fixed by Article 22, without prejudice to the power of the Secretary-General to appoint temporary officials. Provided always that officials of the Third Division may, during the first seven years of service, be discharged at any time by the Secretary-General on giving three months' notice.

3. Officials appointed as provided above are described in these Regulations as "permanent officials", other officials as "temporary officials".

4. (*a*) The salary scales provided in Annex I for permanent non-locally-recruited officials of the Second Division are applicable to officials for whom employment at Geneva involves expatriation and who are appointed to posts for which the Assembly has approved payment of salary on one of the said scales.

(*b*) Persons of Swiss nationality who, at the moment of becoming candidates for the post to be filled, are not resident in French-speaking Switzerland (*la Suisse romande*) or in French territory within a radius of twenty-five kilometres from Geneva, will be assimilated to officials for whom employment at Geneva involves expatriation.

(*c*) Persons who, at the moment of their candidature, have been resident for at least five years in French-speaking Switzerland (*la Suisse romande*) or in French territory within a radius of twenty-five kilometres from Geneva, will be treated as locally recruited; provided always that Swiss nationals residing in French-speaking Switzerland (*la Suisse romande*) or within the zone of twenty-five kilometres from Geneva within French territory, and French nationals residing in this latter zone, will be treated as locally recruited, irrespective of the duration of such residence.

(*d*) The three preceding sub-paragraphs (*a*), (*b*) and (*c*) shall apply only to persons entering the service after September 30th, 1932.

(*e*) The Secretary-General's decision as to the application of the rules contained in the above sub-paragraphs (*a*), (*b*) and (*c*) shall be binding upon the candidate.

[2]The maximum periods for which the appointments of Principal Officers may be renewed are as follows: Secretary-General: 3 years; Deputy-Secretaries-General: 5 years; Under-Secretaries-General and Legal Adviser: 7 years; Directors: Indefinite, but for periods not exceeding 7 years.

5. Permanent officials of the First Division below the rank of Chief of Section will normally be appointed between the ages of 23 and 35 (inclusive) and permanent officials of the Second Division between the ages of 21 and 30 (inclusive); but the Secretary-General may fix different age-limits for appointment in particular cases. In the case of vacancies in the Third Division, the Secretary-General will fix the minimum and maximum ages for appointment in accordance with the nature of the duties attaching to the post.

6. Temporary appointments may be made for such periods and subject to such notice as may be fixed by the Secretary-General.

7. Temporary officials will be appointed at such salaries as may be fixed by the Secretary-General: provided always that, if the appointment is made for at least five years, the salary scale on which a permanent official would have been engaged for the work in question shall be applicable, but the salary may be increased by such increase as may be considered reasonable where the appointment is not pensionable.

8. The categories of temporary officials known as Specialists and Temporary Collaborators are subject to the special rules set out in Annex I, paragraph 1, sub-paragraphs D and E, as regards all the points dealt with in those rules, and in all other respects to the provisions of the present Regulations.

APPOINTMENT AND PROMOTION

ARTICLE 9

All positions on the Secretariat shall be open equally to men and women as provided in Article 7 of the Covenant.

ARTICLE 10

Recruitment in the First Division shall be effected with special regard to the international character of the Secretariat and the importance of securing the collaboration on its staff of nationals of the various Members of the League.

ARTICLE 11

1. The staff of the Secretariat are appointed by the Secretary-General with the approval of the Council.

2. Definitive appointments may be made by the Secretary-General at initial rates of salary not exceeding 8,000 Swiss francs per annum, or the equivalent in any other currency, without submission of each case to the Council.

3. The name of any person engaged to hold an appointment on the Secretariat at a rate of salary higher than the above-mentioned rate shall be submitted to the Council for approval at the first ordinary session following the engagement. The engagement shall become a definitive appointment on receiving the approval of the Council; but shall be provisional only until such approval is given, and, if not approved, shall be terminated as from such date and on such terms as the Council may direct.

4. An appointment approved by the Council remains subject to the provisions as to medical examination and probation contained in these Regulations or in its terms.

Article 12

1. The following Committees shall be established to assist the Secretary-General in regard to the appointment of officials, their promotion and their discharge (except on grounds of invalidity) and in regard to the organisation of the staff:

2. (a) The *Committee on Appointments and Promotion* shall consist of officials nominated by the Secretary-General, who shall not be of lower rank than that of Director and shall be of different nationalities. Subject to paragraph 2 (b), it shall advise in all cases of appointments, promotions, increases of salary under Article 25, paragraph 2, and Article 29, discharge of probationer officials, confirmation or non-confirmation of appointments, suspension of annual increments, resignations, discharge of officials in case of abolition of posts or reduction or reorganisation of staff, and as to the action to be taken upon the septennial reports as to officials' services, conduct and capacity provided for in Article 62. The Secretary-General shall be Chairman of the Committee on Appointments and Promotion.

(b) The *Sub-Committee on Appointments and Promotion* shall consist of officials nominated by the Secretary-General, who may be of lower rank than that of a Director but shall be of different nationalities. This body shall deal with questions falling within the competence of the Committee on Appointments and Promotion, where the salary of the post or official is on a scale not rising above 11,250 Swiss francs per annum or is at a fixed rate not above that sum. It shall present its report either directly to the Secretary-General or to the Committee on Appointments and Promotion, as the Secretary-General may decide. The officer in charge of Internal Administration shall be Chairman of the Sub-Committee on Appointments and Promotion.

(c) The term "Committee on Appointments and Promotion," as used in the present Regulations, means either the body referred to in paragraph 2 (a) or that referred to in paragraph 2 (b), according to the circumstances of the case.

(*d*) For the purposes of the examination of any question directly affecting a particular service, the official responsible for the direction of the service shall form part of the Committee on Appointments and Promotion.

(*e*) Before recommending the discharge of a probationer official or the non-confirmation of an appointment, and before recommending what action should be taken upon a report made under Article 62 where the report is unfavourable to the official, the Committee shall give the official an opportunity to state his case.

(*f*) Before a question of appointment or promotion is finally dealt with by the Committee on Appointments and Promotion, the qualifications of the candidates shall be investigated and a report be made to that Committee by a Selection Board of from three to five members, appointed for the purposes of the particular case. The Selection Board shall be appointed by the Secretary-General or, in the case of appointments or promotions falling within the competence of the Sub-Committee on Appointments and Promotion, by the officer in charge of Internal Administration; the Director or head of service of any section or service directly interested shall form part of the Board.

3. The *Re-grading Committee* shall consist of not less than three nor more than five members nominated by the Secretary-General so as to consist of officials of different nationalities. The officer in charge of Internal Administration shall *ex officio* be Chairman, and at least one other member shall be of the rank of Director or of higher rank. The Treasurer shall attend the meetings in an advisory capacity. This Committee shall advise the Secretary-General in regard to the creation and grading of new posts and the abolition or re-grading of existing posts. It shall be competent, not merely to investigate any questions of this nature which are referred to it by the Secretary-General, but also to make recommendations upon any such question which have come to its notice. It shall have the right to obtain from officials in charge of services any information necessary for the performance of its work.

ARTICLE 13

1. Officials shall be engaged by the delivery and acceptance in writing of a letter of appointment signed by the Secretary-General or, when authorised by the Secretary-General, by the officer in charge of Internal Administration.

2. The letter of appointment shall state:

(*a*) That the appointment is subject to the provisions of the Staff Regulations applicable to the category of appointment in question;

(*b*) The nature of the appointment;

(c) The date at which the official is required to enter upon his duties;

(d) The period of the appointment, or the notice required to terminate it, and the period of probation;

(e) The commencing rate of salary and, if annual increments are allowable, the scale of increments and the maximum attainable;

(f) Any special conditions which may be applicable.

3. Where an appointment is subject to submission to the Council for approval in accordance with Article 11, the letter shall state that the appointment is provisional until the Council's approval has been obtained.

4. In accepting appointment, the person engaged shall state that he has been made acquainted with and agrees to the conditions laid down in the Staff Regulations. A copy of these Regulations will be transmitted to him with the letter of appointment.

5. For all purposes of these Regulations, the period of an official's appointment and his service with the Secretariat shall be reckoned from the date on which he actually enters upon his duties, and, unless the terms on which the official is appointed provide for payment of salary from an earlier date, the official's salary will be payable from the day on which he actually enters upon his duties until the day on which he finally leaves his duties.

ARTICLE 14

1. Before making an appointment, the Secretary-General will normally hold an examination or competition. Appointments will not necessarily be made solely on the basis of the results of such examination or competition.

2. The Secretary-General may offer any post of a special character or special importance to a person whose qualifications render him particularly suitable for appointment.

ARTICLE 15

1. (a) No person shall be appointed for seven years or more until the Secretary-General has been satisfied by a certificate from a duly qualified medical practitioner that the person is in good health, that he is free from any defect or disease likely to interfere with the proper discharge of his duties, and that there is no pathological, personal or family history of, or definite predisposition to, any disease which might result in premature invalidity or premature death.

(b) The certificate shall, wherever possible, be obtained from the Medical Referee of the Secretariat or his substitute.

(c) Where the appointment is made on a certificate from any other medical practitioner,[3] it shall be provisional until the person appointed has been examined by the Medical Referee or his substitute and, if the report is unfavourable and the person so desires, by a medical board which shall be constituted and the expenses of which shall be paid in the same manner as is provided in paragraph 2 (*a*) below. If, as the result of such further examination, the official is not certified to be fit for appointment, the Secretary-General shall terminate the appointment on such terms as he considers just, subject in any case to payment of not less than one month's salary.

2. (*a*) At the end (or, where the Secretary-General considers it desirable, during the course) of his first year of service the official shall be re-examined, at the expense of the Secretariat, by a medical practitioner, or, if the Secretary-General so decides or the official so requests, by a medical board, for the purpose of finally determining whether he is physically fit for employment in the Secretariat. The medical board shall consist of three medical practitioners of whom one shall be appointed by the Secretary-General, one by the official and the third by the two members so chosen. The official may be required to pay the extra expenditure resulting from his appointing on the medical board a practitioner who is not resident in the place where the examination takes place.

(*b*) If, as the result of the examination, the Secretary-General is satisfied that the official is not fit for employment, he shall terminate the appointment on such terms as he considers just, subject, in any case, to payment of not less than one month's salary. The application of this paragraph shall not be affected by any decision which has been taken as to confirming the official's appointment or exempting him from probation (Article 23), but an appointment subject to one year's probation shall not ordinarily be confirmed until the decision as to the official's permanent physical fitness has been taken.

3. Temporary officials shall be appointed after medical examination in accordance with paragraph 1 above, unless the appointment is for less than six months. The provisions of paragraph 2 shall apply if the appointment is for two years or longer. Where the Secretary-General decides to appoint or retain in a temporary capacity the services of a person whose health is below the required standard, he may impose special conditions with regard to the granting of sick leave.

ARTICLE 16

1. Subject in the case of the First and Second Divisions to the maintenance of the international composition of the staff, vacancies shall be filled by promotion of officials in preference to appointment from

[3]The cost of obtaining such a certificate is not paid by the Secretariat.

outside the Secretariat, and, as between candidates of equal merit from outside the Secretariat, preference shall be given, first, to officials of the International Labour Office or the Registry of the Permanent Court of International Justice, and, secondly, to candidates who have in some other capacity been associated with the work of the League of Nations.

2. Other considerations being equal, weight will be attached to seniority in the service.

3. At least two weeks' notice of vacancies shall be given within the Secretariat and to the Director of the International Labour Office and the Registrar of the Permanent Court. Any applicant who is an official of the Secretariat shall be entitled to require that the official in charge of the service in which he is employed shall make a report upon his qualifications which shall be shown to him at his request.

4. Where it is desirable to secure candidates from outside the Secretariat, the International Labour Office and the Registry of the Permanent Court, appropriate publicity shall be given to the intention to make the appointment and as long time as possible be allowed for the submission of applications.

5. Any vacancy may be restricted to candidates of nationalities not adequately represented in the Secretariat or in the category of official in question.

6. A register shall be kept of those applications for employment in the Secretariat which appear to merit consideration, and the claims of persons entered therein who possess suitable qualifications shall be examined whenever it is proposed to make a new appointment to the Secretariat.

7. The present Article shall not apply to vacancies which are filled by the transfer of an official of the appropriate category.

ARTICLE 17

When an official appointed for a fixed period of years is promoted to a rank or position tenable by officials appointed for a shorter period, the latter period shall be substituted for the residue of his original period of appointment.

ARTICLE 17 *bis*

1. (*a*) All officials who are appointed on or after January 1st, 1938 (or on or after that date reach the end of their period of appointment and are continued in the service) are obliged to be members of the Staff Insurance Association against Accident and Illness, provided that they are eligible under the Statutes of the Association, and subject always to the provisions of those Statutes regarding lapsing of membership and expulsion.

(*b*) The official (if not already a member of the Association) shall, as soon as he is eligible, take the necessary steps to obtain admission to the Association in accordance with its Statutes and if his membership lapses shall resume it as soon as possible.

2. If the official is not appointed as a member of the staff employed at Geneva, or if he ceases to be a member of such staff, he shall not be obliged to belong to the Association in virtue of the present article unless he is transferred or returns to regular employment at Geneva.

TERMINATION OF APPOINTMENTS AND RESIGNATION

ARTICLE 18

1. The appointment of any official may be terminated by the Secretary-General if the necessities of the service require a re-organisation of the staff, provided always that regard shall be had to the legitimate interests of the official as assured to him by the present Regulations. If an official is entitled to the compensation prescribed in Article 73 below, he shall receive notice of termination of contract not exceeding one month. If he is not entitled to such compensation, he shall receive from one to three months' notice according to the period for which he was appointed.

2. Compensation for termination of an appointment under this Article shall be payable as prescribed in Article 73.

3. The opinion of the Committee established by Article 67 (Judicial Committee) shall be taken upon the proposed termination of appointment if the official so requests.

ARTICLE 19

In the case dealt with in Articles 8 (paragraph 2 (*b*), 11 (paragraph 3), 15, 22, 24, 25, 39, 40, 62 and 64, appointments may be terminated in accordance with the provisions of the applicable articles.

ARTICLE 20

Wherever the giving of notice is necessary for the termination of an appointment, salary may be paid in lieu of notice.

ARTICLE 21

1. An official may resign from the Secretariat at any time on giving the Secretary-General six month's notice in writing, or, in the case of temporary officials whose terms of appointment provide for a special period of notice, such notice as is thereby provided.

2. The Secretary-General may accept a shorter period of notice.

ARTICLE 22

1. Officials shall retire from the Secretariat on attaining the age of sixty years; provided always that the Secretary-General may retain the services of an official up to the age of sixty-five years.

2. The Secretary-General may for special work engage or retain in the service persons above the age of sixty-five years.

ARTICLE 23

1. All permanent officials of the Secretariat shall be on probation during the first year of their service.

2. Temporary officials shall be on probation for the first year of their service if they are appointed for a longer period than three years, and in other cases for such period as is specified in their terms of engagement.

3. The Secretary-General may shorten or dispense with the period of probation; he may prolong the period of probation, provided always that the total period shall not exceed two years.

ARTICLE 24

An official on probation may be discharged at one month's notice if he fails to perform his duties in a satisfactory manner.

ARTICLE 25

1. On the expiration of the official's period of probation, a decision shall be taken in accordance with the procedure provided in Article 12 in regard to the confirmation or termination of the appointment or the extension of the period of probation. If the appointment is terminated, it shall cease on the date fixed by the Secretary-General, which shall not be earlier than the thirtieth day following the communication of the decision to the official.

2. In confirming an official's appointment, the Secretary-General may, in exceptional cases, make him a special award of one or more annual increments, if he considers that the rate of salary as originally fixed under the appointment is lower than is warranted by the official's qualifications and duties.

ARTICLE 26

In these Regulations the term "probation" and the rules applicable to officials on probation do not relate to a period of trial which an official already on the staff may be required to undergo on being transferred or promoted to a different position in the Secretariat.

SALARIES

ARTICLE 27

1. The salaries of officials of the Secretariat shall, in the absence of a decision of the Secretary-General to the contrary, be payable at the end of each calendar month in respect of the past month.

2. In the event of the death of an official, a grant equal to one month's salary shall be paid to his widow or such other member of his family as the Secretary-General may determine.

ARTICLE 28[4]

1. Annual increments of salary will be granted in the case of officials working under the direction of the head of a service only on a certificate from him that they have given satisfaction during the past year, and in the case of other officials only on a like certificate by the Secretary-General.

2. The first increment allowable under any salary scale shall normally be due at the close of one year's service on such scale, but if at that date the official's appointment on the scale in question has not been finally confirmed, the increment will not normally be due until the appointment is finally confirmed.

3. If an increment certificate does not warrant the grant of increment, it may be decided to accord such increment only at a later date, in which case one or other of the two following courses shall be adopted: either (a) the loss to the official will be limited to the sum which he would have received between the ordinary due date of the increment and that to which it is postponed, or (b) the postponement of increment will continue to affect the official's salary in subsequent years, one increment only being allowable at the end of the period of postponement and subsequent increments being allowable at the end of successive years starting from the end of the period of postponement. If, notwithstanding the penalisation of the official as provided at (a) above, he continues not to give satisfaction, his increment may

---

[4]The Report of the Fourth Committee, which was approved by the 1933 Assembly, states: "The Committee agreed with the Supervisory Commission that any official might reach the maximum salary of his class by annual increments, but was not entitled to his increment unless he had given satisfaction during the past year. The Administration could rightly consider that, in order to give satisfaction, an official must not merely have avoided giving grounds for criticism, but also have increased his efficiency with his experience until he was fit to perform all the duties normally assignable to officials of his class."

be adjourned for further periods on the same terms. On the other hand, in the case provided for at (*b*), if the official's behaviour subsequently justifies that course, his salary may be raised to the rate which he would normally have attained if there had been no postponement of increment and the official be made eligible for subsequent increments on the dates on which he would normally have been eligible for increment.

4. Where sick leave has extended for over two months in the course of the incremental year, payment of increment shall automatically be postponed for a period corresponding to the amount by which such sick leave has exceeded two months, on the terms provided at (*a*) above.

5. A grant of special leave under Article 47, either with or without pay, shall have the same effect as sick leave as regards postponement of grant of increment, but subject to the provision that the period mentioned in the last preceding paragraph shall commence to run from the first date of absence.

6. Any case in which an official is refused an increment under the third paragraph of the present Article shall, if the official so requests, be submitted for enquiry to the Committee established by Article 67 (Judicial Committee.)

ARTICLE 29

Where, after consideration of the case by the Committee on Appointments and Promotion, the Secretary-General is satisfied that there has been a permanent change in an official's duties which imposes upon him responsibilities greater than correspond to the salary which he is receiving, but do not warrant his promotion to a higher category, the Secretary-General may make such increase in the official's salary as he considers just within the limits of the salary scale on which the official stands.

ARTICLE 30

1. The salaries of all officials who are pensionable under the Staff Pensions Regulations of the League of Nations are payable subject to deduction of the contributions prescribed by those Regulations.

2. The salaries of all officials who, after the entry into force of the Staff Pensions Regulations, remain members of the Staff Provident Fund are payable subject to deduction of the prescribed contribution to that Fund.

3. The salaries of officials who are members of the Staff Insurance Association against Accidents and Illness are payable subject to deduction of the subscriptions due from them to that Association.

MODIFICATION OF APPOINTMENTS IN CONSEQUENCE OF DECISIONS OF THE ASSEMBLY

ARTICLE 30 *bis*

1. All appointments made after October 15th, 1932, and all appointments made before that date with the proviso that their terms may be modified by the Assembly, are subject to such modifications of their terms as may be necessary to bring them into conformity with any decision of the Assembly, relating to the conditions of employment of officials (or of particular categories of officials) or to particular special posts, which the Assembly may decide to apply to officials already in the service.

2. In all cases of promotions made after October 15th, 1932, or made before that date with the proviso that their terms may be modified by the Assembly, it is implied that the promoted officials shall thenceforward be subject to decisions of the Assembly fixing the rates of salary.

SICK LEAVE AND MATERNITY LEAVE

ARTICLE 31

1. No official may be absent on the ground of illness for more than three consecutive days without producing a certificate from a duly-qualified medical practitioner stating the nature of the illness and that he is unable to perform his duties and the probable duration of incapacity.

2. If the official is on leave, the provisions of Article 51 shall not apply to days claimed as days of sick leave, however numerous, in respect of which a medical certificate is not produced.

3. If the number of days during which an official is absent in any calendar year without producing a medical certificate shall exceed twelve in the aggregate, the number of days in excess of twelve may be deducted from the amount of annual leave which would normally be due him under these Regulations.

ARTICLE 32

1. On production of a certificate in accordance with Article 31, sick leave on full or half pay may be granted in accordance with the following rules:

(*a*) In the case of officials on probation, the amount of sick leave to be allowed shall be proportionate to the period of probation and be at the rate of thirty working-days on full pay and thirty working-days on half pay in the year. The period of probation may be extended by the amount of leave allowed if such leave exceeds four weeks.

(b) In case of permanent officials whose appointment has been finally confirmed, the amount of sick leave to be allowed shall not exceed an aggregate of 18 months in any four consecutive years, of which the first nine months shall be on full pay and the remainder on half pay, but subject to the provisions that, after six months continuous leave on full pay has been granted, sick leave for the remainder of the same illness will ordinarily be on half pay, and that not more than six months' sick leave on full pay will ordinarily be granted in respect of different illnesses in any twelve consecutive months.

(c) A temporary official engaged for a period exceeding one year shall be treated for the purposes of this Article as though his appointment were not temporary, and other temporary officials may be allowed such sick leave as the Secretary-General may determine in each case.

2. For the purposes of this Article the term "year" shall mean a period of twelve consecutive months.

Article 33

In maternity cases, special leave, which shall not count as sick leave, shall be allowed not exceeding six weeks before and six weeks after confinement.

Article 34

An official shall at once notify any case of contagious disease occurring in his household. An official who is directed not to attend his office in consequence of the presence of disease in his household shall receive his full salary for the period during which he is required to be absent; he may be required to perform such work as he can reasonably do without attending at the office.

Article 35

1. An official applying for sick leave may be required to submit to examination by a medical practitioner named by the Secretary-General.

2. If the applicant is at Geneva, the examination will normally be made there by the medical adviser of the Secretariat. The applicant must not leave Geneva until the sick leave has been granted: if he does so, sick leave may be refused or he may be required to return to Geneva at his own expense for examination.

ARTICLE 36

1. An official to whom sick leave has been granted will be expected to return to his duties as soon as he is capable of performing them, notwithstanding that the period of sick leave granted to him has not expired; and may be required at any time to submit a medical certificate as to his condition, or to undergo examination by a medical practitioner named by the Secretary-General, and the leave may be withdrawn if the Secretary-General is not satisfied that the official in unable to return to his duties.

2. On the expiration of a period for which sick leave has been granted, additional sick leave will only be allowed on the production of a further medical certificate.

ARTICLE 37

An official who receives more than nine weeks' sick leave in the aggregate in any calendar year may, if the circumstances justify this course, be required to forgo not more than half the annual leave which would normally be allowed to him in respect of that year, and an official who receives more than fifteen weeks' sick leave in the aggregate in such a period may similarly be required to forgo up to three-quarters of his annual leave. No official may be required to forgo annual leave under this Article except after consultation of the Administrative Committee.

ARTICLE 38

The termination of an official's appointment shall, as from the date at which the appointment ends, terminate any claim which the official may have to sick leave under these Regulations.

ARTICLE 39

1. Where the nature of an official's illness is or becomes such as to render him incapable of returning to his duties during the period of his appointment, or liable to relapses so frequent as to prevent him from satisfactorily performing his duties, the Secretary-General may terminate his appointment on the ground of invalidity, notwithstanding that the sick leave allowable to him has not been exhausted.

2. In such circumstances, the official is entitled to an equitable indemnity in respect of his unexpired sick leave, when the Regulations of the Pensions Fund do not render him eligible for an invalidity pension. This indemnity shall be independent of any grant which can be made to the official under the Regulations of the Staff Provident Fund of the League of Nations.

ARTICLE 40

On the exhaustion of the sick leave on full and half-pay allowable to an official under these Regulations, the Secretary-General may, subject to the provision of the Staff Pensions Regulations:

(a) Grant additional sick leave without pay;

(b) Terminate the official's appointment on the ground of invalidity.

ARTICLE 41

No official shall be discharged on the ground of invalidity until the majority of a medical board, consisting of three practitioners of whom one shall be appointed by the Secretary-General, one by the official and the third by the two practitioners so chosen, shall have certified that the official is incapable of performing his duties in a satisfactory manner.

HOLIDAYS AND ANNUAL LEAVE

ARTICLE 42

1. Subject to the provisions of Article 7, paragraph 1 (c), all officials employed at the seat of the League will have leave on the following public holidays, which will not be considered as part of their annual leave, viz.:

(a) From Good Friday to Easter Monday inclusive;

(b) Whit-Monday and Ascension Day;

(c) New Year's Day and Christmas Day, together with the working day preceding or following these holidays.

2. The Secretary-General will fix the public holidays for officials of the League offices outside Geneva, taking into consideration the customs of the countries in which they are situated.

ARTICLE 43

1. Permanent officials are entitled to ordinary annual leave in accordance with the following provisions:

(a) Officials of the First and non-locally-recruited officials of the Second Division are entitled to thirty-six working-days' annual leave in each year.

(b) Locally-recruited officials of the Second Division are entitled to thirty-three working-days' annual leave in each year.

(c) Officials of the Third Division under thirty years of age are entitled to fifteen working-days' annual leave in each year. Those over thirty are entitled to 21 working-days.

2. An official who, availing himself of the provisions of paragraph

1 of Article 54, spends all or part of his annual leave in the country in which the place recognised as his home for the purposes of Article 54 is situated, is entitled to add to his leave the time required for the journey to the said home and back, or to the place to which he goes, whichever is the nearer, by the quickest route (excluding aerial navigation) or by an approved route.

This paragraph shall not apply to locally-recruited officials of the Second Division or to officials of the Third Division.

3. The official must take at least half of his annual leave in the course of the year in respect of which the leave is due. The remainder of the leave due for the year may be carried forward and added to the leave which he takes in a subsequent year, provided always that the total amount of ordinary annual leave, including such deferred leave, taken in any year may not exceed three months, except in the case of officials returning on leave to their homes and entitled to have their travelling expenses paid only once in every two or three years (Article 54).

ARTICLE 44

1. On marrying, an official shall be entitled to six working-days' leave.

2. An official shall be entitled to the same amount of leave on the death of a near relation. By near relation, for the purpose of the present Article, is meant the official's father, mother, wife or husband and children; the Secretary-General may in exceptional cases include other persons in the category of near relations.

ARTICLE 45

1. An official entering or quitting the service during the course of a year shall only be entitled in respect of that year to an amount of ordinary annual leave proportionate to the period served by him during the year.

2. On quitting the service for any reason except dismissal for misconduct, an official, in so far as he has not received the ordinary annual leave which is allowable to him at that date under Article 43 and the present Article in respect of his past service, shall be granted either a number of days' leave on full pay equivalent to such arrears of leave or an equivalent sum of money in lieu thereof.

ARTICLE 46

1. A temporary official appointed or having served for one year shall be entitled to the same period of ordinary annual leave as if his appointment were not temporary.

2. The provisions of the preceding paragraph do not apply to officials under 21 years of age engaged under the conditions contemplated in Annex I to these Regulations, who will be entitled to twenty-four working-days' annual leave if appointed in the Second Division and to fifteen working-days' annual leave if appointed in the Third Division.

3. Temporary officials appointed for less than one year shall not be entitled to any annual leave unless they are retained in the service for not less than six months, in which case they shall be allowed leave at the rate of six working-days for each three months of service if they are officials of the First or Second Divisions, and at the rate of three working-days for each three months of service if they are officials of the Third Division.

ARTICLE 47

Special leave of absence with or without pay may, at the request of the official, be granted by the Secretary-General for urgent and exceptional reasons. Normally, such leave will not exceed six months on full or half pay, or twelve months without pay.

ARTICLE 48

With the consent of the official concerned, the Secretary-General may second an official on such terms as he considers proper to permit him to perform work outside the Secretariat or in detachment from the League of Nations.

ARTICLE 49

For the purpose of the articles of the present Regulations relating to leave, save as provided in Article 32, paragraph 2, the term "year" means the calendar year and Saturday shall be counted as a complete working-day.

ARTICLE 50

All arrangements as to leave are subject to the exigencies of the service. The personal circumstances and preferences of individual officials will, as far as possible, be considered. An official may not be recalled from leave without the express sanction of the Secretary-General.

ARTICLE 51

Save as provided in Article 47, days on which an official is sick shall not be counted in calculating leave or holidays of any kind, subject always to the applicable provisions regarding the production of medical certificates.

TRAVELLING AND REMOVAL EXPENSES AND SUBSISTENCE ALLOWANCES

ARTICLE 52

1. The travelling expenses of officials authorised to travel on the business of the League shall be defrayed by the Secretariat.

2. Officials travelling on the business of the League, or employed at a distance from the League office in which they are ordinarily employed, shall be entitled during such displacement to receive a daily subsistence allowance reasonably sufficient to defray the extra personal expenditure necessitated by the displacement.

3. Where the fare paid for the official by the League includes subsistence during the journey, subsistence allowance will not be paid in addition to the fare, but special allowances at fixed rates will be granted to cover necessary out-of-pocket expenditure.

ARTICLE 53

1. The travelling expenses of an official entering the service of the League shall be defrayed by the Secretariat from the place at which the official was residing at the time of his engagement to the place at which he is required to enter upon his duties.

2. The official shall further be entitled during this journey to receive subsistence allowance under Article 52, paragraph 2, or the special allowances provided for in Article 52, paragraph 3.

3. This Article shall not apply to locally-recruited officials of the Second Division or to officials of the Third Division.

ARTICLE 54

1. A permanent official is entitled every year, every two years or every three years, according to the distance between his home and the office in which he is employed, to be paid the cost by sea and rail of one journey to and from his home for the purpose of spending his leave there, provided always that an official appointed after March 1st, 1932, shall not be entitled to any payment under this paragraph while he is on probation, and that no more than one payment of expenses under the paragraph will be authorised in any calendar year.

2. An official who has abstained from exercising the privilege above provided for may, if he so requests, on the next occasion on which it is exercised, also be allowed travelling expenses for a member of his family who is dependent on him. No travelling expenses will be allowed for any servant who may accompany the official or member of his family.

3. The travelling expenses allowed to an official under the first paragraph of this Article shall, in his third year of service, and thereafter not more often than once in any three consecutive years, be increased, if the official so requests, so as to cover the cost of a journey to and from the official's home for his wife and his children under the age of 21 years. The same privilege shall be accorded to a woman official in respect of her husband, provided he is dependent on her, and of her children.

4. Where a husband and wife are both in the service of the League (*i.e.*, where both are officials of the Secretariat or one is an official of the Secretariat and the other an official of the International Labour Office or the Registry of the Permanent Court of International Justice), payment to the wife of travelling expenses every year, every two years or every three years under the first paragraph of this Article shall be conditional on her husband's not receiving travelling expenses for her in the period in question under the third paragraph of this Article, and payment of travelling expenses for children may not be made to both the husband and the wife in any period of three years.

5. The Secretary-General shall determine in each case what place shall be considered to be an official's "home" for the purposes of this Article, having regard to the nationality of the official and to his personal circumstances at the time of his engagement. For exceptional reasons the Secretary-General may permit a different place to be substituted, for the purposes of this Article only, for the place originally fixed as an official's home.

6. An official who desires to spend his leave at a place within the country in which his home is situated other than the place determined as his home may be paid his fares to and from such place up to and not exceeding the amount of the fares to and from his home.

7. The obligations of the Secretariat under this Article may be discharged, as regards the official himself, by allowing an official who is sent to his home on official business at the expense of the League to take his leave there before or on the conclusion of his mission and by paying the cost of his return journey. If the official takes his leave in this manner, the return journey shall be treated as official.

8. The benefit of this Article shall extend to temporary officials as though their appointments were not temporary, subject to the following conditions:

(*a*) Where the official, if his appointment were not temporary, would be entitled to the cost of his journey once in each year, the Article shall only apply if he is appointed or has served for not less than two years;

(*b*) Where the official, if his appointment were not temporary, would be entitled to the cost of his journey every two years, the

Article shall only apply if he is appointed or has served for not less than three years;

(c) Where the official, if his appointment were not temporary, would be entitled to the cost of his journey every three years, the Article shall only apply if he is appointed or has served for not less than five years.

9. The Secretary-General, after consultation of the Administrative Committee, shall determine in each case to what extent service prior to January 1st, 1931, may be taken into account in calculating the three-yearly periods mentioned in the third paragraph of this Article in connection with travelling expenses for the official's wife and children.

10. The present Article shall not apply to locally recruited officials of the Second Division or to officials of the Third Division.

ARTICLE 55

1. On final confirmation of his appointment after the completion of his period of probation, a permanent official shall be entitled to payment of the travelling expenses of his family and of the cost of removal of his furniture and effects from the place where he was ordinarily resident at the time of his engagement to the place at which he is stationed.

2. The term "family" shall mean the official's wife and such of his children as are wholly or mainly dependent upon him and may be extended according to the circumstances of the case, if the Secretary-General so decides, to include: (a) other members of the official's family who are wholly or mainly dependent upon him, and (b) a female servant who is necessary to take charge of the official's children.

3. The term "furniture and effects" shall mean any furniture and personal and household effects which the official may desire to remove for the purpose of establishing himself in the place where he is stationed, within the quantity permitted by the regulations to be made by the Secretary-General under Article 61.

4. Where an official is exempted from undergoing a period of probation, he shall be entitled to the benefit of this Article immediately upon his engagement.

5. The Secretary-General may in special cases:

(a) Allow payment to a probationer official of the travelling expenses of his family, but not the cost of removal of furniture and effects, where the Secretary-General has been informed in advance of the official's desire to be accompanied or joined by his family.

(b) Extend the benefit of this Article to temporary officials.

(c) Permit furniture and effects which were the property of the official before his engagement to be brought from more than one place, provided the maximum quantity allowable to the official is not exceeded.

6. This Article shall not apply to locally recruited officials of the Second Division or to officials of the Third Division.

ARTICLE 56

1. A permanent official who was not married at the date of confirmation of his appointment and who marries a person ordinarily resident in the country in which his home is recognised to be situated shall be entitled to be paid the travelling expenses of his wife from her place of residence to the place where the official is stationed up to, but not exceeding, the cost of travelling expenses from the place recognised as the official's home.

2. In no case may more than one payment of travelling expenses be made under this Article.

3. This Article shall not apply to locally recruited officials of the Second Division or to officials of the Third Division.

ARTICLE 57

1. An official who is obliged to change his residence in consequence of being transferred, permanently or for a substantial period, from an office of the Secretariat in which he has been definitely appointed to a position to another office of the Secretariat shall be entitled to be paid the travelling expenses of his family and the cost of removal of his furniture and effects.

2. The terms "family" and "furniture and effects" shall have the same meaning as in Article 55.

ARTICLE 58

1. A permanent or temporary official shall, on leaving the service of the Secretariat, be entitled to be paid his travelling expenses from the place at which he is stationed to any place to which he may desire to go, but not exceeding the expenses which would be payable if he returned to the place where he was ordinarily resident at the time when he was engaged, unless the Secretary-General, for special reasons in an exceptional case, shall expressly sanction the exceeding of this limit. The official shall further be entitled to subsistence allowance for the number of days for which his travelling expenses are payable by the Secretariat, subject to the provisions of Article 52, paragraph 3.

2. Where the official has been not less than two years in the service, he shall be further entitled to payment of the travelling expenses of

his family and of the cost of removal of his furniture and effects, as defined in Article 55, to any place to which he may desire to remove them, but so as not to exceed the cost of returning them to the place where he was ordinarily resident at the time of his engagement, unless the Secretary-General, for special reasons in an exceptional case, shall expressly sanction the exceeding of this limit.

3. The Secretary-General may allow payment to be made in whole or in part, under the second paragraph of this Article, notwithstanding that the official has not served the prescribed period, if in his opinion it would be a hardship for such payment not to be made; and may exempt temporary officials engaged for less than two years from the conditions as to two years' service.

4. Provided that:

(*a*) In the case of voluntary resignation of his appointment, an official shall not be entitled under this Article to any payment in respect of the travelling expenses of his family or the cost of removal of his furniture and effects, unless he has completed not less than six years' service if his appointment is for more than seven years, and in any other case not less than three years' service; or to payment of his own travelling expenses unless he has completed one year's service if the sum involved is less than 500 francs, and two years' service if the sum involved exceeds that amount. Payment may be refused if the official resigns sooner than six months after the expiry of the last period of leave in respect of which he received payment of travelling expenses from the League.

(*b*) The Secretary-General, after taking the advice of the Committee established by Article 67 (Judicial Committee), may exclude from the benefit of this Article an official who is dismissed under Article 64 or 65 for misconduct.

(*c*) In the case of an official leaving the service who is, within the meaning of the present Article, a member of the family of another official who is also leaving the service, expenses shall not be payable on both grounds, but only on one or other ground, as the person concerned may choose.

5. The present Article shall not apply to locally recruited officials of the Second Division or to officials of the Third Division.

ARTICLE 59

In the event of an official's death, his family, as defined in Article 55, shall be entitled to any travelling and removal expenses which could have been claimed by the official under Article 58 if on the day of his death he had quitted the service through normal expiration of his appointment, and to any payments which the Secretary-General could have allowed to the official under the latter Article, and the provisions of the Article shall be applied accordingly. At the request of the family, the body shall be repatriated at the expense of the League.

ARTICLE 60

Travelling expenses within the meaning of these Regulations include the cost of transport on the journey of such amount of personal luggage as is reasonable in the circumstances of the case.

ARTICLE 61

1. All payments of travelling and removal expenses and subsistence allowance provided for by Articles 52 to 60 shall be governed by, and be made in accordance with, such detailed regulations as the Secretary-General may from time to time prescribe.
2. The regulations contained in Annex III shall apply pending any further or contrary decision by the Secretary-General.

SEPTENNIAL REPORTS ON OFFICIALS' CONDUCT AND CAPACITY

ARTICLE 62

1. A report shall be made by the chief of the service concerned, at the end of each period of seven years of service, on every official of the Secretariat appointed for a term exceeding seven years. The report shall contain an opinion on the official's work, conduct and capacity. It shall be examined by the Committee on Appointments and Promotion in accordance with Article 12.
2. If either the official's work or conduct or the capacity shown by him is not satisfactory, the Secretary-General may decide that, for a period not exceeding three years, the official shall be deprived of annual increments of salary in accordance with one or other of the procedures laid down in Article 28, paragraph 3.
3. If the official has proved to be clearly incapable and his output of work inadequate, the Secretary-General may terminate his appointment, subject to due regard to the legitimate interests of the official as assured to him by the present Regulations.
4. In case of special merit, the Secretary-General may make the official a special award of not more than three annual increments.
5. Notice of the termination of an appointment under this Article shall be given in writing to the official at least six months in advance; he shall be informed of the reason for the termination of the appointment. The termination shall not disqualify the official from receiving

any benefit to which his age and length of service entitle him under the Staff Pensions Regulations.

6. The opinion of the Judicial Committee established by Article 67 shall be taken upon the proposed termination of appointment if the official so requests.

DISCIPLINARY MEASURES IN CASE OF MISCONDUCT OR INEFFICIENCY

ARTICLE 63

Subject to the provisions of the present Regulations, the tenure of all appointments and positions on the Secretariat is conditional upon the good conduct of the official and the efficient discharge by him of his duties.

ARTICLE 64

1. An official guilty of misconduct or wilful failure or negligence in the discharge of his duties may, according to the gravity of the case, be subjected by the Secretary-General to the following penalties or treatment, which may be cumulative:

(*a*) A reprimand by the Secretary-General, which shall be in writing and shall be added to the official's personal file;

(*b*) Transfer from the position occupied by him to another position;

(*c*) Reduction of salary or transfer to a lower scale of salary;

(*d*) Suspension from duty, with or without salary;

(*e*) Dismissal with such notice as may be decided or without notice, accompanied, if the Secretary-General so decides, by forfeiture, in accordance with the provisions of Article 16 of the Staff Pensions Regulations, of the official's right to the benefits provided by those Regulations.

2. Conduct by an official, unconnected with his official duties, tending to bring the Secretariat into public discredit, and, in particular, any use or attempt to make use of his position as an official for his own pecuniary advantage, may constitute misconduct.

ARTICLE 65

1. If a charge of grave misconduct is made against an official and the Secretary-General considers that the charge is *prima facie* well founded and that the official's continued discharge of his functions pending investigation of the charge would prejudice the servite, the

Secretary-General may suspend the official from his functions pending investigation, such suspension to be without prejudice to the rights of the official.

2. All such cases shall without avoidable delay be referred for investigation to, and be reported upon by, the Judicial Committee established by Article 67.

3. The powers of the Secretary-General under the present Article may be exercised by the official in charge of the secretariat of any conference or meeting held by the League outside the seat of the League in respect of the staff attending such conference or meeting. The Secretary-General shall immediately be informed.

ARTICLE 66

No action shall be taken against an official in virtue of Article 64 until the Secretary-General shall have referred the case for enquiry to the Judicial Committee established by Article 67 and shall have received and considered the Committee's report.

PARITATIVE ADVISORY COMMITTEES

ARTICLE 67

1. The Judicial Committee shall consist of two members nominated by the Secretary-General, two members elected by the staff of the Secretariat by such method as the staff may from time to time adopt and as may be approved by the Secretary-General, and a fifth member elected by the other four members.

2. The Secretary-General and the staff shall each respectively nominate or elect two substitutes to replace their representatives in the event of their being unable to sit, and the Committee shall elect one substitute to replace the member elected by it.

3. The members and substitute members of the Committee shall be nominated or elected in January of each year and shall hold office for one year from February 1st following.

4. If the composition of the Judicial Committee changes while a case is pending before it, any retiring member who has already begun to hear the case shall continue to sit as a member for the purpose of dealing with the case, if he is still an official of the Secretariat, unless the new Committee, the question having been raised by one of its members, shall otherwise decide.

5. The Committee shall elect its own Chairman, and, if it desires, also a Vice-Chairman or Vice-Chairmen, and shall determine its own

rules of procedure, subject always to the provisions that a person against whom a complaint is made and the person making the complaint in any case brought before the Committee shall, if they so wish, be heard by the Committee before its report is made and shall have access to all papers relating to the case which are submitted to the Committee.

6. The Committee, which shall be guided solely by legal considerations, shall advise the Secretary-General upon:

(a) All cases in which an official may be guilty of misconduct or wilful failure or negligence in the discharge of his duties, or be incapable of performing his duties, and become accordingly liable to disciplinary measures; and

(b) Any complaint by an official alleging that he has been treated in a manner inconsistent with the provisions of the Staff Regulations or the terms of his appointment, or that he has been subjected by a superior official to treatment which was unjustifiable or unfair.

7. The Committee's competence as regards complaints of unjustifiable or unfair treatment shall extend to cases of refusal or suspension of annual increment of salary or of dismissal of an official at the end of a seven-year period.

Article 68

1. For the purpose of advising the Secretary-General in the application of these Regulations in regard to all matters not placed within the competence of the Committees established by Article 12 (Committee on Appointments and Promotion and Re-grading Committee) or the Judicial Committee established by Article 67, or of a medical board, there shall be created a paritative advisory committee known as the Administrative Committee.

2. The Administrative Committee shall consist of one member appointed by the Secretary-General, and one elected by each of the three Divisions of the staff for the same period as the members of the Judicial Committee, and a fifth member elected by the four other members. The Treasurer shall attend meetings in an advisory capacity.

3. The Secretary-General shall appoint, and each Division of the staff shall elect, a substitute to replace their respective representatives in the event of their being unable to sit, and the Committee shall elect one substitute to replace the member elected by it.

4. The Committee shall elect its own Chairman, and, if it desires, also a Vice-Chairman or Vice-Chairmen, and determine its own rules of procedure.

5. The Administrative Committee may make proposals to the Secretary-General for the amendment of those provisions of these Regulations with which it is concerned.

STAFF COMMITTEE

ARTICLE 69

1. A committee appointed by the staff, to be known as the Staff Committee, shall be established for the purpose of ensuring continuous contact between the staff and the Secretary-General. The Committee shall be entitled to make proposals for improvements in the situation of officials, both as regards their conditions of work and their general conditions of life in Geneva.

2. The Staff Committee shall be composed in such a way as to afford equitable representation to each of the three Divisions of the staff.

ALLOWANCES BY WAY OF COMPENSATION OR ASSISTANCE

ARTICLE 70

1. An official receiving a physical injury or incurring a disease in the course and in consequence of his employment as an official shall be allowed reasonable compensation.

2. Should the official's death result from the injury or disease, reasonable compensation shall be paid to members of the official's family who were wholly or partially dependent upon him at the time of his death or, but for the injury or disease, would have been so dependent.

3. In fixing the compensation to be given, reasonable account shall be taken of any pension or capital sum which may be payable under the Staff Pensions Regulations or the Regulations of the Staff Provident Fund.

4. Claims for compensation must be submitted within a reasonable time of the date on which the accident or illness is alleged to have occured.[5] Any accident in which an official has been injured and which occurred in the course and in consequence of his employment should be notified to the Secretary-General as soon as possible. For this purpose the official must, if possible, use a prescribed form which can be obtained from the Personnel Office and must comply with the directions on the Form.

5. The application of the present Article is subject to the interpretation adopted by the Assembly in 1932.[6]

[5] In the grounds for its judgment No. 14, the Administrative Tribunal recognised that this principle "seems to answer to a legal necessity, inasmuch as, while reconciling the interests of the officials with those of the Administration, it gives the latter an opportunity of verifying the facts alleged to be the cause of the damage to be made good."
[6] This interpretation is as follows (see report of the Supervisory Commission, document

ARTICLE 71

1. A probationer official who is dismissed during the period of probation under the provisions of Article 24, after completing not less than four month's service, may be given by the Secretary-General a grant not exceeding one month's salary.

2. No grant may be given on the expiration of the period of probation.

ARTICLE 72
(Cancelled)

ARTICLE 73

1. A permanent official whose appointment is terminated under the provisions of Article 18 shall be paid a sum equal to six months' salary if he has served less than seven years and one year's salary if he has served more than seven years.

2. The provisions of the present Article shall not affect the application of the Staff Pensions Regulations.

3. The sum mentioned in paragraph 1 shall be paid in annual instalments. Each instalment shall be equal to three months' salary, or, if the instalment would then be less than 1,200 Swiss francs, to a sum as near as possible to 1,200 francs within the limits of the total amount due.

4. If an official's contract has been suspended, the payment made on suspension shall be deducted from the total amount payable under this Article.

ARTICLE 74

1. In case of discharge or resignation on grounds of health and in case of death, where the causes of the ill-health or death are not imputable to the service, no payments may be made by the Secretary-General to the official or his representatives or dependants beyond such payments as may be assured by the Regulations of the Staff

A.5(b).1932.X, page 7, adopted by the Assembly on October 17th, 1932). "The applicant for compensation must prove both that the accident or illness was incurred while he was engaged in executing his duty and also that it was the materialisation of a risk involved in the nature of the work which he was performing or the circumstances in which he was performing it, and not, for example, of a quite general risk or a risk to which by his own act or negligence he had unnecessarily exposed himself. The idea that it is sufficient to prove that the accident or illness would not have been incurred if the official's work had not led to his being in a particular place at the moment when it was incurred must be rejected. Moreover, there cannot be any liability on the League of Nations where the official brings an injury upon himself or incurs a disease by wilful negligence or misconduct in performing a work of a perfectly safe kind on premises and with appliances which are perfectly suited to their purpose."

Provident Fund of the League of Nations or the Staff Pensions Regulations, except always in the case contemplated by Article 39 of the present Regulations.

2. The Secretary-General may, however, in cases of retirement through ill-health, or of death, of officials who are neither members of the Staff Provident Fund nor subject to the Pensions Regulations, grant a limited sum as financial assistance to the official or his dependants.

MISCELLANEOUS PROVISIONS

ARTICLE 75

In these Regulations and the Annexes thereto, words importing either gender include the other, except where the contrary intention appears from the context.

ARTICLE 76

A personal file shall be kept for each official, containing the originals or copies of the documents constituting his appointment, and of all documents relating to his service or conduct which constitute official action or of which official notice has been taken. The file shall be shown to the official at his request.

ARTICLE 77

The present Regulations do not apply to employees, whether working on the premises of the Secretariat or not, who do not hold appointments as officials of the Secretariat.

ARTICLE 78

1. Nothing in the present Regulations shall be interpreted as preventing the Secretary-General from appointing officials with terms of service different from those contemplated in the present Regulations, in execution of decisions of the Council or the Assembly, or where he considers that the interests of the service so require. In the event of any difference or conflict between the present Regulations and the terms of service agreed upon with a particular official, the latter shall prevail.

2. Any case in which the Secretary-General may be led to take, in regard to any official, any measure different from what is provided in the present Regulations shall be notified to the Supervisory Commission established by the Regulations for the Financial Administration of the League of Nations, in so far as such measure entails expenditure which would not otherwise be incurred.

3. No exceptional measure not in conformity with the present Regulations may be taken except with the agreement of the official concerned and subject to its not being prejudicial to any other official or to any category of official.

ARTICLE 79

The powers of the Secretary-General under these Regulations are exercised on his behalf by the officer in charge of Internal Administration: provided always that a final decision regarding action on a recommendation of any of the advisory committees referred to in these Regulations, and amendments of the Regulations or the Annexes thereto, shall require the approval of the Secretary-General.

ARTICLE 80

The present Regulations and their Annexes may be amended by the Secretary-General, without prejudice always to the acquired rights of officials. Any amendments that the Secretary-General may have introduced shall be reported to the Assembly at its next ordinary session.

FINAL ARTICLE

The present Regulations shall come into force on January 1st, 1931, and shall supersede the Staff Regulations in force before that date. Existing terms of appointment shall be maintained except in so far as new terms shall by agreement be substituted therefor.

V. DIPLOMATIC IMMUNITIES ACCORDED TO THE STAFF OF THE LEAGUE OF NATIONS AND OF THE INTERNATIONAL LABOR OFFICE

1. COMMUNICATIONS FROM THE SWISS FEDERAL COUNCIL CONCERNING DIPLOMATIC IMMUNITIES TO BE ACCORDED TO THE STAFF OF THE LEAGUE OF NATIONS AND OF THE INTERNATIONAL LABOUR OFFICE

Report by M. Titulesco, adopted by the Council on September 20th, 1926.[1]

Certain questions relating to the application of Article 7, paragraph 4, of the Covenant (diplomatic immunities) were laid before the Council, which decided at its session in March last to adjourn discussion of these questions to a later session, in order to allow the Swiss Federal Government and the Secretary-General to continue the negotiations

[1]Document [C.558.1926.V.]. Reprinted from *Official Journal*, October, 1926, p. 1422. See also the following major Conventions on Privileges and Immunities which have been adopted by the General Assembly of the United Nations: (1) "Resolution [22(I)A] Relating to the Adoption of the General Convention on Privileges and Immunities of the United Nations, and Text of the Convention," adopted on February 13, 1946, in *Resolutions Adopted by the General Assembly during the First Part of Its First Session*, United Nations Document A/64, July 1, 1946, p. 25–28. (2) "Interim Arrangement on Privileges and Immunities of the United Nations Concluded between the Secretary-General of the United Nations and the Swiss Federal Council. Signed at Berne, on 11 June 1946, and at New York, on 1 July 1946. Approved by the General Assembly of the United Nations on 14 December 1946," in United Nations, *Treaty Series*, Vol. I (1946–1947), p. 163–179. (3) "Agreement between the United Nations and the United States of America regarding the Headquarters of the United Nations," adopted by Resolution 169(II) of the General Assembly of the United Nations on October 31, 1947, in *Official Records of the Second Session of the General Assembly. Resolutions*, United Nations Document A/519, January 8, 1948, p. 91–102. (4) (a) "Resolution [22(I)C] on the Privileges and Immunities of the International Court of Justice," adopted on February 13, 1946, in *Resolutions Adopted by the General Assembly during the First Part of Its First Session*, United Nations Document A/64, July 1, 1946, p. 33. (b) "Agreement Concerning the Privileges and Immunities of the Court, the Registrar and the Staff of the Registry in the Netherlands, Dated June 26th, 1946," in *International Court of Justice. Series D. No. 1* (1946), p. 84–87. For text of the "General Principles," supplemented by "Rules of Application" of May 22, 1928 relating to the "External Status of Members of the Permanent Court of International Justice," see *Official Journal* (July, 1928), p. 985–987; see also *ibid.*, p. 866, and *Permanent Court of International Justice. Series E. No. 4*, p. 57–63. (5) "Agreement of March 11, 1946,

which they had begun with a view to reaching a satisfactory arrangement.

For the history of this question, I beg to refer you to the following documents:

Memorandum addressed to the Secretary-General by M. G. Motta, Federal Councillor, Head of the Federal Political Department (document C.92.1926.V);

Extract from the Correspondence exchanged between the Federal Political Department at Berne and the Secretary-General (document C.66.1926.V);

Observations presented by the Secretary-General on the Memorandum by the Federal Political Department (document C.127. 1926.V).

The negotiations, after a second adjournment ordered by the Council at its June session, have resulted in a fresh arrangement for the exercise in Switzerland of the diplomatic immunities laid down by Article 7 of the Covenant.

Avoiding all discussion on the legal interpretation of Article 7, paragraph 4, of the Covenant, the agreement contains practical rules on all of which the Swiss Federal Government, the Secretary-General of the League of Nations and the Director of the International Labour Office have declared their agreement. The Council will no doubt be glad to find that the negotiations, for which it had decided to adjourn the examination of this question, have resulted in a satisfactory solution and that the matter can be struck off its agenda. I would therefore simply propose that the Council should take note of the arrangement agreed to (Annex 911 a) and should thank the representative of Switzerland for the good-will he has constantly shown in the settlement of this matter.

---

between the Swiss Federal Council and the International Labour Organization Concerning the Legal Status of the International Labour Organization in Switzerland and Arrangement for the Execution of the Agreement," in *International Labour Office. Official Bulletin*, Vol. XXXIX, No. 1 (August 31, 1946), p. 48. (6) (*a*) "Resolution [22(I)D] on the Co-ordination of the Privileges and Immunities of the United Nations and the Specialized Agencies," adopted on February 13, 1946 by the General Assembly of the United Nations, in *Resolutions Adopted by the General Assembly during the First Part of Its First Session*, United Nations Document A/64, July 1, 1946, p. 33. (*b*) "Convention on the Privileges and Immunities of the Specialized Agencies," adopted by Resolution 179(II) of the General Assembly of the United Nations on November 21, 1947, in *Official Records of the Second Session of the General Assembly. Resolutions*, United Nations Document A/519, January 8, 1948, p. 112–130.

It should be noted that in United Nations Document A/519 the texts of Annex V (The International Monetary Fund) and Annex VI (The International Bank for Reconstruction and Development) are not final. The final form of these Annexes were filed with the United Nations by the Bank and the Fund in April, 1949 and May, 1949, respectively.

2. COMMUNICATIONS FROM THE SWISS FEDERAL COUNCIL CONCERNING THE DIPLOMATIC IMMUNITIES TO BE ACCORDED TO THE STAFF OF THE LEAGUE OF NATIONS AND OF THE INTERNATIONAL LABOUR OFFICE

Note by the Secretary-General, submitted to the Council on September 20th, 1926.[2]

Geneva, September 18th, 1926.

The Secretary-General has the honour to submit to the Council the text of a new *modus vivendi* concerning the diplomatic immunities of the staff of the League organisations at Geneva. This text has been accepted both by the Federal Government and by the Secretary-General and the Director of the International Labour Office.

I

The Swiss Federal Government recognises that the League of Nations, which possesses international personality and legal capacity, cannot, in principle, according to the rules of international law, be sued before the Swiss Courts without its express consent.

II

The premises in which the services of the League of Nations (Secretariat and International Labour Office) are installed (in the case of buildings entirely occupied by League offices, the buildings themselves, together with gardens and annexes) are inviolable, that is to say, no agent of the public authority may enter them, in the exercise of his duties, without the consent of the Secretariat or of the International Labour Office.

III

The archives of the League of Nations are inviolable.

IV

The Secretary-General of the League of Nations and the Director of the International Labour Office are entitled to use couriers for the reception and despatch of official correspondence with the Members of the League of Nations and its agents outside Switzerland.

[2]Document [C.555.1926.V.]. Reprinted from *Official Journal*, October, 1926, p. 1422–1424.

V

Customs exemption is granted to the League of Nations in respect of all objects, whether intended to form an integral part of a building or not, which are the absolute property of the League and are destined for its exclusive use.

VI

The League of Nations shall enjoy complete fiscal exemption in respect of its bank assets (current and deposit accounts) and its securities.

In particular, it shall be exempted from the stamp duty on coupons instituted by the Federal Law of June 25th, 1921. The exemption shall be effected by the repayment to the League of Nations of the duty levied on its assets.

VII

Subject to the provisions of Article IX below, officials of the organisations of the League of Nations at Geneva who are members of the staff of the first category or extra-territorial staff shall enjoy immunity from civil and criminal jurisdiction in Switzerland, unless such immunity is waived by a decision of the Secretary-General or of the Director of the International Labour Office.

The members of the staff of the second category shall enjoy the same privileges in respect of acts performed by them in their official capacity and within the limits of their functions. They shall remain subject to local laws and jurisdiction in respect of acts performed by them in their private capacity.

It is clearly understood, however, that the organisations of the League of Nations at Geneva will endeavour to facilitate the proper administration of justice and execution of police regulations at Geneva.

VIII

Officials of the organisations of the League of Nations who are members of the staff of the first category enjoy fiscal immunity. Consequently, they are exempted, in accordance with international practice, from all direct taxes, with the exception of the charges attaching to immovable property (the land tax). They are liable for the payment of indirect taxes and charges. The expression "direct taxes" shall be understood to mean taxes which are levied directly upon the taxpayer. "Charges"—whatever the expression employed in the regulations governing the matter may be—shall only be understood to mean payments in return for the rendering of a special and definite service by the administration to the person who pays them, together with those which are paid in order to cover special expenditure necessitated by an act of the taxpayer.

Members of the staff of the second category are exempted:

(1) From the tax (*taxe*) on salary (*revenu professionnel*);

(2) From the tax (*taxe*) on capital (*fortune*) or income (*revenu*);

(3) From the Emergency Federal War Tax.

IX[3]

In the case of members of the staff of Swiss nationality, the following exceptions are instituted:

1. Officials of Swiss nationality may not be sued before the local courts in respect of acts performed by them in their official capacity and within the limits of their official duties.

2. The salaries paid to them by the League of Nations are exempted from cantonal and municipal direct taxes.

X

The Customs examination of packages, etc., addressed to the officials of the organisations of the League of Nations shall be effected in accordance with the regulations (*prescriptions*) the text of which was communicated to the Secretary-General of the League by the Head of the Federal Political Department on January 10th, 1926.

XI

If the exigencies of training and the interests of the country permit, exemptions from or postponements of military service shall be granted to officials of Swiss nationality incorporated in the Federal Army in cases in which their compliance with an order calling them up for military service would be likely seriously to interfere with the normal working of the services of the League.

XII

Correspondence relating to the application of the rules of the *modus vivendi* between the organisations of the League of Nations and the Swiss authorities shall be exchanged through the intermediary of the Federal Political Department, except in cases in which some other procedure has been prescribed.

[3]As regards the Federal War Tax, see annexed note on page 478, following.

XIII

The present provisions complete or summarise, but do not abrogate, the rules previously established by an exchange of notes between the organisations of the League of Nations and the Federal Political Department.

XIV

As long as the present arrangement remains in force, the examination of the legal arguments set forth in the notes of February 24th and March 5th, 1926, shall not be proceeded with.

The above rules of the *modus vivendi* can only be modified by agreement between the organisations of the League of Nations and the Federal Political Department. If, however, an agreement cannot be reached, it shall always be open to the Federal Government or to the organisations of the League of Nations to denounce the whole or part of the rules of the *modus vivendi*. In this case, the rules mentioned in the denouncement shall remain in force for one year from the date of such denouncement.

NOTE CONCERNING THE FEDERAL WAR TAX (MEMBERS OF THE STAFF OF SWISS NATIONALITY).

As regards the exemption from the Federal War Tax granted to members of the staff of Swiss nationality, the present position is as follows:

A letter of July 17th, 1926, from the Federal Political Department shows that the Federal Council is prepared to exempt from this tax the salary of officials of Swiss nationality until the expiration of the contracts of service which the persons concerned at present hold and which make provision for a salary payable free of taxes. By means of this temporary exemption, the Federal Council desires to prevent the possibility of the payment of the Federal War Tax resulting, through the operation of the clauses of the contracts in force, in imposing, even indirectly, any charge upon the budget of the League of Nations. In view of the character and special object of the Federal War Tax and certain considerations of principle, the Federal Council does not feel able to contemplate permanent exemption.

As the Secretary-General has accepted the arrangement proposed by Federal Council as regards the contracts at present in force, but considers it necessary to give further consideration to the various legal and administrative difficulties which might arise from differentiations in contracts, a final solution has not up to now been reached.

3. CIRCULAR REGARDING THE RIGHTS CONFERRED AND THE OBLIGATIONS IMPOSED UPON MEMBERS OF THE SECRETARIAT OF THE LEAGUE OF NATIONS BY ARTICLE 7 OF THE COVENANT[4]

This Circular is issued for the purpose of calling the attention of the Staff of the Secretariat to the special status of the officials of the League of Nations, and of supplying them with the necessary information regarding the diplomatic privileges and immunities to which they are entitled.

The Secretary-General is confident that the officials of the Secretariat will always scrupulously observe the provisions set out below, and that they will constantly bear in mind the obligations which their privileged position imposes upon them. He would further remind the members of the staff that, notwithstanding the immunities which they enjoy, they are bound to observe the laws and regulations in force in Switzerland and that, in particular, they must scrupulously comply with all provisions regarding public safety and the maintenance of order (traffic regulations, police regulations for streets and public places, etc.).

I. OFFICIALS OF NATIONALITY OTHER THAN SWISS

The staff is divided into two categories:

A. Members of the first category (in possession of pink identity cards).

B. Members of the second category (in possession of blue identity cards).

A.—Members of the First Category, "Extra-territorial Staff"

This part of the staff enjoys in principle the same diplomatic privileges and immunities as are granted to the Diplomatic Corps at Berne, *i.e.*:

(1) Immunity from civil and criminal jurisdiction in Switzerland unless such immunity is waived. Should the question of waiver arise, the Secretary-General should be consulted beforehand by the official concerned.[5]

It need hardly be added that administrative or disciplinary action involving, in certain contingencies, even the dismissal of the official, may be taken, if necessary, by the Secretary-General.

This immunity does not preclude the lodging of a complaint with the official's national authorities should such action appear desirable,

---

[4] A classified document, dated Geneva, May 1st, 1928, distributed exclusively to the Secretariat. Footnotes 5, 6, 7, and 8 are as in the original document.
[5] For all details see Official Circular 5/1927. of January 30th, 1927.

although it is of course always understood that the officials of the League of Nations are not in any way responsible, as regards their duties, to any national government.

(2) Fiscal immunity: general exemption from direct personal taxes and taxes on luxuries, general taxes on property whether in the form of capital or income, and from war-taxes (*décimes de guerre*).

This does not apply to charges *in rem* on immovable property (land tax) and to death duties to which they may be liable as heirs or legatees of a person who has died in Switzerland, or as beneficiaries by a gift *inter vivos*, where the donor was domiciled in Switzerland, it being understood that the transfer *mortis causa* or by gift *inter vivos* of property belonging to officials enjoying diplomatic privileges continues to be exempted from all taxation.

By a Decree dated June 14th, 1921, of the Council of State of the Republic and Canton of Geneva, the members of the first category of the staff are exempt within the Canton of Geneva from the payment of:

(*a*) The tax on professional revenue (*traitement*) *i.e.*, earned income (salaries).

(*b*) Tax on fortune or revenue, *i.e.*, property or income.

(*c*) *Taxes accessoires* or *somptuaires*, *i.e.*, incidental taxes and taxes on luxuries, not including shooting and fishing licenses.

The staff of the Secretariat are, moreover, exempt from the Emergency Federal War-Tax. (Federal Decree dated September 28th, 1920.)

All charges due to the Swiss authorities for services rendered must be paid should application for such payment be made. For example, the cost price of a motor-car plate, charges for inspecting motor-cars and boats, registry-office fees and Chancellery fees (legal documents, issue of deeds), fees for registration of marriage particulars and for entries in the land register, and Court fees may be mentioned.

(3) Privileges regarding Customs and visa formalities:

The following are permitted to introduce free of Customs duty all articles intended for their personal use: the Secretary-General of the League of Nations, the Assistant Secretary-General, Under-Secretaries-General and Directors. The baggage of these officials is also, in principle, not subject to examination by Customs officers.

The members of the first category of the staff, excluding the Secretary-General, the Assistant Secretary-General, Under-Secretaries-General and Directors, are entitled to introduce free of duty only new articles required when they first establish a home (*première installation*), etc. (To obtain this franchise, please consult the Establishment Officer.)[6] The formalities connected with the examination of the

---

[6]For regulations regarding Customs see Office Circulars 56 and 56a of October 5th, 1926.

luggage of such officials by Customs officers are, however, to be limited to what is absolutely necessary.

The members of this category of the Staff are entitled to diplomatic visas on their passports.

(4) Permits for temporary or permanent residence (*permis de séjour ou d'établissement*).

Members of the Staff are exempt from the obligation of reporting in person to the police authorities directly and submitting their identity papers.

Any person who claims exemption from the obligation of reporting to the police and submitting his papers, but whose name does not appear in the official lists communicated by the Secretariat, can be called upon to furnish evidence of his status as an official. In such a case the identity card issued by the Federal Political Department, or an official statement on the part of the Secretariat, will be regarded as sufficient evidence.

The wife, children, parents and parents-in-law of an official in this category enjoy the same privileges as the official in regard to *permis de séjour ou d'établissement*, provided they reside with the official and do not exercise any vocation.

Domestic employees of this category of the staff (governesses, housekeepers, domestic servants, private secretaries) are subject to the Federal and Cantonal regulations with regard to temporary or permanent residence.

Only the domestic employees of the high officials mentioned below are, provisionally, exempt from the obligation of reporting in person to the police authorities: the Secretary-General, the Assistant Secretary-General, Under-Secretaries-General and Directors.

The wife and children of an official of the first category are, as a general rule, granted the same status as the head of the family, provided they reside with him and do not exercise any vocation in Geneva.

In order to afford the families of members of the Secretariat of the first category facilities for staying in Switzerland elsewhere than at Geneva, the Federal Political Department at Berne has kindly consented, upon receiving notice from the Secretariat, to inform the cantonal authority concerned directly, in order to prevent requests to take out *permis de séjour*, claims for taxation, etc., from being sent to such persons.

Any officials of the Secretariat intending to send members of their family for more than three months to a place in Switzerland other than Geneva are accordingly recommended to give notice beforehand to the Establishment Office, which will forward such information to Berne. The Federal Political Department recommends that persons taking advantage of these facilities should see that their passports, which will be visaed by the Federal Political Department, are in order, and requests them to hand them to the authorities on demand.

B.—Members of the Staff of the Second Category[7]

(a) Complete immunity in respect of acts performed in their official capacity and within the limits of their duties.

They are, however, subject to local laws and jurisdiction in respect of acts performed in their private capacity.

(b) Permits of residence (permis de séjour):

Officials of this category are exempt from the obligation of reporting in person to the police authorities and submitting their identity papers.

The wife, children, parents and parents-in-law of a member of the staff of the second category enjoy the same privileges, provided they reside with him and do not exercise any vocation.

What is said above with regard to officials of the first category whose names do not appear in the list of the staff applies equally to the second category of the staff.

The ruling given above concerning families of members staying in Switzerland elsewhere than at Geneva also applies in this case.

(c) Fiscal immunity:

In accordance with the Federal Decree dated September 28th, 1920, and the Decree dated June 14th, 1921, of the Council of the State of the Canton of Geneva, staff of the second category are exempt from the payment of:

1. Tax on professional revenue (traitement), i.e., earned income (salaries).
2. Tax on "fortune," i.e., property or income.

The members of this category are, moreover, exempt from payment of the Emergency Federal War-Tax imposed by the Federal Decree, dated September 28th, 1920.

The same regulations as for officials of the first category apply to payment of charges due to the Swiss authorities for services rendered (see above).

The wife and children of a member of the staff of the second category are, as a general rule, granted the same status as the head of the family, provided they reside with him and do not exercise any vocation in Geneva.

II. Swiss Members of Staff

Members of the Secretariat who are Swiss nationals are regarded by the Swiss Government as occupying a position distinct from that of the so-called "extra-territorial" staff and the second category of

[7]For regulations regarding Customs see Office Circulars 56 and 56a of October 5th, 1926.

staff. As a general rule, therefore, they do not enjoy the same advantages and privileges as attach to those grades.

It should, however, be mentioned that Swiss nationals who are officials of the League of Nations enjoy the following privileges:

(1) Immunity from jurisdiction in respect of acts performed in their official capacity and within the limits of their duties;

(2) Exemption, under the Decree of the Council of State, dated June 14th, 1921, within the Canton of Geneva, from the payment of the taxe sur le revenue professionnel on the salary which they receive from the League of Nations.[8]

Further, subject to the fulfilment of all the formalities prescribed in the legal provisions relating to votes and elections (deposit of certificates of origin, declaration, etc.) they are exempt from the obligation to take out a *permis de séjour* or a *permis d'établissement*.

III. TRAFFIC REGULATIONS AND PUBLIC SAFETY

The *Règlement général* (General Regulations) for traffic and public safety applies to all officials and employees of the League of Nations.

Officials of the Secretariat, to whatever class they may belong, are therefore bound, particularly for purposes of travel in the Canton of Geneva and throughout Switzerland, to carry out the usual formalities (driving tests and inspection of cars in the case of motor-cars, inspection of boats, number-plates for motor-cars and bicycles).

It is understood, however, that officials holding international motor-car licences issued by their national authorities, or driving licences from their national authorities which entitle them to international motor-car licences without further driving test, may, on presentation of these documents, when such documents have been issued after a driving test has been passed before the national authority, take out the Geneva licence without a further driving test.

Cars belonging to officials of the first category are provided with a distinctive mark in addition to the usual number-plate; this distinctive mark, however, is optional.

IV. OFFENCES

The extra-territorial staff (Category 1) is not liable to appear before the Swiss Courts. If, however, breaches of the Swiss laws and regulations should take place, the Secretary-General will not fail to take administrative or disciplinary measures, including dismissal if necessary, against the delinquents.

[8] For the Federal War-Tax and Federal Military Tax see Office Circular 57/1926 of October 7th, 1926, which also gives information about military service.

V. Miscellaneous

Officials of the League of Nations are particularly requested (though no arrangement has been made on this subject with the Federal or the Cantonal Government) to take every precaution to avoid incurring, by contract, any liability for the fulfilment of obligations which might be incompatible with their position in the Secretariat at Geneva.

It seems desirable, for instance, that a special clause should be inserted in leases to provide for the cancellation of the lease as a result of an unexpected departure, whether due to removal of the seat of the League of Nations outside the Canton of Geneva or to the despatch of the official on other League of Nations duty, or in case of the death or dismissal of the lessee.

Lists of members of the staff enjoying diplomatic immunities will be drawn up from time to time by the Establishment Office. These lists will be sent to the authorities at Berne, who will circulate them to the various administrative services of the Confederation and the Canton of Geneva.

As it is highly desirable that the lists in the possession of the Swiss authorities should be as complete as possible, officials of the Secretariat are particularly requested to keep the Establishment Office informed of alterations, changes of address, etc.

(*signed*) ERIC DRUMMOND.

VI. STATUTE OF THE LEAGUE OF NATIONS ADMINISTRATIVE TRIBUNAL. ADOPTED AT GENEVA, SEPTEMBER 26, 1927[1]

Art. 1. There is established by the present Statute a Tribunal to be known as the "League of Nations Administrative Tribunal."

Art. 2—1. The Tribunal shall be competent to hear complaints alleging non-observance, in substance or in form, of the terms of appointment of officials of the Secretariat or of the International Labour Office, and of such provisions of the Staff Regulations as are applicable to the case.

2. The Tribunal shall be competent to settle any dispute concerning the compensation provided for by Articles 43 or 71 of the Staff Regulations of the Secretariat or Articles 96 *bis* or 61 *ter* of the Staff Regulations of the International Labour Office and to fix finally the amount of compensation, if any, which is to be paid.

3. The Tribunal shall be open:

(a) To the official, even if his employment has ceased, and to any person on whom the official's rights have devolved on his death:

(b) To any other persons who can show that he is entitled to some right under the terms of appointment of a deceased official or under provisions of the Staff Regulations on which the official could rely.

4. Any dispute as to the competence of the Tribunal shall be decided by it.

Art. 3.—1. The Tribunal shall consist of three judges and three deputy-judges, who shall all be of different nationalities. The judges and deputy-judges shall be appointed by the Council of the League of Nations for the period of three years, subject to the establishment by the Council of transitional measures to permit part only of the Tribunal to be renewed each year. The Tribunal shall elect a President and Vice-President from among the judges.

2. A meeting of the Tribunal shall be composed of three members, of whom one at least must be a judge.

Art. 4. The Tribunal shall hold ordinary sessions at dates to be fixed by the Rules of Court, subject to there being, in the opinion of the President, of a character to justify holding the session. An extraordinary session may be convened at the request of the Acting Presi-

[1] In force, September 26, 1927. Text from League of Nations Document T.A.4.

dent of the Council or of the Chairman of the Governing Body of the International Labour Office.

Art. 5. The Tribunal shall decide in each case whether the oral proceedings before it or any part of them shall be public or in camera.

Art. 6. The Tribunal shall take decisions by a majority vote; judgments shall be final and without appeal. The reasons for a judgment shall be stated. The judgment shall be communicated in writing to the head of the administration concerned and to the complainant.

Judgments shall be drawn up in two copies, one of which shall be filed in the archives of the Secretariat and the other in the archives of the International Labour Office, where they shall be available for consultation by any person concerned.

Art. 7. A complaint shall not be receivable unless the decision impugned is a final decision and the person concerned has exhausted such other means of resisting it as are open to him under the applicable Staff Regulations.

To be receivable, a complaint must also have been filed within ninety days after the complainant was notified of the decision affecting a class of officials, after the decision was published.

Where the administration fails to take a decision upon any claim of an official within sixty days from the notification of the claim to it, the person concerned may have recourse to the Tribunal and his complaint shall be receivable in the same manner as a complaint against a final decision. The period of ninety days provided for by the last preceding paragraph shall run from the expiration of the sixty days allowed for the taking of the decision by the Administration.

The filing of a complaint shall not involve suspension of the execution of the decision impugned.

Art. 8. No action shall be taken upon a complaint unless the complainant deposits with the administration concerned, within the ninety days allowable under Article 7, an amount equal to one-fifth of his annual salary (net salary).

The Tribunal, when pronouncing judgment, will order the refund of the deposit to the complainant if and in so far as it considers that there were sufficient grounds for presenting the complaint.

Art. 9. In cases falling under Article 2, paragraph 1, the Tribunal, if satisfied that the complaint was well founded, shall order the rescinding of a decision or execution of an obligation is not possible or advisable, the Tribunal shall award the complainant compensation for the injury caused to him.

Art. 10.—1. The administrative arrangements necessary for the operation of the Tribunal shall be made by the Secretariat and the International Labour Office in consultation with the Tribunal.

2. Expenses occasioned by sessions of the Tribunal, other than expenses attributable to the hearing of particular complaints, shall be

divided between the Secretariat and the International Labour Office in equal shares or in such proportion as the Assembly may determine. The expenses attributable to the hearing of a complaint shall be borne by the administration against which the complaint is made.

3. Any compensation awarded by the Tribunal shall be chargeable to the budget of the administration concerned.

Art. 11. Subject to the provisions of the present Statute, the Tribunal shall draw up Rules of Court covering:

The election of the President and Vice-President;

The convening and conduct of its sessions;

The rules to be followed in presenting complaints and in the subsequent procedure, including intervention in the proceedings before the Tribunal by persons whose rights as officials may be affected by the judgment;

And, generally, all matters relating to the operation of the Tribunal which are not settled by the present statute.

The Tribunal may amend the Rules of Court.

Art. 12. If the decision impugned was notified to the person concerned or was published after December 31st, 1927 but before the date at which the Tribunal first constituted itself, such decision, for the purposes of Article 7, shall be deemed to have been notified or published at the date at which the Tribunal first constituted itself.

The present Statute shall remain in force during the pleasure of the Assembly.

VII. GENERAL REGULATIONS ON COMMITTEES[1]

1. DURATION OF COMMITTEES

1. Committees shall continue for the period necessitated by the character of their task.

2. If a Committee has not met for two consecutive years, the Council of the League of Nations shall consider whether this Committee should continue in existence. To this end, the Secretary-General shall communicate to the Council at its January session a complete list of Committees, at the same time indicating any which are in this position.

This rule shall, of course, not apply if the statutes of the Committee give it a permanent character.

2. DUTIES OF COMMITTEES

The duty of Committees is to study the questions in their province as defined by a Convention or by the Assembly's or Council's terms of reference, and advise the Council on these questions.

3. REPORTS OF COMMITTEES

Committees shall report to the Council on the work of each of their sessions.

In the absence of any decision to the contrary by the Committee in a particular case, the report shall be communicated simultaneously to the Council and to the Members of the League.

4. PROGRAMMES OF WORK

In reporting to the Council, Committees must indicate their programme of work for the subsequent year or any other suitable period, this programme being drawn up on the basis of their terms of reference. They shall make special mention of any new work which they may propose to undertake.

5. REQUESTS FOR INFORMATION

1. Within the limits of their competence, Committees may ask the

[1]Reprinted from *Official Journal*, February, 1936, p. 131–133.

Secretary-General, or through him, for any information necessary for the performance of their task. They may, in particular, ask for consultations of experts.

2. If the obtaining of this information necessitates any outlay, Committees must make a proposal to this effect to the Secretary-General. The Secretary-General may act on this proposal in so far as budgetary credits permit.

3. Committees may not proceed to a general consultation of Governments without the Council's approval.

6. Chairmen

1. Each Committee shall appoint its chairman.

2. The Committee shall fix the chairman's term of office, while bearing in mind the necessity for making possible reasonably frequent changes.

The term of office shall not be less than one year.

7. Bureaux and Sub-Committees

1. Committees may appoint a bureau, sub-committees, etc. from among their members. The bureau and sub-committees shall report to the Committee. They may not send reports direct to the Council without the latter's consent. The Council's consent shall also be necessary before the bureau or sub-committees can assume the duties belonging to the Committee itself.

2. Committees may not appoint permanently or temporarily sub-committees or delegations consisting, in whole or in part, of persons other than members of the Committee, without the Council's authorisation.

3. Cases in which it is merely desired to ask an expert to provide information or conduct an enquiry are governed by Article 5.

8. Publicity of Meetings

1. Committees shall decide whether their meetings are to be public.

2. If meetings are private, Committees may decide to admit permanent delegates or other representatives of the Members of the League, duly authorised by their Governments, to attend their proceedings.

3. Such delegates or representatives shall be required to observe the discretion which, in any case, is incumbent upon the members of the Committee.

9. Appointment of Members

1. The Council shall appoint the members of Committees, as far as possible, at its January session.

2. Appointments shall be made by the Council on the nomination of the Rapporteur to the Council in consultation with the Secretary-General. Proposals for appointments to technical Committees working in closely related spheres[2] shall be submitted by the Rapporteur jointly.

3. The Rapporteur or Rapporteurs in making their nomination, and the Council in taking its decision, shall bear in mind the nationality and personal position of the candidate (official or private occupations, age, etc.) from the standpoint of the experience, influence and activity he can bring to the Committee's service.

4. The principles of the foregoing paragraph should also be borne in mind by Governments when appointing their delegates to Governmental committees.

10. Tenure of Office of Members

1. *Committees composed of Government representatives.*—The mandate is conferred on a Government. It shall last for not more than three years. It shall be renewable, unless the Council, in order to facilitate rotation, has decided otherwise.

2. *Committees consisting of members appointed in their personal capacity.*—The term of office shall be not more than three years, but shall be renewable. The Council shall nevertheless bear in mind the necessity of ensuring reasonably frequent renewal of the membership of Committees.

11. Resignation

The resignation of a member of a Committee shall take effect as from the date on which the Secretary-General has received notice of resignation from the member concerned.

12. Prolonged Absence

A Government which has not sent a representative for two years to a Committee consisting of Government representatives, or a person belonging to a Committee in his individual capacity who has not attended a meeting for two years, shall cease to form part of the Committee.

[2] As in the case of the Financial, Economic and Communications Committees.

13. Replacement during Term of Office

If, during a term of office, a Government or person member of a Committee ceases to belong thereto, such Government or person shall be replaced for the remainder of the term of office.

14. States Withdrawing from the League

1. A Government which has been appointed member of a Committee in its capacity as Member of the League, shall cease to be a member of the Committee if it ceases to belong to the League.

2. Nevertheless, in the case of a Committee to which States not members of the League may belong, the Council may reappoint the Government in question.

15. Substitutes

1. *Committees consisting of representatives of Governments.*—Governments represented on a Committee may at any time change or replace their representative on giving notice to the Committee.

2. *Members appointed in an individual capacity.*—(*a*) If the Council or the Assembly has appointed substitutes, titular members may only be replaced by the substitute members thus appointed.

(*b*) A titular member who falls ill or is prevented from attending may send a temporary substitute to replace him, with the consent of the chairman of the Committee and of the Secretary-General.

If the titular member has not proposed a substitute, the latter may be appointed by the President of the Council after consultation with the Rapporteur to the Council.

The substitute member should, in principle, possess the same qualifications as the titular member.

(*c*) The replacement of a titular member by a substitute member shall not involve expenditure materially greater than previously allowed for.

16. Associate or Correspondent Members and Assessors

1. Associate or correspondent members and assessors may in special cases be appointed by the Council or by the Committee with the Council's authorisation.

2. Such members or assessors shall not be entitled to vote.

17. Members' Allowances

1. The expenses of members of Committees appointed in a personal

capacity shall be paid out of the budget of the League of Nations under the conditions laid down by the Assembly.

2. It shall be for the Governments themselves to pay the expenses of their representatives on Governmental Committees.

18. APPLICATION OF THE PRESENT REGULATIONS

1. The above rules shall apply to all the Committees of the League of Nations in the absence of any provision to the contrary in their statutes or regulations.

2. Committees already possessing a statute or rules of procedure shall submit them to the Council during the year 1936 and, if possible, before the seventeenth ordinary session of the Assembly, in order that their provisions may be brought into line with the above rules.

Committees shall submit all necessary proposals in this connection.

3. The Council may authorise derogations to the above rules. Certain derogations are already provided for in Part IV of the report.

4. Committees which may be set up in future shall submit their draft rules of procedure for endorsement by the Council.

VIII. THE REGISTRATION AND PUBLICATION OF TREATIES AS PRESCRIBED UNDER ARTICLE 18 OF THE COVENANT OF THE LEAGUE OF NATIONS. MEMORANDUM APPROVED BY THE COUNCIL OF THE LEAGUE OF NATIONS, MEETING IN ROME, ON MAY 19, 1920[1]

1. One of the important innovations in International Law established by the Covenant for Members of the League of Nations consists in the Registration and Publication of every Treaty or International Engagement entered into by any Member of the League.

Article 18 of the Covenant of the League of Nations, by which this has been provided for, reads as follows:—

"Every Treaty or International Engagement entered into hereafter by any Member of the League shall be forthwith registered with the Secretariat and shall as soon as possible be published by it. No such Treaty or International Engagement shall be binding until so registered."

It is hardly necessary to dwell on the importance of an arrangement whereby publicity of Treaties and other International Engagements—and, as a preliminary thereto, their registration—will be secured.

Publicity has for a long time been considered as a source of moral strength in the administration of National Law. It should equally strengthen the laws and engagements which exist *between nations*. It will promote public control. It will awaken public interest. It will remove causes for distrust and conflict. Publicity alone will enable the League of Nations to extend a moral sanction to the contractual obligations of its Members. It will, moreover, contribute to the formation of a clear and indisputable system of International Law.

Since the satisfactory execution of the principles of Article 18 of the Covenant depends in the first place on the co-operation of the Governments of the Members of the League of Nations, the Secretary-General begs to present to the Members of the League in the following memorandum some suggestions whereby, in his opinion, the application of Article 18 may best be secured. The arrangements suggested have, of course, only a provisional character. Experience may, in the future, suggest modification and revision.

2. If the application of Article 18 is to conform to the best advantage with the objects of the League of Nations, an extensive inter-

[1]Reprinted from 1 *Treaty Series*, p. 7–13.

pretation of its provisions should be adopted. The details of its applications have accordingly been worked out with this principle in view.

The aim of the following suggestions is to establish as far as possible a complete and reliable survey of the whole system of Treaties and International Engagements entered into after the coming into force of the Covenant of the League.

3. The provision that "every Treaty of International Engagement shall be forthwith registered with the Secretariat" leads to the following conclusions as regards the material which requires registration.

This material comprises not only every formal Treaty of whatsoever character and every International Convention, but also any other International Engagement or Act by which nations or their Governments intend to establish legal obligations between themselves and another State, Nation or Government.

Agreements regarding the revision or the prolongation of Treaties form separate International Engagements; they also should be registered under Article 18.

It is proposed, moreover, that the denunciation of any Treaty or Agreement should, if only for the sake of completeness, be included in the scheme of registration.

4. Article 18 refers to Treaties, etc., entered into "hereafter." It is thereby understood that registration is necessary for *all* Treaties, etc., which become, or *have* become finally binding so far as the acts between the Parties *inter se* are concerned, after the date of the coming into force of the Covenant (January 10th, 1920).

Treaties or Engagements which have finally come into force at an earlier date are not included; but the International Secretariat is authorised, if this appear desirable to the Contracting Parties, to extend the system of Treaty Registration so as to include Treaties and Engagements of an earlier date.

5. As no Treaties or International Engagements will be binding until registration with the International Secretariat has taken place, the latest date at which they should be presented for registration will be the date when, so far as the acts of the Parties *inter se* are concerned, they receive final binding force, and are intended to come into operation. It may prove convenient, however, for various reasons, for the Parties to present a Treaty or International Engagement for Registration as soon as the text has been finally decided upon, even if exchange of ratifications between them still has to take place at a later date. The Secretary-General will, of course, have to see that, if a Treaty or Engagement be published at this stage, it is made clear that the Parties have not yet finally entered into the Treaty or Engagement.

In event of a Treaty or Engagement being presented for registration before it is finally entered into, the Parties will no doubt inform the Secretariat of the later act by which they definitely bring the Treaty into force.

6. It is suggested as a general principle that the Parties presenting a Treaty or Engagement for registration should do so by depositing a textual and complete copy thereof with all appurtenant declarations, protocols, ratifications, etc., at the Treaty Registration Bureau of the International Secretariat, accompanying it with an authentic statement that this text represents the full contents of the Treaty or Engagement into which the Parties intend to enter.

In case of necessity, the contents of a Treaty or Engagement can of course be transmitted to the International Secretariat by other means—for instance, by telegram—so long as it is established that the text is indisputably the one agreed upon between the Parties.

7. A Certificate of Registration will be delivered to the Parties concerned, under the signature of the Secretary-General of the League of Nations, or of his Deputy.

Certificates thus issued will be numbered consecutively.

8. Treaties or International Engagements may be presented for Registration by one Party only, either in the name of all the Parties at the same time, or of that Party alone, as long as it is established that the text is that which has been agreed upon between the Parties.

9. Publication of a Treaty or Engagement registered with the Secretariat will be secured automatically and as soon as possible, by its inclusion in the Treaty Part of the League of Nations Journal. Copies of this Journal will be regularly forwarded to the Governments of all States Members of the League.

It is intended to give that part of the Journal in which the publication of Treaties and Engagements is effected a special form, convenient for placing separately in Law Libraries and in private studies.

The separate index for this Treaty Part of the League of Nations Journal will be published at regular intervals.

10. The Secretary-General of the League proposes to organise his system of Registration in the following manner, hoping that it may prove convenient alike to the Parties and to all those interested in the contents of Treaties and the relevant details.

A Register will be kept in chronological order, stating, with regard to each Treaty or other Engagement or International Act, the Parties between which it has been concluded, the title (short title if any), the dates of signature, ratification and presentation for registration, and finally, the number under which it has been registered.

The actual texts presented to the Secretariat will be kept as an annex to this Register, each text being marked *ne varietur* by the Secretary-General or his Deputy.

Apart from the chronological Register, a second Register will be kept which will form to some extent an *état civil* of all Treaties and Engagements concerned. For every Treaty or Engagement a special page will be set apart as in a ledger, where all the data concerning it will be noted—including not only the Parties' signatures and ratifications, but also later adhesions, denunciations, etc. Notes relative to preparatory matter, discussions, and internal legislation arising out of the Treaties, etc., may also be added.

The Secretariat may on occasion be requested to deliver to States, Courts of Justice or private persons interested, certified extracts from this Register, attesting the existence and the status of International Treaties and Engagements, the moment of their coming into force, their ratification, their denunciations, the reservations entered in respect of them, etc., etc. The Secretary-General intends to make the Treaty Registration Office available for this purpose, but no legal liability for the contents of such extracts can be assumed by the Secretariat.

A general Index will be made to the Collection of Treaties and Engagements. It will be arranged in a way convenient for consultation.

11. The Treaty Registers of the International Secretariat will, moreover, include a special series of those Treaties and Conventions which, by some special provision or with some special object in view, are placed under the care of the Secretary-General. An instance of such a provision will be found in Article 405 of the Treaty of Versailles, according to which Draft Labour Conventions will be deposited with the Secretariat. The same applies to Labour Recommendations.

To these may be added other Draft Conventions and Recommendations, which may be made by analogous organisations under the League of Nations.

12. It should be noted that by the provisions of Article 18 not only Treaties between Members of the League of Nations have to be registered, but also Treaties or Engagements entered into by a Member of the League with a State which has not yet been admitted into the League.

13. In connection with this last point, it has been suggested that the system of Registration of Treaties by the Secretariat of the League of Nations should from the beginning be so extended as to admit of the registration of Treaties, etc., made by and between States or Communities that have not yet been admitted as Members of the League of Nations. This would serve to complete the Registration of Treaties and the public collection of Treaties which will be formed by the Treaty Part of the League of Nations Journal. The Secretary-General therefore proposes, although the Registration will be for this part absolutely voluntary, to accept applications for the Registration of

Treaties, etc., even if none of the Parties is at the time a Member of the League of Nations.

The Secretary-General of the League of Nations trusts that experience may show that the system of registration and publication of Treaties on the lines suggested in this Memorandum will work satisfactorily. He will be glad to receive suggestions for possible modifications of the present scheme.

IX. PREPARATORY PROCEDURE TO BE FOLLOWED IN THE CASE OF GENERAL CONVENTIONS TO BE NEGOTIATED UNDER THE AUSPICES OF THE LEAGUE OF NATIONS[1]

The Assembly adopts the following amended text for Section IV of Resolution No. 1, adopted by the eleventh Assembly on October 3rd, 1930:

That, in the case of all general conventions to be negotiated under the auspices of the League of Nations, the following preparatory procedure should, in principle, be followed, except in the cases where previous conventions or arrangements have established a special procedure or where, owing to the nature of the questions to be treated or to special circumstances, the Assembly or the Council consider other methods to be more appropriate:

1. Where an organ of the League of Nations recommends the conclusion of a general convention on any matter, it shall prepare a memorandum explaining the objects which it is desired to achieve by the conclusion of the convention and the benefits which result therefrom. Such memorandum shall be submitted to the Council of the League of Nations.

2. If the Council approves the proposal in principle, a first draft convention shall be prepared and communicated, together with the explanatory memorandum, to Governments, with the request that, if they feel that the draft should be taken into consideration, they shall inform the Secretary-General of their views, both with regard to the main objects or the suggested means of attaining them, and also with regard to the draft convention. In some cases, it may be desirable to annex a specific questionnaire.

3. The draft convention and the observations of Governments (together with the answers to the questionnaire, if any) shall be communicated to the Assembly, and the Assembly shall then decide whether the subject appears *prima facie* suitable for the conclusion of a convention.

4. If the Assembly considers the subject *prima facie* suitable for the conclusion of a convention, the Council shall arrange for the preparation of a draft convention in the light of the replies received from Governments, and the new draft convention (together with the replies of

[1]Assembly Resolution of September 25, 1931. Reprinted from *Official Journal*, Special Supplement No. 92, p. 11-12.

other Governments) shall be transmitted to each Government with a request for their opinion on the provisions of the draft and any observations on the above-mentioned replies of other Governments.

5. In light of the results of this second consultation of the Governments, the Assembly shall decide whether a convention should be concluded and, if so, whether the draft should be submitted to a conference, the date of which it will request the Council to fix.

6. The Council, in fixing the date for the convocation of a conference, shall endeavour, as far as possible, to avoid two League of Nations conferences being held simultaneously, and to ensure the lapse of a reasonable time between two conferences.

7. The procedure set out in the preceding paragraphs will be followed, as far as possible, in the case of draft conventions the desirability of which is recognised by a decision of the Assembly either on its own initiative or as the result of a proposal by a Government. In these cases, the Council will instruct either the Secretariat or some other organ of the League or specially selected experts to prepare the above-mentioned report, which shall subsequently be submitted to the Council.

X. AGREEMENT BETWEEN THE SWISS FEDERAL COUNCIL AND THE SECRETARY-GENERAL OF THE LEAGUE OF NATIONS CONCERNING THE ESTABLISHMENT AND OPERATION IN THE NEIGHBOURHOOD OF GENEVA OF A WIRELESS STATION[1]

In view of the resolution of the League of Nations Assembly dated September 24th, 1929, relating to the establishment of a wireless telegraph station destined to ensure independent communications for the League of Nations in times of emergency,

The Swiss Federal Council, hereinafter termed the "Swiss Government"

and

The Secretary-General of the League of Nations, hereinafter termed the "Secretary-General," acting in virtue of the powers granted him under the above-mentioned resolution,

Have agreed upon the following provisions:

ARTICLE I

1. In conformity with the provisions of the present Agreement and of the special Convention to be concluded between the Secretary-General and the Société Radio-Suisse, hereinafter termed "Radio-Suisse," a wireless station, destined chiefly to meet the needs of the League of Nations in normal times and to ensure independent communications to the League in times of emergency, shall be established in the neighbourhood of the seat of the League.

2. This station, known as "Radio-Nations" and established on land and in buildings belonging to the Radio-Suisse, shall, in particular, include, firstly, a central telegraph office and a long-wave post already in operation, constructed at the cost of the Radio-Suisse and the property of the latter; and, secondly, a short-wave post to be established as soon as possible at the cost of the League, whose property it shall be.

3. The Radio-Nations station shall be operated in normal times by the Radio-Suisse and in times of emergency shall pass under the exclusive management of the League.

[1]Document [C.191.M.91.1930.VIII.] (1930.VIII.2.).

ARTICLE 2

1. The Swiss Government shall take the necessary steps to enable the Radio-Suisse to discharge any obligations devolving upon it in virtue of the above-mentioned special Convention.

2. If, during the existence of the present Agreement and of the Convention between the Secretary-General and the Radio-Suisse, the Swiss Government exercises any right of reversion with regard to the Radio-Suisse or repurchases by mutual agreement the buildings and installations of the Radio-Suisse, the latter's rights and obligations arising out of the Agreement and Convention shall pass to the new proprietor, who will be either the Swiss Administration or a new Swiss company under the control of the Swiss Government.

3. The Swiss Government guarantees the execution of the provisions of the above-mentioned Convention by the Radio-Suisse or by any other concessionnaire or administration.

ARTICLE 3

The Swiss Government shall give the station and the installations connected therewith, at all times, the same protection and the same security as it gives to the premises of the League of Nations. The legal status of the station in times of emergency shall be the same as that of the buildings of the League of Nations.

ARTICLE 4

As soon as the Secretary-General notifies the Swiss Government that a period of emergency has begun, the Radio-Nations station shall pass under the exclusive management of the League of Nations. The latter shall, at its own risk, take possession of the whole of the installations, including the long-wave transmitter and all other wireless installations with which the station may subsequently be supplied.

ARTICLE 5

While the state of emergency lasts, the staff of the station shall be placed at the disposal of the Secretary-General and shall be regarded as League of Nations Secretariat staff. This provision shall apply even in the case of the mobilisation of the Swiss army. Nevertheless, the Swiss Government may, as an exceptional measure and after previous notice, withdraw a part of the staff from the station.

ARTICLE 6

1. The Secretary-General shall, in times of emergency, take any measures relating to management which he may consider desirable;

in particular, as regards the increase and replacement of the staff. Nevertheless, in order to facilitate the resumption of normal operations by the Radio-Suisse on the termination of the period of emergency, the replacement of permanent staff shall be effected only as an exceptional measure, *i.e.*, in cases where the Secretary-General deems it necessary in order to ensure the satisfactory working of the station or the independence of the communications of the League of Nations.

2. The Secretary-General shall equitably compensate any permanent official of the station whose contract is suspended and for whom other employment cannot be provided by the Radio-Suisse or the Swiss Administration.

ARTICLE 7

1. In times of emergency the station shall be primarily intended for the despatch and receipt of official communications of the League of Nations (messages from or to the Secretariat of the League, the International Labour Office, the official representatives of the States Members of the League and delegations to the Council, the Assembly and Conferences of the League).

2. Nevertheless, the Secretary-General shall endeavour to ensure the transmission of all other communications in so far as this does not interfere with the official communications of the League. It is understood, however, that non-official communications shall be subject to all measures of control existing in Switzerland. Accordingly, such telegrams may be handed in only at a Swiss telegraph office, and, after receipt by Radio-Nations, shall be transmitted to the addressee only through the agency of a Swiss telegraph office. Non-official telephone calls shall be effected through the agency of a Swiss central telephone office.

ARTICLE 8

1. During the period of emergency, the cost of the station, including charges for amortisation and the interest on the capital, shall be borne entirely by the League of Nations.

2. The League of Nations shall collect the total revenue from official communications despatched by Radio-Nations without the assistance of the Swiss Administration. In the case of non-official communications, which must be exchanged with the assistance of the Swiss Administration in accordance with the preceding article, and in the case of official communications exchanged with that assistance, the League of Nations shall receive through the Swiss Administration the total revenue from the share of the transit charges accruing to the station, the terminal charge being retained by the Swiss Administration.

3. Any net profit from the operation of the station shall be divided between the League of Nations and the Radio-Suisse proportionately to the revenue from official and non-official communications.

ARTICLE 9

1. In conformity with the resolution adopted on September 24th, 1929, by the Assembly of the League of Nations, concerning the establishment of a wireless station, the Swiss Government shall in times of emergency, be represented at the station by an observer, whose duties will be those defined by the Council of the League of Nations in its resolution of March 9th, 1929.

2. The Secretary-General shall give this observer every facility for carrying out his mission. The Secretary-General shall, in particular, supply him with full information as to the origin of messages transmitted by the station and the destination of messages received by the station. The same facilities shall, if necessary, be given to the observer's assistants.

3. The Secretary-General and the services controlled by him shall refrain from transmitting through the station any communication of a nature to affect the regime of the neutrality of Switzerland as defined in the Declaration of London of February 13th, 1920.

4. The Swiss Government, in conformity with the resolution of the Council of the League of Nations dated March 9th, 1929, reserves the right to ask for explanations from the Council regarding any activity of the station in times of emergency which appear to it to affect the essential interests of Switzerland.

ARTICLE 10

Immediately on the termination of the period of emergency, the station shall be handed back to the Radio-Suisse, which shall resume operation thereof in accordance with the provisions of the Convention to be concluded with the Secretary-General.

ARTICLE 11

It is understood that, as regards the official communications of the League of Nations, the Radio-Nations station shall not be deemed to be a party to the Telegraph Union as coming under the Swiss Confederation; nor, as regards the installations which are the property of the League of Nations, shall it be a party to the Radio-Telegraphic Union as coming under the Swiss Confederation.

ARTICLE 12

1. Disputes which may arise concerning the interpretation or application either of the present Agreement or of the Convention to be concluded between the Secretary-General and the Radio-Suisse shall be deemed to be disputes between the parties to the present Agreement. Should it prove impossible within a reasonable time to settle them by amicable agreement, they shall be submitted, subject to the provisions of paragraph 2 of the present Article, to an arbitral tribunal; such tribunal, unless otherwise agreed between the parties, shall consist of three members appointed by the Chamber for Summary Procedure of the Permanent Court of International Justice. The arbitral procedure shall be governed by the provisions of the Convention for the Pacific Settlement of International Disputes of October 18th, 1907.

2. Should the dispute, in the opinion of one of the parties, relate to the interpretation or application of the Declaration of London of February 13th, 1920, it shall be examined by the Council of the League of Nations. Should such examination not result in the settlement of the dispute by amicable agreement, recourse shall be had to the arbitral procedure provided for above, unless it has been possible to submit the question at issue to the Permanent Court of International Justice.

3. The present Agreement and the Convention between the Secretary-General and the Radio-Suisse shall be interpreted in accordance with the general principles of law.

ARTICLE 13

1. The present Agreement shall enter into force immediately upon its signature and shall cease to have effect on the expiry of a period of ten years as from the date on which the short-wave transmission post is officially opened for operation.

2. Unless it is denounced two years before the expiry of this period of ten years, the Agreement shall remain in force until denounced by either party subject to two years' previous notice being given. In such a case, however, the denunciation shall take effect only at the end of the current financial year.

3. On the expiry of the present Agreement, a settlement shall be effected in conformity with the provisions of the Covention to be concluded between the Secretary-General and the Radio-Suisse.

IN FAITH WHEREOF the undersigned have concluded the present Agreement.

DONE in duplicate at Geneva, on the 21st day of May, one thousand nine hundred and thirty.

(*Signed*) ERIC DRUMMOND.   (*Signed*) MOTTA.

XI. MEMBERS AND FORMER MEMBERS OF THE LEAGUE AS OF APRIL 18, 1946

1. LIST OF MEMBERS AS OF APRIL 18, 1946

On April 18, 1946, the day of the termination of the League's activities, the League was composed of the following 44 members.[1] The dates in parentheses indicate the day of entry into the League.

Afghanistan (September 27, 1934)
Albania (December 17, 1920)
Argentine (January 10, 1920)
Australia (January 10, 1920)
Belgium (January 10, 1920)
Bolivia (January 10, 1920)
Bulgaria (December 16, 1920)
Canada (January 10, 1920)
China (July 16, 1920)
Colombia (February 16, 1920)
Cuba (March 8, 1920)
Czechoslovakia (January 10, 1920)
Denmark (March 8, 1920)
Dominican Republic (September 29, 1924)
Ecuador (September 28, 1934)[2]
Egypt (May 26, 1937)
Estonia (September 22, 1921)

[1]See also Walther Schücking and Hans Wehberg, *Die Satzung des Völkerbundes* (3rd ed., Berlin, 1931), p. 239–372; and *The Treaty of Versailles and After: Annotations of the Text of the Treaty* (Washington, 1947), p. 72–78. On Austria's status, see above, p. 19.

[2]See also *Official Journal*, November 1934, p.1468–1469. "The Secretary-General informed the Council that he had just received a telegram which was evidently intended for the Assembly, but since the Assembly was now over, he asked permission to read it to the Council. It was from the Government of Ecuador. To understand its contents it might perhaps be well to recall the fact that Ecuador was an original Member of the League of Nations and that her name appeared in the first part of the Annex to the Covenant. The telegram was as follows:

"'Quito, September 27th, 1934.

"'By the authority of the Senate of the Republic, I have the honour to inform you, and through you the League of Nations, that Ecuador has decided to become a member of that distinguished Institution which is generously and continually working for peace among the peoples. I take this opportunity to extend a greeting, on behalf of the Government and people of Ecuador, to the great and friendly nations which are so worthily represented in the Assembly. His Excellency M. Gonzalo Zaldumbide, Envoy Extraordinary and Minister Plenipotentiary, will represent Ecuador in the League, and I trust that the latter will believe what he will say in the name of the Republic, espe-

Ethiopia (September 28, 1923)
Finland (December 16, 1920)
France (January 10, 1920)
Greece (March 30, 1920)
India (January 10, 1920)
Iran (Persia) (January 10, 1920)
Iraqu (October 3, 1932)
Ireland (Irish Free State) (September 10, 1923)
Latvia (September 22, 1921)
Liberia (June 30, 1920)
Lithuania (September 22, 1921)
Luxembourg (December 16, 1920)
Mexico (September 12, 1931)[3]

cially when he expresses the earnest desire of the people of Ecuador for peace, freedom and justice.

> (*Signed*) J. M. Velasco Ibarra
> Constitutional President of the Republic
> (*Signed*) M. Sotomayor Luna
> Minister for Foreign Affairs'

"It would be seen from this telegram that Ecuador, an original Member of the League of Nations, was now acceding to the Covenant. There was therefore no question of an admission or election. The Secretary-General was sure that the Council would be willing to consider Ecuador forthwith as a Member of the League of Nations, with all the rights and duties arising out of this capacity . . . The President said that he had requested the representative of Ecuador to sit at the Council table in order to inform him that the Council had taken cognisance of the telegram which his Government had just sent to the Secretary-General regarding its accession to the Covenant of the League of Nations."

[3]On the admission of Mexico, see Assembly Resolution of September 12, 1931, *Official Journal*, Special Supplement No. 93, p.92–93. It reads as follows: "Translation: The Assembly has noted with great satisfaction the acceptance by Mexico of the invitation which is unanimously sent to her to accede to the Covenant and become a Member of the League.

The General Committee has carefully considered the reply received from Mexico and has unanimously asked me to propose the following resolution:

The Assembly,

Having by its resolution of September 8th, 1931, considered as an omission, which should in justice be repaired, the fact that Mexico is not mentioned in the Annex of the Covenant enumerating the countries invited to accede thereto;

Having unanimously decided to repair that omission and therefore to invite Mexico to accede to the Covenant and to lend its valuable support to the League as though it had been invited from the outset;

Having by this exceptional invitation—which must not be regarded as establishing a precedent—formally indicated that it accepts as having been fulfilled from the outset in the case of Mexico the conditions governing the entry of States into the League as set forth in Article 1 of the Covenant;

Noting the reply of the Government of Mexico dated September 10th, 1931, by which it agrees without reservation to enter the League on the terms announced:

Declares Mexico to have become a Member of the League of Nations and invites the representatives of Mexico to take part as soon as possible in the work of the present session of the Assembly. . .

The draft resolution was adopted."

Netherlands (March 9, 1920)
New Zealand (January 10, 1920)
Norway (March 9, 1920)
Panama (November 25, 1920)
Poland (January 10, 1920)
Portugal (April 8, 1920)
Siam (Thailand) (January 10, 1920)
Sweden (March 9, 1920)
Switzerland (March 8, 1920)[4]
Turkey (July 18, 1932)
Union of South Africa (January 10, 1920)
United Kingdom (January 10, 1920)[5]
Uruguay (January 10, 1920)
Yugoslavia (Serb-Croat-Slovene State) (February 10, 1920)

[4]On Switzerland's accession to the Covenant, see Council Resolution of February 13, 1920, which reads in part as follows: "The Council of the League of Nations, while affirming that the conception of neutrality of the Members of the League is incompatible with the principle that all Members will be obliged to co-operate in enforcing respect for their engagements, recognises that Switzerland is in a unique situation, based on a tradition of several centuries, which has been explicitly incorporated in the Law of Nations; . . . It is in this sense that the Council of the League has taken note of the declaration made by the Swiss Government in its Message to the Federal Assembly of 4th August, 1919, and in its Memorandum of 13th January, 1920, which declarations have been confirmed by the Swiss delegates at the meeting of the Council and in accordance with which Switzerland recognizes and proclaims the duties of solidarity which membership of the League of Nations imposes upon her, including therein the duty of co-operating in such economic and financial measures as may be demanded by the League of Nations against a Covenant-breaking State, and is prepared to make every sacrifice to defend her own territory under every circumstance even during operations undertaken by the League of Nations, but will not be obliged to take part in any military action or to allow the passage of foreign troops or the preparation of military operations within her territory.

In accepting these declarations, the Council recognises that the perpetual neutrality of Switzerland and the guarantee of the inviolability of her territory as incorporated in the Law of Nations, particularly in the Treaties and in the Act of 1815, are justified by the interests of general peace and as such compatible with the Covenant . . . The resolution was carried unanimously." *Council, Second Session, Sixth Meeting*, p.23–25.
[5]The Annex to the Covenant lists "British Empire" in addition to Canada, Australia, South Africa, New Zealand, India. By contrast, the Final Report of the Board of Liquidation refers in many places to "United Kingdom." See Document [C.5.M.1947.]

2. List of Members Whose Membership Was Terminated Prior to April 18, 1946[6]

State	Period of Membership	Ceased to be a Member on
Austria	1920–1938	March 18, 1938
Brazil	1920–1928	June 13, 1928
Chile	1920–1940	June 1, 1940
Costa Rica	1920–1926	Jan. 1, 1927
Germany	1926–1935	Oct. 19, 1935
Guatemala	1920–1938	May 25, 1938
Haiti	1920–1944	April 8, 1944
Honduras	1920–1938	July 9, 1938
Hungary	1922–1941	April 10, 1941
Italy	1920–1939	Dec. 10, 1939
Japan	1920–1935	March 27, 1935
Nicaragua	1920–1938	June 26, 1938
Paraguay	1920–1937	Feb. 23, 1937
Peru	1920–1941	April 8, 1941
Roumania	1920–1942	July 10, 1942
Salvador	1920–1939	Aug. 9, 1939
Spain	1920–1941	May 8, 1941
Union of Soviet Socialist Republics	1934–1939	Dec. 14, 1939
Venezuela	1920–1940	July 11, 1940

[6]The Final Report of the Board of Liquidation [C.5.M.5.1947.] lists on p. 31 Austria as a non-member. It is controversial whether Austria had ceased to be a member of the League as of March 18, 1938 as indicated in the Report. See the Assembly Resolution of April 12, 1946 in *Official Journal*, Special Supplement No. 194, p. 277.

XII. REGULATIONS FOR THE FINANCIAL ADMINISTRATION OF THE LEAGUE OF NATIONS.[1] EDITION ISSUED IN SEPTEMBER 1945, AND INCORPORATING AMENDMENTS IN FORCE ON THE DATE OF ISSUE

THE ASSEMBLY of the League of Nations

Adopts the following resolution concerning the financial administration of the League of Nations:

DEFINITIONS

In these Regulations:

The *League* includes the Secretariat and all autonomous and non-autonomous organisations.

Assembly means the Assembly of the League of Nations.

Council means the Council of the League of Nations.

Autonomous Organisations include the International Labour Organisation, the Permanent Court of International Justice, and any autonomous organisation hereafter created by the Assembly.

The word "autonomous" has reference solely to the separation of the financial administration of such organisations from that of the Secretariat and does not imply any wider consequences.

Competent authority means, (*a*) in the case of the Secretariat and non-autonomous organisations, the Council; (*b*) in the case of the International Labour Organisation, the Governing Body of the Labour Office; and, (*c*) in the case of the Permanent Court of International Justice, the Court or, by delegation from the Court, its President.

Competent official means, (*a*) in the case of the Secretariat and non-autonomous organisations, the Secretary-General; (*b*) in the case of the International Labour Organisation, the Director of the Labour Office; and, (*c*) in the case of the Permanent Court of International

---

[1]Reprinted from *Regulations for the Financial Administration of the League of Nations. Edition Issued in September 1945 and Incorporating Amendments in Force on the Date of Issue* [C.81.M.81.1945.X.]. The document (in English and French) also contains an annex, "Model Estimates," p. 31, and an index, p. 49–60. The footnotes, with the exception of the present one, are those of the document.

Justice, the Registrar of the Court; or the duly authorised deputies of these officials.

Non-autonomous organisations include all organisations of the League (other than the autonomous organisations) which do not form part of the general services of the Secretariat.

Commission means the Supervisory Commission.

Rapporteur means the Rapporteur of the Commission.

CHAPTER I.　THE SUPERVISORY COMMISSION

ARTICLE 1[2]

1. There shall be a Supervisory Commission to perform the duties assigned to it by these Regulations, and to deal with any other special matters referred to it by the Assembly or the Council.

2. As from January 1st, 1939, the Commission shall be composed of seven members. One member at least shall be a financial expert. The members shall be appointed by the Assembly, which, in selecting members, shall include among them persons belonging to countries Members of the League which are not represented on the Council.

3. (*a*) The term of office of members of the Commission shall be three years, corresponding to three financial years of the League.

(*b*) A person who has served two consecutive full terms of office on the Commission shall not, during the next three years, be eligible for re-election to the Commission.

(*c*) The members of the Commission shall retire in rotation and not simultaneously. The system of rotation shall be that resulting from the report regarding the composition of the Supervisory Commission approved by the Assembly on September 30th, 1937 (document [A.7.1937.X.]), the recommendations of which shall have effect notwithstanding that they derogate from the provisions of the present article.

(*d*) Any vacancy caused by the death or resignation of a member before the end of his term of office shall be filled by appointing a member to hold office until the end of the term of office of the member deceased or resigning.

ARTICLE 2

1. The Commission shall appoint from its members a Chairman, a Vice-Chairman and a Rapporteur for each financial year. They shall be eligible for reappointment.

[2]The 1939 Assembly approved a proposal of the Supervisory Commission (see Third Report of the Commission to the 1939 Assembly, document [A.5(*b*).1939.X.]) temporarily to suspend paragraphs 2 and 3 of Article 1.

2. The Rapporteur shall be generally responsible for the preparation of the work of the Commission before its plenary meetings. He shall ascertain that the decisions taken by the Commission at its meetings are carried out, and shall execute all duties placed upon him by these Regulations or by the Commission.

ARTICLE 3

1. The Commission shall hold its sessions at Geneva, or, exceptionally and subject to the condition that greater expenditure will not be incurred, at such other place as may be decided by a vote of its members. Suitable office accommodation, as required, shall be provided by the Secretary-General for the Commission and the Rapporteur.

2. The Secretary-General shall place the necessary clerical assistance at the disposal of the Commission and the Rapporteur. An official of the Secretariat, who shall be assisted by an official of the International Labour Office, shall act as Secretary of the Commission.

ARTICLE 4

1. An auditor, who shall be a person in no way in the service of any of the organisations of the League, shall be appointed by the Council on the proposal of the Commission.

2. The auditor shall be appointed for a period of five years, and shall not be removable except by the Council and on the proposal of the Commission, with reasons stated.

3. During his presence at the seat of any League organisation for the purposes of an audit, the auditor shall receive subsistence allowance and such other allowances as the Commission may determine, and his necessary travelling expenses shall be refunded on production of a duly certified statement.

4. The Council shall, if necessary, appoint a deputy auditor to assist and replace the auditor in case of need. Paragraphs 1 and 3 of the present article, and Articles 41, 44, 45, 46, 47 and 48, shall apply to the deputy auditor.

ARTICLE 5

1. The competent officials shall, on their request, be heard by the Commission, whenever it is in session, and shall appear before the Commission at its request. Other officials shall appear before and give information to the Commission on a request to that effect being addressed by the Commission to the competent officials.

2. While the Commission is not in session, the Rapporteur, if pres-

ent at the seat of the League or of one of its organisations for the discharge of his duties, shall be entitled to obtain information from officials in accordance with the preceding paragraph. The Rapporteur shall submit to the Chairman of the Commission any question which the competent officials request him so to submit.

3. The Commission shall supply the Council with any information relating to its work which the Council may require.

CHAPTER II. FINANCIAL ADMINISTRATION OF LEAGUE ORGANISATIONS

ARTICLE 6

All organisations of the League, autonomous and non-autonomous, and all temporary organisations hereafter created under the auspices of the League, whether their expenditure is or is not, in whole or in part, met out of the votes of the Assembly, shall comply with these regulations and with every decision of the Assembly governing financial and budgetary administration.

ARTICLE 7

1. The financial administration of autonomous organisations shall be independent of the financial administration of the Secretariat, subject always to the provisions of the Regulations.

2. The financial administration of the non-autonomous organisations shall be an integral part of the financial administration of the Secretariat.

3. The Secretary-General, acting in consultation with the Advisory Committee of the organisation (if any), shall be responsible for estimating the financial requirements of the non-autonomous organisations and for submitting such estimates. He shall likewise be responsible for the expenditure of all funds voted for these organisations, and for the appropriation of such expenditure to the proper items of the Budget.

4. In the case of an autonomous organisation, the responsibilities dealt with in paragraph 3 shall rest upon the competent official or competent authority.

5. The adoption by the Assembly or the Council of a report of an advisory committee containing proposals which may directly or indirectly involve expenditure, either immediately or in the future, shall not be made the ground for asking for a credit if the report does not contain, as an annex to its text, an estimate of the expenditure involved.

CHAPTER III. DRAWING UP THE BUDGET

ARTICLE 8

The financial year of the League shall be the calendar year.

ARTICLE 9

1. For every financial year, estimates shall be made of the expenditure to be incurred by the League.

2. The estimates shall be divided into separate *Parts:* (*a*) for the Secretariat, (*b*) for each autonomous organisation, and (*c*) for the Working Capital Fund, when it is necessary to ask for contributions to this fund, in accordance with the model shown in the annex.

3. Each *Part* (except that relating to the Working Capital Fund) shall be divided into two *Sections*, one for ordinary expenditure and the other for capital expenditure.

4. The Sections referred to in paragraph 3 shall be subdivided into *Chapters* corresponding to the various services or categories of expenditure. The different organisations shall aim at uniformity of arrangement.

ARTICLE 10

1. There shall be included in the part of the Budget dealing with the expenses of the Secretariat the cost of sessions of the Council and the Assembly, the cost of all non-autonomous organisations, and any expenses of a bureau or commission which the Council may decide so to include in the expenses of the Secretariat in accordance with Article 24 of the Covenant.

2. There shall be separate Chapters for each of these categories of expenditure and for the general expenses of the Secretariat.

ARTICLE 11

The general Budget of the League shall be preceded by a summary of the estimated income and expenditure for all the organisations covered by the Budget. This statement shall set out the amount required to cover:

(*a*) Ordinary expenditure,
(*b*) Capital expenditure,
(*c*) Contributions, when necessary, to the Working Capital Fund.

1. Each Part of the Budget, as defined in Article 9, shall consist of:

(*a*) A summary of Chapters;

(*b*) A full statement of items, showing for each, in addition to the sum asked for, the sum voted for the current year, and the sum voted for and the amount actually expended in the preceding year;

(*c*) Wherever possible, detailed schedules and explanatory statements. The schedules shall be subdivided in accordance with the principles of Article 9.

2. Important differences in the amounts estimated during successive years for the same items shall be fully explained by means of notes.

ARTICLE 13

A list showing the names of the officials of the Secretariat and of other organisations, and setting out their nationalities, duties, salaries, and entertainment and house allowances (if any), shall be confidentially circulated to the Members of the League at the same time as the Budget, and to the Assembly at its regular annual session.

ARTICLE 14

Cancelled

CHAPTER IV. ADOPTION OF THE BUDGET

ARTICLE 15

1. The Secretary-General shall arrange for the Budget and the Annexes, as described in the preceding Chapter, together with a general introduction, to be submitted to the Commission before May 1st of each year.

2. In order to enable the Secretary-General to comply with the provisions of paragraph 1, the competent officials of the autonomous organisations shall supply the Secretary-General with the data required on or before a date to be fixed by the Secretary-General in agreement with the officials concerned.

ARTICLE 16

1. The Commission shall annually examine the Budget and prepare a report thereon in time for both documents to be despatched

to the Council and the Members of the League three months before the regular annual session of the Assembly.

2. The observations of the Council upon the Budget and upon the report of the Commission shall be despatched to the Members of the League in time for them to be received at least one month before the regular annual session of the Assembly.

3. When the Commission is considering their respective Budgets, the autonomous organisations shall be represented before the Commission in such manner as they may decide and the Commission approve. A non-autonomous organisation shall be represented by the Secretary-General, assisted by one of the officials especially responsible for its work, and, if so requested, by a member of the Advisory Committee.

4. The Commission may not amend the Budget, as presented to it, but may propose modifications. The Commission will discuss such modifications (if any) with the competent official or authority, and report its conclusions to the Council and the Assembly.

5. Proposed credits which in the opinion of the Commission require special examination by the Assembly may form the object of special reports by the Commission which shall be dealt with by the procedure laid down in Article 16c below. If the credit forms part of the budget of an autonomous organisation, the special report shall be communicated to the competent authority of the organisation.

ARTICLE 16*a*

1. A proposal for expenditure on a purpose for which provision is not made in the Budget as communicated to the Members of the League must be placed in the hands of the Secretary-General at least one month before the date fixed for the opening of the Assembly's session.

If such a proposal is received later than one month before the opening of the session or made during the session, it shall be dealt with as follows:

(*a*) It shall be submitted directly by the Secretary-General to the Supervisory Commission for a report upon its general financial consequences;

(*b*) Unless, after considering the report of the Supervisory Commission, the Assembly or the Finance Committee, by a special resolution adopted by a two-thirds majority, decides to take it into consideration during the current session, the proposal shall be adjourned until the next session of the Assembly;

(*c*) If it is decided to deal with the proposal during the current session, the ordinary procedure laid down for supplementary credits should be followed, with the exception that the voting of a credit by the Finance Committee shall require a two-thirds majority.

2. The Secretary-General shall incorporate the estimates referred to in paragraph 1 above, and estimates for any increases in the Budget of the Secretariat which he himself considers it necessary to propose, in a single supplementary budget, which shall be circulated to the Members of the League and to the Supervisory Commission not later than two weeks before the opening of the Assembly's session.

ARTICLE 16*b*

A session of the Supervisory Commission shall be held each year during the session of the Assembly.

ARTICLE 16*c*

1. Proposed credits upon which a special report has been made by the Supervisory Commission under Article 16, paragraph 5, and the various estimates included in the supplementary budget, shall be dealt with by the following procedure:

(*a*) Where consideration of the objects for which the proposed credit is required is referred by the Assembly to a Committee other than the Finance Committee, all the relevant documents shall be placed before such Committee, which, in so far as it reports in favour of the said objects, shall examine the estimate of expenditure and, if necessary, modify it to correspond to the recommendations which it makes. The Committee's report, if it recommends a credit, shall be passed directly to the Supervisory Commission for verification of the estimated expenditure and be then submitted to the Finance Committee with a report by the Supervisory Commission. The report of the Committee concerned (other than the Finance Committee) must, however, be received by the Supervisory Commission within fifteen days from the opening of the session of the Assembly. If it is received later, the examination of the credit shall be adjourned to the next session of the Assembly, unless the Finance Committee, by a decision taken by a two-thirds majority, shall otherwise resolve, in which case the credit shall be referred to the Supervisory Commission for examination and report at the earliest possible moment.

(*b*) In other cases, the proposed credits shall be referred to the Finance Committee with the observations of the Supervisory Commission.

2. The rules contained in paragraph 1 (*a*) above shall also apply in all cases where: (1) a proposal for expenditure for a purpose for which provision is not made in the Budget or Supplementary Budget is referred by the Assembly to one of its Committees other than the Finance Committee: (2) a Committee other than the Finance Committee of its own motion adopts proposals capable of involving an increase in the Budget as originally communicated to the Members of the League.

ARTICLE 16*d*

A decision of the Finance Committee shall be reconsidered if a request to that effect is formulated by one-quarter of the members of the Finance Committee or by the competent official of the organisation affected or by a vote of another committee of the Assembly affected thereby.

Such reconsideration shall not take place until after an interval of at least twenty-four hours from the time when the request was made or was communicated to the Finance Committee.

ARTICLE 16*e*

Subject to the above provisions, the Budget and Supplementary Budget shall be referred to the Finance Committee, which shall place them before the Assembly in the form approved by it, preferably in a single document.

ARTICLE 17

Cancelled

ARTICLE 18

1. When the Assembly or its Finance Committee discusses the Budget of any autonomous organisation, such organisation may delegate one representative to assist at the meetings of the Assembly and as many representatives as the Finance Committee may approve to assist at the meetings of the Finance Committee. Such representative or representatives may be heard, but shall not address the meeting except on the invitation of the President.

2. The Advisory Committee of a non-autonomous organisation may, in like manner, send a representative to attend at meetings of the Finance Committee of the Assembly at which its Budget is discussed.

ARTICLE 19

Cancelled

CHAPTER V. COLLECTION OF FUNDS

ARTICLE 20

The expenses of the League shall be borne by the Members of the League in the manner prescribed by the Covenant.

ARTICLE 21

1. As soon as possible after the Assembly has adopted the Budget and the total amount voted has been apportioned among the Members of the League in the manner prescribed by the Covenant, the Secretary-General shall transmit all relevant documents to the Members of the League and request them to remit their contributions as soon as possible after the beginning of the financial year for which they are due. The Secretary-General shall, at the same time, request each Member of the League to state which of the following methods it desires to employ for such remittance:

(*a*) By direct remittance to the League either in instalments or in one sum; the dates of payment must be stated;

(*b*) By remittance of negotiable Treasury Bills, payable at such bank as the Government may designate and the Treasurer of the League of Nations may approve; the proportion of the contribution which will be covered by each bill, the dates at which the bills will be remitted and the dates at which they will be payable must be stated;

(*c*) By authorising the Treasurer of the League to draw upon it bills, up to the amount of the contribution, negotiable at such bank or banks as the Government and the Treasurer of the League of Nations may approve. In this case, the Government must indicate the number of bills to be drawn, the dates on which they are to be payable and the proportion of its contribution for which each bill is to be drawn, and, if it is necessary under its law that the bills should be stamped, should supply the necessary number of stamped sheets or stamped draft bills or the necessary stamps.

The Treasurer is authorized to endorse and to draw bills as above contemplated on behalf of the League of Nations so as to bind the League by such endorsement or drawing of bills.

2. If a Member of the League has not paid its contribution and has not furnished the information requested by the Secretary-General by the first day of April following, the Secretary-General shall repeat his request. He shall again repeat his request at the end of three months and at the end of a further three months, if the information requested has still not been given and if payment of the contribution has not in the meantime been made.

3. If the date or dates proposed for the payment of the contribution of a Member of the League are too late to meet the needs of the League, the Secretary-General shall explain the position to the Member concerned.

4. At the first session of the Council held after each of the dates mentioned in paragraph 2, the Secretary-General shall present to the Council a statement on the general financial position and on the

steps which he has taken. A similar statement shall annually be presented to the Assembly. The Assembly will take such action as it may deem proper.

5. Any payment in respect of contributions made by a Member of the League which has not paid in full its contributions for previous financial years shall, unless the Assembly decides otherwise in particular cases, be credited against the earliest in date of such arrears, notwithstanding any expression of intention to the contrary by the debtor Member. Where arrears have been consolidated, a Member of the League is required to pay its annual instalment in respect of arrears in full before liquidating its current contribution for the year in question.[3]

ARTICLE 22

1. States not Members of the League which have been admitted Members of any autonomous organisation of the League shall contribute towards the expenses of the autonomous organisation concerned in the proportion in which they would contribute to such expenses if they were Members of the League.

The contributions of States not Members of the League, which shall be calculated on the total outlay of the autonomous organisations to which they have been admitted Members, shall be applied exclusively to the expenses of such autonomous organisations.

2. The amounts receivable in accordance with paragraph 1 shall be shown separately in the Budget; they shall be entered as revenue in the Budget for the financial year for which they have been fixed, and shall be applied to reduce the sums to be contributed by the Members of the League. They shall be collected by the autonomous organisations themselves, which shall, in so doing, be guided by the rules laid down in Article 21; the competent officials shall supply the Secretary-General with the necessary information as to the results obtained.

3. States not Members of the League which either (a) have been admitted Members of any non-autonomous organisation or (b) participate in the work of the League in the sense of being represented at conferences convened by, or at the expense of, the League or of having official representation upon committees set up by the League and maintained at its expense, shall contribute towards the cost of such organisation or work, in the same proportion as if they were Members of the League.

4. The amounts receivable in accordance with paragraph 3 shall

[3]The Supervisory Commission, at its session held in September 1944, approved the suspension of Articles 21(5) and 33b for the year 1945 in regard to the appropriation of contributions in arrears (see document [C.27.M.27.1944.X.]).

be calculated on the total outlay which such non-autonomous organisation or such work involves for the League in any given year, irrespective of the budget heads to which the relevant expenditure has been charged.

The Secretary-General shall assess the contributions due from the non-member States in accordance with the provisions of this paragraph on the basis of the completed accounts; he shall take the steps prescribed in Article 21 which shall apply *mutatis mutandis* to the collection of contributions from the non-member States. The amounts received shall be inserted in the first Budget under preparation thereafter, in reduction of the total sum chargeable, for the year in question, to the Members of the League.

ARTICLE 23

1. Receipts other than contributions payable by Governments, such as receipts from the sale of publications and other miscellaneous sources and interest, shall, as far as possible, be estimated in advance and be deducted, as appropriations-in-aid, from the estimates put forward in the Budget, save as otherwise provided in the present Regulations or decided by the Assembly.

1. (*a*) The same shall apply to the contribution payable to the expenses of the Permanent Court of International Justice, under Article 35, paragraph 3, of the Statute of the Court, by States which are parties to disputes before the Court and are not Members of the League of Nations.

2. A summary of such receipts, if any, arising under each part of the Budget shall be set out as an appendix to the part under which they arise.

3. Any interest or gains earned by funds held by the League for special purposes (shown in the accounts as extra-budgetary or as suspense accounts) shall be added annually to the capital of the funds, unless the Assembly otherwise decides on a report by the Supervisory Commission.

ARTICLE 23*a*

1. Gifts which may directly or indirectly involve an immediate or ultimate financial liability for the Members of the League may only be accepted after authorisation by the Assembly.

2. Gifts not involving any financial liability for the Members of the League may be accepted by the Council or, where offered to an autonomous organisation, by the competent authority of the organisation, if the Council or the authority is satisfied that acceptance will not undesirably affect the general character of the League or the

special organisation in question and is in accordance with the general policy which should be pursued.

CHAPTER VI. APPROPRIATION OF FUNDS

ARTICLE 24

The adoption of a Budget by the Assembly shall constitute an authorisation to the competent officials or authorities to incur expenditure, during the year to which the Budget relates, for the purposes for which money has been voted in the Budget up to, but not exceeding, the amounts so voted.

ARTICLE 25

The competent officials shall not allow any money to be expended for any purpose in excess of the amount provided in the Budget for such purpose. In order to prevent any such excess of expenditure, they shall cause all payments, as made, to be appropriated to the proper item of the Budget, and shall keep a record of such appropriations and of liabilities incurred showing at all times the amount available under each item.

ARTICLE 26

1. On the receipt of each contribution, the Secretary-General shall distribute to the competent officials of the autonomous organisations the proportional amount to which each organisation is entitled. The share of each autonomous organisation shall bear the same proportion to the whole contribution as the estimates of such organisation bear to the whole estimates of expenditure of the League for the year to which the contribution relates.

2. The Secretariat and the autonomous organisations shall share in the Working Capital Fund in a proportion determined, *mutatis mutandis*, on the principle of paragraph 1.

3. Where the current requirements of the Secretariat, or of an autonomous organisation, within the limits of its Budget, cannot be met out of its proportional share of the contributions hitherto received or other income, the Secretary-General shall make advances to meet such requirements out of the Working Capital Fund up to the amount of the organisation's proportional share in the fund. An organisation may be advanced more than its proportional share of the fund as a temporary loan with the consent of the competent officials of the organisations whose shares are thereby diminished.

ARTICLE 27

1. Where the advances which can be made under the preceding article are not sufficient, the Secretary-General shall have power to contract loans within the limits of the Budget and with the approval of the Council, or, if the Council is not in session, of the President of the Council.

2. The interest on such loans shall be charged to the various organisations in the proportion in which they benefit from them; but, if any organisation has already received more than its proportional share of the Working Capital Fund, it shall, as from the date of contracting the loan, be charged interest on such excess as though it were money derived from the loan, and an equal amount of the loan shall be available, without interest, for the organisations whose shares of working capital have been depleted.

3. The Secretary-General shall not borrow for any organisation in any year more than its proportional share (calculated on the same principle as its proportional share in contributions) of the total amount which he estimates that he can borrow during such year.

ARTICLE 28

When a sum is voted in the Budget by the Assembly without specification of the precise purposes for which it is to be applied, no part of such sum shall be expended until a detailed statement as to the nature and object of the expenditure has been considered and approved by the competent authority.

ARTICLE 29

1. Transfers from one item to another of the same chapter of the Budget may be effected by a decision of the Supervisory Commission in the case of the Secretariat, and of the competent authority in the case of the other autonomous organisations.

2. Except as provided in Article 33, no transfer other than those mentioned in paragraph 1 above shall be made. Nevertheless, for the 1940 financial year, transfers from one chapter to another may be effected by a decision of the Supervisory Commission.[4]

3. The decisions taken in pursuance of paragraphs 1 and 2 above shall at once be communicated to all Members of the League and to the Assembly at the beginning of its regular annual session.

[4]By successive decisions the Supervisory Commission approved the application of Article 29(2) for the years 1941, 1942, 1943, 1944, and 1945.

ARTICLE 30

1. Payments in respect of transactions for which provision is made in the Budget of the particular year, and which take place before December 31st of that year, may be charged to the accounts of that year if they are made not later than January 31st of the following year.

2. Persons to whom any payment is due out of the Budget for any year shall be requested to submit their accounts in good time before January 31st of the following year, and shall, so far as is possible, be tendered payment before that date.

3. There shall be included in each Part of the Budget for each year a fund, known as the "Unpaid Liabilities Fund," for the purpose of enabling the competent officials to pay debts which are due in respect of transactions covered by the Budget for previous years, but which could not be paid in time to be chargeable to such years owing to unavoidable or excusable delay in the presentation or settlement of the accounts.

4. Creditors who, after their attention has been called to the provisions of this article, neglect to present their accounts in time to allow of payment by the prescribed date, if they cannot be paid out of the Unpaid Liabilities Fund without preventing payment therefrom of creditors who satisfy the requirements of paragraph 3, shall be informed that their accounts cannot be paid until the necessary sum has again been voted by the Assembly.

CHAPTER VII. THE WORKING CAPITAL FUND: INVESTMENT OF FUNDS

ARTICLE 31

1. The Working Capital Fund is a fund established for the purposes mentioned in Article 33 below, and constituted by monies voted by the Assembly and payable by the Members of the League, in addition to the sum voted for the expenses of a year.

2. The sums paid by Members of the League since January 10th, 1920, for the purpose of constituting or augmenting the Working Capital Fund shall be carried to the credit of the Members which have paid such sums.

3. The Assembly may liberate all or part of the sums constituting the Working Capital Fund, and the sums so liberated shall be returned to the Members which have contributed to the Fund in proportion to their respective contributions.

4. Subject to a decision of the Assembly, the States which for any reason cease to be Members of the League shall be entitled to the re-

imbursement of the total amount of their contributions to the Working Capital Fund.

5. Members joining the League after November 15th, 1920, are entitled to increase their contributions to the Working Capital Fund or to contribute thereto in the proportion of payments made by other Members, even if the Working Capital Fund reaches the maximum limit fixed for it. This provision shall be communicated by the Secretary-General to all the Members which entered the League after November 15th, 1920.

ARTICLE 32

1. The Working Capital Fund shall be administered as a separate account. As soon as a Member pays its contribution, the Working Capital Fund Account shall be immediately credited with a portion of the contribution corresponding to the ratio between the amount voted in respect of the Working Capital Fund for the year and the total amount voted for the year.

2. The amount shall be debited with the amounts withdrawn in accordance with these Regulations.

ARTICLE 33

1. In accordance with Article 26, paragraph 2, the Working Capital Fund is primarily applicable to meet temporarily normal requirements of regular organisations of the League which cannot be paid out of income at the time when they are due to be met. Such organisations shall have the first claim to assistance from the fund. The assistance shall be given in the form of advances from the fund to the competent officials of the organisations, and such advances shall be repaid to the fund as soon as the necessary income is available.

2. Recoverable advances required for work undertaken by the League may be made from the Working Capital Fund if the money is not required for the regular organisations. Such advances must be authorised by a special resolution of the Council, which shall keep the Members of the League fully informed with regard to all such resolutions and advances.

3. Repayments of recoverable advances shall be paid into the fund from which the advances were drawn pending a decision by the Assembly as to their final disposal.

4. Sums drawn from the Working Capital Fund by way of recoverable advances under the terms of paragraph 2 above, but which the Council subsequently decides cannot, in fact, be recovered, shall be repaid to the fund, either by means of a transfer approved by the Council from some other part of the Budget for the current year or

by means of a specific vote for the purpose in the Budget for the year following that in which they were declared by the Council to be irrecoverable.

Article 33a

1. There shall be a special fund known as the Guarantee Fund which shall be administered and utilised as provided in the present article and may not be diverted from such use.

2. (a) Where the Assembly, on a report from the Supervisory Commission, considers it to be probable that the actual expenditure under a chapter of a part of the Budget concerning the Secretariat or an autonomous organisation may be less than the total amount which it is desirable to vote in order to provide for all contingencies, it may:

(i) Vote the credits without reduction, and

(ii) Direct that part only of the total amount of the chapter shall be collected in contributions from the Members of the League and that the balance, if it should become necessary to spend it, shall be provided from the Guarantee Fund.

(b) Reductions of contributions may be effected under sub-paragraph (a) only to the extent to which they are covered by sums available in the Guarantee Fund.

3. In the case of the Secretariat, the Guarantee Fund shall be drawn upon directly by the Treasurer. In the case of the autonomous organisations, the competent officials shall apply to the Secretary-General, who shall give effect to their requests.

4. The application to the Secretariat and the autonomous organisations of the provisions of the present article is subject to the supervision provided for in Chapter X of the present Regulations.

5. The Guarantee Fund shall be alimented by the sums which the Assembly shall decide to have paid into it. It shall not form part of the Budget as referred to in Chapter III of the present Regulations and shall be administered as a distinct account. A statement showing the position of the Fund and audited by the Auditor shall be annexed to the annual accounts presented to the Assembly.

6. (a) If the statement shows any withdrawals from the Guarantee Fund, the amounts withdrawn shall be made good to the Fund from the Budget within two years from the date of their withdrawal, unless the Assembly otherwise decides.

(b) If, at the end of the financial year, the amounts shown in the statement as standing to the credit of the Guarantee Fund, together with any sums withdrawn from the Fund and still outstanding, exceed the amounts which the Assembly has decided from time to time to have paid into it, the amount of such excess shall be withdrawn from the Fund and treated as a receipt for that financial year.

ARTICLE 33*b*⁵

1. There shall be a Reserve Fund, the object of which shall be to ensure that the expenses of the League of Nations are duly met within the limits of the Budget voted by the Assembly.

2. The Reserve Fund shall be constituted by: (*a*) the sums which are received from Members of the League in respect of financial periods anterior by two or more years to the current financial period; (*b*) any other sums which the Assembly may cause to be paid into it; and (*c*) any interest earned on the investments of the Fund.

3. The Fund shall not be drawn upon except in virtue of express authorisation by the Supervisory Commission, which shall make a special report to the Assembly.

4. The Reserve Fund shall be administered as a separate account. A statement showing the position of the Fund, audited by the Auditor, shall be submitted each year to the Assembly.

ARTICLE 34

The Secretary-General may place the Working Capital Fund, and any other funds not immediately required for use, on deposit at interest with the bankers of the League, or in other banks of internationally recognised standing, for such periods as he may consider desirable. The interest received shall be dealt with in accordance with Article 23.

CHAPTER VIII. THE ACCOUNTS

ARTICLE 35

The annual accounts shall consist of two parts:

1. A budget account showing for each item: (*a*) the original vote, (*b*) the vote as modified by any transfers which may have been approved by the competent authority, (*c*) the actual expenditure incurred.

2. A statement of assets and liabilities as at December 31st.

ARTICLE 36

1. A statement showing the position of the Working Capital Fund, based on the account mentioned in Article 32, shall be attached to the accounts as an annex.

⁵The Supervisory Commission, at its session held in September 1944, approved the suspension of Articles 21(5) and 33*b* for the year 1945 in regard to the appropriation of contributions in arrear (see document [C.27.M.27.1944.]).

2. A statement showing for the past financial year (*a*) any recoverable advances made from the Working Capital Fund, and (*b*) any expenses borne on a vote for unforseen expenses incurrable only by special resolution of a competent authority, shall be annexed to the accounts.

3. There shall be attached to the accounts as annexes: a memorandum showing for the past financial year the resolutions of the Council with reference to (*a*) any recoverable advances made from the Working Capital Fund and (*b*) any advances originally thought to be recoverable and ultimately considered by the Council to be irrecoverable; and of the competent authority with reference to (*c*) any expenses borne on a vote for unforseen expenses incurrable only by special resolution of a competent authority and (*d*) any transfers made in the Budget.

ARTICLE 37

1. The procedure prescribed in Chapter IV with regard to the Budget shall, *mutatis mutandis*, apply also to the accounts.

2. The Secretary-General shall see that accounts and the annexes for each year reach the Commission before April 1st of the following year.

3. The provisions of Chapter IV concerning the representation of the various organisations at meetings of the Commission and the Assembly or its Finance Committee shall also apply to the submission and discussion of the accounts.

ARTICLE 38

1. The Assembly shall finally pass the expenditure and income accounts. It may disallow any item which it may consider improper and may direct the corresponding amendment of the accounts. The accounts, with the modifications (if any) made by the Assembly, shall be adopted by the Assembly.

2. If the Assembly disallows any item in the accounts, it shall, at the same time, decide what steps shall be taken to deal with the matter.

ARTICLE 38*a*

The difference between the actual receipts and the expenditure for each completed financial year shall be entered in the Budget of the second year following. If the difference constitutes a credit balance, it shall be used to effect a corresponding reduction of the sum to be collected from the Members of the League by way of contribution for the year in the Budget of which it is entered; if the difference represents a deficit, the sum to be contributed by Members of the League for such year shall be increased by the amount of the deficit.

CHAPTER IX.　INTERNAL CONTROL

ARTICLE 39

The competent officials shall designate the officials who may incur liabilities and make payments on behalf of, or out of the funds of, the respective organisations. They shall make rules to secure: (*a*) that no liabilities are incurred or payments made except by such officials, (*b*) that no liabilities are incurred which are not provided for in the Budget, (*c*) that no payment is made for which the liability has ceased, and (*d*) generally to establish strict control enforcing observance of the rule of this article.

ARTICLE 40

1. The competent officials shall make rules to ensure the exercise of the greatest economy in incurring liabilities.

2. In all cases in which it seems to be desirable, and in any event in the case of any single purchase of supplies likely to exceed 10,000 Swiss francs in cost, tenders shall be invited by advertisement in at least two leading newspapers belonging to different countries, and in the *Monthly Summary* of the League or an official publication of any autonomous organisation concerned.

3. The competent officials shall determine who may open and accept tenders, and make rules for guidance in accepting tenders.

ARTICLE 41

In order to ensure economy, the competent officials shall cause an accurate record to be kept of all capital acquisitions, and of all supplies purchased and used during each year, and shall submit to the auditor, with their accounts, a statement showing the stores in hand at December 31st, distinguishing stores purchased from capital and stores purchased from revenue.

ARTICLE 42

1. The competent officials shall make rules prohibiting the use of the property or the services of the League for private purposes, except with due authorisation given in the interests of the League and subject to specific regulations.

2. Such regulations shall provide for payment, unless there is a reason to forgo payment in the interest of the League, and shall contain the necessary provisions to ensure that all payments due are regularly collected.

CHAPTER X. EXTERNAL SUPERVISION

ARTICLE 43

1. The provisions of the following articles are without prejudice to the provisions of other Chapters defining the supervision exercisable by the Commission.

2. The following articles are without prejudice to the power of the Commission under other Chapters, where no special mention is made of the rapporteur or the auditor, to delegate to them powers and duties by the regulations which the Commission makes for the conduct of its business.

ARTICLE 44

1. The accounts of the League shall be audited by the auditor after the closing of the accounts for each year, and, in addition, three times during the course of each year.

2. The three audits which are to be performed during the year shall be at such time as the Commission may determine, but reasonable notice shall be given in advance to the competent officials of the organisations concerned.

3. The auditor shall report to the Commission upon each audit. The audit of the closed accounts of each year shall be completed and be submitted, with the auditor's report thereon, to the Commission not later than April 15th in the year following.

ARTICLE 45

The auditor shall be entitled to see, on demand, any document which is relevant to his examination of the accounts or other duties. Not later than the 10th of each month, a statement of receipts and expenditure for the preceding month shall be forwarded to him, together with the report of the Internal Control Officer.

ARTICLE 46

For the purpose of each of the audits, the competent officials shall furnish to the auditor, at the seat of the organisation concerned, budget accounts, with vouchers, showing all receipts and payments for every completed month since the last audit down to the close of the preceding month.

ARTICLE 47

1. The auditor shall verify whether the receipts and payments are in accordance with the Budget and with the regulations.

2. With respect to the payments, he shall in particular ascertain whether any sums have been paid which were not due and whether any double or over-payments have been made.

3. Any question which the auditor may raise with regard to any receipt or payment, and upon which he is not satisfied by such verbal explanation as he may receive from the competent official, shall be put to such official and be answered by him in writing, and the question shall, if the reply is not satisfactory to the auditor, be placed before the Commission.

ARTICLE 48

1. The auditor shall include in his report upon the closed accounts for each year a statement dealing with:

   (*a*) The receipts of the League during the year.

   (*b*) The amounts receivable at December 31st.

   (*c*) The amounts recoverable at December 31st.

   (*d*) The stores in hand at December 31st.

   (*e*) The liabilities at December 31st.

   (*f*) Any other items which the Commission may deem it necessary to add hereto.

2. In addition to the reports referred to in Article 44, the auditor may, if he thinks fit, report to the Commission from time to time, and shall so report if the Commission so determines.

ARTICLE 49

1. After considering the reports submitted by the auditor, the rapporteur shall draft a general report on the accounts of each year for the consideration of the Commission. This report shall deal in detail with all matters likely to be of interest concerning the financial administration of the League during the year in question.

2. The rapporteur shall at once send to the competent official copies of the parts of his draft report relating to their organisations

FINAL PROVISIONS

ARTICLE 50

1. Rules made by the competent officials, in order to carry out the provision of these Regulations, shall be communicated to the

Commission in due time before the next session of the Commission.

2. The rules of internal financial administration hitherto in force in the various organisations shall be brought into conformity with these Regulations.

ARTICLE 51

These Regulations shall not be amended except by the Assembly acting upon the advice of its Finance Committee; but, where it is proved to the Commission that some alteration or addition is urgently required, the Commission is authorised to approve and to put into temporary operation such alteration or addition, but shall report thereon to the Council and the Assembly as soon as possible for final decision by the latter.

ARTICLE 52

The present Regulations shall come into force on January 1st, 1923.

XIII. THE BUDGET OF THE LEAGUE

The following table of budget figures for financial periods lists in Column I total expenditures for all League activities, which include expenditures for the Permanent Court of International Justice (Column II) and the International Labor Organization (Column III). The figures concerning the International Labor Organization in Column III indicate only the amount of the International Labor Organization budget borne by States Members of the League; the budget of the International Labor Organization differed from these figures (see Column IV) since in actual practice membership in the International Labor Organization was independent of membership in the League.

The budgets of the League of Nations covering the Second (1920) to the Eighteenth Financial Period (1936) were computed in gold francs adopted by the League of Nations. This gold franc was equivalent to 0.3225806 of a gram of gold 90 per cent fine, or to 0.2903225 of a gram of gold fine. From 1923 to 1936—to be exact, to September 26, 1936—this gold franc was on a parity with the Swiss franc. In 1921 and 1922 the gold franc rated slightly higher than the Swiss franc (1921 rate: 1 gold franc = 1.196322 Swiss francs; 1922 rate: 1 gold franc = 1.06121-25 Swiss francs). Beginning with the Nineteenth Financial Period all League budget estimates were expressed in Swiss francs. The preliminary estimates of the Permanent Court of International Justice were computed in Dutch guilders. As indicated in Column V, the first budget of the League was drawn up in English pounds sterling.

Year	Financial[a] Period	I Total Expenditures	II Permanent Court of International Justice	III International Labor Organization *League* *Expenditures*	IV International Labor Organization *Total* *Expenditures*	V Mone- tary Unit
1920	Organization[b]	250,000	100	33,000		Pounds sterling
1920	Second[c]	10,000,000	150,000	3,250,000		Gold francs
1921	Third[d]	20,650,000	1,500,000	7,000,000[e]	8,762,500	”
1922	Fourth	20,873,945	1,500,000	6,135,610	8,159,325	”
1923	Fifth	25,673,508	1,880,000	8,200,462	8,744,212	”
1924	Sixth	23,233,635.70	1,920,168	7,032,295	7,077,295	”
1925	Seventh	22,658,138	1,908,209	7,340,595	7,355,595	”
1926	Eighth	22,930,633	1,907,691	7,114,938	7,469,720	”
1927	Ninth	24,512,341	2,143,777	7,431,724	7,812,490	”
1928	Tenth	25,333,817	1,171,104	7,958,470	8,098,470	”
1929	Eleventh	27,026,280	2,255,555	8,612,640	8,782,640	”
1930	Twelfth	28,210,248	2,267,981	8,552,011	8,860,011	”
1931	Thirteenth	31,637,501	2,712,668	8,661,652	9,157,715	”
1932	Fourteenth	33,687,994	2,663,702	8,792,290	9,287,290	”
1933	Fifteenth	33,429,132	2,660,196	8,351,972	9,065,442	”
1934	Sixteenth	30,827,805	2,538,827	8,257,876	8,737,505	”
1935	Seventeenth	30,639,664	2,535,646	8,686,046	8,932,110	”
1936	Eighteenth[f]	28,279,901	2,321,200	6,699,450	9,919,093	”
1937	Nineteenth	29,184,128	2,561,333	7,608,662	9,708,009	Swiss francs
1938	Twentieth[g]	22,827,081.19	1,878,035.38[h]	5,408,135.82[j]		Gold francs
		32,273,251	2,894,516[i]	8,335,272[k]	10,261,003	Swiss francs
1939	Twenty-first[l]	22,799,327[m]	1,799,437.46[n]	5,319,321.10[p]		Gold francs
		32,234,012	2,839,689[o]	8,394,243[q]	10,399,779	Swiss francs
1940	Twenty-second	15,172,790.95[r]	1,685,962.72[t]	4,492,528.15[v]		Gold francs
		21,451,408[s]	2,383,638[u]	6,351,600[w]	7,858,000	Swiss francs
1941	Twenty-third[x]	10,659,711	500,000	3,253,000.	4,224,000	”
1942	Twenty-fourth[y]	9,647,462[z]	500,000	3,169,302	4,224,000	”
1943	Twenty-fifth[aa]	11,388,376[bb]	456,608	4,588,187	5,224,000	”
1944	Twenty-sixth[cc]	10,089,049	471,465	3,725,534	5,463,000	”
1945	Twenty-seventh[dd]	14,868,409	471,226	8,513,016	11,525,505	”
1946	Twenty-eighth[ee]	17,883,849	3,016,424	8,618,015	11,521,510[ff]	”

[a]The term varied in the early years of the League. The first budget was for the "Organisation Period"; "Fiscal Period" was the term used for the second, fourth, and fifth budgets (1920, 1922, 1923); the third (1921) was simply the "Third Budget." Beginning with the sixth (1924) the budget was for a "Financial Period."

[b]This so-called first budget of the League (see Council Minutes, 5th Sess., p. 239) covered the expenses and receipts of the League for the months April, May, and June. 1920, plus the expenses incurred up to March 31, 1920. In contrast to all the other

figures, which are given in gold francs or in Swiss francs (see Column V), the first budget figures were in English pounds sterling.

cCovered the period July 1 to December 31, 1920. See Council Minutes, 5th Sess., p. 253.

dCovered the calendar year 1921.

eOn this amount, see also footnote in *Official Journal*, October, 1920, p. 453.

fSee *Official Journal*, October, 1935, p. 1014.

gFor computation in both gold and Swiss francs, see *Official Journal*, October, 1935, p. 705 and 708.

hNet sum allocated among the League members; see *ibid.*, p. 705.

iEstimate for 1938 in Swiss francs; see *ibid.*, p. 708.

jNet sum allocated among the League Members:; see *ibid.*, p. 705.

kEstimate for 1938; see *ibid.*, p. 708.

lSee *Official Journal*, October, 1938, p. 703.

mSee *ibid.*

nNet sum allocated among the League members; see *ibid.*

oEstimates for 1939 in Swiss francs; see *ibid.*, p. 706.

pNet sum allocated among the League Members; see *ibid.*, p. 703.

qEstimates for 1939 in Swiss francs; see *ibid.*, p. 706.

rSee *Official Journal*, November–December, 1939, p. 429.

sSee *ibid.*

tSee *ibid.*

uReduced estimate in Swiss francs; see *ibid.*, p. 432.

vSee *ibid.*, p. 429.

wReduced estimate in Swiss francs; see *ibid.*, p. 432.

xEstimates for 1941 in Swiss francs; see Document [C.153.M.140.1940.X.], p. 4.

yEstimates for 1942 in Swiss francs; see Document [C.54.M.51.1941.X.], p. 4.

zEquivalent to 6,823,713 gold francs.

aaEstimates for 1943 in Swiss francs; see Document [C.81.M.81.1942.X.], p. 4.

bbEquivalent to 8,055,073 gold francs.

ccEstimates for 1944 in Swiss francs; see Document [C.24.M.24.1943.X.], p. 4.

ddEstimates for 1945 in Swiss francs; see Document [C.28.M.28.1944.X.], p. 4.

eeEstimates for 1946 in Swiss francs; see Document [C.102.M.102.1945.X.], p. 4.

ffFor 1947 and 1948, estimated total expenditures, in Swiss francs, of the International Labor Organization were 15,952,980 and 18,942,983, respectively.

Appendix Two

DOCUMENTS RELATING TO THE INTERNATIONAL LABOR ORGANIZATION AND THE PERMANENT COURT OF INTERNATIONAL JUSTICE

I. STATUTE OF THE INTERNATIONAL LABOUR ORGANISATION[1]

SECTION I. ORGANISATION OF LABOUR

PREAMBLE

Whereas the League of Nations has for its object the establishment of universal peace, and such a peace can be established only if it is based upon social justice;

And whereas conditions of labour exist involving such injustice, hardship and privation to large numbers of people as to produce unrest so great that the peace and harmony of the world are imperilled; and an improvement of those conditions is urgently required: as, for example, by the regulation of the hours of work, including the establishment of a maximum working day and week, the regulation of the labour supply, the prevention of unemployment, the provision of an adequate living wage, the protection of the worker against sickness, disease and injury arising out of his employment, the protection of children, young persons and women, provision for old age and injury, protection of the interests of workers when employed in countries other than their own, recognition of the principle of freedom of association, the organisation of vocational and technical education and other measures;

Whereas also the failure of any nation to adopt humane conditions of labour is an obstacle in the way of other nations which desire to improve the conditions in their own countries;

The High Contracting Parties, moved by sentiments of justice and humanity, as well as by the desire to secure the permanent peace of the world, agree to the following: —

CHAPTER I.—ORGANISATION

ARTICLE 387

A permanent organisation is hereby established for the promotion of the objects set forth in the Preamble.

[1]Officially, Part XIII of the Treaty of Versailles and of the corresponding sections of the peace treaties concluded with the other Central Powers after World War I. The numbering here is that of Part XIII of the Treaty of Versailles. For subsequent amendments to the Constitution of the ILO see above, p. 356–357.

The original Members of the League of Nations shall be the original Members of this organisation, and hereafter membership of the League of Nations shall carry with it membership of the said organisation.

ARTICLE 388

The permanent organisation shall consist of (I) a General Conference of Representatives of the Members and (II) an International Labour Office controlled by the Governing Body described in Article 393.

ARTICLE 389

1. The meetings of the General Conference of Representatives of the Members shall be held from time to time as occasion may require, and at least once in every year. It shall be composed of four Representatives of each of the Members, of whom two shall be Government Delegates and the two others shall be Delegates representing respectively the employers and the workpeople of each of the Members.

2. Each Delegate may be accompanied by advisers, who shall not exceed two in number for each item on the agenda of the meeting. When questions specially affecting women are to be considered by the Conference, one at least of the advisers should be a woman.

3. The Members undertake to nominate non-Government Delegates and advisers chosen in agreement with the industrial organisations, if such organisations exist, which are most representative of the employers or workpeople, as the case may be, in their respective countries.

4. Advisers shall not speak except on a request made by the Delegate whom they accompany and by the special authorisation of the President of the Conference, and may not vote.

5. A Delegate may by notice in writing addressed to the President appoint one of his advisers to act as his deputy, and the adviser, while so acting, shall be allowed to speak and vote.

6. The names of the Delegates and their advisers will be communicated to the International Labour Office by the Government of each of the Members.

7. The credentials of Delegates and their advisers shall be subject to scrutiny by the Conference, which may, by two-thirds of the votes cast by the Delegates present, refuse to admit any Delegate or adviser whom it deems not to have been nominated in accordance with this Article.

ARTICLE 390

1. Every Delegate shall be entitled to vote individually on all matters which are taken into consideration by the Conference.

2. If one of the Members fails to nominate one of the non-Government Delegates whom it is entitled to nominate, the other non-Government Delegate shall be allowed to sit and speak at the Conference, but not to vote.

3. If in accordance with Article 389 the Conference refuses admission to a Delegate of one of the Members, the provision of the present Article shall apply as if that Delegate had not been nominated.

ARTICLE 391

The meetings of the Conference shall be held at the seat of the League of Nations, or at such other place as may be decided by the Conference at a previous meeting by two-thirds of the votes cast by the Delegates present.

ARTICLE 392

The International Labour Office shall be established at the seat of the League of Nations as part of the organisation of the League.

ARTICLE 393

1. The International Labour Office shall be under the control of a Governing Body consisting of 24 persons, appointed in accordance with the following provisions:

2. The Governing Body of the International Labour Office shall be constituted as follows: —

Twelve persons representing the Governments,

Six persons elected by the Delegates to the conference representing the employers;

Six persons elected by the Delegates to the Conference representing the workers.

3. Of the 12 persons representing the Governments eight shall be nominated by the Members which are of the chief industrial importance, and four shall be nominated by the Members selected for the purpose by the Government Delegates to the Conference, excluding the Delegates of the eight Members mentioned above.

4. Any question as to which are the Members of the chief industrial importance shall be decided by the Council of the League of Nations.

5. The period of office of the members of the Governing Body will be three years. The method of filling vacancies and other similar questions may be determined by the Governing Body subject to the approval of the Conference.

6. The Governing Body shall, from time to time, elect one of its members to act as its Chairman, shall regulate its own procedure and

shall fix its own times of meeting. A special meeting shall be held if a written request to that effect is made by at least 10 members of the Governing Body.

ARTICLE 394

1. There shall be a Director of the International Labour Office, who shall be appointed by the Governing Body, and, subject to the instructions of the Governing Body, shall be responsible for the efficient conduct of the International Labour Office and for such other duties as may be assigned to him.

2. The Director or his deputy shall attend all meetings of the Governing Body.

ARTICLE 395

The staff of the International Labour Office shall be appointed by the Director, who shall, so far as is possible with due regard to the efficiency of the work of the Office, select persons of different nationalities. A certain number of these persons shall be women.

ARTICLE 396

1. Functions of the International Labour Office shall include the collection and distribution of information on all subjects relating to the international adjustment of conditions of industrial life and labour, and particularly the examination of subjects which it is proposed to bring before the Conference with a view to the conclusion of international conventions, and the conduct of such special investigations as may be ordered by the Conference.

2. It will prepare the agenda for the meetings of the Conference.

3. It will carry out the duties required of it by the provisions of this Part of the present Treaty in connection with international disputes.

4. It will edit and publish in French and English, and in such other languages as the Governing Body may think desirable, a periodical paper dealing with problems of industry and employment of international interest.

5. Generally, in addition to the functions set out in this Article, it shall have such other powers and duties as may be assigned to it by in the Conference.

ARTICLE 397

The Government Departments of any of the Members which deal with questions of industry and employment may communicate directly with the Director through the Representative of the Government on the Governing Body of the International Labour Office, or failing any such Representative, through such other qualified official as the Government may nominate for the purpose.

ARTICLE 398

The International Labour Office shall be entitled to the assistance of the Secretary-General of the League of Nations in any manner which it can be given.

ARTICLE 399

1. Each of the Members will pay the travelling and subsistence expenses of its Delegates and their advisers and of its Representatives attending the meetings of the Conference or Governing Body, as the case may be.

2. All the other expenses of the International Labour Office and of the meetings of the Conference or Governing Body shall be paid to the Director by the Secretary-General of the League of Nations out of the general funds of the League.

3. The Director shall be responsible to the Secretary-General of the League for the proper expenditure of all moneys paid to him in pursuance of this Article.

CHAPTER II.—PROCEDURE

ARTICLE 400

The agenda for all meetings of the Conference will be settled by the Governing Body, who shall consider any suggestion as to the agenda that may be made by the Government of any of the Members or by any representative organisation recognised for the purpose of Article 389.

ARTICLE 401

The Director shall act as the Secretary of the Conference, and shall transmit the agenda so as to reach the Members four months before the meeting of the Conference, and, through them, the non-Government Delegates when appointed.

ARTICLE 402

1. Any of the Governments of the Members may formally object to the inclusion of any item or items in the agenda. The grounds for such objection shall be set forth in a reasoned statement addressed to the Director, who shall circulate it to all the Members of the Permanent Organisation.

2. Items to which such objection has been made shall not, however, be excluded from the agenda, if at the Conference a majority of two-

thirds of the votes cast by the Delegates present is in favor of considering them.

3. If the Conference decides (otherwise than under the preceding paragraph) by two-thirds of the votes cast by the Delegates present that any subject shall be considered by the Conference, that subject shall be included in the agenda for the following meeting.

ARTICLE 403

1. The Conference shall regulate its own procedure, shall elect its own President, and may appoint committees to consider and report on any matter.

2. Except as otherwise expressly provided in this Part of the present Treaty, all matters shall be decided by a simple majority of the votes cast by the Delegates present.

3. The voting is void unless the total number of votes cast is equal to half the number of the Delegates attending the Conference.

ARTICLE 404

The Conference may add to any committees which it appoints technical experts, who shall be assessors without power to vote.

ARTICLE 405

1. When the Conference has decided on the adoption of proposals with regard to an item in the agenda, it will rest with the Conference to determine whether these proposals should take the form: (a) of a recommendation to be submitted to the Members for consideration with a view to effect being given to it by national legislation or otherwise, or (b) of a draft international convention for ratification by the Members.

2. In either case a majority of two-thirds of the votes cast by the Delegates present shall be necessary on the final vote for the adoption of the recommendation or draft convention, as the case may be, by the Conference.

3. In framing any recommendation or draft convention of general application, the Conference shall have due regard to those countries in which climatic conditions, the imperfect development of industrial organisation, or other special circumstances make the industrial conditions substantially different, and shall suggest the modifications, if any, which it considers may be required to meet the case of such countries.

4. A copy of the recommendation or draft convention shall be authenticated by the signature of the President of the Conference and of

the Director, and shall be deposited with the Secretary-General of the League of Nations. The Secretary-General will communicate a certified copy of the recommendation or draft convention to each of the Members.

5. Each of the Members undertakes that it will, within the period of one year at most from the closing of the session of the Conference, or if it is impossible owing to exceptional circumstances to do so within the period of one year, then at the earliest practicable moment and in no case later than 18 months from the closing of the session of the Conference, bring the recommendation or draft convention before the authority or authorities within whose competence the matter lies, for the enactment of legislation or other action.

6. In the case of a recommendation, the Members will inform the Secretary-General of the action taken.

7. In the case of a draft convention, the Member will, if it obtains the consent of the authority or authorities within whose competence the matter lies, communicate the formal ratification of the convention to the Secretary-General and will take such action as may be necessary to make effective the provisions of such convention.

8. If on a recommendation no legislative or other action is taken to make a recommendation effective, or if the draft convention fails to obtain the consent of the authority or authorities within whose competence the matter lies, no further obligation shall rest upon the Member.

9. In the case of a federal State, the power of which to enter into conventions on labour matters is subject to limitations, it shall be in the discretion of that Government to treat a draft convention to which such limitations apply as a recommendation only, and the provisions of this Article with respect to recommendations shall apply in such case.

10. The above Article shall be interpreted in accordance with the following principle: —

11. In no case shall any Member be asked or required, as a result of the adoption of any recommendation or draft convention by the Conference, to lessen the protection afforded by its existing legislation to the workers concerned.

ARTICLE 406

Any convention so ratified shall be registered by the Secretary-General of the League of Nations, but shall only be binding upon the Members which ratify it.

ARTICLE 407

1. If any convention coming before the Conference for final consideration fails to secure the support of two-thirds of the votes cast by

the Delegates present, it shall nevertheless be within the right of any of the Members of the Permanent Organisation to agree to such convention among themselves.

2. Any convention so agreed to shall be communicated by the Governments concerned to the Secretary-General of the League of Nations, who shall register it.

ARTICLE 408

Each of the Members agrees to make an annual report to the International Labour Office on the measures which it has taken to give effect to the provisions of conventions to which it is a party. These reports shall be made in such form and shall contain such particulars as the Governing Body may request. The Directors shall lay a summary of these reports before the next meeting of the conference.

ARTICLE 409

In the event of any representation being made to the International Labour Office by an industrial association of employers or of workers that any of the Members has failed to secure in any respect the effective observance within its jurisdiction of any convention to which it is a party, the Governing Body may communicate this representation to the Government against which it is made and may invite that Government to make such statement on the subject as it may think fit.

ARTICLE 410

If no statement is received within a reasonable time from the Government in question, or if the statement when received is not deemed to be satisfactory by the Governing Body, the latter shall have the right to publish the representation and the statement, if any, made in reply to it.

ARTICLE 411

1. Any of the Members shall have the right to file a complaint with the International Labour Office if it is not satisfied that any other Member is securing the effective observance of any convention which both have ratified in accordance with the foregoing Articles.

2. The Governing Body may, if it thinks fit, before referring such a complaint to a Commission of Enquiry, as hereinafter provided for, communicate with the Government in question in the manner described in Article 409.

3. If the Governing Body does not think it necessary to communicate the complaint to the Government in question, or if, when they

have made such communication, no statement in reply has been received within a reasonable time which the Governing Body considers to be satisfactory, the Governing Body may apply for the appointment of a Commission of Enquiry to consider the complaint and to report thereon.

4. The Governing Body may adopt the same procedure either of its own motion or on receipt of a complaint from a Delegate to the Conference.

5. When any matter arising out of Articles 410 or 411 is being considered by the Governing Body, the Government in question shall, if not already represented thereon, be entitled to send a representative to take part in the proceedings of the Governing Body while the matter is under consideration. Adequate notice of the date on which the matter will be considered shall be given to the Government in question.

Article 412

1. The Commission of Enquiry shall be constituted in accordance with the following provisions: —

2. Each of the Members agrees to nominate within six months of the date on which the present Treaty comes into force three persons of industrial experience, of whom one shall be a representative of employers, one a representative of workers, and one a person of independent standing, who shall together form a panel from which the members of the Commission of Enquiry shall be drawn.

3. The qualifications of the persons so nominated shall be subject to scrutiny by the Governing Body, which may by two thirds of the votes cast by the representatives present refuse to accept the nomination of any person whose qualifications do not in its opinion comply with the requirements of the present article.

4. Upon the application of the Governing Body, the Secretary-General of the League of Nations shall nominate three persons, one from each section of this panel, to constitute the Commission of Enquiry, and shall designate one of them as the President of the Commission. None of these three persons shall be a person nominated to the panel by any Member directly concerned in the complaint.

Article 413

The Members agree that, in the event of the reference of a complaint to a Commission of Enquiry under Article 411, they will each, whether directly concerned in the complaint or not, place at the disposal of the Commission all the information in their possession which bears upon the subject-matter of the complaint.

ARTICLE 414

1. When the Commission of Enquiry has fully considered the complaint, it shall prepare a report embodying its findings on all questions of fact relevant to determing the issue between the parties and containing such recommendations as it may think proper as to the steps which should be taken to meet the complaint and the time within which they should be taken.

2. It shall also indicate in this report the measures, if any, of an economic character against a defaulting Government which it considers to be appropriate, and which it considers other Governments would be justified in adopting.

ARTICLE 415

1. The Secretary-General of the League of Nations shall communicate the report of the Commission of Enquiry to each of the Governments concerned in the complaint, and shall cause it to be published.

2. Each of these Governments shall within one month inform the Secretary-General of the League of Nations whether or not it accepts the recommendations contained in the report of the Commission; and if not, whether it proposes to refer the complaint to the Permanent Court of International Justice of the League of Nations.

ARTICLE 416

In the event of any Member failing to take the action required by Article 405, with regard to a recommendation or draft Convention, any other Member shall be entitled to refer the matter to the Permanent Court of International Justice.

ARTICLE 417

The decision of the Permanent Court of International Justice in regard to a complaint or matter which has been referred to it in pursuance of Article 415 or Article 416 shall be final.

ARTICLE 418

The Permanent Court of International Justice may affirm, vary or reverse any of the findings or recommendations of the Commission of Enquiry, if any, and shall in its decision indicate the measures, if any, of an economic character which it considers to be appropriate, and which other Governments would be justified in adopting against a defaulting Government.

ARTICLE 419

In the event of any Member failing to carry out within the time specified the recommendations, if any, contained in the report of the Commission of Enquiry, or in the decision of the Permanent Court of International Justice, as the case may be, any other Member may take against that Member the measures of an economic character indicated in the report of the Commission or in the decision of the Court as appropriate to the case.

ARTICLE 420

The defaulting Government may at any time inform the Governing Body that it has taken the steps necessary to comply with the recommendations of the Commission of Enquiry or with those in the decision of the Permanent Court of International Justice, as the case may be, and may request it to apply to the Secretary-General of the League to constitute a Commission of Enquiry to verify its contention. In this case the provisions of Articles 412, 413, 414, 415, 417 and 418 shall apply, and if the report of the Commission of Enquiry or the decision of the Permanent Court of International Justice is in favour of the defaulting Government, the other Governments shall forthwith discontinue the measures of an economic character that they have taken against the defaulting Government.

CHAPTER III.—GENERAL

ARTICLE 421

1. The Members engage to apply conventions which they have ratified in accordance with the provisions of this part of the present Treaty to their colonies, protectorates and possessions, which are not fully self-governing:

(1) Except where owing to the local conditions the convention is inapplicable, or

(2) Subject to such modifications as may be necessary to adapt the convention to local conditions.

2. And each of the Members shall notify to the International Labour Office the action taken in respect of each of its colonies, protectorates and possessions which are not fully self-governing.

ARTICLE 422

Amendments to this Part of the present Treaty which are adopted by the Conference by a majority of two-thirds of the votes cast by the Delegates present shall take effect when ratified by the States whose representatives compose the Council of the League of Nations and by three-fourths of the Members.

Article 423

Any question or dispute relating to the interpretation of this Part of the present Treaty or of any subsequent Convention concluded by the Members in pursuance of the provisions of this Part of the present Treaty shall be referred for decision to the Permanent Court of International Justice.

CHAPTER IV.—TRANSITORY PROVISIONS

Article 424

1. The first meeting of the Conference shall take place in October, 1919. The place and agenda for this meeting shall be as specified in the Annex hereto.

2. Arrangements for the convening and the organisation of the first meeting of the Conference will be made by the Government designated for the purpose in the said Annex. That Government shall be assisted in the preparation of the documents for submission to the Conference by an International Committee constituted as provided in the said Annex.

3. The expenses of the first meeting and of all subsequent meetings held before the League of Nations has been able to establish a general fund, other than the expenses of Delegates and their advisers, will be borne by the Members in accordance with the apportionment of the expenses of the International Bureau of the Universal Postal Union.

Article 425

Until the League of Nations has been constituted all communications which under the provisions of the foregoing Articles should be addressed to the Secretary-General of the League will be preserved by the Director of the International Labour Office, who will transmit them to the Secretary-General of the League.

Article 426

Pending the creation of a Permanent Court of International Justice, disputes which in accordance with this Part of the present Treaty would be submitted to it for decision will be referred to a tribunal of three persons appointed by the Council of the League of Nations.

ANNEX

First Meeting of Annual Labour Conference, 1919

1. The place of meeting will be Washington.
2. The Government of the United States of America is requested to convene the Conference.
3. The International Organising Committee will consist of seven members, appointed by the United States of America, Great Britain, France, Italy, Japan, Belgium and Switzerland. The Committee may, if it thinks necessary, invite other Members to appoint representatives.
4. Agenda —
(1) Application of principle of the 8-hours day or of the 48-hours week.
(2) Question of preventing or providing against unemployment.
(3) Women's employment:
(*a*.) Before and after child-birth, including the question of maternity benefit.
(*b*.) During the night.
(*c*.) In unhealthy processes.
(4) Employment of children:
(*a*.) Minimum age of employment.
(*b*.) During the night.
(*c*.) In unhealthy processes.
(5) Extension and application of the International Conventions adopted at Berne in 1906 on the prohibition of night work for women employed in industry and the prohibition of the use of white phosphorus in the manufacture of matches.

SECTION II. GENERAL PRINCIPLES

ARTICLE 427

The High Contracting Parties, recognising that the well-being, physical, moral, and intellectual, of the industrial wage-earners is of supreme international importance, have framed in order to further this great end, the permanent machinery provided for in Section I, and associated with that of the League of Nations.

They recognise that differences of climate, habits and customs, of economic opportunity and industrial tradition, make strict uniformity in the conditions of labour difficult of immediate attainment. But, holding as they do, that labour should not be regarded merely as an article of commerce, they think that there are methods and principles for regulating labour conditions which all industrial communities should endeavour to apply, so far as their special circumstances will permit.

Among these methods and principles, the following seem to the High Contracting Parties to be of special and urgent importance:—

First.—The guiding principle above enunciated that labour should not be regarded merely as a commodity or article of commerce.

Second.—The right of association for all lawful purposes by the employed as well as by the employers.

Third.—The payment to the employed of a wage adequate to maintain a reasonable standard of life as this is understood in their time and country.

Fourth.—The adoption of an eight-hours day or a forty-eight-hours week as the standard to be aimed at where it has not already been attained.

Fifth.—The adoption of a weekly rest of at least twenty-four hours, which should include Sunday wherever practicable.

Sixth.—The abolition of child labour and the imposition of such limitations on the labour of young persons as shall permit the continuation of their education and assure their proper physical development.

Seventh.—The principle that men and women should receive equal remuneration for work of equal value.

Eighth.—The standard set by law in each country with respect to the conditions of labour should have due regard to the equitable economic treatment of all workers lawfully resident therein.

Ninth.—Each State should make provision for a system of inspection in which women should take part, in order to ensure the enforcement of the laws and regulations for the protection of the employed.

Without claiming that these methods and principles are either complete or final, the High Contracting Parties are of opinion that they are well fitted to guide the policy of the League of Nations; and that, if adopted by the industrial communities who are Members of the League, and safeguarded in practice by an adequate system of such inspection, they will confer lasting benefits upon the wage-earners of the world.

II. STATUTE OF THE COURT PROVIDED FOR BY ARTICLE 14 OF THE COVENANT OF THE LEAGUE OF NATIONS AS AMENDED IN ACCORDANCE WITH THE PROTOCOL OF SEPTEMBER 14TH, 1929[1]

ARTICLE I

A Permanent Court of International Justice is hereby established, in accordance with Article 14 of the Covenant of the League of Nations. This Court shall be in addition to the Court of Arbitration organized by the Convention of The Hague of 1899 and 1907, and to the special Tribunals of Arbitration to which States are always at liberty to submit their disputes for settlement.

CHAPTER I. ORGANIZATION OF THE COURT

ARTICLE 2

The Permanent Court of International Justice shall be composed of a body of independent judges, elected regardless of their nationality from amongst persons of high moral character, who possess the qualifications required in their respective countries for appointment to the highest judicial offices, or are jurisconsults of recognized competence in international law.

ARTICLE 3*

The Court shall consist of fifteen members.

ARTICLE 4*

The members of the Court shall be elected by the Assembly and by the Council from a list of persons nominated by the national groups in

[1]Reprinted from Permanent Court of International Justice, Series D, No. 1, *Statute and Rules of Court and Other Constitutional Documents, Rules or Regulations* (3d ed., Leyden, 1936). "The amended text of the Statute is reproduced from the League of Nations Document C. 80. M. 28. 1936. V. The new articles and those which have been modified under the Protocol of September 14th, 1929, are however indicated by an asterisk."

the Court of Arbitration, in accordance with the following provisions.

In the case of Members of the League of Nations not represented in the Permanent Court of Arbitration, the lists of candidates shall be drawn up by national groups appointed for this purpose by their governments under the same conditions as those prescribed for members of the Permanent Court of Arbitration by Article 44 of the Convention of The Hague of 1907 for the pacific settlement of international disputes.

The conditions under which a State which has accepted the Statute of the Court but is not a Member of the League of Nations, may participate in electing the members of the Court shall, in the absence of a special agreement, be laid down by the Assembly on the proposal of the Council.

Article 5

At least three months before the date of the election, the Secretary-General of the League of Nations shall address a written request to the members of the Court of Arbitration belonging to the States which join the League subsequently, and to the persons appointed under paragraph 2 of Article 4, inviting them to undertake, within a given time, by national groups, the nomination of persons in a position to accept the duties of a member of the Court.

No group may nominate more than four persons, not more than two of whom shall be of their own nationality. In no case must the number of candidates nominated be more than double the number of seats to be filled.

Article 6

Before making these nominations, each national group is recommended to consult its Highest Court of Justice, its Legal Faculties and Schools of Law, and its National Academies and national sections of International Academies devoted to the study of Law.

Article 7

The Secretary-General of the League of Nations shall prepare a list in alphabetical order of all the persons thus nominated. Save as provided in Article 12, paragraph 2, these shall be the only persons eligible for appointment.

The Secretary-General shall submit this list to the Assembly and to the Council.

Article 8*

The Assembly and the Council shall proceed independently of one another to elect the members of the Court.

ARTICLE 9

At every election, the electors shall bear in mind that not only should all the persons appointed as members of the Court possess the qualifications required, but the whole body also should represent the main forms of civilization and the principal legal systems of the world.

ARTICLE 10

Those candidates who obtain an absolute majority of votes in the Assembly and in the Council shall be considered as elected.

In the event of more than one national of the same Member of the League being elected by the votes of both the Assembly and the Council, the eldest of these only shall be considered as elected.

ARTICLE 11

If, after the first meeting held for the purpose of the election, one or more seats remain to be filled, a second and, if necessary, a third meeting shall take place.

ARTICLE 12

If, after the third meeting, one or more seats still remain unfilled, a joint conference consisting of six members, three appointed by the Assembly and three by the Council, may be formed, at any time, at the request of either the Assembly or the Council, for the purpose of choosing one name for each seat still vacant, to submit to the Assembly and the Council for their respective acceptance.

If the Conference is unanimously agreed upon any person who fulfils the required conditions, he may be included in its list, even though he was not included in the list of nominations referred to in Articles 4 and 5.

If the joint conference is satisfied that it will not be successful in procuring an election, those members of the Court who have already been appointed shall, within a period to be fixed by the Council, proceed to fill the vacant seats by selection from amongst those candidates who have obtained votes either in the Assembly or in the Council.

In the event of an equality of votes amongst the judges, the eldest judge shall have a casting vote.

ARTICLE 13*

The members of the Court shall be elected for nine years. They may be re-elected.

They shall continue to discharge their duties until their places have been filled. Though replaced, they shall finish any cases which they may have begun.

In the case of the resignation of a member of the Court, the resignation will be addressed to the President of the Court for transmission to the Secretary-General of the League of Nations.

This last notification makes the place vacant.

ARTICLE 14*

Vacancies which may occur shall be filled by the same method as that laid down for the first election, subject to the following provision: the Secretary-General of the League of Nations shall, within one month of the occurrence of the vacancy, proceed to issue the invitations provided for in Article 5, and the date of the election shall be fixed by the Council at its next session.

ARTICLE 15*

A member of the Court elected to replace a member whose period of appointment has not expired, will hold the appointment for the remainder of his predecessor's term.

ARTICLE 16*

The members of the Court may not exercise any political or administrative function, nor engage in any other occupation of a professional nature.

ARTICLE 17*

No member of the Court may act as agent, counsel or advocate in any case.

No member may participate in the decision of any case in which he has previously taken an active part as agent, counsel or advocate for one of the contesting parties, or as a member of a national or international Court, or of a commission of enquiry, or in any other capacity.

Any doubt on this point is settled by the decision of the Court.

ARTICLE 18

A member of the Court cannot be dismissed unless, in the unanimous opinion of the other members, he has ceased to fulfil the required conditions.

Formal notification thereof shall be made to the Secretary-General of the League of Nations, by the Registrar.

ARTICLE 19

The members of the Court, when engaged on the business of the Court, shall enjoy diplomatic privileges and immunities.

ARTICLE 20

Every member of the Court shall, before taking up his duties, make a solemn declaration in open Court that he will exercise his powers impartially and conscientiously.

ARTICLE 21

The Court shall elect its President and Vice-President for three years; they may be re-elected.

It shall appoint its Registrar.

The duties of Registrar of the Court shall not be deemed incompatible with those of Secretary-General of the Permanent Court of Arbitration.

ARTICLE 22

The seat of the Court shall be established at The Hague.

The President and Registrar shall reside at the seat of the Court.

ARTICLE 23*

The Court shall remain permanently in session except during the judicial vacations, the dates and duration of which shall be fixed by the Court.

Members of the Court whose homes are situated at more than five day's normal journey from The Hague shall be entitled, apart from the judicial vacations, to six month's leave every three years, not including the time spent in travelling.

Members of the Court shall be bound, unless they are on regular leave or prevented from attending by illness or other serious reason duly explained to the President, to hold themselves permanently at the disposal of the Court.

ARTICLE 24

If, for some special reason, a member of the Court considers that he should not take part in the decision of a particular case, he shall so inform the President.

If the President considers that for some special reason one of the members of the Court should not sit on a particular case, he shall give him notice accordingly.

If in any such case the member of the Court and the President disagree, the matter shall be settled by the decision of the Court.

ARTICLE 25*

The full Court shall sit except when it is expressly provided otherwise.

Subject to the condition that the number of judges available to constitute the Court is not thereby reduced below eleven, the Rules of Court may provide for allowing one or more judges, according to circumstances and in rotation, to be dispensed from sitting.

Provided always that a quorum of nine judges shall suffice to constitute the Court.

ARTICLE 26*

Labour cases, particularly cases referred to in Part XIII (Labour) of the Treaty of Versailles and the corresponding portions of the other treaties of peace, shall be heard and determined by the Court under the following conditions:

The Court will appoint every three years a special Chamber of five judges, selected so far as possible with due regard to the provisions of Article 9. In addition, two judges shall be selected for the purpose of replacing a judge who finds it impossible to sit. If the parties so demand, cases will be heard and determined by this Chamber. In the absence of any such demand, the full Court will sit. In both cases, the judges will be assisted by four technical assessors sitting with them, but without the right to vote, and chosen with a view to ensuring a just representation of the competing interests.

The technical assessors shall be chosen for each particular case in accordance with rules of procedure under Article 30 from a list of "Assessors for Labour Cases" composed of two persons nominated by each Member of the League of Nations and an equivalent number nominated by the Governing Body of the Labour Office. The Governing Body will nominate, as to one-half, representatives of the workers, and, as to one-half, representatives of employers from the list referred to in Article 412 of the Treaty of Versailles and the corresponding articles of the other treaties of peace.

Recourse may always be had to the summary procedure provided for in Article 29, in the cases referred to in the first paragraph of the present Article, if the parties so request.

In Labour cases, the International Office shall be at liberty to furnish the Court with all relevant information, and for this purpose the Director of that Office shall receive copies of all written proceedings.

ARTICLE 27*

Cases relating to transit and communications, particularly cases referred to in Part XII (Ports, Waterways and Railways) of the Treaty of Versailles and the corresponding portions of the other treaties of peace, shall be heard and determined by the Court under the following conditions:

The Court will appoint every three years a special Chamber of five judges, selected so far as possible with due regard to the provisions of Article 9. In addition, two judges shall be selected for the purpose of replacing a judge who finds it impossible to sit. If the parties so demand, cases will be heard and determined by this Chamber. In the absence of any such demand, the full Court will sit. When desired by the parties or decided by the Court, the judges will be assisted by four technical assessors sitting with them, but without the right to vote.

The technical assessors shall be chosen for each particular case in accordance with rules of procedure under Article 30 from a list of "Assessors for Transit and Communications Cases" composed of two persons nominated by each Member of the League of Nations.

Recourse may always be had to the summary procedure provided for in Article 29, in the cases referred to in the first paragraph of the present Article, if the parties so request.

ARTICLE 28

The special chambers provided for in Articles 26 and 27 may, with the consent of the parties to the dispute, sit elsewhere than at The Hague.

ARTICLE 29*

With a view to the speedy despatch of business, the Court shall form annually a Chamber composed of five judges who, at the request of the contesting parties, may hear and determine cases by summary procedure. In addition, two judges shall be selected for the purpose of replacing a judge who finds it impossible to sit.

ARTICLE 30

The Court shall frame rules for regulating its procedure. In particular, it shall lay down rules for summary procedure.

ARTICLE 31*

Judges of the nationality of each of the contesting parties shall retain their right to sit in the case before the Court.

If the Court includes upon the Bench a judge of the nationality of one of the parties, the other party may choose a person to sit as judge. Such person shall be chosen preferably from among those persons who have been nominated as candidates as provided in Articles 4 and 5.

If the Court includes upon the Bench no judge of the nationality of the contesting parties, each of these parties may proceed to select a judge as provided in the preceding paragraph.

The present provision shall apply to the case of Articles 26, 27 and 29. In such cases, the President shall request one or, if necessary, two of the members of the Court forming the Chamber to give place to the members of the Court of the nationality of the parties concerned, and, failing such or if they are unable to be present, to the judges specially appointed by the parties.

Should there be several parties in the same interest, they shall, for the purpose of the preceding provisions, be reckoned as one party only. Any doubt upon this point is settled by the decision of the Court.

Judges selected as laid down in paragraphs 2, 3 and 4 of this Article shall fulfil the conditions required by Articles 2, 17 (paragraph 2), 20 and 24 of this Statute. They shall take part in the decision on terms of complete equality with their colleagues.

ARTICLE 32*

The members of the Court shall receive an annual salary.

The President shall receive a special annual allowance.

The Vice-President shall receive a special allowance for every day on which he acts as President.

The judges appointed under Article 31, other than members of the Court, shall receive an indemnity for each day on which they sit.

These salaries, allowances and indemnities shall be fixed by the Assembly of the League of Nations on the proposal of the Council. They may not be decreased during the term of office.

The salary of the Registrar shall be fixed by the Assembly on the proposal of the Court.

Regulations made by the Assembly shall fix the conditions under which retiring pensions may be given to members of the Court and to the Registrar, and the conditions under which members of the Court and the Registrar shall have their travelling expenses refunded.

The above salaries, indemnities and allowances shall be free of all taxation.

ARTICLE 33

The expenses of the Court shall be borne by the League of Nations, in such a manner as shall be decided by the Assembly upon the proposal of the Council.

CHAPTER II. COMPETENCE OF THE COURT

ARTICLE 34

Only States or Members of the League of Nations can be parties in cases before the Court.

ARTICLE 35*

The Court shall be open to the Members of the League and also to States mentioned in the Annex to the Covenant.

The conditions under which the Court shall be open to the other States shall, subject to the special provisions contained in treaties in force, be laid down by the Council, but in no case shall such provisions place the parties in a position of inequality before the Court.

When a State which is not a Member of the League of Nations is a party to a dispute, the Court will fix the amount which that party is to contribute towards the expenses of the Court. This provision shall not apply if such State is bearing a share of the expenses of the Court.

ARTICLE 36

The jurisdiction of the Court comprises all cases which the parties refer to it and all matters specially provided for in treaties and conventions in force.

The Members of the League of Nations and the States mentioned in the Annex to the Covenant may, either when signing or ratifying the Protocol to which the present Statute is adjoined, or at a later moment, declare that they recognize as compulsory *ipso facto* and without special agreement, in relation to any other Member or State accepting the same obligation, the jurisdiction of the Court in all or any of the classes of legal disputes concerning:

(a) the interpretation of a treaty;

(b) any question of international law;

(c) the existence of any fact which, if established, would constitute a breach of an international obligation;

(d) the nature or extent of the reparation to be made for the breach of an international obligation.

The declaration referred to above may be made unconditionally or on condition of reciprocity on the part of several or certain Members or States, or for a certain time.

In the event of a dispute as to whether the Court has jurisdiction, the matter shall be settled by the decision of the Court.

ARTICLE 37

When a treaty or convention in force provides for the reference of a matter to a tribunal to be instituted by the League of Nations, the Court will be such tribunal.

ARTICLE 38

The Court shall apply:

1. International conventions, whether general or particular, establishing rules expressly recognized by the contesting States;
2. International custom, as evidence of a general practice accepted as law;
3. The general principles of law recognized by civilized nations;
4. Subject to the provisions of Article 59, judicial decisions and the teachings of the most highly qualified publicists of the various nations, as subsidiary means for the determination of rules of law.

This provision shall not prejudice the power of the Court to decide a case *ex æquo et bono,* if the parties agree thereto.

CHAPTER III. PROCEDURE

ARTICLE 39*

The official languages of the Court shall be French and English. If the parties agree that the case shall be conducted in French, the judgment will be delivered in French. If the parties agree that the case shall be conducted in English, the judgment will be delivered in English.

In the absence of an agreement as to which language shall be employed, each party may, in the pleadings, use the language which it prefers; the decision of the Court will be given in French and English. In this case the Court will at the same time determine which of the two texts shall be considered as authoritative.

The Court may, at the request of any party, authorize a language other than French or English to be used.

ARTICLE 40*

Cases are brought before the Court, as the case may be, either by the notification of the special agreement or by a written application addressed to the Registrar. In either case the subject of the dispute and the contesting parties must be indicated.

The Registrar shall forthwith communicate the application to all concerned.

He shall also notify the Members of the League of Nations through the Secretary-General, and also any States entitled to appear before the Court.

ARTICLE 41

The Court shall have the power to indicate, if it considers that circumstances so require, any provisional measures which ought to be taken to reserve the respective rights of either party.

Pending the final decision, notice of the measures suggested shall forthwith be given to the parties and the Council.

ARTICLE 42

The parties shall be represented by agents.

They may have the assistance of counsel or advocates before the Court.

ARTICLE 43

The procedure shall consist of two parts: written and oral.

The written proceedings shall consist of the communications to the judges and to the parties of Cases, Counter-Cases and, if necessary, Replies; also all papers and documents in support.

These communications shall be made through the Registrar, in the order and within the time fixed by the Court.

A certified copy of every document produced by one party shall be communicated to the other party.

The oral proceedings shall consist of the hearing by the Court of witnesses, experts, agents, counsel and advocates.

ARTICLE 44

For the service of all notices upon persons other than the agents, counsel and advocates, the Court shall apply direct to the government of the State upon whose territory the notice has to be served.

The same provision shall apply whenever steps are to be taken to procure evidence on the spot.

ARTICLE 45*

The hearing shall be under the control of the President or, if he is unable to preside, of the Vice-President; if neither is able to preside, the senior judge shall preside.

ARTICLE 46

The hearing in Court shall be public, unless the Court shall decide otherwise, or unless the parties demand that the public be not admitted.

ARTICLE 47

Minutes shall be made at each hearing, and signed by the Registrar and the President.

These minutes shall be the only authentic record.

ARTICLE 48

The Court shall make orders for the conduct of the case, shall decide the form and time in which each party must conclude its arguments, and make all arrangements connected with the taking of evidence.

ARTICLE 49

The Court may, even before the hearing begins, call upon the agents to produce any document, or to supply any explanations. Formal note shall be taken of any refusal.

ARTICLE 50

The Court may, at any time, entrust any individual, body, bureau, commission or other organization that it may select, with the task of carrying out an enquiry or giving an expert opinion.

ARTICLE 51

During the hearing any relevant questions are to be put to the witnesses and experts under the conditions laid down by the Court in the rules of procedure referred to in Article 30.

ARTICLE 52

After the Court has received the proofs and evidence within the time specified for the purpose, it may refuse to accept any further oral or written evidence that one party may desire to present unless the other side consents.

ARTICLE 53

Whenever one of the parties shall not appear before the Court, or shall fail to defend his case, the other party may call upon the Court to decide in favor of his claim.

The Court must, before doing so, satisfy itself, not only that it has jurisdiction in accordance with Article 36 and 37, but also that the claim is well founded in fact and law.

ARTICLE 54

When, subject to the control of the Court, the agents, advocates and counsel have completed their presentation of the case, the President shall declare the hearing closed.

The Court shall withdraw to consider the judgment.

The deliberations of the Court shall take place in private and remain secret.

ARTICLE 55

All questions shall be decided by a majority of the judges present at the hearing.

In the event of an equality of votes, the President or his deputy shall have a casting vote.

ARTICLE 56

The judgment shall state the reasons on which it is based.

It shall contain the names of the judges who have taken part in the decision.

ARTICLE 57

If the judgment does not represent in whole or in part the unanimous opinion of the judges, dissenting judges are entitled to deliver a separate opinion.

ARTICLE 58

The judgment shall be signed by the President and by the Registrar. It shall be read in open Court, due notice having been given to the agents.

ARTICLE 59

The decision of the Court has no binding force except between the parties and in respect of that particular case.

ARTICLE 60

The judgment is final and without appeal. In the event of dispute as to the meaning or scope of the judgment, the Court shall construe it upon the request of any party.

ARTICLE 61

An application for revision of a judgment can be made only when it is based upon the discovery of some fact of such a nature as to be a decisive factor, which fact was, when the judgment was given, unknown to the Court and also to the party claiming revision, always provided that such ignorance was not due to negligence.

The proceedings for revision will be opened by a judgment of the Court expressly recording the existence of the new fact, recognizing that it has such a character as to lay the case open to revision, and declaring the application admissible on this ground.

The court may require previous compliance with the terms of the judgment before it admits proceedings in revision.

The application for revision must be made at latest within six months of the discovery of the new fact.

No application for revision may be made after the lapse of ten years from the date of the sentence.

ARTICLE 62

Should a State consider that it has an interest of a legal nature which may be affected by the decision in the case, it may submit a request to the Court to be permitted to intervene as a third party.

It will be for the Court to decide upon this request.

ARTICLE 63

Whenever the construction of a convention to which States other than those concerned in the case are parties is in question the Registrar shall notify all such States forthwith.

Every State so notified has the right to intervene in the proceedings: but if it uses this right, the construction given by the judgment will be equally binding upon it.

ARTICLE 64

Unless otherwise decided by the Court, each party shall bear its own costs.

CHAPTER IV. ADVISORY OPINIONS

ARTICLE 65*

Questions upon which the advisory opinion of the Court is asked shall be laid before the Court by means of a written request, signed either by the President of Assembly or the President of the Council of the League of Nations, or by the Secretary-General of the League under instructions from the Assembly or the Council.

The request shall contain an exact statement of the question upon which an opinion is required, and shall be accompanied by all documents likely to throw light upon the question.

Article 66*

1. The Registrar shall forthwith give notice of the request for an advisory opinion to the Members of the League of Nations, through the Secretary-General of the League, and to any States entitled to appear before the Court.

The Registrar shall also, by means of a special and direct communication, notify any Member of the League or State admitted to appear before the Court or international organization considered by the Court (or, should it not be sitting, by the President) as likely to be able to furnish information on the question, that the Court will be prepared to receive, within a time-limit to be fixed by the President, written statements, or to hear, at a public sitting to be held for the purpose, oral statements relating to the question.

Should any Member or State referred to in the first paragraph have failed to receive the communication specified above, such Member or State may express a desire to submit a written statement, or to be heard; and the Court will decide.

2. Members, States, and organizations having presented written or oral statements or both shall be admitted to comment on the statements made by other Members, States, or organizations in the form, to the extent and within the time-limits which the Court, or, should it not be sitting, the President, shall decide in each particular case. Accordingly, the Registrar shall in due time communicate any such written statements to Members, States, and organizations having submitted similar statements.

Article 67*

The Court shall deliver its advisory opinions in open Court, notice having been given to the Secretary-General of the League of Nations and to the representatives of Members of the League, of States and of international organizations immediately concerned.

Article 68*

In the exercise of its advisory functions, the Court shall further be guided by the provisions of the Statute which apply in contentious cases to the extent to which it recognizes them to be applicable.

III. RULES OF COURT[1]

PREAMBLE

The Court,
Having regard to the Statute annexed to the Protocol of December
16th, 1920, and the amendments to this Statute annexed to the Pro-
tocol of September 14th, 1929, in force as from February 1st, 1936;
Having regard to Article 30 of this Statute;
Adopts the present Rules:

HEADING I. CONSTITUTION AND WORKING
OF THE COURT

SECTION 1. CONSTITUTION OF THE COURT

Judges and Technical Assessors

ARTICLE 1

The term of office of members of the Court shall begin to run on
January 1st of the year following their election, except in the case of
an election under Article 14 of the Statute, in which case the term of
office shall begin on the date of election.

ARTICLE 2

1. Members of the Court elected at an earlier session of the Assembly and of the Council of the League of Nations shall take precedence
over members elected at a subsequent session. Members elected during
the same session shall take precedence according to age. Judges nominated under Article 31 of the Statute of the Court from outside the
Court shall take precedence after the other judges in order of age.

2. The Vice-President shall take his seat on the right of the President. The other judges shall take their seats on the left and right of
the President in the order laid down above.

ARTICLE 3

1. Any State which considers that it possesses and which intends to
exercise the right to nominate a judge under Article 31 of the Statute

[1]Reprinted from Permanent Court of International Justice, Series D, No. 1, *Statute
and Rules of Court and Other Constitutional Documents, Rules or Regulations* (3d ed.,
Leyden, 1936).

of the Court shall so notify the Court by the date fixed for the filing of the Memorial. The name of the person chosen to sit as judge shall be indicated, either with the notification above mentioned, or within a period to be fixed by the President. These notifications shall be communicated to the other parties and they may submit their views to the Court within a period to be fixed by the President. If any doubt or objection should arise, the decision shall rest with the Court, if necessary after hearing the parties.

2. If, on receipt of one or more notifications under the terms of the preceding paragraph, the Court finds that there are several parties in the same interest and that none of them has a judge of its nationality upon the Bench, it shall fix a period within which these parties, acting in concert, may nominate a judge under Article 31 of the Statute. If, at the expiration of this time -limit, no notification of a nomination by them has been made, they shall be regarded as having renounced the right conferred upon them by Article 31 of the Statute.

ARTICLE 4

Where one or more parties are entitled to nominate a judge under Article 31 of the Statute, the full Court may sit with a number of judges exceeding the number of members of the Court fixed by the Statute.

ARTICLE 5

1. The declaration to be made by every judge in accordance with Article 20 of the Statute of the Court shall be worded as follows:
   "I solemnly declare that I will exercise all my powers and duties as a judge honourably and faithfully, impartially and conscientiously."
2. This declaration shall be made at the first public sitting of the Court at which the judge is present after his election or nomination. A special public sitting of the Court may be held for this purpose.
3. At the public inaugural sitting held after a new election of the whole Court the required declaration shall be made first by the President, next by the Vice-President, and then by the remaining judges in the order laid down in Article 2 of the present Rules.

ARTICLE 6

For the purpose of applying Article 18 of the Statute of the Court the President, or if necessary the Vice-President, shall convene the members of the Court. The member affected shall be allowed to furnish explanations. When he has done so the question shall be discussed and a vote shall be taken, the member in question not being present.

If the members present are unanimous, the Registrar shall issue the notification prescribed in the above-mentioned Article.

ARTICLE 7

1. The President shall take steps to obtain all relevant information with a view to the selection of the technical assessors to be appointed in a case. For cases falling under Article 26 of the Statute of the Court, he shall consult the Governing Body of the International Labour Office.

2. Assessors shall be appointed by an absolute majority of votes by the full Court or by the Chamber which has to deal with the case in question, as the case may be.

3. A request for assessors to be attached to the Court under Article 27, paragraph 2, of the Statute must at latest be submitted with the first document of the written proceedings. Such a request shall be complied with if the parties are in agreement. If the parties are not in agreement, the decision rests with the full Court or the Chamber, as the case may be.

ARTICLE 8

Before taking up their duties, assessors shall make the following solemn declaration at a public sitting:
"I solemnly declare that I will exercise my duties and powers as an assessor honourably and faithfully, impartially and conscientiously, and that I will scrupulously observe all the provisions of the Statute and of the Rules of Court."

The Presidency

ARTICLE 9

1. The President and the Vice-President shall be elected in the last quarter of the last year of office of the retiring President and Vice-President. They shall take up their duties on the following January 1st.

2. After a new election of the whole Court, the election of the President and of the Vice-President shall take place at the commencement of the following year. The President and Vice-President elected in these circumstances shall take up their duties on the date of their election. They shall remain in office until the end of the second year after the year of their election.

3. Should the President or the Vice-President cease to belong to the Court before the expiration of his normal term of office, an election

shall be held for the purpose of appointing a successor for the unexpired portion of his term of office.

4. The elections referred to in the present Article shall take place by secret ballot. The candidate obtaining an absolute majority of votes shall be declared elected.

ARTICLE 10

The President shall direct the work and administration of the Court; he shall preside at the meetings of the full Court.

ARTICLE 11

The Vice-President shall take the place of the President, if the latter is unable to fulfil his duties. In the event of the President ceasing to hold office, the same rule shall apply until his successor has been appointed by the Court.

ARTICLE 12

1. The discharge of the duties of the President shall always be assured at the seat of the Court, either by the President himself or by the Vice-President.

2. If at the same time both the President and the Vice-President are unable to fulfil their duties, or if both appointments are vacant at the same time, the duties of President shall be discharged by the oldest among the members of the Court who have been longest on the Bench.

3. After a new election of the whole Court, and until the election of the President and the Vice-President, the duties of the President shall be discharged by the oldest member of the Court.

ARTICLE 13

1. If the President is a national of one of the parties to a case brought before the Court, he will hand over his functions as President in respect of that case. The same rule applies to the Vice-President or to any member of the Court who might be called on to act as President.

2. If, after a new election of the whole Court, the newly elected President sits, under Article 13 of the Statute of the Court, in order to finish a case which he had begun during his preceding term of office as judge, the duties of President, in respect of such case, shall be discharged by the member of the Court who presided when the case was last under examination, unless the latter is unable to sit, in which case the former Vice-President or the oldest among the members of

the Court who have been longest on the Bench shall discharge the duties of President.

3. If, owing to the expiry of a President's period of office, a new President is elected, and if the Court sits after the end of the said period in order to finish a case which it had begun to examine during that period, the former President shall retain the functions of President in respect of that case. Should he be unable to fulfil his duties, his place shall be taken by the newly elected President.

The Registry

ARTICLE 14

1. The Court shall select its Registrar from amongst candidates proposed by members of the Court. The latter shall receive adequate notice of the date on which the list of candidates will be closed so as to enable nominations and information concerning the nationals of distant countries to be received in sufficient time.

2. Nominations must give the necessary particulars regarding age, nationality, university degrees and linguistic attainments of candidates, as also regarding their judicial and diplomatic qualifications, their experience in connection with the work of the League of Nations and their present profession.

3. The election shall be by secret ballot and by an absolute majority of votes.

4. The Registrar shall be elected for a term of seven years reckoned from January 1st of the year following that in which the election takes place. He may be re-elected.

5. Should the Registrar cease to hold his office before the expiration of the term above mentioned, an election shall be held for the purpose of appointing a successor. Such election shall be for a term of seven years.

6. The Court shall appoint a Deputy-Registrar to assist the Registrar, to act as Registrar in his absence and, in the event of his ceasing to hold the office, to perform the duties until a new Registrar shall have been appointed. The Deputy-Registrar shall be appointed under the same conditions and in the same way as the Registrar.

ARTICLE 15

1. Before taking up his duties, the Registrar shall make the following declaration at a meeting of the full Court:

"I solemnly declare that I will perform the duties conferred upon me as Registrar of the Permanent Court of International Justice in all loyalty, discretion and good conscience."

2. The Deputy-Registrar shall make a similar declaration in the same conditions.

ARTICLE 16

The Registrar is entitled to two months' holiday in each year.

ARTICLE 17

1. The officials of the Registry, other than the Deputy-Registrar, shall be appointed by the Court on proposals submitted by the Registrar.

2. On taking up their duties, such officials shall make the following declaration before the President, the Registrar being present:

"I solemnly declare that I will perform the duties conferred upon me as an official of the Permanent Court of International Justice in in all loyalty, discretion and good conscience."

ARTICLE 18

1. The Court shall determine or modify the organization of the Registry upon proposals submitted by the Registrar.

2. The Regulations for the staff of the Registry shall be drawn up having regard to the organization decided upon by the Court and to the provisions of the Regulations for the staff of the Secretariat of the League of Nations, to which they shall, as far as possible, conform. They shall be adopted by the President on the proposal of the Registrar, subject to subsequent approval by the Court.

ARTICLE 19

In case both the Registrar and the Deputy-Registrar are unable to be present, or in case both appointments are vacant at the same time, the President, on the proposal of the Registrar or the Deputy-Registrar, as the case may be, shall appoint the official of the Registry who is to act as substitute for the Registrar until a successor to the Registrar has been appointed.

ARTICLE 20

1. The General List of cases submitted to the Court for decision or for advisory opinion shall be prepared and kept up to date by the Registrar on the instructions and subject to the authority of the Presi-

dent. Cases shall be entered in the list and numbered successively according to the date of the receipt of the document bringing the case before the Court.

2. The General List shall contain the following headings:

     I. Number in list.
     II. Short title.
     III. Date of registration.
     IV. Registration number.
     V. File number in the archives.
     VI. Nature of case.
     VII. Parties.
     VIII. Interventions.
     IX. Method of submission.
     X. Date of document instituting proceedings.
     XI. Time-limits for filing documents in the written proceedings.
     XII. Prolongation, if any, of time-limits.
     XIII. Date of termination of the written proceedings.
     XIV. Postponements.
     XV. Date of the beginning of the hearing (date of the first public sitting).
     XVI. Observations.
     XVII. References to earlier or subsequent cases.
     XVIII. Result (nature and date).
     XIX. Removal from the list (nature and date).
     XX. References to publications of the Court relating to the case.

3. The General List shall also contain a space for notes, if any, and spaces for the inscription, above the initials of the President and of the Registrar, of the dates of the entry of the case, of its result, or of its removal from the list, as the case may be.

ARTICLE 21

1. The Registrar shall be the channel for all communications to and from the Court.

2. The Registrar shall ensure that the date of despatch and receipt of all communications and notifications may readily be verified. Communications and notifications sent by post shall be registered. Communications addressed to the agents of the parties shall be considered as having been addressed to the parties themselves. The date of receipt shall be noted on all documents received by the Registrar, and a receipt bearing this date and the number under which the document has been registered shall be given to the sender.

3. The Registrar shall, subject to the obligations of secrecy attach-

ing to his official duties, reply to all enquiries concerning the work of
the Court, including enquiries from the Press.

4. The Registrar shall publish in the Press all necessary information as to the date and hour fixed for public sittings.

ARTICLE 22

A collection of the judgments and advisory opinions of the Court,
as also of such orders as the Court may decide to include therein, shall
be printed and published under the responsibility of the Registrar.

ARTICLE 23

1. The Registrar shall be responsible for the archives, the accounts
and all administrative work. He shall have the custody of the seals
and stamps of the Court. The Registrar or the Deputy-Registrar shall
be present at all sittings of the full Court and at sittings of the Special
Chambers and of the Chamber for Summary Procedure. The Registrar shall be responsible for drawing up the minutes of the meetings.

2. He shall undertake, in addition, all duties which may be laid upon him by the present Rules.

3. The duties of the Registry shall be set forth in detail in a list of
instructions submitted by the Registrar to the President and approved
by him.

The Special Chambers and the Chamber for Summary Procedure

ARTICLE 24

1. The members of the Chambers constituted by virtue of Articles
26, 27 and 29 of the Statute of the Court and also the substitute
members shall be appointed at a meeting of the full Court by secret
ballot and by an absolute majority of votes.

2. The election shall take place in the last quarter of the year and
the period of appointment of the persons elected shall commence on
January 1st of the following year.

3. Nevertheless, after a new election of the whole Court, the election
shall take place at the beginning of the following year. The period of
appointment shall commence on the date of election and shall terminate, in the case of the Chamber referred to in Article 29 of the
Statute, at the end of the same year and, in the case of the Chambers
referred to in Articles 26 and 27 of the Statute, at the end of the second
year after the year of election.

4. The Presidents of the Chambers shall be appointed at a sitting
of the full Court. Nevertheless, the President of the Court shall preside

ex officio over any Chamber of which he may be elected a member; similarly, the Vice-President of the Court shall preside *ex officio* over any Chamber of which he may be elected a member and of which the President of the Court is not a member.

SECTION 2. WORKING OF THE COURT

ARTICLE 25

1. The judicial year shall begin on January 1st in each year.

2. In the absence of a special resolution by the Court, the dates and duration of the judicial vacations are fixed as follows: (*a*) from December 18th to January 7th; (*b*) from the Sunday before Easter to the second Sunday after Easter; (*c*) from July 15th to September 15th.

3. In case of urgency, the President can always convene the members of the Court during the periods mentioned in the preceding paragraph.

ARTICLE 26

1. The order in which the leaves provided for in Article 23, paragraph 2, of the Statute of the Court are to be taken shall be laid down in a list drawn up by the Court for each period of three years. This order can only be departed from for serious reasons duly admitted by the Court.

2. The number of members of the Court on leave at any one time must not exceed two. The President and the Vice-President must not take their leave at the same time.

ARTICLE 27

Members of the Court who are prevented by illness or other serious reasons from attending a sitting of the Court to which they have been summoned by the President, shall notify the President who will inform the Court.

ARTICLE 28

1. The date and hour of sittings of the full Court shall be fixed by the President of the Court.

2. The date and hour of sittings of the Chambers referred to in Articles 26, 27 and 29 of the Statute of the Court shall be fixed by the Presidents of the Chambers respectively. The first sitting, however, of a Chamber in any particular case is fixed by the President of the Court.

ARTICLE 29

If a sitting of the full Court has been convened and it is found that there is no quorum, the President shall adjourn the sitting until a quorum has been obtained. Judges nominated under Article 31 of the Statute shall not be taken into account for the calculation of the quorum.

ARTICLE 30

1. The Court shall sit in private to deliberate upon disputes which are submitted to it and upon advisory opinions which it is asked to give.

2. During the deliberations referred to in the preceding paragraph, only persons authorized to take part therein and the Registrar or his substitute shall be present. No other person shall be admitted except by virtue of a special decision taken by the Court.

3. Every judge who is present at the deliberations shall state his opinion together with the reasons on which it is based.

4. Any judge may request that a question which is to be voted upon shall be drawn up in precise terms in both the official languages and distributed to the Court. Effect shall be given to any such request.

5. The decision of the Court shall be based upon the conclusions adopted after final discussion by a majority of the judges voting in an order inverse to the order laid down by Article 2 of the present Rules.

6. No detailed minutes shall be prepared of the private meetings of the Court for deliberation upon judgments or advisory opinions; the minutes of these meetings are to be considered as confidential and shall record only the subject of the debates, the votes taken, the names of those voting for and against a motion and statements expressly made for insertion in the minutes.

7. After the final vote taken on a judgment or advisory opinion, any judge who desires to set forth his individual opinion must do so in accordance with Article 57 of the Statute.

8. Unless otherwise decided by the Court, paragraphs 2, 4 and 5 of this Article shall apply to deliberations by the Court in private upon any administrative matter.

HEADING II.   CONTENTIOUS PROCEDURE

ARTICLE 31

The rules contained in Sections 1, 2 and 4 of this Heading shall not preclude the adoption by the Court of particular modifications or additions proposed jointly by the parties and considered by the Court to be appropriate to the case and in the circumstances.

SECTION I. PROCEDURE BEFORE THE FULL COURT

I. GENERAL RULES

Institution of Proceedings

ARTICLE 32

1. When a case is brought before the Court by means of a special agreement, Article 40, paragraph 1, of the Statute of the Court shall apply.

2. When a case is brought before the Court by means of an application, the application must, as laid down in Article 40, paragraph 1, of the Statute, indicate the party making it, the party against whom the claim is brought and the subject of the dispute. It must also, as far as possible, specify the provision on which the applicant founds the jurisdiction of the Court, state the precise nature of the claim and give a succinct statement of the facts and grounds on which the claim is based, these facts and grounds being developed in the Memorial, to which evidence will be annexed.

3. The original of an application shall be signed either by the agent of the party submitting it, or by the diplomatic representative of that party at The Hague, or by a duly authorized person. If the document bears the signature of a person other than the diplomatic representative of that party at The Hague, the signature must be legalized by this diplomatic representative or by the competent authority of the government concerned.

ARTICLE 33

1. When a case is brought before the Court by means of an application, the Registrar shall transmit forthwith to the party against whom the claim is brought a copy of the application certified by him to be correct.

2. When a case is brought before the Court by means of a special agreement filed by one only of the parties, the Registrar shall notify forthwith the other party that it has been so filed.

ARTICLE 34

1. The Registrar shall transmit forthwith to all the members of the Court copies of special agreements or applications submitting a case to the Court.

2. He shall also transmit through the channels indicated in the Statute of the Court or in a special arrangement, as the case may be, copies

to Members of the League of Nations and to States entitled to appear before the Court.

ARTICLE 35

1. When a case is brought before the Court by means of a special agreement, the appointment of the agent or agents of the party or parties lodging the special agreement shall be notified at the same time as the special agreement is filed. If the special agreement is filed by one only of the parties, the other party shall, when acknowledging receipt of the communication announcing the filing of the special agreement, or failing this, as soon as possible, inform the Court of the name of its agent.

2. When a case is brought before the Court by means of an application, the application, or the covering letter, shall state the name of the agent of the applicant government.

3. The party against whom the application is directed and to whom it is communicated shall, when acknowledging receipt of the communication, or failing this, as soon as possible, inform the Court of the name of its agent.

4. Applications to intervene under Article 64 of the present Rules, interventions under Article 66 and requests under Article 78 for the revision, or under Article 79 for the interpretation, of a judgment, shall similarly be accompanied by the appointment of an agent.

5. The appointment of an agent must be accompanied by a mention of his permanent address at the seat of the Court to which all communications as to the case are to be sent.

ARTICLE 36

The declaration provided for in the Resolution of the Council of the League of Nations dated May 17th, 1922, shall be filed with the Registry at the same time as the notification of the appointment of the agent.

Preliminary Measures

ARTICLE 37

1. In every case submitted to the Court, the President ascertains the views of the parties with regard to questions connected with the procedure; for this purpose he may summon the agents to a meeting as soon as they have been appointed.

2. In the light of the information obtained by the President, the Court will make the necessary orders to determine *inter alia* the num-

ber and order of the documents of the written proceedings and the time-limits within which they must be presented.

3. In the making of an order under the foregoing paragraph, any agreement between the parties is to be taken into account so far as possible.

4. The Court may extend time-limits which have been fixed. It may also, in special circumstances and after giving the agent of the opposing party an opportunity of submitting his views, decide that a proceeding taken after the expiration of a time-limit shall be considered as valid.

5. If the Court is not sitting and without prejudice to any subsequent decision of the Court, its powers under this Article shall be exercised by the President.

ARTICLE 38

Time-limits shall be fixed by assigning a definite date for the completion of the various acts of procedure.

Written Proceedings

ARTICLE 39

1. Should the parties agree that the proceedings shall be conducted wholly in French, or wholly in English, the documents of the written proceedings shall be submitted only in the language adopted by the parties.

2. In the absence of an agreement with regard to the language to be employed, the documents shall be submitted in French or in English.

3. Should the use of a language other than French or English be authorized, a translation into French or into English shall be attached to the original of each document submitted.

4. The Registrar shall not be bound to make translations of the documents of the written proceedings.

ARTICLE 40

1. The original of every document of the written proceedings shall be signed by the agent and filed with the Court accompanied by fifty printed copies bearing the signature of the agent in print.

2. When a copy of a document of the written proceedings is communicated to the other party under Article 43, paragraph 4, of the Statute of the Court, the Registrar shall certify that it is a correct copy of the original filed with the Court.

3. All documents of the written proceedings shall be dated. When a document has to be filed by a certain date, it is the date of the receipt of the document by the Registry which will be regarded by the Court as the material date.

4. If the Registrar at the request of the agent of a party arranged for the printing, at the cost of the government which this agent represents, of a document which it is intended to file with Court, the text must be transmitted to the Registry in sufficient time to enable the printed document to be filed before the expiry of any time-limit which may apply to it.

5. When, under this Article, a document has to be filed in a number of copies fixed in advance, the President may require additional copies to be supplied.

6. The correction of a slip or error in a document which has been filed is permissible at any time with the consent of the other party, or by leave of the President.

Article 41

1. If proceedings are instituted by means of a special agreement, the following documents may, subject to Article 37, paragraphs 2 and 3, of the present Rules, be presented in the order stated below:

a Memorial, by each party within the same time-limit;
a Counter-Memorial, by each party within the same time-limit;
a Reply, by each party within the same time-limit.

2. If proceedings are instituted by means of an application, the documents shall, subject to Article 37, paragraphs 2 and 3, of the present Rules, be presented in the order stated below:

the Memorial by the applicant;
the Counter-Memorial by the respondent;
the Reply by the applicant;
the Rejoinder by the respondent.

Article 42

1. A Memorial shall contain: a statement of the facts on which the claim is based, a statement of law, and the submissions.

2. A counter-Memorial shall contain: the admission or denial of the facts stated in the Memorial; any additional facts, if necessary; observations concerning the statement of law in the Memorial, a statement of law in answer thereto, and the submissions.

Article 43

1. A copy of every document in support of the arguments set forth therein must be attached to the Memorial or Counter-Memorial; a

list of such documents shall be given after the submissions. If, on account of the length of a document, extracts only are attached, the document itself or a complete copy of it must, if possible, and unless the document has been published and is of a public character, be communicated to the Registrar for the use of the Court and of the other party.

2. Any document filed as an annex which is in a language other than French or English, must be accompanied by a translation into one of the official languages of the Court. Nevertheless, in the case of lengthy documents, translations of extracts may be submitted, subject, however, to any subsequent decision by the Court, or, if it is not sitting, by the President.

3. Paragraphs 1 and 2 of the present Article shall apply also to the other documents of the written proceedings.

ARTICLE 44

1. The Registrar shall forward to the judges and to the parties copies of all the documents in the case, as and when he receives them.

2. The Court, or the President if the Court is not sitting, may, after obtaining the views of the parties, decide that the Registrar shall hold the documents of the written proceedings in a particular case at the disposal of the government of any Member of the League of Nations or State which is entitled to appear before the Court.

3. The Court, or the President, if the Court is not sitting, may, with the consent of the parties, authorize the documents of the written proceedings in regard to a particular case to be made accessible to the public before the termination of the case.

ARTICLE 45

Upon the termination of the written proceedings, the case is ready for hearing.

ARTICLE 46

1. Subject to the priority resulting from Article 61 of the present Rules, cases submitted to the Court will be taken in the order in which they become ready for hearing. When several cases are ready for hearing, the order in which they will be taken is determined by the position which they occupy in the General List.

2. Nevertheless, the Court may, in special circumstances, decide to take a case in priority to other cases which are ready for hearing and which precede it in the General List.

3. If the parties to a case which is ready for hearing are agreed in

asking for the case to be put after other cases which are ready for hearing and which follow it in the General List, the President may grant such an adjournment; if the parties are not in agreement, the President decides whether or not to submit the question to the Court.

Oral Proceedings

ARTICLE 47

1. When a case is ready for hearing, the date for the commencement of the oral proceedings shall be fixed by the Court, or by the President if the Court is not sitting.

1. If occasion should arise, the Court or the President, if the Court is not sitting, may decide that the commencement or continuance of the hearings shall be postponed.

ARTICLE 48

1. Except as provided in the following paragraph, no new document may be submitted to the Court after the termination of the written proceedings save with the consent of the other party. The party desiring to produce the new document shall file the original or a certified copy thereof with the Registry, which will be responsible for communicating it to the other party and will inform the Court. The other party shall be held to have given its consent if it does not lodge an objection to the production of the document.

2. If this consent is not given, the Court, after hearing the parties, may either refuse to allow the production or may sanction the production of the new document. If the Court sanctions the production of the new document, an opportunity shall be given to the other party of commenting upon it.

ARTICLE 49

1. In sufficient time before the opening of the oral proceedings, each party shall inform the Court and, through the Registry, the other parties, of the names, Christian names, description and residence of witnesses and experts whom it desires to be heard. It shall further give a general indication of the point or points to which the evidence is to refer.

2. Similarly, and subject to Article 48 of these Rules and to the preceding paragraph of this Article, each party shall indicate all other evidence which it intends to produce or which it intends to request

the Court to take, including any request for the holding of an expert enquiry.

ARTICLE 50

The Court shall determine whether the parties shall address the Court before or after the production of the evidence; the parties shall, however, retain the right to comment on the evidence given.

ARTICLE 51

The order in which the agents, counsel or advocates shall be called upon to speak shall be determined by the Court, unless there is an agreement between the parties on the subject.

ARTICLE 52

1. During the hearing, which is under the control of the President, the latter, either in the name of the Court or on his own behalf, may put questions to the parties or may ask them for explanations.
2. Similarly, each of the judges may put questions to the parties or ask for explanations; nevertheless, he shall first apprise the President.
3. The parties shall be free to answer at once or at a later date.

ARTICLE 53

1. Witnesses and experts shall be examined by the agents, counsel or advocates of the parties under the control of the President. Questions may be put to them by the President and by the judges.
2. Each witness shall make the following solemn declaration before giving his evidence in Court.:
"I solemnly declare upon my honour and conscience that I will speak the truth, the whole truth and nothing but the truth."
3. Each expert shall make the following solemn declaration before making his statement in Court:
"I solemnly declare upon my honour and conscience that my statement will be in accordance with my sincere belief."

ARTICLE 54

The Court may invite the parties to call witnesses or experts, or may call for the production of any other evidence on points of fact in regard to which the parties are not in agreement. If need be, the Court shall apply the provisions of Article 44 of the Statute of the Court.

ARTICLE 55

The indemnities of witnesses or experts who appear at the instance of the Court shall be paid out of the funds of the Court.

ARTICLE 56

The Court, or the President should the Court not be sitting, shall, at the request of one of the parties or on its own initiative, take the necessary steps for the examination of witnesses or experts otherwise than before the Court itself.

ARTICLE 57

1. If the Court considers it necessary to arrange for an enquiry or an expert report, it shall issue an order to this effect, after duly hearing the parties, stating the subject of the enquiry or expert report, and setting out the number and appointment of the persons to hold the enquiry or of the experts and the formalities to be observed.

2. Any report or record of an enquiry and any expert report shall be communicated to the parties.

ARTICLE 58

1. In the absence of any decision to the contrary by the Court, or by the President if the Court is not sitting at the time when the decision has to be made, speeches or statements made before the Court in one of the official languages shall be translated into the other official language; the same rule shall apply in regard to questions and answers. The Registrar shall make the necessary arrangements for this purpose.

2. Whenever a language other than French or English is employed with the authorization of the Court, the necessary arrangements for a translation into one of the two official languages shall be made by the party concerned; the evidence of witnesses and the statements of experts shall, however, be translated under the supervision of the Court. In the case of witnesses or experts who appear at the instance of the Court, arrangements for translation shall be made by the Registry.

3. The persons making the translations referred to in the preceding paragraph shall make the following solemn declaration in Court:
"I solemnly declare upon my honour and conscience that my translation will be a complete and faithful rendering of what I am called upon to translate."

ARTICLE 59

1. The minutes mentioned in Article 47 of the Statute of the Court shall include:

    the names of the judges present;

    the names of the agents, counsel or advocates present;

    the names, Christian names, description and residence of witnesses and experts heard;

    a statement of the evidence produced at the hearing;

    declarations made on behalf of the parties;

    a brief mention of questions put to the parties by the President or by the judges;

    any decisions delivered or announced by the Court during the hearing.

2. The minutes of public sittings shall be printed and published.

ARTICLE 60

1. In respect of each hearing held by the Court, a shorthand note shall be made under the supervision of the Registrar of the oral proceedings, including the evidence taken, and shall be appended to the minutes referred to in Article 59 of the present Rules. This note, unless otherwise decided by the Court, shall contain any interpretations from one official language to the other made in Court by the interpreters.

2. The report of the evidence of each witness or expert shall be read to him in order that, under the supervision of the Court, any mistakes may be corrected.

3. Reports of speeches or declarations made by agents, counsel or advocates shall be communicated to them for correction or revision, under the supervision of the Court.

II. OCCASIONAL RULES

Interim Protection

ARTICLE 61

1. A request for the indication of interim measures of protection may be filed at any time during the proceedings in the case in connection with which it is made. The request shall specify the case to which it relates, the rights to be protected and the interim measures of which the indication is proposed.

2. A request for the indication of interim measures of protection

shall have priority over all other cases. The decision thereon shall be treated as a matter of urgency.

3. If the Court is not sitting, the members shall be convened by the President forthwith. Pending the meeting of the Court and a decision by it, the President shall, if need be, take such measures as may appear to him necessary in order to enable the Court to give an effective decision.

4. The Court may indicate interim measures of protection other than those proposed in the request.

5. The rejection of a request for the indication of interim measures of protection shall not prevent the party which has made it from making a fresh request in the same case based on new facts.

6. The Court may indicate interim measures of protection *proprio motu*. If the Court is not sitting, the President may convene the members in order to submit to the Court the question whether it is expedient to indicate such measures.

7. The Court may at any time by reason of a change in the situation revoke or modify its decision indicating interim measures of protection.

8. The Court shall only indicate interim measures of protection after giving the parties an opportunity of presenting their observations on the subject. The same rule applies when the Court revokes or modifies a decision indicating such measures.

9. When the President has occasion to convene the members of the Court, judges who have been appointed under Article 31 of the Statute of the Court shall be convened if their presence can be assured at the date fixed by the President for hearing the parties.

Preliminary Objections

ARTICLE 62

1. A preliminary objection must be filed at the latest before the expiry of the time-limit fixed for the filing by the party submitting the objection of the first document of the written proceedings to be filed by that party.

2. The preliminary objection shall set out the facts and the law on which the objection is based, the submissions and a list of the documents in support; these documents shall be attached; it shall mention any evidence which the party may desire to produce.

3. Upon receipt by the Registrar of the objection, the proceedings on the merits shall be suspended and the Court, or the President if the Court is not sitting, shall fix the time within which the party against whom the objection is directed may present a written statement of its

observations and submissions; documents in support shall be attached and evidence which it is proposed to produce shall be mentioned.

4. Unless otherwise decided by the Court, the further proceedings shall be oral.

5. After hearing the parties the Court shall give its decision on the objection or shall join the objection to the merits. If the Court overrules the objection or joins it to the merits, it shall once more fix time-limits for the further proceedings.

Counter-Claims

ARTICLE 63

When proceedings have been instituted by means of an application, a counter-claim may be presented in the submissions of the Counter-Memorial, provided that such counter-claim is directly connected with the subject of the application and that it comes within the jurisdiction of the Court. Any claim which is not directly connected with the subject of the original application must be put forward by means of a separate application and may form the subject of distinct proceedings or be joined by the Court to the original proceedings.

Intervention

ARTICLE 64

1. An application for permission to intervene under the terms of Article 62 of the Statute of the Court shall be filed with the Registry at latest before the commencement of the oral proceedings.

2. The application shall contain:
   a specification of the case;
   a statement of law and of fact justifying intervention;
   a list of the documents in support of the application; these documents shall be attached.

3. The application shall be communicated to the parties, who shall send to the Registry their observations in writing within a period to be fixed by the Court, or by the President, if the Court is not sitting.

4. The application to intervene shall be placed on the agenda for a hearing, the date and hour of which shall be notified to all concerned. Nevertheless, if the parties have not, in their written observations, opposed the application to intervene, the Court may decide that there shall be no oral argument.

5. The Court will give its decision on the application in the form of a judgment.

ARTICLE 65

1. If the Court admits the intervention and if the party intervening expresses a desire to file a Memorial on the merits, the Court shall fix the time-limits within which the Memorial shall be filed and within which the other parties may reply by Counter-Memorials; the same course shall be followed in regard to the Reply and the Rejoinder. If the Court is not sitting, the time-limits shall be fixed by the President.

2. If the Court has not yet given its decision upon the intervention and the application to intervene is not opposed, the President, if the Court is not sitting, may, without prejudice to the decision of the Court on the question whether the application should be granted, fix the time-limits within which the intervening party may file a Memorial on the merits and the other parties may reply by Counter-Memorials.

3. In the cases referred to in the two preceding paragraphs, the time-limits shall, so far as possible, coincide with those already fixed in the case.

ARTICLE 66

1. The notification provided for in Article 63 of the Statute of the Court shall be sent to every Member of the League of Nations or State which is a party to a convention invoked in the special agreement or in the application as governing the case referred to the Court. A Member or State desiring to avail itself of the right conferred by the above-mentioned Article shall file a declaration to that effect with the Registry.

2. Any Member of the League of Nations or State, which is a party to the convention in question and to which the notification referred to has not been sent, may in the same way file with the Registry a declaration of intention to intervene under Article 63 of the Statute.

3. Such declarations shall be communicated to the parties. If any objection or doubt should arise as to whether the intervention is admissible under Article 63 of the Statute, the decision shall rest with the Court.

4. The Registrar shall take the necessary steps to enable the intervening party to inspect the documents in the case in so far as they relate to the interpretation of the convention in question, and to submit its written observations thereon to the Court within a time-limit to be fixed by the Court or by the President if the Court is not sitting.

5. These observations shall be communicated to the other parties and may be discussed by them in the course of the oral proceedings; in these proceedings the intervening party shall take part.

Appeals to the Court

ARTICLE 67

1. When an appeal is made to the Court against a decision given by some other tribunal, the proceedings before the Court shall be governed by the provisions of the Statute of the Court and of the present Rules.

2. If the document instituting the appeal must be filed within a certain limit of time, the date of the receipt of this document in the Registry will be taken by the Court as the material date.

3. The document instituting the appeal shall contain a precise statement of the grounds of the objections to the decision complained of, and these constitute the subject of the dispute referred to the Court.

4. An authenticated copy of the decision complained of shall be attached to the document instituting the appeal.

5. It lies upon the parties to produce before the Court any useful and relevant material upon which the decision complained of was rendered.

Settlement and Discontinuance

ARTICLE 68

If at any time before judgment has been delivered, the parties conclude an agreement as to the settlement of the dispute and so inform the Court in writing, or by mutual agreement inform the Court in writing that they are not going on with the proceedings, the Court will make an order officially recording the conclusion of the settlement or the discontinuance of the proceedings; in either case the order will prescribe the removal of the case from the list.

ARTICLE 69

1. If in the course of proceedings instituted by means of an application, the applicant informs the Court in writing that it is not going on with the proceedings, and if, at the date on which this communication is received by the Registry, the respondent has not yet taken any step in the proceedings, the Court will make an order officially recording the discontinuance of the proceedings and directing the removal of the case from the list. A copy of this order shall be sent by the Registrar to the respondent.

2. If, at the time when the notice of discontinuance is received, the respondent has already taken some step in the proceedings, the Court, or the President if the Court is not sitting, shall fix a time-limit within which the respondent must state whether it opposes the discontinuance of the proceedings. If no objection is made to the discontinu-

ance before the expiration of the time-limit, acquiescence will be presumed and the Court will make an order officially recording the discontinuance of the proceedings and directing the removal of the case from the list. If objection is made, the proceedings shall continue.

SECTION 2. PROCEDURE BEFORE THE SPECIAL CHAMBER AND THE CHAMBER FOR SUMMARY PROCEDURE

ARTICLE 70

Procedure before the Chambers mentioned in Articles 26, 27 and 29 of the Statute of the Court shall, subject to the provisions of the Statute and of these Rules relating to the Chambers, be governed by the provisions as to procedure before the full Court.

ARTICLE 71

1. A request that a case should be referred to one of the Chambers mentioned in Articles 26, 27 and 29 of the Statute of the Court, must be made in the document instituting proceedings or must accompany that document. Effect will be given to the request if the parties are in agreement.

2. Upon receipt by the Registry of the document instituting proceedings in a case brought before one of the Chambers mentioned in Articles 26, 27 and 29 of the Statute, the President of the Court shall communicate the document to the members of the Chamber concerned. He shall also take such steps as may be necessary to assure the application of Article 31, paragraph 4, of the Statute.

3. The President of the Court shall convene the Chamber at the earliest date compatible with the requirements of the procedure.

4. As soon as the Chamber has met in order to go into the case submitted to it, the powers of the President of the Court in respect of the case shall be exercised by the President of the Chamber.

ARTICLE 72

1. The procedure before the Chamber for Summary Procedure shall consist of two parts: written and oral.

2. The written proceedings shall consist of the presentation of a single written statement by each party in the order indicated in Article 41 of the present Rules; to it must be attached the documents in support. The Chamber may however, if the parties so request or in view of the circumstances and after hearing the parties, call for the presentation of such other written statement as may appear fitting.

3. The written statements shall be communicated by the Registrar

to the members of the Chamber and to opposing parties. They shall mention all evidence, other than the documents referred to in the preceding paragraph, which the parties desire to produce.

4. When the case is ready for hearing, the President of the Chamber shall fix a date for the opening of the oral proceedings, unless the parties agree to dispense with them; even if there are no oral proceedings, the Chamber always retains the right to call upon the parties to supply verbal explanations.

5. Witnesses or experts whose names are mentioned in the written proceedings must be available so as to appear before the Chamber when their presence is required.

ARTICLE 73

Judgments given by the Special Chambers or by the Chamber for Summary Procedure are judgments rendered by the Court. They will be read, however, at a public sitting of the Chamber.

SECTION 3. JUDGMENTS

ARTICLE 74

1. The judgment shall contain:
   the date on which it is pronounced;
   the names of the judges participating;
   a statement of who are the parties;
   a summary of the proceedings;
   the submissions of the parties;
   a statement of the facts;
   the reasons in point of law;
   the operative provisions of the judgment;
   the decision, if any, in regard to costs;
   the number of the judges constituting the majority.

2. Dissenting judges may, if they so desire, attach to the judgment either an exposition of their individual opinion or a statement of their dissent.

ARTICLE 75

1. When the judgment has been read in public, one original copy, duly signed and sealed, shall be placed in the Archives of the Court and another shall be forwarded to each of the parties.

2. A copy of the judgment shall be sent by the Registrar to members of the League of Nations and to States entitled to appear before the Court.

ARTICLE 76

The judgment shall be regarded as taking effect on the day on which it is read in open Court.

ARTICLE 77

The party in whose favour an order for the payment of the costs has been made may present his bill of costs after judgment has been delivered.

SECTION 4. REQUESTS FOR THE REVISION OR INTERPRETATION OF A JUDGMENT

ARTICLE 78

1. A request for the revision of a judgment shall be made by the application.
   The application shall contain:
   a specification of the judgment of which the revision is desired;
   the particulars necessary to show that the conditions laid down by Article 61 of the Statute of the Court are fulfilled;
   a list of the documents in support; these documents shall be attached to the application.
2. The request for revision shall be communicated by the Registrar to the other parties. The latter may submit observations within a time-limit to be fixed by the Court, or by the President if the Court is not sitting.
3. If the Court makes the admission of the application conditional upon previous compliance with the judgment to be revised, this condition shall be communicated forthwith to the applicant by the Registrar and proceedings in revision shall be stayed pending receipt by the Court of proof of compliance with the judgment.

ARTICLE 79

1. A request to the Court to interpret a judgment which it has given may be made either by the notification of a special agreement between the parties or by an application by one or more of the parties.
2. The special agreement or application shall contain:
   a specification of the judgment of which the interpretation is requested;
   mention of the precise point or points in dispute.
3. If the request for interpretation is made by means of an application, the Registrar shall communicate the application to the other

parties, and the latter may submit observations within a time-limit to be fixed by the Court, or by the President if the Court is not sitting.

4. Whether the request be made by special agreement or by application, the Court may invite the parties to furnish further written or oral explanations.

ARTICLE 80

If the judgment to be revised or to be interpreted was rendered by the full Court, the request for its revision or for its interpretation shall be dealt with by the full Court. If the judgment was pronounced by one of the Chambers mentioned in Articles 26, 27 or 29 of the Statute of the Court, the request for revision or for interpretation shall be dealt with by the same Chamber.

ARTICLE 81

The decision of the Court on requests for revision or interpretation shall be given in the form of a judgment.

HEADING III. ADVISORY OPINIONS

ARTICLE 82

In proceedings in regard to advisory opinions, the Court shall, in addition to the provisions of Chapter IV of the Statute of the Court, apply the provisions of the articles hereinafter set out. It shall also be guided by the provisions of the present Rules which apply in contentious cases to the extent to which it recognizes them to be applicable, according as the advisory opinion for which the Court is asked relates, in the terms of Article 14 of the Convenant of the League of Nations, to a "dispute" or to a "question."

ARTICLE 83

If the question upon which an advisory opinion is requested relates to an existing dispute between two or more Members of the League of Nations or States, Article 31 of the Statute of the Court shall apply, as also the provisions of the present Rules concerning the application of that Article.

ARTICLE 84

1. Advisory opinions shall be given after deliberation by the full Court. They shall mention the number of judges constituting the majority.

2. Dissenting judges may, if they so desire, attach to the opinion of the Court either an exposition of their individual opinion or the statement of their dissent.

ARTICLE 85

1. The Registrar shall take the necessary steps in order to ensure that the text of the advisory opinion is in the hands of the Secretary-General at the seat of the League of Nations at the date and hour fixed for the sitting to be held for the reading of the opinion.

2. One original copy, duly signed and sealed, of every advisory opinion shall be placed in the archives of the Court and another in those of the Secretariat of the League of Nations. Certified copies thereof shall be transmitted by the Registrar to Members of the League of Nations, to States and to international organizations directly concerned.

FINAL PROVISION

ARTICLE 86

The present Rules of Court which are adopted this eleventh day of March, 1936, repeal, as from this date, the Rules adopted on March 24th, 1922, as revised on July 31st, 1926, and amended on September 7th, 1927, and February 21st, 1931.

Done at The Hague, this eleventh day of March nineteen hundred and thirty-six.

(*Signed*) CECIL J. B. HURST, *President*
(*Signed*) A. HAMMARSKJÖLD, *Registrar*

ANNEX TO ARTICLE 36

RESOLUTION ADOPTED BY THE COUNCIL ON MAY 17th, 1922

The Council of the League of Nations, in virtue of the powers conferred upon it by Article 35, paragraph 2, of the Statute of the Permanent Court of International Justice, and subject to the provisions of that article,

RESOLVES:

1. The Permanent Court of International Justice shall be open to a State which is not a Member of the League of Nations or mentioned in the Annex to the Convenant of the League, upon the following condition, namely: that such State shall previously have deposited with the Registrar of the Court a declaration by which it accepts the juris-

diction of the Court, in accordance with the Convenant of the League of Nations and with the terms and subject to the conditions of the Statute and Rules of the Court, and undertakes to carry out in full good faith the decision or decisions of the Court and not to resort to war against a State complying therewith.

2. Such declaration may be either particular or general.

A particular declaration is one accepting the jurisdiction of the Court in respect only of a particular dispute or disputes which have already arisen.

A general declaration is one accepting the jurisdiction generally in respect of all disputes or of a particular class or classes of disputes which have already arisen or which may arise in the future.

A State in making such a general declaration may accept the jurisdiction of the Court as compulsory, *ipso facto*, and without special convention, in conformity with Article 36 of the Statute of the Court; but such acceptance may not, without special convention, be relied upon vis-à-vis Members of the League or States mentioned in the Annex to the Covenant which have signed or may hereafter sign the "optional clause" provided for by the additional protocol of December 16th, 1920.

3. The original declarations made under the terms of this Resolution shall be kept in the custody of the Registrar of the Court, in accordance with the practice of the Court. Certified true copies thereof shall be transmitted, in accordance with the practice of the Court, to all Members of the League of Nations, and States mentioned in the Annex to the Covenant, and to such other States as the Court may determine, and to the Secretary-General of the League of Nations.

4. The Council of the League of Nations reserves the right to rescind or amend this Resolution by a Resolution which shall be communicated to the Court; and on the receipt of such communication and to the extent determined by the new Resolution, existing declarations shall cease to be effective except in regard to disputes which are already before the Court.

5. All questions as to the validity or the effect of a declaration made under the terms of this Resolution shall be decided by the Court.

Appendix Three

DOCUMENTS RELATING TO THE TRANSFER OF LEAGUE OF NATIONS ASSETS AND FUNCTIONS TO THE UNITED NATIONS

I. REPORT OF THE LEAGUE OF NATIONS COMMITTEE TO THE GENERAL ASSEMBLY. TRANSFER OF CERTAIN FUNCTIONS, ACTIVITIES AND ASSETS OF THE LEAGUE OF NATIONS[1]

Rapporteur: Mr. H. T. Andrews (Union of South Africa)

The General Assembly in its Eighteenth Plenary Meeting held on 26 January 1946, referred to the League of Nations Committee the question of the possible transfer of certain functions, activities and assets of the League of Nations.

After having considered these questions on the basis of Chapter XI of the Report of the Preparatory Commission of the United Nations and of the Report of the Committee set up by the Preparatory Commission to discuss and establish with the Supervisory Commission of the League of Nations a Common Plan for the transfer of the assets of the League of Nations, (see Documents A/18; A/18/Add/1; A/18/Add/2), the League of Nations Committee has approved the following resolutions, the adoption of which I have the honour to propose:[2]

I. FUNCTIONS AND POWERS BELONGING TO THE LEAGUE OF NATIONS UNDER INTERNATIONAL AGREEMENTS

Under various treaties and international conventions, agreements and other instruments, the League of Nations and its organs exercise, or may be requested to exercise, numerous functions or powers for the continuance of which after the dissolution of the League, it is, or may be, desirable that the United Nations should provide.

Certain Members of the United Nations, which are parties to some of these instruments and are Members of the League of Nations, have informed the General Assembly that at the forthcoming session of the Assembly of the League they intend to move a resolution whereby the Members of the League would, so far as this is necessary, assent and give effect to the steps contemplated below.

[1]Adopted on February 12, 1946; see *Journal* No. 30, p. 526–527, and *Journal* No. 34, p. 706–709. Reprinted from United Nations Document A/28, February 4, 1946.
[2]Text of these Resolutions, subsequently considered as one resolution subdivided into four sections and numbered as Resolution 24(1), also in *Resolutions Adopted by the General Assembly during the First Part of Its First Session*, United Nations Document A/64, 1 July 1946, p. 35–36.

THEREFORE

1. The General Assembly reserves the right to decide, after due examination, not to assume any particular function or power, and to determine which organ of the United Nations or which specialized agency brought into relationship with the United Nations should exercise each particular function or power assumed.

2. The General Assembly records that those Members of the United Nations which are parties to the instruments referred to above assent by this Resolution to the steps contemplated below and express their resolve to use their good offices to secure the co-operation of the other parties to the instruments so far as this may be necessary.

3. The General Assembly declares that the United Nations is willing, in principle and subject to the provisions of this Resolution and of the Charter of the United Nations, to assume the exercise of certain functions and powers previously entrusted to the League of Nations, and adopts the following decisions, set forth in A, B, and C below.

A. Functions Pertaining to a Secretariat

Under certain of the instruments referred to at the beginning of this Resolution, the League of Nations has, for the general convenience of the parties, undertaken to act as custodian of the original signed texts of the instruments, and to perform certain functions, pertaining to a secretariat, which do not affect the operation of the instruments and do not relate to the substantive rights and obligations of the parties. These functions include: the receipt of additional signatures and of instruments of ratification, accession and denunciation; receipt of notice of extension of the instruments to colonies or possessions of a party or to protectorates or territories for which it holds a mandate; notification of such acts to other parties and other interested states; the issue of certified copies; and the circulation of information or documents which the parties have undertaken to communicate to each other. Any interruption in the performance of these functions would be contrary to the interests of all the parties. It would be convenient for the United Nations to have the custody of those instruments which are connected with activities of the League of Nations and which the United Nations is likely to continue.

THEREFORE

The General Assembly declares that the United Nations is willing to accept the custody of the instruments and to charge the Secretariat of the United Nations with the task of performing for the parties the functions, pertaining to a secretariat, formerly entrusted to the League of Nations.

B. Functions and Powers of a Technical and Non-Political Character

Among the instruments referred to at the beginning of this Resolution are some of a technical and non-political character which contain provisions, relating to the substance of the instruments, whose due execution is dependent on the exercise, by the League of Nations or particular organs of the League, of functions or powers conferred by the instruments. Certain of these instruments are intimately connected with activities which the United Nations will or may continue.

It is necessary, however, to examine carefully which of the organs of the United Nations or which of the specialized agencies brought into relationship with the United Nations should, in the future, exercise the functions and powers in question, in so far as they are maintained.

THEREFORE

The General Assembly is willing, subject to these reservations, to take the necessary measures to ensure the continued exercise of these functions and powers, and refers the matter to the Economic and Social Council.

C. Functions and Powers Under Treaties, International Conventions, Agreements and Other Instruments Having a Political Character

The General Assembly will itself examine, or will submit to the appropriate organ of the United Nations, any request from the parties that the United Nations should assume the exercise of functions or powers entrusted to the League of Nations by treaties, international conventions, agreements and other instruments having a political character.

II. NON-POLITICAL FUNCTIONS AND ACTIVITIES OF THE LEAGUE OF NATIONS OTHER THAN THOSE MENTIONED IN I

1. The General Assembly requests the Economic and Social Council to survey the functions and activities of a non-political character which have hitherto been performed by the League of Nations in order to determine which of them should, with such modifications as are desirable, be assumed by organs of the United Nations or be entrusted to specialized agencies which have been brought into relationship with the United Nations. Pending the adoption of the measures decided upon as the result of this examination, the Council should, on or before the dissolution of the League, assume and continue provisionally the work hitherto done by the following League departments: The Economic, Financial and Transit Department, particularly the research and statistical work; the Health Section, particularly the epidemiological service; the Opium Section and the secretariats of the Permanent Central Opium Board and Supervisory Body.

2. The General Assembly requests the Secretary-General to make provision for taking over and maintaining in operation the Library and Archives and for completing the League of Nations Treaty Series.

3. The General Assembly considers that it would also be desirable for the Secretary-General to engage for the work, referred to in paragraphs 1 and 2 above, on appropriate terms, such members of the experienced personnel by whom it is at present being performed as the Secretary-General may select.

III. Transfer of the Assets of the League of Nations to the United Nations

The General Assembly having considered the Report of the Committee set up by the Preparatory Commission to discuss and establish with the Supervisory Commission of the League of Nations a Common Plan for the transfer of the assets of the League of Nations, approves of both the Report of the Committee set up by the Preparatory Commission and of the Common Plan submitted by it.

IV. Appointment of a Negotiating Committee

The General Assembly approves of the setting up of a small negotiating committee to assist the Secretary-General in negotiating further agreements in connection with the transfer of certain assets in Geneva, and in connection with the premises in the Peace Palace in the Hague. This Committee shall consist of one representative designated by the delegations, if they so desire, of each of the same eight Members as previously constituted the Committee created by the Preparatory Commission: Chile, China, France, Poland, South Africa, the Soviet Union, the United Kingdom and the United States of America.

II. REPORT OF THE COMMITTEE SET UP BY THE PREPARATORY COMMISSION TO DISCUSS AND ESTABLISH WITH THE SUPERVISORY COMMISSION OF THE LEAGUE OF NATIONS A COMMON PLAN FOR THE TRANSFER OF THE ASSETS OF THE LEAGUE OF NATIONS[1]

1. The Committee was set up by the Preparatory Commission on 18 December 1945 and consists of one representative designated by the Delegations of each of the following eight Members: Chile, China, France, Poland, South Africa, the Soviet Union, the United Kingdom and the United States of America.

The Committee's terms of reference were to enter on behalf of the Preparatory Commission, into discussions with the League Supervisory Commission, for the purpose of establishing a common plan for the transfer of the assets of the League to the United Nations on such terms as are considered just and convenient. The duly authorized representative of the International Labour Organization were to be consulted on questions connected with the transfer which affected that Organization.

The Committee was instructed to have regard to the views expressed by the Executive Committee in paragraphs 24, 25, 28–31 of the "Report on the Transfer of Certain Functions, Activities and Assets of the League of Nations" (Report by the Executive Committee, pages 112–114).

The Committee was not called on to make recommendations on the transfer of functions and activities of the League which is the subject of a separate recommendation of the Preparatory Commission. The Committee, however, calls attention to the desirability of acting on this matter promptly in order to facilitate the termination of the League as soon as possible.

The Preparatory Commission recommended that the plan developed by the Committee should be submitted for approval to the General Assembly, if possible during the First Part of the First Session.

2. The Committee held conversations with the Supervisory Commission of the League of Nations and consulted duly authorized representatives of the Governing Body of the International Labour Organization. The Committee has received all possible assistance from

[1]Reprinted from United Nations Document A/18, January 28, 1946.

these bodies who share the Committee's desire that the necessary steps should be taken with the greatest possible speed.

3. The main concern of the United Nations Committee was to survey the present position of the assets of the League and to determine how the assets taken over should be evaluated and how any financial settlement should be effected.

The Supervisory Commission was, however, concerned with a number of other questions connected with the liquidation of the League, and indirectly affecting the transfer of assets. Therefore, the Common Plan established contains several points not immediately of interest to the United Nations.

4. The Committee recommends that the United Nations should, in order to facilitate the early dissolution of the League of Nations in definite and proper conditions, take over all material assets of the League of Nations. These material assets include:

(a) the buildings in Geneva holding the offices of the Secretariat, the Assembly Hall with the committee rooms and the library, together with the transferable rights of the League of Nations to use the land on which the building stands, the land within one hundred metres of the buildings and the roads leading to the buildings:

(b) the surrounding grounds belonging to the League of Nations including fields, woodlands and four villas purchased to maintain the amenities of the immediate surroundings;

(c) the furniture fittings and equipment belonging to the League;

(d) the stocks of stationery, printing paper and publications, office supplies and equipment of the League;

(e) the books belonging to the League;

(f) the League archives.

A more precise specification is set out in column I of the Schedule attached to the Common Plan.

The Committee is of the opinion that the cost of maintenance of the fixed assets mentioned under (a) and (b) should not be excessive in relation to their value.

The question of the premises of the Court of Justice in the Hague is referred to in paragraph 11.

5. In accordance with its terms of reference the Committee was to find a value which should "in principle imply neither profit nor loss for the United Nations." The Committee and the Supervisory Commission agreed that in general a "just and convenient" evaluation of these assets today would be the price they had cost the League of Nations.

For the movable assets the cost price is certainly on balance favourable to the United Nations. It should be noted that the inventory of movable assets is subject to minor changes, since the figures given are based on a survey made in July 1945. It is understood that all gifts, many of which have a high artistic and monetary value, will be transferred without any pecuniary consideration.

As regards the fixed assets a method of evaluation on any basis other than that recommended by the Committee was found to be extremely difficult in view, amongst other things, of the uncertainty of the future use of the buildings. Postponement of valuation until a later date was considered by the Committee, but this plan was regarded by the Supervisory Commission as impracticable due to the uncertainties involved and to the need for a more definite and clear cut arrangement if the League is to be terminated at an early date. Further this procedure might involve the United Nations in financial dealings with States non-Members.

The Committee recommends that the valuation at cost price set out in column II of the Schedule attached to the Common Plan, with the reservations as to revision set out in the notes appended, be accepted.

6. The Common Plan agreed with the Supervisory Commission proposes the following procedure for a financial settlement.

The shares in the total credit established in settlement of the transfer should be distributed between the States entitled to participate, in accordance with percentages to be laid down by the League at its next Assembly. The fixing of these percentages is a matter to be decided exclusively by the League of Nations Assembly. The shares, thus established, of such of those States as are Members of the United Nations shall be credited to them respectively in the books of the United Nations. These credits should be translated into dollar currency at the rate effective on the day of transfer of the material assets. The claims of States non-Members of the United Nations should be dealt with otherwise by the League of Nations.

As regards the credits booked to the Members of the United Nations, the General Assembly should decide on the purposes to which these credits shall be applied and on the dates on which they shall be so applied. It is, however, agreed that these credits should, in any event, begin to be available not later than 31 December 1948. This provision preserves the budgetary freedom of the General Assembly, but it gives some guarantee to the recipient states that the settlement of their claims will not indefinitely be postponed.

This procedure provides for a financial settlement within the United Nations and avoids all payments or transfers of credit to non-Members of the United Nations or to the League. The Committee, therefore, recommends that it be accepted.

7. In view of the legal, financial and administrative arrangements to be made, 1 August 1946 appears to be the earliest date that can be fixed for the legal transfer of the material assets. It is, however, prudent to provide for some degree of elasticity to prevent embarrassment for the administrations concerned. Therefore, the Committee

recommends that the transfer be effected on or about 1 August 1946, the precise date to be determined by the administrative authorities of the two organizations.

8. It may not be convenient for the League of Nations to set free certain premises or equipment on the date selected for the legal transfer. On the other hand the United Nations may wish to use the premises or equipment of the League before that date. It is understood that in either case the Administration of the Organization legally entitled to the ownership will make all reasonable arrangements to accommodate the other Administration without any charge.

9. The Supervisory Commission of the League of Nations has agreed to recommend to the League Assembly that the assets mentioned in paragraph 4 be transferred to the United Nations. The Supervisory Commission will also recommend that all other questions relating to the liquidation of the League of Nations shall be handled exclusively by the League of Nations, the United Nations having no voice in these matters nor responsibility for them. The League of Nations would, therefore, make arrangements:

(a) to discharge all its obligations as soon as practicable;

(b) to settle the question of contributions of Member States in arrears;

(c) to separate the interests of the International Labour Organization in the assets of the League before transfer to the United Nations; (It is understood that the International Labour Organization building at Geneva will be transferred to that Organization.)

(d) for the continued administration of the Staff Pensions Fund, and with regard to the pensions of the Judges of the Permanent Court of International Justice;

(e) when it has discharged all its obligations and made the necessary dispositions concerning the Working Capital Fund and regarding outstanding contributions, for crediting or distributing the remaining liquid assets to Members of the League under a scheme to be determined by it.

Though the question of contributions in arrears of Members of the League of Nations does not directly concern the United Nations, the Supervisory Commission stated that a satisfactory solution of the question would be of considerable assistance in expediting the final settlement and liquidation of the League.

10. The Supervisory Commission has done all that is possible to separate the interests of the International Labour Organization in the assets of the League. The International Labour Organization has, however, some interests in the material assets that are to be transferred to the United Nations that could not be separated. These interests had to be discussed.

The International Labour Organization is interested in the continued use of the Assembly Hall at Geneva for its conferences and in the continued use of the League library. The Committee recommends that the United Nations should agree that the International Labour Organization may use the Assembly Hall, together with the necessary committee rooms, office accomodation and other facilities connected therewith at times and on financial terms to be agreed from time to time between the United Nations and the International Labour Organization; and further that the International Labour Organization may use the library under the same conditions as other official users thereof.

The Committee is of the opinion that the detailed arrangements necessary in this connection should be made by the competent authorities of the two organizations.

The following suggestions, which have been tentatively put forward by the International Labour Organization, might afford an appropriate basis for these negotiations.

A share of the cost of maintaining the Assembly Hall corresponding to its period of use in the course of the year, together with any additional charges incurred in respect of meetings held under the auspices of the International Labour Organization should be borne by that Organization.

The International Labour Organization should notify the United Nations at least three months in advance of the date on which the International Labour Organization wishes to make use of the Hall and the initial and terminal dates for such use shall be agreed between the competent authorities of the International Labour Organization and of the United Nations.

The United Nations and the International Labour Organization should agree upon the most convenient period of the year at which the Assembly Hall shall normally be available for meetings of the International Labour Conference.

11. In connection with the transfer of certain assets in Geneva agreements must be made with the Swiss authorities. A small negotiating committee to assist the Secretary-General should be appointed to make these agreements.

As to the premises for the use of the new Court in the Hague, arrangements must be made with the Carnegie Foundation.

In this context it should be noted that the premises in the Peace Palace in the Hague were considerably altered to house the Permanent Court of International Justice. The United Nations will have the advantage of this arrangement for which several instalments on two loans obtained from the Carnegie Foundation are still due.

The Committee recommends that the small committee mentioned above should be sent to the Hague to make the necessary arrangements.

12. The League of Nations will, during the liquidation and the transfer of assets, take all steps necessary to assist in the assumption and continuance, under the auspices of the Economic and Social Council of the United Nations, of those League activities which the United Nations decides to assume and continue. Any ex-official of the League of Nations subsequently engaged temporarily or otherwise by the United Nations should enter service under conditions of employment established by the United Nations.

The League agrees to transfer the archives, particularly those dealing with current matters, as soon as desired. The two Secretaries-General should be empowered to make detailed arrangements. The archives should be located where they could best serve the work of the United Nations.

1. ANNEX TO THE REPORT OF THE UNITED NATIONS COMMITTEE ON LEAGUE OF NATIONS ASSETS. COMMON PLAN FOR THE TRANSFER OF LEAGUE OF NATIONS ASSETS ESTABLISHED BY THE UNITED NATIONS COMMITTEE AND THE SUPERVISORY COMMISSION OF THE LEAGUE OF NATIONS[2]

1. The League of Nations agrees to transfer to the United Nations, and the United Nations agrees to receive on or about 1 August 1946, the precise date to be determined by the administrative authorities of the two Organizations, all material assets of the League of Nations shown in column I of the attached Schedule at the valuation shown in column II.

The League of Nations agrees that the shares in the total credit thus established shall be distributed between States entitled to participate, in accordance with percentages to be laid down by the League at its next Assembly.

The United Nations agrees:

(a) that the shares, thus established, of such of these States as are Members of the United Nations shall be credited[3]to them respectively in the books of the United Nations: and

(b) that the General Assembly shall decide on the purposes to which these credits shall be applied and on the dates on which they shall be so applied; and further that these credits shall in any event, begin to be available not later than 31 December 1948.

The United Nations further agrees:

(a) that the International Labour Organization may use the Assembly Hall, together with the necessary committee rooms, office ac-

---

[2]Reprinted from United Nations Document A/18/Add/1, January 28, 1946.
[3]These credits shall be translated into dollar currency at the rate effective on the day of transfer of the material assets referred to in par. 1.

commodation and other facilities connected therewith at times and on financial terms to be agreed from time to time between the United Nations and the International Labour Organization;

(*b*) that the International Labour Organization may use the library under the same conditions as other official users thereof.

2. The League of Nations shall take steps to discharge all its obligations as soon as practicable.

3. The League of Nations shall take steps to settle the question of contributions of Member States in arrears.

4. The League of Nations shall take steps to separate the interests of the International Labour Organization in the assets of the League, before transfer to the United Nations. It is understood that the International Labour Organization building at Geneva will be transferred to that Organization.

5. Any ex-officials of the League of Nations subsequently engaged by the United Nations shall enter service under conditions of employment established by the United Nations, and it will be for the League of Nations to take the necessary steps to make this possible.

6. It is understood that the League of Nations shall make arrangements, independently of the United Nations, with regard to the continued administration of the Staff Pension Fund and with regard to the pensions of the Judges of the Permanent Court of International Justice.

7. When the League has discharged all its obligations and made the necessary dispositions concerning the Working Capital Fund and regarding outstanding contributions, the remaining liquid assets shall be credited or distributed to Members of the League under a scheme to be determined by it.

8. Both the United Nations and the League of Nations shall authorize competent authorities to make any necessary agreements with the Swiss Authorities on all matters connected with the transfer of assets of the League of Nations to the United Nations.

2. *APPENDIX TO THE COMMON PLAN FOR THE TRANS-FER OF LEAGUE OF NATIONS ASSETS ESTABLISHED BY THE UNITED NATIONS COMMITTEE AND THE SUPER-VISORY COMMISSION OF THE LEAGUE OF NATIONS*[4]

SCHEDULE

I	II
Secretariat building and Assembly Hall....................	38,553,914.03[5]
Library building.................	..........[6]

[4]Reprinted from United Nations Document A/18/Add/2, January 28, 1946. The figures in this schedule are given in Swiss francs. The footnotes, with the exception of the present one, are those of Document A/18/Add/2.

Real estate belonging to the League
of Nations having an area of
203,446 square meters and comprising four villas and other build-
ings............................... 2,889,453.45
Furniture, fittings, typewriters, etc.
for the use of the Secretariat, including the branch offices, and for
the other buildings in Geneva....
Total according to the annexed inventories...................... 3,329,978.70
Total included under Secretariat
building and Assembly Hall to be
deducted...................... 1,429,185.02   1,900,793.68[7]
Furniture, fittings, typewriters, etc.
for the use of the Court of Justice
in the Hague...................   278,615.20[7]
Stocks of stationery, printing paper
and publications, office supplies
and equipment, in Geneva and
branch offices..................   199,657.25[8]
Books, stocks of stationery, printing
paper and publications, office supplies and equipment for the Court
in the Hague...................   291,596.00[8]
Gifts..............................   ....[9]
Library: Books etc. in Geneva ac-
cording to the annexed inventory   3,518,089.00[10]
Archives of the League of Nations
and of the Permanent Court of
International Justice............   ....

TOTAL..............................   47,631,518.61

[5]Cost of building and equipment of the Secretariat and the Assembly Hall. The League
has a transferable right to use the land on which the buildings stand, the land 100 meters
around it and the two roads leading to the buildings. The League further has a non-
transferable right to use the remainder of the plot of land in Ariana Park in which the
buildings stand. No value is placed on these rights in the schedule.
[6]The cost of this building given by Mr. Rockefeller was 5,564,206.22 Swiss francs.
[7]Owing to possible changes before the date of transfer these figures are provisional and
subject to revision.
[8]Owing to possible changes before the date of transfer these figures are provisional and
subject to revision. Deduction might also be made for gifts included in this figure.
[9]The nominal value of the gifts should be put at 1,234,640 Swiss francs.
[10]This figure includes gifts and will therefore be revised, a deduction being made for
gifts.

III. NON-POLITICAL FUNCTIONS AND ACTIVITIES OF THE LEAGUE OF NATIONS

RESOLUTION OF THE ECONOMIC AND SOCIAL COUNCIL OF FEBRUARY 16, 1946[1]

1. In its resolution of 12 February 1946, on the Transfer of Certain Functions, Activities and Assets of the League of Nations, the General Assembly has requested that:

(a) the Economic and Social Council survey the functions and activities of a non-political character which have hitherto been performed by the League of Nations in order to determine which of them should, with such modifications as are desirable, be assumed by organs of the United Nations or be entrusted to specialized agencies which have been brought into relationship with the United Nations; and

(b) the Council, pending the adoption of the measures decided upon as the result of this examination, assume and continue provisionally the work hitherto done by the following League departments: The Economic, Financial and Transit Department, particularly the research and statistical work; the Health Section, particularly the epidemiological service; the Opium Section, and the Secretariats of the Permanent Central Opium Board and Supervisory Body.

2. The Economic and Social Council accordingly,

(a) Requests the Secretary-General to undertake the survey called for by the General Assembly and to report at an early date to the Economic and Social Council.

(b) Directs the Secretary-General acting in accordance with the Resolution of the General Assembly, to take the steps necessary to the provisional assumption and continuance of the work hitherto done by the League departments named above.

RESOLUTION OF THE GENERAL ASSEMBLY OF DECEMBER 14, 1946[2]

In accordance with the resolution adopted by the General Assembly on 12 February 1946 and the resolution adopted by the Economic

[1] Reprinted from United Nations Document E/19, February 15, 1946. Text of this Resolution, which was adopted by the Economic and Social Council on February 16, 1946, also in *Journal of the Economic and Social Council*, First Year, No. 12 (April 10, 1946), p. 133.
[2] Resolution 51(I), *Transfer to the United Nations of Certain Non-political Functions*

and Social Council on 16 February 1946, the Secretary-General submitted to the Economic and Social Council, at its third session, a report dated 26 September 1946 concerning the provisional assumption and continuation of certain non-political functions and activities of the League of Nations, other than those exercised pursuant to international agreements.

The Economic and Social Council took note of the Secretary-General's report on 2 October 1946 and has transmitted it to the General Assembly.

The General Assembly recognizes that it is desirable for the United Nations to assume and continue the non-political functions and activities of the League of Nations which are described in the report of the Secretary-General dated 26 September 1946.

The General Assembly, therefore,

Authorizes and requests the Secretary-General to assume and continue the non-political functions and activities of the League of Nations previously performed by the League of Nations Secretariat, with the exception of:

(*a*) Those functions and activities exercised pursuant to international agreements;

(*b*) Those functions and activities entrusted to specialized agencies which have been, or are to be, brought into relationship with the United Nations, under Articles 57 and 63 of the Charter.

The Secretary-General shall exercise the functions and activities authorized by this paragraph, subject to such policies as may be established by the Economic and Social Council.

Authorizes and requests the Economic and Social Council to assume and continue the non-political functions and activities of the League of Nations previously performed by the various committees and commissions of the League with the exception of:

(*a*) Those functions and activities exercised pursuant to international agreements;

(*b*) Those functions and activities entrusted to specialized agencies, which have been, or are to be brought into relationship with the United Nations, under Articles 57 and 63 of the Charter.

This resolution shall not affect any decision of the General Assembly with respect to functions and activities exercised by the League of Nations pursuant to international agreements.

Sixty-fifth plenary meeting,
14 December 1946

and Activities of the League of Nations, Other than Those Pursuant to International Agreements. Text in United Nations Document A/64/Add.1, January 31, 1947, p. 78.

IV. TRANSFER OF THE ASSETS OF THE LEAGUE OF NATIONS. REPORT OF THE FIFTH COMMITTEE[1]

Rapporteur: Mr. T. Aghnides (Greece)

1. In accordance with instructions given by the General Assembly at its forty-sixth plenary meeting, held on 31 October 1946, the Fifth Committee has considered the question of the transfer of the assets of the League of Nations to the United Nations as outlined in a memorandum by the Secretary-General (document A/172).

2. In the course of the discussion, several delegations submitted representations that their Governments were entitled to participation in the total credit accruing from the transfer of the assets of the League of Nations to the United Nations. The Committee considered these representations in relation to the scheme drawn up for the distribution of this credit pursuant to the resolution of the General Assembly approving the Common Plan. A proposal was put forward by certain delegations that those Member States which are former members of the League of Nations and are entitled under this scheme to share in the credit, should, when their share has been established, consult together to consider an arrangement under which all former members of the League of Nations now Members of the United Nations could be allocated a share in the credit on a basis comparable with that applicable to members of the League of Nations as set out in the League of Nations scheme of distribution. The Committee took note of the intention to arrange for such discussions before the General Assembly has to take decisions under Paragraph 1 (b) of the Common Plan.

3. The Committee approved, by thirty-four votes to nil, the conclusions of the report presented by the Secretary-General on the transfer of certain assets, together with an Agreement concerning the Execution of the Transfer to the United Nations of certain Assets of the League of Nations and a Protocol concerning the Execution of various Operations in the Transfer to the United Nations of certain Assets of the League of Nations.

4. The Fifth Committee recommends, therefore, that the General Assembly adopt the following resolution:[2]

[1] Reprinted from United Nations Document A/214, December 5, 1946.
[2] This Resolution was adopted, as proposed, by the General Assembly on December 7, 1946. Text of this Resolution, including Annex I and Annex II, also published as

TRANSFER OF THE ASSETS OF THE LEAGUE OF NATIONS

The General Assembly resolves that:

1. The Agreement concerning the execution of the Transfer to the United Nations of certain Assets of the League of Nations and the Protocol concerning the Execution of various Operations in the Transfer to the United Nations of certain Assets of the League of Nations, arrived at in accordance with the provisions of the Common Plan with respect to the transfer of certain assets of the League of Nations, are approved as they appear in Annexes I and II to this resolution.

2. The Secretary-General is authorized to prepare a definite schedule for establishing a final valuation of these assets, in accordance with the terms of the Common Plan, in consultation with the Advisory Committee on Administrative and Budgetary Questions and the League authorities; and therefore that such a schedule agreed upon by the Advisory Committee, the League authorities and the Secretary-General shall be considered as final.

I. ANNEX I. AGREEMENT CONCERNING THE EXECUTION OF THE TRANSFER TO THE UNITED NATIONS OF CERTAIN ASSETS OF THE LEAGUE OF NATIONS, SIGNED ON 19 JULY 1946[3]

Whereas the General Assembly of the United Nations, by a resolution adopted on 12 February 1946, and the Assembly of the League of Nations, by a resolution adopted on 18 April 1946, respectively approved the Common Plan[4] for the transfer to the United Nations of certain assets of the League of Nations, on the financial conditions mentioned in the aforesaid Plan,

The League of Nations, represented by Mr. Sean Lester, Secretary-General, and the United Nations represented by M. Wlodzimierz Moderow, Director, representative of the Secretary-General of the United Nations at Geneva, have concluded the present Agreement for the purpose of determining the details of the transfer of the ownership of the assets in question, apart from the financial conditions mentioned in the Common Plan.

Resolution 79(I) in *Resolutions Adopted by the General Assembly during the Second Part of Its First Session*, United Nations Document A/64/Add.1, January 31, 1947, p. 139–144.

[3]Text of this Agreement also in United Nations, *Treaty Series*, Vol. I (1946–1947), p. 109–117. For "Arrangement Concluded between the United Nations and the League of Nations to Give Practical Effect to Certain Provisions of the Agreement of July 19th, 1946 Dealing with the Execution of the Transfer of League Assets to the United Nations. Signed at Geneva on 31 July 1946," see *ibid.*, p. 119–129.

[4]Cf.: For the United Nations, document A/18 of 28 January 1946. For the League of Nations, document A/32 (1).1946.X—Appendix. (Footnote as in Document A/214.)

ARTICLE 1

The transfer of rights in respect of immovable property shall relate to the following items.

1. All transferable rights which, in virtue of the Agreement concluded on 26 March 1929, between the Swiss Confederation and the League of Nations, the latter possesses over the Ariana site and the buildings erected by it on that site;

2. The rights possessed by the League of Nations in respect of the Sécheron property, as defined in the Agreement of 26 March 1929, referred to in paragraph 1 above;

3. The full ownership enjoyed by the League of Nations in properties situated in Geneva and at Pregny, with an area of 203,446 square metres, consisting of various plots of land with four villas and their outbuildings;

4. The following rights:

(a) The servitudes constituted in favour of the League of Nations in the Bill of Sale dated 14 June 1938, by which the Latvian Government acquired a property situate in the Commune of Geneva (Petit-Saconnex district), and the right of pre-emption reserved to the League of Nations;

(b) The servitudes constituted in favour of the League of Nations in the Bill of Sale dated 7 March 1940, concluded between the Société immobilière de la Place des Nations and the League of Nations, and the right of purchase reserved to the League of Nations.

ARTICLE 2

The transfer of rights in respect of movable property shall relate to the following items:

(a) The fittings, furniture, office equipment and books, and the stock of supplies which are in the aforementioned premises and which are the property of the League of Nations;

(b) The books and collections of the Library;

(c) The fittings, furniture, office equipment and books, and the stock of supplies for the use of the Permanent Court of International Justice which are the property of the League of Nations;

(d) The fittings, furniture, office equipment and books and the stock of supplies which are or were in the branch offices of the League of Nations and which have remained the property of the League of Nations;

(e) Any fittings, furniture, office equipment, books and stock of supplies which would become the property of the League of Nations in consequence of the dissolution of organizations or institutes subsidiary thereto;

(f) The stocks of supplies held by suppliers, which are the property of the League of Nations;

(g) The archives of the League of Nations and of the Permanent Court of International Justice;

(h) All other corporeal property belonging to the League of Nations.

ARTICLE 3

It is understood that gifts presented to the League of Nations by Governments, public bodies or private individuals, whether they have become part of the buildings or whether they have retained the character of movable property, shall be transferred to the United Nations on the same terms as those on which the said gifts were presented.

ARTICLE 4

It is recalled that, in accordance with the terms of the Common Plan:

(a) The International Labour Organization may use the Assembly Hall, together with the necessary committee rooms, office accommodation and other facilities connected therewith at times and on financial terms to be agreed from time to time between the United Nations and the International Labour Organization: and

(b) The International Labour Organization may use the Library under the same conditions as other official users thereof.

ARTICLE 5

The United Nations shall assume the following obligations which the League of Nations has undertaken to transfer to the acquirers of certain of its immovable property, namely:

(a) As provided in the Act of 2 July 1940, by which the Republic and Canton of Geneva sold to the League of Nations the landed property situate in the Commune of Geneva, Petit-Saconnex district (plot 7033, sheet 4, with an area of 19 ares and 91 metres), the buyer, in the event of re-sale, shall undertake not to exercise his right to build on the said plot otherwise than in conformity with the legal provisions relevant in the matter;

(b) As provided in Article 3 of the Agreement of 20 February 1941, between the Services industriels de Genève and the League of Nations, obligations in respect of underground mains shall be transferred to the acquirer of the land;

(c) As provided in Article 6 of the Arrangement of 18 July 1942, between the Swiss Postal and Telegraph Services and the League of Nations, obligations in respect of underground mains shall be transferred to the acquirer of the land.

ARTICLE 6

The movable objects transferred shall be listed in an inventory drawn up by the League of Nations and verified jointly by the United Nations at the time of the transfer.

ARTICLE 7

The transfers provided for in the present Agreement shall take place on 1 August 1946.

Article 8

1. In conformity with item 8 of the report by the Committee of the United Nations accompanying the Common Plan (United Nations document A/18, 28 January 1946), the United Nations shall, during the liquidation of the League of Nations, allow the latter to use without any charge the premises and the furniture and equipment with which they are provided, together with the supplies necessary for the continuation of its activities until the date of the transfer of the said activities to the United Nations or of their termination.

2. Subsequently, for the work of liquidation of the League of Nations, until the completion of that liquidation, the United Nations shall grant, free of charge, the use of the premises and the furniture and equipment with which they are provided and available supplies in reasonable quantities.

ARTICLE 9

A protocol shall be drawn up between the League of Nations and the United Nations in order, if need be, to supplement the present Agreement and to settle any practical questions arising out of the transfer.

ARTICLE 10

The present Agreement shall enter into force on the date on which it shall have been signed by the Secretary-General of the League of Nations and the Secretary-General of the United Nations, or by their representatives.

Done and signed at Geneva on 19 July 1946, in four copies, two in French and two in English, the texts in both languages being equally authentic, of which two texts, one French and one English were handed to the representatives of the League of Nations and the two remaining texts to the representatives of the United Nations.

For the League of Nations: For the United Nations:
    (*Signed*) SEAN LESTER   (*Signed*) W. MODEROW

2. ANNEX II. PROTOCOL [NO. I] CONCERNING THE EXE-CUTION OF VARIOUS OPERATIONS IN THE TRANSFER TO THE UNITED NATIONS OF CERTAIN ASSETS OF THE LEAGUE OF NATIONS, SIGNED 1 AUGUST 1946[5]

MR. SEAN LESTER, Secretary-General of the League of Nations, and M. WLODZIMIERZ MODEROW, Director, Representative of the Secretary-General of the United Nations in Geneva:

Note that, in application of the Common Plan, approved by a resolution of the General Assembly of the United Nations, dated 12 February 1946, and by a resolution of the Assembly of the League of Nations, dated 18 April 1946, and of a subsequent Agreement dated 19 July 1946, concerning the execution of the transfer to the United Nations of certain assets of the League of Nations, the following operations were effected on 1 August 1946:

1. The transfer of rights in respect of the League of Nations buildings and other immovable property was effected on 1 August 1946, and the necessary entries having been made this day in the Land Register of the Republic and Canton of Geneva.

2. The transfer of the ownership and possession of the movable property was also effected on 1 August 1946.

In accordance with Article 6 of the Agreement of 19 July 1946, the movable objects transferred have been listed in an inventory drawn up by the League of Nations which is in course of being verified by the United Nations. A protocol will be drawn up placing on record the completion of this operation.

3. A final valuation of the assets will be made in accordance with the terms of the Common Plan. It will be the subject of a special protocol.

Geneva, 1 August 1946   (*Signed*) SEAN LESTER
                                              W. MODEROW

3. PROTOCOL NO. II ON THE TRANSFER OF CERTAIN SERVICES FROM THE LEAGUE OF NATIONS TO THE UNITED NATIONS. SIGNED AT GENEVA ON 1 AUGUST 1946[6]

MR. SEAN LESTER, Secretary-General of the League of Nations, and MR. WLODZIMIERZ MODEROW, Director, Representative of the Secretary-General of the United Nations in Geneva,

[5]Also in United Nations, *Treaty Series*, Vol. I (1946–1947). p. 131, as "Protocol (No. I)."
[6]Reprinted from United Nations, *Treaty Series*, Vol. I (1946–1947), p. 135. This supplements Protocol No. I (see note 5, above).

Note that, in accordance with a resolution of the General Assembly of the United Nations dated 12 February 1946 and a resolution of the Assembly of the League of Nations dated 18 April 1946;

The following services, together with their staff, have been transferred by the League of Nations to the United Nations:

1. The Library, Internal Service, Household, General Stenographic Service, and Roneo and Multigraph Service have been transferred in accordance with the conditions laid down by an Arrangement of 31 July 1946.

2. The Economic Intelligence Service and a part of the transit and communication section have been transferred by virtue of an exchange of letters dated 29 and 31 July 1946.

(Signed) SEAN LESTER

Geneva, 1 August 1946   W. MODEROW

V. INTERIM ARRANGEMENTS ON THE PRIVILEGES AND IMMUNITIES OF THE UNITED NATIONS CONCLUDED WITH THE SWISS FEDERAL COUNCIL AND ON AGREEMENTS CONCERNING THE ARIANA SITE. JOINT REPORT OF THE SECRETARY-GENERAL AND THE NEGOTIATING COMMITTEE[1]

Report of the Sixth Committee
Rapporteur: Professor K. H. Bailey (Australia)

1. The report of the Secretary-General on negotiations with the Swiss Federal Council (document A/175) contains the Interim Arrangement on Privileges and Immunities of the United Nations in Switzerland and the Agreement on the Ariana Site, which were drawn up in April by the Negotiating Committee on League of Nations Assets and representatives of the Swiss Federal Council, and which entered into force on the date of their signature by the Secretary-General (1 July 1946). The report also contains a review of later discussions between the Secretary-General and the Swiss Federal authorities and the text of two letters dated 22 October 1946 from the Head of the Political Department, the first dealing with a point of interpretation of the Interim Arrangement on Privileges and Immunities and the second dealing with the question of radio facilities for the United Nations in Switzerland.

2. The General Assembly, at its forty-sixth plenary meeting on 31 October 1946, referred the Secretary-General's report to the Sixth Committee; it was given detailed consideration by a Sub-Committee. The report of this Sub-Committee was presented to the Sixth Committee by its Rapporteur, Jonkherr G. Baelaerts van Blokland.

3. The Committee is of the opinion that the Interim Arrangement on Privileges and Immunities and Agreement on the Ariana Site are entirely satisfactory, and that an expression of the General Assembly's appreciation of the results obtained should be conveyed to the Secretary-General and to the Negotiating Committee on League of Nations Assets, as well as to the Swiss Federal authorities. In view of the purposes which it is proposed that the United Nations Office in Geneva should serve, the Committee is further of the opinion that it can recommend approval of the interpretation of the Interim Arrangement

[1]Reprinted from United Nations Document A/257, December 12, 1946.

contained in the letter from the Head of the Federal Political Department referred to above.

4. The question of radio facilities for the United Nations in Switzerland has legal as well as administrative aspects. The Committee does not feel it necessary to discuss the matter at this stage, in the hope that assurances concerning the transfer to the United Nations of wave-lengths previously registered for the use of Radio-Nations may shortly be received from the Swiss Federal authorities, as requested by the Secretary-General. Once the assurances have been received, the matter of radio facilities will fall entirely within the competence of the Fifth Committee.

5. The Sixth Committee recommends the adoption by the General Assembly of the following resolution:

INTERIM ARRANGEMENTS ON THE PRIVILEGES AND IMMUNITIES OF THE UNITED NATIONS CONCLUDED WITH THE SWISS FEDERAL COUNCIL AND ON AGREEMENTS CONCERNING THE ARIANA SITE

THE GENERAL ASSEMBLY

HAS TAKEN NOTE with satisfaction of the report by the Secretary-General on the negotiations with the Swiss Federal Council.

CONSIDERS THAT the documents set out in that report, including the letter of 22 October 1946 from the Head of the Swiss Federal Political Department relating to the use of the United Nations buildings in Geneva, constitute a satisfactory basis for the activities of the United Nations in Switzerland;

THEREFORE APPROVES the arrangements concluded with the Swiss Federal Council.

VI. RESOLUTION FOR THE DISSOLUTION OF THE LEAGUE OF NATIONS[1]

The Assembly o the League of Nations,

Considering that the Charter of the United Nations has created, for purposes of the same nature as those for which the League of Nations was established, an international organisation known as the United Nations to which all States may be admitted as Members on the conditions prescribed by the Charter and to which the great majority of the Members of the League already belong;

Desiring to promote, so far as lies in its power, the continuation, development and success of international co-operation in the new form adopted by the United Nations;

Considering that, since the new organisation has now commenced to exercise its functions, the League of Nations may be dissolved; and

Considering that, under Article 3, paragraph 3, of the Covenant, the Assembly may deal at its meetings with any matter within the sphere of action of the League:

ADOPTS THE FOLLOWING RESOLUTION:

DISSOLUTION OF THE LEAGUE OF NATIONS

1. (1) With effect from the day following the close of the present session of the Assembly, the League of Nations shall cease to exist except for the sole purpose of the liquidation of its affairs as provided in the present resolution.

(2) The liquidation shall be effected as rapidly as possible and the date of its completion shall be notified to all the Members by the Board of Liquidation provided for in paragraph 2.

2. (1) The Assembly appoints the persons named in the Annex to form a "Board of Liquidation," hereinafter called the Board, which shall represent the League for the purpose of effecting its liquidation. Subject to the provisions of this resolution and other relevant decisions taken by the Assembly at the present session, the Board shall have full power to give such directions, make such agreements and

[1]Reprinted from *Official Journal*, Special Supplement No. 194, p. 269–272; see also *ibid.*, p. 133. This Resolution was adopted on April 18, 1946, at the final plenary meeting of the Twenty-first Session of the Assembly of the League of Nations. For detailed background information on this Resolution see Denys P. Myers, "Liquidation of League of Nations Functions," *American Journal of International Law*, Vol. 42 (April, 1948), p. 330–332.

take all such measures as in its discretion it considers appropriate for this purpose.

(2) Vacancies on the Board shall be filled by co-option. Provided that the number of members be not reduced below five, the Board may refrain from filling particular vacancies.

(3) The Board shall elect a chairman and vice-chairman and adopt rules of procedure. Five members shall form a quorum and all decisions shall be taken by a majority.

(4) The members of the Board shall be entitled to travelling and subsistence allowances on the scale at present in force for members of the Committees of the League and shall draw fees for their services at the rate of 3,000 Swiss francs per month for the Chairman and 2,000 Swiss francs per month for the other members of the Board.

(5) The members of the Board, in the exercise of their functions, and the staff referred to in paragraph 4 (1) below shall be deemed to be officials of the League within the meaning of Article 7 of the Covenant.

(6) The expenditure incurred by the Board for the year 1946 shall be met from the Budget of the Secretariat for that year and, if the Board continues to function subsequently, it shall adopt a Budget and make appropriations to meet the expenditure involved from the Guarantee Fund or other funds of the League.

3. The Secretary-General shall be responsible to the Board. He shall retire from office on the completion of the liquidation. If for any reason he should cease to act, the Board shall appoint another person to carry out his duties.

4. (1) The officials of the Secretariat having received notice of the termination of their engagements as from July 31st next, such staff shall be employed as may be required for the purpose of carrying out the liquidation and for maintaining in operation the departments and services of the Secretariat to whatever extent is necessary in order that the United Nations may, under the best possible conditions, assume those activities hitherto performed by the League which it decides to assume and take over the material assets which are to be transferred to it.

(2) The Board may employ such professional assistance as it may deem expedient.

5. The Assembly approves and directs that effect shall be given in the manner set out in the Report of the Finance Committee to the "Common Plan for the Transfer of League of Nations Assets," which was drawn up jointly by a United Nations Committee and the Supervisory Commission, acting respectively on behalf of the United Nations and the League of Nations, and was approved by the General Assembly of the United Nations on February 12th, 1946.

6. Nothing in this resolution shall relieve any Member or former Member of the League of Nations from any pecuniary liability incurred by it towards the League of Nations, whether under the Budget for 1946 or under previous Budgets or in virtue of agreements with the League of Nations or in any other manner whatsoever; but the Board may, where in its discretion it considers this course to be justifiable, make a composition with any debtor Government for a lesser sum than is due, on condition that such a sum or the agreed instalments thereof shall be paid as promptly as possible. The report provided for in paragraph 21 shall give particulars of the debts which have been collected in full, those in regard to which a composition or only a partial payment has been made and those, if any, towards which no payment has been made. If any amounts due in respect of the International Labour Organisation remain unpaid at the date of the completion of the liquidation, a report on the collection of such contributions shall be communicated by the Board to the International Labour Organisation and such amounts shall be recoverable by that Organisation.

7. (1) Subject to the provisions of sub-paragraph (2) below and of any relevant decisions embodied in the Report of the Finance Committee, any cash balances resulting from the liquidation shall be divided among the Members of the League in the manner set out in the Report of the Finance Committee.

(2) Balances to the credit of the Reserve Fund and of the Fund to cover exchange losses shall be paid to the Staff Pensions Fund, and the balances in respect of the various funds, extra-budgetary and suspense accounts, enumerated in the Report of the Supervisory Commission on the Work of its One-hundredth Session (document A.19. 1946.X) shall be dealt with as recommended in the Commission's report.

8. The Auditor of the League shall remain in office until he has audited the final closed accounts of the League of Nations and of the Board of Liquidation and drawn up a report thereon for communication to the Members of the League. If for any reason he should be unable to act, the Board shall appoint another Auditor.

9. The Board shall, as soon as possible after the transfer of the material assets, and every three months thereafter, make interim reports on the progress of its work and shall take into consideration any observations thereon made by the Members of the League.

10. The present High Commissioner for Refugees shall remain in office until the end of the year 1946, or such earlier date as may appear to the Board desirable, and his expenses shall be met out of the provision made for this purpose in the Budget of the Secretariat.

INTERNATIONAL LABOUR ORGANISATION

11. The present resolution shall not in any way prejudice the continued existence of the International Labour Office or the measures taken or to be taken by the International Labour Organisation to make in its Constitution such changes as may be required as the result of the dissolution of the League, or the enjoyment by the International Labour Organisation of the privileges and immunities provided by Article 7 of the Covenant pending elaboration of and acceptance by the Members of the Organisation of other provisions dealing with this matter.

12. The amount collected for the expenses of the International Labour Organisation in the Budget of 1946 shall remain available for that purpose down to and after the end of the year.

13. (1) The Board shall in due course transfer to the International Labour Organisation its appropriate share in the Renovation Fund and any other fund in which it may have an interest.

(2) The balances of the International Labour Organisation for the financial years 1941, 1943 and 1944 shall be transferred from the suspense account in which they are at present placed to a special reserve fund for the International Labour Organisation.

14. An agreement to cause the full ownership of the land and buildings at present occupied by the International Labour Organisation to vest in that Organisation shall be concluded between the Secretary-General of the League and the Acting Director of the International Labour Office and all the steps which, under the law of the Republic and Canton of Geneva or of the Swiss Confederation, are necessary to give effect to the agreement shall be taken as soon as possible.

ADMINISTRATIVE TRIBUNAL

15. The following amendments are hereby made in the Statute of the League of Nations Administrative Tribunal:

(1) Wherever the words "League of Nations Administrative Tribunal" occur in the Regulations, they shall be replaced by the words "International Labour Organisation Administrative Tribunal."

(2) Paragraph 1 of Article 3 shall read as follows:

"(i) The Tribunal shall consist of three judges and three deputy judges who shall all be of different nationalities.

"(ii) Subject to the provisions set out at (iii) below, the judges and deputy judges shall be appointed by the appropriate organ of the International Labour Organisation.

"(iii) The terms of office of the judges and deputy judges who were in office on January 1st, 1940, are prolonged until April 1st, 1947, and thereafter until otherwise decided by the appropriate organ of the International Labour Organisation. Any vacancy which occurs during the period in question shall be filled by the said organ."

(3) As from October 31st, 1946,[2] but subject always to sub-paragraph (4) below, the Administrative Tribunal shall have no jurisdiction in regard to (a) complaints of non-observance of the terms of appointment of officials of the Secretariat or of the Secretariat's Staff Regulations, (b) disputes concerning the compensation provided for by Articles 45 or 70 of the Secretariat Staff Regulations or (c) complaints of non-observance of the provisions of Article 1 of the Staff Pensions Regulations, in so far as that Article provides for persons who have been appointed as officials of the Secretariat or the Registry of the Permanent Court becoming subject to those Regulations, but the Tribunal shall otherwise retain its existing jurisdiction under its Statute and under Article 26 of the Staff Pensions Regulations.

(4) Complaints already transmitted to the Registrar of the Tribunal shall be heard and determined notwithstanding the provisions of sub-paragraph (3).

(5) In order to enable the International Labour Organisation to make by action of its appropriate organ the changes in the Statute necessitated by sub-paragraphs (1) and (2) above and such other amendments as it may from time to time consider desirable, the third paragraph of Article 12 of the Statute is amended to read as follows: "The present Statute shall remain in force during the pleasure of the General Conference of the International Labour Organisation. It may be amended by the Conference or such other organ of the Organisation as the Conference may determine."

STAFF PENSIONS FUND

16. (1) Subject to the agreement of the International Labour Organisation, the following measures shall be taken in regard to the Staff Pensions Fund:

(a) Liability for making the contributions due from the League under Article 7 of the Staff Pensions Regulations and, subject to (c) below, the guarantee given by the League under Article 13 of the Regulations shall be assumed by the International Labour Organisation.

(b) The accumulated assets of the Fund (including any amount

[2]"Note.—This date is selected as giving sufficient time for adjudication of any disputes which may arise out of the notices of dismissal which have been given to the officials of the Secretariat and which take effect on July 31st, 1946. In the unlikely event of a dispute between the Administration and those officials who remain in service after July 31st, who will be on a purely temporary basis, the Board of Liquidation may be trusted to find a just and equitable solution."

added by the Assembly at its present session or by the Board of Liquidation) shall be transferred to the International Labour Organisation for application in accordance with the Regulations.

(*c*) Retired officials of the Secretariat and the Registry of the Permanent Court and their widows and children shall continue to receive the benefits due to them from the Fund, but, if the payment of these benefits involves a deficit for the Fund which has to be met by additional contributions from the International Labour Organisation, the amounts involved shall be divided among and form part of the contributions of those Members of the Organisation which were Members of the League at the date of the present resolution in the proportions in which those Members contribute to the other expenses of the International Labour Organisation.

(*d*) In order to enable the International Labour Organisation to amend the Regulations of the Fund and, in particular, to make the changes rendered necessary by the dissolution of the League and the Permanent Court, the last sentence of Article 31 of the Regulations is amended to read as follows:

"The Regulations may be amended by the appropriate financial authority of the International Labour Organisation, with due regard to the rights of the beneficiaries."

This amendment shall not take effect until the agreement of the International Labour Organisation to the provisions of the present sub-paragraph has been secured.

(2) If the International Labour Organisation's agreement is not secured to the provisions of sub-paragraph (1) above, the Board of Liquidation shall make the best provision that it can for giving effect to the rights of the beneficiaries of the Fund and shall have power for that purpose to amend or annul all or any part of the Regulations.

17. Any surplus remaining after the discharge of all claims upon the Staff Pensions Fund shall belong to the International Labour Organisation, if it has accepted the task of administering the Fund.

PENSIONS FUND FOR THE MEMBERS OF THE PERMANENT
COURT OF INTERNATIONAL JUSTICE

18. (1) The Regulations for the Administration of the Pensions Fund for the Members of the Permanent Court of International Justice are hereby abrogated.

(2) If the International Labour Organisation consents, responsibility for the administration of the Fund, as augmented by the Assembly during the present session or by the Board of Liquidation, and the responsibility for paying the pensions shall be transferred to the Organisation on the understanding that, (*a*) if the Fund is inadequate for its purpose, those Members of the Organisation which are at pres-

ent League Members shall contribute to make good the deficiency, which shall be divided among them and form part of their contributions in the proportions in which those Members contribute to the other expenses of the International Labour Organisation, and (*b*) any surplus remaining after pensions to the judges have ceased to be payable shall belong to the International Labour Organisation.

(3) Failing such agreement, the Board shall make such other provision for the administration of the Fund and payment of the pensions or for the purchase of annuities for the judges as it may find it possible to arrange.

REGULATIONS FOR THE FINANCIAL ADMINISTRATION OF THE LEAGUE OF NATIONS

19. (1) As from the entry into force of the present resolution, the Regulations for the Financial Administration of the League of Nations shall apply only in so far as they concern the International Labour Organisation or are considered by the Board to be relevant to the liquidation.

(2) Article 51 of the Regulations is hereby amended to read as follows:

"These Regulations may be amended by the appropriate financial authority of the International Labour Organisation."

WORKING CAPITAL FUND

20. Subject to maintenance of the existing rights to repayment of the States which own shares therein, the whole balance of the Working Capital Fund shall be transferred to the International Labour Organisation for use as working capital.

FINAL ARTICLE

21. On the completion of its task, the Board shall make and publish a report to the Governments of the Members of the League giving a full account of the measures which it has taken, and shall declare itself to be dissolved. On the dissolution of the Board, the liquidation shall be deemed to be complete and no further claims against the League shall be recognised.

Annex.—MEMBERS OF THE BOARD OF LIQUIDATION

M. Emile Charveriat (France)
Sir Atul Chatterjee (India)
Mr. F. T. Cheng (China)

M. Adolfo Costa du Rels (Bolivia)
M. Carl Joachim Hambro (Norway)
Mr. Seymour Jacklin (Union of South Africa)
—from August 1st, 1946
Sir Cecil H. Kisch (United Kingdom)
Dr. Jaromír Kopecký (Czechoslovakia)
M. Daniel Secretan (Switzerland)

VII. RESOLUTIONS ADOPTED ON THE REPORTS OF THE FIRST COMMITTEE OF THE LEAGUE OF NATIONS ASSEMBLY [1]

1. DISSOLUTION OF THE PERMANENT COURT OF INTERNATIONAL JUSTICE

The Assembly of the League of Nations,

Considering that, by Article 92 of the Charter of the United Nations, provision is made for an International Court of Justice which is to be the principal judicial organ of the United Nations and which is to be open to States not members of the United Nations on terms to be determined by the United Nations;

Considering that the establishment of this Court and the impending dissolution of the League of Nations render it desirable that measures for the formal dissolution of the Permanent Court of International Justice shall be taken;

Considering that the Preparatory Commission of the United Nations, in a resolution of December 18th, 1945, declared that it would welcome the taking of appropriate steps by the League of Nations for the purpose of dissolving the Permanent Court, and that this resolution records the assent to the dissolution of the Permanent Court of all the Members of the United Nations which are parties to the Protocol of Signature of the Statute of the Permanent Court, whether members of the League of Nations or not;

Considering that all the Judges of the Permanent Court have resigned and that on the dissolution of the League no machinery will exist for the appointment of new Judges:

Resolves:

That the Permanent Court of International Justice is for all purposes to be regarded as dissolved with effect from the day following the close of the present session of the Assembly, but without prejudice to such subsequent measures of liquidation as may be necessary.

[*Resolution adopted on April 18th, 1946 (morning).*]

2. THE ASSUMPTION BY THE UNITED NATIONS OF FUNCTIONS AND POWERS HITHERTO EXERCISED BY THE LEAGUE UNDER INTERNATIONAL AGREEMENTS

The Assembly of the League of Nations,

Having considered the resolution on the assumption by the United

[1] Reprinted from *Official Journal*, Special Supplement No. 194, p. 269–272; see also *ibid.*, p. 133.

Nations of functions and powers hitherto exercised by the League of Nations under international agreements, which was adopted by the General Assembly of the United Nations on February 16th, 1946,

Adopts the following resolutions:

1. *Custody of the Original Texts of International Agreements*

The Assembly directs that the Secretary-General of the League of Nations shall, on a date to be fixed in agreement with the Secretary-General of the United Nations, transfer to the Secretariat of the United Nations, for safe custody and performance of the functions hitherto performed by the Secretariat of the League, all the original signed texts of treaties and international conventions, agreements and other instruments, which are deposited with the Secretariat of the League of Nations, with the exception of the Conventions of the International Labour Organisation, the originals of which and other related documents shall be placed at the disposal of that Organisation.

2. *Functions and Powers Arising out of International Agreements of a Technical and Non-political Character*

The Assembly recommends the Governments of the Members of the League to facilitate in every way the assumption without interruption by the United Nations, or by specialised agencies brought into relationship with that organisation, of functions and powers which have been entrusted to the League of Nations, under international agreements of a technical and non-political character, and which the United Nations is willing to maintain.

[*Resolution adopted on April 18th, 1946 (afternoon).*]

3. THE ASSUMPTION BY THE UNITED NATIONS OF ACTIVITIES HITHERTO PERFORMED BY THE LEAGUE

The Assembly directs the Secretary-General of the League of Nations to afford every facility for the assumption by the United Nations of such non-political activities, hitherto performed by the League, as the United Nations may decide to assume.

[*Resolution adopted on April 18th, 1946 (afternoon).*]

4. MANDATES

The Assembly,

Recalling that Article 22 of the Covenant applies to certain territories placed under mandate the principle that the well-being and development of peoples not yet able to stand alone in the strenuous conditions of the modern world form a sacred trust of civilisation;

1. Expresses its satisfaction with the manner in which the organs of the League have performed the functions entrusted to them with respect to the mandates system and in particular pays tribute to the work accomplished by the Mandates Commission;

2. Recalls the role of the League in assisting Iraq to progress from its status under an "A" Mandate to a condition of complete independence, welcomes the termination of the mandated status of Syria, the Lebanon, and Transjordan, which have, since the last session of the Assembly, become independent members of the world community;

3. Recognises that, on the termination of the League's existence, its functions with respect to the mandated territories will come to an end, but notes that Chapters XI, XII and XIII of the Charter of the United Nations embody principles corresponding to those declared in Article 22 of the Covenant of the League;

4. Takes note of the expressed intentions of the Members of the League now administering territories under mandate to continue to administer them for the well-being and development of the peoples concerned in accordance with the obligations contained in the respective Mandates, until other arrangements have been agreed between the United Nations and the respective mandatory Powers.

[*Resolutions adopted on April 18th, 1946 (afternoon*).]

5. INTERNATIONAL BUREAUX AND OTHER ORGANISATIONS PLACED UNDER THE DIRECTION OF THE LEAGUE OF NATIONS OR BROUGHT INTO RELATION THEREWITH

1. The Assembly directs the Secretary-General to thank the international bureaux and other organisations named in this resolution for their collaboration with the League of Nations in the past, and to inform them that the relation with the League which was established in accordance with Article 24 of the Covenant must be regarded as coming to an end on the dissolution of the League, with effect from the day following the close of the present session of the Assembly.

This resolution shall apply to the following organisations:

The International Bureau for Information and Enquiries regarding Relief to Foreigners (Paris);

The International Hydrographic Bureau (Monaco);

The Central International Office for the Control of the Liquor Traffic in Africa (Brussells);

The International Commission for Air Navigation (Paris);

The International Exhibitions Bureau (Paris);.

2. The Assembly directs the Secretary-General to address a similar communication to the International Relief Union (Geneva), which, though it was not placed under the direction of the League, was brought into relation with the League under the Convention of July 12th, 1927, which created the Union.

[*Resolution adopted on April 18th, 1946 (afternoon*).]

6. INTERNATIONAL INSTITUTE OF INTELLECTUAL CO-OPERATION

1. The Assembly thanks the International Institute of Intellectual Co-operation (Paris) for the valuable collaboration which, since 1925, it has given to the League of Nations as the organ for the execution of the decisions and recommendations of the International Committee on Intellectual Co-operation.

2. The Assembly,

Being desirous of facilitating by all the means in its power the continuity of the work of intellectual co-operation;

Considering that paragraph 7 of the letter of December 8th, 1924, from the French Government to the President of the Council of the League of Nations provides that, in the event of the abolition of the Institute, any articles and, in particular, the archives and collections of documents deposited in the premises by the Governing Body, as well as any property which has been acquired by the Institute during its period of operation, shall remain the property of the League of Nations:

Resolves to transfer the right of property mentioned above to the United Nations;

Instructs the Secretary-General of the League of Nations to take in due time, in conjunction with the Directorate of the Institute, the necessary measures for the execution of the present resolution.

[*Resolution adopted on April 18th, 1946 (afternoon).*]

VIII. AGREEMENT BETWEEN THE UNITED NATIONS AND THE SWISS FEDERAL GOVERNMENT CONCERNING RADIO FREQUENCIES FORMERLY USED BY THE LEAGUE OF NATIONS[1]

Memorandum by the Secretary-General

In his reports of 4 November and 11 December 1946 (documents A/175 and A/247) the Secretary-General informed the General Assembly of his exchange of communications with the Swiss Federal authorities on the subject of the transfer to the United Nations of the wave-lengths originally registered by *Radio Suisse* for *Radio Nations*, the station which had been utilized by the League of Nations. It did not prove possible at that stage to reach a definite solution of the problem but an appropriate procedure for reaching such a solution was agreed. The Secretary-General stated that he would report to the second regular session of the General Assembly such results as might in the meantime be achieved.

Negotiations undertaken in Switzerland early this year led to the signature on behalf of the Swiss Federal Government and the Secretary-General of a draft protocol, modus vivendi and additional protocol concerning the transfer to the United Nations of the rights on, and the use of, certain frequencies formerly used by the League of Nations. These documents, the texts of which are reproduced in the attached Annex, were duly ratified by the Swiss Federal Government on 11 April 1947 and approved on 31 July by the Secretary-General under the special powers granted to him by the General Assembly at the first part of its first session. The agreements reached fully meet the prospective requirements of the United Nations and the Secretary-General desires to express his warm appreciation of the co-operative attitude of the Swiss authorities which made these agreements possible.

The Bureau of the International Telecommunications Union was duly informed of the agreement and requested to reserve the frequencies concerned for the United Nations, pending the admission of the United Nations Operating Service as a Member of the International Telecommunications Union. After the United Nations Operating Service was recognized as a special Member of the Telecommuni-

[1]Reprinted from United Nations Document A/C.5/207, 8 November 1947.

cations Union at the Atlantic City Conference, these frequencies were formally registered for the United Nations by the Bureau.

As stated in the Secretary-General's Memorandum on United Nations Telecommunications (document A/C.5/. . .), final implementation of the agreement between the Swiss Federal Government and the United Nations is however dependent on the General Assembly's approval of the establishment of a United Nations Telecommunications system.[2]

ANNEX

TRANSLATION

Protocol

M. Ph. Zutter, Counsellor of Legation, on behalf of the Swiss Federal Political Department, and Mr. G. F. van Dissel, Member of the United Nations Advisory Committee on Telecommunications, on behalf of the United Nations, together with

M. F. Rothen,   Director of Radio-Suisse, and

MM. E. Metzler and

     Ch. Chappius,   of the General Board of the Swiss Posts, Telegraphs and Telephones,

on behalf of the Swiss authorities, and

Mr. A. B. Elkin,   Assistant Director in the Geneva Office of the United Nations, and

Mr. K. Erim,   Member of the United Nations Secretariat,

on behalf of the United Nations,

have on 5, 6, and 7 March 1947, at the Palais des Nations at Geneva, and on 13 and 14 March at the Palais Fédéral at Berne, examined various questions relating to the United Nations telecommunications in Switzerland and the use by the United Nations Stations of certain wave-lengths originally reserved for the Radio-Nations Station, and at present reserved for and used by the Swiss Administration of Posts, Telegraphs and Telephones, and Radio-Suisse, S. A. These questions have been the subject of correspondence between the Secretary-General of the United Nations and the Swiss Government, particularly in the course of the month of December 1946.

Having considered these matters, they have agreed as follows:

Without prejudice to the legal validity of the considerations advanced in the said correspondence, the attached texts of a Provisional

[2]On November 20, 1947, the General Assembly adopted the following resolution: "The General Assembly directs the Secretary-General to take all steps necessary to ensure that the United Nations can proceed with negotiations now in progress for obtaining the wave-lengths (frequencies), call signs, rights and privileges necessary for the operation of a United Nations telecommunications system, and to report and submit appropriate recommendations to the General Assembly at its third regular session." See U.N. General Assembly, *Assembly Resolutions Adopted on November 20, 1947: Resolutions Adopted on Reports of the Fifth Committee*, p. 8.

Working Arrangement and of the Additional Protocol shall be submitted for approval, without prejudice to a final settlement of the general question of the telecommunications of the Geneva Office of the United Nations in Switzerland, by Mr. van Dissel to the Secretary-General of the United Nations, and by M. Zutter to the Swiss Federal Political Department and to the other Swiss authorities concerned.

Done at Berne on 14 March 1947.

Provisional Working Arrangement

Article 1

1. The group of frequencies included in List 1, attached hereto, shall be subdivided into two separate categories, viz.:
   (a) the frequencies used by the Swiss Administration of Posts, Telegraphs and Telephones and by Radio-Suisse for their broadcasts;
   (b) the frequencies used by the Swiss Administration of Posts, Telegraphs and Telephones and by Radio-Suisse for their regular services.

2. Group (a) shall be reserved for the world broadcasting services of the United Nations.

3. The United Nations is only concerned in group (b) for "point to point" telecommunications services between New York and Geneva.

Article 2

As regards the use of the frequencies referred to in Article 1, subparagraph (a) above, it is agreed that:

1. The United Nations shall have the exclusive right to use waves of this category in whatever direction and for whatever period it may deem it necessary for its services;

2. Nevertheless, by virtue of paragraph 4 of the letter addressed to the Secretary-General of the United Nations on 9 December 1946 by the Swiss Delegation in New York, it is understood that the Swiss Administration of Posts, Telegraphs and Telephones will have subsidiary priority to use these frequencies so far as the United Nations programme permits, and in whatever direction and for whatever period the said Administration may consider it most suitable. It is, however, clearly understood that the Swiss Administration of Posts, Telegraphs and Telephones shall take the necessary steps in this connection to avoid any interference with United Nations broadcasts.

Article 3

By way of reciprocity, the Swiss Administration of Posts, Telegraphs and Telephones shall have the exclusive right to use all the other frequencies not included in List 1, group (a) and reserved for its broadcasting services, in whatever direction and for whatever period it may deem it necessary. The United Nations shall, however, have subsidiary priority to use this wave-group in whatever direction and for whatever period it may deem it necessary, provided that this does not in any way interfere with the broadcasts of the Swiss services.

Article 4

By virtue of the principle of reciprocity on which the present Provisional Working Arrangement is based, both Parties shall be entitled to protect their mutual interests as defined in the present document. In particular, they agree jointly to uphold their mutual interests within the framework of arrangements and conventions already in existence or which may be concluded hereafter.

Article 5

As regards group (*b*) referred to in Article 1 above, both Parties agree that only such frequencies as are likewise included in List 2 shall be used by the United Nations for telecommunications services between New York and Geneva.

Article 6

As regards the other frequencies of group (*b*) not covered by Article 5, the following rule shall apply: the frequencies used or reserved by the Swiss Administration of Posts, Telegraphs and Telephones or Radio-Suisse for their telecommunications services shall remain at their disposal. Nevertheless, the United Nations shall have the right to use these frequencies provided that this in no way interferes with the telecommunications of the Swiss Administration of Posts, Telegraphs and Telephones and of Radio-Suisse. Such frequencies may be used by the United Nations only after consultation with the Swiss Administration of Posts, Telegraphs and Telephones and Radio-Suisse.

Article 7

It is agreed that the frequencies referred to in List 1, group (*a*) and in List 2 shall be registered by the International Telecommunications Office in Berne in the name of the United Nations.

Article 8

Both Parties agree to reconsider the question, if need be, should the decision taken by the forthcoming International Conference on Tele-communications necessitate the revision of the present arrangement.

List No. 1

Frequencies in kilocycles/sec. listed for the League of Nations service and used by the Swiss Administration of Posts, Telegraphs and Telephones and the Société Radio-Suisse.

GROUP (a)

Frequencies used by the Swiss Administration of Posts, Telegraphs and Telephones and Radio-Suisse for *broadcasting purposes*.

9515)
9545)   in the international broadcasting band
9595)   9500-9700 kilocycles/sec.
9655)
11715   in the international broadcasting band 11,700-11,900 Kc/sec.
17770   in the international broadcasting band 17,700-17,900 Kc/sec.

GROUP (b)

Frequencies used by the Swiss Administration of Posts, Telegraphs and Telephones and Radio-Suisse for their regular *services*.

3615	9345	14538	17585
5395	9975	14717	18450
6675	10145	14945	18480
7443	10338	15395	18950
7454 4	11402	15420	18970
7565	11465	15692	19190
7696	11505	15827	19375
7797	12030	15855	19610
8064	12965	16195	19730
9225	13205	17170	20730
9285	14462	17565	

List No. 2

Frequencies in kilocycles/sec. to be used by the United Nations for its regular service between New York and Geneva.

7443	12030
8064	15827
9185	17170
9923	17565
10145	19375
11505	19730

These frequencies are all shown in GROUP (*b*), LIST 1, with the exception of the frequency 9923 and the frequency 9185.

Additional Protocol

1. Radio-Suisse is prepared to place at the disposal of the United Nations until such time as the latter has installed its own station, the short wave (Marconi) transmitter formerly owned by the League of Nations, together with the appropriate aerials for any communications the United Nations may wish to establish. Only a certain proportion of the costs involved, namely, the cost of power and of transmitter valves, will be charged by Radio-Suisse to United Nations account.

As regards the times and duration of the use of these installations by the United Nations, a special arrangement shall be concluded between the Parties concerned according to requirements.

2. The competent Swiss authorities are willing to effect transmissions for the United Nations over the broadcasting and wireless telephone installations belonging to the Swiss Administration of Ports, Telegraphs and Telephones in so far as domestic requirements permit.

Done at Berne on 14 March 1947.

IX. DISTRIBUTION OF ASSETS[1]

The assets with which the Board has been called upon to deal consist of two parts:

(a) Credits in respect of material assets to be dealt with under the terms of the "Common Plan";

(b) Liquid assets distributable to States Members on the completion of the liquidation.

Swiss francs

The total value of the assets available for apportionment among States Members at the close of the liquidation is 61,433,363.61

split up as follows:

Material assets 46,194,569.29
Cash.   15,238,794.32

In the matter of allocating credits and cash assets among States Members entitled to participate, the Board has followed the scheme laid down in 1946 by the Assembly, which decided that the shares of the States Members in the aggregated assets of the League should be based upon the proportion of the contributions paid.[2]

In the case of States Members of the League not members of the United Nations, their claims in respect of material assets have, in accordance with the "Common Plan", been discharged in cash for a total of Swiss francs 4,626,182.28, compensation being afforded to League States also Members of the United Nations by an appropriate augmentation of their share in the credits. The residue of these assets available in cash, Swiss francs 10,612,612,04 has been apportioned among the States entitled to participate. The final result of the distribution among States is shown in the following table, which takes into account the allocation to participating States not members of the United Nations of cash in lieu of a credit in the material assets.

[1]Reprinted from Board of Liquidation, *Final Report*, p. 8–10 [C.5.M.5.1947.]. The footnotes, with the exception of the present one, are those of the *Final Report*.
[2]Records of the Twenty-first Ordinary Session of the Assembly, Annex 26, General Report of the Second (Finance) Committee, *Official Journal*, Special Supplement No. 194, page 267. See also Part II of this Report, Chapter 9.

LIST OF PARTICIPATING STATES	(a) Percentage of total assets	SHARE OF EACH STATE IN		
		(b) Material assets	(c) Liquid assets	(d) Total assets
Afghanistan	0.070937	35,170.80	8,408.06	43,578.86
Union of South Africa	2.968866	1,471,978.70	351,895.49	1,823,874.19
Argentine	3.599993	1,784,895.—	426,702.04	2,211,597.04
Australia	4.768950	2,364,469.47	565,256.72	2,929,726.19
Belgium	2.652537	1,315,141.43	314,401.41	1,629,542.84
Bolivia	0.277115	137,395.71	32,846.22	170,241.93
United Kingdom	17.348335	8,601,392.44	2,056,273.13	10,657,665.57
Canada	6.285744	3,116,503.54	745,040.10	3,861,543.64
China	4.002465	1,984,442.59	474,406.43	2,458,849.02
Cuba	0.890378	441,453.72	105,535.17	546,988.89
Czechoslovakia	3.853633	1,910,650.75	456,765.56	2,367,416.31
Denmark	1.838814	911,693.17	217,951.97	1,129,645.14
Dominican Republic	0.109203	54,143.51	12,943.71	67,087.22
Ecuador	0.032213	15,971.41	3,818.19	19,789.60
Egypt	0.633323	314,004.77	75,066.87	389,071.64
Finland	1.507624	—	926,184.20	926,184.20
France	11.754286	5,827,834.75	1,393,218.63	7,221,053.38
Greece	0.936791	504,225.36	71,276.55	575,501.91
India	9.345315	4,633,454.36	1,107,686.67	5,741,141.03
Iran	0.466494	286,583.09	—	286,583.09
Iraq	0.264381	131,081.64	31,336.72	162,418.36
Ireland	1.530307	—	940,118.84	940,118.84
Luxemburg	0.191608	95,000.16	22,711.01	117,711.17
Mexico	0.516574	317,348.46	—	317,348.46
Netherlands	3.443749	1,707,428.33	408,182.64	2,115,610.97
New Zealand	1.570779	778,800.16	186,182.15	964,982.31
Norway	1.496884	742,162.87	177,423.54	919,586.41
Panama	0.207788	103,022.39	24,628.80	127,651.19
Poland	4.370420	2,166,876.26	518,019.55	2,684,895.81
Portugal	1.398596	—	859,204.66	859,204.66
Siam	1.234638	612,139.94	146,339.90	758,479.84
Sweden	3.347232	1,659,574.77	396,742.61	2,056,317.38
Switzerland	3.093880	—	1,900,674.58	1,900,674.58
Turkey	0.881271	436,938.72	104,455.80	541,394.52
Uruguay	0.740221	367,005.31	87,737.30	454,742.61
Yugoslavia	2.368656	1,365,785.71	89,359.10	1,455,144.81
Total	100.00	46,194,569.29	15,238,794.32	61,433,363.61

The calculations in the above table have been examined by the Auditor of the League, who has certified that the scheme of distribution gives effect to the decisions of the Assembly.

The share of States in the material assets is, in accordance with the "Common Plan", being reported to the United Nations for attribution to them in the books of that organisation in terms of U.S. dollars at the rate of exchange effective on the date of transfer of the material assets— viz., August 1st, 1946.[3] The liquid assets consist mainly of

[3]In the accounts of the United Nations, the rate of exchange is shown at $23.40 for Swiss francs 100.

Swiss francs, but partly of U.S. dollars. The distribution of the share of States between these two currencies is shown on page 50 of Part II of this Report, and States Members are being advised of the amounts in question.

The following table exhibits in summary form the material assets and funds disposed of by transfer in accordance with the final Resolution of the Assembly and the balance of the liquid assets refunded to States, Members at the close of the liquidation.

1. To the United Nations   *Swiss francs*
(*a*) Material assets (land, buildings,
    furniture, equipment, etc.)   46,194,569.29
(*b*) Library Building (donation of Mr.
    John D. Rockefeller, Jnr.)   gratis
    (Construction costs: Swiss francs
    5,609,168.32)
(*c*) Funds (transferred to the manage-
    ment of the United Nations)
                             Swiss francs
    Library Endowment Fund 2,395,221.56
    International Press House Fund . . 109,464.10
    Donation from the Administrative
      Board of the Carnegie Foundation
      (Wateler Peace Prize, 1935) . . . 14,285.30
    Darling Foundation 12,926.75
    Léon Bernard Fund 16,165.55
                                     2,548,063.26
        Total transferred to United Nations 48,742,632.55
(*d*) Works of art, furniture, etc. (gifts)   gratis

2. To the International Labour Organisation
(*a*) Material assets (buildings, etc.)   3,646,485.87
(*b*) Funds:
    Working Capital Fund 3,797,661.95
    Renovation Fund (share) 105,078.75
    Cash surplus 1946 . . . . 1,737,558.511
    Contributions remitted since
      January 1st, 1947 . . . . . . 3,583,491.76
    Staff Pensions Fund (transferred to
      the Management of the I.L.O.) 25,507,672.
    Judges' Pensions Fund (transferred
      to the Management of the I.L.O.) 2,447,504.65
      Total transferred to the Inter-
      national Labour Organisation ————————40,825,453.49

3. *To the World Health Organisation*
Balance of account of the Eastern
Health Bureau, Singapore 92,030.60

4. *States Members*
Balance of liquid assets refunded
to States Members of the League   15,238,794.32
Grand total 104,898,910.96

Conclusion

The liquidation has shown the financial stability of the organisation and the Board trusts that States Members of the League will find the result satisfactory. In the Board's view, all valid claims have been met and the affairs of the League of Nations have terminated in good order.

In conclusion, the Board desires to place on record its appreciation of the services of the Secretary-General and the small but highly skilled staff serving under him. The Board was dependent upon them for information and advice on the whole range of complex matters which came before it and has benefited throughout its work from their knowledge, competence and loyalty.

Having thus concluded the task imposed upon it by the Assembly Resolution, and having rendered its Final Report to States Members, the Board hereby declares itself to be dissolved.

C. J. Hambro, *Chairman.*   Atul Chatterjee. S. Jacklin.
Cecil Kisch, *Vice-Chairman.* F. T. Cheng.   J. Kopecky.
E. Charvériat.   A. Costa du Rels. Daniel Secrétan.
July 31st, 1947.

X. FINAL SCHEDULE[1]

approved on behalf of the League of Nations by the Board of Liquidation and on behalf of the United Nations by the Advisory Committee on Administrative and Budgetary Questions and by the Secretary-General of the United Nations.

	Swiss francs
(1) Secretariat Building and Assembly Hall[2]	38,742,999.43
(2) Library Building[3] . . .	Nil
(3) Real estate belonging to the League of Nations having an area 203,446 sq. metres and comprising four villas and other buildings	2,889,453.45
(4) Furniture, fittings, typewriters, etc., for the use of the Secretariat, including the Branch Offices[4] and for the other buildings in Geneva:	

Total according to the
inventories 3,332,922.61
To be deducted: *Swiss francs*
(a) Amounts included
    under Secretariat
    building 1,454,080.45
(b) Amount in respect
    of extra-budgetary
    (Rockefeller Grant)   25,782.99

[1]Reprinted from Board of Liquidation, *Final Report*, p. 60 [C.5.M.5.1947.]. The footnotes, with the exception of the present one, are those of the *Final Report*.

[2]Cost of building and equipment of the Secretariat and the Assembly Hall. The League had a transferable right to use the land on which the buildings stand, the land 100 metres around it and the two roads leading to the buildings. The League further had a non-transferable right to use the remainder of the plot of land in Ariana Park in which the buildings stand. No value has been placed on these rights in the schedule.

[3]The cost of this building given by Mr. Rockefeller was 5,564,206.22 Swiss francs.

[4]*Including* London, Princeton, Washington, New Delhi and Singapore, but *excluding* Paris.

(c) Amounts in respect of the Library Endowment Fund. . . 4,514.15

1,484,377.59

1,848,545.02

(5) Furniture, fittings, typewriters, etc., for the use of the Permanent Court of International Justice in The Hague 199,810.55

(6) (a) Stocks of stationery, printing paper and the office supplies and equipment in Geneva and Branch Offices . 132,625.54

(b) Publications in Geneva and Branch Offices . . . . 400,000.—

(7) Books, stocks of stationery, printing paper and publications, office supplies and equipment of the Permanent Court of International Justice in The Hague 55,562.35

(8) Gifts[5] . . . . Nil

(9) Library: Books, etc., in Geneva[6] 1,925,572.95

(10) Archives of the League of Nations and of the Permanent Court of International Justice . . . . . Nil

Total 46,194,569.29

[5]Gifts include paintings, sculptures and other works of art which cannot be valued in terms of money. They also comprise furnishings, etc., estimated at Swiss francs 1,234, 640.

[6]Not including books acquired by gift or exchange and estimated at Swiss francs 1,592,516.05.

XI. RESOLUTION NO. 250 OF THE THIRD SESSION OF THE UNITED NATIONS. TRANSFER OF THE ASSETS OF THE LEAGUE OF NATIONS[1]

The General Assembly

1. Resolves that,

In accordance with the provisions of:

(i) The Common Plan for the transfer to the United Nations of certain assets of the League of Nations, as approved by the General Assembly at the first part of its first session [resolution 24(I)],[2] and,

(ii) Resolution 79(I)[3] adopted by the General Assembly at the second part of its first session,

The credits in the amount of $10,809,529.21,[4] arising from the transfer of the assets of the League of Nations to the United Nations, shall be made available to the Member States designated by the League of Nations in the percentages determined by the League of Nations, as detailed in annex A; and resolves that the following procedure shall be adopted;

(a) The amount of $9,741,994, which relates to the permanent capital assets, shall be liquidated in fifteen equal annual instalments, and the credits required for this purpose shall be provided by the inclusion of an item in the annual budget estimates for each of the years 1951–1965 inclusive;

(b) The amount of $1,067,535.21 which relates to other than permanent capital assets, shall be liquidated in two instalments, on the following basis:

(i) An amount of $533,768 shall be included as an item in the supplementary budget estimates for the year 1948 and covered by assessments jointly with the assessments for the 1949 budget, in accordance with regulation 17 of the Provisional Financial Regulations.

(ii) An amount of $533,767.21 shall be included as an item in the budget estimates for the year 1950;

(c) The credits shall not be liquidated in cash, but for the Members who have credits to be liquidated, the amount of each yearly instalment (i.e., liquidation of credits) shall be applied first as a

---

[1]Text of Resolution 250(III) and of Annex A and Annex B from United Nations Document A/810, December, 1948, p. 143–147.
[2]See above, p. 597, footnote 2.
[3]See above, p. 611, footnote 2.
[4]All sums mentioned in this Resolution are in U.S. dollars.

credit against the amount assessable against the Member on account of the acquisition of the assets, and any balance against or other contributions to the budget of the Organization;

(d) The scale of contributions for the annual budget each year shall be used as the basis of assessment to cover the instalment due in each year under sub-paragraph (a) above; new Members shall become liable to contribute only towards such instalments as fall due after the date of their admission, and no retroactive adjustments shall be made; a permanent record shall be maintained of assessments and actual contributions of each Member towards the permanent asset portion of the acquisition;

2. (a) Recommends that the Member States designated by the League of Nations as entitled to credits as a result of the transfer of the material assets of the League of Nations should make available to nine additional Member States shares in these credits in accordance with annex B attached, and that Member States should for this purpose surrender a pro rata share of their credits as set forth in annex A, in order to provide for credits in favour of the nine additional Member States;

(b) Requests Member States to communicate to the Secretary-General before the end of the first part of the current session of the General Assembly their decisions in this regard, and authorizes the Secretary-General to make the necessary adjustments.[5]

> Hundred and eighty-sixth plenary meeting,
> 11 December 1948.

[5]See also: *Transfer of the Assets of the League of Nations. Report of the Fifth Committee.* Rapporteur: Mr. O. P. Machado (Brazil). United Nations Document A/797, December 10, 1948. This report, exclusive of the Resolution, reads as follows:

"1. In accordance with the instructions given by the General Assembly on 24 September 1948, the Fifth Committee, at its 173rd meeting held on 8 December 1948, considered the question of the credits arising as a result of the transfer of the material assets of the League of Nations. The Committee had before it the report of the Secretary-General (A/604), an amendment of the United States of America (A/C.5/281) to the draft resolution included in the report and a draft resolution submitted by France and the United Kingdom (A/C.5/285).

"2. The Committee took note in this connexion of the provisions of the Common Plan (A/18/Add.1), which was approved by the General Assembly on 12 February 1946, and particularly of the following paragraphs:

" 'The League of Nations agrees that the shares in the total credit thus established shall be distributed between States entitled to participate, in accordance with percentages to be laid down by the League at its next Assembly.

" 'The United Nations agrees;

" '(a) That the shares, thus established, of such of these States as are Members of the United Nations snall be credited to them respectively in the books of the United Nations; and

" '(b) That the General Assembly shall decide on the purposes to which these credits shall be applied and on the dates on which they shall be so applied; and further that these credits shall, in any event, begin to be available not later than 31 December 1948.'

"3. The Committee also recalled the observations contained in its report to the General Assembly at the second part of the first session, as follows:

" 'In the course of the discussion, several delegations submitted representations that their Governments were entitled to participation in the total credit accruing from the transfer of the assets of the League of Nations to the United Nations. The Committee considered these representations in relation to the scheme drawn up for the distribution of this credit pursuant to the resolution of the General Assembly approving the Common Plan. A proposal was put forward by certain delegations that those Member States which are former Members of the League of Nations and are entitled under this scheme to share in the credit should, when their share has been established, consult together to consider an arrangement under which all former members of the League of Nations now Members of the United Nations could be allocated a share in the credit on a basis comparable with that applicable to Members of the League of Nations as set out in the League of Nations scheme of distribution. The Committee took note of the intention to arrange for such discussions before the General Assembly has to take decisions under paragraph 1(b) of the Common Plan.'

"4. In the course of the consideration of the draft resolution submitted by France and the United Kingdom the representative of the Netherlands requested that the opinion of his delegation should be recorded to the effect that the proposals made should be considered a final settlement of the question of the credits. The representative of the Union of Soviet Socialist Republics stated that, in the event that any nation formerly a member of the League of Nations should, upon admission to membership in the United Nations, make application for a share in the credits, the Union of Soviet Socialist Republics reserved the right to support such an application.

"5. On a roll-call vote, the joint draft resolution submitted by France and the United Kingdom, was approved by 33 votes to none, with 3 abstentions. The voting was as follows:

"*In favour:* Afghanistan, Argentina, Australia, Belgium, Bolivia, Brazil, Burma, Byelorussian SSR, Canada, Chile, China, Czechoslovakia, Denmark, Ecuador, Egypt, France, India, Iran, Iraq, Liberia, Mexico, Netherlands, New Zealand, Norway, Peru, Philippines, Poland, Ukrainian SSR, Union of Soviet Socialist Republics, United Kingdom, Uruguay, Venezuela, Yugoslavia.

"*Against:* Nil.

"*Abstaining:* Sweden, Union of South Africa, United States of America.

"6. The Committee took note of the fact that thirty of the thirty-two Member States designated by the League of Nations as entitled to credits had already indicated their agreement to surrender the *pro rata* shares set forth in Annex A, and agreed that this should constitute acceptance of the General Assembly's recommendation.

"7. The Committee then proceeded to consider the draft resolution submitted by the Secretary-General (A/604) and the amendment proposed by the United States of America (A/C.5/281). Following discussion of the proposed amendment, the representative of the United States agreed to change the terms of his proposal to provide for liquidation over a period of fifteen years from 1951 to 1965; and a further amendment was also accepted to change paragraph (b) in order to provide for liquidation of the amount of $1,067,535.21 over a period of two years.

"8. The Fifth Committee, therefore, decided to recommend to the General Assembly the adoption of the following resolution:..."

ANNEX A

LIST PREPARED BY THE SECRETARY-GENERAL OF THE LEAGUE OF NATIONS SHOWING CREDITS OF UNITED NATIONS MEMBERS ARISING FROM THE TRANSFER OF ASSETS OF THE LEAGUE OF NATIONS

	MATERIAL ASSETS	
STATE[a]	Swiss francs	Dollars (U.S.)
1. Afghanistan	35,170.80	8,229.97
2. Argentina	1,784,895.00	417,665.43
3. Australia	2,364,469.47	553,285.85
4. Belgium	1,315,141.43	307,743.09
5. Bolivia	137,395.71	32,150.60
6. Canada	3,116,503.54	729,261.83
7. China	1,984,442.59	464,359.57
8. Cuba	441,453.72	103,300.17
9. Denmark	911,693.17	213,336.20
10. Egypt	314,004.77	73,477.12
11. Ecuador	15,971.41	3,737.31
12. France	5,827,834.75	1,363,713.33
13. Greece	504,225.36	117,988.73
14. India	4,633,454.36	1,084,228.32
15. Iraq	131,081.64	30,673.10
16. Iran	286,583.09	67,060.44
17. Luxembourg	95,000.16	22,230.04
18. Mexico	317,348.46	74,259.54
19. Norway	742,162.87	173,666.11
20. New Zealand	778,800.16	182,239.24
21. Panama	103,022.39	24,107.24
22. Netherlands	1,707,428.33	399,538.23
23. Poland	2,166,876.26	507,049.04
24. Dominican Republic	54,143.51	12,669.58
25. United Kingdom	8,601,392.44	2,012,725.83
26. Siam	612,139.94	143,240.75
27. Sweden	1,659,574.77	388,340.50
28. Czechoslovakia	1,910,650.75	447,092.27
29. Turkey	436,938.72	102,243.66
30. Union of South Africa	1,471,978.70	344,443.02
31. Uruguay	367,005.31	85,879.24
32. Yugoslavia	1,365,785.71	319,593.86
	46,194,569.29	10,809,529.21

[a] Listed in French alphabetical order here and in annex B following.

ANNEX B

STATEMENT SHOWING THE CREDITS ESTABLISHED BY THE LEAGUE OF
NATIONS AND THE ADJUSTMENTS REQUIRED TO MAKE CREDITS
AVAILABLE TO NINE ADDITIONAL PARTICIPANTS

(*Expressed in U.S. dollars*)

MEMBER STATES ENTITLED TO PARTICIPATE IN THE CREDITS AS ESTABLISHED BY THE LEAGUE OF NATIONS	Amount of credit as established by the League of Nations	Shares recommended to be made available to additional participants	Amounts to be surrendered by original participants in order to make credits available to additional participants	Adjusted amounts of credits
1. Afghanistan	8,229.97		394.35	7,835.62
2. Argentina	417,665.43		20,012.84	397,652.59
3. Australia	553,285.85		26,511.22	526,774.63
4. Belgium	307,743.09		14,745.80	292,997.29
5. Bolivia	32,150.60		1,540.53	30,610.07
6. Canada	729,261.83		34,943.28	694,318.55
7. China	464,359.57		22,250.23	442,109.34
8. Cuba	103,300.17		4,949.73	98,350.44
9. Denmark	213,336.20		10,222.21	203,113.99
10. Egypt	73,477.12		3,520.73	69,956.39
11. Ecuador	3,737.31		179.08	3,558.23
12. France	1,363,713.33		65,343.63	1,298,369.70
13. Greece	117,988.73		5,680.42	112,308.31
14. India	1,084,228.32		51,951.84	1,032,276.48
15. Iraq	30,673.10		1,469.73	29,203.37
16. Iran	67,060.44		4,446.96	62,613.48
17. Luxembourg	22,230.04		1,065.17	21,164.87
18. Mexico	74,259.54		5,642.04	68,617.50
19. Norway	173,666.11		8,321.38	165,344.73
20. New Zealand	182,239.24		8,732.17	173,507.07
21. Panama	24,107.24		1,155.12	22,952.12
22. Netherlands	399,538.23		19,144.26	380,393.97
23. Poland	507,049.04		24,295.74	482,753.30
24. Dominican Republic	12,669.58		607.08	12,062.50
25. United Kingdom	2,012,725.83		96,441.69	1,916,284.14
26. Siam	143,240.75		6,863.52	136,377.23
27. Sweden	388,340.50		18,607.70	369,732.80
28. Czechoslovakia	447,092.27		21,422.85	425,669.42
29. Turkey	102,243.66		4,899.10	97,344.56
30. Union of South Africa	344,443.02		16,504.33	327,938.69
31. Uruguay	85,879.24		4,114.98	81,764.26
32. Yugoslavia	319,593.86		15,386.45	304,207.41

ADDITIONAL MEMBER STATES
ADMITTED TO SHARES IN THE
CREDITS BY AGREEMENT
AMONG THE ORIGINAL PAR-
TICIPANTS

1. Chile	120,537.57	120,537.57
2. Guatemala	7,567.24	7,567.24
3. Haiti	20,085.51	20,085.51
4. Honduras	4,793.08	4,793.08
5. Nicaragua	2,671.20	2,671.20
6. Peru	38,180.60	38,180.60
7. El Salvador	11,789.47	11,789.47
8. Union of Soviet Socialist		
Republics	256,392.68	256,392.68
9. Venezuela	59,348.81	59,348.81

10,809,529.21	521,366.16	521,366.16	10,809,529.21

INDEX

INDEX

676 INDEX

Schücking, Walther, and Hans Wehberg, *Die Satzung des Völkerbundes*, 145*n*, 399, 505*n*

Schüller, Richard, on tariff level indices, 225

Schwarzenberger, Georg, *International Law*, 399; *The League of Nations and World Order*, 399

"Science in the United States," 346

Sea, employment at, 369, 373, 374, 379; products of, exploitation of, 274

Seamen, I.L.O. Convention *No. 9* on, 369, *Nos. 22 and 23* on, 370, Draft Conventions *Nos. 52, 54, 55, 56* on, 372, Conventions *Nos. 70–74* on, 373, Recommendations *Nos. 9 and 10* on, 375, *No. 48* on, 377, *Nos. 75, 76* on, 379

Secretariat, activities on economic matters, 29; child welfare, 201; diplomatic immunity: 88, 91, text of *modus vivendi* with Switzerland, 473–84; income tax questions, 115; information of, to be spread, 112; Internal Administrative Services, 13*n*, 15; instructions to, as to minutes: of Committees, 14, of Council meetings, 13*n*; model rules for engagement, 112; office rules, 88; organization, 86–90; Princeton Mission, 29, 215, 240; publishing activities, 115, 338; Sections: 86, general, 86–87, special, 86; sections for: administrative commissions, 145–46, 188, health, 162, intellectual cooperation, 333*n*; mandates, 188*n*, 198, minorities, 187–88, opium traffic, 179, 184, transit and communications, 259; merger of sections, 215 (*see also* Information Section; Library; Legal Section); slavery questions, 198; staff, 87: allowances and indemnities to, 115, 116; voluntary contributions of, 116; staff lists, 103; Staff Regulations, 30, 31*n*, 88, 109*n*, 116, text, 440–72; Staff Pensions Fund, 59, 90, 114, 115, 116, 624–25; Staff Provident Fund, 58, 90, 115, 116; Supervisory Commission's report on, 111; *see also* Administrative Tribunal; Publications Committee; Ranshofen-Wertheimer

Secretary-General, allocation of expenses, 98–99; armaments truce, letters on, 301; authority over sections, 259*n*; circular and note on diplomatic immunity, text, 475–84; consent required

for publication of subcommittee meetings, 14; to be consulted on financial and administrative consequences of certain publication proposals, 15*n*; financial situation, memoranda on, 60, 98–100, 102; mandate of Acting ——, 58*n*, 60, 61; notes on economic situation, 128, 129; persons who held position as, 87; political functions of, 87, 308*n*; Publications Committee advisory to, 15; Radio-Nations, agreements and note concerning, 124–25; refugees, functions on behalf of, 191, 192, 197; reports: annual, 30, list of annual, 126–29, special, 93, 99, 115, on improvement in penal administration, 210–11, on work of League during war, 16, 24*n*, 36*n*, 38*n*, 58–59, 129, 215*n*; extension of treaty-registration, memorandum on, 277*n*, 287, text, 493–97; supervision of treaties, charged with, 26

Securities, suppression of falsification of, 247

Security, 294–97; treaties of mutual, 294–97

Serbian Loans, Permanent Court's judgment on, 393

Serbs, Croats and Slovenes, minorities treaty with, 189

Serological conference and studies, 169–70

Serruys, D., on tariff systems, 224

Sèvres, Treaty of, 152*n*

Sex hormones, standardization of, 170

Shipbuilding, 223

Ships: I.L.O. Convention *No. 8* on, 369, *Nos. 28 and 32* on, 370, Draft Conventions *Nos. 53 and 57* on, 372, Conventions *Nos. 69, 75, 76* on, 373, Recommendations *Nos. 26 and 27* on, 376, *Nos. 40 and 49* on, 377, *No. 78* on, 379

—— government, employed in commerce, legal status of, 285

Shotwell, James T., on security, 292*n*, 295*n*

—— and Francis Deák, *Turkey at the Straits*, 331*n*

—— and Marina Salvin, on lessons on security from League's history, 274*n*

Sickness insurance, 231; I.L.O. Conventions *Nos. 24 and 25* on, 370, Draft Convention *No. 56* on, 372

016. 34113
A918g